Encyclopedia of Parapsychology

Courtney M. Block

ROWMAN & LITTLEFIELD
Lanham • Boulder • New York • London

To the daughters, the dreamers, and the ghosts.
And to Sam, Allie, and Jenny—you inspire me more than you'll ever know.

Published by Rowman & Littlefield
An imprint of The Rowman & Littlefield Publishing Group, Inc.
4501 Forbes Boulevard, Suite 200, Lanham, Maryland 20706
www.rowman.com

86-90 Paul Street, London EC2A 4NE

Copyright © 2022 by Courtney M. Block

All rights reserved. No part of this book may be reproduced in any form or by any electronic or mechanical means, including information storage and retrieval systems, without written permission from the publisher, except by a reviewer who may quote passages in a review.

British Library Cataloguing in Publication Information Available

Library of Congress Cataloging-in-Publication Data

Names: Block, Courtney M., 1986– author.
Title: The encyclopedia of parapsychology / Courtney M. Block.
Description: Lanham : Rowman & Littlefield Publishers, [2022] | Includes
   bibliographical references and index. | Summary: "This work provides an
   encyclopedic overview of the field of parapsychology, including
   prominent researchers, seminal studies, topics, figures, and more. It
   also includes a chapter on the intersection of parapsychology and pop
   culture to highlight the many, nuanced ways that the psychical is
   intertwined into our culture"— Provided by publisher.
Identifiers: LCCN 2022014892 (print) | LCCN 2022014893 (ebook) | ISBN
   9781538155455 (cloth) | ISBN 9781538155462 (epub)
Subjects: LCSH: Parapsychology—Encyclopedias.
Classification: LCC BF1029 .B5596 2022 (print) | LCC BF1029 (ebook) | DDC
   133.3—dc23/eng/20220328
LC record available at https://lccn.loc.gov/2022014892
LC ebook record available at https://lccn.loc.gov/2022014893

Contents

Foreword		v
Preface		vii
Acknowledgments		xv
1	A History of Parapsychology	1
2	Prominent Figures in Parapsychology	25
3	What Does the Research Say? A Core Annotated Bibliography of Parapsychological Resources through the Decades	139
4	Criticisms of Parapsychology	237
Appendix A: Topical Bibliographies to Get You Started!		243
Appendix B: Journals Where You Can Find Parapsychology-Related Topics		249
Appendix C: Parapsychological Research Organizations		251
Glossary		253
Bibliography of Resources Found in Glossary		309
Bibliography		321
Index		339
Person Index		343
About the Author		349

Foreword

Psi exists and it belongs to everyone.

This position statement accompanied the 2021 reboot of the website that I created at PublicPara psychology.org. Back in 2006, even without a formal science degree, my efforts to bring academic parapsychology to the public's attention got me into the office of the Parapsychological Association, and eventually to the front of the organization as its executive director. After many years of almost exclusively serving the needs of professionals in the field, I recently returned a portion of my time to Public Parapsychology to support the trending movements of citizen and participatory team science.

Public participation in science may be trending, but it is certainly not new. Consider the historic "men and women of leisure" such as Isaac Newton, Florence Nightingale, Benjamin Franklin, and Charles Darwin who made major contributions to scientific knowledge outside of academia. Florence Nightingale probably best embodied the radical spirit of citizen science as she challenged gender roles and used her passion for statistics to pioneer evidence-based nursing. Today's citizen scientists are ushering in discoveries in astronomy, documenting ecological and social change, and affecting public policy. Citizen science is no longer just a hobby for the rich, it is becoming a civic virtue.

Meanwhile, one of the greatest scientific mysteries that we all possess, and quite possibly take for granted, is consciousness itself. It is unlikely that scientists will develop an adequate theory of how consciousness works until we understand its stranger and seemingly anomalous events such as precognitive dreams, ghostly encounters, and out of body experiences, just to name a few.

It took a while to gather the courage to finally do what I had already warned a few colleagues that I would do with my Public Parapsychology reboot: not just admit to the reality of psi (or "psychic") ability, but to acknowledge that, on some level, we all have a personal relationship with it. There is over 150 years of rigorous research supporting the statement "psi exists," much of which is published in peer-reviewed journals and likely sitting on the shelves at your local public university, if not freely available online.

Proof-oriented research on extrasensory perception (ESP) has demonstrated—at the very least—statistical anomalies relating to human behavior that persist even in the most rigorous laboratory settings. However, Courtney M. Block rightly points out that "not all endeavors at understanding parapsychological events are undertaken in a lab with research scientists and academics. . . . For many people, the goal of engaging with parapsychological concepts isn't to end up being published in a peer-reviewed journal." The drive to create, to intuit, to shape, to investigate, and to rationalize are innate to all humans. Psi does not belong only to career scientists or to established practitioners. It belongs to everyone.

Perhaps, however, you are considering a career in science and wish to study parapsychological topics; perhaps you are already well-acquainted with the literature of parapsychology but want to access lesser-known work from the women of early psychical research. Maybe you are a paranormal researcher who wants to level up your theoretical understanding. Or maybe you work in a traditional clinical setting and wish to better understand the "impossible" events that sometimes happen around trauma. Perhaps with a strong grasp of the history of parapsychology you will change the world, or maybe it is enough just to deepen your own relationship with psi.

Congratulations on finding this encyclopedia. So many decades of psi research around the globe leaves a lot to untangle, and not every public library has a knowledgeable librarian such as Ms. Block to help you navigate it. With the help of guides such as this, career and citizen scientists alike may be deterred from re-inventing the wheel—that is, inventing more and more elaborate ways to prove that psi exists. Accessing this rich history of research will likely inspire more questions about the processes underlying psi itself. Together we can shape a field of parapsychology that not only validates the lived experiences of individuals, but can interpret and use psi in ways that may positively impact ourselves and our world.

Annalisa Ventola
Founder, Public Parapsychology
Executive Director, Parapsychological Association

Preface

Existing physical science contains several huge puzzles. One of them is consciousness.[1]

The figure floating above me has dirt on the hem of its dress. My body is frozen in place. My eyes are wide open as I stare at the dirty hem while a growing sense of dread builds within me. I know that there is something gruesome attached to it, but I'm too afraid to look. Everything else in the room appears normal. There's the closet, with its tangle of scarves and clothes. There's the bedroom door, the security light in the hallway glowing through the crack in the frame. There are the paintings on the wall to my right. My eyes start to slowly scan the entity above me, moving from the dirty hem to the tattered white bodice of a nightgown, until I finally look all the way up and see its face. I scream internally for my body to "just wake up, just wake up," but I'm paralyzed, unable to move even a finger. With what feels like tremendous effort, I turn my head to the right and squeeze my eyes shut. When I open them, the figure is gone. My body can move. The sense of dread has left, even though my heart still beats rapidly, and I scan the room twice before I convince myself that nothing is there. Sleep paralysis has come once again.

Fortunately for us, researchers around the globe investigate the mind and consciousness, diving into the mysteries of experiences like the one I outline above. Researcher David E. H. Jones, in his book *Why Are We Conscious?* muses, "I suspect that the unconscious mind sometimes makes contact with an unknown world 'outside our diving bell,'" and "that unknown world may contain much information never accessed by physical science."[2] The question he ponders about the nature of consciousness is raised time and again by fellow researchers worldwide, and it's a question that has been pondered for centuries. It's even a question that transcends the realm of science and permeates nearly every avenue of society—literature, film, spirituality, and philosophy have grappled with the connotations of consciousness on the human experience. You have probably paused at some point or another to wonder about the link between consciousness and the physical world. Have you ever dreamt of something, no matter how mundane, before it has happened? Perhaps you've encountered that pervasive phenomenon known as déjà vu, or have gotten an intuition of who is calling before looking at your phone? Oftentimes we chalk this up to nothing more than coincidence, and we think no further about it because the realm of coincidence is safe. How many of us, though, stop and wonder *what if* there's something more than coincidence lurking just below the surface?

This book highlights the work of those who asked, *"what if"* and dove into these questions, merging them with research and experimentation. These experiments, often lumped under the realm of parapsychology (or an older term, psychical science), seek to expand our understanding of the ways in which our mind interacts with the world around us. As a result of people asking these questions, we now have a large and international body of work on various parapsychological topics. This work continues today.

Parapsychology is, as defined by the Parapsychological Association, "the scientific and scholarly study of three kinds of unusual events—ESP, mind-matter interaction, and survival."[3] ESP is the acronym used to refer to extrasensory perception. Survival, as the association uses it, refers to the survival of consciousness after death. Mind-matter interactions refer to other types of psychical phenomena like precognition, psychokinesis, and more. Another way to talk about parapsychology is to refer to "psychical" phenomena, or the more modern equivalent, "psi," which is phenomena of or related to the mind. Essentially, parapsychologists believe that there is more to the mind-matter connection than we currently are aware.

As I mention above, and fortunately for those interested in learning more about this topic, there is a long history of scholarly inquiry into parapsychology, which has not come without obstacles. Even today there exists, among some, a fervent disagreement about the value of scholarly inquiry into psychical phenomena, not to mention paranormal phenomena at large. Even though the topic of parapsychology sometimes continues to be a contentious topic among researchers, noted researcher and academic Dr. Jeffrey Kripal outlines the importance of having an intellectual imagination[4] when it comes to these topics and hopes that the academy is on the verge of a flip in attitude. In his 2019 work, appropriately titled *The Flip*, Dr. Jeffrey Kripal discusses the epiphanies people have after encountering anomalous experiences—epiphanies that made them question their fundamental materialist worldview. He writes, "The general materialistic framework of the sciences at the moment is not wrong. It is simply half-right. We know that mind is mattered. What these stories suggest is that matter is also minded."[5]

Dr. Kripal goes on to discuss how, for many in the academy, it takes an extremely powerful personal experience to "flip" their attitude regarding the value of psi research. He also reminds us that this type of research doesn't devalue the knowledge the science already gives us. In fact, he writes that the academy can engage in it "without surrendering an iota of our remarkable scientific and medical knowledge about the material world and the human body."[6] My work here is an attempt to bolster Dr. Kripal's words by showing readers the vast amount of information regarding parapsychology—information which may, in fact, challenge some to question certain assumptions and/or beliefs.

OUR PSYCHICAL LIVES: THE POWER OF THE SUBJECTIVE EXPERIENCE

The extremely powerful subjective experience that Dr. Kripal mentions is a perfect example of how the psi phenomena can affect our lives. While laboratory parapsychology takes place in controlled environments organized by research scientists and academics, it's clear that it's not the only environment in which psi is at play. Some other ways it manifests are through very intense encounters like a near-death experience, or in more subtle ways through intuition, déjà vu, or synchronicity. These experiences often leave a mark on a person, lingering with them long after the event has concluded.

The personal experience I share at the beginning of this preface is one of the reasons I became interested in parapsychology. Having always been a vivid dreamer, it wasn't until a few years ago that I started experiencing bouts of sleep paralysis. Anyone who has experienced this will immediately know what I'm talking about, but for those who are unfamiliar, sleep paralysis happens when your mind awakens before your physical body, resulting in a type of paralysis that exists somewhere between being fully awake and fully asleep. Quite often, a symptom of sleep paralysis also includes feelings of immense dread and/or seeing strange figures as if they are in the room with you. The scariest thing about sleep paralysis is that you cannot separate the dream state from the waking state—in other words, any hallucinations you have in this state seem as real as if you were fully awake and aware. During yet another episode, I saw a green goblin with shocking red hair crouched on my bed. On yet another occasion, I saw a black horned figure standing next to me as I slept.

Because of my intense dream experience, I began keeping a dream journal. In doing so, I started to notice that I dreamt about things before they happened. Before you get too excited, no, I never dreamt about winning lottery numbers. The things I dreamt of were mundane, like a scene in book I would read later in the week or of conversations that would happen a day or two later. And as mundane as these dreams were, nevertheless, the experience left me wondering what this means about the intersection of consciousness and our physical world.

This brings me to an important point. While it is beneficial to scientifically study the various phenomena related to parapsychology, it is equally important to muse upon (and make space for) the subjective power of the paranormal experience. The laboratory setting of the paranormal experiment and the powerful, subjective nature of the paranormal experience are equal in value. While the scientific view can help us add to our scope of knowledge about the world around us, the subjective experience does that too *while also* activating a personal sense of wonder and reverence for the mystical. Our subjective experiences can even motivate us to become citizen scientists, spurred on by our own personal encounters to learn more about the anomalous, which brings me to another important point. Not all endeavors at understanding parapsychological events are undertaken in a lab with research scientists and academics. People just like you can explore the mysteries of the psychical through conducting your own experiments. For many people, the goal of engaging with parapsychological concepts isn't to end up being published in a peer-reviewed journal. Their goal is, perhaps, to simply deepen their personal relationship between the known and unknown and for many, myself included, it contains a spiritual element as well.

A MAGICAL MINDSET: SOCIETY AND THE PARANORMAL FROM ANTIQUITY

Before diving into chapter 1, a history of parapsychology, let's delve further into the sense of wonder and mysticism for a moment. Remember, magic was once viewed as part and parcel of daily life. We see one example of this in ancient Greek society. The Greeks made regular employ of women known as oracles. At Delphi, this oracle was referred to as Pythia. These women would divine messages for prominent members of the community. Researcher Libby Ruffle tells us that these oracles were key members of society and "connected the human to the divine."[7] The oracles remained important figures of society, particularly at Delphi, and prophesized from 800 BC to 380 AD.[8] Of course, in this example, the act of divination is intimately connected to religious life, but nevertheless this serves as a reminder that mystical abilities connected to *seeing beyond* one's normal capacity have existed since antiquity.

Figure P.1. The Oracle at Delphi Entranced by Heinrich Leutemann
CC-PD-Mark via WikiCommons

Of course, this example from Greek culture is not the only case of magical practices from antiquity. In tombs, Egyptians carved messages and spells to aid the buried along on their afterlife journey. In Babylonia, breaking the legs on a small sculpture symbolized intent to keep evil spirits at bay. Mayan culture utilized psychotropic substances to enter a trance-like state to commune with spirits, and in ancient Rome "curse tablets" would be used to inscribe ill wishes—the idea being that even words themselves had power to affect the world around us.[9] The point here is, from humankind's beginning, we have held beliefs that we can interact with forces and spirits of an invisible world around us. And while many of these beliefs seem to get tied up in attitudes and rituals surrounding death and the afterlife (and therefore, religion), some of these practices (like the aforementioned curse tablets or figurine-smashing), are performed to achieve some outcome in the present moment. It is in *these* practices that we inch closer to a demarcation between magic and religious belief. Parapsychologists of the modern world seek to understand the ways in which our minds and consciousness affect our physical world, so in a way, when we study psychical phenomena, we study practices as old as humankind itself.

In addition to these examples from antiquity, folk magic and occult practices also remind us of humankind's long, complex history of the psychical timeline. Psychologist John Beloff reminds us that "before the advent of the Scientific Revolution of the seventeenth century, the distinction between what was normal and paranormal was too fluid to justify distinguishing a separate discipline devoted to the latter. Magic and the occult arts, were, after all, still part of received knowledge."[10] Beloff reminds us that the Renaissance was rife with interest in and practice of magic and occult rituals, and that it was "the sophisticated magic of a learned and dedicated elite."[11] Practitioners concerned themselves with one of two types of magical practices: natural and supernatural. Natural magic refers to the belief that everything in the world contains a soul, and that everything is connected to one another. It is illustrated most readily through alchemy and astrology, and the belief that every plant, substance, or animal contains some "sympathetic relationship" with the cosmos.[12] Some of the influential "natural-magic"

practitioners, known as magi (magic practitioners), include Henry Cornelius Agrippa, of Germany, who wrote *De Occulta Philosophia*, a seminal text of Renaissance magic. Another German, Phillipus Bombastus, was a physician who believed, contrary to the zeitgeist of his time, that ailments were caused by nature and not by forces of evil. Giordano Bruno, from Italy, believed in intelligent life beyond Earth and even served in the court of Queen Elizabeth in the sixteenth century.[13] Another member of the queen's court was astrologer John Dee, described as "the most celebrated magus of the period."[14] William Gilbert was another interesting figure. He was the queen's physician and wrote a treatise on the relationship between magnets and psychical phenomena nearly two hundred years before Franz Mesmer began his own experiments into magnetism.[15]

Supernatural magic, on the other hand, involves the use of certain spells to summon noncorporeal beings for assistance. The supernatural magic of the Renaissance time was influenced by Judaic philosophies and sources such as the cabala and *Sefer Yezirah*, mystical traditions and works that discuss, among many things, the power of using the Hebrew alphabet to summon spirits.[16] This also gave rise to the practice of numerology, since the Hebrew alphabet has numerical counterparts. The aforementioned astrologer John Dee kept detailed journals on the séances he conducted to summon angels using this alphabet, but here is where researcher John Beloff reminds us that though these practices occurred, it was not until some two hundred years later that we begin to see people using séances to contact deceased loves ones.[17]

So far, our discussion spans the magical mindset from antiquity to the Renaissance. It is this long history of integration of the magical into culture and belief that blurs the edges of where parapsychological inquiry began. Beloff muses about the difficulty in pinpointing an exact beginning because humankind has always had a relationship with what we collectively coin the paranormal. It's a particularly muddy question to ask, especially, since, as Beloff tells us, the key tenet of both parapsychology *and* magic is whether or not humans, through their own intent and faculty, can influence the physical world around them to achieve some desired outcome.[18] The fundamental motivation, then, between magic and the psychical, is one and the same—the key difference being that one is more palatable for laboratory study and the other remains relegated to the realm of mysticism, religion, culture, and personal practice. When researching the history of parapsychology, though, it is useful to be aware of the history of humankind's fascination with the mysterious and the various ways in which it manifests in our lives.

Scholar Owen Davies helps us understand magic folk practices of the past, in particular those of the cunning folk of England. The term "cunning folk" describes men and women who were "multi-faceted practitioners of magic who healed the sick and the bewitched, told fortunes, identified thieves, induced love," and much more.[19] Existing since the Middle Ages, cunning folk were influential in their communities. Davies reinforces this point by reminding us that "for centuries [they were] as integral to English life as the clergyman, constable, and doctor."[20] Davies further points to the etymology of the word "cunning" to describe how these men and women were viewed within society. Cunning, coming from the Anglo Saxon *cunnan* means "to know." Even the term "wizard," which was sometimes used (though only in particular parts of England and only when referring to males) comes from *wis*, an Old English root meaning "wise." In other words, as Davies shows us, cunning folk were noted for "possessing more knowledge than those around them, knowledge that was acquired either from a supernatural source, from an innate . . . ability, or from being able to understand writing."[21]

These cunning folk occupied a liminal space that existed somewhere between the auspices of "high" and "low" magic. High magic refers to the ceremonial, ritualistic practices emanating from a shared philosophy and set of established practices whereas low magic refers to practical applications passed down from generation to generation, with no rule book or set of unifying principles, and which was employed merely as a means to achieve a certain task.[22] Cunning folk, Davies tells us, were people who possessed knowledge of both types of magic.

Though cunning folk became oft-consulted members of society, their activities were often not condoned by government or the church. The reality of that dynamic has seemed to ebb and flow throughout history. Up through the Viking era, "Various secular and ecclesiastical legal codes condemned people for using charms to cure the sick, [foretell] the future, and [procure] love."[23] There weren't, however, any secular laws against the practice of magic during the twelfth century, a period that saw dismissive reception from government yet an increased irritation by the church toward folk magic. Acceptance in different ways during different eras makes these cunning folk liminal people themselves, occupying a trade that was tolerated at best and persecuted at worst. England is, of course, just one country among many with a rich history of folk magic. This example illustrates how humans have both engaged in and been fascinated by our ability to metaphysically influence the physical world around us since the beginning.

Not surprisingly, there is myriad of folk magic practices that exist today, spanning the globe. In rural Pakistan, for example, tona is a magico-religious practice used in the healing of certain ailments.[24] Wiccans perform rituals based on the seasons of the year and perform spells for desired outcomes like attracting good luck, cutting cords, or divination.[25] In Mongolia, shamans today continue a forty-thousand-year-old tradition of inducing trance to commune with spirits.[26] In Seoul, South Korea, the folk tradition Muism is reminiscent of the Pythia of Delphi. In Muist practices (a modern resurgence of an ancient Korean practice dating back to the fourth century), women divine answers to common questions surrounding jobs, health, money, relationships, and more.[27]

This brief foray into magic and folk practices reminds us that humans have had (and continue to have) a magical mindset regarding our ability to influence the world. That, in a nutshell, *is* psi at its simplest—an ability to influence the physical world through mind, consciousness, and intent. Any conversation about parapsychology would be remiss without at least a nod to the magical mindset that continues to guide our quest for knowledge. It also reminds us that these inquiries are not foreign—they are not merely modern conventions but are instead deeply rooted in the human experience. These examples also remind us to have a sense of mysticism about the whole endeavor, for as much as we may uncover, numerous questions spill in to take their place.

HOW TO USE THIS BOOK

In the *Encyclopedia of Parapsychology*, I provide an international compendium of researchers, notable research, and common terms associated with the field of parapsychology. There are multiple works on this topic (including some wonderful encyclopedias), so my goal is not to duplicate these works, but rather to create a guide targeted at the everyday person, the beginner new to this topic who is fascinated by strange phenomena and simply wants to know more. As such, my goal is to provide a modern supplement from which readers can jumpstart their research into this topic. I do, of course, include historical figures and research to provide readers with the historical context of this field as well.

This work is also international in scope, highlighting key figures, researchers, and institutions from across the globe and particularly including those who have often been left out of the conversation, known perhaps only to seasoned scholars in the field. This work is intended for those who are entirely (or relatively) new to the topic of parapsychology. It is targeted at those who want to know more about the scientific pursuit of the anomalous and it is *especially* targeted at students within the academy who may sometimes feel as if they have to censor their interest in the strange and mysterious.

It is important to note that not all the researchers presented in this work are necessarily parapsychologists. Some of the people I include would probably not call themselves a parapsychologist at all, in fact. If they are included, it is because they engage in research that has some connection to topics surrounding parapsychology. For example, near-death experience can be considered an aspect of parapsychology, so you may find mention of a neuroscientist or cardiologist who studies near-death experiences. The doctor themself is not a parapsychologist, but the work they do is inherently centered around parapsychological aspects. My goal, through including a diverse range of researchers, it to highlight the intersectional nature of the psychical.

On that note keep the same caveat in mind when you consult the notable research portion of this work. There are many phenomena that fall under the umbrella of parapsychology, so you will see a wide swath of research topics. Know that all resources are included because of an inherent connection to parapsychology. This section reflects and reveals the complex, intersectional nature of parapsychological research. Additionally, the research hails from myriad range of sources that run the gamut from the obvious *Journal of Parapsychology* to the not-so-obvious *Journal of the American Medical Association* to everything in between.

Readers may, at any point, skip back and forth to different chapters of this book. It is not necessary to read in any linear order, though it may help contextualize the information you find in subsequent chapters. It is my goal to provide enough background information to set the stage for information you find later in this work. Chapter 1 provides an overview of parapsychological research from the 1700s. Chapter 2 is an extensive biographical treatment of seminal figures in parapsychology—historic, modern, and international in scope. Chapter 3 is a core annotated bibliography of parapsychology-related research from the late 1800s to the 2020s. In that chapter you will find annotations of a wide range of resources, from journal articles, monographs, and more. Chapter 4 is a discussion of the common critiques of parapsychological research, an important discussion to be aware of. The appendices highlight international research organizations, topical bibliographies, and a list of some obvious (and not-so-obvious) journals to consult to find even more parapsychological resources. There is a glossary of terms within parapsychology (like poltergeist, ESP, Global Consciousness Project, etc.) that also contains a robust amount of "further reading" resources. Throughout this work you will find countless "further reading" additions that are intended to help readers easily locate additional relevant resources, which are included so that readers have an overwhelming number of resources located within *one* work.

It is my hope that this work provides readers with a starting point for their interest in parapsychology. This work will be palatable enough even for high school readers and is certainly beneficial for those who may even have a small understanding of this topic to begin with. It is not necessarily meant to supplement an expert's bookshelf, though I'll never discourage any reader. A librarian by trade, my skill set includes locating information and presenting it to people. That's what I do. Where readers choose to take this information is their own choice. I am not a parapsychologist and I make no claim to be one. In this work I take what I'm good at, which is finding resources, and merge it with a personal interest. It isn't my goal to convince anyone of anything, though I do hope it raises questions. I hope that in addition to providing information, it emphasizes the beauty of moving through this world with a little bit of mysticism in your mindset.

I used to spend a fair amount of time worried about the implications of being a tenure-track academic who openly promotes the importance of paranormal research. I used to worry that not conforming 100 percent to the dominating materialist agenda of higher education would put a target on my back. But then I realized the importance of revealing myself as a *weirdo* to students or perhaps even colleagues who are interested in these same topics. If others see me openly engaging the paranormal within a higher-education setting, perhaps it will encourage others to embrace their weird as well, and to see the value of what they can contribute. Most importantly, I realize that there must be enough of us who are comfortable sitting in the borders, who can save a seat for others to show them that the outer edges are a valid, and often necessary place to be.

NOTES

1. David E. H. Jones, *Why Are We Conscious? A Scientist's Take on Consciousness and Extrasensory Perception* (Singapore: Pan Stanford Publishing, 2017), 3.

2. Ibid., 3.

3. "What is Parapsychology?" (February 11, 2011). The Parapsychological Association. Accessed January 4, 2021 from https://parapsych.org/articles/36/76/what_is_parapsychology.aspx.

4. Jeffrey J. Kripal, *The Flip: Epiphanies of Mind and the Future of Knowledge* (New York: Bellevue Literary Press, 2019), 13.

5. Ibid., 12.

6. Ibid.

7. Libby Ruffle, "The Oracle at Delphi: Vessels of the Gods," *History Today* 67, no. 5 (May 2017): 50–52.

8. Ibid.

9. Kathryn Hennessy, Rose Blackett-Ord, Anna Fischel, and Megan Douglass, eds., *A History of Magic, Witchcraft, and the Occult* (New York: DK Publishing, 2020), 12–13.

10. John Beloff, *Parapsychology: A Concise History* (New York: St. Martin's Press, 1993), ix.

11. Ibid., 2.

12. Ibid., 3.

13. Ibid., 4–5.

14. Ibid., 5.

15. Ibid.

16. Ibid., 6. Kaufmann Kohler and Louiz Ginzberg, "Cabala." Accessed March 10, 2021, from https://www.jewishencyclopedia.com/articles/3878-cabala.

17. Beloff, *Parapsychology*, 6–7.

18. Ibid., 1.

19. Owen Davies. *Cunning-Folk: Popular Magic in English History* (London: Hambledon and London, 2003), vii.

20. Ibid.

21. Ibid., vii–viii.

22. Ibid., xii.

23. Ibid., 1.

24. Azher Hameed Qamar, "Tona, the Folk Healing Practices in Rural Punjab, Pakistan," *Journal of Ethnology & Folkloristics* 9, no. 2 (July 2015): 59.

25. Hennessy et al., *A History of Witchcraft, Magic, and Occult*, 264–72.

26. Ibid., 278.

27. Ibid., 280.

Acknowledgments

This book would not have been possible without the support systems that surround me. From family, friends, loved ones, colleagues, and everyone in between, there have been so many ways that folks helped, from offering encouragement, locating resources, bringing me dinner, engaging in late-night brainstorming and philosophical musings (Suzanne, I'm looking at you), and much more. Thanks to my parents and sisters for being the best cheerleaders. Thanks to my community of paranormal friends, both online and in-person, who champion and celebrate weirdness and inspire me every day. Thanks to Charles "Chris" Isaacs, graduate student and photographer, for teaching me how to use Photoshop. Thanks to my editors Charles and Erinn for their guidance and patience. Thanks to Amy, Ann Marie, Becky, and Jay, for our journeys through the infinite space and magic of the dreamscape. And last, but certainly not least, thanks Grandma Rose, for sharing your ghost stories with me.

1

A History of Parapsychology

I would venture a guess that nearly every parapsychologist is drawn to the field because, at some point in their life, they had at least one experience, mysterious and powerful, which they cannot deny, bury, and explain away."[1]

Parapsychology is most simply defined as the study of the mind's influence on matter. In other words, this field attempts to understand the nuances of the mind-matter connection. For many readers this likely conjures images of ESP (extrasensory perception), or perhaps any number of scenes in movies, television, and literature where people display supernatural abilities. Topics that fall under the umbrella of parapsychology include near-death experiences, hauntings, psychokinesis, and poltergeist activity, just to name a few. Essentially, parapsychology subsumes any phenomena in which consciousness *may* play a role in influencing our physical world. As you can imagine, the topic is extremely complex.

Human beings have been intrigued by parapsychological phenomena for millennia. Oftentimes, we ascribe spiritual or religious meanings when we encounter mysterious events. Some of us take our intrigue and questions into the laboratory to ferret out as much scientific knowledge as we can about strange phenomena. Regardless of the meanings we ascribe or the reactions we have during these moments, one thing is abundantly clear: these phenomena have been documented and questioned throughout the history of humankind. These encounters and inquiries often leave us with no tidy answers, yet weave themselves into the very fabric of our daily lives, whether that is through popular culture, spirituality, philosophy, or science.

Quite simply, the parapsychological makes us question the role and influence of consciousness in our physical world.

Some of you may wonder, and rightfully so, that if there are no tidy answers, then what is the importance of this field? If there is no concrete explanation and scientific mapping of consciousness that we can point to, even after all our pursuits and philosophical musings, then why the continued chase? Ingrid Kloosterman, a faculty member in the school of Social and Behavioural Sciences at Utrecht University in the Netherlands, has a response that helps us answer this question. In a 2012 publication for the journal *History of the Human Sciences*, Kloosterman points out that parapsychology incites revolution.[2] In fact, their article points out that social scientists are particularly intrigued by parapsychology and its role within the academy because "it might provide the live-witnessing of a scientific revolution."[3] As many of us know, scientific revolutions can bring with them a new era of understanding and progress. Parapsychology is revolutionary in nature because it pushes back against the dominant materialist philosophy that tells us we can only understand the world around us *in certain ways.* Furthermore, Kloosterman reminds us that parapsychology can serve as a bridge between science and religion, and many ascribe merit to that.[4] Of course, this also reveals why parapsychology sits on the sideline of the sciences today. This wasn't always the case, though, and the section below on the historical roots of parapsychology will reveal just how opposite this once was.

This chapter provides some answers to that "So what?" question posed above by highlighting the history of parapsychological inquiry. It begins with a philosophical discussion on the liminal (or, in-between) nature of the field. This discussion is important to begin with as it helps readers better understand the tensions that have existed (and continue to exist) throughout parapsychology's timeline. It then delves into a historical overview of parapsychological work since the 1700s, moving chronologically from mesmerism, Spiritualism, and the global formation of academic institutions studying psi. This chapter also includes a section on the modern criticisms of parapsychology research and a brief discussion of its current relationship with the academy. I end this chapter by highlighting some modern parapsychologists and the work that continues today. This chapter demonstrates that our questions and experiments with the psychical echo outward from the depths of human history and continue to shape our worldviews today. With that, let us dive into the discussion by acknowledging the liminal space in which parapsychology so often finds itself.

LIMINAL SPACES: FINDING COMFORT IN THE IN-BETWEEN

Tracing a historical timeline of parapsychology may not necessarily look like what you expect. Keep in mind that humankind's fascination with the paranormal and with potential powers of the mind have been around since our beginning. As you can imagine, historical context affects how each era views the psychical, and in addition to these ever-changing paradigms, *many* different phenomena exist under the realm of parapsychology. Further complicating this matter is the fact that the paranormal was once regarded as a widely accepted fact—in fact, occult magic and folk practices were not relegated to the peripheries of acceptable knowledge until the seventeenth century.[5] It becomes clear rather quickly that obtaining a comprehensive historical understanding of this topic is a very complex matter.

Early in this chapter I note that researcher Ingrid Kloosterman comments on the revolutionary characteristic of parapsychology—that is, its potential to take our current scientific knowledge and expand it even further. Noted parapsychologist, scholar, and author Dr. Dean Radin muses about this as well. In

an October 2020 episode of the podcast *Nite Drift*, Dr. Radin tells us,

> You can't throw away materialism because it's just way too successful. [Throwing it away] doesn't make any sense. If you go towards idealism, it doesn't mean that you're throwing away materialism. It means what science has always done—to expand it. You keep what's good and you expand it, and so the parts of materialism that work, we absolutely want to keep, but I think it can be expanded and the way you expand it is imagining it's a bubble, and the outside of the bubble has a new layer, and that layer is called consciousness.[6]

Through this quote, Dr. Radin reminds us that scientific research and the paranormal don't have to be mutually exclusive. In fact, he tells us that engaging in psychical research is simply following the path that science promotes, which is learning more about that which we do not know or understand. In this podcast, he muses about his work with the Institute of Noetic Sciences, an organization that studies profound and anomalous human experiences. He reflects that while he's grateful to be able to conduct such research, there aren't as many institutes dedicated to these questions—but not for a lack of interest. Dr. Radin says "even though the world is saturated with interest in these topics (psi phenomena), there's almost no funding for it . . . and that's a pity."[7] This is a stark reminder of the schism that exists between the paranormal and the academy. Even though research has unveiled surprising facts about consciousness, it still seems to exist on the fringes of acceptable science and inquiry.

Further complicating the intersection of parapsychology and the academy, Dr. Radin reminds us that in the Western world, we are introduced to the paranormal primarily through pop culture and media. As a result, the paranormal often gets "dismissed as something that is not quite real."[8] Since our institutions are dominated by a materialist philosophy, many anomalous phenomena are dismissed as "not quite real" without any second thought or experimentation. Dr. Radin discusses how this Western, materialist worldview of the paranormal trickles into laboratory research that is often dismissed or trivialized by other scientists, even when it shows evidence of anomalous effect.

Nevertheless, Dr. Radin stresses the importance of engaging in parapsychological research. It helps reveal more about the world around us, he says, even if it so often leaves us with more questions than answers. We can't even begin to fathom how much there is that we still don't know. He likens this to sitting in front of a bonfire. "If you're around a tiny little bonfire, you can't see how much darkness there is. You need a pretty big bonfire to suddenly realize, 'Holy crap, I'm in a huge amount of ignorance here.'"[9]

The trajectory of parapsychology exists on a spectrum that, in centuries past, started with acceptance, integration, and belief. Now, at least in our institutions of higher education, the pendulum has swung and exists at a point of skepticism and dismissal, if not sometimes outright hostility. Running alongside this spectrum is the general societal attitude toward anomalous phenomena, which Dr. Radin references and is supported by statistics like this one: in 2017, a *USA Today* article cites a survey that reveals 45 percent of people in the United States believe in ghosts.[10]

Since the topic of parapsychology is a very divisive one, it is a field that exists in a liminal, in-between state. Credible, highly credentialed researchers conduct scientific parapsychological experiments within institutions dominated by materialist philosophy that, while extremely necessary and useful, sometimes doesn't understand the value of paranormal research. This creates a liminal space in which both the topic and the researcher become liminal. This in-between state carries great meaning, though. The liminal state is where things are deconstructed and re-created. In the case of parapsychology, researchers deconstruct assumptions about our world in order to recreate a new understanding. In this process, they also deconstruct stereotyped notions about what it means to be an academic person. Scholars who take up the plight of paranormal research don't do so because it's going to make them popular at their university. I hope that changes soon, and there certainly seem to be more supportive institutions than others. When a researcher engages in this work, they actively place themselves in a liminal space and through their work, challenge conventional notions of how to behave as an academic. This decon-

struction helps pave the way for more researchers, and is, I hope, a stepping-stone toward more open-mindedness within the academy. When we look at it this way, then, there is beauty in the in-between. The liminal space offers a new perspective and energy with which to engage in topics. It's not restrictive or stereotyped and provides opportunities for ingenuity and experimentation.

Because parapsychology exists in a liminal space, there is also ample room for nonacademics to creatively engage with this field. In fact, lay researchers and citizen scientists seem to be directing the popular parapsychological theories that abound among the general public. Citizen science creates a sense of play with the paranormal because experimentation is not so strictly regulated or bound. This sense of play invites ingenuity and encourages people to think deeper about the world around them in very creative ways. Regardless of your credentials, this is a worthy endeavor. And in today's world, with an overwhelming number of podcasts and web series, people can share their theories, experiments, and engage with others in a matter of seconds. The creative energy that people manifest in today's world is unparalleled and serves, I think, to support the overall mission of learning more about the psychical mysteries of the world. This brings me to another point. Experimentation is not relegated to scientists in lab coats or those with university affiliations. Anyone can investigate the topics presented in this book. Sure, those investigations might not end up in the pages of a scientific or academic journal, but that doesn't mean that the effort isn't valuable or that it has no impact on how we, as a society, interact with and understand parapsychological phenomena. Again, this is the beauty of the liminal space. It deconstructs stereotyped notions of authority and fosters creativity. Because the liminal space is a place of destruction and re-creation, when we get comfortable being in this space, we collectively continue to progress our understanding of this strange world. I hope that anyone interested in engaging with parapsychological topics feels empowered to play among the mystery because there are deeply meaningful personal experiences to be had. Let's turn now to a discussion on the ways in which others through history have engaged with the unknown.

HISTORICAL ROOTS:
A MESMERIZING BEGINNING (1778–1847)

Conversations regarding a starting point on the historical roots of parapsychology always seem to come back to Franz Anton Mesmer. Mesmer was an Austrian physician to whom we credit the word "mesmerism." He believed that an invisible fluid surrounds our bodies and is susceptible to the gravitational pull of the planets, which could be demonstrated by the placement of magnets upon the body. Furthermore, he believed that strategic placement of these magnets could cure certain diseases.[11] Charles Richet, author and psychical researcher, uses Mesmer as a delineation point in the timeline of parapsychology in his 1923 work titled *Thirty Years of Psychical Research: Being a Treatise on Metaphysics.*[12] Researcher John Beloff, introduced above, struggles with choosing a definitive starting point to this topic and settles on the emergence of Mesmer and his foray into mesmerism as a starting point that indicates a scientific- and laboratory-based approach to the field of parapsychology.[13] Let's dive into the four eras of psychical research that Charles Richet outlines in his 1923 treatise to see exactly where Mesmer fits in.

Richet, a psychical researcher and member of the Society for Psychical Research, a scientific organization dedicated to the study of psychical phenomena, wrote, in 1923, a lengthy tome outlining the past thirty year's work of research into these various phenomena. While certain ideologies espoused by Richet are problematic, he outlines four key eras of attitudes toward the psychical, which I find useful in providing historical context. Richet tells us that the first stage of public thought and attitude toward the psychical is the mythical stage, which runs from antiquity up till 1778, when Mesmer and his notions of hypnotism arrive on the scene.[14] This stage is dominated by the paranormal (which includes any psychical phenomena) being viewed as inseparable from both folklore and religion. In other words, oral traditions and religious texts outline all sorts of paranormal phenomena but there's no possible way it can ever be tested. This era of paranormal attitude, then, is more helpful to the historian than the laboratory scientist. What Richet does is essentially the same thing that John Beloff does—he identifies Mesmer as the turning point of scientific inquiry into the paranormal rather than *only* a realm of folklore and religion. The second stage is the magnetic stage, ushered in from 1778 till 1847 with the emergence of the Fox sisters, a trio of siblings from Hyde Park who popularized Spiritualism in the United States. Just as Mesmer indicated a turning point in paranormal thought, so too did the Fox sisters, who ushered in the third stage that Richet identifies as the spiritist stage. This third stage is marked by the rise of Spiritualism, fraud, and the paranormal as entertainment and profit. Richet's fourth era is the scientific stage, which he outlines as 1872 to the time of publication, 1923.[15]

These four stages of thought represent the various shifts in how humans have approached the paranormal. Since multiple sources point to Mesmer as the first scientific turning point of parapsychology, let's take a deeper look at him. As we know, Mesmer was an Austrian physician who, in the late 1700s, believed that there was an aura, or force field, of animal magnetism surrounding our bodies. He believed that it was affected not only by the gravitational pull of celestial bodies, but also that it could be influenced by magnets. Essentially, he believed that transferring, via magnets, the force field of a healthy person to that of an ill one would assist in curing ailments. Though he had a steady stream of patients, the Austrian medical community did not applaud Mesmer's experiments and he eventually found his way to Paris, where his beliefs were more welcomed.[16] Mesmer began his work with magnets but, as it continued, he "soon discovered that he could obtain the same results using a system of stroking or making passes with the hands across the patient's body."[17] An unintended consequence of this practice resulted in patients being lured into a trance-like state. Often, these states found the patients impervious to pain, and as Beloff points out, this was a time before the advent of "chemical anesthesia," and for that reason alone this tactic proved useful.[18]

Another thing that Mesmer and his practitioners noticed, though, is that in these trance-like states, patients would sometimes exhibit psychical abilities. This explains why Beloff tells us that Mesmer is the natural precursor of parapsychology. Mesmerists found that while in a trance-like state, patients would exhibit "eyeless sight," or the ability to identify items they could not possibly know, like reading a passage from a book they've never read or identifying the contents of a sealed envelope.[19] One of Mesmer's followers, the aristocratic French soldier Marquis de Puységur, is credited with bringing attention to the somnambulism that Mesmer's practices could evoke. Puységur used Mesmer's techniques and discovered, while treating a patient, that they not only entered a trance-like state but would act like a completely different person, walking around and exhibiting fluent speech while at all other times being severely tongue-tied. The patient had no memory of what occurred once brought out of the trance.[20]

While Mesmer and his associates were eventually discredited, and the medical community urged physicians against believing in an invisible, magnetic fluid surrounding the body, the impact of Mesmer's work cannot be denied. Beloff even argues that Mesmer's work proved to be the forerunner of modern psychiatry because it discovered, albeit unintentionally, that humans could measure the depths of their subconscious. Many practitioners, in addition to Puységur, abandoned the idea of the magnetic force field and instead focused on the implications of the somnambulist, trance-like state. In fact, it was the Scottish surgeon John Braid who used Mesmer's notions to come up with his own theory of "nervous sleep," which later became known as hypnotism.[21] The physicians who ran with the notion of trance and hypnotism continued to witness their patients display curious, psychical behavior. One example from 1846 involves a patient who was treated with mesmerism by Dr. J. W. Haddock, a general practitioner from Lancashire. Not only did the patient develop "eyeless sight," but they also developed the ability to expand it beyond the confines of the doctor's office, and even used it to identify lost and stolen money on more than one occasion.

Another interesting case study that arises from the halls of mesmerism surrounds a young German woman, Friedericke Hauffe, who was known as the Seeress of Prevorst.[22] Friedericke fell ill and was put under the care of Justus Kerner, the local physician (and interestingly, the scientist to whom we credit the discovery of botulism). She didn't respond to conventional medical treatments so Kerner decided to try magnetism, as he himself had once been successfully treated with mesmerist techniques. As a result, Friedericke began to "propound cosmological and theological teachings which even managed to impress some of Kerner's learned friends."[23] She

foretold certain deaths and even exhibited physical abilities like telekinesis. Throughout all of this, she even spoke about worlds and beings beyond ours. Her case remains an example of what Beloff tells us is the "mystical mesmerism" tradition that flourished in Germany in the 1800s. Unfortunately, Friedericke eventually succumbed to her illness in 1829. Just a few short years later in 1832, Kerner published a case study of her life and the treatments he gave, becoming what has been dubbed the first book-length case study in the field of "dynamic psychiatry."[24] Kerner's publication elicited so many responses that he established two journals dedicated to the inquiry. These publications ran from 1831 to 1853 and some muse that they were the first parapsychological journals in existence.[25]

Mesmerism and its practical applications began to die out in the 1850s. And while, as Beloff tells us, mesmerism always tried to insert itself within the realm of medical science, certain governing authorities denounced its application. In 1784, in fact, the Royal Commission chalked the effects of mesmerism up as nothing more than the placebo effect. However, researcher Alan Gauld muses that the effects that mesmerism produced are simply too curious to be chalked up to *merely* the power of suggestion. He presumes that perhaps mesmerist techniques have more in common with the modern practices of acupuncture and qigong, and point to the untapped powers of the human mind.[26] Mesmerism provides us the first scientific foray into the psychical world, and even though it fizzled out in the 1850s, the impact it left upon the scientific community cannot be denied. With its slow demise in the latter half of the nineteenth century, we then saw the rise of the next era of psychical history, Spiritualism.

SPIRITUALISM AND MEDIUMS ON THE PARAPSYCHOLOGICAL TIMELINE (1847–1882)

After the slow demise of mesmerism, we begin to see the beginning of a new era on the parapsychological timeline: the era of Spiritualism. Researcher Ingrid Kloosterman reminds us of the two key components that have been central to the scientific pursuit of parapsychology from the very beginning: proof and fraud.[27] This reminder is perhaps the best place to begin our discussion of Spiritualism because it was an era which, though it raised immense awareness of psi phenomena, rampant fraud occurred. John Beloff tells us that this deceit perhaps had a silver lining: it necessitated an increase of scientific inquiry into certain psychical phenomena, like mediumship. Beloff tells us that a second contribution of Spiritualism to the field of parapsychology is that it brought new life and energy to the questions surrounding life after death.[28] He also reminds us that Spiritualism arose after the Romantic era of thought had receded. Society now placed an emphasis on science and proof and Spiritualism sought to deliver proof of life after death. Furthermore, Victorian society was grappling with the disillusionment of religion. Researcher Janet Oppenheim tell us,

> Victorians themselves were fully aware that the place of religion in the cultural fabric of their times was scarcely secure. In an effort to counter that insecurity, to calm their fears, and to seek answers where contemporary churches were ambiguous, thousands of British men and women in the Victorian and Edwardian eras turned to spiritualism and psychical research.[29]

Oppenheim also tells us that while Spiritualism is notable due to the abundance of mediums, it also became a widespread activity of women. Oppenheim even tells us that the spiritualist zeitgeist was so embedded in the fabric of society that "indeed mediumship could be, in its fashion, as domesticated and feminine an art as embroidery."[30]

The fascination with Spiritualism begins, most agree, in 1848 with the Fox sisters of New York. Oppenheim even tells us that the activities of these sisters seemed to fan the flames of spiritualist intrigue in Britain.[31] Margaret, Kate, and Leah Fox claimed to hear strange rapping noises coming from a wall in their home in Hydesville. They began to interact with the strange noises and concluded that they were communicating with the spirit of a man who was buried on the property. Word spread about the strange goings-on at the Fox household and soon neighbors and community members flocked to the house to investigate for themselves. Nobody could find a reason for these strange noises, and soon the sisters were invited to tell their tales and communicate with spirits outside their home.[32]

Figure 1.1. The Fox Sisters (from left, Margaret, Kate, and Leah)
Lithograph Titled "Mrs. Fish and the Misses Fox: The Original Mediums of the Mysterious Noises at Rochester Western, N.Y." by N. Currier. (New York, 1852), Library of Congress

While the Fox sisters helped set off the spark of Spiritualism in the United States, other figures were making their rounds in Europe. A few mediums from the United States were already on the scene in Britain, but the séance scene really seemed to take off when Daniel Dunglas Home returned to his homeland. Home, who was born in 1833 in Scotland, migrated with his family to the United States in the 1840s where he began to display curious abilities. He began performing these skills in séances, and in 1855, he traveled to England. For the next twenty years, he spent time in Europe dazzling prominent figures with his séances—figures such as Napolean III, Queen Sophia of Holland, Elizabeth Barrett Browning, and more.[33]

At this point, some readers may wonder what took place at a Victorian séance. Typical occurrences would be levitation of tables or other objects in the room, musical instruments appearing to play by themselves, objects disappearing and then reappear-

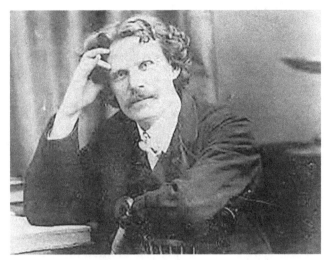

Figure 1.2. Daniel Dunglas Home
From CC-PD-Mark via WikiCommons

ing, levitation of the medium themself, and even the appearance of phantom limbs (most often hands or faces). Often, the rooms that a séance took place in would be dimly lit. Sometimes the medium would be placed in a special closet or small room behind curtains (a room referred to as the cabinet).[34] These séances would be held in a variety of settings—from people's homes to hotel rooms.

As we can see from the examples above, Spiritualism was intimately connected with entertainment and, because of this, it was just as intimately connected to fraud. Perhaps one of the more well-known and controversial mediums was Florence Cook, a young woman who held séances that generated full-fledged "apparitions" that were known to socialize with séance guests. Florence herself had a frequent guest apparition dubbed Katie King, who would appear and walk around the room. During one séance in 1880, a guest grabbed the apparition of Katie King after observing modern accessories under her muslin-like gown. Other guests searched the closet where Florence reportedly retreated to in order to manifest these apparitions, and found it absent of Florence's presence but filled with many of her discarded garments.[35] Florence Cook was not the only medium who performed acts of materializations, of course. She and other medium-entertainers helped boost the convictions of people who were eager to accept these acts as proof of the afterlife. They even drew the attention of renowned scientists who were eager to study their claims and examine any truthfulness that could be found for support of psychical phenomena. The Victorians embodied the phrase "I want to believe" long before Fox Mulder uttered his ubiquitous tagline.

Scientists who studied these mediums were interested, of course, in potential psychical phenomena, but they were also interested from a psychological perspective. Another well-known and controversial medium who drew the attention of the public and academic communities is Eusapia Palladino. Palladino was born in Italy in 1854 and was orphaned by age twelve. When she was thirteen years old she stayed with a local family. They reported that strange occurrences took place in Eusapia's presence, such as table-turnings and strange knocking sounds.[36] The family told the young girl that she could stay with them longer if she continued to perform these abilities for guests. During her séances, objects would be seen moving of their own accord, items would go missing only to be discovered later, and more of the strange knocks and rapping would continue. Soon, more and more people began attending Eusapia's séances, and she eventually grew to international fame. Eusapia soon become a professional medium and in 1888, Ercole Chiaia wrote to Cesare Lombroso, a renowned Italian criminologist and physician, imploring him to study the strange phenomena that surrounded Eusapia. Lombroso did not immediately reply to Chiaia's letter, but he eventually did meet and study Eusapia's abilities. It was this meeting that eventually brought Eusapia to the attention of seven scientists who met in Milan in 1892 to study her abilities further.[37] She was the center of even more studies in Poland, Rome, and Naples, which included scientists from various arenas of study, even zoology. These scientists were often left either convinced of supernatural ability or dubious of some sort of trickery and fraud.

One particular series of experiments were held at the home of French physiologist Charles Richet. Richet invited various other scientists, including researchers from England, Warsaw, and Germany. They made efforts to secure the hands of Eusapia during her séances and to have enough light to see if there were any trickery involving her legs and feet. During one such sitting, the scientists witnessed a melon levitate and float from a chair behind Eusapia and to the table in front of them. They admitted no ability to explain it other than supernatural abilities, though others, after reading

Figure 1.3. Eusapia Palladino
From Théodore Flournoy's *Spiritism & Psychology* (New York: Harper & Brothers, 1911).

the reports, proposed an alternative hypothesie that suggested Eusapia was a skilled magician and an expert in the sleight-of-hand.[38] Additional séances and tests were held, and scientists even went as far as holding the hands *and* feet of Eusapia as she somehow still exhibited supernatural ability. Her abilities seemed to cause a rift between these scientists, many of whom were members of the Society for Psychical Research, and accounts would seem to go back-and-forth on the genuineness of Eusapia's abilities. What was clear, however, was the need for tools beyond mere physical observation—tools that could measure things beyond the scope of the human eye and which were not susceptible to human fallibility and suggestion. In this way, then, the scrutiny of mediums helped advance the efforts of psychical researchers who were forced to evaluate their scientific methods.

As we can see, the actions of mediums drew the attention of scientists around the globe. In the United States, Robert Hare, a chemistry professor at the University of Pennsylvania, was an ardent denouncer of Spiritualism and set out to debunk the abilities of Daniel Dunglas Home. Hare developed a device that he called a "spiritscope," which he used to test the credibility of table-tipping. The spiritscope was a disc containing an arrow and all letters of the alphabet. The spiritscope would spin and rotate in the event that its balance was disturbed. Hare's thought process seemed to be that if table-tipping were merely a random bit of physical trickery, then the spiritscope would simply spell out nonsense. If there were more supernatural phenomena at play, the spiritscope would respond intelligently, being manipulated by the subtle motions of the table. When Hare implemented this spiritscope at Home's séances, he set it up in such a way that only Hare himself could view the device, thereby eliminating the chance of Home purposefully spelling out certain messages. What Hare discovered is that he not only received intelligent responses, but he also discovered that he was able to seemingly influence the board himself, making him wonder about his own medium-like abilities. Hare wrote a book about this device and his experiments after being convinced that there was more to Spiritualism than meets the eye, and but unfortunately, he was mocked and discredited by his peers. He even

Figure 1.4. One of Robert Hare's Séance Devices
From S. R. Morgan's *Index to Psychic Science* (Swarthmore, 1950): PD US not renewed

attempted to discuss his research on the spiritscope at a conference of the American Association for the Advancement of Science in 1854, but he was mocked there as well and shortly after resigned his post at the university.[39]

Hare wasn't the only researcher who wrote about experiments on the physical phenomena present at séances. In France, Count Agenor de Gasparin conducted a series of experiments on table-tipping and determined that he could not replicate the type of tippings that occurred during popular séances. He never indicated *what* might be making the tables tip, and instead merely wrote an 1854 manuscript about how his experiments failed to replicate the phenomena. Marc Thury, a physics professor in Geneva, expanded upon Gasparin's work and conducted similar experiments that came to the same conclusion: he was unable to replicate the table-tippings that occurred in séances. Thury, however, went a bit further than Gasparin and proposed the idea of a "psychode," or "[the ability of the mind to act on material objects]."[40] These examples help illustrate that for many, Spiritualism was simply a form of entertainment. Indeed, there were many who staunchly opposed the idea that there could be anything *except* entertainment at play. There were others, however, who saw an opportunity to investigate the psychological and supernatural aspects of this movement. As I mention above, the blatant fraud that occurred during this time helped pave the way for the next era of paranormal inquiry because it revealed the necessity of more nuanced tools for researchers hoping to obtain objective evidence of strange phenomena. Spiritualism, while perhaps the most controversial point on the parapsychological timeline, deserves inclusion because of this fact as well as because it advanced the research of mediumistic ability and the inquiry into life after death.

To help wrap-up our discussion of Spiritualism, researcher John Beloff reminds us that there are two eras. The first is filled with concern regarding the legitimacy of physical manifestations, like the aforementioned tests that sought to debunk Eusapia Palladino. The second, however, is marked by a focus on the messages imparted by mediums and the implication that those messages could indicate evidence of life after death.[41] Beloff lists Daniel Dunglas Home as the forerunner of the physical mediumship era, while the medium who marks the

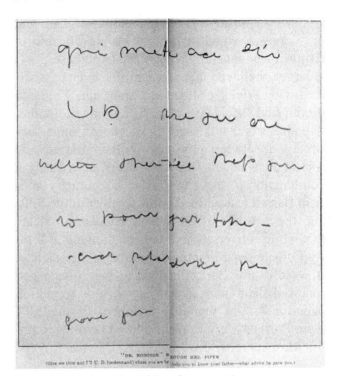

Figure 1.5. Automatic Writing of Leonora Piper
From Théodore Flournoy's *Spiritism & Psychology* (New York: Harper & Brothers, 1911).

shift from physical to mental mediumship is Leonora Piper. Piper attracted the attention of psychical researcher William James in 1884. She became a test subject of the Society for Psychical Research (SPR). Let's now take a closer look at the SPR, a group of scholars who, spurred not only by the onset of Spiritualism, set out to scientifically investigate psychical phenomena.

THE RISE OF THE SOCIETY FOR PSYCHICAL RESEARCH AND A GLOBAL FASCINATION WITH PARAPSYCHOLOGY (1882–1935)

The Society for Psychical Research was founded in England in 1882. During this time period, "late Victorian England was plunged into the fateful aftermath of the Darwinian doctrine" and many of SPR's founders were perhaps attracted to the study of psychical phenomena because of "the hope it offered of a universe that might not, after all, be the soulless machine which the new scientific materialism was propagating."[42] Their philosophy, as outlined in their publication titled *Journal of the Society for Psychical Research*, is defined as such: "To examine without prejudice or prepossession and in a scientific spirit those faculties of man, real or supposed, which appear to be inexplicable in terms of any generally recognized hypotheses."[43] It is largely believed that a group of scholars associated with Trinity College in Cambridge, England, established the idea for the SPR, though another hypothesis is that the society was born from a conversation between physicist William Barrett and a journalist named Dawson Rogers. It is likely a combination of these two, as in his obituary William Barrett is described as the founder of the SPR, and the writings of other SPR members indicate that while conversations had been brewing at Trinity College regarding the formation of this society, it wasn't until Barrett arrived at the college and renewed their interest that any serious formation occurred.[44] The founding members of the SPR were Barrett, Mary Boole, Edmund Gurney, Stainton Moses, Frederic W. H. Myers, Dawson Rogers, Henry Sidgwick, and Hensleigh Wedgwood. Interestingly, Mary Boole resigned from the council after only six months, citing her reason for doing so as "being the only lady on Council,"[45] which is curious, but no further explanation has been given. Fortunately, though, there are other prominent women in the early history of the SPR, such as Eleanor Sidgwick. Eleanor's husband, Harry, became the first president of the SPR and together they have been described as extremely influential components of the SPR's founding.[46]

Some of the earliest studies of SPR involved inquiries into thought transference. Experiments were set up involving cards, patterns, and even geometric shapes to see if one person could send an impression to another. Interestingly, these early experiments also studied how those impressions were received—for example, did the receiver seem to obtain messages with an *image* or a *word* that

Figure 1.6. Trinity College: It is largely believed that a group of scholars associated with Trinity College in Cambridge established the idea for the British SPR

From Robert Willis' *The Architectural History of the University of Cambridge, and of the Colleges of Cambridge and Eton*, vol. 2. (Cambridge University Press: 1886): CC PD Mark via WikiCommons

popped into the mind?[47] Other early inquiries focused on clairvoyance, haunted houses, dreams, coincidences, and gathering eyewitness testimonies. The proceedings of their first studies, published the same year in which they were founded, not only brought with it the creation of the word "telepathy," but also a philosophical discussion of the infancy of scientific psychical research and the difficulties the field faced in the absence of any precedent or guidelines.[48] One year later, in 1883, the SPR had amassed more than ten thousand pages of evidence into the aforementioned phenomena.

In 1885, Eleanor Sidgwick published a report titled "Notes on the Evidence, Collected by the Society, for Phantasms of the Dead," in which she outlines types of hauntings and ghost experiences.[49] It is one of the earliest comprehensive surveys of these phenomena and yielded lots of information. For example, she discovered, through her own work collecting ghost stories, that there are vastly different types of experiences—some people witness apparitions of those still living. Other people see apparitions of those long dead. Part of her research also included weeding out instances of outright fraud and/or exaggeration, considering things like people's vision and environmental factors that could perhaps lead to hallucinations. Her research also included surveys of haunted houses in Europe and India. She discovered that the age of a home has no real bearing on likelihood of haunting experience. Furthermore, she discovered that ghosts are seen just as often in the daytime, and that most encounters seem to be random instead of on a looping, predictable schedule.[50]

All this work led to SPR's first manuscript, *Phantasms of the Living*, published in 1886. This work, penned by Edmund Gurney, F. W. H. Myers, and Frank Podmore, includes case studies and instances of telepathy, hypnosis, and extrasensory perception. It outlines various experiments and methods that people used to communicate telepathically. The authors discuss the statistical probabilities of phenomena occurring simply at random and assert that the overwhelming number of telepathic experiences points to its existence. They stop short, however, of positing *how* these phenomena occur, going only as far to say that these phenomena seem to suggest that the mind and brain are two separate entities.[51]

Following this, the SPR organized a Census of Hallucinations, an international survey that sought to compile not just experiences of hallucinations but also the likelihood of hallucinations being the result of misidentification or sheer coincidence.[52] A few years after this report was published, F. W. H. Myers's posthumous work *Human Personality and its Survival of Bodily Death* is published and the organization continued their early work of sifting through fraudulent or exaggerated reports and attempted to develop a baseline of empirical evidentiary practices.[53]

The interest in psychical phenomena had already spread to other parts of the world, and in 1885, an American branch of the SPR was founded by psychologist William James. SPR's early work focused on gathering reports of experiences on telepathy, haunting experiences, investigation of mediums, and establishing techniques for studying these types of phenomena. Once some groundwork had been laid, an era of experimentation began. SPR researcher Renée Haynes tells us that "during the first decades of the twentieth century, the Society's intense interest in apparitions and phantasms diminished, to be outshone by interest in the psychology, the data, and the implications of mediumship."[54] Eleanor Sidgwick published a new edition of *Phantasms of the Dead* in 1918 and for a while, the society focused on amassing data through small-scale studies. In addition to medium studies, the SPR also began branching into consciousness studies. For example, the British physicist George Tyrell experimented with consciousness and various ways to induce altered states. While Tyrell was conducting these experiments in England, the scientific exploration of psi phenomena, which refers to events of or relating to a psychic nature in the United States blossomed under the leadership of J. B. Rhine. In 1947, the society sent out another survey on hallucinations in an attempt to supplement the data from the original survey, and they discovered that these experiences continued to happen just as frequently.[55]

Many works discussing the history of parapsychology naturally spend a great deal of time discussing the SPR. While this group is touted as the first organization formally created to scientifically study psychical phenomena, the United Kingdom was far from the *only* country scientifically concerned with it. Many countries, in addition to the United Kingdom, were grappling with notions of psychical science at the turn of the nineteenth century, and others began independently investigating these notions even earlier, such as Germany's Franz Mesmer. It is a German, in fact, by the name of Max Dessoir who coins the phrase "parapsychology" that was later popularized by the American J. B. Rhine.[56] In France, Charles Richet was a forerunner of the psychical research movement, while Germany's Hans Driesch and the United States' William James led their country's efforts in this field.[57] This section provides a brief overview of international psychical research, both historic and modern, so that you can begin to understand the global interest in and contributions to parapsychology. This section is not an exhaustive treatise on the international contributions to the field, but for additional inclusion of an international scope, you can find more information in chapters 2 and 3.

In addition to the British SPR, the Institut Métaphysique International (International Metaphysics Institute) was also an early and respected research organization. Founded in France in 1919 by Jean Meyer and Gustave Geley, its first president was the aforementioned physiologist Charles Richet.[58] France was a forerunner of psychological research in the nineteenth century, especially in regard to abnormal psychology and hypnotism. Professor Régine Plas tells us that early psychological research in France focused on experimental psychology, sometimes referred to as the "pathological method."[59] These early psychologists discovered that hypnotism had very interesting psychological implications and it became the basis for many of these early experiments. Thus, Plas points out that "in this context, their early works, though satisfying all scientific criteria, surprise the contemporary reader, for they seem more closely linked with parapsychology than to psychology as we know it today."[60] Additionally, French psychological research organizations founded at this time, including the Institut Métaphysique International, often included founding members who openly investigated psi phenomena.

As we know, Charles Richet was a member of the British SPR, but he was also a seminal figure in the creation of the Society of Physiological Psychology in 1885, about thirty years prior to the creation of the Institut Métapsychique International. One of the case studies of this society involved a woman named Léonie. She exhibited, while placed in a hypnotic state, an ability to read people's minds and guess the contents of sealed envelopes. Researchers also later discovered that, while in these states, Léonie exhibited three distinct personalities, and one of her main researchers became convinced that while her abilities were curious, there was some deeper mental pathology at play—one which was brought to light when hypnosis was applied. Early experiments of psychical researchers, then, had the unintended consequence of revealing more about our minds than we have ever known before, and for that reason alone, psi researchers play a significant role in the history of psychology.[61] For a brief period of time it appeared that psychical researchers and traditional psychologists were working peacefully side by side, but nonetheless the Society for Physiological Psychology disbanded in 1890 when the notion that the subconscious was largely responsible for psi phenomena took hold.

From this period on, psychical research was not considered a legitimate subset of psychology, and various instances of fraud amid mediums of the time certainly did not help its case. France saw a rise in Spiritualism in the post–World War I era, though, which helped revive interest in the 1919 formation of the Institut Métaphysique International. This revived interest saw an increased focus of using preestablished scientific methods applied to psychical phenomena, mostly involving the abilities of mediums.[62] In fact, one of the more controversial (and perhaps entertaining) moments in psychical history emanated from one of the institute's founding members, Gustave Geley. Geley, in the course of his work with Polish medium Franek Kluski, created "ectoplasmic mouldings" of hands and feet that would mysteriously appear at Kluski's séances.[63] The veracity of those moldings has been largely discredited, but in the years since this incident, the work of the institute continues today through conferences and supporting research endeavors.

The divide between the psychical and psychological was not just limited to France. Dr. Heather Wolffram outlines the debates between animism and spiritism that were occurring simultaneously in Germany.[64] Debates in Germany seemed to center around whether the field of psychology should focus *only* on waking consciousness, since it's much easier to objectively and physiologically study, versus states of unconsciousness like hypnotism, in which the category of mediums fell. These debates were exacerbated when physicist Johann Karl Friedrich Zöllner joined forces with his colleagues to conduct experiments with Henry Slade, a notorious American medium. Through these experiments, in which Slade produced physical phenomena much akin to those described earlier in this chapter, Zöllner was convinced that the phenomena were a result of "beings occupying a fourth dimension,"[65] and used this claim as the foundation to advocate for a new science called transcendental physics. Zöllner's claim created a lot of backlash, most notably from Germany's leader of experimental psychology, Wilhelm Wundt, who decreed that any legitimate psychological science *must* relegate itself to "ordinary states of consciousness."[66] This response was an attempt to distance the new, growing field of psychology from Zöllner's claims and to establish some form of academic boundaries.

While this Wundt-Zöllner debate raged on, another was raging between scientists regarding the boundaries of psychology. In 1885, the philosopher Eduard von Hartmann published *Der Spiritismus (Spiritism)*, in which he offered shared hallucination as an explanation for the phenomena that so often occurred in séances. This work provoked the editor of the spiritist publication *Psychische Studien (Psychical Studies)*, Alexander Aksakof, who wrote two volumes arguing against von Hartmann's theory. Aksakof's response even decried a field of experimental psychology that was dominated by materialism, such as that espoused by Wilhelm Wundt. The most ironic part of this is that Hartmann wasn't saying that psychical (or even physical) phenomena weren't possible or didn't have a place within the field of psychology. He was merely saying that the idea of phenomena being the result of anything beyond the faculties of a living person's unconsciousness was the problem.[67]

Where Hartmann differs from Wundt, however, is that Wundt dismissed certain phenomena as outright fraud while Hartmann theorized that they occurred due to a natural, yet undiscovered, human ability. Furthermore, Hartmann's arguments created a bridge between the attitudes of the academy and the general public in regard to psi phenomena. He believed that society in general needed (and would benefit) from public, academic inquiries into these topics. He even stated that it was the government's duty to temper the public's fanatical beliefs in the occult with scientific data. Wolffram sums up Hartmann's attitude best:

> Hartmann argued that while an epidemic belief in spirits was dangerous because it promoted gullibility and fanaticism and provided multiple opportunities for swindlers, the a priori rejection of such phenomena advocated by Enlightenment dogmatists also represented a form of superficiality and lack of criticalness that did nothing to address this problem.[68]

Aksakof, in his response to Hartmann's theories, did not necessarily reject the idea that séance phenomena were partially due to the unconscious abilities of the medium. Aksakof simply took this a step further and stated that it was a combination of the medium's natural abilities (personism) with "unconscious psychical phenomena . . . beyond the limits of the medium's body," (animism).[69] These two things worked in tandem with "spiritism" (intelligence from the spirit world). In Aksakof's view, psychical phenomena required all three things to be present.

While Hartmann and Aksakof continued debating with one another, philosopher Carl du Prel entered the scene. du Prel was a founder of Psychologische Gesellschaft (Psychological Society), the first German society dedicated to psychical research. Another early psychical organization, based out of Berlin, was the Gesellschaft für Experimental-Psychologie (Society for Experimental Psychology). These two research groups existed during the same time, and both had a mission of studying psychology in more than simply a physiological way. Both groups, then, included psychical phenomena as an important category of inquiry. What's interesting, however, is that the same tensions as discussed above existed in these groups as well, with some researchers believing wholeheartedly in spiritism and others adhering to a theory of natural, yet misunderstood powers of a living person's unconscious. Even though these groups sometimes differed even among their own members, they all agreed that the accepted psychology being espoused by the universities was too narrow and restrictive. The above organizations, existing outside the formal boundary of the academy, had much more freedom to incorporate a multidisciplinary outlook to the psychical. Researchers like Wolffram point out that these multiple dividing points shed fascinating light on the birth and growth of both psychology and parapsychology in Germany.

A rather interesting stop on the historic international timeline of parapsychology takes us to Japan. Professor Miki Takasuna tells us that Spiritualism in Japan came in two waves, which is not unlike the situation in other countries.[70] The first wave, lasting about twenty years, was marked mainly by the practice of hypnotism. Psi was also seen as entertaining in Japan, primarily through a Ouija-like game called *kokkuri-san*. The emergence of female mediums known as *itako* was also seen during this first wave—these itako were typically blind women primarily consulted for health questions. Interestingly, hypnotism fell squarely in the realm of legitimate psychotherapy techniques in Japan, the only debate seeming to be whether it should be encouraged among lay practitioners. The second wave of Spiritualism in Japan occurred in the early 1900s and was marked by a growing interest in psychical research. In fact, many psychical publications were created at this time, and newspapers often included discussions about psi phenomena or synopses of research from the SPR.[71]

During the second wave of Spiritualism, Japan's preeminent parapsychologist emerged, Tomokichi Fukurai, who was influenced by the work of William James. He began studying hypnotism after graduating from Tokyo Imperial University with a psychology degree. Fukurai went on to complete a dissertation on the research behind hypnosis at the same university and two years later became a faculty member of abnormal psychology. Shortly thereafter he published *Saimin shinrigaku* (Hypnotic Psychology), which was considered "to be the only scientific textbook on hypnosis in existence"[72] until the 1940s. While teaching, he also conducted studies on various psychical phenomena like clairvoyance, even coining the word "thoughtography" due to one test subject's apparent ability to mentally transfer an image on film. One of Fukurai's test subjects was Chizuko Mifune, a young woman who had been hypnotized by her brother, during which he implanted the belief that she was clairvoyant. Her abilities persisted even beyond those sessions

and began to draw attention. In one of their early experiments in 1910, Mifune correctly guessed the entire wording of 65 percent of small pieces of paper tucked inside tin cans. She went on to participate in additional experiments where she continued to display telepathic abilities, though not everyone was convinced there was not some fraudulent behavior. Unfortunately, Mifune committed suicide one short year later, and some have suggested that public criticism of her abilities played a role in this.

Fukurai had additional clairvoyant test subjects, including Ikuko Nagao, Sadako Takahashi, and Koichi Mita. Nagao was the first subject who claimed the ability of mentally transcribing images onto undeveloped film. Various experiments seemed to be successful, but she came under intense scrutiny when, similar to Mifune's case, Nagao claimed she could only perform successfully when left alone in the room. Fukarai's work with Nagao marked the beginning of his academic downfall and a growing skepticism among the general public toward psychical phenomena.[73]

At this point, colleagues attempt to persuade Fukurai away from psychical research, and when he didn't heed their call, he was placed on leave in 1913. A new chair of psychology was appointed, who called upon the university to "regain lost credibility"[74] by only focusing on objective psychological issues. Here again we see a philosophical divide on the accepted boundaries of psychological research. In fact, Takasuna tells us that "Fukurai's ousting was part of the process of modernizing psychology in Japan, to declare psychology a science and to distinguish between authentic psychological research and the pseudoscience of parapsychology."[75] Even though Fukurai was removed from his academic post, he continued psychical research on his own, and even attended conferences where he gave presentations. The Tohoku Psychical Research Society was founded in his honor in 1960, and today is now an institution called Fukurai Institute of Psychology, which, among other things, offers lectures on parapsychology.[76] Additionally, the Japanese Society for Parapsychology, founded in 1968, publishes the *Japanese Journal of Parapsychology*, holds annual conferences, and promotes research.[77]

The next stop on this overview takes us from Japan to the Netherlands. In her 2012 article, Ingrid Kloosterman discusses the history of parapsychology in the Netherlands and reminds us of that country's unique contributions to the field. In fact, Kloosterman tells us that the world's first academic chair of a parapsychology program was the Dutch parapsychologist Willhelm Tenhaeff, who taught at Utrecht University.[78] Two figures were key in the early development of the Netherland's relationship with parapsychology. Psychiatrist Frederik van Eeden gave lectures to the SPR in England, while psychologist Gerard Heymans established, in 1892, the Netherland's first psychical laboratory. Heymans also became the first president of the Dutch Society for Psychical Research after it was founded in 1920. In 1892, he established his laboratory and in 1920 conducted well-known tests on telepathy. Heymans was a professor at Groningen University, which means that this academic affiliation with psychical research predates America's J. B. Rhine by about ten years, leading some to posit that Heyman's research was the earliest psychical research "to be carried out under university auspices."[79] Then, in the 1930s, Wilhelm Tenhaeff begins work at Utrecht University and is appointed chair of parapsychology in 1953. This program existed in various fashions until 2006 when it was abolished at Utrecht University. However, members of the Dutch SPR collaborated with the University for Humanistics in Utrecht to create an "exceptional human experiences" program which exists still today.[80] In the case of the Netherlands, then, "Dutch parapsychology managed to retain a foothold on academic ground even after the 1920s."[81]

In Spain, researchers were closely following (and sometimes working with) French psychical researchers. The zeitgeist of spiritualism had made its way to Spain, and in the second half of the nineteenth century, a growing number of groups and publications formed to discuss psi phenomena. Like in many other countries, however, there were differing schools of thought when it came to the place of psychical research within society. The psychologist Emili Mira i López was especially critical of commercial mediumship, because it created confusion among the general public in regard to the differences between Spiritualism and scientific psychical research.[82]

An intriguing case of telepathy from Spain involved the son of the Marquis of Santa Cara. The marquis' son, Joaqúin, apparently developed the ability of metasomoscopy, or the ability to see through metal containers, which he used to intuit the objects within. He gained the attention of psychical researchers in 1922, and soon the idea developed that Joaqúin was able to see through solid objects by using a special band of vision he could produce. In 1924, Joaqúin and the marquis visited researchers at the American SPR where they were put to the test by none other than Harry Houdini. Houdini, who was employed by the American SPR, would put his knowledge of illusion and sleight-of-hand to ferret out fraudulent instances of psychical ability. Houdini was unconvinced that Joaqúin's abilities were genuine, however, and even expressed his dubiousness to the newspapers.[83]

The above examples represent merely a glimpse into the international scope of parapsychological history. A desire to scientifically understand the phenomena that seemed to explode on the scene with the rise of Spiritualism affected researchers across the globe. At the same time, the field of psychology as a new science was just entering the scene and trying to navigate its new place within the academy. Naturally, tensions often rose between those who viewed psychical research as a subset of psychology, while others adamantly refused to believe that psi research had any relevancy. Tensions even arose among members of the same institutions, illustrating that this time period was a confusing and constantly evolving era marked by the struggle to create clear boundaries of accepted science *and* a growing fascination among the general public about the reality of supernatural phenomena. Additional discussions of the international contributions to parapsychology can be found in chapters 2 and 3 as well as appendix C.

J. B. RHINE, THE DUKE PARAPSYCHOLOGY LABS, AND THE PARAPSYCHOLOGICAL ASSOCIATION (1935–1957)

Joseph Banks (J. B.) Rhine was an American botanist who founded the Duke Parapsychology Labs in 1930 at Duke University in North Carolina. His colleagues and cofounders include William McDougall, Dr. Helge Lundholm, and Dr. Karl Zener.[84] Motivated by the curious dismissal within the academy to study psychical phenomena, Rhine and his colleagues set out to study all manner of extrasensory perception. Rhine's wife, Dr. Louisa Rhine, also studied psi phenomena and went on to author several books and scholarly articles on this topic. Early studies at the Duke Parapsychology Labs focused on hypnotism, and whether students displayed heightened telepathic abilities while hypnotized. These initial studies, which weren't overwhelmingly successful, transitioned to all manner of experiments designed to study psi. For example, Rhine and Zener collaborated to create a deck of cards known still today as Zener cards. These cards contain a mixture of different symbols (circle, square, star, squiggly line, and plus sign). Study participants would enter a room that included only a table, chairs, and this deck of cards. One person would pull a card and attempt to telepathically send the image to the other person. Rhine and Zener, in the course of establishing this experiment, determined that the probability of correct guesses being due to chance were 5 in 25, and thus used this marker as a control to test for significant results. They launched a large-scale study using these cards in 1931 and discovered that the average correct guess rate of participants was 6.5 of 25, odds that they calculated were 1 in 250,000. Student Hubert Pearce once heard about Rhine's studies and attempted the cards himself, correctly guessed twenty-five cards in a row, eliciting a response from Rhine that it was the most phenomenal feat he had witnessed.[85]

Considered by many to be the "Father of Modern Parapsychology," throughout his research career, Rhine and the Duke Parapsychology Labs had, after only ten years, created thirty-three different experiments that included at least one million trials. A large part of these experiments involved eliminating the potential for sensory bias. For example, in the Zener card scenario above, to help eliminate any bias between participants, one variant of this test is to place people behind physical barriers or in completely separate rooms. Of the thirty-three experiments Rhine helped develop and implement, twenty-seven of them yielded statistically significant results. These experiments have also been replicated by other unaffiliated scientists who have discovered significant results.[86]

In June 1957, at the behest of Rhine, the Parapsychological Association was founded.[87] This international organization exists to scientifically examine

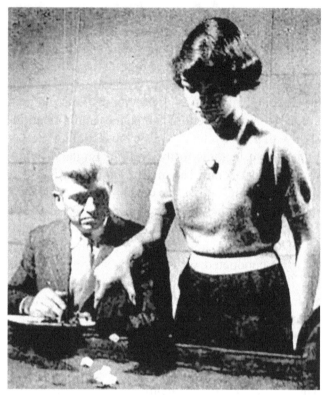

Figure 1.7. J. B. Rhine Oversees a Psychical Experiment Using Dice
From: Aldous Huxley, "A Case For ESP, PK and Psi," *Life Magazine* (January 11, 1954). PD US not renewed

psi phenomena, collaborate on research, and publish findings in both the scholarly literature and to the general public. On their website you can even find a list of universities that offer educational programs relating to psi topics.[88] Rhine continued his research until retirement in 1965, at which time the Duke Parapsychology Labs were disbanded. Researchers continued the work begun at the Duke Parapsychology Labs and in 1965 Rhine established the Foundation for Research on the Nature of Man, which eventually became the Rhine Research Center—an organization that still exists today.[89]

CRITICISMS OF PARAPSYCHOLOGY AND MODERN RELATIONSHIP WITH THE ACADEMY

As we just learned, parapsychology and the study of psychical phenomena have been wrought with criticism and tension that have played out on an international scale. Much of this tension existed between the academy and unaffiliated researchers, both vying for their opinion on what accepted scientific endeavor should look like. Andreas Sommer, in an article published by the *History of Human Sciences*, reminds us that psychology was a fledgling scientific discipline at the turn of the nineteenth century.[90] This, of course, was the same time that saw the formation of both the British and American branches of the SPR. This time period also saw the sweeping popularity of Spiritualism and mediumship, much of which involved blatant fraudulent activities interspersed with curious, unexplainable phenomena. Sommer notes that it is often a conveniently misplaced fact that the father of American psychology, William James, was an ardent believer and researcher of psychical phenomena. James advocated for bringing psychical phenomena such as extrasensory perception, into the broader arena of psychology, while others, like Wilhelm Wundt (German psychologist and founder of experimental psychology), adamantly denounced psychical phenomena as having any place within the psychological academic arena. Sommer tells us that this tension between psychical science and psychology is even more ironic since early psychical researchers helped pave the way for psychological advancement. For example, psychical researchers "contributed important empirical findings by conducting the first experiments investigating the psychology of eyewitness testimony . . . and empirical and conceptual studies illuminating mechanisms of dissociation and hypnotism."[91] Sommer tells us that this divide was so deeply entrenched during the formation of American psychology that some psychologists latched onto an antipsychical research stance to help form a psychological identity. In other words, they latched on to this attitude to help define the borders of accepted psychological science.

These divisive attitudes were so pervasive that some psychologists set out with a personal mission of debunking certain studies by psychical researchers in order to claim victory over the boundaries of this emerging discipline. For example, Hugo Münsterberg (a student of Wilhem Wundt), set out to expose Eusapia Palladino as a fraud and Andreas Sommer tells us that these efforts "have been celebrated as victories of American scientific psychology over psychical research."[92] Münsterberg's efforts, in other words, were seminal in furthering the academic divide between psychology and psychical science. Readers interested in learning just how vitriolic this divide was need only look for the correspondence between William James and Hugo Münsterberg, which lasted well into the twentieth century. It wasn't until 1969 that parapsychology was even recognized as a field of study by the American Association for the Advancement of Science.[93] In this way, parapsychology still remains a new and emerging science trying to find its foothold within the academy.

Figure 1.8. An early séance laboratory, 1926
From: Harry Price. "A Model Psychic Laboratory." Journal of Psychical Research (Vol. 1, No. 1, May–June, 1926). PD US not renewed

It is also worth noting that criticism even came from within and among psychical researchers themselves. Some researchers were quick to point out that since there was no formal training or recognized mechanism through which verified psychical techniques could be taught, this left even the researchers themselves susceptible to incompetence at best and fraud at worst.[94] And while we know that an early aim of the SPR was to ferret out instances of paranormal fraud, this shows that doubt and skepticism were a cornerstone of the emerging science of psychical research. Other early psychical researchers thought that efforts to integrate this new science within the academy was a waste of time, given the sheer amount of backlash that existed. They proposed merely carrying on with their own research without academic affiliation.[95]

Controversy and criticism of psychical research's modern equivalent, parapsychology, still continue today. Even Spiritualism itself has only recently been discussed as an important cultural component of the Victorian era. For example, "In 1998 Alison Winter was one of the first cultural historians to

Figure 1.9. Debunking a Card-Guessing Experiment
From: A. J. Lorraine, "What is There in Telepathy?" *Popular Science* (July 1920).

write about mesmerism as something essential to Victorian culture, instead of as an interesting but marginal oddity."[96]

Most critics of parapsychology today claim that it is nothing more than a pseudoscience masquerading as research adhering to scientific methods. A large point of contention to this debate holds that parapsychologists always have an explanation for "null results."[97] In other words, when an experiment fails to produce evidence of psi phenomena, some criteria is pointed to as simply not being psi-conducive. Another point that critics adhere to is an overall low number of experiments with significant positive indications of psi phenomena. And while some researchers acknowledge that psi data may not be profuse and overwhelming, critics always seem to forget the fact that there have been experiments that yielded positive results.[98]

Perhaps the most well-known and outspoken modern critic of parapsychology is the Committee for the Scientific Investigation of Claims of the Paranormal.[99] Scientists and researchers noticed, in the 1970s, a growing popularity and interest in the paranormal—so much interest, in fact, that the academic community saw fit to create a committee in 1976 that could contribute scientifically to this growing interest. They espouse, like some others in the historical timeline, a responsibility to promote advanced critical thinking when it comes to the paranormal. The committee publishes an international journal, the *Skeptical Inquirer*, and has contributed thousands of articles of inquiry into paranormal topics. It doesn't just relegate itself to the academic arena, either. In fact, it's largely concerned with educating the general public about the science of the paranormal. For example, the committee has called out *Readers Digest* and NBC for publishing pseudoscientific information. It also critiques and points out weaknesses in scientific methodologies, which is the crux of its frustration as concerns parapsychological research within the academy. And while it has been accused of being a scientific vigilante, it stands by its claim that it's less concerned about the subject matter and more concerned about the quality of methodologies.[100] It is, perhaps, the modern manifestation of that historical tension between those fighting to draw the boundaries of acceptable science.

Overall, today's relationship of parapsychology and the academy seems to at least be better than it was at the turn of the nineteenth century. Antiparapsychology attitudes are still very much present, but there is a robust and growing body of literature that focuses on psi phenomena. In fact, there are a number of universities today where you can enroll in parapsychological programs or study various aspects of the paranormal. The University of Edinburgh, for example, houses the Koestler Parapsychology Unit within their School of Psychology. The University of Greenwich in the United Kingdom offers programs on anomalistic psychology and parapsychology. Lund University in Sweden has a Center for Research on Consciousness and Anomalous Psychology, and the University of Colorado houses the Psibotics Lab. These are merely three examples—you can also find academic parapsychological opportunities in Germany, France, the Czech Republic, Hungary, Italy, Sweden, the United States, and Australia.[101]

Additionally, you can find research about parapsychological phenomena in all varieties of scholarly journals, including the *British Journal of Psychology*, the *Journal of Abnormal Psychology*, the *Journal of Scientific Exploration, Sociology of Religion*, and the *Journal of Near-Death Studies*. Prominent scholarly databases such as SocINDEX, ProQuest Dissertations and Theses, PsycARTICLES, and Academic Search Complete all contain citations to additional journals that discuss various psychical phenomena. Additionally, there are countless scholarly books that discuss both the theories of and science behind parapsychological phenomena. Today, there are more and more scientists willing to research these topics and admit that a bias toward materialist philosophy keeps us, perhaps, from knowing more about the strange connections between consciousness, the mind, and the physical world.

WHAT THE RESEARCH POINTS TO TODAY

Parapsychological research continues today and fortunately shows no indication of stopping. Some of the most compelling evidence, in my opinion, comes from near-death studies, though this is certainly not the only subject that parapsychologists study. Other topics include extrasensory perception, poltergeist activity, haunted houses, ghosts, psychokinesis, and much more. The crux of the research always seems to point back to the question of consciousness surviving beyond bodily death, and it seems that science has repeatedly illustrated that consciousness transcends the boundaries of our physical bodies. In this section, I briefly touch on some modern psi research to help reveal the current state of the field. As with all sections, you will find more on what is mentioned in this section later in this work, particularly in chapter 3.

Dr. Pim van Lommel is a Dutch cardiologist who has spent more than twenty years studying the near-death experiences of his patients. What I find most compelling about Dr. van Lommel heard his patients discussing strange experiences, and decided to put these experiences to the test, and created controlled environments with qualified medical practitioners to begin gathering data.[102] This study was eventually published in *The Lancet,* a scholarly and prestigious medical journal. The crux of that study centered around the statement that "the current materialistic view of the relationship between the brain and consciousness held by most physicians, philosophers and psychologists is too restricted for a proper understanding of this phenomena."[103]

Dr. Dean Radin is another modern figure in the world of parapsychology. He is the chief scientist at the Institute of Noetic Science (IONS), an organization whose mission "is to reveal the interconnected nature of reality through scientific exploration and personal discovery."[104] In other words, IONS is dedicated to using principles of science to understand phenomena that is experienced but not yet understood. One study that Dr. Radin and colleagues undertook examined the effect of healing intentions on water. In this study, they discovered that focusing healing intention on water affected its hydrogen-oxygen covalent bond. Furthermore, this bond was also affected when distilled water was placed in a small container and worn around the neck of a practitioner delivering a healing practice to a patient.[105] The authors indicate, of course, that more research is needed, but that initial studies seem to indicate that conscious intent somehow impacts the physical world around us.

Another modern scholar is Dr. Jeffrey Kripal. He examines the intersection of mysticism, consciousness, and supernatural phenomena. Dr. Kripal is the associate dean of humanities at Rice University and the chair of philosophy and religious thought.[106] He coauthored a book in 2016 with UFO-experiencer Whitley Strieber in which they discuss the philosophy behind the supernatural. In this work, they argue that our world is inherently a supernatural one, and they "address the major materialist concerns that are so often at the heart of paranormal criticism . . . and provide a wide range of philosophical and practical arguments advocating . . . that the paranormal . . . has been part of our world all along."[107]

Concerning haunting phenomena, an extremely interesting article by a group of seven authors from Australia, Portugal, the United Kingdom, and the United States proposes the existence of "Haunted People Syndrome (HP-S)."[108] The authors state that this syndrome occurs when people "invoke labels of ghosts or other supernatural agencies to explain a specific set of anomalous events that are perceived recurrently."[109] These anomalous events can include both subjective and objective events, and takes into consideration the role that culture plays in informing the subjective nature of a paranormal experience. Furthermore, the authors comment that HP-S seems to be triggered by "the right people in the right settings."[110] This article combines social science and psychology with psi phenomena, offering a multifaceted explanation for why and how people experience and interpret paranormal phenomena.

Concerning both haunted houses and mediums, researcher Michaeleen C. Maher conducted an interesting study at a General Wayne Inn in Pennsylvania rumored to be haunted.[111] Maher asked three people who identified themselves as "sensitive" to walk through the property of a haunted inn and, using provided floorplans, mark where they sensed an apparition. Maher then asked three people who did not identify as sensitive to do the same thing. In addition, Maher provided a list of phenomena that occurred at this property and interspersed it with phenomena that had never been reported. Without indicating that any of the items on that list were made up, she asked all participants to mark which phenomena they sensed had occurred on the location. The results indicated that one of the sensitives significantly and correctly identified both the locations and the phenomena. As a total group, all three sensitives showed an indication of correct indications, whereas the control group showed no significant indication to either location of ghosts reported or phenomena. Maher muses, in this article, whether the ability of sensitives to correctly identify locations and phenomena were markers of picking up on past experiences of those working and visiting the inn *or* if perhaps it indicates a genuine ability to intuit spirits.

A fascinating example of modern parapsychological research emanates from Brazil. In 2019, a group of researchers at the University of São Paulo and the Universidade Federal de Juiz de Fora joined forces to investigate the curious case of medium Francisco (Chico) Cândido Xavier.[112] Xavier, who was born in rural Brazil in 1910, claimed to have the ability of psychography, which is the mediumistic phenomena of writing under the influence of nonliving persons. In other words, Xavier would write and claim that these writings were coming to him from psychical impressions of dead people. During his lifetime, he wrote more than 450 books and penned an estimated ten thousand personal letters all attributed to

the influence of spirits. Interestingly, Xavier did not take payment for any of these works even though his books were translated into ten languages and sold millions of copies, instead choosing to donate his royalties to charity. As you can imagine, many people have analyzed Xavier's writings, looking for examples that indicate either proof or fraud. Researchers analyzed a selection of poems, for example, that Xavier attributed to well-known deceased poets and concluded that Xavier's writings indicated an advanced and sophisticated level of literary understanding that Xavier did not seem to possess. Other studies analyzing Xavier's writings came to similar conclusions.[113]

The group of researchers from the aforementioned universities set out to analyze the content of thirteen letters Xavier wrote and attributed to one spirit in particular, that of José Roberto Pereira da Silva, an eighteen-year-old who passed away in 1972. They analyzed all thirteen letters and identified ninety-nine points that could be used as "verifiable information"[114]—information that could not be deduced by fraud, chance, or accessible public or private data. Of these thirteen letters, they selected one letter to focus on and created rankings that listed the likelihood of certain verifiable information being known to Xavier. The letter they chose was one of the very first written to da Silva's family, thereby mitigating any contact between the medium and the family. In interviews with da Silva's family, researchers discovered some curious points within the letter: the fact that Xavier knew da Silva's cause of death was a traumatic head injury when that information was never released, that he had a fascination with time-keeping, his motivations for attending medical school, and some facts about da Silva's extended family, such as the name of a priest who was a godfather to da Silva's grandmother.[115] The researchers concluded, after spending more than twenty hours interviewing da Silva's family, that Xavier displayed an ability to obtain information he could not likely have known. Further adding to Xavier's case is that in the nearly seventy years he was active, no known instances of fraud were discovered or even alleged against him. Furthermore, Xavier was not a rich man to begin with—he was not someone who perhaps didn't *need* money, and nevertheless he donated it to charity, choosing to live on a meager salary until his death.[116]

In addition to these scholars, parapsychological associations continue their work around the globe. The SPR is still an active organization, for example, as is the Parapsychological Association. Another modern parapsychology organization that continues to study psi phenomena is located in Germany. The Wissenschaftliche Gesselschaft zur Förderung der Parapsychologie (Scientific Society for the Furtherance of Parapsychology, or WGFP)[117] was founded in 1981 by psychology chair Johannes Mischo of Freiburg University. One of WGFP's missions is the "journalistic promotion of qualified parapsychological research at universities and institutes."[118] Members of the WGFP also manage a parapsychology counseling center that helps those who have encountered parapsychology phenomena. The WGFP offer regular workshops, lectures to the general public, and even training for psychology professionals, all while conducting their own field work and research.[119]

This is an extremely topical overview of the state of modern psi research and is merely intended to provide a brief glimpse into the world of current parapsychological research and thought before readers dive into the more comprehensive resources found in the following chapters. These subsequent chapters will include many additional researchers and studies and will help form more of a comprehensive understanding of this field. The vignettes of researchers I provide here hopefully illustrate the diversity of phenomena and topics within parapsychology, and the diversity of researchers themselves. Parapsychological research is not bound by geography or culture, and researchers across the globe study a wide range of phenomena that fall under the psi umbrella. This chapter also illustrates that psi phenomena has captivated humankind through the ages and is a curiosity that doesn't appear to be dwindling. Even though there still exists some tension within the academy, psi research is gaining more of a foothold and has immense implications for all manner of disciplines—from the medical sciences to the humanities.

NOTES

1. Thelma Moss, *The Body Electric: A Personal Journey into the Mysteries of Parapsychological Research, Bioenergy, and Kirlian Photography.* Los Angeles: J. P. Tarcher, 1979: 12.

2. Ingrid Kloosterman, "Psychical Research and Parapsychology Interpreted: Suggestions from the International Historiography of Psychical Research and Parapsychology for Investigating its History in the Netherlands," *History of the Human Sciences* 25, no. 2 (2012): 7.

3. Ibid., 8.

4. Ibid., 9.

5. John Beloff, *Parapsychology: A Concise History.* New York: St. Martin's Press, 1993: ix.

6. Jim Perry and Tim Rothschild, "Dr. Dean Radin on Real Magic and the Secret Power of the Universe." *Nite Drift* (October 19, 2020).

7. Ibid.

8. Ibid.

9. Ibid.

10. Ashley May, "How Many People Believe in Ghosts or Dead Spirits?" *USA Today* (October 25, 2017). Retrieved February 23, 2021 from https://www.usatoday.com/story/news/nation-now/2017/10/25/how-many-people-believe-ghosts-dead-spirits/794215001/.

11. Courtney M. Block, *Researching the Paranormal: How to Find Reliable Information about Parapsychology, Ghosts, Astrology, Cryptozoology, Near-Death Experiences, and More.* Lanham, MD: Rowman & Littlefield, 2020: 52–53.

12. Charles Richet, *Thirty Years of Psychical Research: Being a Treatise on Metaphysics.* New York: Macmillan Company, 1923: 15.

13. Beloff, *Parapsychology*, ix.

14. Richet, *Thirty Years*, 15.

15. Ibid., 15–30.

16. Ibid., 18.

17. Beloff, *Parapsychology*, 16.

18. Ibid., 17.

19. Ibid., 24.

20. Ibid., 21.

21. Ibid., 23.

22. Ibid., 33.

23. Ibid., 33.

24. Ibid., 34.

25. Ibid.

26. Ibid., 35–36.

27. Kloosterman, *Psychical Research*, 6.

28. Beloff, *Parapsychology*, 38.

29. Janet Oppenheim, *The Other World: Spiritualism and Psychical Research in England: 1850–1914*. London: Cambridge University Press, 1985: 1.

30. Oppenheim, *The Other World*, 9.

31. Ibid., 11.

32. Block, *Researching the Paranormal*, 21–22.

33. Oppenheim, *The Other World*, 11–12.

34. Beloff, *Parapsychology*, 42.

35. Oppenheim, *The Other World*, 17–19.

36. Eric J. Dingwall, *Very Peculiar People: Portrait Studies in the Queer, the Abnormal and the Uncanny*. New York: University Books, 1962: 178.

37. Ibid., 180–84.

38. Ibid., 186–88.

39. Beloff, *Parapsychology*, 45–46.

40. Ibid., 46.

41. Ibid., *Parapsychology*, 41.

42. Ibid., 65.

43. Renée Haynes, *The Society for Psychical Research: 1882–1982, A History*. London: MacDonald & Co., 1982: xiii.

44. Ibid., xiii, 4–5.

45. Ibid., 6.

46. Ibid., 9.

47. Ibid., 11.

48. Ibid., 27.

49. Eleanor Sidgwick, "Notes on the Evidence, Collected by the Society, for Phantasms of the Dead." Proceedings of the Society for Psychical Research 3 (April 24, 1885): 69–150.

50. Haynes, *The Society for Psychical Research*, 28–31.

51. Ibid., 35–43.

52. "Our History" (2018). The Incorporated Society for Psychical Research. Accessed March 29, 2021 from https://www.spr.ac.uk/about/our-history.

53. Ibid.

54. Haynes, *The Society*, 44.

55. Ibid., 48–49.

56. Kloosterman, "Psychical Research," 4.

57. Ibid.

58. Beloff, *Parapsychology*, 93–94.

59. Régine Plas, "Psychology and Psychical Research in France around the End of the 19th Century," *History of the Human Sciences* 25, no. 2, (2012): 92.

60. Plas, "Psychology and Psychical," 92.

61. Ibid., 96.

62. Ibid., 99.

63. "Historical Overview of IMI's Activities" (2021). Institut Métaphysique International. Accessed March 31, 2021 from https://www.metapsychique.org/apercu-historique-des-activites-de-limi/.

64. Heather Wolffram, "Hallucination of Materialization? The Animism versus Spiritism Debate in Late 19th-Century Germany," *History of the Human Sciences* 25, no. 2 (2012): 45–66.

65. Ibid., 47.

66. Ibid.

67. Ibid., 47–48.

68. Ibid., 50.

69. Ibid., 54.

70. Miki Takasuna, "The Fukarai Affair: Parapsychology and the History of Psychology in Japan." *History of the Human Sciences* 25, no. 2 (2012): 150.

71. Ibid., 150–51.

72. Ibid., 152.

73. Ibid., 154.

74. Ibid., 156.

75. Ibid., 157.

76. Ibid., 153.

77. "Japanese Society for Parapsychology." Accessed April 1, 2021 from http://j-spp.umin.jp/english/jspp_e.htm.

78. Ibid., 3.

79. Beloff, *Parapscyhology*, 237.

80. Kloosterman, "Psychical Research," 14–15.

81. Ibid., 16.

82. Annette Mülberger and Mónica Balltondre, "Metaphysics in Spain: Acknowledging or Questioning the Marvellous?" *History of the Human Sciences 25*, no. 2 (2012): 115.

83. Ibid., 119–20.

84. Block, *Researching the Paranormal*, 102.

85. Ibid., 103.

86. "J.B. Rhine." The Parapsychological Association (2021). Accessed March 30, 2021 from https://www.parapsych.org/articles/0/257/jb_rhine.aspx.

87. "History of the Parapsychological Association." The Parapsychological Association. (2021). Accessed March 30, 2021 from https://www.parapsych.org/articles/1/14/history_of_the_parapsychological.aspx.

88. Ibid.

89. Block, *Researching the Paranormal*, 104.

90. Andreas Sommer, "Psychical Research and the Origins of American Psychology: Hugo Münsterberg, William James and Eusapia Palladino," in *History of the Human Sciences* 25, no. 2 (2012): 23.

91. Ibid., 24.

92. Ibid., 25.

93. Kloosterman, "Psychical Research," 4.

94. Ibid., 6.

95. Ibid., 7.

96. Ibid., 11.

97. Johann Baptista and Max Derakhshani, "Beyond the Coin Toss: Examining Wiseman's Criticisms of Parapsychology." *Journal of Parapsychology* 78, no. 1 (Spring 2014): 56.

98. Ibid., 57.

99. "History of CSICOP." Center for Inquiry, Inc. (2021). Accessed April 1, 2021 from https://skepticalinquirer.org/history-of-csicop/.

100. Ibid.

101. "University Education in Parapsychology" (2021). The Parapsychological Association. Accessed April 1, 2021 from https://www.parapsych.org/section/34/university_education_in.aspx.

102. Pim van Lommel, "Consciousness Beyond Life, the Science of the Near-Death Experience." Accessed March 29, 2021 from https://pimvanlommel.nl/en/consciousness-beyond-life/.

103. Ibid.

104. "About: Weaving Together Knowledge and Knowing." Institute of Noetic Sciences, 2021. Accessed March 29, 2021 from https://noetic.org/about/.

105. Dean Radin, Yount Garret, Arnaud Delorme, Loren Carpenter, and Helané Wahbeh, "Spectroscopic Analysis of Water Treated by and in Proximity to Energy Medicine Practitioners: An Exploratory Study." *Explore: The Journal of Science & Healing* 17, no. 1 (January 2021): 27–31.

106. Jeffrey J. Kripal, "Life." 2018. Accessed March 29, 2021 from https://jeffreyjkripal.com/life/.

107. Block, *Researching the Paranormal*, 226.

108. Ciaran O'Keeffe, James Houran, Damien J. Houran, Neil Dagnall, Kenneth Drinkwater, Lorraine Sheridan, and Brian Laythe, "The Dr. John Hall story: A case study in putative 'Haunted People Syndrome,'" *Mental Health, Religion & Culture* 23, no. 7 (December 2019): 532–49.

109. Ibid., 533.

110. Ibid., 534.

111. Michaeleen C. Maher, "Quantitative Investigation of the General Wayne Inn." *Journal of Parapsychology* 64, no. 4 (December 2000): 365–90.

112. Denise Paraná, Alexandre Caroli Rocha, Elizabeth Schmitt Freire, Francisco Lotufo Neto, and Alexander Moreira-Almeida, "An Empirical Investigation of Alleged Mediumistic Writing: A Case Study of Chico Xavier's Letters." *The Journal of Nervous and Mental Disease* 207, no. 6 (June 2019): 497–504.

113. Ibid., 498.

114. Ibid.

115. Ibid., 499–500.

116. Ibid., 499.

117. Eberhar Bauer, Gerd H. Hövelmann, and Walter Von Lucadou, "Betraying the Present by Distorting the Past: Comments on Parker's Tendentious Portrait of German Psychical Research." *Journal of the Society for Psychical Research* 77, no. 910 (January 2013): 34.

118. "Scientific Society for the Promotion of Parapsychology." Accessed April 1, 2021 from http://www.parapsychologische-beratungsstelle.de/WGFP/.

119. Ibid.

2

Prominent Figures in Parapsychology

Ignorance is the only limitation that reins us back. The battle against the unknown is gradually being lost or rather won by the new generation of scientists who are finding themselves more and more in Alice's Wonderland where nothing is impossible."[1]

To have a well-rounded understanding of a topic, it is useful to know key historic and modern figures throughout its history. In this chapter, you will find biographical entries on a range of international scholars and mediums throughout the timeline of parapsychology. These entries are organized into two categories. The first set of biographies include figures, both historic and modern (and international in scope), who engage in parapsychological research. This includes people like Dr. Louisa Rhine, Dr. J. Ricardo Musso, Dr. Dean Radin, Dr. Caroline Watt, and others. Most of these figures are affiliated with the academy and their work is found in scholarly publications. However, some of the people in this category are not affiliated with the academy but are included because they worked closely with parapsychologists and/or their impact in raising awareness about the field is particularly notable.

An important point to keep in mind is that not every person in this category may call themselves a parapsychologist—remember, too, that the very term "parapsychology" wasn't in fashion until the 1940s and 1950s. Therefore, you see labels such as "psychical researcher" in the first half of this category. In fact, there were not any academic parapsychology programs until the second half of the twentieth century, so figures early in this timeline are, by default, not referred to as parapsychologists.

Most historic figures are noted by some other profession who *just happen* to also engage in parapsychological research.

Keep in mind, too, that not all the modern figures in this section necessarily refer to themselves as a parapsychologist or even attended a parapsychology-specific program. As a result, this category includes researchers from many disciplines whose research represents a wide variety of psi topics. For example, Dr. Pim van Lommel is a cardiologist who *also* researches the near-death experience. For that reason, he is a figure included in our discussion of parapsychology. The focus, then, is the *work* that people do, not the label to which they subscribe.

This first category is separated into two subcategories that reflect both historic and contemporary scholars. I include these subcategories to reflect change and growth in the field, but also to provide an easily accessible list of modern researchers who may not be discussed in other encyclopedic works on this topic. Tracing biographies chronologically can help illustrate these shifts and trends. Using John Beloff's assertion of Franz Mesmer as a marker of the formation of parapsychology as a formal scientific field of study, historic figures are those whose contributions range from approximately 1800 to the mid-1900s. Contemporary modern figures are those whose work appears from the 1950s to present day. Both categories of researchers are comprehensive and international in scope, and any omission from this category is not intentional. It is my goal merely to provide a core yet comprehensive list upon which readers new to this topic can *continue* to build.

The second category of biographies includes the mediums, or people who exhibited psi behavior, and who often found themselves at the center of inquiry. This includes people like Leonora Piper, D. D. Home, Chizuko Mifune, Lajos Pap, and Eusapia Palladino. The inclusion of mediums from the spiritualist era may perhaps seem a bit controversial because as we know, many in that era engaged in fraudulent behavior. However, they are central to the foundation of parapsychology as a formal field of study. The field may never have blossomed, in fact, without the incentive they created to ferret out the real from the fraudulent. Additionally, this category includes figures at the center of psychical case studies—people who may not have publicly engaged in performances like mediums but rather those whose psychical abilities drew the attention of researchers. Both categories of people are arranged alphabetically by last name. A further reading section is found after many entries that includes references to works affiliated with that person.

PARAPSYCHOLOGISTS THROUGH HISTORY: FROM THE 1800s TO THE 1950s

A

Aksakof, Alexander (1832–1903, Imperial Councilor): Alexander Aksakof was a Russian psychical investigator and imperial councilor to Czar Nicholas II. Aksakof was fascinated by the inquiry of life after death and was particularly inspired by the writings of Emanuel Swedenborg. Because publications discussing psychical phenomena were censored by the Russian government, Aksakof submitted his research to German publications. In fact, he created the parapsychology journal *Psychische Studien* in 1874 and served more than twenty years as its editor. He attended séances of many mediums including Eusapia Palladino and D. D. Home. He is perhaps most known for his discussions of dematerialization, inspired by a séance in which the lower portion of the medium's body seemed to disappear—an event which was hotly contested by some of Aksakof's contemporaries.[2]

Further Reading:

Alexander Aksakof, *A Case of Partial Dematerialization of the Body of a Medium.* Boston: Banner of Light, 1898.

Allison, Lydia Winterhalter (1880–1959, Psychical Researcher): Lydia Winterhalter Allison's husband died in 1920, and though he was an ardent believer in life after death, Lydia herself was not. His death, however, left her curious so she attended séances in hopes of connecting with him. She reported her experiences with mediums Gladys Osborne Leonard and Minnie Soule to the American Society for Psychical Research (ASPR). She helped establish the Boston Society for Psychic Research in 1925 after a rift between members of ASPR. The Boston SPR produced many publications of psychical research. In 1941, Lydia helped rejoin these two organizations under the authority of the ASPR.[3]

Further Reading:

L. W. Allison, *Leonard and Soule Experiments in Psychical Research.* Boston: Boston Society for Psychic Research, 1929.

B

Balfour, Arthur James (1848–1930, Prime Minister): Arthur Balfour was the prime minister of England from 1902–1905 and a student of psychical researcher Henry Sidgwick. It is perhaps this study and his time at Trinity College that sparked an interest in psychical studies—a spark that only grew after some poignant personal psychical experiences. He served as president of the British Society for Psychic Research in 1893 and was one of the earliest members.

Figure 2.1. Alexander Aksakof
From: Library of Congress Prints & Photographs Online Catalog. Photo by Vezenberg & Co.; PD US

He is noted for his connection to the Palm Sunday case. Balfour was engaged to Mary Catherine Lyttleton. In 1875, before they married, Mary passed away on Palm Sunday. This affected Balfour greatly and, as an ode to her passing, he spent every Palm Sunday with Mary's family. Thirty-seven years after Mary's passing, one of the mediums involved in the cross-correspondences (a decades-long study involving automatic writers intuiting messages from spirits), appeared to create a message that came from Mary herself. Balfour was convinced of the genuineness of the message and believed it was a sign of life after death.[4]

Balfour, Gerald (1853–1945, Politician and Psychical Researcher): Gerald Balfour was Eleanor Sidgwick's brother and a past president of the SPR. He attended Trinity College where he became acquainted with many future members of the SPR. His most notable contribution to the field of parapsychology is his involvement in the nearly thirty-year study of cross-correspondences. The cross-correspondences involved writings produced by automatists (automatic writers) that were believed to be messages from spirits. As part of this work, he lived with other primary investigators, including his sister, while they conducted this long-term study.[5]

Further Reading:
A. C. Pigou, "Cross-Correspondences: A Reply to Mr. Gerald Balfour." *Journal of the Society for Psychical Research* 15 (May 1911): 66–70.

Barlow, Fred (?–1964, Photographer): Fred Barlow was a member of the SPR. As a photography expert, the SPR relied on him to analyze reported instances of spirit photography. Barlow was also a member of the short-lived Society for the Study of Supernormal Pictures, making him the perfect go-to when determining the validity of curious photographs. He was open to the idea of psychical phenomena, but when it came to spirit photographs he did not believe that any of them were genuine examples of spectral visitors. He was able to point out how certain elements always seemed to be a superimposition of an image in another photograph or even a painting. Upon Barlow's death, his work was catalogued and preserved by researcher Eric Dingwall and was later donated to the British Museum.[6]

Barrett, Sir William (1844–1925, Physicist): Sir William F. Barrett was one of the founding members of the British Society for Psychic Research. A British physicist, he taught at the Royal College of Science in Dublin, Ireland. Shane McCorristine reminds us that to simply refer to Barrett as a physicist is an incomplete portrait. He was "a scientist, educationalist, populariser of physics, psychical researcher, and lobbyist for various domestic reform movements."[7]

In 1882, Barrett was approached by spiritualist E. Dawson Rogers, who wanted to help enhance the reputation of Spiritualism by inviting respected members of the academy to investigate various phenomena. Rogers knew that Barrett might be willing to listen to his plea, as Barrett had already been engaged in some psychical research of his own.[8]

Barrett's interest in psychical phenomena likely developed (or at least grew) after his meeting with Irish scientist John Wilson in the 1860s. At this time, Barrett was employed at London's Royal Institution. Physicists of this time period were engaging in boundary work, that is, proposing theories and ideas that pushed the limits of accepted scientific knowledge. This resulted in a type of backlash in other academic circles, especially in the Royal Institution where Barrett found himself. From his meeting with John Wilson, Barrett discovered that scientists in Ireland were much more open to this type of boundary work, and the two men began investigating hypnotism and thought-transference.[9]

In one of Barrett's hypnotism experiments, he asked a hypnotist to place a subject into a trance. The subject would then be left in a room by themself while the hypnotist would be placed in a separate, but adjoining room. Standing directly between rooms so that Barrett could observe, the subject was asked to identify certain tastes or sensations. These sensations would correlate to something the hypnotist was consuming in the adjoining room. Though neither person could see one another, Barrett's experiment yielded positive results and he was encouraged to continue his research into extrasensory perception, or what he called thought-transference.[10]

Another early investigation involved the Creery family, who lived in Buxton, England, in 1881. Reverend Creery had been inspired by a popular guessing game played at the time, and set out to investigate the possibility of thought-transference. A group of people would gather to play. One person would leave the room while the others decided collectively on an object which that person must successfully identify upon reentry. Of course, the person reentering relied on subtle clues like body language and facial expressions to try and correctly guess the object, but Reverend Creery was curious to know if it would still work without any clues from body language. If so, he believed this would be evidence for thought-transference (extrasensory perception). He began testing his theory with his daughters and maid, and eventually wrote to Barrett about their wild success. Barrett came to the Creery house to conduct his own studies and removed the element of body language in different ways. In some tests, one person would walk into another room while those remaining would collectively think about an object. The lone person would then be required to return to the group with the object in hand. Another version involved the "guesser" keeping their back to everyone once reentering a room, to take visual body language cues out of the mix. In Barrett's studies, the guesses were correct in a significant number of attempts.

To remove the possibility of conspiracy, Barrett enlisted two of his SPR colleagues to come and study at the Creery house. Instead of the family members, they asked neighbors to participate. They achieved lesser but still notable results using non-family members as well. The phenomena slowly died down over time, seeming to wane the more the family participated. Nevertheless, the results were curious, and Barrett even published his work on this case in the scholarly journal *Nature*.[11] Harvey J. Irwin, researcher and parapsychologist himself, points out that these early telepathy experiments were also notable for their inclusions of statistical probabilities. Barrett and his colleagues calculated chance probabilities and marked a movement "in the development of a paradigmatic ESP experiment."[12]

The hypnotism and Creery cases were experiments that Barrett was known for and soon he began recruiting colleagues to create a more formal and organized group of people to investigate various psi phenomena. The SPR was born.[13] Specifically, its beginnings can be traced to January 6, 1882, when Barrett held a psychical conference in London to discuss just such matters.[14]

A committee founded in the beginning years of the SPR was the Committee on Thought Reading. Barrett led the charge for this committee, having done relevant work on the topic. In the committee's report, Barrett and colleagues outlined the Creery experiments, but a few short years later in 1888, the girls admitted to using signals devised among themselves.[15] The work done during this experiment wasn't all for naught, however. Remember, these early experiments were notable for their inclusion of statistical probability, thus helping to pave the way for more scientific inquiries of psychical phenomena. This case also inspired methods for future studies.

It is worth noting that even though the Creery girls were able to elude some of Barrett's inquiry, Barrett was not completely blind or ignorant of the rampant spiritualist fraud that was so prevalent at this time period. He writes in his own work, *On the Threshold of the Unseen*, "Unforunately, where there is good

Figure 2.2. William Barrett (left), Miss Scatcherd, and Stanley de Brath (the floating visage was thought to be that of Letty Hyde).
From: Helen C. Lambert's *A General Survey of Psychical Phenomena*. (New York: Knickerbocker Press, 1928).

coin there is also false, and Spiritualism has suffered from a fraudulent imitation trading on the credulity of the ignorant or uncritical."[16]

Through his research and connections made in England, Ireland, and the United States, Barrett played a pivotal role not only in the formation of the British SPR, but in the formation of branches in Dublin and the United States as well.[17] Throughout his studies, Barrett became convinced of the validity of psychical phenomena. In fact, he concluded a few remarkable things near the end of his professional career. Rudolf Steiner, in his *Dictionary of the Psychic, Mystic, Occult,* reminds us that some of Barrett's last writings included his summation of what psychical research reveals: "The existence of a spirit world," "survival after death," and "occasional communication with those passed over."[18]

Further Reading:

William Barrett, *On the Threshold of the Unseen: An Examination of the Phenomena of Spiritualism and of the Evidence for Survival After Death.* London: Kegan, Paul, Trench, Trubner, & Co, 1917.

Shane McCorristine, "William Fletcher Barrett, Spiritualism, and Psychical Research in Edwardian Dublin." *Estudios Irlandeses,* no. 6 (2011), 39–53.

Bender, Hans (1907–1991, Psychologist): Dr. Hans Bender was a German psychologist who served as chair of Germany's first academic parapsychology program at Albert-Ludwig University.[19] In his youth, Bender had a memorable experience involving automatic writing and a Ouija board. He was impressed by the activity and the information retrieved but skeptical that it was the result of any outside agency or spirit.[20] In his twenties, Bender attended university in Paris and was greatly influenced by the French psychologist Pierre and his ideas on the subconscious. Bender decided to investigate the intersection of the subconscious and extra-sensory perception and even wrote his PhD thesis on this topic.[21] Bender also had meaningful relationships with Carl Jung and J. B. Rhine. Rhine, in fact, preferred controlled laboratory settings whereas Bender thrived on the spontaneous, real-world settings of phenomena like hauntings and poltergeist activity.[22]

Throughout his career, Bender served as president of the Parapsychological Association, helped establish scholarly journals that published psychical research, and led parapsychology programs in multiple universities.[23] One of his most notable accomplishments was the founding of the Institute for Border Areas of Psychology and Mental Hygiene (aka The Bender Institute) in Germany, an organization that supported psychical research as well as the public dissemination of psychical knowledge. In a tribute to Bender after his death in 1991, Eberhard Bauer wrote that this institute was Bender's "most personal creation,"[24] and that many psychical researchers began their careers within its walls. Additionally, Bauer writes,

> Among the visitors were mediums and magicians, astrologers and ufologists, dowsers and numerologists, witches and healers, gurus and charlatans, spiritualists and hostile sceptics, psychotics and serious scientists; classes of students, TV teams and hard-nosed journalists—they all came to Freiburg to see and to talk to the famous professor.[25]

His seminars drew the attendance of not only researchers and students, but large swaths of the general public as well, all of whom clamored to listen to his tales. Undoubtedly, they were enthralled by listening to some of Bender's most noteworthy research, that of the poltergeist.

In 1968, the small Bavarian town of Nickelheim was host to some peculiar occurrences. A family with a teenage daughter reported strange knocking sounds and stones falling from the ceiling. Bender came to the home to investigate, hanging his coat inside the house. When he later went to retrieve it, he found his coat to be missing. On further investigation, it was laying outside in the snow. Others, including a family priest and lawyer, reported strange teleportation of items as well.[26] One year prior to the Nickelheim incident, in 1967, a law firm in Rosenheim, a city in Bavaria, was plagued by inexplicable phenomena. Hundreds of phantom phone calls were made from the office, light bulbs constantly exploded, the copiers malfunctioned, and electrical fuses blew. Naturally, electricians were called in but could not determine the cause. Bender was eventually called in, theorizing that the events were due to psychokinetic activity emanating in poltergeist form through a nineteen-year-old employee of the law firm. She seemed to trigger heightened activity when physically present in the office, and curiously, the activity seemed to stop after she quit working there.[27]

Bender's contributions to the field of parapsychology are immense, and he was particularly impactful in the realm of qualitative field work. He believed that psi phenomena emanated from human beings, and that certain "affective" states need be present in order to trigger psychical phenomena in the first place. Bauer tells us "it was impossible for him to separate the paranormal phenomenon he was after from the persons who were experiencing it."[28]

Further Reading:

Martin Ebon, "Hans Bender: A Life in Parapsychology." *Journal of Religion and Psychical Research,* vol. 18, no. 4 (October 1995): 187–95.

Bergson, Henri (1859–1941, Philosopher): Henri Bergson was a French philosopher who theorized on matters relating to time, memory, and perception. He believed that there was more than just chronological, or clock, time, and that humans also experienced what he referred to as "lived time." In his 1896 book *Matter and Memory* "he concluded that memory—mind or soul—is independent of the body,"[29] which is clearly a theory relevant to psychical researchers. In fact, Bergson delivered the presidential address to the 1913 meeting of the SPR.

Bergson also believed that since consciousness and the mind were not bound by the physical body, the human mind was capable of psychical phenomena like telepathy. His metaphysical outlook on the power of the human mind gave new perspectives on the inquiry into psychical phenomena. For example, Bergson theorized that there are multiple "channels" of consciousness that operate around us simultaneously, and that instances of psi phenomena (like telepathy) are simply moments in which we have transcended the boundaries of our own channel and tapped into another concurrent channel at the same time.[30] He even went beyond this to say that memory is woven into the collective channels of consciousness, and that because consciousness is not linear

Figure 2.3. Henri Bergson
From the Library of Congress' George Granthan Bain Collection; PD-US

and humankind shares a collective consciousness, that our memories can ebb and flow between us. Because collective consciousness exists, though, Bergson proposed that our minds are equipped with filters that keep all those concurrent channels from bleeding into our own experience, but perhaps when those filters malfunction, strange things happen. This is, then, where phenomena like clairvoyance or clairsentience come into play.

Bergson researcher William G. Barnard tells us this of the French philosopher: "Do not . . . take Bergson lightly. This is philosophy with a kick, philosophy that might, little by little, rearrange your comfortable mental world in unexpected ways."[31]

Further Reading:

William G. Barnard, *Living Consciousness: The Metaphysical Vision of Henri Bergson.* Albany State University of New York Press, 2011.

Besterman, Theodore (1904–1976, Psychical Researcher): Theodore Besterman was a librarian and editor with the Society for Psychical Research. He was known for his outspoken criticisms of his colleagues and their experimental designs and was particularly critical of studies involving mediums. Besterman designed a study to investigate the fallibility of eyewitness testimony during séances (or sittings as they are sometimes called) and discovered that eyewitnesses were only about 33 percent reliable. As such, he believed that no human testimony from a séance was useful, and this belief even kept him from discussing some of his own psychical experiences at séances. Sir Arthur Conan Doyle was so disgusted with Besterman's intense criticism of psychical researcher Ernesto Bozzano and his work with Italian medium Eusapia Palladino, that Doyle Besterman resigned from the SPR. Besterman resigned from all work with the SPR in 1935.[32]

Further Reading:

Theodore Besterman, *Collected Papers on the Paranormal.* New York: Garrett Publications, 1968.

Bird, James Malcolm (1886–1964, mathematician): James M. Bird was an American psychical researcher and a controversial figure in the history of parapsychology. He was the associate editor of *Scientific American.* In the 1920s, *Scientific American* organized a committee tasked with finding proof of psychical phenomena. As part of this inquiry, the committee held sittings with medium Mina Crandon, and it was Bird who gave her the pseudonym that she is often referred to as: Margery. The committee was divided on their thoughts regarding the genuine nature of Mina, though Bird was absolutely convinced of her abilities. He published a book about Mina's abilities, though it has been highly criticized as unreliable and sensational. This is perhaps where Bird's reputation began to suffer. Though he was slowly becoming a controversial figure, he was appointed as a coresearch officer of the ASPR alongside fellow researcher Walter Prince. Prince was extremely frustrated that the ASPR would promote Bird to this position, and it resulted in Prince's resignation from that organization. In fact, multiple other members of ASPR were so offended at that posting that they joined Prince in resignation and formed their own psychical research organization, the Boston Society for Psychic Research.[33] Bird faded into obscurity in the 1930s.

Further Reading:

James Bird, *"Margery" the Medium.* Boston: Small, Maynard, and Co., 1925.

Boirac, Emile (1851–1917, Philosopher): Emile Boirac was a French philosopher and psychical researcher who is credited with coining the term "déjà vu." He described it, in an article published by the journal *Revue Philosophique*, as an illusion of memory. In this article, he writes that he noticed a familiar sensation when visiting a new city, and even noticed this same sensation when having conversations with people—the sensation, as we all are likely familiar, of having encountered. He discovered that many other people had this same experi-

Figure 2.4. Emile Boirac
From: *La Psychologie Inconnue* by Emile Boirac, CC-PD-Mark

ence of familiarity during new encounters.[34] He was also inspired by Franz Mesmer's animal magnetism theory and theorized that this invisible field that surrounded humans was responsible for psi abilities like extrasensory perception.[35]

Further Reading:

Emile Boirac, *Psychic Science: An Introduction and Contribution to the Experimental Study of Psychical Phenomena.* London: W. Rider & Son, 1918.

Boole, Mary (1832–1916, Mathematician): Mary Boole was a self-taught mathematician and one of the founding members of the British SPR. She was, in fact, the sole female founding member. She remained with the SPR for about six months at which point she left the group, leaving some to wonder if being the lone female voice in a group otherwise dominated by men left her feeling unheard. Others have postulated that she perhaps stepped away from the SPR to devote her time to the various social causes to which she was dedicated. Mary was actively devoted to promoting the role of women not just in society, but in education as well. She was the author of children's math books, and also promoted the merits of psychical research.[36] In 1908, she wrote a nearly three hundred-page book titled *The Message of Psychic Science to the World* in which she urges the academy not to dismiss the merits of knowledge gleaned from psychical pursuits. In this book, we learn that Mary's father was an occultist who also urged his colleagues to seriously consider trance and mesmerism.[37]

Further Reading:

Mary Everest Boole, *The Message of Psychic Science to the World.* London: C. W. Daniel, 1908.

Bozzano, Ernesto (1862–1943, Psychical Researcher): Ernesto Bozzano was an Italian psychologist interested in psychical research. He became interested in it after reading works by Charles Richet and articles in the journal *Annales des Science Psychique.* In 1893, he received through a medium what he believed was a message from his mother. This event led to his interest in mediumship. Bozzano was part of a group that sat with Eusapia Palladino over the course of five years. He had no

Figure 2.5. Ernesto Bozzano
From: S. R. Morgan's *Index to Psychic Science* (Swarthmore, 1950); PD-US-not renewed

formal training in the scientific method and so didn't serve as a leading experimentalist. Rather, his work consisted of compiling, classifying, and organizing cases of various psychical phenomena. Through this work, Bozzano discovered some curious patterns. For example, he noticed that apparitions of the deceased were seen beyond the confines of where they once lived, helping to expand the body of knowledge about haunt phenomena. He also gathered ethnographies of paranormal experiences among different cultures and his compilation on deathbed visions was particularly insightful.

Further Reading:

Carlos S. Alvarado, "Ernesto Bozzano on the Phenomena of Bilocation." *Journal of Near-Death Studies,* vol. 23, no. 4 (Summer 2005): 207–38.
Giovanni Iannuzzo, *Ernesto Bozzano: La Vita e l'Opera.* Verona: Luce e Ombra, 1983.

Bucke, Richard Maurice (1837–1902, Psychiatrist): Richard Maurice Bucke was a Canadian psychiatrist who coined the term "cosmic consciousness," something he wrote about after having his own intensely personal and mystical experience in which he encountered "a new dimension of consciousness far above his normal one."[38] In 1894, he published his work on cosmic consciousness and even read it to those attending a convention of the American Medico-Psychological Association in Philadelphia. In this work, Bucke lays out his theory of a cosmic consciousness. A profound passage at the beginning of this work reads:

Twenty years' study has shown me clearly that the human mind has been slowly evolved by a species of unfolding or growth, extending over millions of years. Not that the *human* mind has existed as long as that, but that the mind which we possess today, in its human and its ante-human forms, extends back for unknown ages and eons into the geologic past of the planet, sending its roots and drawing its sap today from the lives of tens of thousands of generations of our prehuman as well as human ancestors. And, it may be said in passing, it is apparently this almost infinite experience, treasured up and handed down the ages in the form of instincts, monitions of conscience and delicate phases of emotion, that gives to the human mind of the present time many of its most profound and subtle qualities.[39]

Through his publications and research, Bucke brought the importance of mystical experiences to the attention of the academy.[40]

Further Reading:

Cyril Greenland, "Richard Maurice Bucke, M.D., 1837–1902: The Evolution of a Mystic." *Canadian Psychiatric Association Journal* 11, no. 2 (April 1966): 146–54.

C

Canavesio, Orlando (1915–1957, Physician): Orlando Canavesio was an Argentinian physician who served as the chief of psychiatry at the University of Córdoba. Canavesio was intrigued by psychical phenomena, which led him to establish the Argentine Metapsychic Medical Association in 1946. He was known for his research using electroencephalographs and extrasensory perception. His medical association is credited as the first formal association that urged medical practitioners to consider the merits of extrasensory perception. He also served as director of Argentina's Institute of Applied Psychopathology; an institute administered by the Department of Health. This institute was charged with investigating the impact of Spiritualism on physical health.[41]

Carington, Walter (1884–1947, Psychical Researcher): Walter Carington was a scientist and psychical researcher who advocated for enhanced quantitative studies of psychical phenomena. He believed that not only would this fill a gap in the data on psi phenomena, it would also help these topics gain more of a foothold within the scientific community. To advocate for this he wrote "The Quantitative Study of Trance Personalities," which was a series of articles published regularly from 1935–1939. He believed in the cosmic consciousness theory and also espoused the idea that all humans were capable of telepathy.[42]

Carrington, Hereward (1880–1958, Psychical Researcher): Hereward Carrington was an author, researcher, and member of both the British and American SPR. Much of his research centered on mediums, and in 1907 he published a book outlining the rampant fraud among mediums titled *Physical Phenomena of Spiritualism*. He was part of a panel of researchers tasked with studying the abilities of Eusapia Palladino, and while he wasn't entirely convinced about her, he did nonetheless end up believing that she had *some* psychical abilities. He also founded the American Psychical Institute and Laboratory.

Perhaps his most notable work involved his inquiry into the mediumship of Canadian Mina Crandon, referred to simply as Margery. In the 1920s, Mina began exhibiting mediumship abilities during séances hosted by her husband, Dr. Crandon, a Boston surgeon at Harvard Medical School, who was intrigued by Spiritualism. Upon exhibiting these abilities, Margery was constantly invited and encouraged to attend sittings with various people, and eventually she drew the attention of some of her husband's colleagues at Harvard. Knowledge of her abilities continued to draw attention and culminated in her entry to a $5,000 contest hosted by *Sci-*

Figure 2.6. Hereward Carrington
From: How Much Does Your Soul Weigh? *Leslie's Weekly*. Volume 133. July-December, 1921.; PD-US-expired

entific American in 1924. The goal of this contest was to offer a reward for anyone who could prove psychic abilities. A committee of investigators was assigned to Margery's entry and included not only Hereward but also Harry Houdini, psychologist William McDougall, and a few others. During sittings, she appeared to display violent psychokinetic activity, but the committee assigned to her was very dubious. Houdini, as a hardened skeptic of any psi behavior, was adamant that there was fraud involved and Hereward eventually became the sole voice of belief in this case. Inquiry into Margery's abilities continued and still leave a divide among the community today.[43]

Further Reading:

Hereward Carrington, *The Physical Phenomena of Spiritualism*. Boston: Small, Maynard, & Co., 1908.

Charcot, Jean-Martin (1825–1893, Physician): Dr. Charcot was a French physician who defied the notion that hypnotism and mesmerism had no place in modern science. Mesmerism, a theory proposed by Franz Mesmer in the late 1700s, was often looked upon with scorn by the medical community and some institutions even placed formal bans restricting physicians from using it in their practice. Charcot, however, saw the potential benefit of hypnotism in his patients suffering from hysterics. He established a clinic at the Saltpêtrière Hospital in Paris to examine this and other neurologic conditions. When placing patients suffering from hysterics under hypnosis, Charcot discovered that their symptoms abated significantly. Once he helped those suffering from neurological conditions, Charcot tested the limits of hypnosis and found that he could convince perfectly healthy individuals that they were suffering from hysteria. His work showed conclusively that physical disorders can have psychological origins and he helped pave the way for hypnotism to be formally recognized and accepted by the scientific community. Psychical researcher Pierre Janet studied under Charcot as did Sigmund Freud.[44]

Further Reading:

Maria Teresa Brancaccio, "Between Charcot and Bernheim: The Debate on Hypnotism in *Fin-de-Siècle* Italy." *Notes and Records* 71 (2017): 157–77.

Chari, Cadambur T. K. (1909–1993, Philosopher): Cadambur T. K. Chari was a philosopher at Madras Christian College in India and one of the country's foremost parapsychology philosophers. As a young man, he was influenced by readings of psychical researchers, in particular that of Stainton Moses. His writings on the philosophies of parapsychology can be found in scholarly journals worldwide, including the United Kingdom, Italy, France, the United States, Germany, and more.[45]

Further Reading:

C. T. K. Chari, "ESP and the 'Theory of Resonance.'" *British Journal for the Philosophy of Science* 15, no. 58 (1964): 137–40.

Cox, William (1915–1994, Mechanical Engineer): William Cox was a mechanical engineer with an interest in psychokinesis. In the 1950s, he conducted research for the Duke Parapsychology Labs, and even developed multiple methods and devices for testing psychokinesis. One of these methods is known as the "PK-placement" test, a setup in which objects are mechanically released onto a platform and subjects are tasked with mentally altering the typical trajectory of that item. Some have mused that William's work helped keep psychokinesis from falling out of interest to psychical research.[46]

Further Reading:

W. E. Cox, "Whither Today's Psi Sensitives?" *Journal of the American Society for Psychical Research* 87, no. 2 (1993): 125–32.

Crawford, William Jackson (1881–1920, Mechanical Engineer): William Crawford was a British engineer and mechanical engineering professor at Queen's University in Belfast, Ireland, noted for his six-year study of the medium Kathleen Goligher and her family—investigations that came to be known as the Goligher Circle. William believed that mediums obtained their psychical powers through the energy of those in attendance. He also believed in an ectoplasmic theory for levitation of objects during séances, known as the psychic rod theory. Crawford's theory, which merged notions of mechanical engineering with Spiritualism, posited that invisible, but dense, rods emanated from the medium and sitters and acted as cantilevers to make objects in the room move. He added evidence to this theory by pointing out an average weight loss before and after séances in both the medium

Figure 2.7. William Jackson Crawford
From: F. W. Warrick's *Experiments in psychics; practical studies in direct writing, supernormal photography and other phenomena, mainly with Mrs. Ada Emma Deane.* New York: Dutton, 1939; PD US not renewed

and their attendees. His work has not been without criticism, but nevertheless remains an intriguing part of psychical history.[47]

Further Reading:

W. J. Crawford, *The Reality of Psychic Phenomena: Raps, Levitations, Etc.* New York: E. P. Dutton & Company, 1919.

Crookes, William (1832–1919, Physicist): William Crookes was a British physicist and psychical researcher. He is known for having discovered thallium and joined many prestigious organizations such as the Royal Society, the Institution of Electrical Engineers, and many more. He also served as president for the Society for Psychical Research and on the psychical front is perhaps most noted for his investigations of mediums D. D. Home and Florence Cook. Crookes's interest in psychical phenomena began after he attended several séances and was curious about the abilities displayed during those sittings. He publicly announced that he would immerse himself in an investigation of Spiritualism, and though he professed a belief that we don't know everything and shouldn't assume as such, his public statement appeared to imply that he expected to uncover that all phenomena associated with Spiritualism was "worthless residuum."[48]

After his first scientific tests with medium D. D. Home, Crookes published a statement saying that he was convinced about the reality of psychical phenomena. Most interesting, however, is the fact that he scrambled to find a publication willing to report his findings after the Royal Society refused to publish his paper since it contained positive psychical sentiments. Such was the antipsychical attitude espoused by some members of the academy at the time. He nevertheless found publication in the *Quarterly Journal of Science.*

Crookes investigated the controversial medium Florence Cook and the spirit that often manifested itself at her séances, Katie King. During his studies, conducted at his own home, he maintained that the manifestation seemed genuine, causing an uproar among the scientific community. After these two psychical studies, he retreated back to his regular work, feeling dismayed by the reaction against him. Throughout the rest of his life, he maintained belief in both the procedures he used and the phenomena he encountered with these two mediums.[49]

Further Reading:

William Crookes, "Notes of an Enquiry into the Phenomena Called Spiritual, During the Years 1870–73." *Quarterly Journal of Science* (January 1874).

D

Delanne, Gabriel (1857–1926, Psychical Researcher): Gabriel Delanne was a leading figure in French spiritism. He was particularly intrigued by reincarnation and the studies of medium Eusapia Palladino. During her cases, she appeared to psychically alter soft plaster, leaving an impression of faces or other parts of the body, like hands. This inspired him to use paraffin casts during the séances he studied in order to physically capture attributes of any manifestations that might appear. This method

was later used by researcher Gustave Geley in his study of the medium Franek Kluski. Delanne, along with his colleague and fellow spiritist researcher Léon Denis, presented at the 1900 International Congress of Psychology, and urged their colleagues to see the merits of psychical inquiry.[50]

Further Reading:

Gabriel Delanne, *Materialized Apparitions of the Living and of the Dead.* Vol 1: Phantoms of the Living (Paris: Librairie Spirite, 1909). Original French title: *Les Apparitions Matérialisées des Vivants & des Morts. Vol 1: Les Fantômes de Vivants.*

Dessoir, Max (1867–1947, Philosopher and Psychologist): Max Dessoir is credited with coining the term "parapsychology." Born in Germany, he was a philosopher, psychologist, and aesthetician, among many other things. He was a cofounder of the Society for Experimental Psychology, established in Germany in 1888.[51] Dessoir was the first to compile resources on hypnotism in German, and was also a leader in dissociation research. He published some of his research to the journal *Sphinx*, a publication dedicated to the discussion of psychical topics.[52]

Dessoir was active in psychical research during a very interesting time in Germany's development of the field of psychology. In the late 1800s, scientists were establishing the "psychology of occult" to help explain why certain people believe in inexplicable things. A subset of this also focused on the "psychology of deception."[53] These theories and discussions were led by scientists who saw no value in investigating the veracity of psychical phenomena and who certainly also saw no value in merging this study within the academy. To these scientists, psi phenomena was nothing more than either outright trickery or an event explained away by hallucination or misinterpretation.

Nevertheless, there were German researchers who were not satisfied with this dominant view of psychology and who saw the value in scientifically investigating psi phenomena. Realizing the value of such research, Dessoir and his colleague Albert von Schrenk-Notzing cofounded the Society for Experimental Psychology. Through its focus on experimental psychology, they were able to ride that border area between fringe and established science. They were inspired by their colleagues doing experimental psychology involving psi phenomena in England and France, in particular the work being done on hypnotism. Researcher Andreas Sommer tells us that "it is obvious that Schrenk and Dessoir had initially intended to challenge, or at least broaden, the narrow scope of fledgling German psychology [and] by acting as conduits for French and English strands of experimental psychology, they in fact closely followed the example of the founder of American psychology, William James."[54] They were also inspired to cofound this society as a way to distance themselves from other German institutions that focused heavily on metaphysical and philosophical treatments of parapsychology—for Dessoir and Schrenk-Notzing, the focus was first on scientific methods and *then* musing on what the data might suggest or mean for the human condition.[55]

Dessoir and his colleague were convinced of the genuineness of telepathy when they cofounded the Society for Experimental Psychology. A guiding principle of the society was to replicate experiments done by French and English researchers to see if they could also replicate results and contribute to the scholarly literature of the field.[56] Dessoir investigated notable mediums Leonora Piper and Eusapia Palladino and through his studies believed that they displayed some curious, hitherto unexplainable, psychical abilities. A leading figure to the field of parapsychology, especially in Germany's timeline, Max Dessoir's goal was to help advance the cause of scientific parapsychological inquiry.[57]

Further Reading:

Max Dessoir, "Hypnotism in France." *Nature* 9, no. 226 (June 3, 1887): 541–45.

Max Dessoir, *Outlines of the History of Psychology.* Translated by Donald Fisher. New York: The Macmillan Company, 1912.

Andreas Sommer, "Normalizing the Supernormal: The Formation of the 'Gesellschaft Für Psychologische Forschung' ('Society for Psychological Research')": 18–44.

Heather Wolffram, "Parapsychology on the Couch: The Psychology of Occult Belief in Germany, c. 1870–1939." *Journal of the History of the Behavioral Sciences* 42, no. 3 (Summer 2006): 237–60.

Dingwall, Eric (1890–1986, Anthropologist): Dr. Eric Dingwall was a British anthropologist who was intrigued by psychical phenomena. Specifically, he was intrigued by physical mediumship and his interest into this topic led him to serve as the director for the American Society for Psychical Research's Department of Physical Phenomena. He was also a research officer in the British Society for Psychical Research, during which time he engaged in research with mediums such as Mina Crandon (Margery).[58] He also investigated the Polish medium Stefan Ossowiecki, noted for his clairvoyant abilities. In one such study, in 1923, Ossowiecki was presented with a wrapped package presented to him by a third party, that is, someone unconnected to the research and with no knowledge of the contents of the package. This was done to avoid any subtle, unconscious physical hints that Ossowiecki might be able to pick up on. In Dingwall's study, the package contained multiple envelopes, one of which contained a drawing of a bottle of ink and an inscription in French. Ossowiecki was able to correctly identify that the drawing was indeed of an ink bottle but couldn't identify the exact wording of the inscription other than to say it was written in French. In other instances of this same test, Ossowiecki correctly guessed the drawing *and* the inscriptions.[59]

As mentioned, Dingwall was mostly concerned with physical mediumship. One characteristic of physical mediumship is the appearance of manifestations. These manifestations could take effect through apports (the seemingly unexplainable and sudden appearance of physical items) or through manifestations of shapes, substances, hands, and other forms of corporeal imaging. Perhaps the most well-known of these materializations is ectoplasm, a type of filmy substance that emanates from the medium. Most popular during the heyday of Spiritualism, researchers, including Dingwall, studied the occurrence of ectoplasm to determine its origin and veracity. Some believed that physical substances like ectoplasm could be produced, and others believed that mediums could exert invisible forces outward from them to manipulate objects or people in the room.[60] Dingwall's essay "The Plasma Theory" in the *Journal of the American Society for Psychical Research* provides an overview of the theories and studies of ectoplasm that had been performed to date.

Further Reading:

Eric J. Dingwall. "The Plasma Theory." *Journal of the American Society for Psychical Research* 15 (1921): 207–19.

Eric Dingwall. *Some Human Oddities: Studies in the Queer, the Uncanny and the Fanatical.* London: Home & van Thal, 1947.

Driesch, Hans (1867–1941, Philosopher): Hans Driesch was a German philosopher and psychical researcher who, according to Nandor Fodor, was "the most influential psychical investigator in Germany."[61] He was the first German researcher to be named president of the Society for Psychical Research. In 1928, he studied the Brazilian medium Carlos Mirabelli and when a vase was knocked off the table he was convinced that the medium displayed psychokinetic abilities. He also believed that the medium Willie Schneider had genuine psychical abilities.[62]

Stefan Gruner tells us that Driesch made "noteworthy contributions especially to the metaphysics of life (bio-philosophy) and the metaphysics of mind and soul (psycho-philosophy)."[63] Trained as a biologist, he morphed into a philosopher of biology and established the field of theoretical biology. Considered a vitalist, he believed that life was more than simply a clinical mechanism of biology, and he believed that this view could help explain certain psychical phenomena.[64]

Further Reading:

Stefan Gruner, "Hans Driesch Re-Visited After a Century: On 'Leib Und Seele-Eine Untersuchung Uber Das Psychophysische Grundproblem." *Cosmos and History: The Journal of Natural and Social Philosophy* 13, no. 3 (October 2017): 401–24.

E

Ebon, Martin (1917–2006, Author and Researcher): Martin Ebon was an author who worked as an administrative assistant for the Parapsychology Foundation. During his twelve years working for this organization, he was able to help psychical researchers with their own studies and in the process he wrote more than thirty books on various psychical topics including life after death and extrasensory perception. Researchers Arthur and Joyce Berger laud Ebon's writings as upholding the scientific lens of the field instead of sensationalizing topics or cases.[65] He was particularly intrigued by parapsychology in the Soviet Union, and his book *Psychic Warfare* discusses Russian research into extrasensory perception.[66]

Further Reading:

Martin Ebon, *They Knew the Unknown.* New York: World Publishing, 1971.

van Eeden, Frederik (1860–1932, Psychiatrist): Frederik van Eeden was a Dutch psychiatrist who coined the phrase "lucid dreaming."[67] Researcher Ingrid Kloosterman reminds us that van Eeden "was the first Dutchman actively interested in the work of the British SPR."[68] van Eeden became familiar with the work of Frederic Myers and was able to meet with him during a psychology conference. As a result of this meeting, van Eeden's interest in

Figure 2.8. Frederik van Eeden
From: *The World's Work,* edited by Walter H. Page. (Chicago: Doubleday, Page, & Co.). Photo from Underwood & Underwood; PD-US

psychical phenomena grew and he was even invited to give lectures on dreams at meetings of the Society for Psychical Research.[69] van Eeden believed that instances of the paranormal (e.g., haunting experiences) were natural topics to study within the field of psychology, and he was a pioneering figure in the history of Dutch psychology.[70]

Further Reading:

Ilse N. Bulhof, "From Psychotherapy to Psychoanalysis: Frederik van Eeden and Albert Willem van Renterghem." *The History of the Behavioural Sciences* 17, no. 2 (April 1981): 209–21.

Efron, David (1904–1981, Anthropologist): Dr. David Efron was an Argentinian anthropologist and parapsychologist. After receiving his PhD from the University of Buenos Aires in 1929, he was awarded monies to pursue psychical research in France and Germany. While there he studied at the Institut Métapsychique International in Paris, attended séances of the medium Rudi Schneider, and was inspired to return to Argentina to establish his own laboratory. When he returned to the University of Buenos Aires in 1931 after his research and networking abroad, Efron got to work establishing a parapsychology lab. Everything was set in motion for the new department and lab to open, which would have made the University of Buenos Aires the first university to formally incorporate a parapsychological field of study. However, the political climate in Argentina was volatile and a coup that overthrew the government also decimated academic programs, expelling multiple students in the process. Efron's work in establishing the first academic parapsychology lab was lost to that of J. B. Rhine at Duke University.[71]

Further Reading:

Juan Gimeno, "David Efron: Biography of a Forgotten Pioneer in Psychical Research." *Journal of the Society for Psychical Research* 83, no. 2 (April 2019): 102–15.

Ehrenwald, Jan (1900–1988, Psychiatrist): Jan Ehrenwald was a psychiatrist and member of the medical section of the American Society for Psychical Research. Ehrenwald first became interested in parapsychology when he was working at a hospital in Vienna. While there, one of his patients with schizophrenia claimed she was receiving telepathic messages from her mother. This was curious to Ehrenwald, who noted it and began noticing that other patients with the ailment displayed telepathic abilities as well. He believed this characteristic of schizophrenia was important enough to publish, though the backlash to that publication resulted in being fired from his job.[72]

Further Reading:

Jan Ehrenwald, *Telepathy and Medical Psychology*. New York: W. W. Norton & Company, 1948.

Paulina F. Kernberg, "Comments on Jan Ehrenwald, M.D.: Patterns of Neurotic Interaction." *American Journal of Psychotherapy* 50, no. 4 (Fall 1996): 497–98.

F

Ferenczi, Sándor (1873–1933, Psychoanalyst): Sándor Ferenczi was a Hungarian psychoanalyst and a leading figure in Hungary's history of psychical research. In his early professional career, he attended séances and even dabbled in automatic writing, which he found he had a knack for.[73] He began publishing articles that called for a union between spiritism and scientific inquiry.

In particular, Ferenczi saw the need in Hungary for a more scientific approach to psychical phenomena,

Figure 2.9. Sandor Ferenczi
Photo by Aladár Székely; CC-PD-Mark

as previous organizations did not adhere as strictly to scientific methods as Ferenczi would like. Ferenczi wished to model a society based on the methods of people like William James, Charles Richet, and Albert von Schrenck-Notzing, researchers who applied more rigorous methods to their studies.[74] To begin, he established the Budapest School of Psychoanalysis and began searching for mediums to investigate. His studies on psi phenomena actually helped pave the way for modern understandings of thought transference and projection. In that regard, the psychical had direct implications for psychological science that we know today.[75] Ferenczi believed that when the psyche was in a vulnerable or sensitive state, psychical abilities like thought transference were possible, but that these abilities emanated from the unconscious, not necessarily from some outward, spirit world.[76]

Further Reading:

Júlia Gyimesi, "Why 'Spiritism?'" *The International Journal of Psychoanalysis* 97 (2016): 357–83.

Fielding, Everard (1867–1936, Attorney): Everard Fielding was a British attorney and psychical researcher who formed part of a committee tasked with studying the psychical abilities of medium Eusapia Palladino. In November 1908, Fielding, Hereward Carrington, and William W. Baggaly held eleven sessions with Eusapia at the Hotel Victoria in Naples. Frank Podmore, fellow psychical researcher, wrote a report of this committee's findings in his 1911 work *The Newer Spiritualism*. In this work, based on the report given forth by the committee, Podmore states, "Either there was a display of some hitherto unrecognized force or the witnesses were hallucinated."[77] However, Podmore goes on to offer a critical response to the committee's report, one in which he lays out a case of sense deception on Eusapia's part, resulting in seemingly supernatural phenomena that were no more than the result of sleight of hand. Still others seem less critical of the report, and it remains to this day a divisive document of parapsychological history.

Further Reading:

Frank Podmore, *The Newer Spiritualism*. New York: Henry Holt and Company, 1911.

Flournoy, Theodore (1854–1920, Psychologist): Theodore Flournoy was a Swiss psychologist and chair of experimental psychology at the University of Geneva. After a six-year study of the medium Hélène Smith, Flournoy wrote *From India to the Planet Mars*, a textbook outlining the subconscious qualities that manifested Smith's abilities. In this text, Flournoy lays out the case that Smith's subconscious created seemingly strange abilities when placed in a hypnotic state, and he theorized that in this state she was able to access information that was buried in her subconscious.[78]

While he laid out a case that attributed the strange abilities of Ms. Smith to subconscious origins, Flournoy didn't outright discount the curiosity of psychical phenomena. He did believe in telekinesis: some of Eusapia Palladino's abilities made him question the reality of that phenomena. He also supported

Figure 2.10. Theodore Flournoy
From: Theodore Flournoy's *Spiritism and Psychology* (Harper & Brothers, 1911); PD US

the idea of life after death, though not necessarily that living people could communicate with those who are dead. In other words, he believed that the soul continues to live on separate from the body, and this belief perhaps came out of a survey he administered to seventy-two members of a French psychical society. In this survey, he asked about personal experiences with apparitions of the dead and/or dying and published the results in a 1911 work translated into English as *Spiritism and Psychology*.[79]

Further Reading:

Theodore Flournoy, *Spiritism and Psychology*. New York: Harper and Brothers Publishing, 1911.

Flügel, John Carl (J. C.) (1884–1955, Psychologist and Psychoanalyst): J. C. Flügel was a psychology professor and psychoanalyst at the University College of London. While attending school at Oxford University, he began exploring his interest in psychical phenomena. He conducted séances and even joined the Society for Psychical Research. Once he became a professor at University College, he joined a group of scholars who teamed up with paranormal investigator Harry Price to help spread knowledge about psychical research and phenomena. Harry Price had set up a laboratory designed for scholars and laypeople alike, and Flügel regularly attended séances there.[80]

Further Reading:

J. C. Flügel. *A Hundred Years of Psychology: 1833–1933*. London: G. Duckworth, 1945.

Fodor, Nandor (1895–1964, Psychoanalyst): Nandor Fodor was a Hungarian psychical researcher and psychoanalyst. He published multiple books on psychical topics and authored a seminal reference work in this field titled *An Encyclopedia of Psychic Science*. He helped establish the International Institute for Psychical Research in England and served as a correspondent for the American Society for Psychical Research. In this role, he had a column titled "A Letter from London" that was published in the society's professional journal. The books he wrote and columns he wrote helped create vast amounts of indexing on psychical work, including information on the researchers themselves, notable cases, events, publications, and more. Furthermore, some of his books even advanced psychical theories of the time, as he examined psychical topics through his psychoanalyst background.[81]

Fodor also engaged in psychical research and published his findings in the scholarly literature. Carlos Alvarado tells us that Fodor first became intrigued by psi phenomena when he attended séances conducted by various mediums in New York in the 1920s. He became so intrigued by these events that in 1934 he published a book chronicling the lives of various mediums titled *Mysterious People*.[82] One year prior, in 1933, when Fodor considered himself to be formally part of the psychical movement when he became an assistant editor to the journal *Light*. From that point he began devoting time to researching and writing about mediums.[83]

Fodor was particularly interested in physical mediumship and the occurrence of apports, which are objects that mysteriously appear out of thin air. He studied the Hungarian medium Lajos Pap, known

Figure 2.11. Nandor Fodor
From: Hereward Carrington and Nandor Fodor's *Haunted People: The Story of the Poltergeist down the Centuries* (Dutton, 1951); PD-US-not renewed

for producing extensive apport phenomena.[84] Lajos was a medium who was the subject of extensive studies done by Hungarian chemist and psychical researcher Elemér Chengery Pap. Fodor was present at some of these séances and was impressed by the apports that Lajos seemed to produce. Fodor invited both Lajos and Elemér to London for additional study and during this visit, Fodor discovered that Lajos wore a hidden pouch that was mysteriously never reported during the Hungarian séances at Elemér's laboratory.[85]

Though Fodor discovered this potentially fraudulent behavior, he nevertheless remained intrigued by psi phenomena. For instance, Fodor also studied the intersection of psychology and the poltergeist phenomenon. He was, in fact, one of the first researchers who applied a psychoanalytical point of view to this topic.[86] Fodor believed, as did earlier German parapsychologists, that poltergeist behavior emanated from the living, not from the dead—specifically that children going through puberty were able to psychokinetically produce poltergeist activity.[87] Fodor's work on poltergeist research and theory even earned him the support of Sigmund Freud, notably due to his involvement with the Thornton Heath poltergeist case.[88]

Further Reading:

Carlos S. Alvarado, "Early Psychological Research Reference Works: Remarks on Nandor Fodor's *Encyclopedia of Psychic Science. Journal of Scientific Exploration*" 34, no. 4 (December 2020): 717–54.

Nandor Fodor, *Between Worlds*. West Nyack, NY: Parker Publishing Co., 1964.

Forwald, Haakon (1897–1978, Electrical Engineer): Born in Norway in 1897, Haakon Gabriel Forwald was an electrical engineer. He was also "perhaps the most successful PK [psychokinesis] experimenter of modern times."[89] He served as an engineer for a prestigious Swedish electrical company and held more than five hundred patents for his designs. He became interested in psychical phenomena after a table-tilting incident with friends. After this, Forwald was intrigued by the phenomenon of psychokinesis and designed experiments to study this topic. He devoted twenty years to studying this phenomenon, even working alongside researcher Joseph G. Pratt. Their research garnered them the McDougall Award for Distinguished Work in Parapsychology. The crux of his experiments involved "placement" tests with dice. Essentially, he was curious if he could somehow influence the location in which the dice would land—placement that would directly refute the statistical probability of where the dice should land. As an engineer, he initially suspected that there were some physical explanations that might explain psychokinesis, but he ultimately concluded that the only seeming explanation was his mental projection. In this sense, then, Forwald became both researcher and subject simultaneously.[90] He carried out large numbers of placement tests with various types of dice and was even invited to Duke University's parapsychology labs under the directorship of psychical researcher J. B. Rhine.[91]

Further Reading:

R. A. McConnell and H. Forwald, "Psychokinetic Placement: II. A Factorial Study of Successful and Unsuccessful Series." *Journal of Parapsychology* 31 (1967): 198–213.

Fukurai, Tomokichi (1869–1952, Psychologist): Tomokichi Fukurai was a psychology professor at Tokyo Imperial University. He was Japan's preeminent parapsychologist and was heavily influenced by the work of William James. He was interested in hypnotism, writing about it during his doctoral thesis and also publishing a comprehensive work on it that was considered to be the only academic textbook on the topic until the 1940s.[92] He coined the term "thoughtography," which is a medium's ability to mentally imprint an image onto film.[93] One of the mediums he studied, Ikuko Nagao, claimed to have the ability to mentally transcribe images onto film. As she drew the attention of other researchers, though, both Nagao and Fukurai came under scrutiny as she claimed she could only successfully perform when left completely alone in a room. Naturally, this made people doubtful and unfortunately marked the beginning of Fukurai's decline. He was asked to vacate his post at the university but continued nevertheless to study psychical phenomena on his own. A parapsychology research institute was established in his honor in 1960.[94]

Figure 2.12. Tomokichi Fukurai
From: Kyōiku Jissei Kai's *Meiji Seidai Kyōikuka Meikan, Daiippen (A directory of educators in the Meiji era, Volume 1)*. 1912 (reprint, Yumani Shobō, 1990).

Further Reading:

Miki Takasuna, "The Fukurai Affair: Parapsychology and the History of Psychology in Japan." *History of the Human Sciences* 25, no. 2 (2012): 149–64.

G

Geley, Gustave (1868–1924, Physician): Gustave Geley was a French physician who, after the publication of his second book outlining psychical theories, left his post as physician to devote his time to parapsychological inquiry.[95] This second book, *From the Unconscious to the Conscious*, "is considered by many as the most important contribution to psychical research since Myers' (Frederic W. H. Myers) *Human Personality*."[96] In this book Geley lays out a scientific theory for things like reincarnation and communication with the dead. In the preface he writes, "To build up my demonstration I have endeavored to take account

Figure 2.13. Gustave Geley
From: S. R. Morgan's *Index to Psychic Science* (Swarthmore, 1950); PD-US-not renewed

of all known facts whether in the natural sciences, in general biology, or in admitted data relating to the physiological and psychological constitution of the individual."[97]

Geley was also the director of the Institut Métaphysique International (International Metaphysical Institute) who, while still practicing as a physician, often came under attack and scrutiny for his psychical interests by his medical colleagues. In addition to his publications, some of his other notable work includes making plaster casts of mysterious hands that appeared during the séances involving medium Franek Kluski. Geley also investigated the medium Marthe Béraud, known more commonly as Eva Carrière. Though Geley believed Béraud's mediumship to be authentic, her séances were later discredited as fraudulent.

Further Reading:

Gustave Geley, *From the Unconscious to the Conscious*. Translated by S. De Brath. New York: Harper and Brothers, 1919.

Goldney, Kathleen M. (1894–1992, Psychical Researcher): Kathleen M. Goldney was a British psychical researcher and early member of the Society for Psychical Research. She coauthored the Shackleton Report, "Considered for decades one of the most important series of experiments ever conducted in parapsychology."[98] The Shackleton Report refers to the South African psychic Basil Shackleton. Having been gifted with psychic abilities his entire life, he was in London at the same time as researcher Samuel Soal. Shackleton learned of the research Soal was doing in regard to ESP, and reached out to him. Soal enlisted his colleague Kathleen Goldney and together they performed over four thousand tests in which Shackleton, guessing cards with various animals imprinted on them, exhibited a large amount of positive and statistically significant hits. However, in 1978 it was revealed the Goldney's research partner Soal had manipulated data and unethically published that fraudulent data, leaving us to wonder about the true abilities of Shackleton.[99]

In addition to the Shackleton Report, Goldney investigated the medium Eileen Garrett, specifically the physiological aspects of Garrett's trance state. Goldney also investigated Garrett's reports of receiving precognitive visions of the R-101 plane crash in 1930.[100]

Gurney, Edmund (1847–1889, Psychologist): Edmund Gurney was one of the founding members of the British SPR. Along with his fellow SPR cofounders Frank Podmore and Frederic W. H. Myers, he authored a seminal text on psychical and haunt phenomena titled *Phantasms of the Living*. In fact, most of the authorship of this work is attributed to Gurney, with Myers contributing the introduction and Podmore in charge of case studies and evidentiary support.[101] This work, still considered an important document in parapsychology, contains the case studies of approximately seven hundred people who experienced seeing or hearing a living person who could not possibly have been in that physical location at the time. This would be like seeing your cousin, who resides in Alaska, suddenly walk down your hallway one day. Gurney's work on *Phantasms of the Living* helped establish that there was a large occurrence of people who seemed to be experiencing some spectral hallucination that, through the details and instances of each experience, could not be explained away through illness or misidentification—in fact, statistician Francis Y. Edgeworth worked with Gurney to determine what role chance could even play in such detailed encounters as these.[102] In many instances, these experiences were classified as "crisis apparitions" because the sighting (or sound) of the person often coincided very near a time in which they were encountering severe danger or even death. Researchers Berger and Berger summarize it nicely when they write, "The authors of the book believed that crisis apparitions were created by a telepathic message from the one undergoing the crisis that causes the recipient of the message to have an hallucination."[103]

In addition to his work on *Phantasms of the Living*, Gurney was highly interested in hypnotism. After becoming intrigued by both psychology and philosophy, he met fellow psychologist and psy-

Figure 2.14. K. M. Goldney
Anonymous photo, 1940s.

chical researcher William James, and he already knew the parapsychologists Frederic W. H. Myers and Henry Sidgwick from his Trinity College days. As his fascination with psychology and associated professional connections grew, he devoted his time to the SPR and psychical investigations, many of which involved hypnotism.[104] According to psychical historian and researcher Nandor Fodor, Gurney had "devised a large number of experiments by which he proved that there is sometimes, in the induction of hypnotic phenomena, some agency at work which is neither ordinary nervous stimulation, nor suggestion conveyed by any ordinary channel to the subject's mind."[105] Inspired by the findings in *Phantasms of the Living*, Gurney helped develop the Census of Hallucinations, an international research study conducted by members of the SPR that investigated the phenomena of crisis apparitions. Researchers in this study gathered nearly seventeen thousand reports from those who reported seeing apparitions of living people. His contributions to the intersection of hallucination, hypnotism, and consciousness cannot be overstated.[106]

Further Reading:

Gordon Epperson, *The Mind of Edmund Gurney*. Madison, NJ: Fairleigh Dickinson University Press, 1997.

Andreas Sommer, "Professional Heresy: Edmund Gurney (1847–1888) and the Study of Hallucinations and Hypnotism." *Medical History* 55 no. 3 (July 2011): 383–88.

H

Heymans, Gerardus (1857–1930, Psychologist and Philosopher): Gerardus Heymans was a leading figure in Dutch parapsychology. He was a philosopher, psychologist, and forerunner of experimental parapsychology. Researcher Ingrid Kloosterman reminds us that Dutch parapsychology didn't blossom until 1919 when the Dutch Society for Psychical Research was founded, with Heymans as its first president. Heymans believed in and promoted the idea of psychic monism, which posits that "only the psychical exists, since everything physical is nothing more than how the psychical is perceived."[107] At the crux of this view is the notion of shared consciousness, and that all living beings

Figure 2.15. Gerardus Heymans
Photo by A. S. Weinberg, June 1909; CC-PD-Mark

share consciousness. This was a view espoused by others at the time as well.

Further Reading:

T. T. ten Have, "Essentials of Heymans' Philosophy." *Synthese* 5, no. 11/12 (March–April 1947): 526–41.

Heywood, Rosalind (1895–1980, Psychical Researcher): Rosalind Heywood was a psychic and member of the British SPR. She noticed that she had extrasensory abilities when she served as a nurse's aide in World War I. Resorting to unconventional methods to save patients, Heywood couldn't describe how she received the knowledge, but knew that it came from outside herself. She continued having telepathic encounters and joined the SPR in 1938 to learn more about her own experiences and contribute to the knowledge of the field. She contributed to the society's experiments and literature, and even published multiple books, one being an autobiography.[108]

Figure 2.16. Rosalind Heywood
Anonymous photo, California, 1966; PD-US-no notice

Further Reading:

Rosalind Heywood, *Beyond the Reach of Sense: An Inquiry into Extrasensory Perception.* New York: Dutton, 1959.

Rosalind Heywood, *ESP: A Personal Memoir.* New York: Dutton, 1964.

Hodgson, Richard (1855–1905, Psychical Researcher): Richard Hodgson was an Australian researcher who, after obtaining his law degree in Melbourne, Australia, moved to England to continue his law studies at Cambridge. While there he joined the Ghost Society and subsequently became interested in the SPR. He became one of SPR's earliest members. Due to his legal background, he was particularly poised to ferret out instances of fraud among mediums. Perhaps his most well-known work in that regard is his unmasking of notable medium Madam Blavatsky. In November 1884, during a trip to India, he unveiled a large-scale fraud operation at the core of her performances.

In addition to Madam Blavatsky, Hodgson also investigated medium Leonora Piper, though this inquiry had much different results. After his work unveiling the Blavatsky mediumship, he was offered the role of secretary for the American SPR. He accepted the offer and soon got to work not only publishing papers but also investigating the authenticity of Leonora Piper. Though he was skeptical of psychical phenomena, he spent fifteen years studying Leonora and concluded that her abilities were genuine. During one sitting with her, in fact, he learned through her of the untimely passing of his former love—a fact that was later verified and which left a lasting impact on him. His fifteen-year study of this medium was considered to be one of the greatest contributions to parapsychology at that time. He passed away suddenly in 1905, and shortly after, Leonora Piper claimed to receive messages from him.[109]

Further Reading:

Richard Hodgson, "Spiritism and Mrs. Piper." *Medico-Legal Journal* 19, no. 4 (1901–1902): 741–45.

Humphrey, Betty (1917–, Parapsychologist): Betty Humphrey is the author of *Handbook of Tests in Parapsychology*, published in 1948 by the Parapsychology Labs at Duke University. Humphrey became interested in parapsychology while engaging in psychical research during her undergraduate studies an Earlham College in Indiana. Because of her interest in this topic, she pursued graduate work at Duke University, knowing that, at the time, they had an established lab devoted to parapsychological study. Naturally, she befriended J. B. Rhine who asked her to continue her research in a formal position at the parapsychology labs. Along with her husband and fellow parapsychologist J. Fraser Nicol, Humphrey's research uncovered a link between extroversion and psychical abilities. In other words, she discovered that those with extrasensory abilities often have extroverted personalities, and she also discovered a link between mood and psychical ability, noting that participants in a calmer mood often exhibited higher rates of psi ability.[110] These methods and more can be found in the handbook listed below.

Further Reading:

Betty M. Humphrey, *Handbook of Tests in Parapsychology.* Durham, NC: Duke University, 1948.

Hyslop, James (1854–1920, Psychical Researcher): James Hyslop was an early researcher of the American SPR and an ethics professor at Columbia University. Prior to his work at Columbia, he taught at Lake Forest and Bucknell Universities. His ill health forced him into an early retirement from Columbia and it was then that he began devoting much of his time to psychical studies. He became interested in parapsychology mostly through his friendship with William James and encounters with the medium Leonora Piper.[111] Hyslop was a key investigator, in fact, into the mediumship of Leonora Piper and held numerous sessions with her. After his twelfth reading with her, he was convinced that her telepathic abilities were genuine and that he was communicating with his dead relatives, most notably his father and brothers.[112] In 1904, he founded the American Institute for Scientific Research, an organization whose aim was psychical research. He is the author of several books on psychical topics.

Further Reading:

James Hyslop, *Contact with the Other World: The Latest Evidence as to Communication with the Dead.* New York: The Century Co., 1919.

James Hyslop, *Life After Death.* New York: E. P. Dutton & Co., 1918.

Michael Tymn, "Difficulties in Spirit Communication Explained by Dr. James Hyslop." *The Journal of Spirituality and Paranormal Studies* 33, no. 4 (2010): 195–209.

J

James, William (1842–1910, Psychologist and Philosopher): Dr. William James is considered by many to be the father of American psychology. Researcher Daniel W. Bjork tells us that James had many interests and pursuits, though. He was at various times involved in many different fields, including the two for which he is most well-known, psychology and philosophy.[113] The oldest son of Henry James and Mary Walsh, James perhaps took after his father who is described as mystical and someone who engaged in a lifelong spiritual journey. Born and raised in New York, at the age of thirteen James and his family traveled abroad and lived in various places including Geneva, Paris, and London. While in Europe, James attended various schools or was taught by private tutors, and it was during this time that his early passion for art was greatly enhanced.[114] This artistic interest continued to grow and eventually became a vocational calling for him, much to the disappointment of his father. After some studies, however, James gave up on artistry to pursue science, but maintained his creative outlook. Bjork tells us that "his was an eclectic, omnivorous intelligence, an intelligence that explored various interpretations of natural, social, and metaphysical reality while simultaneously searching for a suitable medium of creative expression."[115]

James enrolled in the Lawrence Scientific School in 1861 and earned his medical degree from Harvard in 1869. A few short years later, in 1873, he was appointed as anatomy and physiology professor at Harvard.[116] In 1878, James published his earliest scholarly articles that discussed consciousness. To James, consciousness involved an "interested, dissociative mind willfully selecting rather than simply reacting to environmental stimuli."[117] His interest in the intersection of psychology, physiology, and philosophy blossomed over the next decade.

During a trip to England in 1882, James met with some of the founders of the British SPR and became inspired by their work. As a researcher open to the possibility of psychical phenomena himself, this meeting and inspiration led him to create an American branch of the SPR in 1884. A year later, in 1885, James learned of the medium Leonora Piper. James's mother-in-law had attended one of Leonora's séances and told him what an amazing experience she'd had. He decided to attend one of the séances himself and over a series of months, he and one of his colleagues continued to attend multiple séances through which he became convinced of Leonora's genuine supernatural abilities. James's fascination with Ms. Piper's abilities manifested into an enormous survey on trance and hallucinations. A survey, the Census of Hallucinations, gathered more than seventeen thousand responses. To him, psychopathological states and psychical abilities like mediumship were closely connected. And much like it seems researchers still do today, he spent a great deal of time trying to persuade the academy and his colleagues to see the value in psychical study.[118]

In fact, "from the early 1880s until his death in 1910, James immersed himself in" psychical study.[119] He continued collaborating with his British colleagues and in 1894 even served as president of the British SPR. At the time of this presidency, his interest in psychical phenomena reached its height. In 1896, for example, he gave lectures at the Lowell Institute at Huntington Hall. This lecture series, which focused on notions of the unconscious, included topics such as dreams, hypnotism, possession, multiple personality, and automatism.[120]

Interestingly, Bjork points out that some of James's contemporaries (and some still in psychology today) viewed James's psychical interests with disdain, dismissing it as nothing more than a fanciful interest that he entertained. Even James's own son asked for his father's psychical works to be excluded from an exhibit at Harvard.[121] Researcher Krister Dylan Knapp reminds us, however, that James was neither an automatic believer nor an adamant denier of psychic phenomena. Rather, he was interested in what these phenomena could reveal to us about the human mind and consciousness. In fact, Knapp tells us that "his purpose . . . was neither to advance a religious cause not to undermine one but rather to understand and hypostatize psychic phenomena."[122] It was the aforementioned encounter with medium Leonora Piper that really seemed to launch William's scholarly inquiry into mediumistic abilities, and in particular with telepathy. In the early 1900s, he became involved in studies with the Italian medium Eusapia Palladino, and he traveled extensively to lecture on these topics, especially to Europe. His writings on psychical matters were published in the *American Journal of Psychology*, *Psychological Review*, *The Atlantic*, and more.[123] All this work supported his creation of the sublime conscious theory and the notion of a subliminal self, a theory which posits that the existence of psychical ability in trance states points to the reality of "extra-consciousness."[124] His work helped set the stage for future psychical researchers and advanced ideas of the power of the human mind and consciousness.

Further Reading:

Daniel W. Bjork, *William James: The Center of His Vision.* Washington, DC: American Psychological Association, 1997.

William James, "What Psychical Research Has Accomplished." *Forum* (August 1892): 727.

Krister Dylan Knapp, *William James: Psychical Research and the Challenge of Modernity.* Chapel Hill: The University of North Carolina Press, 2017.

Janet, Pierre (1859–1947, Psychologist): Pierre Janet was a French psychologist and physician and one of the founders of French psychology. As a founder of psychology when it was a growing discipline, Janet practiced psychology during a

Figure 2.17. Pierre Janet
Bibliothèque de la Sorbonne, Unknown author, CC BY-SA 4.0 <https://creativecommons.org/licenses/by-sa/4.0>

time in which psychical phenomena were not *quite* relegated to their own subdiscipline. Topics like telepathy and clairvoyance, and particularly the phenomena of mediumship, were research topics of many leading psychologists of the time.[125]

Janet was interested in the ways that hypnosis could be used to treat illnesses, particularly mental illnesses. He was "among the first to observe that psi was closely connected to altered states of consciousness."[126] In his studies, he found that those in hypnotic states exhibited ESP, and he also discovered that hypnosis could be induced from a long distance.[127]

Further Reading:

Renaud Evrard, Erika Annabelle Pratte, and Etzel Cardeña, "Pierre Janet and the Enchanted Boundary of Psychical Research." *History of Psychology* 21, no. 2 (2018): 100–25.

Jephson, Ina (189?–1961, Psychologist): Ina Jephson was a British psychologist who coined the notion of the decline effect. In 1928, Jephson designed an experiment in which more than 240 people, in pairs, would attempt to correctly identify playing cards held by one participant. She noticed, through the course of this experiment, that the statistical significance of correct guesses seemed to follow a certain pattern. Correct guesses began occurring early in the test, then fell off only to have a slight surge again toward the end of the experiment.[128] Jephson also referred to this as the "fatigue effect," and her experiments on telepathy were highly regarded by the SPR, in which she became a member in 1920.[129]

Johnson, Alice (1860–1940, Zoologist): Alice Johnson was a research officer for the SPR and secretary of fellow parapsychologist Eleanor Sidgwick when they were both working at Newnham College. In her research, Johnson was involved in the inquiries into both Leonora Piper and Eusapia Palladino. Johnson also spent decades studying the curious phenomena of cross-correspondences, which refers to instances in which the speech or writing of two separate and unconnected mediums are either a direct match or appear to answer one another. Many cross-correspondences occurred during automatic writing sessions and were sometimes signed off with the name of a deceased person. To Johnson

and her fellow researchers, cross-correspondences indicated the survival of life after death.

In addition to her research, Johnson was editor of the *Proceedings of the Society for Psychical Research* and helped posthumously complete Frederic W. H. Myer's *Human Personality and its Survival of Bodily Death.*[130]

Further Reading:

Alice Johnson, "Coincidences." *Proceedings of the Society for Psychical Research* 14 (1898–99): 158–330.
Emily Williams Kelly, "Some Directions for Mediumship Research." *Journal of Scientific Exploration,* vol. 24, no. 2 (2010): 247–82.

Jung, Carl (1875–1961, Psychiatrist): Dr. Carl Jung was a Swiss psychiatrist who, in addition to his immense contributions to the field of psychology, had lifelong experience with the paranormal. As a young man, Jung experienced telepathy, precognitive dreams, and even a near-death experience. To the field of parapsychology, he is perhaps most known for two concepts: the collective unconscious and synchronicities. The collective unconscious refers to a "trans-psychicism" that is shared by all living beings—that is, the notion that all knowledge is shared by all beings. It has been used as a theory to explain certain psychical phenomena like telepathy, clairvoyance, and especially the abilities demonstrated by mediums.[131]

"Synchronicity," a term many readers have likely heard, refers to those coincidences that seem to be accompanied by significant meaning. Jung believed that synchronicities occurred when a physical manifestation seemed to coincide with either normal psychological or anomalous psychical events. For example, Jung himself experienced a striking synchronicity when he was meeting with a patient who had been having recurring dreams of a scarab beetle. During one of these meetings, Jung heard a noise at his window and looked over to see a scarab beetle perched on his ledge.[132] Michael Fordham, in the preface to Jung's *Synchronicity,* tells us that "Jung introduced the idea of synchronicity to strip off the fantasy, magic, and superstition which surround and are provoked by unpredictable, startling, and impressive events that, like these, appear to be connected. They are simply 'meaningful coincidences.'"[133]

Further Reading:

Carl Jung, *Synchronicities*. New York: Bollingen, 1960.

K

Kilner, Walter John (1847–1920, Physician): Walter Kilner was a British physician noted for being the first researcher to investigate the presence of a human aura. He even designed special glasses that would allow wearers to see these invisible fields around the body. His work (and the concept) are controversial, but Kilner is notable for being the first to venture into experimentation with auras.[134]

Further Reading:

Walter J. Kilner, *The Human Aura*. Secaucus, NJ: Citadel Press, 1965 (a reprint of the original 1911 title *The Human Atmosphere*).

L

Lodge, Sir Oliver (1851–1940, Physicist): Researcher Nandor Fodor tells us that "Sir Oliver Lodge [was] the first great thinker who brought the transcendental world into close relationship with the physical one."[135] Lodge was a British physicist and early member of the SPR. Researcher John Beloff, in his introductory chapter in the *Handbook of Parapsychology*, reminds us that when the SPR was founded, it made particular effort to include people from many backgrounds, but most certainly those from scientific backgrounds. Sir Oliver Lodge was one of these early scientific members of the SPR, joining after befriending both Edmund Gurney and Frederic W. H. Myers.[136]

Lodge became convinced of the reality of psychical phenomena during his investigations with mediums. The first well-known medium he investigated was Italian medium Eusapia Palladino. Lodge attended four séances with Eusapia and published his favorable findings in the *Journal of the Society for Psychical Research*. Even when Eusapia's abilities were attacked as fraudulent a year later, Lodge stood by his conclusion, commenting that there were vast differences between the two studies, further adding to the complex enigma of Eusapia herself.[137]

Figure 2.18. Sir Oliver Lodge
Lafayette Studio, CC BY 4.0 <https://creativecommons.org/licenses/by/4.0>

While the inquiry into Eusapia was marked by controversy, the medium Leonora Piper ultimately sealed his belief in psychical abilities. He attended more than twenty sessions and concluded that her abilities seemed to be a result of some ability not yet known to science. He continued his research with mediums and was introduced in the early 1900s to medium Gladys Osborne Leonard and her cross-correspondences.[138] In fact, "it was through her that [he] claimed to have made contact with his son Raymond, killed in action in 1915."[139]

Lodge served as the president of the British SPR during a tenuous time in the organization's history—some even say that his leadership helped ensure the continued operation of the group.[140]

Further Reading:

Sir Oliver Lodge, "Possible Automatism of Young Children." *Journal of the Society for Psychical Research* 14 (March 1909): 60–64.

James Mussell and Graeme Gooday, *A Pioneer of Connection: Recovering the Life and Work of Oliver Lodge*. Pittsburgh: University of Pittsburgh Press, 2020.

M

McDougall, William (1871–1931, Psychologist): William McDougall was a British American psychologist and the chair of psychology at Harvard University. He argued for the scientific acceptance of the soul in his book *Body and Mind*, which also includes a chapter on psychical phenomena and the implications of cross-correspondence to science.

Though he believed in the reality of psychical phenomena, he wasn't blind to the fraud that often accompanied séances. In fact, during one of the first séances McDougall attended, he revealed one of the medium's fraudulent tactics. He also believed that the infamous medium "Margery" (Mina Crandon) to be a fraud as well. These encounters didn't dampen his belief in the existence of anomalous phenomena, and in 1920 he was appointed president of the British SPR. Just one short year later he was also appointed president of the American branch of the SPR. He was an active proponent of bringing psychical studies into college curriculums, and in 1927 when he became chair of the psychology department at Duke University, his work and ethos "helped pave the way for [J. B.] Rhine's work and the creation of the Parapsychology Laboratory."[141]

Further Reading:

Egil Asprem, "A Nice Arrangement of Heterodoxies: William McDougall and the Professionalization of Psychical Research." *Journal of the History of Behavioral Sciences* 46, no. 2 (Spring 2010): 123–43.

William McDougall, "The Need for Psychical Research." *Journal of the American Society for Psychical Research* 17, no. 1 (January 1923): 4.

J. G. Pratt, "William McDougall and Present-Day Psychical Research." *Journal of the American Society for Psychical Research* 64, no. 4 (October 1, 1970): 385.

J. B. Rhine, "The Importance of Parapsychology to William McDougall." *Journal of Parapsychology* 35, no. 3 (September 1, 1971): 169–88.

Morselli, Enrico (1852–1929, Psychiatrist): Enrico Morselli was an Italian psychiatrist who was involved in studies of various mediums like Eusapia Palladino. Although interested in the merits of hypnotism, Morselli was highly skeptical of physical mediumship and was dedicated to exposing fraud wherever he could. In a 2014 dissertation for the University of California, Daphne Rozenblatt tells us that "he adamantly opposed spiritism and in fact, might be regarded as its most vocal enemy in Italy."[142] Morselli conducted more than thirty séances with Eusapia Palladino, the results of which he published a two-volume study and in addition to this work, authored numerous other works on his theories and research into spiritist practices.[143]

Further Reading:

Enrico Morselli, *Psicologia e "Spiritismo": Impressioni e Note Critiche sui Fenomeni Medianici di Eusapia Palladino*. Two volumes. Turin: Fratelli Bocca, 1908.

Daphne Claire Rozenblatt, "Madness and Method: Enrico Morselli and the Social Politics of Psychiatry, 1852–1929." PhD diss., University of California, 2014.

Moser, Fanny H. (1872–1953, Biologist): Dr. Fanny Moser was a Swiss biologist credited as one of the first scientists to link psychical phenomena with altered states of consciousness. Her publication *Okkultismus* outlines twenty-seven of her most memorable cases.[144]

Münsterberg, Hugo (1863–1916, Psychologist): Dr. Hugo Münsterberg was a German American psychologist. He was very critical of psychical phenomena and a vocal opponent of psychical phenomena having any place within the fledgling discipline of psychology. After repeated attempts by psychologist William James for Münsterberg to attend a séance and consider the evidence for himself, he finally relented in December 1909 and agreed to consider the mediumship of Eusapia Palladino. Researcher Andreas Sommer reminds us, though, that Hugo Münsterberg was a popular figure among the press and "must have known that his verdict on any controversial matter related to the study of the human mind would be snapped up by the media and

Figure 2.19. Hugo Münsterberg
From: Münsterberg's *Grundzüge der Psychologie*, 1900; CC-PD-Mark

accepted as the official verdict of scientific psychology."[145] Perhaps Münsterberg accepted the invitation to study Eusapia as an opportunity to officially declare a statement on psychical phenomena. Indeed, his resulting publication "revealed his determination to cleanse academic psychology from any occult connotations."[146] His publication outlining the fraud that he exposed during Eusapia's séance indicates not only the nuanced and curious case of Eusapia herself, but the vitriolic divide within the academy regarding acceptable boundaries of psychological research.

Further Reading:

Andreas Sommer, "Psychical Research and the Origins of American Psychology: Hugo Münsterberg, William James and Eusapia Palladino." *History of the Human Sciences* 25, no. 2 (2012): 23–44.

Myers, Frederic W. H. (1843–1901, Psychical Researcher): Dr. Frederic W. H. Myers was a founding member of the British SPR. His interest in psychical phenomena can partly be attributed to his friendship with SPR cofounder Henry Sidgwick. Myers had a role in nearly every aspect of the early work of the SPR—in fact, he is credited with coining the terms "telepathy" and "supernormal."[147] One of the early works of the SPR (and one of Myers' star contributions to parapsychology that has been hailed as a landmark publication) was the publication of *Phantasms of the Living*, a publication that compiled more than seven hundred case studies of people who experienced telepathic sounds or visions. This publication challenged assumptions of haunt phenomena when the authors discovered that many instances of haunt experience involved visions of living people, hence the term "phantasms of the living."[148]

In addition, Myers was a key figure in the organization of the International Congress of Psychology, served leadership roles within that organization, and regularly published research in periodicals.[149] In his work, one key theory stands out: the notion of "the subliminal self." Myers' theory of "the subliminal self" predates organized theories about the unconscious and posits that "below the threshold of consciousness, exists another hidden strata of our being in which is found material more precious than that repressed from consciousness."[150] One of his most notable accomplishments and contributions to the field of parapsychology was his publication *Human Personality and its Survival of Bodily Death*, which outlines this notion of the subliminal self. Myers began this work while still alive and it was posthumously finished by his colleagues, most notably Alice Johnson. Researcher Nandor Fodor describes this work by telling us that "it is an exposition of the potential powers of the subliminal self . . . a vast psychic organism of which the ordinary consciousness is but an accidental fraction, the life of the soul, not bound up with the life of the body, of which the supernormal faculties are the ordinary channels of perception."[151]

Throughout his involvement with the SPR, Myers conducted many studies of mediums, including Eusapia Palladino, Rosalie Thompson, C. E. Wood, Annie Fairlamb, and more. In fact, it was his work with Rosalie Thompson that sealed his conviction of life after death, and he even presented that viewpoint at an International Congress of Psychology.[152] Myers was admired by his colleagues and his contributions to parapsychology echo still today.

Further Reading:

Frederic W. H. Myers, *Human Personality and its Survival of Bodily Death.* London: Longmans, Green, and Co., 1919.

N

Nash, Carroll Blue (1914–1998, Biologist): Dr. Nash was the chair of the biology department at St. Joseph's College in Philadelphia and an eminent parapsychologist. Having developed an interest in psychical topics since childhood (his mother was particularly interested in such topics and it seems this was passed to her son), he even attended a handful of séances in his youth. After receiving his doctorate and taking a post at St. Joseph's College, Dr. Nash also created a parapsychology lab on campus where he could continue his interest in psychical matters from a scholarly perspective. He would go on to author multiple parapsychology textbooks and more than one hundred articles.[153]

Further Reading:

Carroll B. Nash, "The Effect of Subject-Experimenter Attitudes on Clairvoyance Scores." *Journal of Parapsychology* 24, no. 3 (September 1, 1960): 189–98.
Dorothy H. Pope, "Obituary: Carroll Blue Nash." *Journal of Parapsychology* 62, no. 4 (December 1998): 361–62.

Newbold, William R. (1865–1926, Philosopher): Dr. William R. Newbold was a philosophy professor at the University of Pennsylvania and a member of the American SPR. His research into psychical phenomena included cases of possession, dream studies, and mediumship studies. He is credited with introducing the medium Leonora Piper, a medium with whom he had more than twenty studies with and of whom he was convinced had genuine psychical abilities, to his colleague James Hyslop.[154]

O

Ochorowicz, Julian (1850–1917, Psychologist and Philosopher): Dr. Julian Ochorowicz was a Polish psychologist and philosopher who studied at Warsaw University and obtained his PhD at the University of Leipzig. He was particularly interested in hypnotism, mediumship, and altered states of consciousness. As Zofia Weaver tells us in her biographical article, Ochorowicz came to believe that hypnotism was neither a pathological state nor a mere trick of suggestion. Rather, he believed it was anomalous. In 1887, he published a book outlining the experiments that he and other psychical researchers had conducted regarding hypnotism. In it, he also discusses some of the anomalous phenomena that seem correlated with this altered state of consciousness, such as clairvoyance and table-tilting—phenomena that Ochorowicz believed were rooted in the subconscious and not from an otherworldly spectral influence.[155]

Further Reading:

Zofia Weaver, "Julian Ochorowicz and his Contribution to Psychical Research." *Journal of Parapsychology* 83, no. 1 (Spring 2019): 69–78.

Osterreich, Traugott Konstantin (1880–1949, Philosopher): Traugott K. Osterreich was a German philosopher who was among the first academics to discuss the prevalence of possession and trance experiences in cultures across the globe. He was also an early German scientist who attempted to advance the cause of formal psychical studies within the academy. He was a contemporary of Hans Driesch, a fellow German parapsychologist, but unfortunately both he and Driesch were forced to resign their posts and pause their research during World War I.[156]

Osty, Eugene (1874–1938, Physician): Eugene Osty was a French physician who is often referred to as a founder of French psychical research alongside his contemporary Charles Richet. Osty was involved in research with mediums Gerard Croiset, Pascal Forthuny, Franek Kluski, and Rudi Schneider. He

Figure 2.20. Eugene Osty
Photo by anonymous, circa 1930

wrote an entire book, in fact, on Forthuny and was convinced of the legitimacy of physical manifestations of paraffin hands at the séances of Kluski.

The first significant encounter Osty had with psychical phenomena was in 1909 during a visit to a palm reader. During the session, the palmist gave curiously accurate descriptions of people Osty knew, convincing him of no normal explanation for knowing this information. This encounter sparked Osty's curiosity and led him down a path of scientific inquiry into clairvoyance. He published some of this research in French scientific journals such as *Les Annales des Sciences Psychiques* and *Psychica*. In 1924, he became president of the Institut Métaphysique International (International Metaphysical Institute). During his leadership, he was concerned with developing better instrumentation to study psychical phenomena. Human observation was a good start, but Osty realized the fallible nature of the human mind, so he worked closely with his engineer son to develop instruments that could eliminate the potential of human subjectivity in psychical research.[157] Researcher Nandor Fodor tells us that "in 1931 and 1932, with the collaboration of his son, Marcel Osty, he employed, for the first time in mediumistic research, infrared and ultraviolet rays in the study of Rudi Schneider."[158] Schneider seemed to display psychokinetic abilities during his séances, that is, the ability to move/affect physical items telepathically. In order to ferret out any instance of fraud, Osty developed a system of infrared rays placed around the séance room that would reveal any tampering by unnoticed human hands.[159]

Another researcher, Carlos Alvarado, reminds us of Osty's theories on out-of-body experiences in a 2016 article in the *Journal of the Society for Psychical Research*. In it, Alvarado discusses the research and case studies of people who experienced anomalous visions of living people such as the phenomena outlined in *Phantasms of the Living*. Osty believed that experiences of "visions of the self" were equally as important as visions of others.[160] In a 1930 article, Osty describes case studies of people who experienced seeing apparitions of themselves during the course of their normal day, but he also goes on to describe case studies of those who saw themselves during an out-of-body experience, such as during a medical procedure, crisis, or moment of extreme emotional distress. Osty believed that the occurrence of "an exteriorization of the self" had important psychological implications and that, perhaps, the same subconscious mechanisms that occur during sleep can also occur during wakefulness. Osty's research helped pave the way for generations of future psychical researchers both in France and abroad.

Further Reading:

Carlos Alvarado, "Eugene Osty on Out-of-Body Experiences." *Journal of the Society for Psychical Research* 80, no. 2 (2016): 122–25.

Eugene Osty, *Supernormal Faculties in Man: An Experimental Study*. London: Methuen & Co., 1923.

P

Pagenstecher, Gustav (1855–1942, Physician): Dr. Gustav Pagenstecher was born in Germany and later moved to Mexico to practice medicine. A patient of his, María Reyes de Zierold, was the catalyst who made him believe in psychical phenomena. When Reyes de Zierold sought out Dr. Pagenstecher for therapy, he employed the use of hypnotism, and in so doing discovered that she displayed psychic abilities. Specifically, she displayed psychometric abilities, which occurs when a person obtains psychic impressions and information from merely touching a physical object.[161] In one such instance, Reyes de Zierold gleaned information from a letter found in a bottle that had been tossed to sea from a ship that had sunk during World War I. The information that she received when handling the letter (which was in a sealed envelope), was fact-checked against historical records. Pagenstecher was able to identify which ship and even which passenger it was from. He presented his findings on this research at conferences, and even though his colleagues were a bit dubious about the value of such research, he was nevertheless elected as president of the Mexican Medical Society.[162]

Further Reading:

G. Pagenstecher, "A Notable Psychometric Test." *Journal of the American Society for Psychical Research* 14, no. 8 (August 1920): 386.
Walter Franklin Prince, "Psychometric Experiments with María Reyes de Z." *Journal of the American Society for Psychical Research* 26 (1922): 5–40.

Pap, Elemér Chengery (1869–?) (Chemist): Elemér Chengery Pap was a Hungarian chemist who studied physical mediumship and wrote one of the largest single-author works on experimental parapsychology.[163] Researcher Michael Nahm tells us that while Elemér contributed detailed studies into physical mediumship, unfortunately his work is known to few outside the academy, indicating perhaps a bias toward parapsychological literature from the United Kingdom and United States. Born into a family interested in Spiritualism, it is perhaps no surprise that Elemér became interested in related topics as well. Using his background as a chemist, Elemér created a laboratory designed to strictly control test conditions and conducted research there with two mediums: Tibor Molnar and Lajos Pap.[164] The laboratory also included a room that housed a museum of apported objects, which have unfortunately been lost in the aftermath of World War II. Elemér also attended séances conducted by the noted Austrian medium Maria Silbert, sometimes with Molnar in tow.

While Elemér briefly worked with medium Molnar, the overwhelming majority of research conducted in his lab involved Lajos Pap. During the mediumship experiments conducted at his laboratory, Elemér maintained strict procedures. Everyone present was checked to ensure they carried no hidden objects, and only after everyone was checked were people allowed in the laboratory. At this point, though, participants were required to check the room, ensuring that all doors were locked and all items in the room were thoroughly checked for hidden features. Once the séance participants were checked, some of whom were physicians, the medium Lajos could enter and was subject to a comprehensive physical overview to ensure that there were no hidden items on his person: he would sometimes even undress completely. At this point, all persons present were given robes that had luminescent ribbons sewn around the wrists and ankles, allowing for observance of hands and feet at all times. From 1928–1938, these procedures were implemented during all 194 tests involving Lajos. It was during these séances that some of the most intense apport phenomena was reported. During some of these séances, objects would apport into the locked séance room. Some of these items came from other rooms in the lab, while some came from Elemér's home. Twice the scientist's turtle even mysteriously apported beneath the bound hands of Lajos.[165] For a more detailed overview of these experiments, and for a critique involving a hidden belt that was never revealed by Elemér to séance participants, see the further reading section.

Further Reading:

Michael Nahm, "Out of Thin Air? Apport Studies Performed between 1928 and 1938 by Elemér Chengery Pap." *Journal of Scientific Exploration* 33, no. 4 (2019): 661–705.

Piddington, John George (1869–1952, Psychical Researcher): John George Piddington was a British parapsychologist who joined the SPR in 1890. He helped gather support to create a research endowment fund that would allow the SPR to obtain a full-time psychical researcher. In 1924, he became president of the British SPR and delivered a speech that addressed the tensions apparent in the society during that decade—tensions that seemed to emanate from a difference of opinion in experimental standards and that caused many members to cease their support.

For three decades, he and his colleagues (including but not limited to Gerald Balfour, Eleanor Sidgwick, and Alice Johnson) compiled research on cross-correspondences. This refers to writings and letters obtained by automatic writers that appeared to correspond to one another. For example, a letter obtained by one automatic writer appearing to answer or add to some information in writings obtained by another automatic writer. Most often, these cross-correspondences seemed to be delivered through the mediums by spirits of deceased individuals.[166] Researcher points out that "the cross-correspondences are, in the opinion of some eminent psychical researchers who studied them for years, the most convincing evidence of intelligent communication from the 'dead.'"[167]

Further Reading:

J. G. Piddington, "A Discussion of Cross-Correspondences." *Journal of the Society for Psychical Research* 14, no. 274 (December 1910): 400.

Podmore, Frank (1856–1910, Psychical Research): Frank Podmore was an early member and researcher with the British SPR. He is perhaps most well known for his involvement in the publication *Phantasms of the Living*, which compiled hundreds of case studies of people who experienced anomalous visions of living people. Podmore, in fact, is credited as the main researcher and investigator who compiled these case studies. He held a different belief in psychical abilities than some of his contemporaries. For example, he believed that telepathy was the only genuine psychical phenomena and that all else was merely a case of misidentification or outright fraud. Podmore also believed that telepathy only occurred between living minds. That is, he did not believe that deceased spirits could psychically relay information to a living person. A significant point to his credit is that he urged his colleagues to be wary of their social biases against anyone not of a certain social and economic class.[168]

Further Reading:

Frank Podmore, *Apparitions and Thought-Transference.* London: The Walter Scott Publishing Co., 1892.

Frank Podmore, *The Newer Spiritualism.* New York: Henry Holt & Co., 1911 (published posthumously).

Price, Harry (1881–1948, Author, Journalist, and Psychical Investigator): Harry Price was a British author, photographer, and researcher who wrote about and studied various paranormal phenomena and places. He is known for helping to bring an awareness of psychical phenomena to the general public, though he was and remains a controversial figure in the field. Price, though a believer in psychical phenomena, assumed that most abilities demonstrated by mediums were the result of fraud. He believed this adamantly and became a vocal opponent of such mediums as Rudi Schneider and Margery (Mina Crandon). Of course, his popularity and writings in such magazines as *Light* and his own series of books only helped to spread this criticism far and wide.

One of the things Harry Price is most well known for is his investigation of the Borley Rectory. Psychical historians Arthur and Joyce Berger tell us that it is "the most famous ghost story in the history of psychical research."[169] It is also a prime example of the folklore that can create a paranormal shroud over a place. Borley Rectory was built in Essex, England, in 1863 by the Reverend Henry Bull. Upon his death, the rectory was passed down to Henry's son, Harry (also a reverend), and it remained in the family's possession until 1927. The parish of Borley, at this point, tried in vain to find a new rector but it took thirteen attempts before they were successful. Their offers were repeatedly turned down by priests who had heard the rumors of the haunted Borley Rectory. These rumors include a story about the rectory being haunted by a priest and a nun who had an illicit affair and who were gruesomely executed upon the discovery of their actions.

No records have ever verified those rumors, and fortunately for the Borley parish, in 1928, Reverend G. E. Smith became the new priest and moved into Borley. He did, however, soon learn about the building's sordid reputation and had trouble hosting gatherings at the rectory. He had so much trouble, in fact, that "he contrived the idea of getting psychical researchers to make an investigation that would clear the rectory's name."[170] A reporter from a local newspaper heeded Reverend Smith's request and visited the rectory to see what all the fuss was

Figure 2.21. Harry Price (right) with medium Rudi Schneider (left)

From *Rudi Schneider: A Scientific Examination of His Mediumship* (Methuen, 1930). PD-US not renewed

about. This reporter claims to have heard phantom footsteps and became convinced of the supernatural aura of the place. This reporter alerted Harry Price to the reverend's request and in 1929 Price set out on what would be a decades-long investigation into Borley Rectory.

Though the building had its own folklore that was not rooted in factual evidence, multiple people nevertheless reported strange happenings at the location. The Bull family themselves reported seeing apparitions dressed in black, a student living there once reported seeing apparitions as well, and another family who occupied the building in the 1930s reported hearing strange bells ringing, apparitions, and poltergeist phenomena. When Price arrived in 1929, though, it spelled disaster for the family living there. Due to his popularity and the power of the press, hundreds of visitors flocked to the house every day and it proved too much for Reverend Smith and his family, who fled the home. Price himself lived there briefly and hosted multiple séances and investigations.[171] The veracity of those investigations remains in question to this day, but the fact remains that Borley Rectory is perhaps one of the earliest examples of media-induced paranormal tourism.

Aside from the Borley Rectory, Price is known for his 1923 establishment of the National Laboratory of Psychical Research. Opened in London under rental space owned by the London Spiritualist Alliance, Price created this laboratory as a place for researchers to investigate mediums. Just a few short years later, in 1925, he was elected to be a research officer with the American SPR. His laboratory ran until 1937, and though it had a reputation as more entertainment than science, its library and equipment were donated to the University of London.[172]

Further Reading:

Harry Price, *Confessions of a Ghost Hunter*. London: Putnam, 1936.

Harry Price, *The End of Borley Rectory, 'The Most Haunted House in England.'* London: G. G. Harrap & Co., 1946.

Paul Tabori, *Harry Price: The Biography of a Ghost-Hunter*. London: Sphere, 1974.

Price, Margaret M. (Birth/Death N/A, Research Assistant at Duke Parapsychology Lab): Margaret M. Price was an early research assistant at the Duke Parapsychology Labs. Throughout her time with the laboratory, she conducted research and published scholarly literature in partnership with J. G. Pratt and J. B. Rhine. In a few of her articles, Price investigated extrasensory perception among blind individuals. She found that blind participants scored slightly higher in success rates than seeing participants and also found differences in the methods used. For example, participants were more successful in correctly identifying targets when cards were sealed in opaque envelopes versus being held (yet concealed) in front of them.[173]

Further Reading:

Margaret M. Price, "A Comparison of Blind and Seeing Subjects in 'ESP' Tests." *Journal of Parapsychology* 2, no. 4 (December 1, 1938): 273–86.

Prince, Walter Franklin (1863–1934, Priest and Psychical Researcher): Walter F. Prince was an American priest and psychical researcher. He served as director of research for the American SPR and editor of the organization's scholarly journal. He also served as a researcher for the Boston SPR and twice held the post of president of the British SPR.[174]

His is an interesting path to psychical research. When Prince was a priest in Pittsburgh, a member of his congregation was a young girl named Doris who would visit the priest regularly. Prince soon noticed the drastic swings in Doris's personality and began writing down his observations. Doris would display multiple personalities, one of them claiming to be a spirit. Researchers Arthur and Joyce Berger tell us that Prince's "observations of Doris culminated in the most prolonged, unusual, and detailed study of multiple personality ever recorded."[175] When the spirit personality continued to reveal itself, Prince contacted psychical researcher James Hyslop, and the two began working together to solve this seemingly psychical puzzle. From this point on, Prince's psychical research experience grew, and he conducted experiments on an international scale, especially on psychometry. He also studied the medium Margery (Mina Crandon) and was not convinced that her abilities were genuine.[176]

Further Reading:

Walter Franklin Prince, *Noted Witnesses for Psychic Occurrences*. Boston: Boston Society for Psychic Research, 1928.

R

Rhine, Joseph Banks (J. B.) (1895–1980, Botanist and Parapsychologist): Joseph Banks (J. B.) Rhine was an American botanist hailed as the father of modern parapsychology. In his early career, Rhine was a botanist at West Virginia University. He received his doctorate in philosophy at the University of Chicago, which marks the point when his professional career began turning toward psychical research. Rhine, along with his wife, Louisa, left their current postings and began working for noted psychical researcher William McDougall in the psychology department at Duke University. McDougall had already made some progress at integrating psychical studies into the academic curriculum, making Rhine's eventual success a bit easier. In fact, under McDougall's guidance, Rhine and a handful of his psychology colleagues established the Duke

Parapsychology Labs in 1930. As a result, Duke University is recognized as the first university in the United States to formally integrate a parapsychology lab into its programs.[177] The lab, which existed into the 1960s, conducted more than nine thousand psychical experiments.[178]

Much of Rhine's psychical research in the Duke labs involved extrasensory perception, though the earliest work involved hypnotism. Specifically, Rhine and his associates wondered if a posthypnotic state enhanced someone's telepathic abilities, so they designed studies around this query. The results did not seem statistically significant, so they transitioned their focus to developing experiments that tested extrasensory perception.[179]

To facilitate these experiments, Rhine cocreated a special set of cards with his colleague Karl Zener. The Zener cards, as they came to be known, are marked with certain symbols (like wavy lines, a circle, a plus sign, etc.) and are used to test the sending and receiving of telepathic impressions. Not only did Rhine and his colleagues obtain statistically significant results, they also advanced procedures and standards for the field. In fact, "for almost fifty years, [Rhine] produced for parapsychology terms, concepts, and standardized research procedures the field continues to employ."[180] In 1937, Rhine cofounded the *Journal of Parapsychology*, which to this day publishes scholarly literature of the field, and in 1957 he helped establish the Parapsychological Association, which also exists to this day.[181]

In 1965, when Rhine retired from Duke University, the Parapsychology Labs were also disbanded. Rhine did not let this discourage him, however, as this same year he created the Foundation for Research on the Nature of Man, which was renamed in 1995 to the Rhine Education Center, as it is known and operates today.[182]

Further Reading:

J. B. Rhine, *New Frontiers of the Mind: The Story of the Duke Experiments*. New York: Farrar & Rinehart, 1937.

Rhine, J. B. and Betty M. Humphrey, "The PK Effect: Special Evidence from Hit Patterns." *Journal of Parapsychology* 8, no. 1 (March 1, 1944): 18–60.

Rhine, Louisa (1891–1983, Botanist and Parapsychologist): Similar to her husband, J. B. Rhine,

Further Reading:

Louisa E. Rhine, "Hallucinatory Psi Experiences I: An Introductory Survey." *Journal of Parapsychology* 20, no. 4 (December 1, 1956): 233–56.
Louisa Rhine, *Hidden Channels of the Mind* (New York: William Slone Associates, 1961).
Louisa Rhine, *PSI, What is It? The Story of ESP and PK.* (New York: Harper & Row, 1975).

Richet, Charles (1850–1935, Physiologist): Charles Richet was a French physician who, aside from his psychical contributions, is well known for his work on anaphylaxis—work that earned him a Nobel Prize in 1913.[184] He contributed to many disciplines including psychology, pathology, statistics, and much more. Richet lived in France during a time in which not only was psychology as a discipline blossoming, but so, too, were questions about consciousness during altered states like hypnosis. Some of Richet's early psychical writings discuss hypnosis and the observation of personality changes in this state. Researcher Carlos S. Alvarado tells us that an 1884 article of Richet's is a "classic of nineteenth-century ESP literature," and discusses the idea of thought transference and even the ability to place someone under a trance from a distance. The core idea of this article is that our thoughts and mental energies manifest themselves beyond our own consciousness.[185]

When investigating psychical phenomena, Richet employed strict scientific protocols that advanced and influenced experimentation in general. In fact, "Richet introduced his research program on divination using double-blind (or masked) protocols and statistical analyses, offering tools that would become standard in experimental human and social sciences."[186]

In 1891, he cocreated the scholarly journal *Annales des Sciences Psychiques*, a publication that encouraged international scholarship and discussion of psychical matters.[187] Some of these discussions naturally centered around mediumship, which Richet also studied. He attended séances with Eusapia Palladino, Eva Carriere, and Franek Kluski. He believed that *some* of their abilities were genuine even though these mediums were cloaked in controversy. In 1905, he served as president of the British SPR.[188]

One of his lasting contributions to parapsychological history is his 1923 publication *Thirty Years*

Figure 2.22. Louisa E. Rhine
Photo by anonymous, 1914; PD US expired

American parapsychologist Louisa Rhine began her professional career as a botanist. She eventually found her way to Duke University under the mentorship of parapsychologist William McDougall. Her husband cofounded the Parapsychology Labs at Duke University in 1930 and she began investigating psychical phenomena under its auspices. Much of her research portfolio involves investigations of psychokinesis (PK), that is, the ability of the mind to affect physical matter. As her interest in this phenomenon grew, she began, in 1948, to collect spontaneous PK instances that people sent in to her. It's estimated that she compiled nearly fifteen thousand cases. Some of these were instances of PK and others instances of nonphysical psi phenomena, such as clairvoyance or precognition. She wrote numerous articles for the *Journal of Parapsychology* and also published a handful of books, which were lauded for their approachable nature, essentially bringing psychical science to the general public.[183]

of Psychical Research in which he uses the term "metaphysics" to refer to psychical phenomena. He also outlines the major epochs of psychical research and outlines a hope that the future will reveal more psychical knowledge.[189]

Further Reading:

Carlos S. Alvarado, "Fragments of a Life in Psychical Research: The Case of Charles Richet." *Journal of Scientific Exploration* 32, no. 1 (2018): 55–78.

Charles Richet, *Thirty Years of Psychical Research.* New York: The Macmillan Company, 1923.

de Rochas, Albert (1837–1914, Colonel and Parapsychologist): Aldert de Rochas was a French colonel and director of the prestigious school École Polytechnique. During a séance with Eusapia Palladino, he discovered how she was evading researchers who believed they were holding her hands to the table. Primarily, however, Rochas was highly intrigued by hypnotism, and researchers Arthur and Joyce Berger recount a strange story involving one of his experiments. One experiment Rochas conducted involved testing whether he could control the movements and actions of those in a hypnotic state simply by speaking to them while in that state. They didn't all respond to these suggestions, but Rochas found that some of them did. One day he suggested to his hypnotized participant that three plus two equals four. Believing that he had brought the participant fully out of hypnosis, he was alarmed to discover that the participant had not expunged that suggestion from his mind when he learned the man was at risk of being fired from his job over simple accounting errors. Rochas immediately rehypnotized the man to reverse the previous suggestion, and all was well after that.[190]

S

Salter, Helen (1883–1959, Parapsychologist): Helen Salter was a research officer and editor within the SPR. She served on its council alongside her husband, William Salter, who also engaged in psychical research. She was also the daughter of Margaret Verrall, a famous British automatic writer. Through the connections of her parents, Salter grew up surrounded by key figures in parapsychology, and even became an automatic writer herself—an ability that she practiced for nearly thirty years. She was one of the automatic writers involved in the decades-long study of cross-correspondences, and her research appeared in many journals including the *Journal of the Society for Psychical Research* and the *Journal of Parapsychology.*[191]

Saltmarsh, H. F. (1881–1943, Parapsychologist): One of H. F. Saltmarsh's contributions to the field of parapsychology occurred in 1938 when he published a work explaining, in lay terms, the thirty-year study of cross-correspondences. Publications and information on this study prior to this were technical and difficult for those not within the academy to understand.[192]

Schrenk-Notzing, Albert von (1862–1929, Psychiatrist): Albert von Shrenck-Notzing was a German psychiatrist, aristocrat, and psychical researcher. He is credited with popularizing the term "parapsychology" when he renamed a popular scholarly publication *Zeitschrift für Parapsychologie* (*Journal for Parapsychology*, today called the *Journal for Parapsychology and Border Areas of Psychology*). Among other things, he is known for his inquiries of physical mediums, most notably Eusapia Palladino, Eva Carriere (Eva C.), and the Schneider brothers, Rudi and Willi.

Schrenk-Notzing engaged in research during a tense time in Germany's psychological timeline as, similar to other countries, there was a turf war of sorts between psychologists who saw no place for psychical studies and those who saw it as a natural subtopic within the overall discipline.[193] The divide in Germany was a vitriolic one, and some critics pointed at Shrenck-Notzing as the ringleader of this new, antiscientific parapsychology movement. Frustrated that scholars were being swayed by psychical notions, some academics went so far as to accuse Shrenck-Notzing as being a "hypnotic enchanter," willfully charming people due to his status in society. Critics of parapsychology believed that Shrenck-Notzing's experiments created sensational environments that caused people to succumb to hypnotic suggestion.[194] Since Schrenk-Notzing was a member of the aristocracy, he had a large home suitable for use as a gathering place for study and experimentation, and his critics argued that "his palatial home and aristocratic title predisposed the professors who attended his séances to abandon logic in favor of their desire to believe."[195] Even though psychical research was making better progress in other parts of the world and was viewed by many scholars as a worthy inquiry, it certainly didn't help that Shrenck-Notzing had too much pride to admit when one of his mediums, Ladislaus Lalzlo, was caught in a fraudulent act.[196]

Schrenck-Notzing was a contemporary of Frederic W. H. Myers, Charles Richet, and Henry Sidgwick. He investigated the Italian medium Eusapia Palladino alongside Charles Richet, and eventually attended more than fifty of her séances. He discovered fraudulent acts in some of their sessions but was still convinced that *some* of her abilities were genuine and unexplainable. He was absolutely convinced of the genuine mediumistic abilities of Eva C. (Eva Carriere, a.k.a. Marthe Béraud), and was certain that ectoplasm was a genuine paranormal physical manifestation.[197]

Further Reading:

Andreas Sommer, "Tackling Taboos—From *Psychopathia Sexualis* to the Materialisation of Dreams: Albert von Schrenck-Notzing (1862–1929)." *Journal of Scientific Exploration* 23, no. 3 (2009): 299–322.

Albert von Schrenck-Notzing, *Phenomena of Materialization*. Translated by E. E. Fournier d'Albe. London: Kegan Paul, Trench, Trubner, & Co., 1923.

Sidgwick, Eleanor (1845–1936, President of Newnham College and Psychical Researcher): Eleanor Sidgwick was a Scottish psychical researcher, and according to researcher Carlos S. Alvarado, "was one of the most productive psychical researchers" in the early days of the British SPR.[198] She joined the SPR in 1884 but had been involved in psychical studies of mediums alongside Frederic W. H. Myers, her husband, Henry Sidgwick, and Edmund Gurney, to name a few. One short year after joining the SPR, Sidgwick undertook a massive task to analyze almost four hundred case reports the society had received regarding haunt phenomena, or as the SPR would be wont to say, "phantasms of the dead."[199] Her ability to organize, analyze, and classify was unparalleled, and from this work she identified patterns of hauntings, ferreted out cases

Figure 2.23. Portrait of Eleanor Sidgwick (1889) by James Jebusa Shannon. Oil on canvas.
Image © Newnham College, University of Cambridge.

of misidentification or fraud, and presented theories to explain the genuine cases that were left. As others have noted, "The amount of detail and critical analysis presented by Sidgwick had no precedent in the previous literature examining apparitions of the dead."[200] Her work analyzing these hundreds of haunt cases not only shed light on patterns of haunt phenomena, but also helped create a standard set of criteria for ferreting out genuine cases of haunt phenomena moving forward.[201]

A few years after her work on that project, Sidgwick assumed the role of primary investigator on the SPR's Census of Hallucinations, a survey sent to seventeen thousand people over the course of three years. It investigated waking hallucinations, that is, it asked people if they had ever, while being fully awake and conscious, seen an apparition, heard a phantom noise, or even felt something that wasn't physically there. Eleanor and her secretary, Alice Johnson, are the two who are credited with analyzing and organizing all the data, and the Census of Hallucinations wouldn't be the amazing document it is without their hard work.[202] Eleanor undertook this work while simultaneously serving as president of Newnham College in Cambridge.

In addition to the work above, she also created experiments designed to study telepathy and even presented her research at the International Congress of Experimental Psychology. There, she proclaimed that while there was an overwhelming amount of case studies and examples of telepathy, little had been done by science to seriously examine the nuances of this phenomena. She was also a key investigator in the thirty-year study of cross-correspondences, which involved automatic writers.[203] Her contributions to the field of parapsychology are immeasurable and she is a shining example of one of the earliest female members of the SPR.

Further Reading:

Carlos S. Alvarado, "Eleanor M. Sidgwick (1845–1936)." *Journal of Parapsychology* 82, no. 2. (2018): 127–31.

Christopher Keep, "Evidence in Matters Extraordinary: Numbers, Narratives, and the Census of Hallucinations." *Victorian Studies* 61, no. 4 (Summer 2019): 582–607.

Eleanor Sidgwick, "Notes on the Evidence Collected by the Society, for Phantasms of the Dead." *Proceedings of the Society for Psychical Research* 3 (1885): 69–150.

Sidgwick, Henry (1838–1900, Philosopher and Psychical Researcher): Henry Sidgwick was a British philosopher who, along with his colleagues Frederic W. H. Myers and Edmund Gurney, was one of the cofounders of the British SPR. He was also the first president of this society. Historians Arthur and Joyce Berger tell us that "his intelligence, integrity, tact, patience and the extremely high standards of evidence he insisted on were his most important contributions to psychical research."[204] In this regard, he was much like his wife and fellow psychical researcher, Eleanor Sidgwick, who also had a reputation for holding data and experimentation to extremely high standards.[205] In fact, the two made a great academic pair and often worked together on projects like the Census of Hallucinations and the thirty-year study of cross-correspondences.

In 1894, he joined his fellow psychical researchers at Charles Richet's home in France to undergo a series of studies involving the Italian medium Eusapia Palladino. At the time, he was convinced of her genuine psychical abilities, but when deceptive tactics were later discovered in one of her séances, he denounced any value of previous studies involving the medium. He did, however, remain convinced of the mediumship of Leonora Piper.[206] In addition to his psychical work he has been described as "the most influential professor at Cambridge,"[207] and he was a vocal advocate of advanced educational opportunities for women.[208]

Further Reading:

Arthur Sidgwick, *Henry Sidgwick: A Memoir.* London: Macmillan & Co. Limited, 1906.

Stuart, Charles E. (1907–1947, Parapsychologist): Charles Stuart was an undergraduate at Duke University when he became familiar with J. B. Rhine and the work of the Parapsychology Labs. Upon graduation, he continued his studies in the psychology department, even working in the Parapsychology Labs. In 1941 he received his doctorate. His thesis involved an experimental study of extrasensory perception and was the first doctorate awarded based on a thesis of this subject matter. His research is notable for the examination of statistical methods to investigation extrasensory perception.[209]

Further Reading:

C. E. Stuart, "The Willoughby Test of Clairvoyant Perception." *Journal of Applied Psychology* 19, no. 5 (1935): 551–54.

Sudre, René (1880–1968, Psychical Researcher and Journalist): René Sudre was a French journalist and psychical researcher who first became interested in psychical phenomena while writing an article for the periodical *L'Avenir*. In the process of writing this article (about a boxer who claimed to have strange abilities), Sudre befriended psychical research Gustav Geley, director of the psychical research organization Institut Métapsychique International. Geley introduced him to the organization and Sudre's fascination with the topic skyrocketed. He became a research assistant and even translated notable psychical works into French.[210]

Sudre was an extensive contributor to journals both in France and abroad. His subject matter spanned nearly every aspect of parapsychology and his writings included topics such as levitation, clairvoyance, the subconscious, mediumship, and much more. Sudre also presented his writings at various international parapsychology conferences. One of his main beliefs was that psychical science needed a unifying theory for more scientists to take it seriously. He believed that if there were a theory that encompassed the whole of psychical phenomena, that the academy would not be nearly as divisive about psychical research. He even suggested his own theory of "l'esprit,'" which posited that "all paranormal phenomena can be subsumed under a great creative power that permeates all life."[211]

Further Reading:

Renaud Evrard, "René Sudre (1880–1968): The Metapsychist's Quill."*Journal of the Society for Psychical Research* 73, no. 897. (October 2009): 207–22.

T

Tenhaeff, Wilhelm (1894–1981, Psychologist): Wilhelm Tenhaeff was a key figure in the history of parapsychology in the Netherlands. After the Dutch SPR was founded in 1920, Tenhaeff helped establish the society's scholarly journal *Tijdschrift voor Parapsychologie*. In 1953, he became chair of parapsychology at Utrecht University, the first academic chair, in fact, of a formal parapsychology program.[212] He helped advance the field of parapsychology in the Netherlands, but his reputation was tarnished during his inquiry of the medium Gerard Croiset when fellow researchers discovered that he was fabricating and/or sensationalizing data.[213]

Further Reading:

W. H. C. *Telepathie en Helderziendheid (Telepathy and Clairvoyance)*. Antwerp: Zeist, 1958.

Thomas, Charles D. (1867–1953, Minister and Psychical Researcher): Charles D. Thomas was a British minister who also engaged in psychical research. As a minister, it is likely no stretch of the imagination to believe that he was interested in the question of life after death. He also began attending sessions with and studying mediums, such as Gladys Osborne Leonard, for twenty years. During these studies he developed the "book" and "newspaper" tests, which were designed to test the psychical abilities of mediums. Specifically, the newspaper test required the medium to provide a headline or information of what would be in the paper the next day. The book test required the medium to psychically intuit a book and passage with meaningful significance to the sitters.[214]

Thouless, Robert Henry (1894–1984, Psychologist): Robert H. Thouless was a noted British parapsychologist and psychology professor at universities in Manchester, Cambridge, and Glasgow. He served as president of the SPR 1942 to 1944, and had numerous articles published in the *Journal of the Society for Psychical Research*. He is credited with the creation of the term "psi." He came up with it in order to have a term that took out some of the loaded connotations of the words "psychical" and "parapsychology." As we learned in chapter 1, when parapsychology as a field of study developed simultaneously as psychology, there was a much divisiveness regarding if parapsychology was a legitimate field. In reducing these phenomena to a newer term, Thouless was introducing, hopefully, a more neutral and encompassing term.

Using Thouless's terms, "psi" refers to extrasensory perception and psychokinesis. He further used "psi Gamma" and "psi Kappa" to refer to mental and physical phenomena, respectively. He also developed the cipher test, which was applied to mediums who claimed they had psychic messages from deceased individuals. One concern about these instances was the worry that mediums were simply picking up, telepathically, on information being projected by one of the sitters who knew the deceased and was perhaps thinking about them at the time. This would still indicate some psi phenomena, of course, but it wouldn't indicate survival of consciousness beyond death. In order to mitigate the possibility of psi between living minds, the cipher test was developed. Essentially, anyone who expressed a desire to try to communicate via mediums after their passing would encrypt a message that they would attempt to send. The sitters or the medium would not know the contents of the encrypted message, so if the medium did relay that exact message, it could indicate possible communication with a deceased spirit.[215]

Further Reading:

Robert Thouless, *From Anecdote to Experience in Psychical Research*. London: Routledge & Kegan Paul, 1972.

Tillyard, Robin (1881–1937, Zoologist and Psychical Researcher): Robin Tillyard was a British Australian zoologist and psychical researcher who studied various mediums including Mina Crandon and Eleonore Zugan. He died suddenly in 1937 in a car crash, which was interestingly prophesized nearly nine years earlier by a medium. Tillyard contributed psychical research not only to publications in the field, but also to the scholarly journal *Nature*.[216]

Tischner, Rudolf (1879–1961, Historian, Ophthalmologist, and Psychical Researcher): Rudolf Tischner was a German historian and ophthalmologist with an interest in psychical studies. His main contribution to the field of parapsychology is through his numerous works on the history of various topics and figures in the field. For example, some of his works include biographical treatments of D. D. Home, William Crookes, and Franz Mesmer. In addition to these works, Tischner also wrote a book about his experiments with telepathy. That work, titled *Telepathie und Hellsehen* (Telepathy and Clairvoyance), was a groundbreaking work on the subject. His library and collections were unfortunately destroyed during World War II.[217]

Further Reading:

Rudolf Tischner, *Telepathy and Clairvoyance*. London: K. Paul, Trench, Trubner, & Co., 1925.

Tyrell, G. N. M. (George Nugent Merle) (1879–1952, Physicist and Psychical Researcher): George Tyrell was a physicist, engineer, and psychical researcher who also served as president of the SPR from 1945–1946. His daughter, Gertrude, displayed ESP so he devised experiments to test her abilities. His laboratory was destroyed during World War II. After this period he turned to philosophical discussions about the nature of psychical phenomena and coined the term "mediating vehicles."[218]

V

Varley, Cromwell Fleetwood (1828–1883, Engineer and Psychical Researcher): Cromwell Varley was a British engineer whose "inventions dealing with submarine cables made the construction of the transatlantic cable possible."[219] He became interested in psychical research through his exposure to

Figure 2.24. Cromwell Fleetwood Varley
Photo by Anonymous; PD US

spiritualism and was particularly drawn to mediums. He studied Kate Fox, Florence Cook, and D. D. Home, to name a few. Coupling his psychical interests with his background in electrical engineering, Varley created an electric device to use during séances, which could help ferret out instances of fraud. The device would be put in place at the beginning of a séance and if its electrical circuits were broken, could indicate tampering, movement, and potential fraudulent behavior.[220]

Further Reading:

Cromwell F. Varley. *Description of the Translating Apparatus and Universal Galvanometer Invented by Cromwell F. Varley*. London: Waterlow and Sons, 1863.

Vasiliev, Leonid L. (1891–1966, Physiologist and Psychical Researcher): Leonid L. Vasiliev was a pioneer of Soviet psychical research. He was a physiology professor at the University of Leningrad and had an interest in both extrasensory perception and hypnosis. Vasiliev was greatly inspired by the work of Pierre Janet and began to replicate some of Janet's experiments. He was able to prove that someone could be placed in a trance telepathically during an experiment that placed the sender and receiver nearly one thousand miles apart.[221]

Historians Arthur and Joyce Berger relay the impact of Vasiliev's work when they tell us that "he conducted research that still stands as among the best pioneering work done in these areas and entitles him to be considered along with Joseph B. Rhine as one of the great figures of the period."[222]

Further Reading:

L. L. Vasiliev, *Experiments in Mental Suggestion.* Hampshire: I.S.M.I. Publications, 1963.

Verrall, Margaret (1859–1916, Medium and Psychical Researcher): Margaret Verrall was one of the first female students at Newnham College in Cambridge, England. After graduating, she became a professor of classical literature there. Verrall was intrigued by psi phenomena after experiencing strange telepathic events with her daughter. As her exposure to the psychical world grew, she attempted automatic writing and discovered that she had a knack for it. She eventually became one of the key figures in the decades-long cross-correspondences study.

In addition to her own psychical abilities, Verrall joined the SPR in 1889. She contributed reports summarizing the work of other researchers and was on the SPR's Committee of Reference, which reviewed submissions for the *Proceedings of the Society for Psychical Research.*[223] Through her involvement in the cross-correspondences and her own research into the mediumship of Leonora Piper, Verrall concluded that "the boundary between the two states—the known and the unknown—is still substantial, but it is wearing thin in places."[224]

W

Wallace, Alfred Russell (1823–1913, Biologist and Psychical Researcher): Alfred Wallace was a British biologist noted for his simultaneous theories of evolution alongside Charles Darwin. He

was dubious about any genuine merit of psychical phenomena until he attended a lecture about mesmerism. He was intrigued by the subject matter, returned home, and successfully attempted his own mesmeric experiments.

After this experience and hearing about the curious phenomena taking place at séances, he began attending sittings hosted by mediums, becoming more convinced about psychical phenomena during his sittings with the medium Mary Marshall. During these sittings, he witnessed psychokinetic phenomena and received telepathic information about his brother's death. Wallace continued attending séances and became familiar with the medium Miss Nichols, who he witnessed levitate noiselessly above a table. A notable event at Miss Nichols's séances was the apportation of flowers. Large quantities of them would appear on the table, and in one instance delivered a six-foot sunflower at the random bequest of one of her sitters.

Wallace was also involved with the Dialectical Society during which he formed a committee to study psychokinesis. He was an advocate for psychical science and tried to persuade some of his colleagues to see its value. He defended the plight of mediums against their critics and even testified to some in legal proceedings.[225]

Further Reading:

Alfred R. Wallace, *On Miracles and Modern Spiritualism: Three Essays.* London: James Burns, 1875.

Walther, Gerda (1897–1977, Psychical Researcher): Gerda Walther was a German psychical researcher who, as a child, experienced telepathy from both living and deceased persons. She began her psychical career as an assistant to fellow psychical researcher Alfred von Schrenck-Notzing. Walther studied the medium Rudi Schneider and believed that he exhibited genuine psychical abilities. She is the author of two notable books on the topic, and she helped spread international awareness of European psychical studies when she contributed summaries to the *Journal of the American Society for Psychical Research.* Interestingly, during World War II Walther was approached by the German government and asked to train psychics to detect enemy submarines, but she refused.[226]

Further Reading:

Niamh Burns, "A Modern Mystic: Philosophical Essence and Poetic Method in Gerda Walther (1897–1977)." *German Life and Letters* 72, no. 2 (April 2020): 246–69.

Warcollier, René (1881–1962, Engineer and Psychical Researcher): René Warcollier was a French engineer and psychical researcher. Throughout his career, he was president of the Institut Métapsychique International and a member of the Boston SPR. He became interested in psychical research when the wave of spiritualism was sweeping the country. He is noted for his experiments on telepathy, and he believed that the receiver was perhaps the more important agent in a telepathic study. Most people at the time held the belief that the "sender" was the most crucial component of telepathy, but Warcollier believed otherwise. In fact, he stated that "a large number of experiments have convinced us that the agent is not always very important, but that his action is not entirely negligible."[227]

Warcollier designed a unique transatlantic experiment in 1923. He partnered with fellow psychical researcher Gardner Murphy to design this study, which placed subjects in New York and Paris who switched back and forth as sender and receiver (also referred to as agent and percipient). Warcollier himself even acted as an agent (sender) and visualized a glass funnel. At that same time in New York, a percipient drew an image of a glass funnel.[228]

Further Reading:

René Warcollier, *Experimental Telepathy*. Gardner Murphy, ed. Translated by Josephine B. Gridley. Boston: Boston Society for Psychic Research, 1938.

Z

Zöllner, Johann Karl Friedrich (1834–1882, Astronomer and Psychical Researcher): Johann K. F. Zöllner was a German astronomer who taught at Leipzig University. He and his colleagues at Leipzig studied the medium Henry Slade and witnessed strange materializations during his séances. Slade was unfortunately discovered engaging in fraudulent activity by the Seybert Commission and,

Figure 2.25. Apparatus Designed by Johann Karl Friedrich Zöllner
From *After Death–What?* by Cesare Lombroso (Boston: Small, Maynard, and Co., 1909). PD-US

as a result, the studies of Zöllner and his colleagues were essentially dismissed by their contemporaries. One of the most unique contributions of Zöllner is his theory of a fourth dimension of space, which he referred to as the "space of four."[229]

Further Reading:

Johann K. F. Zöllner and Charles Carleton Massey, *Transcendental Physics*. Boston: Colby & Rich, 1888.

Zorab, George A. M. (1898–1990, Psychical Researcher): George A. M. Zorab was "the Netherlands' foremost (and oldest) worker in the field of psychical research"[230] and a member of the International Committee for the Study of Spontaneous Paranormal Phenomena.[231] He witnessed séance phenomena at an early age and continued being intrigued by psychical phenomena. Zorab was particularly influenced by *Phantasms of the Living*, and eventually joined both the Dutch and British SPRs. His publication on mediums Florence Cook and Kate Fox was an important contribution on mediumship, and he went on to pen more than three hundred books and articles on psychical topics.[232]

Further Reading:

George A. M. Zorab, *Bibliography of Parapsychology*. New York: Parapsychology Foundation, 1957.

MODERN PARAPSYCHOLOGISTS: THE 1950s TO PRESENT DAY

This section provides a biographical listing of parapsychologists who have mainly been active from the 1950s to the present. Similar to the first section of historical figures, some of the people listed below may straddle the line between pre- and post-1950s. Entries include biographical information, research summaries, and resources for further reading. Where there is no birth/death information, you will find those spaces blank and/or one of the dates marked by a "?" symbol.

A

Adamenko, Victor G. (1936–, Parapsychologist): Dr. Victor G. Adamenko is a Soviet biophysicist and inventor of the tobiscope, a device that measures the electromagnetic fields of acupuncture points. He was also interested in psychokinesis and developed a method for everyday people to practice developing PK abilities. Using Adamenko's method, people would first start out by using electrostatics to influence the physical movement of items that are typically affected (like a Styrofoam cup). Gradually, you replace items susceptible to electrostatic energy with items that are larger and larger and less susceptible to that force. The theory behind this is that you "first build up confidence in the subject by *simulating* PK through normal means, but then gradually wean the subject off the normal to the paranormal,"[233] thereby positing the notion that people can learn PK. When the Soviet Union became hostile to parapsychological research, Adamenko left the country to teach psychobiophysics at Crete University in Greece.[234]

Alvarado, Carlos S. (1955–, Parapsychologist): Carlos S. Alvarado is a parapsychologist and member of the American SPR and the Parapsychological Association. Alvarado has written a vast number of publications on psychical topics, and a large portion of his work provides historical insight into topics such as mediumship in France, biographical sketches, nineteenth-century attitudes toward psychical phenomena, book reviews, and much more. Born in Puerto Rico in 1955, he was a psychology professor at the University of Puerto Rico before going to California to pursue a parapsychology program at John F. Kennedy University. After he earned his degree from that university, he went on to work for the parapsychology program at the University of Virginia.[235]

In his 2014 article in the *Journal of Parapsychology* titled "Mediumship, Psychical Research, Dissociation, and the Powers of the Subconscious Mind," Alvarado discusses the differing historical viewpoints of scientists regarding mediumship and its origins.[236] This article, the goal of which "is to reacquaint contemporary students of dissociation and of mediumship with this nearly forgotten past,"[237] traces the historical train of thought about the subconscious mind and its connection to mediumship. He points out that there were two schools of thought regarding mediums and their associated phenomena. Some researchers believed that mediumship could be explained merely as a byproduct of dissociation and other components of psychopathology, but others believed that it spoke more to the evidence for "supernormal" abilities. Alvarado outlines the work and theories of researchers who advocated for the idea of supernormal attributes, including Frederic W. H. Myers and Eduard Von Hartmann.

Alvarado's contributions to the field are immense, and what is particularly notable is the vast amount of historical information Alvarado provides about topics, researchers, and events (all on an international scope) in the parapsychological timeline. In 2010, Alvarado founded the Alvarado Zingrone Institute for Research and Education alongside fellow parapsychologist Nancy Zingrone, which also offers access to publications and resources on parapsychology.[238]

Further Reading:

Carlos S. Alvarado, "Mediumistic Materializations in France During the Early 1920s." *Journal of Scientific Exploration* 35, no. 1 (2021): 209–23.

Nancy L. Zingrone and Carlos S. Alvarado, "On Women in Parapsychology." *Journal of Parapsychology* 83, no. 2. (Fall 2019): 286–89.

Anderson, Margaret L. (1920–1986, Educator and Parapsychologist): Margaret L. Anderson was a past president of the Parapsychology Association who received her PhD in education from the University of Pittsburgh. She was a parapsychologist interested in extrasensory perception of children, especially instances of ESP in children in school settings. In the 1950s she worked at the Duke Parapsychology Labs and began developing experiments designed to test ESP. She theorized that this phenomenon could be fostered through promoting imagination and fantasy in children. She created classroom environments that actively encouraged these types of behaviors through games and other activities finding that instances of ESP increased during these activities. Anderson worked closely with fellow researchers Rhea White and Robert A. McConnell on some of these studies. She was a recipient of the McDougall Award for Distinguished Work in Parapsychology.

Further Reading:

M. Anderson, "The Use of Fantasy in Testing for Extrasensory Perception." *Journal of the American Society for Psychical Research* 60 (1966): 150–63.

Atwater, P. M. H. (1937–, Researcher on Near-Death Experiences): P. M. H. Atwater earned a LhD (Doctor of Humane Letters) for her work on near-death experiences (NDEs). After experiencing three NDEs of her own in 1977, she began, one year later, to seriously examine this phenomenon.[239] I include NDEs into this broader discussion of parapsychology because they are a phenomenon that seem to indicate a survival of consciousness beyond bodily death. In fact, then, NDEs really strike at the core of what the SPR set out to examine in 1882.

Throughout the course of her research, Atwater realized that studies centered largely on the near-

death experiences of adults, with little research being devoted to the NDEs of children. She set out to conduct her own studies and even developed a new model to investigate the unique experience of children who go through these experiences. She discovered remarkable occurrences during these studies and presented that research at the 2007 annual conference of the Academy of Spirituality and Paranormal Studies. In this presentation, Atwater presented 277 case studies of children who had experienced an NDE. For example, she discovered that, unlike most adults, children reported a "dark light" experience at vastly higher percentages than adults, which is sometimes also referred to as the "living dark."[240] What is even more intriguing is that 96 percent of children who experienced an NDE under the age of fifteen months tested at "genius levels of intelligence without genetic markers to account for this."[241] Atwater's research reveals not only the unique NDEs of children, but adds to our knowledge of the complexity of this phenomena.

Further Reading:

P. M. H. Atwater, *The Big Book of Near-Death Experiences.* Charlottesville, VA: Hampton Roads, 2007.

P. M. H. Atwater, "Near-Death Experiences in Children." *Journal of Religion and Psychical Research* 25, no. 1 (January 2002): 26–29.

Auerbach, Loyd (1956–, Parapsychologist): Loyd Auerbach is a parapsychologist, professor at Atlantic University, and member of various organizations including the Parapsychological Association and the Rhine Education Center. He previously volunteered at the J. Allen Hynek Center for UFO Studies. On the website of the Parapsychological Association, Auerbach's biography outlines how, in 1989, he established a research organization of his own after J.F.K. University ended their graduate parapsychology program. In fact, that university is where Auerbach not only received his graduate degree but also where he served as faculty member in that same program until it disbanded. One of Auerbach's goals is to bridge the divide between amateur and professional researchers of the paranormal.[242]

Auerbach's articles can be found in a variety of publications including but not limited to the *Journal of Parapsychology* and the *Journal of Scientific Ex-*

ploration. In addition to articles, he has written nine books on parapsychological topics as well. Many of his articles provide in-depth historical vignettes on events or figures throughout the timeline of parapsychology. Auerbach has also coauthored book chapters, including a one in *Extrasensory Perception: Support, Skepticism, and Science.* The chapter, titled "Anomalous Cognition/ESP and Psychokinesis Research in the United States," provides a brief overview of the modern status of ESP research followed by an historical overview of the studies, figures, and research of ESP in the United States through the ages.[243]

Further Reading:

Loyd Auerbach, *Hauntings and Poltergeists.* Oakland, CA: Ronin Publishing, 2004.

B

Barrington, Mary Rose (1926–2020, Lawyer and Parapsychologist): Mary R. Barrington was a British lawyer and parapsychologist who joined the SPR in 1957. Her primary research interests were in spontaneous psi cases and mediumship, though she was also a keen researcher of poltergeist phenomena. In fact, she contributed to the theories on why poltergeist activity occurs, especially after her involvement in the "flying thermometer" case she studied alongside Maurice Grosse. Through the course of her research into spontaneous psi phenomena, she created the "Just One of Those Things" theory, referred to as JOTT. This refers to moments when objects disappear and then reappear in mysterious ways, and though the phrase sounds flippant, it was anything but. As researcher Zofia Weaver tells us, JOTT is a "collective name for various kinds of spatial discontinuity, and perhaps [makes] the case for the inclusion of such phenomena in the 'bigger picture' of reality."[244]

Further Reading:

M. R. Barrington, "The Case of the Flying Thermometer." *Journal of the Society for Psychical Research* 43 (1965–1966): 11–20.

M. R. Barrington. *JOTT: When Things Disappear . . . and Come Back or Relocate—and Why It Really Happens.* San Antonio, TX: Anomalist Books, 2018.

Batcheldor, Kenneth J. (1921–1988, Psychologist): Kenneth Batcheldor was a British psychologist who brought the Victorian séance back into the modern world. He was curious what would happen if he gathered a group who had no preconceived Victorian notions with no medium present. What Batcheldor discovered was that strange phenomena occurred anyway such as levitations and cold spots, which occurred even in the modern séance. What he realized is that "if the right conditions to affect mood and belief are set up, psychokinesis and physical phenomena can occur in a small and informal group meeting regularly . . . without the help of a medium."[245] Batcheldor's research suggests that group dynamics play a large role in the production of psi phenomena, and that these things don't necessarily need a medium present in order to occur.

Further Reading:

Kenneth J. Batcheldor, "Contributions to the Theory of PK Induction from Sitter-Group Work." *Journal of the American Society for Psychical Research* 78, no. 2 (1984): 105–22.

Bayless, Raymond (1920–2004, Painter and Parapsychologist): Raymond Bayless was an American painter and parapsychologist who is credited with being the first person to discover what we would later call "electronic voice phenomena." In his obituary in the *Journal of Near-Death Studies*, we learn that "it [was] note widely known that Bayless was the first to report the reception of whispers, voices, and raps received in silence on tape."[246] In the 1970s, Bayless expanded this concept in a two-year study with parapsychologist D. Scott Rogo in which they investigated cases of people receiving phone calls from the deceased *or* phone calls from people who could not possibly have made the call at the time it was received. Bayless and Rogo gathered fifty cases of these phantom phone calls and conducted in-depth interviews with the people who experienced them. They discovered four types of anomalous phone calls that people reported. The first category of phantom calls is labeled "simple calls" and refers to short phone calls originating from the deceased person, and which last only a few seconds, with just a few words spoken and no real back-and-forth conversation. The second category is labeled "prolonged calls" and refers to cases where the recipient of the phone call does not realize that the person on the other end of the line is deceased at the time of the call. These calls typically last at least thirty minutes and involve normal conversation. The third category of phone calls is "answer calls" and occurs when someone living calls a person not knowing they are dead. Though they are dead at the time of the phone call, they answer and, like the second category, are usually prolonged as well. Bayless and Rogo note that there seems to be a correlation between length of phone call and realization by the living person that they are/should be talking to a deceased individual. Interestingly, they also discovered a fourth type of anomalous phone call that is labeled as the "intention call." This does not involve any deceased individual but rather occurs when someone *intends* to call someone, but the recipient is adamant that, though the person never called, the phone conversation did in fact take place.[247] Bayless and Rogo's work was published in a 1979 book and researchers in 2014 attempted to replicate and extend their work.

Further Reading:

Callum E. Cooper, "An Analysis of Exceptional Experiences Involving Telecommunication Technology." *Journal of Parapsychology* 78, no. 2 (September 2014): 209–22.

D. S. Rogo and R. Bayless, *Phone Calls from the Dead: The Results of a Two-Year Investigation into an Incredible Phenomenon.* Englewood Cliffs, NJ: Prentice-Hall, 1979.

Beischel, Julie (Pharmacologist and Parapsychologist): Julie Beischel is a pharmacologist who engages in parapsychological work through her studies of mediums and the psi phenomena often associated with them. She is also the research director at the Windbridge Research Center which she founded in 2017 alongside her husband and fellow psi researcher Mark Boccuzzi. This research organization, built upon an institute that both Beischel and Boccuzzi started in 2008, engages in "peer-reviewed research on the topics of life after death and after-death communication."[248] Together, they edit and publish the open-access scholarly journal *Threshold: Journal of Interdisciplinary Consciousness Studies.* Beischel also wrote an entry for SPR's

online psi encyclopedia that provides an overview of modern mediumship research.[249]

Further Reading:

Julie Beischel, *Among Mediums: A Scientist's Quest for Answers.* Tucson, AZ: The Windbridge Institute, 2013.

Beischel, Julie, "Contemporary Methods Used in Laboratory-Based Mediumship Research." *Journal of Parapsychology* 71 (Spring 2007): 37–68.

Beloff, John (1920–2006, Psychologist): Dr. John Beloff was a British psychologist who helped establish the Koestler Chair of Parapsychology at Edinburgh University. Beloff himself was a parapsychologist along with his colleague Arthur Koestler, who the chair position of the program is named after. He was a member and past president of the Parapsychological Association and he served as editor of the *Journal of the Society for Psychical Research* for many years. Beloff was a psychology professor at the University of Edinburgh. He who wrote numerous articles on various psi phenomena, figures, and events. He believed that parapsychological study could help reveal more about the world and even expand (undoubtedly challenge) current scientific understandings. Beloff also believed that psi phenomena didn't need to be grandiose and spectacular in order to provide proof. He also believed that the cases of certain mediums of the nineteenth century should be reexamined, especially the cases of Mina Crandon (Margery), Florence Cook, and Carlos Mirabelli. His book *Parapsychology: A Concise History* is a main contributor to the introductory chapter in this book.

Further Reading:

John Beloff, *Parapsychology: A Concise History.* New York: St. Martin's Press, 1993.

John Beloff, ed., *New Directions in Parapsychology.* London: Elek Science, 1974.

Bem, Daryl (1938–, Psychologist): Dr. Daryl Bem is a social psychologist who, at least in the field of parapsychology, is perhaps most known for his 2011 article in the *Journal of Personality and Social Psychology* that discusses retrocognition and claims to present direct evidence for psi phenomena.[250] In this article, Bem focuses on both precognition and premonition since they both seem to indicate "a retroactive influence of some future event on an individual's current responses."[251] Motivated by these particular psi phenomena, Bem designed nine experiments involving more than one thousand participants that "time-reversed" certain sociocognitive processes to see if "the individual's responses are obtained before the putatively causal stimulus events occur."[252] One of Bem's goals in writing this article was to provide simple and clear methods for fellow researchers to replicate, acknowledging the fact that one of the main criticisms of psi research is the replicability of studies. In fact, future researchers did use Bem's methods to replicate in their own studies and they also found statistically significant psi results.[253]

Bem's nine experiments showed statistically significant results in all but one design. One of the experiments involved participants seated and facing a computer screen. On the screen were two images of a curtain, side by side. Behind one curtain was a blank wall and behind the othern was a sexually explicit image. The goal of the participants was to choose the curtain that concealed the explicit image. Bem discovered that participants were able to correctly identify which curtain concealed the explicit image at rates higher than that of chance.[254] Interestingly, the experiments in Bem's study used methods that were familiar to and frequently used in social psychology experiments. The only difference is that Bem reversed the order in which the experiment was designed (in order to test for precognitive abilities, that is). This gave his study a bit more credibility because he was using methods already accepted by the academic community and merely flipping them, but it also resulted in a huge amount of controversy.

This article he wrote about this generated so much controversy that the editors of the journal published an editorial comment introducing Bem's article. In this comment, they assured readers that Bem's article was reviewed with the same peer review rigor they apply to all submissions and wrote that "we openly admit that the reported findings conflict with our own beliefs about causality and that we find them extremely puzzling."[255] They end by reminding readers that "our obligation as journal editors is not to endorse particular hypotheses but

to advance and stimulate science through a rigorous review process."[256] The editors also chose to simultaneously publish a response article from other researchers alongside Bem's original article to facilitate discussion around these findings, but this act also shows how controversial this 2011 article was (and remains).

Further Reading:

D. J. Bem, "Feeling the Future: Experimental Evidence for Anomalous Retroactive Influence on Cognition and Affect." *Journal of Personality and Social Psychology* 100 (2011): 407–25.

Bengston, William (1950–, Sociologist): Dr. William Bengston is a sociology professor at St. Joseph's College, president of the Society for Scientific Exploration, and an editor of the *Journal of Alternative and Complementary Medicine.*

As a young man, Bengston befriended Bennett Mayrick, a gentleman who exhibited psi abilities. Specifically, Mayrick exhibited psychometry, or the ability to intuit information about something/someone by placing your hands on that item or person. As their friendship grew, and as Bengston became more and more convinced of the genuineness of Mayrick's ability, he convinced Mayrick to submit to studies conducted by the parapsychologist Karlis Osis of the American SPR. During these studies, in which Mayrick exhibited psi phenomena, brain scans showed curious and simultaneous productions of beta and theta waves that seemed to indicate Mayrick was in a deep meditative trance. Shortly after the experiment with Osis, and as Mayrick continued giving psychic readings for people, he discovered a seeming ability to reduce pain when he touched people. Bengston collaborated with a hospital in New York to design a double-blind test that examined this curious ability of Mayrick. During this study, Mayrick was able to correctly describe the physical symptoms of patients in a display of psychometry.[257]

Bengston was so intrigued by Mayrick's ability that he began testing psychometry on himself and discovered that he could also display this ability. He went on to conduct several psychometry studies of cancer in mice that curiously revealed high survival rates. His experience with Mayrick and his subsequent psychometric studies led Bengston to create a theory of resonant bonding. This theory "posits that living creatures share an energetic bond by which they can influence each other's health."[258] Bengston's research has been met with ambivalence by his academic colleagues, which has led him to publish articles musing about the willingness of the academy to engage in the strange.

Further Reading:

William Bengston, *The Energy Cure: Unraveling the Mystery of Hands-On Healing.* Boulder, CO: Sounds True, 2010.

Sarah Beseme, Loren Fast, William Bengston, Michael Turner, Dean Radin, and John McMichael, "Effects Induced In Vivo by Exposure to Magnetic Signals Derived from a Healing Technique." *Dose-Response: An International Journal* (January 2020): 1–10.

Berger, Arthur S. (1920–, Attorney and Historian): Dr. Arthur S. Berger is an American historian, lawyer, and parapsychologist who is particularly interested in the question of survival after death. He wrote an encyclopedia of parapsychology alongside his wife, Joyce Berger, which has been a vital resource for the creation of this book. He designed the "dictionary test," which was inspired by the cipher test. In the dictionary test, a person chooses a word and its definition at random from the dictionary and uses a formula to encipher both. The idea is that, upon death and via a medium, the keys to decipher that message would be revealed, thereby providing evidence for the survival of consciousness beyond death.[259]

Further Reading:

A. S. Berger, *The Aristocracy of the Dead: New Findings in Postmortem Survival.* Jefferson, NC: McFarland & Co., 1987.

Bierman, Dick (1943–, Psychologist): Dr. Dick Bierman is a Dutch psychologist and parapsychologist who has taught at the University of Amsterdam, the University of the Southe Pacfic, the University of Groningen, and within the parapsychology department at the University of Utrecht. Before entering the realm of psi, Bierman was first a scientist in the realm of atomic and molecular physics. After his work with

physics, he began investigating artificial intelligence and learning systems that led him down an eventual path to altered states of consciousness. Bierman's research includes studies of presentiment, psychokinesis, and particularly the effort to replicate studies to advance the reputation of data in parapsychology.[260]

Further Reading:

Dick Bierman, "Consciousness Induced Restoration of Time Symmetry (CIRTS): A Psychophysical Theoretical Perspective." *Journal of Parapsychology* 74, no. 2 (Fall 2010): 273–99.

Dick Bierman and Jacob J. Jolij, "Dealing with the Experimenter Effect." *Journal of Scientific Exploration* 34, no. 4 (2020): 703–09.

Biondi, Massimo (1952–, Psychiatrist): Dr. Massimo Biondi is an Italian psychiatrist and parapsychologist. Most interested in instances of spontaneous psi, he conducted much research between the 1970s and 1980s. Dr. Biondi is also an editor for the Italian journal *Quaderni di Parapsicologia.*[261]

Further Reading:

Carlos Sl. Alvarado, Massimo Bionid, and Wim Kramer, "Historical Notes on Psychic Phenomena in Specialised Journals." *European Journal of Parapsychology* 21, no.1 (2006): 58–87.

Blackmore, Susan (1951–, Psychologist): Dr. Susan Blackmore is a British psychologist and has been a member of the SPR, the Association for the Study of Anomalous Phenomena, and the Parapsychological Association. Her curiosity for parapsychology grew when she attended the University of Oxford. While there, Blackmore served as president of the Oxford University SPR. She went on to obtain her PhD in parapsychology from Surrey University. Blackmore was particularly interested in ESP and, though she conducted a multitude of studies, repeatedly found no significant results that indicated the presence of psi phenomena. Her resulting theory is that people are encountering spontaneous cases that they *interpret* as psi, but she reinforced that these are important psychological experiences to study nevertheless.[262] Her 1984 article on out-of-body experiences (OBEs), for example, posits that OBEs are simply a result of an altered state of consciousness created by the mind due to a sudden change in normal stimuli and not the result of a psychical separation of consciousness and the physical body.[263]

Blackmore began stepping back from parapsychological research in the early 2000s. On her website, she provides a variety of reasons for this, one being the effort needed to maintain an open mind. It is certainly easy to understand as maintaining an open mind takes in the face of phenomena and experiences that challenge what we know, and which especially challenges what we know in the academy.[264] She continues to publish work related to the field though, especially in the realm of consciousness studies and her contributions to the field of parapsychology are numerous.

Further Reading:

Susan J. Blackmore, *Consciousness: An Introduction.* London: Hodder & Stoughton, 2003.

Susan J. Blackmore, "A Psychological Theory of the Out-of-Body Experience." *Journal of Parapsychology* 48, no. 3 (September 1984): 201–18.

Bleksley, Arthur E. H. (1908–1984, Astrophysicist and Mathematician): Dr. Arthur E. H. Bleksley was a South African astrophysicist and mathematician and served as president of the South African SPR. He was also the director of research for the South African Institute for Parapsychological Research. His most notable research involved sleep and long-distance ESP. Bleksley was contacted by a man who claimed he had the ability to wake up at random times. This of course doesn't sound paranormal, as we all likely find ourselves waking up randomly during the night, but what makes this case different is that this gentleman, W. van Vuurde, could awaken at random times chosen by others and unknown to him. van Vuurde eventually contacted Bleksley asking him to help shed light on this strange ability, and eventually Bleksley designed an experiment to test this phenomenon. This first experiment was hundreds of miles away from van Vuurde, yet Bleksley discovered statistically significant results. In one stretch, van Vuurde awoke ten consecutive nights "within one minute of the target time."[265]

Further Reading:

A. E. H. Bleksley, "An Experiment of Long-Distance ESP During Sleep." *Journal of Parapsychology* 21, no. 1 (March 1963).

Braud, William G. (1942–2012, Psychologist): Dr. William Braud was an American psychologist and member of the American SPR, the Parapsychological Association, and the American Association for the Advancement of Science. Braud's PhD was in experimental psychology, and after obtaining this degree, he taught at the University of Houston where he also engaged in research involving memory, psychophysiology, and more. In 1975, he began working for the Mind Science Foundation in Texas, an organization that studies topics like creativity and Alzheimer's, but which also conducts research on remote viewing and psychokinesis. Braud oversaw these branches of parapsychological inquiry. From 1992–2010, he was the research director at the Institute of Transpersonal Psychology (today known as Sofia University). At this institute, he also served as dissertation mentor and engaged in research into exceptional human experiences. He wrote more than 290 publications including books, book chapters, and articles.[266]

In a book he coauthored with Rosemarie Anderson in 2011 titled *Transforming Self and Others through Research*, Braud and Anderson discuss the unconscious and its relation to "direct knowing." They discuss ways in which you can access information and a sense of direct knowing through unconscious processes. In one chapter, Braud outlines how dreams are important unconscious processes for him and how he prompts the "dream maker" to provide information and clarity on certain issues or problems.[267] In another portion of this chapter, and in a more blatant parapsychological vein, Braud discusses several psychical processes that enable us to have (or grow the ability to have) "direct knowing." He outlines an exercise involving two people. One sits quietly and relives a poignant moment in their life while the other person also sits quietly in a meditative state (perhaps in another room or even a different location) attempting to psychically receive impressions, visions, feelings, sounds, etc. related to the person reliving and projecting their experience.[268]

In addition to the unconscious, Braud was particularly interested in psychokinesis. His research portfolio includes multiple publications on this topic. For example, in a 1989 article in the journal *Perceptual and Motor Skills*, Braud and his coauthor Stephen Dennis point out that multiple studies have shown a correlation between ESP and low geomagnetic field (GMF) levels. Braud and his coauthor began wondering if there is a correlation between geomagnetic field activity and psychokinesis (PK) and they theorized that positive PK events would correspond to days of higher geomagnetic activity based in part on research others had done noting that poltergeist activity seemed to correspond with higher levels of GMF activity. They ran analyses of four studies involving positive PK and ran them against GMF levels on the corresponding dates and discovered that PK did indeed seem to correspond to higher GMF levels.[269]

Further Reading:

William G. Braud and Stephen P. Dennis, "Geophysical Variables and Behavior: LVIII. Autonomic Activity, Hemolysis, and Biological Psychokinesis: Possible Relationships with Geomagnetic Field Activity." *Perceptual and Motor Skills* 68, no.3 (June 1989): 1243–54.

Braude, Stephen E. (1945–, Philosopher): Dr. Stephen Braude is an American philosopher and parapsychologist. A core part of Braude's research focuses on the philosophy, future, and implications of parapsychology. In his works, Braude ponders the limits of quantitative data when it comes to psi phenomena.[270] Quantitative data can reveal if something is happening, perhaps, but we still don't really understand how that thing is happening yet. Qualitative data, on the other hand, perhaps better reflects the chaotic and spontaneous nature of psi phenomena. Braude, in addressing the attitudes of some against parapsychology, also reminds us that psi is a worthy inquiry even though it is perhaps not yet very well understood. He elucidates on some of these philosophical quandaries of parapsychology in his 2021 article in the *Journal of Scientific Exploration*. Braude tells us "to remember that science started with, and has always been driven by, the desire to explain what we've already and undeniable observed to occur."[271] He continues to advocate for the study of psi phenomena as he continues to tell us that "the crucial point here is that our explanatory uncertainty was never a barrier to forming and using the concepts in the meantime, even if that meant we had to define the concepts for a while with respect to some level of ignorance."[272] Braude's article

exemplifies an academic open-mindedness that acknowledges and values materialist science that isn't flippant or disdainful about the merits of psychical research. His works provide overviews of progress to date, detailed discussions of data and experimentation, and provide a wonderfully intriguing and philosophical lens to the field of parapsychology.

Further Reading:

Stephen E. Braude, *Crimes of Reason: On Mind, Nature, and the Paranormal.* Lanham, MD: Rowman & Littlefield, 2014.

Stephen E. Braude, *ESP and Psychokinesis: A Philosophical Examination.* Philadelphia: Temple University Press, 1979.

Stephen E. Braude, *The Limits of Influence: Psychokinesis and the Philosophy of Science.* New York: Routledge & Kegan Paul, 1986.

Brier, Robert (1943–, Egyptologist): Dr. Robert Brier is an American Egyptologist and parapsychologist who has worked alongside J. B. Rhine and held membership in the British and American SPR. Among his research portfolio is an inquiry into extrasensory perception. In a 1968 article for the *Journal of Parapsychology*, Brier and his coauthor investigated if scorers of precognition tests can psychically influence the outcome. Acknowledging the unconscious influences at play during psi phenomena, Brier and his coauthor Sara R. Feather write, "Because of the apparent tendency of psi processes to transcend both time and space, many bizarre possibilities arise concerning what might be influencing the subject as [they are] taking a precognition test."[273] They posit that a test subject might score differently if they know who the scorer is, and that perhaps they are psychically picking up on expectations.

In their experiments, participants were told that a certain researcher (Feather) would be checking half of the tests and that an unidentified colleague would be checking the other half. Participants were asked to indicate which of their four tests they believed Feather would be checking, and what the researchers discovered is that, on those who correctly identified that Feather would be checking their results, the psi scores were statistically significant. On those who incorrectly identified the checker, psi scores were not positive. This data led them to conclude that there is an "ESP differential effect relating to who checked the data and whom the subjects expected to check the data."[274] For the complete overview of these studies, consult the Further Reading section below.

Further Reading:

Sara R. Feather and Robert Brier, "The Possible Effect of the Checker in Precognition Tests." *The Journal of Parapsychology* 32, no. 3 (September 1968): 167–75.

Broughton, Richard S. (1946–, Parapsychologist): Dr. Richard S. Broughton is an American parapsychologist and past president of both the Parapsychological Association and the SPR. His teaching and research have taken place in the United States, the Netherlands, and the United Kingdom. Broughton studied ESP and was particularly interested in cognitive processes that occur in the brain during this phenomenon.[275]

With fellow parapsychologist John Beloff, Broughton helped to create the first computer game designed to test psychokinesis. In fact, Broughton believed that the use of computers could help with data control and improve the overall reliability of certain studies. Like parapsychologist Robert Brier, Broughton also noticed that the experimenter seems to influence psi studies and designed a test to study this. He concluded, after obtaining similar results as what Brier received, that "either the participants could retrospectively influence their results or he, himself, was the source of the psi effect."[276]

During the writing of his influential work *Parapsychology: The Controversial Science*, Broughton was serving as the research director of the Institute for Parapsychology, the successor of the Duke Parapsychology Labs in North Carolina, today known as the Rhine Research Center.[277] Broughton was instrumental in obtaining the records of the Psycho-Physical Research Laboratories when that organization closed. These records included some of the largest collections of psi research involving ganzfeld methods.[278]

Further Reading:

Richard S. Broughton, *Parapsychology: The Controversial Science*. New York: Ballantine Books, 1991.

R. S. Broughton, Psi and the two halves of the brain. *Journal of the Society for Psychical Research* (1975) 48, no. 765. 133–47

C

Cadoret, Remi J. (1928–2005, Physiologist): Dr. Remi J. Cadoret was a Canadian physiologist and parapsychologist. He contributed to advancing the understanding of generational behaviors, especially regarding psychological attributes passed down to adopted children. Cadoret worked at the parapsychology labs at Duke University in the 1950s. A unique moment in his life was the study of Chris the Wonder Dog, a beagle believed to display psi abilities. This work launched Cadoret into the national news and R. L. Philibert muses that perhaps this moment was the first example of a "television psychiatrist."[279]

In addition to that bit of sensational news, Cadoret also conducted psi studies in which participants were connected to an EEG machine, which is able to detect electrical activity in the brain. This was an attempt to determine the correlation of brain wave activity and psi phenomena.[280] In 1958, Cadoret partnered with a Finnish researcher to study the role of hypnosis on ESP, and they discovered that some participants did seem to perform at higher psi levels under the influence of hypnotism.[281]

Further Reading:

Jarl Fahler and Remi J. Cadoret, "ESP Card Test of College Students with and without Hypnosis." In *Basic Research in Parapsychology*, 2nd edition. Edited by K. Ramakrishna Rao, 251–61. Jefferson, NC: McFarland and Company, 2001.

Cardeña, Etzel (1957–, Psychologist): Dr. Etzel Cardeña is a psychology professor at Lund University in Sweden. Growing up in Mexico, he was influenced by his father's work and research in psychoanalysis and psi phenomena. While working on his psychology dissertation at the University of California, Cardeña became involved with the Foundation for Research on the Nature of Man, an organization led by the psychical researcher J. B. Rhine, today known as the Rhine Research Center. His interest into psi phenomena continued to grow from here and his research has taken him to postings at universities worldwide. Cardeña has also served as editor of the *Journal of Parapsychology* and is the director of the Center for Research on Consciousness and Anomalous Psychology, an organization that studies the neurophenomenology of hypnosis, dissociation, and more.[282]

In a 2020 article in the *Journal of Parapsychology*, Cardeña and his coauthor David Marcusson-Clavertz discuss how altered states of consciousness seem to facilitate psi ability,[283] and provides a wonderful review of past literature on hypnosis and psi. This article discusses the ways in which an altered state of consciousness might affect people who test high on hypnotizibility and who have strong beliefs in their own psi abilities. Additionally, Cardeña and Marcusson-Clavertz tested and compared psi results between hypnosis and a ganzfeld environment, which essentially creates a sensory-deprivation setting. They discovered that psi abilities *did* present themselves in ganzfeld settings. The authors discuss the implications for their findings on hypnosis and muse about future studies regarding altered states of consciousness.[284]

Further Reading:

Etzel Cardeña and D. Marcusson-Clavertz, "Changes in State of Consciousness and Psi in Ganzfeld and Hypnosis Conditions." *Journal of Parapsychology* 84, (2020): 66–84.

E. Cardeña, J. Palmer, and D. Marcusson-Clavertz (eds.) *Parapsychology: A Handbook for the 21st Century.* Jefferson, NC: McFarland, 2021.

Cassirer, Manfred (1920–2003, Author): Manfred Cassirer was a German-born author and parapsychologist. He served as the chair of the Physical Phenomena committee of the British SPR and has published numerous articles in the *Journal of the Society for Psychical Research*.[285] After joining the SPR, he became a research officer at one of the labs where he investigated spontaneous cases of psi phenomena. Cassirer was particularly interested in mediums and his 1996 book *Medium on Trial* discusses the life of Helen Duncan, a Scottish medium. He also wrote about the Italian medium Eusapia Palladino.

In addition to his interest in mediums, Cassirer was an advocate for the study of UFO phenomena and believed that there was a correlation between UFO sightings and psi phenomena, like ESP and apparitions. He also investigated a series of poltergeist hauntings in Bromley, London, and alongside his coinvestigator, they ruled out fraud and natural explanations, leaving them to believe that strange things were indeed happening. This investigation is outlined in yet another of Cassirer's book, the 1993 title *The Persecution of Mr. Tony Elms*.[286]

Further Reading:

Manfred Cassirer, *Medium on Trial: The Story of Helen Duncan and the Witchcraft Act.* Stansted: PN Publications, 1996.

Manfred Cassirer, *Parapsychology and the UFO.* London: M. Cassirer, 1988.

Manfred Cassirer, *The Persecution of Mr. Tony Elms.* London: M. Cassirer, 1993.

Cassoli, Piero (1918–2000, Physician): Piero Cassoli was an Italian physician who cofounded the Centro Studi Parapsicologici (Center for Parapsychological Studies) in Italy. His research confirmed that there is a psychosocial nature to many paranormal events. For example, in his study of a woman who seemed to psychokinetically affect crucifixes and who claimed to see apparitions of holy figures, Cassoli discovered that her family was devoutly religious and had even been connected to a family experiencing similar phenomena.[287]

Further Reading:

Piero Cassoli, *Il Guaritore (The Healer).* Milan: Armenia Editore, 1979.

Chauvin, Rémy (1913–2009, Biologist): Rémy Chauvin was a French biologist who studied animal behavior. He was particularly interested in the potential for animals to exhibit extrasensory perception. From 1968–1986 he published papers on his tests of ESP among mice.[288] Additionally, he authored more than fifty books that have been translated into multiple languages, along with nearly two hundred scholarly publications throughout his career.

In 1959, he befriended J. B. Rhine during a trip to Rhine's parapsychology institute—a trip he took after becoming interested in Zener cards and his own experiments among friends and family. Rémy also worked with the French parapsychology organization the Institut Métephysique International

(IMI). Through his involvement with IMI, he led a committee on comparative parapsychology in which he conducted studies with animals, and he eventually became president of the IMI a number of years later. He helped advance the scientific cause of parapsychology in France and was a mentor to many students interested in the topic. His work on ESP among mice earned him the prestigious McDougall Award and he was the first French researcher awarded the Outstanding Career Award from the Parapsychological Association.[289]

Further Reading:

Renaud Evrard, "Rémy Chauvin." *Journal of Scientific Exploration* 24, no. 2 (2010): 299–303.

Corliss, William R. (1926–2011, Physicist): William R. Corliss was an American physicist, technical writer for NASA, and former programs director of the organization now known as Lockheed Martin. He was interested in and helped advance the field of anomalistics, which is "an interdisciplinary field that seeks scientific discoveries in the lore of the curious and the unexplained."[290] Corliss was inspired by the work of Charles Fort who compiled and presented tales of strange and mysterious events to the public. Corliss was also inspired by an essay written by psychologist (and psychical researcher) William James in which James refers to an "unclassified residuum" that comprises those random, strange events that seem easy to brush off without a second thought. Corliss began compiling his own catalog of strange and curious information that he culled specifically from scientific journals, choosing not to include information from sources that seemed dubious or noncredible. Corliss called this multidecade research the *Sourcebook Project*, which represents information gathered from 1974–2007.

Perhaps one of the sources most relevant to the field of parapsychology is Corliss's *The Unfathomed Mind: A Handbook of Unusual Mental Phenomena.* Published in 1982, this work includes bibliographies of resources on such subjects as automatic writing, hypnotism, altered states of consciousness, and dreams. Especially useful for those just beginning to learn more about parapsychology, the references in Corliss's book are extremely helpful in finding credible resources, and it's easy to see how this book helped Corliss achieve his goal of introducing these

topics to a wider audience. Bibliographic entries include publications from a wide variety of sources including the *Journal of the American Society for Psychical Research, Popular Science,* the *Journal of Abnormal and Social Psychology,* and much more.

Further Reading:

William R. Corliss, *The Unfathomed Mind: A Handbook of Unusual Mental Phenomena.* Glen Arm, MD: The Sourcebook Project, 1982.

Crookall, Robert (1890–1981, Geologist): Dr. Robert Crookall was a British geologist who, in the field of parapsychology, is most noted for his work on astral projection. Crookall surveyed hundreds of people who claimed to have experienced astral projection in an attempt to better understand this phenomenon from a cultural, religious, and even scientific standpoint. In compiling these experiences, Crookall amassed a catalog of astral projection that identifies certain characteristics like "the double" and "the silver cord."

D

Dagnall, Neil (Psychologist): Dr. Neil Dagnall is a psychologist and parapsychologist at Manchester Metropolitan University in England. His publications cover topics such as memory, perception of the paranormal, narcissism, sleep paralysis, conspiracy-believing, and more. In a 2020 article in the scholarly journal *Frontiers in Psychology,* Dagnall coauthored a paper that "contains a narrative overview of the past 20-years of environmental research on anomalous experiences attributed to 'haunted houses.'"[291] In this article, Dagnall and his coauthors discuss the role of environmental psychology (the ways in which surroundings and people affect one another) on haunt experiences. They begin by reminding us that haunting phenomena is perhaps the oldest topic for environmental psychologists to ponder.

Using an identified set of keywords established to obtain relevant results, Dagnall and coauthors conducted a review of the literature on haunt phenomena and environmental factors since 2001 (the date from which the next most recent and relevant survey had been done). Through the course of their review, they identified six environmental factors that act "as either conscious or unconscious stimulants of anomalous experiences."[292] These factors were embedded cues (like portraits hanging in a room where people claim to feel a presence), lighting, air quality, temperature, infrasound ("audio frequency energy that falls below the range of normal hearing"[293]), and electromagnetic fields. These six factors can stimulate haunt phenomena, but Dagnall and his coauthors discuss that the current literature shows that few comprehensively heed these factors in their studies and urge future research that consider these attributes and the ways in which it interacts with and influences haunt phenomena.

Further Reading:

Kenneth Graham Drinkwater, Neil Dagnall, Andrew Denovan, and Christopher Williams, "Differences in Cognitive-Perceptual Factors Arising from Variations in Self-Professed Paranormal Ability." *Frontiers in Psychology* 12 (June 10, 2021): 1–8.

Dalkvist, Jan (Psychologist): Jan Dalkvist is a Swedish psychologist who published many articles of parapsychological research in her time at Stockholm University. In a 2013 article for the *Journal of Parapsychology*, Dalkvist discusses an experiment that tests group telepathy and notes that previous psi research tends to eschew favor to individual versus group tests. As of 2013, this article acknowledges that little to no studies involve both telepathy *and* group design. Dalkvist's group experiments, which she had been conducting since 1993, involve the potential for one group to telepathically send emotional signals to another group. The design of the experiment involves one group of subjects (the senders), viewing certain emotionally charged photographs (positive or negative). A second group of subjects, in a separate room and with no idea as to what the pictures are (the receivers), attempt to pick up on the emotions of the first group by guessing whether each picture is positive or negative. Though only revealing a small statistically significant result, Dalksvist outlines some of the things this study revealed and ways in which future research of this type can be continued.

Further Reading:

Jan Dalkvist, "Performance in Group Telepathy Experiments as a Function of Target Picture Char-

acteristics." *Journal of Parapsychology* 77, no.1 (Spring 2013): 79–105.

Dean, E. Douglas (1916–2001, Parapsychologist): E. Douglas Dean was a British parapsychologist who has been described as "one of parapsychology's most brilliant innovators."[294] He received his masters of electrochemistry from Liverpool University before obtaining his PhD from the Saybrook Institute (called the Humanistic Psychology Institute at the time). Dean was chair of the joint parapsychology and paraphysics program at the International College of Montreal. He also served as assistant research director at the Parapsychology Foundation and served as president of the Parapsychological Association. During his term as president, Dean helped that organization become an affiliate of the American Association for the Advancement of Science.[295]

Some of Dean's key research areas were psychokinesis and healing. Fellow parapsychologist Gertrude Schmeidler describes one of Dean's major studies in regard to healing. Dean theorized that people known as healers could have a psychokinetic effect on water. In other words, he theorized that the psychical processes that healers use during sessions can impact the physical attributes of water. To test this, he designed a study in which healers wore small flasks of water on their body while conducting their healing session. Dean discovered that there were different infrared deflections of water between those that had been held by the healers and water that hadn't. He discovered that these changes were more pronounced the longer the healer possessed the water and began to decrease the longer the healer was separated from it. Gertrude Schmeidler muses about the impact of Dean's study and remarks that one implication "is that it should end the contention, still made by some parapsychologists, that PK cannot produce a physical change."[296]

Further Reading:

E. Douglas Dean, "Precognition and Retrocognition." In *Psychic Exploration* by Edgar D. Mitchell. (Ed. John White). G. P. Putnam's Sons, 1974.

Delanoy, Deborah (Parapsychologist): Dr. Deborah Delanoy is an American parapsychologist. After obtaining her sociology degree, she obtained a masters and PhD in parapsychology from the University of Edinburgh in Scotland under the guidance of fellow parapsychologist Dr. John Beloff. Delanoy held a visiting professorship in Germany for three years before she began teaching and researching at the University of Northampton. It was here that she cofounded the Centre for the Study of Anomalous Psychological Processes. She was coeditor of the scholarly publication *European Journal of Parapsychology*, was a past president of the Parapsychological Association, and was awarded that organization's Lifetime Achievement Award.[297]

A large portion of Delanoy's work involves testing and improving conditions that are conducive to psi abilities. In fact, her work helped inform the ganzfeld experiments still in use today at the Koestler Parapsychology Unit in Edinburgh. In a 2008 article in the *Journal of the Society for Psychical Research*, Delanoy and her coauthors David P. Luke and Simon J. Sherwood theorized that there may be a psi component to luck. Noting that we've all encountered those moments where we attribute some event to good luck, they designed a study to examine if luck is sometimes a psi-mediated instrumental response. Participants in their study exhibited precognitive abilities and they discovered a potential link between psi abilities and a belief in propensity for luck.[298]

Further Reading:

D. L. Delanoy, "Important Psi-Conducive Practices and Issues: Impressions from Six Parapsychological Laboratories." *European Journal of Parapsychology* 13, no. (1997): 62–68.

David P. Luke, Deborah Delanoy, and Simon J. Sherwood, "Psi May Look Like Luck: Perceived Luckiness and Beliefs about Luck in Relation to Precognition." *Journal of the Society for Psychical Research* 72, no. 4 (October 2008): 193–207.

Delorme, Arnaud (Neuroscientist): Arnaud Delorme is a neuroscientist and researcher at the Institute of Noetic Sciences and University of California. In a 2021 article for *Explore: The Journal of Science and Healing*, Delorme and his coauthors investigated energy healing. Specifically, they recruited subjects who had carpal tunnel pain and likewise recruited practitioners of energy healing. Energy healing sessions were delivered in close contact and subjects were analyzed for pain before, during, immediately after, and three weeks after treatment. In addition to identifying reduced pain levels both immediately and three weeks after, subjects also claimed to feel a deeper sense of well-being and calm. Delorme and colleagues conclude that there appears to be a connection between pain, energy healing, and the parasympathetic nervous system but that continued research is needed.[299]

Further Reading:

Garret Yount, Arnaud Delorme, Dean Radin, Loren Carpenter, Kenneth Rachlin, Joyce Anastasia, Meredith Pierson, Sue Steele, Heather Mandell, Aimee Chagnon, and Helané Wahbeh, "Energy Medicine Treatments for Hand and Wrist Pain: A Pilot Study." *Explore: The Journal of Science and Healing* 17 (2021): 11–21.

Drinkwater, Kenneth (Parapsychologist): Dr. Kenneth Drinkwater is a parapsychologist at Manchester Metropolitan University in England. In a 2020 article in the *Journal of Parapsychology*, Drinkwater and coauthors present a study on electronic voice phenomena and cognitive-perceptual attributes such as fantasy proneness, hallucinations, schizotypy, and paranormal belief. The subjects in the study listened to a recording of white and pink noise and were asked to indicate what they heard. The recording was created for purpose of study, not a genuine paranormal artifact. Some participants claimed to hear voices, specifically in the form of the popular holiday song, "White Christmas." The authors discuss the cognitive-perceptual attributes that may impact a person's psychological tendency to experience anomalous sounds.[300]

Further Reading:

Kenneth Drinkwater, Andrew Denovan, Neil Dagnall, and Andrew Parker, "Predictors of Hearing Electronic Voice Phenomena in Random Noise: Schizotypy, Fantasy Proneness, and Paranormal Beliefs." *Journal of Parapsychology* 84, no. 1 (2020): 96–113.

Duplessis, Yvonne (1912–2017, Philosopher and Dermo-Optics Researcher): Dr. Yvonne Duplessis was a French philosopher, dermo-optics researcher, and parapsychologist. She was introduced to Rene

Warcollier in the 1950s and became interested in pursuing her own research. As such, she began conducting her own experiments with the Institut Métapsychique International. Her research involved testing ESP with blind people and creating new cards for people with synesthesia. In a rather unique set of studies, she combined her knowledge of dermo-optics with perception, testing how people can determine the color of objects without the use of their eyes.[301]

E

Eisenbud, Jule (1908–1999, Psychiatrist): Dr. Jule Eisenbud was an American psychiatrist at the Columbia College of Physicians and Surgeons. Eisenbud was fascinated with dreams and the phenomena of precognitive dreaming. Eisenbud himself even had some poignant psychic dreams. When he opened his private practice, Eisenbud's research into dreams and dreaming flourished.[302] He rose to recognition through his research on Ted Serios, a man who claimed to product "thoughtography," or the ability to record his thoughts and dreams on film—polaroid picture film, to be exact. He was a colleague of Jan Ehrenwald and together with other psychiatrists were members of the medical section of the American Society for Psychical Research. In the 1940s, he discussed this topic at a meeting of the New York Psychoanalytic Society that resulted in professional snubbing, which was a blow to his reputation and credibility.[303] Nevertheless, his contribution to parapsychology is notable. His 1970 book *Psi and Psychoanalysis* "was the first comprehensive presentation of the relevance of psi to analytic practice."[304]

Further Reading:

Jule Eisenbud, *Psi and Psychoanalysis: Studies in the Psychoanalysis of Psi-Conditioned Behavior.* New York: Grune and Stratton, 1970.

Ellison, Arthur J. (1920–2000, Electrical Engineer): Dr. Arthur J. Ellison was a British electrical engineer and parapsychologist. He was drawn to parapsychology due to his own experiences with anomalous phenomena including hauntings and out-of-body experiences.[305] He twice served as president of the SPR—once in the 1960s and again

in the 1980s. Ellison taught at various universities included Queen Mary College, the Massachusetts Institute of Technology, and the National University of Engineering in Peru. Ellison investigated a number of mediums, including physical medium Uri Geller, Matthew Manning, and the séance community known as the Scole group.[306]

Further Reading:

Arthur J. Ellison, *Science and the Paranormal: Altered States of Reality.* Edinburgh: Floris Books, 2003.

Erickson, Deborah L. (Psychologist): Dr. Deborah L. Erickson is a psychologist, parapsychologist, and web manager for the British SPR. She obtained her psychology PhD from Saybrook University with a concentration on consciousness and spirituality. In a 2011 article in the journal *NeuroQuantology*, Erickson discusses the phenomenon of interspecies communication. Specifically, she discusses the ways in which meditation can slow brain waves and shift consciousness into a consciousness akin to those in hypnagogic and hypnapompic states, thus allowing us to perhaps tap into a greater, shared consciousness.[307]

Further Reading:

Deborah L. Erickson, "Intuition, Telepathy, and Interspecies Communication: A Multidisciplinary Perspective." *NeuroQuantology* 9, no. 1 (2011): 145–52.

Eysenck, Hans (1918–1997, Psychologist): Dr. Hans Eysenck was a German psychologist and professor at the University of London. He is perhaps most noted for the development of the Eysenck Personality Questionnaire, a measure used widely in parapsychological studies.[308] This personality test measures levels of psychoticism, extraversion, and neuroticism in people.[309] Eysenck believed that extroverts are better at receiving psychical messages due to their lowered levels of cortical stimulation as compared to those of introverts.[310] He firmly believed that parapsychology should not be relegated to the realm of pseudoscience and that the vast amount of learned scholars studying these phenomena give weight to its academic significance, though he urged for more rigorous and scientific methods.[311]

Further Reading:

Hans Eysenck and Carl Sargent, *Explaining the Unexplainable: Mysteries of the Paranormal*. London: Weidenfeld and Nicholson, 1982.

F

Feather, Sally Rhine (Psychologist): Dr. Sally Rhine Feather is an American psychologist and daughter of renowned parapsychologists J. B. and Louisa Rhine. As a child, Feather was a subject in some of her parent's studies, and she went on to serve in a research capacity there as she got older. She engaged in research that observed a "checker" effect in which subject's anticipation of performing well for a known checker appeared to somehow affect psi. Feather also conducted psychokinesis experiments with her mother, Louisa, to study the results when two people attempt PK at once. She has written about both of her parents, and her book *The Gift* goes into particular detail about her mother's experiments.[312]

Further Reading:

Victor Mansfield, Sally Rhine-Feather, and James Hall, "The Rhine-Jung Letters: Distinguishing Parapsychological from Synchronistic Events." *Journal of Parapsychology* 62, no. 1 (March 1998): 3–25.

Ferrari, Diane C. (Psychologist): Dr. Diane C. Ferrari is a psychologist who taught at Princeton University. While there, she coauthored a paper with parapsychologist Dean Radin to analyze fifty-two years' worth of PK studies. Specifically, Ferrari and Radin looked at the well-known studies that used dice to search for instance of PK. Within this fifty-year year time space, seventy-three cases had been published that contained more than two million dice throws and nearly three thousand subjects. After choosing fifty-nine final reports to investigate, Ferrari and Radin tell us that "based primarily on the analysis of a homogenous subset of balanced protocol studies, we conclude that the aggregate evidence suggests the presence of a weak, genuine mental effect."[313]

Further Reading:

Dean I. Radin and D. C. Ferrari, "Effects of Consciousness on the Fall of Dice: A Meta-Analysis." *Journal of Scientific Exploration* 5, no. 1 (1991): 61–83.

Fontana, David (1934–2010, Psychologist): Dr. David Fontana was a British psychologist, parapsychologist, and the author of two books on the topic of survival after death. Fontana also researched electronic voice phenomena and was chair of the Survival Research ommittee of the British SPR. In addition, he investigated cases of poltergeist phenomena and was part of the group of researchers who investigated the Scole group, a group of people who met regularly to host séances.[314]

G

Gauld, Alan (1932–, Psychologist): Dr. Alan Gauld is a British psychologist, parapsychologist, and professor who taught at the University of Nottingham. He became interested in parapsychology during his undergraduate years at Cambridge University, where he served as secretary for the university's SPR. Most interested in spontaneous cases, one of Gauld's major contributions are his publications on the history of the British SPR, poltergeists, and mediumship.

Further Reading:

Alan Gauld, *A History of Hypnotism*. Cambridge: Cambridge University Press, 1992.
Alan Gauld, *Mediumship and Survival*. London: Heinemann, 1982.

Gregory, Anita K. (1925–1984, Parapsychologist): Dr. Anita K. Gregory was a German-British psychologist who obtained her PhD in parapsychology shortly before she died. She served as secretary of the British SPR and focused her work primarily on the mediums Matthew Manning and Rudi Schneider.[315] Gregory also paid close attention to Grosse and Playfair's investigation of the Enfield poltergeist and was critical of the genuineness of the case, believing instead that the researchers had been caught in an elaborate hoax.[316]

Grosse, Maurice (1919–2006, Engineer): Maurice Grosse was a British engineer and inventor who became interested in parapsychology after the death of his daughter. Seeking answers for some of his experiences in the days after her death, Grosse joined the British SPR. He investigated numerous cases through his appointment to the SPR's Spontaneous Cases committee and is most well known for his involvement with the Enfield poltergeist case. Grosse, along with Guy Lyon Playfair, investigated the home and in the course of doing so, recorded hundreds of tapes featuring strange noises and anomalous voices. He investigated a handful of other poltergeist cases after Enfield and soon developed a reputation for his work. People would even mail Grosse their strange photographs of alleged paranormal phenomena.[317]

H

Haraldsson, Erlendur (1931–2020, Psychologist): Dr. Erlendur Haraldsson was an Icelandic psychologist, parapsychologist, and professor at the University of Iceland. In an obituary memorializing the work of Haraldsson, Lance Storm tells us that "Erlendur will be remembered mainly for his reincarnation research, as well as his studies on precognitive dreams, personality, and the psychology of children."[318]

After studying at the University of Munich, Haraldsson worked at J. B. Rhine's Institute for Parapsychology and went on to work with another noted parapsychologist, Hans Bender. His research includes reincarnation, dream recall, cross-cultural death experiences, haunt phenomena, and more.

In a 2009 article in the *Journal of Parapsychology*, Haraldsson interviewed 337 Icelanders who had experienced having an encounter with a deceased person. In his study, he discovered that the vast majority of experiences were visual, followed then by auditory, the least of them being through smell. Less than half the experiences took place in the dark, and he also noticed, most curiously, that a large number of apparitions were those of people who had died in violent ways.[319]

Further Reading:

Erlendur Haraldsson, "Alleged Encounters with the Dead: The Importance of Violent Death in 337 New Cases." *Journal of Parapsychology* 73 (April 2009): 91–118.

Holt, Nicola (Psychologist): Dr. Nicola Holt is a British psychologist and parapsychologist who obtained a PhD exceptional experiences and consciousness studies. Much of her parapsychological research involves the intersection of creativity, consciousness, and anomalous experiences. She has been the winner of numerous awards including the Gertrude R. Schmeidler Outstanding Student Award.[320]

Further Reading:

C. Roe and N. Holt, "Assessing the Role of the Sender as a PK Agent in ESP Studies: The Effects of Strategy ('willing' versus 'absorption') and Feedback (immediate versus delayed) on Psi Performance." *Journal of Parapsychology* 70 (2006): 69–90.

Honorton, Charles (1946–1992, Parapsychologist): Dr. Charles Honorton was an American parapsychologist and recipient of the first federal grant distributed for parapsychological research. In 1967, he joined the research team at the Dream Laboratory at the Maimonides Hospital. He developed and popularized the use of the ganzeld technique to study the intersection of psi and altered states of consciousness.[321]

Further Reading:

C. Honorton and D. B. Ferrari, and G. Hansen, "Future Telling: A Meta-Analysis of Forced-Choice Precognition Experiments, 1935–1987." *Journal of Parapsychology* 53 (1989): 281–308.

J. C. Terry and C. Honorton, "Psi Information Retrieval in the Ganzfeld: Two Confirmatory Studies." *Journal of the American Society for Psychical Research* 70, no. 2 (1976): 207–17.

Houran, James (Psychologist): Dr. James Houran is a psychologist, parapsychologist, managing director at AETHOS Consulting Group, and editorial board member of both the *Journal of the Society for Psychical Research* and *Journal of Parapsychology*. With more than one hundred journal publications, Houran's contribute to parapsychology is vast.[322]

One of Houran's unique contributions is a 2018 article in the *Australian Journal of Parapsychology* in which he discusses the need for a standard operationalization when referring to people who report their paranormal experiences. He reminds us of the importance of words and points out that "the way researchers or authors talk about people who report anomalous or unusual experiences arguably imparts a value judgment that can bias readers' impressions overly or covertly."[323]

In a 2020 article in the *Journal of the Society for Psychical Research*, Houran coauthored a study that investigated the role that architecture plays in haunting cases. An extraordinary architectural experience (EAE) occurs when a building or space fundamentally impacts a person, whether emotionally or physically. These profound experiences often elicit strong physical reactions such as goosebumps or chills, and the authors wondered if the EAEs could hold true with haunted buildings. They discuss six specific environmental and architectural factors that may impact experiences in a haunted location.[324]

Further Reading:

James Houran, Brian Laythe, Ciaran O'Keeffe, Neil Dagnall, Kenneth Drinkwater, and Rense Lange, "Quantifying the Phenomenology of Ghostly Episodes: Part 1—Need for a Standard Operationalization." *Journal of Parapsychology* 83, no. 1 (Spring 2019): 25–46.

James Houran, "'Sheet Happens!' Advancing Ghost Studies in the Analytics Age." *Australian Journal of Parapsychology* 17, no. 2 (December 2017): 187–206.

Hunter, Jack (Anthropologist): Dr. Jack Hunter is a British anthropologist, professor at the University of Chester, and research fellow with the Parapsychology Foundation. Hunter's research includes taking an ecological look at psi, and so accordingly, he created the journal *Paranthropology: Journal of Anthropological Approaches to the Paranormal*.[325]

In a 2011 article in the *Journal of the Society for Psychical Research*, Hunter discusses his fieldwork with the Bristol Spirit Lodge, a group of people who meet regularly to practice mediumship. In this article, Hunter points out that many studies of mediumship naturally tend to focus on the medium themselves, but that the experience of attendees is just as important, especially through a social and anthropological lens.[326]

Further Reading:

Jack Hunter, *Greening the Paranormal: Exploring the Ecology of Extraordinary Experience.* August Night Press, 2019.

I

Irwin, Harvey J. (1943–, Psychologist): Dr. Harvey J. Irwin is an Australian psychologist, parapsychologist, and research fellow at Manchester Metropolitan University. According to researchers Arthur and Joyce Berger, Irwin "has helped put his country on the parapsychological map with a new approach to understanding the out-of-body experience as a psychological rather than a paranormal phenomenon."[327] In addition, Irwin's research focuses on the role of paranormal belief. A 2000 article in the *European Journal of Parapsychology* investigates the psychological needs that might be met from a belief in the paranormal—in particular the feeling of having control over one's life. His study found that some people (mostly women) who prefer to have strict control over their physical environment tend to have positive attitudes toward the paranormal. Irwin reminds us, however, that more studies are needed and the exact relationship between paranormal belief and a locus of control warrants further study.[328]

Further Reading:

Harvey J. Irwin, "Belief in the Paranormal and a Sense of Control Over Life." *European Journal of Parapsychology* 15 (2000): 68–78.

J

Johnson, Martin (1930–2011, Psychologist): Dr. Martin Johnson was a Swedish psychologist and parapsychologist. Johnson grew up in Västerbotton, a northern province in Sweden that is known for its rich shamanic traditions. Johnson's family was full of relatives who had otherworldly abilities. Johnson's grandmother had the reputation of a healer, and his other grandmother often knew who was visiting shortly before they arrived. Johnson's life had been touched by psi from its very beginning so it's not surprising that it was a lifelong topic of interest to him. He attended a lecture by the parapsychologist Wilhelm Tenhaeff, which led Johnson to do a clandestine investigation of the medium Gerard Croiset—clandestine because Johnson first sought to coinvestigate the medium with Tenhaeff but was turned away by the noted parapsychologist. Nevertheless, J. B. Rhine at Duke University heard about this study and invited Johnson to his labs. After working with Rhine and being introduced to other parapsychologists, Johnson returned to the Netherlands where he was appointed as parapsychology professor at the University of Utrecht.[329]

Further Reading:

John Palmer and Martin Johnson, "Defensiveness and Brain Hemisphere Stimulation in a Perceptually Mediated ESP Task." *Journal of Parapsychology* 55, no. 4 (1991): 329–48.

Adrian Parker and Nemo C. Mörck, "Martin Johnson 1930–2011." *Journal of Parapsychology* 75, no. 2 (2011): 353–59.

K

Kappers, Jan (1914–?, Physician): Dr. Jan Kappers was a Dutch physician who was the first to test the effects of psilocybine on psi behavior. The tests showed that the drug could enhance abilities in some cases but overall did not show a significant effect. Kappers was also the first president of the Nederlandse Vereniging Voor Parapsychologie, the Dutch Society for Parapsychology.[330]

Karagulla, Shafica (1914–?, Neuropsychiatrist): Dr. Shafica Karagulla was a Turkish American neuropsychiatrist. Her early research on hallucinations led her to take a post at the State University of New York. She developed a theory of higher senser perception, which she defined as the ability of a person to freely and willfully exhibit ESP-like behavior. Karagulla founded the Higher Sense Perception Research Foundation in California.[331]

Kasahara, Toshio (1947–, Psychologist): Dr. Toshio Kasahara is a Japanese psychologist who "is one of the few writers who has been introducing contemporary parapsychology to Japanese readers."[332] Kasahara has translated works, making them available to Japanese scholars and has also compiled bibliographies of relevant parapsychological research.

Keil, Jürgen (1930–, Psychologist): Dr. Jürgen Keil is a German Australian psychologist and professor at the University of Tasmania. Keil spent a semester at the University of Virginia's Department of Parapsychology where he conducted ESP tests alongside J. Gaither Pratt. During his research with Pratt, the two investigated the mediums Pavel Stepanek and Nina Kulagina.

Further Reading:

Jürgen Keil, "Cases of the Reincarnation Type: An Evaluation of Some Indirect Evidence with Examples of 'Silent' Cases." *Journal of Scientific Exploration* 10, no. 4 (1996): 467–85.

Kelly, Edward F. (Psychiatrist): Dr. Edward F. Kelly, husband of Dr. Emily W. Kelly below, is a psychiatrist and parapsychologist in the Department of Psychiatry and Neurobehavioral Sciences at the University of Virginia. Some of Kelly's research involves reassessments of historical studies. For example, Kelly and colleagues reevaluated a clairvoyance study done in the 1920s and confirmed that the data indicates the presence of psi. In addition to this research, Kelly has coauthored multiple books that seek to expand and challenge our understanding of consciousness. His 2007 coauthored work *Irreducible Mind* discuss a vast array of psychical experiences and his 2015 coauthored work *Beyond Physicalism* brings an interdisciplinary focus to psi.[333]

Further Reading:

E. F. Kelly, A. Crabtree, and P. Marshal, *Beyond Physicalism: Toward Reconciliation of Science and Spirituality.* Lanham, MD: Rowman & Littlefield, 2015.

E. F. Kelly, E. Kelly, A. Crabtree, A. Gauld, M. Grosso, and B. Greyson, *Irreducible Mind: Toward a Psychology for the 21st Century.* Lanham, MD: Rowman & Littlefield, 2007.

Kelly, Emily W. (Parapsychologist): Dr. Emily W. Kelly is a parapsychologist with the Division of Perceptual Studies at the University of Virginia. She joined the university in 1978 after becoming a research assistant to Dr. Ian Stevenson, a leading figure in past-life memories. Her research focuses on consciousness studies and particularly instances of near-death experiences and reincarnation. Through her research, she has added to the body of literature on terminal lucidity, the realization that mental functioning increases in the moments preceding death. In fact, some of Kelly's near-death experience research has shown mental functioning of patients in moments when brain functioning should clinically be impossible.[334]

Further Reading:

E. W. Kelly, "Near-Death Experiences with Reports of Meeting Deceased People." *Death Studies* 25, no. 3 (2001): 229–49.

Kramer, Wim H. (Parapsychologist): Dr. Wim Kramer is a Dutch parapsychologist who has conducted research within the clinical psychology department at the University of Utrecht. He is a coeditor of the 2012 publication *Perspectives of Clinical Parapsychology*. Within that book the first chapter is written by Kramer and in it he discusses the importance of offering counseling to those experiencing psi phenomena.[335]

Further Reading:

Wim H. Kramer, Eberhard Bauer, and Gerd. H. Hövelman, eds., *Perspectives of Clinical Parapsychology: An Introductory Reader.* Bunnik: Stichting Het Johan Borgman Fonds, 2012.

Krieman, Naum (1919–?, Statistician and Parapsychologist): Dr. Naum Krieman was an Argentinian statistician and parapsychologist. He established the scholarly journal *Cuadernos de Parapsicología* and in 1972 established the Instituto de Parapsicología. His 1994 book *Curso de Parapsicología* (Course of Parapsychology) presents an overview of parapsychological research in Latin American (and elsewhere) up through 1970.[336]

Kripal Jeffrey J. (Philosopher and Religious Studies Scholar): Dr. Jeffrey J. Kripal is a professor of philosophy and religion at Rice University. His research investigates the philosophical intersection of mystical, religious, and anomalous experiences.[337] Kripal also publishes history of certain events and people. For example, in the 2015 *Handbook of Spiritualism and Channeling*, Kripal contributes a chapter on remote viewing. This chapter presents information on resources that discuss the

"wide range of paranormal programs and psychical espionage activities" that the United States and Russia engaged in from the 1970s through 90s.[338]

In his 2010 book *Authors of the Impossible,* Kripal offers a philosophical discussion of the paranormal's influence on religious thought through the lens of biographical overviews of figures like Frederic W. H. Myers and Charles Richet, among others.[339]

Further Reading:

Jeffrey J. Kripal, *Authors of the Impossible: The Paranormal and the Sacred.* Chicago: University of Chicago Press, 2010.

Jeffrey J. Kripal, *The Flip: Epiphanies of Mind and the Future of Knowledge.* New York: Bellevue Literary Press, 2019.

Krippner, Stanley (1932–, Psychologist and Parapsychologist): Dr. Stanley Krippner is an American psychologist, parapsychologist, and professor at Saybrook University. He has authored numerous books and articles related to parapsychology. Interested in psi phenomena from an early age, Krippner had his own anomalous experience when he was fourteen and received the premonition of his uncle's passing. While at the University of Wisconsin, Krippner invited parapsychologist J. B. Rhine to campus for a lecture and Krippner's involvement with psi formally began to grow. He served as a research assistant to Gardner Murphy and worked alongside Montague Ullman in the dream labs at Maimonides Hospital.

Krippner's research portfolio includes work on dreams and altered states of consciousness. He is a believer in shared consciousness and also advocates for reducing the assumption that all psi events are rooted in pathology.[340]

Further Reading:

S. Krippner and H. L. Friedman, eds., *Mysterious Minds: The Neurobiology of Physics, Mediums, and Other Extraordinary People.* New York: Gordon & Breach, 1975.

L

Lange, Rense (Psychologist and Data Scientist): Dr. Rense Lange is a psychologist and data scientist whose research also includes topics within parapsychology. For example, in a 1998 article in the *Journal of Nervous and Mental Disease,* Lange and his coauthor James Houran discuss poltergeist phenomena. Specifically, they posit that poltergeist phenomena are the result of cognitive delusions that attempt to make sense of ambiguous stimuli. Various attributes impact the way in which people interpret ambiguous stimuli and include age, gender, and ambiguity tolerance. Furthermore, fear plays a role in stimuli interpretation as well, and they point out that labeling an event/stimuli as paranormal helped experiencers (who had a low tolerance of ambiguity) reduce the fear surrounding that event.[341] Additional parapsychological research of Lange's can be found in journals including *Psychology of Consciousness,* the *Journal of Parapsychology,* and more.

Further Reading:

Rense Lange and James Houran, "Delusions of the Paranormal: A Haunting Question of Perception." *The Journal of Nervous and Mental Disease* 186, no. 10 (October 1998): 637–45.

Lawrence, Madelaine (Health Educator and Author): Dr. Madelaine Lawrence is a health educator and author whose research includes near-death and end-of-life experiences. In a 2017 article in the *American Journal of Hospice and Palliative Medicine,* Lawrence discusses the near-death (NDE) and out-of-body (OBE) experiences that occur not during the end of a terminal illness, but which occur in the midst of natural disaster, war, imprisonment, etc. Within this article are numerous accounts of anomalous and deeply personal experiences during an NDE or OBE. This article is specifically intended for those who are first-responders or medical health professionals. Lawrence points out the lack of information and training available to these people regarding the intense transpersonal events of NDEs and OBEs and not only how to deal with them personally, but how to assist patients or family members through this process.[342]

Further Reading:

Madelaine Lawrence, "Near-Death and Other Transpersonal Experiences Occurring during Catastrophic Events." *American Journal of Hospice and Palliative Medicine* 34, no. 5 (2017): 486–92.

Laythe, Brian (Social Psychologist and Parapsychologist): Dr. Brian Laythe is a social psychologist, parapsychologist, and founder and director of the Institute for the Study of Religious and Anomalous Experience, a research organization located in Indiana. In a 2019 article in the *Journal of the Society for Psychical Research*, Laythe and his coauthor James Houran provide an overview of an investigation at the site of a haunting that involved psychokinesis. They noticed electromagnetic field fluctuations near anomalous movements of objects. These fluctuations were not in line with the normal range of fluctuations that should be present in that space. Specifically, they tell us that "we tentatively assert that a pattern exists here, whereby small EMF fields are being measured contrary to what physics and local sources would seem to theoretically allow."[343]

Further Reading:

Brian Laythe and James Houran, "Concomitant Object Movements and EMF-Spikes at a Purported Haunt." *Journal of the Society for Psychical Research* 83, no. 4 (2019): 212–29.
Cindy Little, Brian Laythe, and James Houran, "Quali-Quantitative Comparison of Childhood Imaginary Companions and Ghostly Episodes." *Journal of the Society for Psychical Research* 85, no. 1 (2021): 1–30.

Lobach, Eva (Mathematician and Psychologist): Eva Lobach is a Dutch mathematician and psychologist who conducted parapsychological research at the University of Amsterdam.[344] In a 2007 article that she coauthored with Dean Radin in *The Journal of Alternative and Complementary Medicine*, they discuss retrocausality in relation to the placebo effect. Specifically, they wonder "what if expectation acts to focus our attention on our potential future states, and allows us to 'select' favorable future paths to pursue?"[345]

Further Reading:

Dean Radin and Eva Lobach, "Toward Understanding the Placebo Effect: Investigating a Possible Retrocausal Factor." *The Journal of Alternative and Complementary Medicine* 13, no. 7 (2007): 734.

Lommel, Pim van (1943–, Cardiologist and Author): Dr. Pim van Lommel is a Dutch cardiologist who worked at the Rijnstate Hospital in the Netherlands. During his work as a cardiologist, Lommel encountered patients who talked about near-death experiences (NDE). Instances of these experiences were pervasive enough that Lommel and his colleagues Ruud van Wees, Vincent Meyers, and Ingrid Elfferich set out to do a longitudinal study on patients who experienced an NDE. They studied 344 cardiac arrest patients at ten hospitals. Of these, 18 percent experienced an NDE. The researchers discovered that NDEs were not correlated to the length of the cardiac arrest, medication, or even the person's fear of dying. Furthermore, they studied these patients two and eight years after the initial experience and discovered certain attributes present among NDE experiencers. Some of these attributes include a deep belief in the afterlife, a reduced fear of death, and enhanced self-awareness. Their study calls for continued inquiry into this phenomenon.[346]

Further Reading:

Pim van Lommel, Ruud van Wees, Vincent Meyers, and Ingrid Elfferich, "Near-Death Experience in Survivors of Cardiac Arrest: A Prospective Study in the Netherlands." *Lancet* 358, no. 9298 (2001): 2039–45.

M

Maher, Michaeleen (Parapsychologist): Dr. Michaeleen Maher is a parapsychologist who has taught at New York's New School University and who researches various phenomena, particularly hauntings. In an article published in 2000 in *The Journal of Parapsychology*, Maher presents a study she conducted at a haunted location, the General Wayne Inn in Merion, Pennsylvania.[347] In this study, Maher gathered three people who identify as sensitive/psychic and three people who claim no psi abilities (controls). Each set of people were given floor plans of the inn and asked to walk through the property. The sensitives were asked to mark where they felt the presence of a ghost and the controls were asked to mark where they thought a person *might* report a ghost. To add to the study, Maher also included a list of one hundred

events that might be common in a haunting case. Of these, thirty-five were examples of reported phenomena at the inn and the other sixty-five had not occurred at the location. Maher's study also took into consideration electromagnetic fields, and she was able to analyze whether those might influence either the sensitives or the controls. Maher's study revealed that sensitive's notations of ghostly phenomena matched eyewitness testimony while the control's notations did not correspond to any of the reported events. Additionally, Maher found no correlation between the locations of haunt phenomena and electromagnetic fields.

In 2004, the *Journal of Religion and Psychical Research* published a series of essays in a series titled "What Happens When We Die: A Philosophical Series." Maher's essay provides a discussion of life, death, and meaning and concludes by saying,

> As we penetrate further into nature's paradoxes, I suspect we will begin to unravel the mystery of death and its survival. In my view, hints are as likely to come from the material world as from the dualist's perspective. . . . I look forward to the time when we can begin to integrate the survival data we have collected into a single grand scheme that incorporates both the physical world and consciousness.[348]

Further Reading:

Michaeleen Maher, "Quantitative Investigation of the General Wayne Inn." *The Journal of Parapsychology* 64, no. 4 (December 2000): 365–90.

Maraldi, Everton (Psychologist): Dr. Everton Maraldi is a Brazilian psychologist and professor at Pontifical Catholic University in São Paulo. He is particularly interested in cross-cultural examinations of psi phenomena and paranormal beliefs. In a 2010 article in the *Journal of Scientific Exploration*, Maraldi and his coauthors Fatima Regina Machado and Wellington Zangari discuss the ways in which spiritualist philosophy has impacted scientific understanding, highlighting the interdisciplinary and complex nature of psi. They point out, for example, that our understanding of the unconscious mind is rooted in spiritist notions that the body and mind can be a vehicle for anomalous communication. This, as we know, spurred researchers to investigate the claims and abilities of mediums and led to a deeper awareness of the subconscious, the unconscious, and how the mind interacts with the world around it. Maraldi and his coauthors point out that the continued examination of psi (like mediumship) should take into consideration the psychosocial implications of those phenomena.[349]

Further Reading:

Everton Maraldi, Fatima Regina Machado, and Wellington Zangari, "Importance of a Psychosocial Approach for a Comprehensive Understanding of Mediumship." *Journal of Scientific Exploration* 24, no. 2 (2010): 181–96.

Marwaha, Sonali (Psychologist): Dr. Sonali Marwaha is a psychologist and parapsychologist from Mumbai. She has a PhD from Andhra University for which she received the J. B. Rhine Biennial Research Award.[350] In a 2015 article in the *Journal of Parapsychology*, Marwaha and coauthor Edwin May discuss a new theory of precognition using physics and neuroscience. Called the multiphasic model of precognition, Marwaha and May's work posits that explanations for psi need to be searched for through an interdisciplinary lens.[351]

Further Reading:

Sonali Bhatt Marwaha and Edwin C. May, "The Multiphasic Model of Precognition: The Rationale." *Journal of Parapsychology* 79, no. 1 (2015): 5–19.

McConnell, Robert A. (1914–2006, Physicist): Dr. Robert A. McConnell was an American physicist, parapsychologist, and professor at the University of Pittsburgh. He coauthored a seminal book on ESP with Dr. Gertrude Schmeidler in 1958 titled *ESP and Personality Patterns*.[352] In a 1967 article in *The Journal of Parapsychology*, McConnell and his coauthor Haakon Forwald reanalyzed a psychokinesis study that had been conducted ten years prior at the Duke Parapsychology Labs.[353] That study, referred to as the Forwald-Durham experiment, involved Haakon Forwald and a machine that would release cubes down a slope and land on a flat surface. During each release of dice, the target goal was the get dice to land in a certain spot. The targeted spot that the dice would land was predetermined by Forwald

as an intent on which to focus. In the original study, Forwald worked with fellow parapsychologist J. Gaither Pratt to analyze and report the findings. McConnell and Forwald reexamined the original data, analyzed the mechanics of devices used, and even interviewed a secretary who assisted with the original study. They found no discrepancies in the data and conclude that the experiment represents a potential display of psychokinesis.[354]

Mossbridge, Julia (Neuroscientist and Psychophysicist): Dr. Julia Mossbridge is a research fellow at the Institute for Noetic Science, a psychology professor at Northwestern University, and a professor of transpersonal psychology at the California Institute of Integral Studies.[355] Mossbridge's research involves consciousness, premonitions, and more. In a 2012 article in *Frontiers in Psychology*, Mossbridge and her coauthors conducted a meta-analysis of previous research on anticipatory effects (some may call this presentiment). In their review, they concluded that previous research collectively shows a small but statistically significant presence of the anticipatory effect—the physiological response of the body to stimulus *before* that stimulus happens.[356]

In a separate article, a 2021 study in the journal *Spirituality in Clinical Practice*, Mossbridge and her coauthors present their work on hypnotism. Specifically, the authors point out that while much research tends to focus on hypnotism and psi "superstars," those people who are screened and known for performing highly on psi. In this study, the researchers wanted to know if placing general subjects in a hypnotic state of unconditional love could enhance precognition and micropsychokinesis (micro-PK). The researchers gave hypnotic suggestions of both unconditional love and precognition to subjects, and they discovered that, prior to the hypnotism, subjects performed above chance on remote-viewing exercises. The hypnotism did not, however, produce significant changes in micro-PK or precognition abilities.[357]

Further Reading:

Theresa Cheung and Julia Mossbridge, *The Premonition Code: The Science of Precognition: How Sensing the Future can Change Your Life*. London: Watkins, 2018.

Julia A. Mossbridge and Dean Radin, "Precognition as a Form of Prospection: A Review of the Evidence." *Psychology of Consciousness: Theory, Research, and Practice* 5, no. 1 (2018): 78–93.

Murphy, Gardner (1895–1979, Psychologist): Gardner Murphy was an American psychologist and professor at Columbia University. He was active in both the Boston SPR and the American SPR and was an editor of the scholarly publication *Journal of Parapsychology*. Murphy was awarded the Hodgson Memorial Fund by the British SPR to conduct psychical research at Harvard. Murphy published more than one hundred works including articles and books, the impact of which lingers still today.[358]

Further Reading:

Gardner Murphy, "Spontaneous Telepathy and the Problem of Survival." *Journal of Parapsychology* 82. Suppl. (2018): 45–53. (originally published in 1943).

Musso, J. Ricardo (1917–1989, Psychologist): Dr. J. Ricardo Musso was an Argentinian psychologist and parapsychologist. Scholar Sergio A. Rueda tells us that Dr. Musso's death "ended an era of personal accomplishments aimed at establishing parapsychology as a scientific discipline in Argentina."[359] Dr. Musso's impact was prolific. In 1953 he founded the Instituto Argentino de Parapsicología and just a few short years later, in 1960, he was part of a landmark moment in parapsychological history. Upon being offered a position at Rosario University, he was asked to teach a parapsychology course that became a requirement for a psychology PhD, a fact significant since it marked the first time a parapsychology class was required for a psychology PhD[360] Collaboration was important to Dr. Musso who once conducted a long-distance ESP study that involved people from twenty different countries.

Further Reading:

J. Ricardo Musso and Mirta Granero, "An ESP Drawing Experiment with a High-Scoring Subject." *Journal of Parapsychology* 37, no. 1 (March 1, 1973): 13–36.

J. Ricardo Musso, *En los Límites de la Psicología: Desde el Espiritismo hasta la Parapsicología.* Buenos Aires: Periplo, 1954.

N

Nahm, Michael (Biologist): Dr. Michael Nahm is a German biologist and parapsychologist with the Institute for Frontier Areas of Psychology and Mental Health in Freiburg. Much of Nahm's research focuses on anomalous death experiences. Some of the anomalous experiences manifest via the near-death experience, but another anomalous event is terminal lucidity, or paradoxical lucidity. This describes moments in which terminally-ill patients with severe neurological conditions display near-perfect lucidity around the time of their death. Nahm and his colleagues discuss paradoxical lucidity in a 2019 article in the scholarly journal *Alzheimer's and Dementia.* Their article concludes, "If systematically verified, the neurobiological implications are that the brain—even in the setting of severe dementia—is capable of accessing functional networks to generate meaningful communication and interaction with the world."[361]

Further Reading:

Michael Nahm, "Reflections on the Context of Near-Death Experiences." *Journal of Scientific Exploration* 25, no. 3 (2011): 453–78.

Michael Nahm, Bruce Greyson, Emily Williams Kelly, and Erlendur Haraldsson, "Terminal Lucidity: A Review and a Case Collection." *Archives of Gerontology and Geriatrics* 55, no. 1 (July/ August 2012): 138–42.

Nelson, Roger (Psychologist): Dr. Roger Nelson is a psychologist and former professor at Johnson State College. While there, he joined the Princeton Engineering Anomalies Research (PEAR) lab. Much of his research at the PEAR lab involved the study of psychokinesis through random mechanical instrumentation. For example, in one study, subjects were asked to influence the placement of foam balls as they were dropped into a random mechanical cascade (RMC). The study indicated, interestingly, the presence of PK when subjects were asked to influence the movement of objects to the left.[362]

One of his most notable accomplishments is the "[development of] the field-REG approach, in which portable random event generators were situated near emotionally-charged public events to investigate collective consciousness effects."[363] His field-REG approach led to the creation of the Global Consciousness Project.

Further Reading:

Roger Nelson, "Coherent Consciousness: Probing the Edges of What we Know." *The Journal of Parapsychology* 76, Suppl. (December 2012): 36–37.

Roger Nelson, "Correlation of Global Events with REG Data: An Internet-Based, Nonlocal Anomalies Experiment." *Journal of Parapsychology* 65, no. 3 (September 2001): 247–71.

Noyes, Ralph (1923–1998, Ministry of Defence): Ralph Noyes was a British officer in the Ministry of Defence who also served as secretary of the SPR. As part of his work with the SPR, he was a founding member of a committee tasked with a project titled "Psychical Research Involving Selected Mediums" (PRISM). The PRISM project comprised seven mediums and seven SPR researchers who were tasked with investigating the presence of psi phenomena. The project included members from the Scole mediumship circle, a group of mediums who met regularly to conduct séances. During this inquiry, Noyes believed that some psi phenomena were genuine, but he also noticed a tendency for some to immediately ascribe "anomaly" to things which might, upon a more critical review, have explainable origins.[364]

O

O'Keeffe, Ciarán (Psychologist and Author): Dr. Ciarán O'Keeffe is a British psychologist and author who has researched various topics such as identifying common environmental attributes present at locations of haunt and poltergeist phenomena. These attributes can possibly contribute to the anomalous experience and include things like temperature, infrasound, electromagnetic fields, and static cues. He has also coauthored studies that identify twenty-eight subjective attributes often present during hauntings. O'Keeffe has also written a handful of books and has appeared on popular paranormal television programs to offer an objective and skeptical perspective to paranormal phenomena.[365]

Further Reading:

C. O'Keeffe, J. Houran, D. J. Houran, N. Dagnall, K. Drinkwater, L. Sheridan, and B. Laythe, "The Dr. John Hall story: a case study in putative "Haunted People Syndrome," *Mental Health, Religion & Culture* 22, no. 9, (2019): 910–29.

Otani, Soji (1924–, Psychologist): Dr. Soji Otani is a psychologist who established the Japanese Society for Parapsychology. In 1964 he gave "the first paper on parapsychology ever presented to Japanese psychologists."[366] His research shows that sound can affect ESP. His contributions to parapsychology are not just an effort to contribute to the core of scholarly literature on this topic, but to help advance the status of parapsychology as a science in Japan.[367]

Further Reading:

Soji Otani, "Relations of Mental Set and Change of Skin Resistance to ESP Score." *The Journal of Parapsychology* 19, no. 3 (September 1955): 164–70.

P

Paulí, E. Novillo (1919–1989, Parapsychologist): E. Novillo Paulí was an Argentinian parapsychologist, priest, and former director of the University of Salvador's Institute for Parapsychology. He wrote a textbook that was for many years the only work on the topic of parapsychology in Argentina. In one experiment, he investigated the presence of bio-psychokinesis (bio-PK) in seeds.[368]

Further Reading:

Enrique Novillo Paulí, *Los Fenómenos Parapsicológicos (The Parapsychological Phenomena).* Buenos Aires: Editorial Kapelusz, 1975.

Persinger, Michael (1945–2018, Psychologist): Dr. Michael Persinger was an American Canadian psychologist at Laurentian University. While there, he established the behavioral neuroscience program and remained its director until his passing. In addition to his other research, Persinger was also interested in parapsychological topics. For example, he discovered that high ESP scores tend to happen on days of low geomagnetic activity, whereas high PK scores tend to occur on days of high geomagnetic activity.[369]

In a 1985 article for the journal *Perceptual and Motor Skills*, Persinger discussed his research into the effect of certain environmental factors on ESP. He studied twenty-five published cases of telepathic phenomena in which the day, month, and year were included. These cases were also published before the first discussions about a possible connection between these two things was discussed in the scholarly or professional literature. Persinger discovered that on the days in which someone experienced a telepathic event, the earth's geomagnetic levels were lower than the typical, average level for that day.[370]

Persinger is also well known for his work on a device that's become known as the "God Helmet." In this study, Persinger and his colleagues discovered that the delivery of low-level magnetic fields through the temporal lobes could facilitate anomalous and mystical experiences.[371]

Further Reading:

Michael A. Persinger, "Geophysical Variables and Behavior: XXX. Intense Paranormal Experiences Occur During Days of Quiet, Global, Geomagnetic Activity." *Perceptual and Motor Skills* 61 (1985): 320–22.

Leslie A. Ruttan, Michael A. Persinger, and Stanley Koren, "Enhancement of Temporal Lobe-Related Experiences During Brief Exposures to Milligauss Intensity Extremely Low Frequency Magnetic Fields." *Journal of Bioelectricity* 9, no. 1 (1990): 33–54.

Playfair, Guy Lyon (1935–2018, Journalist): Guy Lyon Playfair was a British journalist and member of the SPR who participated in various SPR committees such as the spontaneous cases committee, the library committee, and the survival research committee. In his obituary in the *Journal of the Society for Psychical Research*, Alan Murdie tells us that "Guy Playfair exemplified the SPR tradition of independent scholars in the field, operating free of institutional restraint."[372]

While in Brazil working as a freelance journalist, Playfair had a profound experience with a psychic healer. As a result, he was introduced to the Brazilian Institute for Psychobiophysical Research where he was invited to help on investigations. During his few years working closely with that institute, he investigated twenty poltergeist cases in Brazil and wrote extensively about those experiences and his research into automatic writing and materializations. During one of these investigations, Playfair recorded unexplained rapping noises that were later subjected to audio analysis in 2010 and posited to be a sound marker unique to poltergeist cases.[373]

When he returned to England, he continued researching parapsychological topics for the next thirty years. Continuing his research into poltergeist phenomena, he worked alongside researcher Maurice Grosse on the Enfield case. As Alan Murdie tells us, "The Enfield case remains the best documented poltergeist disturbance in the history of the SPR with an excess of 180 recordings, resulting in transcripts running to over 500 pages."[374]

Further Reading:

Guy Lyon Playfair, *This House is Haunted: The True Story of a Poltergeist.* New York: Stein and Day, 1980. Reprinted in 2011 by White Crow Books under the title *This House is Haunted: The Amazing Inside Story of the Enfield Poltergeist.*

Pratt, J. Gaither (1910–1979, Psychologist): Dr. J. Gaither Pratt was an American psychologist who worked at the University of Virginia. As an undergraduate student, he was a student of J. B. Rhine's at Duke University and eventually became a research assistant in Rhine's lab. From here, Pratt's trajectory in parapsychology was established. Berger and Berger tell us that "Pratt was an experimenter in two classic experiments that are invariably cited as scientifically conclusive evidence of the occurrence of ESP."[375] The first case involved another student of Rhine's, Hubert Pearce. Pearce and Pratt were subjects in a study of ESP. Placed in two separate buildings separated by some distance, the results "far exceeded chance expectations."[376] The second test involved Pratt, Joseph L. Woodruff, and a design method called the screen touch matching technique.

In addition to his role as a subject, Pratt conducted research as well, and is particularly noted for his work with the medium Pavel Stepanek. In 1940, he coauthored a book with J. B. Rhine and other researchers that presented an overview of the scientific literature and progress on ESP.

Further Reading:

J. Gaither Pratt, J. B. Rhine, Burke M. Smith, Charles E. Stuart, and Joseph A. Greenwood,

Extrasensory Perception after Sixty Years: A Critical Appraisal of the Research in Extrasensory Perception. New York: Henry Holt & Company, 1940.

Puharich, Andrija (1918–1995, Physician): Dr. Andrija Puharich was an American physician who patented more than fifty items and developed artificial heart and hearing aid devices. In addition to his physician work, Puharich also studied telepathy, the impact of hallucinogens on telepathy, and mediumship. One of his earliest encounters with parapsychology was a meeting with medium Eileen Garrett, who was able to provide information about a physical condition of Puharich's. The physician, through private sponsorships, built his own laboratory on an estate and conducted psi research there with mediums like Peter Hurkos as well as the effect of hallucinogens on psi.[377] The book he wrote on the intersections of hallucinogens and psi boosted his popularity among the general public, and Puharich was even featured on television programs. Due to the fact that Puharich was not tethered to any university affiliations, his research methods have been criticized and some consider him a controversial figure in the field.

Puthoff, Harold E. (1936–, Engineer): Dr. Harold (Hal) Puthoff is an American engineer and parapsychologist. He was a key researcher at the Stanford Research Institute, an organization that investigated remote viewing. Working alongside Richard Targ and Edwin May, Puthoff helped developed protocols for testing ESP, called the ESP Trainer, obtained through remote viewing activities. The work that the three scientists engaged in not only provided decades-long research for the SRI, but today exists in an app that anyone wanting to test their ESP can download on their smartphone.[378]

Further Reading:

Charles T. Tart, Harold E. Puthoff, and Russell Targ, "Information Transmission in Remote Viewing Experiments." *Nature* 284 (March 13, 1980): 191.

R

Radin, Dean (1952–, Engineer and Psychologist): Dr. Dean Radin is an American psychologist

parapsychologist and professor at the California Institute of Integral Studies. He is also the chief scientist at the Institute of Noetic Sciences, an organization dedicated to "[unlocking] the mysteries of the natural world" by "harnessing the best of the rational mind to make advances that further our knowledge and enhance our human experience."[379] As such, Radin advocates viewing psi phenomena through an interdisciplinary lens. He is the author of more than two hundred scholarly and popular journal articles, a handful of books written for scholarly and laypeople alike, and is a frequent presenter on various psychical topics.[380]

Radin has a master's degree in electrical engineering and a PhD in psychology. His experiments on psi phenomena have led him to research posts at various universities such as the University of Edinburgh, Princeton University, the University of Nevada, and more. Radin also worked with the Stanford Research Institute, a government organization conducting confidential psi experiments.

In a 1997 article for the *Journal of Scientific Exploration*, Radin studied the phenomena of presentiment, or the ability to intuit the feeling or knowledge of something before the event occurs. In his study, a computer randomly displayed images to subjects. Certain images were calm and pleasing while other images were graphically disturbing. This study was designed to test if there was a physical bodily response *before* graphic images were presented to the viewer. To determine if a physical response occurred before a picture was displayed, the subject's heart rate, blood volume pulse, and electrodermal activity were monitored. During this study, Radin discovered that some subjects displayed physical responses one second before being shown the graphic, disturbing image while no physical presentiment occurred in the moments before being shown the calming image.[381]

Further Reading:

Dean Radin, *The Conscious Universe: The Scientific Truth of Psychic Phenomena.* New York: HarperOne, 2009.

D. I. Radin, "Unconscious Perception of Future Emotions: An Experiment in Presentiment." *Journal of Scientific Exploration* 11 (1997): 163–80.

Rao, K. Ramakrishna (1932–2021, Psychologist): Dr. K. Ramakrishna Rao was an Indian philosopher, psychologist, and parapsychologist. He was an advocate for experimental parapsychology *and* a proponent of alternative approaches that incorporated Eastern views. J. E. Kennedy tells us that "some of his writings and certainly his comments at parapsychological conventions discussed Eastern ideas and stimulated thinking."[382]

Further Reading:

V. Gowri Rammohan, ed., *New Frontiers of Human Science: A Festschrift for K. Ramakrishna Rao.* Jefferson, NC: McFarland & Co., 2002.

K. Ramakrishna Rao, *Experimental Parapsychology: A Review and Interpretation.* Springfield: Charles C. Thomas, 1966.

Raudive, Konstantin (1909–1974, Philosopher and Psychologist): Dr. Konstantin Raudive was a Latvian philosopher, psychologist, and author who is most known for his work on electronica voice phenomena. Raudive was intrigued by the idea of capturing anomalous audio on recordings after reading about the unexplainable presence of voices in certain situations. He began scanning radio stations and recording the white noise that occurs when the stations are scanning from one to the next. In so doing, he claimed to have recorded seventy thousand spectral voices.[383] When critics raised the point that voice fragments were naturally going to be present in a scan of radio stations, Raudive defended his work by saying that it wasn't necessarily the mere presence of a voice, but *what* the voice said that indicated a potential spectral message.[384]

Further Reading:

D. J. Ellis, "Listening to the 'Raudive Voices.'" *Journal of the Society for Psychical Research* 48, issue 763 (1975): 31–42.

Konstantin Raudive, *Breakthrough: An Amazing Experiment in Electronic Communication with the Dead.* Gerrards Cross: Colin Smythe, 1971.

Rogo, Douglas Scott (1950–1990, Parapsychologist and Author): Douglas Scott (D. Scott) Rogo was an American parapsychologist, author, and member of professional organizations such as the Parapsychological Association, the International Association for Near-Death Studies, and the American SPR. Rogo also authored more than twenty books and nearly ten others that he coauthored and/or edited. He supplemented his knowledge of parapsychology through an education grant from the Parapsychology Foundation. He is the author of multiple articles in scholarly journals and popular magazines, and in the 1970s worked alongside Keith Harary on investigations into out-of-body experiences. Shortly before this, in the late 1960s, Rogo taught a parapsychology course at the University of California. Rogo was a visiting researcher at institutions such as the Psychical Research Foundation and the Maimonides Medical Center's Division for Parapsychology. He wrote and served as editor for popular magazines such as *Fate.* In 1992, the Parapsychology Foundation established a grant in Rogo's name to assist writers with their parapsychological manuscripts.[385]

Further Reading:

D. S. Rogo, *The Return from Silence: A Study of Near-Death Experiences.* Wellingborough: Aquarian Press, 1989.

Roll, William George Jr. (1926–2012, Psychologist): William Roll was a psychologist and parapsychologist who spent his youth and early adulthood in Germany and Denmark before moving to the United States with his father in the 1940s. Roll also studied at Oxford University where he became involved with the Oxford University SPR. J. B. Rhine, director of the Duke Parapsychology Labs, invited Roll to his labs where he started to build his research into poltergeist phenomena.

The first poltergeist case that Roll researched involved a family in New York. Alongside fellow parapsychologist Gaither Pratt, they investigated strange events at a residential home that involved bottles of holy water exploding and objects flying through the room. During this case, Roll and Pratt developed the theory of recurrent spontaneous psychokinesis (RSPK), which they posited were involuntary abilities exhibited by the family's son. Roll continued investigating multiple other poltergeist cases in states like Kentucky, Florida, and Ohio.[386]

In a 2003 article in the *Journal of Scientific Exploration*, Roll discusses the intersection of physical and psychological factors in poltergeist cases, and he also discusses the theory that poltergeist cases are instances of RSPK. He points out, as have others, that physical objects at the center of RSPK often have some sort of psychological connection to a person or place at the center of the poltergeist event.[387]

Further Reading:

William G. Roll, "Some Physical and Psychological Aspects of a Series of Poltergeist Phenomena." *Journal of the American Society for Psychical Research* 62 (1968): 263–308.

Ryzl, Milan (1928–2011): Milan Ryzl was a parapsychologist from Czechoslovakia. His research focused mainly on hypnotism and through his work he "maintained that he had developed a hypnotic procedure to train subjects to use their ESP abilities to such a degree that these powers were amenable to the will and control of experimenters and subjects."[388]

In the 1960s, Ryzl fled Czechoslovakia and established permanent residence in the United States where he began working with fellow parapsychologists such as J. B. Rhine and J. G. Pratt. Ryzl is perhaps best known for his work with Pavel Stepanek, a gentleman who exhibited strong ESP abilities. Over the course of ten years, Ryzl conducted studies with Stepanek.[389]

Further Reading:

Palmer, John, "Milan Ryzl: 1928–2011." *The Journal of Parapsychology* 75, no. 2 (Fall 2011): 359–61.

S

Schmeidler, Gertrude (1912–2009): Dr. Gertrude Schmeidler was an American psychologist and parapsychologist. She was a research officer and past president of the American SPR, past president of the Parapsychological Association (she was, in fact, the first vice president of this organization), and professor emeritus of The City College of New York. She obtained her PhD from Harvard in 1935 and became formally interested in parapsychology after sitting in on a class given by fellow psi researcher Gardner Murphy.[390]

Schmeidler's research included investigations of the medium Ingo Swann. In these experiments, Swann displayed psychokinetic abilities and was able to affect temperatures of thermostats. Schmeidler is perhaps best known for, however, is her sheep-goat experiment. What she discovered is that

subjects in ESP experiments who are open to the possibility of ESP (sheep) are much more likely to score higher and exhibit psi than are those who aren't open to the possibility of psi (goats).[391]

These tests, conducted with the support of Gardner Murphy and a grant from the Richard Hodgson fund, showed that a person's attitude was a key factor in ESP experiments. Once she discovered that belief played a role in a person's ESP scores, the next step was to consider the role that someone's personality might play. In a 1946 article in the *Journal of Experimental Psychology*, Schmeidler and Murphy posit that "it is possible through the use of such methods one might discover the attitudes which facilitate or inhibit the expression of paranormal abilities, and the kinds of personalities most fruitful for parapsychological study."[392]

In an article written shortly after Schmeidler's death, Ruth Reinsel reminds us that the renowned parapsychologist also authored five books on topics related to psi. Reinsel tells us that "all her books endeavored to draw relations between psychic function and other areas of theory and experiment. She sought to show that parapsychology is not a field that exists in isolation from other fields of science or social science."[393]

Further Reading:

Ruth Reinsel, "Obituary: Gertrude R. Schmeidler: 1912–2009." *The Journal of Parapsychology* 73 (Spring 2009): 159–71.
Gertrude Raffel Schmeidler and R. A. McConnell, *ESP and Personality Patterns.* Oxford: Yale University Press, 1958.
Gertrude R. Schmeidler, "The Influence of Attitude on ESP Score." *International Journal of Neuropsychiatry* 2 (1966): 387–97.
Gertrude R. Schmeidler, "Separating the Sheep from the Goats." *Journal of the American Society for Psychical Research* 39 (1945): 47–49.

Schmidt, Helmut (1928–2011, Physicist): Dr. Helmut Schmidt was a German physicist and professor. He also worked for the Boeing Research Laboratory. In a memorial to him in the *Journal of Parapsychology*, Marilyn Schlitz tells us that "Schmidt was one of the first physicists to apply modern technology to the study of psi phenomena."[394] He developed studies that used random number generators (RNG) to test for psychokinetic abilities. His "quantum-mechanical" RNGs involved a box that had four buttons on the top. Subjects were asked to press a button corresponding to which they thought would light up next. The tests showed a slight significant effect. In another series of experiments, Schmidt investigated the concept of retrocausal psychokinesis. In these experiments, he gathered a randomly selected series of numbers before the experiment in order to "[explore] how random events might be influenced by observations from the future."[395]

Further Reading:

Helmut Schmidt, "Precognition of a Quantum Process." *Journal of Parapsychology* 82, Suppl. (2018): 87–95 (originally presented at the December 1967 meeting of the Institute for Parapsychology).

Schouten, Sybo A. (1940–, Psychologist): Dr. Sybo A. Schouten is a Dutch psychologist and parapsychologist who taught at the University of Utrecht in the Netherlands. While at that university, Schouten cofounded the *European Journal of Parapsychology* along with his colleague Martin Johnson. The journal's first edition was published in 1975 and emphasized a focus on quality of design and methodology rather than the data itself. For example, Schouten and Martin urged researchers to submit their detailed design to the journal *before* any data had been collected to eliminate any potential bias of publishing only those worked that showed data favorable to psi.[396]

Further Reading:

Sybo A. Schouten, "The End of the Parapsychology Laboratory of the University of Utrecht." *European Journal of Parapsychology* 7, no. 4 (1989): 95–116.

Servadio, Emilio (1904–1995, Psychoanalyst): Dr. Emilio Servadio was an Italian psychoanalyst and parapsychologist who cofounded the Società Italiana Di Parapsicología (Italian Society of Parapsychology).[397] Servadio was also a researcher with the Italian Psychoanalytical Society.[398]

Servadio believed that psi activity was heightened when our defenses were down. Quite often, those defenses come down during activities like sleep or hypnosis. During these states, Servadio believed that a person could receive telepathic information during these states.[399]

Further Reading:

Emilio Servadio, "A Presumptively Telepathic-Precognitive Dream During Analysis." *The International Journal of Psychoanalysis* 36 (1955): 27–30.

Sheldrake, Rupert (1942–, Biologist): Dr. Rupert Sheldrake is a British biologist who created the concept of morphic resonance, which is the theory that there is a shared, collective memory in nature. This collective memory impacts organisms on a type of biopsychical level, for example, this theory posits that if lab animals learned a new skill in one part of the world, lab animals in another part of the world would soon follow suit, subconsciously tapping into that shared consciousness that runs like a thread through the species.[400]

In addition to his theory of morphic resonance, a theory that has been met with much controversy, Sheldrake has also engaged in telepathy research. For example, in a 2003 article in the *Journal of Parapsychology*, Sheldrake and Pamela Smart designed a study to test the presence of telepathic ability to intuit who is calling on the telephone. Sheldrake and Smart's study revealed possible psi activity between callers known to each other and no statistically significant psi activity between callers unknown to each other.[401]

Further Reading:

Rupert Sheldrake, *The Presence of the Past: Morphic Resonance and the Habits of Nature.* Rochester, NY: Park Street Press, 1988.
Rupert Sheldrake, "The Rebirth of Nature." *RSA Journal* 142 (March 1994): 46–58.

Sommer, Andreas (Historian): Dr. Andreas Sommer is an historian of key figures and organizations throughout the parapsychological timeline. In particular, Sommer has written articles on Edmund Gurney, William James, Eusapia Palladino, and organizations like the German Society for Psychological Research.

His 2013 article in the *Journal of the History of the Behavioral Sciences* discusses the influence of psychical researchers Max Dessoir and Albert von Schrenck-Notzing on the formation of the Gesellschaft für Psychologische Forschung (Society for Psychological Research) in Germany. At the time, this society was formed by researchers who were disillusioned by the psychologist Wilhelm Wundt and his refusal to engage in psychical research. Wanting an avenue of their own to pursue such studies, the society was founded in 1890 and was influenced by the experimental research models coming out of England and France.[402]

Further Reading:

Pascal le Malefan and Andreas Sommer, "Léon Marillier and the Veridical Hallucination in Late-Nineteenth and Early-Twentieth-Century French Psychology and Psychopathology." *History of Psychiatry* 26, no. 4 (December 2015): 418–32.

Andreas Sommer, "Psychical Research and the Origins of American Psychology: Hugo Münsterberg, William James and Eusapia Palladino," in *History of the Human Sciences* 25(2), 23–44.

Stevenson, Ian (1918–2007, Psychiatrist): Dr. Ian Stevenson was a Canadian psychiatrist and professor at the University of Virginia, noted for his research into past-life memories. He was the first director of the University of Virginia's Department of Parapsychology (today called the Division of Perceptual Studies). He was a member of the American SPR and he was a recipient of a research grants from the Parapsychology Foundation.

In his clinical work, he began noticing a pattern of children who seemed to have memories of past lives. Stevenson was so intrigued by this that he began to look even deeper into these events and this initial research was published in the *Journal of the American Society for Psychical Research*. In this research, Stevenson discussed forty-four case studies of children who discussed such minutely detailed memories that a corresponding deceased individual could be identified. This research eventually led Stevenson to locations around the world including Sri Lanka, Brazil, India, the United States, and more, where he continued compiling case studies on reincarnation and past-life memories.

Further Reading:

Ian Stevenson, *Twenty Cases Suggestive of Reincarnation,* 2nd ed. Charlottesville: University Press of Virginia, 1974.

Sugishita, Morihiro (1943–, Neuropsychologist): Dr. Morihiro Sugishita is a Japanese neuropsychologist who has a number of articles in the *Japanese Journal of Parapsychology.* Topics include the out-of-body and near-death experiences. There is a need for translation of Sugishita's work into English, as his parapsychological research is only available in Japanese.

Further Reading:

Morihiro Sugishita, "Neuropsychological Approach to Out of Body Experience." *The Japanese Journal of Parapsychology* (2005): 39–40.

T

Targ, Russell (Physicist): Russell Targ is an American physicist and parapsychologist who is widely known for his research into remote viewing. Targ, along with his colleague Harold Puthoff, coined the term "remote-viewing" and worked to develop a remote viewing program, Star Gate, at the request of the CIA. This program existed from 1972 until 1995 and during this time Targ and Puthoff trained people in remote viewing techniques. The remote viewers gathered intelligence information for various organizations like the CIA, FBI, the Secret Service, the Air Force, the Navy, and more. The viewers in the Star Gate program were able to identify specific buildings, contents of buildings and rooms, and even the contents of drawers and file folders. While the program saw spectacular examples of psi functions, Targ was increasingly frustrated at the emphasis on using psi as a defense tactic instead of studying its nuances for the advancement of science. This, coupled with claims of unsuccessful information in the 1990s, led to the programs closure in 1995.[403]

Further Reading:

Russell Targ and Keith Harary, *The Mind Race: Understanding and Using Psychic Abilities.* New York: Villard Books, 1984.

Russell Targ, "What do We Know About Psi? The First Decade of Remote-Viewing Research and Operations at Stanford Research Institute." *Journal of Scientific Exploration* 33, no. 4 (2019): 569–92.

Tart, Charles (1937–, Psychologist): Dr. Charles Tart is an American psychologist and senior research fellow at the Institute of Noetic Sciences. Tart was interested, even at a very young age, in the intersection of science, consciousness, and spirituality. He was motivated by the work of the British SPR who seemed, to him, to embrace an open-mindedness about the anomalous alongside consideration for the scientific method. Tart studied at the Massachusetts Institute of Technology and while there he established the MIT Psychic Research Society. While he was at MIT, in fact, he conducted his first forays into experimental parapsychology during a hypnosis experiment on his classmates. He obtained his PhD in psychology from the University of North Carolina at Chapel Hill and afterward pursued postdoctoral training in hypnosis.

During the course of his research, Tart believed that one of the main challenges facing parapsychology is the limitations of and replications issues surrounding laboratory experiments. Tart realized that the standard ESP experiments that used items like Zener cards or other such items actually facilitated a decline effect. Instead of providing immediate feedback, these experiments left subjects in the dark quite often and Tart began to experiment with immediate mechanical feedback. This type of feedback facilitates a learning environment that helps people practice and potentially heighten their ESP abilities. This is one example of the ways in which Tart's research has questioned the standards and methods of psi experimentation.[404]

Tart also developed The Archive of Scientists' Transcendent Experiences (TASTE) in 2000 after he realized that colleagues, who were reticent to discuss their experiences before, were comfortable speaking to him about their anomalous experiences. Knowing that Tart openly pursued inquiries involving the anomalous made them feel like they were able to safely have discussions with him, and to facilitate a safe space for those conversations to continue happening, he developed TASTE, a database that is managed today under the auspices of the Academy for the Advancement of Postmaterialist Sciences.[405]

Further Reading:

Charles T. Tart, *The End of Materialism: How Evidence of the Paranormal is Bringing Science and Spirit Together.* Oakland, CA: Noetic Books, 2009.
Charles T. Tart, "Six Studies of Out-of-Body Experiences." *Journal of Near-Death Studies* 17. no. 2 (1998): 73–99.

Thalbourne, Michael (1955–2010, Psychologist): Dr. Michael A. Thalbourne was an Australian psychology professor and parapsychologist at the University of Adelaide. His research focused on multiple topics including kundalini, mystical experiences, and enhancing experimental methods.[406] Thalbourne also discussed the notion of transliminality as it relates to anomalous experiences. In his 2016 article in the *Journal of Parapsychology*, Thalbourne discusses that while anomalous experiences can sometimes be a result of (or influenced by) pathological conditions like depression, dissociation, etc. this doesn't inherently mean that all paranormal or mystical experiences can be explained by a pathological condition. He further points out that paranormal and mystical experiences are mediated by the attributes on the transliminality scale. This scale includes things like magical ideation, creative personality, fantasy proneness, and more. Thalbourne posits that those higher on the transliminal scale are more likely to experience a paranormal or mystical encounter. A high transliminality ranking can also be present in pathological illnesses, too, which makes the intersection of these items even trickier.[407]

Further Reading:

Michael A. Thalbourne, "Psychiatry, the Mystical, and the Paranormal." *Journal of Parapsychology* 70, no. 1 (Spring 2006): 143–65.

Tocquet, Robert (1898–1993, Parapsychologist): Robert Tocquet was the president of the Institut Métapsychique International (IMI) from 1982 to 1987[408] and is the author of the book *The Magic of Numbers.* In this book Tocquet discusses "lightning calculators," which he describes as someone who has "an exceptional memory for numbers [and] the ability to keep them stored in the consciousness in a manner bordering on the supernatural."[409]

Further Reading:

Robert Tocquet, *The Magic of Numbers*. New York: A. S. Barnes, 1963.

Tressoldi, Patrizio E. (Psychologist): Dr. Patrizio E. Tressoldi is an Italian psychologist at the University of Padova where he directs the Consciousness Research Group. Tressoldi's research includes presentiment, psychokinesis, and out-of-body experiences. Presentiment refers to those moments in which knowledge, awareness, or response to an event precedes the actual event. In one study to test the evidence for presentiment, Tressoldi focused on pupillary responses in the eye. Knowing that pupils dilate in size during certain situations, Tressoldi gathered subjects and measured their pupillary response in the moments before playing either a neutral sound or an alarming sound. He discovered that subjects seemed to correctly anticipate when an alarming sound was about to be played, as exhibited through their pupillary response, which occurred at a statistically significant number of times. Additional studies that have been inspired by this have found similar significant results, but this experiment has also succumbed to replication issues since exact replications have not revealed additional significant results.[410]

In a 2021 article in *Advances in Social Sciences Research Journal*, Tressoldi and coauthors discuss the need for a reconceptualization of the way we discuss and classify anomalous experiences. Some of these anomalies might occur via altered states of consciousness, exceptional human experiences, or other strange events. They advocate for using the term "nonordinary mental expressions" to not only allow for more broadness and inclusivity, but to also indicate that these events are not necessarily rooted in some pathological explanation.[411]

Further Reading:

Patrizio E. Tressoldi, Massimiliano Martinelli, Luca Semenzato, and Sara Cappato, "Let Your Eyes Predict: Prediction Accuracy of Pupillary Responses to Random Alerting and Neutral Sounds." *SAGE Open* (July 2011): 1–7.

U

Ullman, Montague (1916–2008, Psychiatrist): Dr. Montague Ullman was an American psychiatrist and parapsychologist. While practicing psychoanalysis, he noticed that some patients seemed to exhibit psi behavior, and so he befriended the parapsychologist Gardner Murphy to help him learn more. Ullman and Murphy began conducting psi experiments using hypnosis techniques, and in 1940 Ullman helped cofound the American SPR's medical section. As psychologists learned more about REM cycles and dreams, Ullman was inspired to conduct telepathic dream experiments. His experiments were gaining so much attention and intriguing data that Gardner Murphy helped him establish the Dream Laboratory at Maimonides Hospital. [412]

Further Reading:

Montague Ullman, Stanley Krippner, and Alan Vaughan, *Dream Telepathy*. New York: Macmillan, 1973.
Montague Ullman and Edward F. Storm, "Dreaming and the Dream: Social and Personal Perspectives." *The Journal of Mind and Behavior* 7 nos. 2/3 (1986): 429–47.

V

Van de Castle, Robert L. (1927–2014, Psychologist): Robert L. Van de Castle was an American psychologist, parapsychologist, and past president of the Parapsychological Association. He investigated, among other topics, dreams and psychokinesis. Dreams, however, were the focus of his body of work. He once worked with J. B. Rhine at the Duke Parapsychology Labs, and he also worked with the Institute of Dream Studies in Florida. Van de Castle also participated, as a subject, in the Maimonides dreams labs in New York, where he exhibited psi abilities of his own.[413]

In addition to his dream research, Van de Castle is known for his studies involving ESP among the Cuna peoples of Panama. In the 1960s, he traveled to Panama to implement research on adolescent boys and girls. In his study, which involved a more culturally-relevant set of Zener cards, so to speak, he discovered that adolescent girls scored above chance while the boys did not exhibit statistically significant results.

Further Reading:

Robert L. Van de Castle, *Our Dreaming Minds.* New York: Ballantine Books, 1994.

Varvoglis, Mario (Parapsychologist): Dr. Mario Varvoglis is an American parapsychologist and current president of the Institut Métapsychique International (IMI) in France. As an undergraduate student, Varvoglis became involved in the studies at the Maimonides Hospital dream labs. There, he helped research dreams, telepathy, and the influence of ganzfeld environments. Shortly after this he worked with parapsychologist Charles Honorton on psychokinesis studies. He eventually moved to France and has been an advocate for the value of parapsychological research.[414]

In a 2016 article in the *Journal of Parapsychology*, Varvoglis and his colleague Peter A. Bancel discuss micro-PK (micro-psychokinesis).[415] Instances of macro-PK are larger disturbances that are visible to the naked eye. These would be things like table tilting, levitation of objects, etc. Micro-PK, on the other hand, are subtler movements often visible only through statistical analysis, like the probability of influencing the movement of a dice one way or another as it rolls. In this article, they discuss previous researchers who believe that micro-PK exists among the general population, albeit in smaller, more less-obvious amounts. Varvoglis and Bancel, however, stress that future research should include studies that intentionally focus on those rarer instances of micro-PK that occurs at higher levels since they believe less in a global micro-PK effect. Additionally, global micro-PK studies that assume an underlying ability present in random participants might reveal the presence of PK, but it is usually a weak correlation—another reason why Varvoglis and Bancel call for future research that intentionally selects PK subjects.[416]

Further Reading:

Mario Varvoglis and Peter A. Bancel, "Micro-Psychokinesis: Exceptional or Universal?" *Journal of Parapsychology* 80, no. 1 (Spring 2016): 37–44.

Ventola, Annalisa (Composer and Parapsychologist): Annalisa Ventola is a composer, parapsy-chologist, and director of the Parapsychological Association—a post that she has held since 2010. In her research, Ventola investigates poltergeist cases, transliminality, and the psychology of those who experience haunt phenomena.[417]

In a 2018 article for the *Journal of the Society for Psychical Research*, Ventola contributed to research into the psychological traits of "haunters:"—those people who have experienced a haunt-type event.[418] The researchers noticed that haunt phenomena exhibits "person-focusing," meaning that hauntings seem to happen around certain people. They set out to analyze the attributes of these people and designed a survey that asked both haunters and nonhaunters questions that elicited information about anxiety, belief, transliminality, intellect, vulnerability, locus of control, and more. What they discovered, contrary to some previous studies by other researchers, is "no evidence that the haunt-type experiences involved obvious cognitive deficits in the respondents . . . and likewise affirm the notion that the phenomenology of haunt-type experiences does not derive purely from external or random forces."[419] They noticed, out of the attributes they studied, that transliminality seemed to be one of the most significant patterns among haunters. Transliminality refers to having permeable mental boundaries or a sensitivity of psychological processes that impact perception and even the physical world around us—a concept identified and developed by Michael Thalbourne. To loosely summarize, the researchers discovered, in this article, that haunt phenomena is perhaps mediated by the right person being in the right place, which also postulates and further supports ideas that hauntings are not solely objective phenomena.[420]

In a 2019 article in the *Journal of the Society for Psychical Research*, Ventola and her coauthors build upon the 2018 research into the psychological traits of "haunters."[421] This article attempts to have a more nuanced understanding and conversation about the nature of poltergeist cases that often seem to focus on claims that psi activity, puberty, and/or childhood trauma are related. In this study, they identified eight attributes common to people in poltergeist cases. This includes things like imagination and fantasy-proneness, rebellious attitude and hostility, low self-esteem, introversion, and more.[422] This research "[lends] further credence and viability to Laythe et.al's (2018) hypothesis that transliminality, in part, mediates 'person-focusing' in anomalous experience attributed to ghosts, haunted houses, and now poltergeist disturbances."[423]

Further Reading:

Brian Laythe, James Houran, and Annalisa Ventola, "A Split-Sample Psychometric Study of 'Haunters.'" *Journal of the Society for Psychical Research* 81, no. 4 (2018): 193–218.

Annalisa Ventola, James Houran, Brian Laythe, Lance Storm, Alejandro Parra, John Dixon, and John G. Kruth, *Journal of the Society for Psychical Research* 83, no. 3 (2019): 144–71.

W

Wahbeh, Helané (Psychologist and Naturopathic Physician): Dr. Helané Wahbeh is a psychologist and naturopathic physician in the neurology department at Oregon Health and Science University. She is also the research director of the Institute for Noetic Sciences.[424] Much of Wahbeh's research focuses on energy healing, channeling, meditation, and the mind-body connection. In a 2021 article in the *Explore: The Journal of Science and Healing*, Wahbeh and her coauthors investigated the potential for environmental factors to influence medical sessions that involve energy healing. The authors begin by acknowledging that doctors already realize that certain environmental factors such as pollution and barometric pressure can influence people's health. In this study, though, Wahbeh and her colleagues investigated the potential for lesser-contemplated factors such as solar activity and geomagnetic field levels to influence healing—specifically energy healing. In total, there were eighteen specific variables of solar activity and GMF attributes that the researchers looked at such as solar wind, lunar illumination, and precipitation. This study identified a possible influence of geophysical attributes like solar radio flux and interplanetary magnetic fields on enhancing the efficacy of energy healing, though Wahbeh and her authors urge for additional studies before a conclusive statement can be made.[425]

Further Reading:

Helané Wahbeh and Bethany Butzer, "Characteristics of English-Speaking Trance Channelers."

Explore: The Journal of Science and Healing 16, no. 5 (September 2020): 304–09.

Watt, Caroline (Psychologist): Dr. Caroline Watt is a psychologist and current Koestler Chair of Parapsychology at the University of Edinburgh's Koestler Parapsychology Unit. A core amount of her research focuses on meta-analyses and discussions that help enhance standards for psi experiments in the future. Additional research includes remote viewing, checker effects and observation theories, and belief and expectancy during psi events like remote view or distance healing.[426] In one study, for example, Dr. Watt and a colleague combined remote viewing and belief to determine the differences between blind and nonblind data analysis. During this research, they asked participants to engage in remote viewing and then rate their level of accuracy. In this nonblind approach where the participant themself was a data analysist, they ranked their accuracy levels very high. When the same data was analyzed in a blind fashion, however, there was no statistically significant data, indicating to Watt and her colleague the presence of confirmation bias. This article serves as a reminder for how necessary blind data analysis is when it comes to remote viewing research.[427]

In another study involving belief and psi events, Dr. Watt designed an experiment to study precognitive dreams. This study looked at both psychological factors *and* parapsychological factors that might be at play. In this study, those who believed that they had experienced precognitive dreaming were asked to intuit a selected, unknown video clip that would randomly be assigned to them. Dr. Watt's study did indicate statistically significant results when dreams were analyzed be independent judges, though they urge making any definite claims about these implications until further studies can be replicated.[428]

Further Reading:

Caroline Watt, Natalie Ashley, Jack Gillett, Megan Halewood, and Rebecca Hanson, "Psychological Factors in Precognitive Dream Experience: The Role of Paranormal Belief, Selective Recall and Propensity to Find Correspondences." *International Journal of Dream Research* 7, no.1 (April 2014): 1–8.

Caroline Watt, *Parapsychology: A Beginner's Guide*. London: Oneworld Publications, 2016.

Weaver, Zofia (1947–, Parapsychologist): Dr. Zofia Weaver is a Polish parapsychologist and associate editor of the *Journal of the Society for Psychical Research*. Weaver's main research interest is Polish mediums, and she is particularly noted for her work on the life of medium Franek Kluski. Weaver is, in fact, working on an English translation of a crucial work on Kluski's life. In addition to that translation, Weaver has also translated work of the Polish parapsychologist Julian Ochorowicz and medium Stefan Ossowiecki.[429]

Further Reading:

Zofia Weaver, M. R. Barrington, and I. Stevenson, *A World in a Grain of Sand: The Clairvoyance of Stefan Ossowiecki*. Jefferson, NC: McFarland, 2005.
Zofia Weaver, *Other Realities? The Enigma of Franek Kluski's Mediumship*. White Crow Books, 2015.

Weiner, Debra H. (1952–, Parapsychologist): Dr. Debra H. Weiner is an American parapsychologist and author of multiple articles and books on such topics as extrasensory perceptions, research methods, and reviews of key figures like Louisa Rhine.

In a 1989 article in the *Journal of Parapsychology*, Weiner and coauthor Nancy L. Zingrone discuss a potential psi event known as the "checker effect."[430] The checker effect is a theory that "checkers" of psi-related experiments actually subconsciously affect the outcome of the data in the experiment. In other words, the checker influences the outcome of actions during the experiment due to their focused observation. What they discovered is that there does seem to be a psychical influence on the part of the checker, but specifically, they replicated other studies that found "checker influence was obtained only under the conditions that allowed checkers to form specific expectations, intentions, and desires for the outcomes."[431]

Further Reading:

D. H. Weiner and J. H. Haight, "Charting Hidden Channels: A Review and Analysis of Louisa E. Rhine's Case Collection Project." *Journal of Parapsychology* 47 (1983): 303–22.

Debra H. Weiner and Jeffery Geller, "Motivation as the Universal Container: Conceptual Problems in Parapsychology." *Journal of Parapsychology* 48, no. 1 (March 1984): 27–37.

West, Donald J. (1924–2020): Dr. Donald J. West was a British psychiatrist, parapsychologist, and professor at Cambridge University. He joined the British SPR in 1941, the same year that he published his first article on a psi topic in the society's journal. West went on to serve as research officer and past president of the SPR. One of his most notable contributions to parapsychology was a 1990 survey in which he reproduced, on a smaller scale, the famous 1894 survey, Census of Hallucinations. In addition to articles, West also published a number of books on psi experimentation and standards.[432]

Further Reading:

Donald J. West and G. W. Fisk, "A Dual ESP Experiment with Clock Cards." *Journal of the Society for Psychical Research* 37 (1953): 185–97
Donald J. West, "A Pilot Census of Hallucinations." *Proceedings of the Society for Psychical Research* 57, no. 215. (1990): 163–207.

White, Rhea A. (1931–2007): Rhea A. White was an American parapsychologist and librarian. In addition to serving as editor of the *Journal of the American Society for Psychical Research*, she also created the Psi Line database, which was an index of journals and articles devoted to psi topics. White also published bibliographies of parapsychological topics and the research of certain key figures in the field.[433]

White herself was a psi researcher and became interested in parapsychology when she chose to work for J. B. Rhine's parapsychology lab instead of attending the path she had previously considered—professional golf. Specifically, White had a near-death experience in college that left her questioning the implications of the near-death experience on meanings of survival, life, and consciousness.[434] To learn more about her own experience, she sought out J. B. Rhine and thus began her professional trajectory as a parapsychologist and archivist of psi resources.

White was, in part due to her own history, interested in the impact of paranormal and anomalous events on people. She referred to them as "exceptional human experiences (EHE)," and in a 1997 article in the *Journal of Religion and Psychical Research*, she outlines what she means by this phrase.[435] She tells us that the anomalous event that lasts a finite amount of time (perhaps even only a few seconds) is just one part of the equation. The lasting effects of that finite experience can ripple outward for years, impacting the way in which that person interacts with and perceives the world around them. Specifically, White tells us that "an exceptional human experience changes the way the experiencer behaves or feels or thinks about [themselves], other people, other organisms, and attitudes toward or ideas about the meaning of self, life, death and other subjects of deep human import."[436] She goes on to discuss how not every anomalous event will necessarily turn into an EHE, but the ones that do became a lifelong journey for the experiencer. White's work not only provides wonderful compendiums of annotations for future researchers, but it also highlights the holistic impact of the paranormal in everyday lives.

Further Reading:

Rhea A. White, "The Human Component in Exceptional Experience." *Journal of Religion and Psychical Research* 20, no. 1 (1997): 23–29.

Rhea A. White, "On Matters Relating to Shared EHEs." *The Journal of Religion and Psychical Research* 17, no. 3. (July 1994): 132–35.

Y

Yount, Garret (Neurobiologist): Dr. Garret Yount is a researcher at the Institute of Noetic Science (IONS). IONS is an organization that researches various unexplainable phenomena in an attempt to learn more about the interconnectedness of the world.[437] Yount holds a PhD in neurobiology and behavior from the State University of New York. His research focuses on biofields and the relationship between them and healing. For example, the ability of one person to somehow impact another person only physically through psychical methods. He is interested in micropsychokinesis as well and has been involved in studies with healers from around the world.[438]

In a 2013 article in *The Journal of Alternative and Complementary Medicine*, Yount and his coauthors set out to investigate the ability of energy medicine to impact cancer cells. In the article, the authors explain their theory that biofields may be impacted by the bioenergetic treatment methods of healers, or those who channel healing intents directed at certain patients. They set out to test two things: first, to test the frequency of directed bioenergies, which could inhibit cancer growth cell and secondly, to determine if the distance between healer and object seemed to impact biofields. They discovered that the first series of tests seemed to indicate a decreased rate of growth in cancer cells in correlation to the number of bioenergy sessions. However, they did not receive the same results upon replication. While their results were inconclusive in this study, it is nevertheless a fascinating experiment and shines light on a core issue of psi studies: the fact that studies are often very hard to replicate exactly. Yount and his colleagues used in vitro methods for this study, but they discuss the potential benefits of continuing this line of bioenergy experimentation on living organisms instead.[439]

Further Reading:

Helané Wahbeh, Garret Yount, Cassandra Vieten, Dean Radin, and Arnaud Delorme, "Measuring Extraordinary Experiences and Beliefs: A Validation and Reliability Study." *F1000Research* 8 (2020): 1–25.

Z

Zingrone, Nancy (1951–, Psychologist): Dr. Nancy Zingrone is a psychology professor at Northcentral University in San Diego, California. She has taught parapsychology courses since the late 1970s, and in the 1980s was a research fellow at the Institute for Parapsychology, known today as the Rhine Research Center. In 2015, after many years of service to the Parapsychological Association, she was awarded the Outstanding Contribution award. Along with her husband and fellow parapsychologist, Carlos S. Alvarado, Zingrone's research focuses on ESP, the experiences of psi events, and experimental psychology.[440]

In a 2015 article in the *Journal of the Society for Psychical Research*, Zingrone and her husband investigated eighty-eight reports of out-of-body experiences (OBEs).[441] In this paper they note that past researchers on OBEs tend to focus on psychological discussions and attributes of experiencers and/or discussions of neurological theories for such experiences. What they point to as lacking, though, is more information on the experience of the OBE itself. From the set of eighty-eight reports, Zingrone and Alvarado discovered some physical and emotional patterns of the OBE event. For example, they discovered that the vast majority have OBEs involuntarily. Interestingly, a small percent (13%) said they could *sometimes* induce an OBE. Furthermore, most OBEs occur when a person was laying on their back, and that most OBEs seem to last only up to five minutes. Zingrone and her Alvarado also discovered patterned physical attributes of the OBE: for example, most respondents indicated seeing their physical body, seeing surroundings as is from above, having a sensation of leaving the body, and remaining in their familiar surroundings.[442] For a complete discussion of her work on OBEs and other psi topics, see the further reading section below.

Further Reading:

- Carlos S. Alvarado and Nancy L. Zingrone, "Features of Out-of-Body Experiences: Relationships to Frequency, Wilfulness of and Previous Knowledge about the Experience." *Journal of the Society for Psychical Research* 79, no. 2 (April 2015): 98–111.
- Carlos S. Alvarado and Nancy Zingrone, "Interrelationships of Parapsychological Experiences, Dream Recall, and Lucid Dreams in a Survey with Predominantly Spanish Participants." *Imagination, Cognition, and Personality* 27, no. 1 (2007/08): 63–69.

MEDIUMS AND THOSE AT THE CENTER OF PSYCHICAL CASE STUDIES

A

Arigo, José (1918–1971): José Arigo was a Brazilian medium who, without any medical training or knowledge, possessed the ability to heal people. Arigo claimed that his healing abilities were channeled through him by the spirit of a deceased German doctor, Dr. Fritz. Arigo would not only diagnose patients, but he would sometimes perform surgical operations on them. Interestingly, these "patients" would not experience pain, blood loss, or infection. The physician and psychical researcher Henry Puharich studied Arigo and was amazed at what he saw, noting that it was a "mind-shattering experience."[443]

B

Bailey, Charles (1870–1947): Charles Bailey (the stage name of Charles Beasmore) was an Australian medium who produced apports in his séances. Apports are physical objects that seem to appear as if from thin air. In fact, psychical researcher and historian Nandor Fodor tells us that Bailey's "archaeological and living apports were animatedly discussed for years both in Australia and in Europe."[444] Bailey was hugely responsible for the spread of spiritualism in Australia due to his

Figure 2.26. Medium Charles Bailey (aka Charles Beasmore)
From *Rigid Tests of the Occult: Being a Record of Some Remarkable Experiences Through the Mediumship of Mr. C. Bailey, with a Critical Examination into the Origin of the Phenomena* by C.W. McCarthy. (Melbourne: J.C. Stephens, 1904). PD-US-expired

infamous séances. During Bailey's séances, wet stones from the sea would appear, as would fish, birds, and once a human skull. Helping spread Bailey's popularity (and the popularity of Australian spiritualism in general) is the fact that he was supported for twelve years by Thomas Welton Stanford, a wealthy spiritualist. Séances were held in Stanford's home and drew the attention of many. Doctors and psychical researchers examined Bailey for hidden objects or pockets, and they even went so far as to enclose him in a bag, leaving only his head and hands free. Still, the apports continued. It wasn't until Bailey's infamy grew and he was invited overseas that his fraudulent acts were uncovered. Not only did this cast further pall on spiritualism, it halted psychical research in Australia for a number of years since researchers were wary of being duped again.[445]

Further Reading:

X, *From Rigid Tests of the Occult: Being a Record of Some Remarkable Experiences Through the Mediumship of Mr. C. Bailey, with a Critical Examination into the Origin of the Phenomena*. Melbourne: J. C. Stephens, 1904.

Béraud, Marthe (Eva C.) (1886–1943): Marthe Béraud was a French medium who is most commonly known by her medium name, Eva C. (or Eva Carriere). In 1903, Béraud began to perform séances during which the apparition of a man would appear. She called this man "Bien Boa" and two short years later, psychical researchers began hearing about the strange medium who seemed to summon apparitions. The French researcher Charles Richet visited Béraud in 1905 and was convinced that her séances, and even the apparitions of Bien Boa, were genuine. So, too, did researcher Albert von Schrenck-Notzing and Gustave Geley. Interestingly, amid these visitations and studies by psychical researchers, a medical doctor and a lawyer claimed to have proof of Béraud's fraud, revealing that she admitted once to them her trickery. Nevertheless, Richet and his colleagues remained convinced.[446]

By 1908, Béraud was in Paris, continuing to perform her séances. Here she was introduced to Juliette Bisson, whom she eventually moved in with after the passing of Bisson's husband. The two women became companions, and as researcher Carlos S. Al-

Figure 2.27. Medium known as Eva Carriere (Eva C.), Marthe Beraud
From *Les Phénomenès dits de Matérialisation: Étude Expérimentale* by Juliette Alexandre-Bisson. (Paris: Librairie Félix Alcan, 1921). PD-US-expired

varado notes in his article "Distortions of the Past," Bisson is one of the oft-overlooked women in the history of parapsychology.[447] She is assumed to have been Béraud's accomplice during séances.

Further Reading:

R. Lambert, "Dr. Geley's Report on the Medium Eva C." *Journal of the Society for Psychical Research* 37 (1954): 380–86.

Blavatsky, Helena Petrovna (1831–1891): Helena Petrovna (H. P.) Blavatsky was a Russian medium and founder of the Theosophical Society, an organization based largely on Hindu philosophy that "investigate[s] unexplained laws of nature and powers of the human being."[448] British researcher Richard Hodgson visited the society's headquarters after hearing multiple reports of psychical phenomena (e.g., letters written by the channeled spirits of the dead). Hodgson concluded that nothing was genuine.[449]

Historian Nandor Fodor outlines the childhood of H. P. Blavatsky, and how through her wild imagination and storytelling abilities, she was able to lure her friends into a state of almost-hypnotism that caused them to suffer hallucinations. After fleeing a marriage and traveling the world, Blavatsky returned to Russia where her mediumistic abilities seemed to have amplified and in one instance she used them to help the local police capture a suspect. She had moments of other clairvoyant abilities, such as finding lost items for people, and though it is believed that close friends of hers aided in some of her séances and that many of her abilities were shadowed by fraud, Fodor remarks that "one can hardly escape the conclusion that imposture occasionally blended with genuine psychic performance."[450]

Author and Blavatsky researcher Marion Meade came to the same conclusion as Fodor in her 1980 biography of the infamous medium. Meade discusses the vast array of phenomena connected to Blavatsky such as levitations, apports, and communion with spirits of the deceased. Meade points out that Blavatsky was caught occasionally in fraudulent behaviors and the assistance of others, but similar to Fodor she writes,

> On the other hand, I do not believe there can be much doubt that she was a genuine sensitive. Members of her family attested to the fact that since early childhood she claimed to see and hear invisible entities, and later as an adult H.P.B. herself supplied detailed accounts of hypnotic states in which other personalities seemed to be colonizing her body.[451]

The case of H. P. Blavatsky is a curious one, though she is necessary to include in the history of parapsychology. Members of the SPR were at times convinced of both her genuineness and her fraud, and she undoubtedly left a mark on the spiritualist scene that propagated interest in and examination of psychical phenomena.

Further Reading:

Marion Meade, *Madame Blavatsky: The Woman Behind the Myth.* New York: G. P. Putnam's Sons, 1980.

C

Cayce, Edgar (1877–1945): Edgar Cayce was an American psychic known as the "sleeping prophet" due to his ability to provide information and healing while in a trance state. Cayce provided information on ailments and suggested treatments to people, even those in faraway states while in these trances.

Many of his treatments seemed to work, though on one occasion he misdiagnosed the daughter of psychical researcher J. B. Rhine. During these trances, Cayce would also provide information on the past lives "of the persons he was helping, some of them hundreds of years before, occasionally with minutely verifiable details."[452] In 1931, Cayce established the Association for Research and Enlightenment, an organization still in existence today. The association's mission is to "provide mind-body-spirit resources for individuals . . . that create opportunities for profound personal change in body, mind, and spirit."[453] Some of these resources include things like meditation, dream work, reincarnation, and intuition.

Further Reading:

K. Paul Johnson, *Edgar Cayce in Context: The Readings: Truth and Fiction.* Albany: State University of New York Press, 1998.

Cook, Florence (1856–1904): Florence Cook was a British medium who produced physical phenomena during her sessions. Historians Arthur and Joyce Berger tell us that "W.H. Salter believed that there was no single episode in psychical research more important than the sittings held between December 1873 and May 21, 1874 by William Crookes with Florence Cook."[454] A wealthy British spiritualist, Charles Blackburn, supported Cook upon learning of her abilities and she conducted many séances in which she channeled an apparition called Katie King. In fact, in some of her séances, the apparition of Katie King herself would physically manifest in the room. On more than one occasion, Cook was caught masquerading as the spirit but even amid this, certain researchers held fast to their belief that Cook was the real deal—Crookes certainly thought so, as did French psychical researcher Charles Richet.[455]

When William Crookes heard about Florence Cook's abilities, he engaged in a six-month-long investigation into her abilities. During these six months, she often stayed at the Crookes's home, sometimes for a week at a time. Crookes remarked that Cook never arrived with more than a small bag and how she was not even permitted to sleep by herself to eliminate as many possible avenues for fraud. During these séances, held in Crookes's library (referred to as the cabinet), Cook often re-

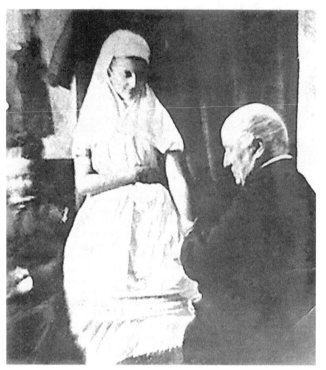

Figure 2.28. Katie King, Channeled Spirit of Florence Cook's Séances
From "Notes of An Enquiry into the Phenomena Called Spiritual During the Years 1870-1873" by William Crookes. Published in *Quarterly Journal of Science*, January 1874, PD-US

mained behind a curtain and the apparition of Katie King would later emerge. Naturally, one would assume that these two figures are the same person, but Crookes noted that certain marks on Florence's face were not present on Katie's, that their hair color was different, and certain other attributes that seemed to imply that these were two different beings. Perhaps the most curious note of Crookes is that during one session, the Katie King apparition asked him to come behind the curtain to help reposition Cook, who had apparently slumped over in an awkward position. Crookes claimed that when he went behind the curtain, he saw two separate beings—one Katie King, and the other Florence, indeed slumped over a small couch and dressed in her usual black attire.[456]

The testimony of Crookes is rife with controversy, though, as nearly fifty years after Cook's passing, her former romantic partner claimed that Cook once admitted that she and Crookes had an affair, and that the séances were part of a coverup to that affair. People have questioned the validity of those claims, and the real details in the case of Florence Cook will perhaps remain a mystery. What adds even more curiosity to Cook's case is that her younger sister, Kate Cook, was also a physical medium. Similar to Florence, Kate appeared to produce an apparition named Lilly during her séances. The wealthy Charles Blackburn also sponsored Kate and actually left the majority of his estate to the Cook family. It is clear in some instances that fraud was evident, and the presence of a large inheritance certainly throws further intrigue into the mix, ensuring that the case of the Cook sisters still remains a curious case to this day.[457]

Further Reading:

Trevor H. Hall, *The Spiritualists: The Story of Florence Cook and William Crookes.* London: G. Duckworth, 1962.

Michael E. Tymn, "An 'Interview' with Sir William Crookes." *Journal of Spirituality and Paranormal Studies* 30, no. 2 (2007): 80–86.

Crandon, Mina (Margery) (1889–1941): Mina Crandon was a physical medium who (similar to other mediums during the spiritualist era) produced ectoplasm during her séances. It would be seen spilling out of her mouth and is thought to have been made out of the lung tissue of an animal.[458] She is a controversial figure, as are many of the spiritualist mediums. During her séances, many strange phenomena occurred such as the appearance of mysterious lights, movement of objects by unseen hands, levitations, "spirit fingerprints," ectoplasm, and more. Mina became known across the United States, drawing hundreds of people eager to attend a session with the famous medium. As her popularity grew, so, too, did the curiosity of psychical researchers including Hereward Carrington, Eric Dingwall, J. B. Rhine, and others. Harry Houdini was even called in to assist researchers at one point, due to his ability as a magician to understand sleight of hand and illusion. Houdini was, in fact, part of a committee organized by *Scientific American* to investigate Crandon. Most of the committee determined that her seeming psi abilities were fake, but a few committee members held fast to their belief in her authenticity. The committee contained members from both the British and American SPR, and the ASPR in particular advocated in defense of Crandon. So divided were researchers on Crandon's case that some of them left the ASPR in disgust over their voracious

Figure 2.29. Mina Crandon and a Materalized Hand
From *The Physical Phenomena of Spiritualism* by Stanley de Brath (London Spiritualist Alliance, 1930). PD-US-Expired

advocacy of her, and formed their own organization, the Boston Society for Psychic Research.

The inquiry into Crandon's mediumship had huge implications, not just for the schism of the ASPR and the creation of a new organization, but also for J. B. Rhine. Rhine, who had sat with Crandon a few times was convinced that she was a fake. Seeing how divided researchers were spurred Rhine to develop alternate ways of testing mediums and their apparent psi phenomenon. It was clear to him that séance observation was not going to help the cause of scientifically advancing the understanding of psi phenomenon, and he set out to set up clinical laboratories to advance psychical study—those labs, as we know, developed into the Duke Parapsychology Labs and exist today as the Rhine Research Center.[459]

Further Reading:

J. B. Rhine and L. E. Rhine, "One Evening's Observation on the Margery Mediumship." *Journal of Abnormal and Social Psychology* 21, no. 4 (1927): 401–21.

Croiset, Gerard (1909 1980): Gerard Croiset was a famous Dutch psychic. He sometimes worked closely with police to help provide information on certain cases and became well known both due to that *and* his involvement with leading Dutch parapsychologist Dr. Wilhelm Tenhaeff. Croiset was referred to as "The Dutchman with the X-Ray Eyes," and the "Wizard of Utrecht," though Dr. Tenhaeff preferred to label Croiset (and others with similar abilities) as a paragnost, translated as "beyond knowledge."[460]

Croiset and Dr. Tenhaeff became acquainted after Croiset attended one of the parapsychologist's lectures in 1945. It wasn't until that lecture that Croiset felt a sense of purpose surrounding his psi abilities. From that point on, Croiset took part in studies by Dr. Tenhaeff and also international researchers who visited the institute for a chance to study the Dutch medium. Dr. Tenhaeff also took Croiset to other parapsychological institutions around the world including those in France, Germany, Italy, Austria, and more. In addition, psychiatrists have examined Tenhaeff's studies of Croiset and one in particular, a researcher at the prestigious Mayo Foundation, called the research revolutionary.[461]

Croiset used psychometry to help intuit information about people and events. Psychometry is the ability to psychically intuit information by touching an object (or even perhaps a person). Upon touching an object, Croiset would go into a sort of trance, speaking until information was exhausted. Most often the information Croiset received was in visualizations, and he would often stop to draw the images coming into his mind. In his 1964 book, author Jack Harrison Pollack provides a detailed overview of the medium's life and discusses some of the curious cases he collaborated on with police.

Further Reading:

Jack Harrison Pollack, *Croiset the Clairvoyant: The Story of the Amazing Dutchman.* Garden City, NY: Doubleday & Company, 1964.

Cummins, Geraldine (1890–1969): Geraldine Cummins was an Irish playwright, journalist, and advocate for women's rights. Along with her fellow playwright Susanne Day and author Edith Somerville, Cummins cofounded the suffragette society Munster Women's Franchise League. She also worked at the National Library in Dublin.[462] Cummins was an automatic writer and psychometrist. She engaged in psychical research with Sir

Rudyard Kipling. She is also known as Mrs. Holland, a pseudonym she used to disguise her psychical work from disapproving family members. Fleming was one of the automatic writers in the nearly thirty-year Cross-Correspondences study. She began engaging in automatic writing in 1898 as a way to produce poetry and soon discovered that she seemed to be receiving messages from beyond the grave. She even believed she received posthumous messages from the spirit of F. W. H. Myers.[468]

Forthuny, Pascal (1872–1962): Pascal Forthuny was a French automatic writer and psychometrist. He discovered his automatic writing ability one day as, while he was consciously writing one of his novels, his hand seemingly took over and wrote words of its own. This, coupled with the precognitive vision of his mother's passing, led him to examine his abilities. In the 1920s he discovered his knack for psychometry, or, psychically obtaining information about objects by touching them. The SPR learned of Flournoy's abilities and subjected him to psychometric tests that he successfully passed.

Fox Sisters (Kate, Leah, Margaret): The Fox sisters, Kate (1836–1892), Leah (1811–1890), and Margaret (1834–1893), who, while living in Hydesville, New York, began experiencing strange rapping and knocks in their home. They began interacting with the sounds and discovered that they seemed to get intelligent responses. When a neighbor learned of the strange goings on, he invited the sisters to his home for a séance, and the popularity of the sisters grew exponentially afterward. Their séances, coupled with the work of medium Andrew Jackson Davis, were responsible for creating the spiritualism movement with its intense focus on mediumship, communication with the dead, and séances. Leah was particularly responsible for coordinating séances and events, while Kate is known as the most mediumistic of the three. Kate was, in fact, studied by psychical researchers Eleanor Sidgwick and Sir William Crookes. They both admitted that some strange occurrences happened during their investigations, but Sidgwick wasn't convinced anything was genuine. In 1888, Margaret Fox publicly stated that the initial rappings at their house in Hydesville were fake, but her sisters Leah and Kate denied this accusation. While most agree that

the Fox sisters seem to rest squarely in the realm of spiritualist entertainment, their séances ushered in a movement that ultimately motivated psychical researchers to dig even deeper into the mysteries of life after death.[469]

G

Garrett, Eileen (1892–1970): Eileen Garett was an Irish American medium and founder of the Parapsychology Foundation, an organization that she established in 1951. As a young child living with her aunt and uncle, she exhibited the ability to intuit information about objects when touching them, which is known as psychometry. In an essay she once described how in her bedroom, there was a dresser that "told [her] stories, as [she] touched the wood caressingly."[470] In this same essay she also talks about seeing the apparitions of two children and sensing items that were beyond her physical grasp.[471] In 1916, she had a vision of her husband's untimely death a week before it happened.[472]

As she grew older and continued to experience strange phenomena, she studied at the British College of Psychic Science to develop her medium abilities. In 1933, she became involved with the American SPR's research.[473] Researchers J. B. Rhine and J. Gaither Pratt, in a study with Garrett, realized that psychic information received via trance wasn't necessarily messages from the dead and perhaps instead indicated an unknown faculty of living consciousness.[474]

Further Reading:

Allan Angoff, *Eileen Garrett and the World Beyond the Senses.* New York: Morrow, 1974.

Geller, Uri (1946–): Uri Geller is an Israeli British physical medium most known for his ability to bend and break things. As a child, Geller noticed that items tended to malfunction or even break around him, and he soon began to notice that he seemed to be able to control them. He began performing these abilities in Israel and eventually turned this into a profitable career path. He attracted the attention of various researchers through the years: parapsychologist Hans Bender, for example, delivered a survey to German residents after a television program displaying Geller's ability seemed to spark a wave of spontaneous psychokinetic events. Hans Bender isn't the only researcher to have studied Geller. Physicists Russell Targ and Harold Puthoff, of the Stanford Research Institute, conducted experiments with Geller and found no evidence of psychokinesis. They did, however, find some small evidence of telepathy, though later replicated designs found none. Geller remains perhaps one of the most controversial physical mediums of today.[475]

Goligher, Kathleen (1898–?): Kathleen Goligher was an Irish medium at whose séances table levitations, strange raps, and ectoplasm occurred. Goligher drew the attention of researcher William Crawford, a British mechanical engineer. He held sittings and studies with Goligher for six years, developing the "rod theory" in which he posited a spectral reason for the table levitations. He theorized that the ectoplasm emanating from Goligher had enough strength to serve as a rod and cantilever for affecting items in the room, like tables. Crawford's theory, while interesting, seems only to have resulted in pictures of what look like man-made rods. Other researchers like Sir William Barrett were initially impressed by Goligher's abilities but later became suspicious of fraud. Crawford's rod theory was all but dismissed though some psychical researchers such as John Beloff and Rose Barrington saw some merit to the theory.[476]

Further Reading:

Tymn, Michael E., "An Interview with Dr. William J. Crawford Concerning the Mediumship of Kathleen Goligher." *Journal of Spirituality and Paranormal Studies* 33, no. 2 (April 2010): 83–93.

Guzyk, Jan (1875–1928): Jan Guzyk was a Polish physical medium who was marked, like many physical mediums of this era, by controversy. When Guyzk was fifteen years old, he was mentored by a spiritualist and began developing psychical abilities. He performed sittings for people and caught the eye of psychical researcher Dr. Gustave Geley in 1921. After conducting fifty sittings with Guzyk, Geley was convinced that the phenomena were genuine. However, other researchers caught Guzyk in undeniable fraudulent acts—in fact, in one instance, researchers snapped a flash photograph in the otherwise dark séance room and discovered Guzyk's hand raised high in the air, manipulating a curtain rod. Some researchers remained open to the idea that *some* of Guzyk's abilities were genuine even amid the fraud, but it seems that the medium's reputation for fraudulent acts had spread far and wide and most dismissed his acts as nothing more than mere entertainment.[477]

H

Home, Daniel Dunglas (1833–1886): Daniel Dunglas (D. D.) Home was a Scottish physical medium. Researchers Arthur and Joyce Berger tell us that he was "reputedly the greatest of all physical mediums and upon whom the case for physical mediumship was said to stand or fall."[478] Born in Scotland, Home moved to Connecticut in his youth where he lived with an aunt. The aunt, being frightened by his psychokinetic behaviors, didn't allow Home to live with her for long, and he ended up primarily staying with neighbors. Word of his

Figure 2.32. Kathleen Goligher
From *The Reality of Psychica Phenomena* by William Jackson Crawford (London: John M. Watkins, 1916). PD-US-Expired

Figure 2.33. Artistic Rendering of a Levitation during a Séance of Daniel Dunglas Home
From *Les Mystères de la Science* by Louis Figuier (Paris: A La Librairie Illustrèe, c. 1880). PD-US-expired

abilities spread and in 1855 a group of spiritualists raised money to send Home to Europe.

During his séances, all manner of strange phenomena occurred: table tipping, musical instruments playing by unseen hands, and perhaps what Home is most infamously known for, levitation, not just of items in the room, but of himself as well. One of the most famous depictions of Home is a drawing that shows him levitating high above a roomful of curious onlookers. In one reported séance, Home levitated himself from a chair in one second-story room, through an open window, across an alley way, and into the chair in the adjacent building. Explanations for this feat have been offered as such, "In order to explain away the apparent phenomena, it has been suggested that Home was a superhypnotist or a supermagician or that those present were all gullible and remembered imperfectly what had actually happened."[479]

Psychical researchers investigated Home, William Crookes among them. Conducting séances at Crookes's London home, the scientist and his colleagues were not able to explain the curious events that took place. Crookes became convinced that Home's abilities were genuine and that they pointed to a new force at work in the universe— a psychic force. Crookes published this theory in leading scientific journals, and it caused an academic uproar.[480] As we have seen time and again in the course of psychical history (especially during the Victorian era), there seemed to be a dividing line between scientists who were open to paranormal phenomena as a new avenue of research and those who believed it was nothing more than fraud and misidentification.

Further Reading:

Harry Houdini, "Daniel Dunglas Home" in *A Magician Among the Spirits.* Cambridge: Cambridge University Press, 2011: 38–49. (Originally published in 1924).

Elizabeth Jenkins, *The Shadow and the Light: A Defence of Daniel Dunglas Home.* London: H. Hamilton, 1982.

Frank Podmore, "Daniel Dunglas Home." In *Modern Spiritualism: A History and a Criticism.* Cambridge: Cambridge University Press, 2012: 223–43. (Originally published in 1902).

Hurkos, Peter (1911–1988): Peter Hurkos was a Dutch medium. At the age of thirty, he fell of a ladder and landed on his head. After the incident, he noticed that he had the ability to psychically obtain information when touching objects. He began performing this ability to crowds and even worked with police to help solve crimes.[481] Hurkos eventually attracted the attention of neurologist and physiologist Dr. Andrija Puharich who invited the medium to his lab (the Round Table Foundation) in Maine. Over the next seven years, Dr. Puharich studied Hurkos who displayed impressive psychometric abilities. At the time, the gold-star of scientific inquiry into psi phenomena was the Duke Parapsychology Labs directed by J. B. Rhine. At the behest of colleagues, Hurkos and Rhine were introduced to each other, but Hurkos was offended when Rhine asked if the medium would submit to a lie detector test about the veracity of his abilities. Hurkos never received an invitation to the labs at Duke, and he seemed content to never work with Rhine.[482]

Further Reading:

Norma Lee Browning, *The Psychic World of Peter Hurkos*. Garden City, NY: Doubleday & Company, 1970.

I

Indridason, Indridi (1883–1912): Indridi Indridason was an Icelandic medium. During his séances, which unlike some others took place in well-lit rooms, Indridason produced apports, materialized strange raps and sounds, levitated objects, and even materializations of spirits. One spirit manifestation, referred to as "Jensen," would appear to the entire room of sitters who could plainly see that Indridason and the spirit were two separate entities. As Indridison's popularity grew, he was studied by the Psychic Experimental Society in Reykjavik.[483] The noted doctor Gudmundur Hannesson was part of this society and a member of a committee who studied Indridason and concluded that the medium's abilities were genuine and "unquestionable."[484] Unfortunately, Indridason passed away at the young age of twenty-nine.[485]

Further Reading:

Loftur R. Gissurarson and Erlendur Haraldsson, "The Icelandic Physical Medium Indridi Indridason." *Proceedings of the Society for Psychical Research* 57 (January 1989): 54–148.

J

Jonsson, Olof (1918–1998): Olof Jonsson was a Swedish psychic who used his abilities to assist police in solving crimes. He was also part of the group who attempted to psychically communicate with astronaut Edgar Mitchell in 1971. Jonsson was studied at the Duke Parapsychology Labs with J. B. Rhine, but those studies were never formally published in the literature. In fact, a 1992 article from the *Journal of Parapsychology* points out that those studies are largely ignored due to inadequate safeguards against fraud.[486] This same article discusses how different methods are needed for those who have high confidence in their psychical abilities and/or who have displayed potentially suspicious psi activities in the past. To put this into action, the authors tested Jonsson using a computer program called the ESPerciser: a program designed to more rigorously test psi ability because it reduces unconscious psychical communication between the experimenter and the subject, and by its nature as a computer program is random and also harder to manipulate. The researchers discovered that Jonsson displayed statistically significant results that seem to indicate the presence of psi phenomena. The authors also discuss Johnsson's previous involvement with J. B. Rhine who had chosen not to publish his studies with the medium. The article discusses some reasons for that: the primary reason being that Jonsson also engaged in public, informal demonstrations of his abilities akin to something like a magic trick. Seeing him as more of an entertainer than a genuine psychic, this impacted some researcher's willingness to publicly comment on studies with Jonsson.[487]

Further Reading:

Norman S. Don, Bruce E. McDonough, and Charles A. Warren, "PSI Testing of a Controversial Psychic Under Controlled Conditions." *Journal of Parapsychology* 56, no. 2 (June 1992): 87–96.

K

Kiyota, Masuaki (1962–): Masuaki Kiyota is a Japanese medium who displays psychokinetic abilities. After appearing on an NBC television show in 1977, which skyrocketed his popularity, Japanese parapsychologists invited Kiyota to participate in studies with them. During these studies, Kiyota continued to display strange metal bending and Polaroid film manipulation. In 1982, psychical researcher Jule Eisenbud studied Kiyota under a controlled laboratory environment and also obtained some evidence of psi ability. Just a few short years later though, in 1984, Kiyota publicly discussed how he was able to bend metal using normal physical processes. This cast a pall on every study involving Kiyota of course, but left some wondering if the pressure to perform had resulted in some fraudulent behavior of an otherwise genuine ability. Even more unfortunate is that Kiyota's admission was a blow to the field of Japanese parapsychology. In fact, historians Arthur and Joyce Berger write that "it produced the kind of hostility and controversy among Japanese scientists and scholars that had not been seen since the heated debates over the work of Tomokichi Fukarai and it had a harmful impact on . . . parapsychologists."[488]

Further Reading:

Jule Eisenbud, "Some Investigations of Claims of PK Effects on Metal and Film by Masuaki Kiyota." *The Journal of the American Society for Psychical Research* 76, no. 3 (1982): 217–50.

Kluski, Franek (1873–1943): Franek Kluski was a Polish medium. Kluski, a pseudonym for Teofil Modrzejewski, has been described as "one of the greatest mediums of all time."[489] As a child, Kluski experienced presentience and haunt phenomena in which apparitions appeared so life-like he thought they were real. He would, in fact, speak to apparitions of both humans and animals. Though these abilities were present from a very early age, Kluski didn't perform séances until he was in his forties, and mostly it was for small groups of friends.[490] Kluski never charged money for his séances and had a genuine respect for science, so it is not shocking that he agreed to participate in studies with psychical researchers. In 1919, the Warsaw SPR conducted studies with Kluski and shortly afterward was introduced to Dr. Gustave Geley and the Institut Métapsychique International (IMI). Kluski's work with Geley is perhaps the best known research on his mediumship. It was during his work with Geley and the IMI that paraffin molds of materializations were captured. During Kluski's séances, melted paraffin wax would be placed on the table and through the course of the séances, molds of hands, feet, and faces would appear in the wax. Geley attempted to reduce the chance of fraud by adding special ingredients to the paraffin, ensuring that no one could secretly sneak a pre-molded figure into the room.[491]

Further Reading:

Gustave Geley, "Experiments in Materialization with M. Franek Kluski." *The Journal of the American Society for Psychical Research* 17, no. 11 (November 1923).

Zofia Weaver, *Other Realities? The Enigma of Franek Kluski's Mediumship.* Hove: White Crow Books, 2015.

Kulagina, Nina (1926–1990): Nina Kulagina was a Russian medium who exhibited psychokinetic abilities. J. B. Rhine, American parapsychologist, had studied psychokinesis in his labs at Duke University. His experiments, using dice, studied the ability of the mind to influence the outcome of a dice roll. If the dice matched the targeted number established before the roll, then the theory was that some sort of brain activity was influencing how those dice rolled. This is a very different type of psychokinesis than what Kulagina possessed. Multiple researchers observed the physical movement of stationary objects placed in front of Kulagina, making it an even more extraordinary occurrence of PK than influencing how an already-moving object will land.

Kulagina attracted the attention of Soviet parapsychologist Leonid Vasiliev in the late 1960s. Once word of her abilities grew, more parapsychologists, physicians, and a host of other scientists were involved in studies regarding her strange abilities. In one observation, researchers witnessed matchsticks move across the table toward her. In another, they watched as she seemed to psychically navigate a glass cylinder through a small bed of gravel.

What's even more interesting about Kulagina's case is the rigor to which Soviet scientists subjected her. Richard S. Broughton tell us that "the Soviets were interested in more than just eliminating fraud. Given the strictly materialist orientation of Soviet science, their scientists worked exceptionally hard to see if some form of normal energy, perhaps present in abnormal quantities, might explain what they were seeing."[492] For seven years, Kulagina was studied by researchers at various organizations: the Institute of Precise Mechanics and Optics, the Baumann Higher School of Technology, and the Research Institute of Radio-Engineering. None of the scientists could explain exactly how Kulagina was able to physically affect stationary items, though they did find that there were strong acoustic and magnetic fields surrounding her hands.

Kulagina, though word of her spread internationally, never sought to use her ability for financial gain. Even though she never capitalized on her ability, critics still existed. When a journal published an article stating that she was a fraud, Kulagina took them to court where scientists from the Soviet Academy of Sciences came to her defense and the journal was ordered to retract their statement. To this day, Kulagina's abilities remain unsolved.[493]

Further Reading:

H. H. Keil, B. Herbert, M. Ullman, and J. G. Pratt, "Directly Observable Voluntary PK Effects: A Survey and Tentative Interpretation of Available Findings from Nina Kulagina and Known Causes of Recent Date." *Proceedings of the Society for Psychical Research* 56 (1976): 197–235.

L

Laplace, Jeanne: Jeanne Laplace was a French medium. She began displaying curious abilities since childhood and eventually became a professional medium before someone familiar with her abilities introduced her to the psychical researcher Eugène Osty. Osty, director of the Institut Métapsychique International (IMI), studied Laplace's abilities from 1927 to 1934. While at IMI, in fact, séances were held with the famous paranormal investigator Harry Price. Laplace's abilities took the form of impressions gathered from tactile hallucinations and even through the senses of taste and smell.[494]

Further Reading:

Caratelli, Giulio and Maria Luisa Felici, "An Important Subject at the Institut Métapsychique International: Jeanne Laplace. The 1927–1934 Experiments." *Journal of Scientific Exploration* 25, no. 3 (2011): 479–95.

Leonard, Gladys Osborne (1882–1967): Gladys Osborne Leonard was a British trance medium who was sometimes referred to as the "British Mrs. Piper," a reference to the American trance medium Leonora Piper.[495] Leonard experienced mediumistic abilities since childhood. She saw visions of landscapes and people that she referred to as the "happy valley," noting that these visions were always serene and felt commonplace for her as a girl. After all, she didn't yet know that these visions weren't the norm. In her teens, she began feeling guided toward spiritualism and attended meetings where she first witnessed mediums channeling spirits of the dead. During one of these meetings, a medium pointed at Leonard and conveyed that Leonard had spirit

Figure 2.34. Gladys Osborne Leonard
From *The History of Spiritualism*, Vol. 2 by Sir Arthur Conan Doyle (New York: George H. Duran, 1926): PD-US

guides watching after her, helping her on her path. This was all curious to Leonard who, other than the "happy valley" hadn't really pursued any mediumistic practice. And since her parents highly disapproved of anything to do with spiritualism, Leonard locked the memory away until years later when, during a hospital stay, she met a nurse who invited her to a séance.[496]

Leonard's involvement with spiritualism and mediumship continued to grow from there, and she was soon introduced, through trance, to her spirit control Feda. Feda claimed to be an ancestor spirit of Leonard's and during séances, Feda would speak through Leonard, and occasionally Leonard seemed to be possessed by a new spirit. In these moments, direct voice phenomena occurred in which a strange voice could be heard in the room, unattributed to any source. Sir Oliver Lodge held sittings with the medium, even publishing a book on his studies in 1916. For a period of time, Leonard's séances were held exclusively for members of the SPR, "and the report that resulted was that she gave good evidence of communicating with discarnate spirits."[497]

Further Reading:

Gladys Osborne Leonard, *My Life in Two Worlds.* London: Cassell & Company, 1931.

M

Mellon, Annie F. (1850–1935): Annie F. Mellon (Annie Fairlamb) was a British medium who, for nearly twenty years, conducted séances in which she materialized apparitions. Her fraudulent acts were discovered when, in Australia in 1894, a sitter at her séance grabbed the materialized apparition and found it to be none other than Mellon herself.[498] Mellon often worked in tandem with fellow medium Catherine Wood. It was common in the spiritualist era that some mediums would either be placed together in cabinets or literally tied to each other, the idea being that together their abilities were enhanced.[499]

Further Reading:

Marlene Tromp, "Queering the Séance: Bodies, Bondage, and Touching in Victorian Spiritualism." In *Handbook of Spiritualism and Channeling,* vol. 9, edited by Cathy Gutierrez, 87–115. Leiden: Brill, 2015.

Mifune, Chizuko (1886–1911): Chizuko Mifune was a Japanese psychic who worked closely with the parapsychologist Tomokichi Fukarai. Using hypnosis, Fukurai convinced Mifune that she had the gift of clairvoyance and it appeared to work. He slowly worked with Mifune to hone those skills to the point that she no longer needed to be placed under hypnosis to receive clairvoyant visions. She was able to identify physical ailments and intuit the contents of sealed envelopes. As her fame grew, she was submitted to more psychical tests. There was some controversy though, as Mifune often asked to be alone in the room when attempting to determine contents of envelopes, tin cans, and more. She claimed that extra persons in the room affected her ability to correctly identify the contents. Some pointed to this as a sure sign of fraudulent activity. Sadly, Mifune committed suicide in 1911.[500]

Mirabelli, Carlos (1889–1951): Carlos Mirabelli was a Brazilian medium who, according to researcher Stephen E. Braude, "is one of the most tantalizing and frustrating [cases] in psychical research."[501] Researchers point to Mirabelli as the most extreme medium case in history, and during his séances, all manner of phenomena occurred: apports, automatic writing, levitation (once of himself in a chair), materialization in broad daylight, speaking in foreign languages, and much more. Some researchers point out that his case wasn't given the same attention as other mediums due perhaps to the exhaustion that researchers felt after decades of studying the spiritualist mediums. It doesn't help that Mirabelli, like so many others, was caught once faking a levitation. Does this one act mar the totality of his s–ances?

Mirabelli, born in 1889 in Brazil, was plagued by strange phenomena from childhood. As a young boy working in a shoe store, strange poltergeist activity routinely happened, once resulting in Mirabelli running out into the street, boxes of shoes flying after him. He was unfortunately admitted to an asylum, since people had no other explanation than to assume he was insane. While at the asylum, doctors studied Mirabelli and determined that he was indeed sane, but that he did possess some rather strange abilities like psychokinesis. He was soon released from the asylum and began conducting séances. His reputation grew. The most notable thing about Mirabelli is that much of his phenomena were displayed in broad daylight—a stark difference from the dark, obscured cabinets of other mediums. He not only engaged in automatic writing, but also in automatic painting, and he was known to create portraits of stranger's dead loved ones.[502]

Researchers in Brazil and with the British SPR studied Mirabelli. The SPR researchers were much more dubious of the medium, giving no credence to his linguistic or automatic writing abilities but slightly more favor to his physical feats such as materializations and psychokinesis. As Stephen E. Braude summarizes, "The case of Mirabelli must be regarded, *at best,* as one of so-called 'mixed-mediumship'—that is combining fraudulent with genuine phenomena."[503]

Molnar, Tibor (1900–?): Tibor Molnar was a Hungarian medium and subject of the psychical researcher Elemér Chengery Pap. When Molnar was in his twenties, he began exhibiting strange psychical phenomena and, being afraid of what was happening to him, sought medical help. The first doctor he went to dismissed Molnar as simply insane, but he sought out another doctor who happened to be familiar with spiritualism. This second doctor did not find Molnar to be insane and instead urged him to meet with spiritualists. Molnar did and thus began fostering his mediumistic abilities. During Molnar's séances, apported objects would appear and items would levitate, even when the medium's hands and feet were bound by sitters. From 1928–1932, Chemgery Pap held séances with Molnar and observed the levitation of objects for himself. Most notable, however, were apported objects, like a chunk of a gravestone or, in one very curious incident, the materialization of an envelope from its charred remains.[504]

Further Reading:

Michael Nahm, "Out of Thin Air? Apport Studies Performed between 1928 and 1938 by Elemér Chengery Pap." *Journal of Scientific Exploration* 33, no. 4 (2019): 661–705.

Moses, William Stainton (1839–1892): William Stainton Moses was a British clergyman, medium, and spiritualist. In 1872, Moses began exhibiting both physical and mental mediumship. He referred to his spirit controls as the "Imperator Band," which comprised forty-nine different entities. As a clergyman and spiritualist interested in mediumistic phenomena, Moses was actually one of the founding members of the British SPR. He left after only four years, though, as he was disgruntled with the strict scientific standards placed upon mediums.[505]

Moses recounted an event to psychical researcher Edmund Gurney regarding a "phantasm of the living." The encounter, in fact, was published in the influential work of that same title. One of Moses's friends had attempted a psychical out-of-body experiment. Not informing Moses of their attempt, they meditated intently on Moses one night and a few days later, while visiting, asked Moses if anything strange had occurred. Moses told him that indeed something strange *had* occurred when he saw a vision of his friend sitting inside his home, only to fade away before his very eyes.[506]

Further Reading:

Michael E. Tymn, "An 'Interview' with the Rev. William Stainton Moses." *Journal of Spirituality and Paranormal Studies* 32, no. 2 (April 2009): 89–100.

Mügge, Kai: Kai Mügge is a German materialization medium who is the resident medium for the Felix Experimental Group, a community of people who meet regularly to hold séances and engage in mediumistic research. Mügge is known around the world for the phenomena displayed during his séances, in particular the production of ectoplasm.[507] In a 2015 article in the *Journal for Spiritual and Consciousness Studies*, researcher Jan Vandersande discusses séances held in Los Angeles in 2014.[508] During these séances, in which Mügge claimed the psychical researcher Hans Bender was his spirit control, sitters witnessed objects move of their own accord, felt strange hands grab their legs, saw a toy trumpet fly around the room, and (perhaps most interestingly) witnessed ectoplasm emanate forth from the medium's mouth. In one of the sittings, they witnessed a puddle of ectoplasm begin to take the shape of a hand, an event that has occurred before during Mügge's séances.[509]

While the aforementioned 2015 article speaks very highly of Mügge, researcher Michael Nahm has pointed out the ways in which he believes the ectoplasm is fraudulently produced and the other shortcomings of Mügge's séances in the articles found below.

Further Reading:

Michael Nahm, "The Development and Phenomena of a Circle for Physical Mediumship." *Journal of Scientific Exploration* 28, no. 2 (2014): 229–83.
Michael Nahm, "Further Comments about Kai Mügge's Alleged Mediumship and Recent Developments." *Journal of Scientific Exploration* 30, no. 1 (2016): 56–62.

Muldoon, Sylvan (1903–1971): Sylvan Muldoon first discovered that he could astral project when he was a young boy. He eventually learned to harness and control this ability, summoning it at his will. Inspired by the works of Hereward Carrington, Muldoon believed that astral projection provided proof that humans actually have two bodies: a physical body and an astral body.[510]

O

Ossowiecki, Stefan (1877–1944): Stefan Ossowiecki was a Polish medium. His mediumistic abilities emerged in childhood when he not only displayed psychokinetic abilities, but also saw people's auras. He was mentored by a yogi who taught him to harness the power of visualization and Ossowiecki's abilities grew even more pronounced. He even developed the ability to intuit information from touching objects, or psychometry. He never took payment from anyone who came to consult him, and he eventually drew the attention of psychical researchers such as Gustave Geley, Charles Richet, Albert von Schrenck-Notzing, and more. None of them could find evidence of fraud. When his safety was threatened by World War II, he refused to leave, feeling a sense of duty to use his psychometry to provide information to his neighbors about their friends and family members. Ossowiecki was unfortunately killed in the Warsaw uprising of 1944.[511]

Further Reading:

Mary Rose Barrington, Ian Stevenson, and Zofia Weaver, *A World in a Grain of Sand: The Clairvoyance of Stefan Ossowiecki.* Jefferson, NC: McFarland & Company, 2005.

P

Palladino, Eusapia (1854–1918): Eusapia (Sapia) Palladino was an Italian medium who was a key figure not only in spiritualism, but in the formation of psychical research. In fact, researcher Andrea Graus reminds us that "without her, the history of spiritism and psychical research would not have developed in the same way."[512] Palladino was born in 1854 in a small village in Italy. Her parents had both died by the time she was twelve, and she became a homeless youth. She briefly lived with an American couple in nearby Naples, but that arrangement fell through, and soon after she moved in with a family who had noticed that strange phenomena seemed to follow the young girl. The family took Palladino in on the requirement that she perform séances for them and their guests. At this same time, the Damianis,

a married spiritualist couple, had attended a séance in which a spirit referred to as "John King" told them that they would find a gifted medium named Eusapia in Naples. They took off in search, found the young girl, and Mr. Damiani became a manager of sorts, arranging séances and helping Palladino's reputation grow substantially. Her next manager was a gentleman named Ercole Chiaia who was determined to introduce psychical researchers to the famous Italian medium.[513]

In 1889, Ercole Chiaia extended an invitation (perhaps more so a challenge) to the psychical researcher Cesare Lombroso, urging him to visit and test Palladino's abilities for himself. When Lombroso declined, Manuel Otero Acevedo (a medical doctor), stepped in. He visited Palladino and outlined the terms of his request: that she produce mediumistic phenomena in broad daylight. Specifically, he placed a bowl of clay in front of her and covered it with a handkerchief. Past séances involved materialization of spirits, and Acevedo wanted proof in the form of impressions left in the clay mold. She went into a deep trance, then yelled an exclamation, and when Acevedo pulled back the handkerchief he was stunned to see the impression of a child's hand in the clay.[514]

Two years after this event, Lombroso did visit Naples to attend sittings with Palladino, in which he was intrigued by some apparent psychokinetic movement of objects. From here, a committee of researchers was formed to investigate the medium, which sparked years of study that took her to such places as Milan, Warsaw, and France. In one study, the researcher Charles Richet hosted Palladino at his home where researchers admitted that, short of trickery, they did not understand how certain phenomena were happening. Their report was highly criticized by SPR member Richard Hodgson who remained convinced that Palladino's abilities were nothing more than fraud.[515]

So divided were members of the SPR regarding Palladino's case that they simply refused to engage in studies with her for nearly ten years. When those ten years had passed, researchers once again held sittings and studies that seemed to renew interest in the famed medium. She was even invited to the American SPR, but she was caught engaging in fraudulent acts.[516] Palladino's case, like so many mediums throughout history, leaves one wondering what, if anything, was genuine phenomena. Could it be that some underlying abilities were genuine and the pressure Palladino was placed under to "perform" resulted in some trickery? The tales from her youth are certainly compelling, as many noted the strange activity that always seemed to follow her. And let's not forget that as a homeless youth, Palladino was offered shelter *on the condition* of performing séances. What was genuine and what was merely a survival mechanism?

Further Reading:

Carlos S. Alvarado, "Eusapia Palladino Anthologized." *Journal of Scientific Exploration* 31, no. 3 (2017): 467–76.

Hereward Carrington, *The American Séances with Eusapia Palladino.* New York: Garrett Publications, 1954.

Pap, Lajos (1883–1938): Lajos Pap was a Hungarian medium and subject of the psychical researcher Elemér Chengery Pap (the two were not related). After being persuaded by friends to attend a séance, Pap gave in even though he was skeptical of the whole topic. During these séances, however, he discovered that he seemingly had mediumistic abilities. The psychical researcher Chengery Pap was introduced to the medium who brought Pap, along with another medium named Tibor Molnar, to his laboratory in Budapest. Chengery Pap was concerned, of course, with ferreting out any potential for fraud and had designed and established certain protocols everyone had to follow during sittings. This included wearing nothing but the same fitted jumpsuit that had fluorescent bands on the wrists and ankles. The most curious thing about Pap was the presence of apported objects during his séances—small items like stones and tacks seemed to appear from nowhere. Pap's reputation took him to Sweden and London before his death in 1938.[517]

Further Reading:

Michael Nahm, "Out of Thin Air? Apport Studies Performed between 1928 and 1938 by Elemér Chengery Pap." *Journal of Scientific Exploration* 33, no. 4 (2019): 661–705.

Parise, Felicia: Felicia Parise was a participant in the Maimonides Dream Laboratory when she first learned about the psychokinetic abilities of Nina Kulagina. Intrigued by Kulagina's abilities, Parise set out to see if she could exhibit psychokinetic abilities as well. Parise practiced her efforts for some time with no success until one day, in a heightened emotional state, she noticed a small vial move beneath her hand. Motivated by this event, Parise continued practicing and eventually revealed her ability to parapsychologist Charles Honorton, who witnessed her PK ability for himself. Similar to the case of Kulagina, multiple tests were set up to try and determine how Parise was exhibiting PK, though no explanations could be found. Honorton even employed the keen eye of a magician who could offer no solid explanation either. Parise collaborated with multiple parapsychologists, but eventually, in her mid-seventies, halted studies and PK due to the energetic toll it had taken.[518] For a more in-depth look into Parise's life and her experiences with both the Maimonides Dream Lab and her PK abilities, see the interview she did with Rosemarie Pilkington in the further reading section.

Further Reading:

C. Honorton, "A Moving Experience." *Journal of the American Society for Psychical Research* 87 (1993): 329–40 (Reprinted in the *Journal of Scientific Exploration* 29, no. 1 [2015]: 62–74).

Rosemarie Pilkington, "Interview with Felice Parise, August 6, 2013." *Journal of Scientific Exploration* 29, no. 1 (2015): 75–108.

Piper, Leonora (1857–1950): Leonora Piper was an American medium who has been described as "one of the most, quite possibly *the* most, remarkable of the very limited number of trance mediums who have merited and submitted to prolonged and serious study."[519] Psychologist and psychical researcher William James first noted that Piper displayed curious abilities during s–ances in which they both attended. Through James, other psychical researchers learned of the American medium and over the course of the next thirty years, she collaborated with both the American and British SPR.[520]

In an 1890 report from the psychical researcher Charles Richet, who sat with Piper at two s–ances in December of that year, we learn how the medium conducted her sittings. Richet points out that Piper used trance to produce her communications. Taking

Figure 2.35. Leonora Piper
From *Spiritism, Hypnotism, and Telepathy as Involved in the Case of Mrs. Leonora E. Piper and the Society for Psychical Research* by Clark Bell (New York: Medico-Legal Journal, 1902). PD-US

hold of the hand of a sitter, Piper took up to fifteen minutes to relax herself into a deep trance. Afterward, her breathing was noticeably different and a few moments later a voice emanated forth sounding decidedly different from the medium's normal tone. At this point, Piper channeled her spirit controls and sitters were free to ask questions of them.[521]

Charles Richet was not the only psychical researcher who wrote about and/or studied Piper. In fact, the most notable research into Piper's mediumship was done by Richard Hodgson. We might remember that Richard Hodgson was a scathing critic of other mediums such as Eusapia Palladino and H. P. Blavatsky, but in his nearly nineteen-year study of Piper, he became not only convinced that her abilities were genuine, but that her information was channeled from spirits of the deceased. Throughout the course of her mediumship, Piper had multiple spirit controls—spirits that were channeled through the medium and provided information during séances. These spirit controls were known as Dr. Phinuit, G. P. (George Pelham), and W. Stainton Moses (the last two of which were known to be spirits of actual people, Dr. Phinuit never being verified as once-living).[522]

Researcher Alan Gauld discussed the "lost years" of Piper's mediumship, those years between 1897 and 1905 in which Piper was not hosting many sittings due primarily to poor health that both her and her husband encountered during that time. Piper's husband actually passed away in 1904 as a result of his illness. Gauld points out that some researchers overlook the few sittings that Piper did manage to have during this time, most notably a sitting with Dr. Samuel Cabot, that seemed to produce remarkably accurate information.[523]

For an extremely thorough inquiry into the Piper mediumship, consult the voluminous work of Eleanor Sidgwick below. Additionally, a 2013 article by Michael Tymn provides a worthy reminder to critics of mediums as viewed through the lens of Mrs. Piper and, interestingly, baseball.

Further Reading:

Eleanor M. Sidgwick, "A Contribution to the Study of Psychology of Mrs. Piper's Trance Phenomena." *Proceedings of the Society for Psychical Research* 28 (1915): 1–657.

Michael E. Tymn, "Debunking Babe Ruth and Leonora Piper." *Journal for Spiritual and Consciousness Studies* 36, no. 4 (October 2013): 182–85

Michael E. Tymn, *Resurrecting Leonora Piper: How Science Discovered the Afterlife*. United Kindom: White Crow Books, 2013.

R

Roberts, Jane (1929–1984): Jane Roberts was an American medium credited with popularizing the new age movement and the use of channeling. Roberts, a woman living in New York, channeled an entity named "Seth" for nearly twenty years. Through her channeled trances with this entity, he dictated to her information that resulted in the publication of ten books. In addition to "Seth," she also claimed to channel the spirit of psychologist and psychical research William James, and she published a book that claimed to be his posthumous thoughts on psi phenomena. Paul F. Cunningham's 2012 article in the *Journal of Parapsychology* provides a detailed overview of Robert's channeling and concludes that "we are led to the possibility that human personality may have a greater reality and awareness than is generally supposed."[524]

Further Reading:

Paul F. Cunningham, "The Content-Source Problem in Modern Mediumship Research." *Journal of Parapsychology* 76, no. 2 (2012): 295–319.

S

Schneider Brothers: Rudi (1908–1957) and Willi (1903–1971): Rudi and Willi Schneider were brothers and Austrian physical mediums. They were studied by psychical researchers such as Albert von Schrenck-Notzing, Eugene Osty, and Theodore Besterman. The researchers seemed much more critical of Rudi's mediumship, especially after Besterman's laboratory studies yielded no evidence of psi phenomena. Willi, however, seems to be more favorable looked upon. Both the brothers were accused of faking their abilities, but especially in the case of Willi Schneider, researchers felt that research environments were suitably controlled and warranted continued inquiry into their abilities.[525]

Silbert, Maria (1866–1936): Maria Silbert was an Austrian physical medium known for her séances that produced levitations, knocks and raps, dematerialization of objects, and phantom engravings that often spelled out the name "Nell." Critics of her mediumship point out the absence of any real scientific control during her sessions. Nevertheless, Hungarian psychical researcher Elemér Chengery Pap held sittings with the medium in 1928 and 1932. During these sittings, he witnessed the levitation of objects, felt strange hands pulling at his back and legs though the medium's hand remained above the table throughout the session, and witnessed psychokinetic movement of personal items belonging to sitters.[526]

Sherman, Harold (1898–1987): Harold Sherman was an American psychic. In perhaps one of the most intriguing displays of psychic demonstration, he attempted to psychically intuit information about the Arctic expedition of Sir Hubert Wilkins. Over a six-month period, Sherman focused on the trip, with 70 percent of his impressions matching the details and experiences of Wilkins, including the phantom sensation of a toothache the same day that Wilkins sought treatment for a dental emergency. Sherman established the ESP Research Associates Foundation in 1963, which held workshops on psychic phenomena.[527]

Slade, Henry (?–1905): Henry Slade was an American automatist who presented spirit messages on slate boards during his séances. Some researchers like Sir William Barrett believed that they had received genuine psychical messages from the deceased, but others were far more critical of Slade's productions.[528] In fact, the divisiveness surrounding this medium seemed to reach a boiling point in 1876 when Slade found himself at the center of "one of the strangest courtroom cases in Victorian England."[529] Edwin Lankester, a zoologist, was deeply frustrated by the rise of spiritualism and mediums, which he saw as a direct threat to the advancement of science. He was so incensed that he sued Slade on the grounds of criminal fraud.

This court case even involved Charles Darwin and Alfred Russell Wallace, the leading figures on natural selection and evolution. Lankester was a student of Darwin and both gentlemen had great disdain for mediums. Wallace, on the other hand, who believed in the merits of psychical investigation,

Figure 2.36. Henry Slade
From *The History of Spiritualism*, Vol. 1 by Sir Arthur Conan Doyle (New York: George H. Duran, 1926): PD-US

served as a character witness for Slade. As Richard Milner describes it, some saw the Slade case "as a public arena where science could score a devastating triumph over superstition. For others, it was the declaration of war between professional purveyors of the 'paranormal' and the fraternity of honest stage magicians." Slade was found guilty of fraud and sentenced to three months of jail time, but before he could serve he fled the country.[530]

Stepanek, Pavel: Pavel Stepanek was a Czechoslovakian psychic. When psychical researchers studied his ESP abilities, he tested consistently well and researchers from Holland, Japan, the United States, and more came to examine his abilities over the course of ten years. Some researchers have, however, criticized the methods by which Stepanek was studied, claiming that they were not well-controlled and were influenced by the celebrity status of Stepanek.[531]

Further Reading:

J. G. Pratt, "A Decade of Research with a Selected ESP Subject: An Overview and Reappraisal of the Work with Pavel Stepanek." *Proceedings of the American Society for Psychical Research* 30, no. 1 (September 1973).

Swann, Ingo Douglas (1933–2013): Ingo Swann was an American artist and psychic who exhibited psi phenomena his entire life. In fact, he remembers having an out-of-body experience at just three years old. In adulthood, researchers became aware of the phenomena that seemed to surround him. Psychical researcher Gertrude Schmeidler designed a test to see if Swann could influence temperature and she successfully demonstrated that he could. This demonstrated Swann's psychokinetic abilities. In another experiment, he successfully demonstrated clairvoyant abilities (and possibly out-of-body experiences as well). In that study, conducted by the American SPR, he was asked to remote view target objects placed eight feet above and obviously out of sight. Swann correctly identified all items, leaving scientists to wonder if it was a result of clairvoyance or a genuine out-of-body experience. He continued remote viewing studies with scientists at the Stanford Research Institute, where he continued to display impressive psi abilities.[532]

Further Reading:

M. A. Persinger, W. G. Roll, S. G. Tiller, S. A. Koren, and C. M. Cook, "Remote Viewing with the Artist Ingo Swann: Neuropsychological Profile, Electroencephalographic Correlates, Magnetic Resonance Imaging (MRI), and Possible Mechanisms." *Perceptual and Motor Skills* 94, no. 3 (2002): 927–49.

T

Thompson, Rosalie (1868–?): Rosalie Thompson was a British medium and key figure in the decades-long Cross-Correspondences study. The psychical researcher F. W. H. Myers held more than 150 sittings with her during which he became convinced that her psi abilities were genuine. During his studies with her, Thompson channeled the spirit of Myers's former romantic partner and he became further convinced that not only were her abilities genuine, but that they were proof that consciousness survives bodily death.[533]

W

Wriedt, Etta (1859–1942): Etta Wriedt was an American "direct-voice" medium from Detroit, Michigan. During her séances she was able to materialize voices of the deceased, which came through

Figure 2.37.   Etta Wriedt
From *The History of Spiritualism*, Vol. 2 by Sir Arthur Conan Doyle (New York: George H. Duran, 1926): PD-US

her and also a trumpet in the room. Sitters would sometimes hear multiple spirit voices coming forth at once. Scientist Sir William Barrett was impressed with and convinced that Wriedt's abilities were genuine and so was Barrett's wife, a lifelong skeptic of mediums until she attended one of Wriedt's séances. Multiple scientists and physicians held sittings with Wriedt, and all were impressed by her direct-voice mediumship.[534] A 2011 article by Michael E. Tymn provides an overview of Wriedt's mediumship and the various researchers who sat with her.

Further Reading:

Michael E. Tymn.,"Etta Wriedt: The Best Medium Ever?" *Journal of Spirituality and Paranormal Studies* 34, no. 4 (2011): 229–38.

Z

Zugun, Eleonore (1913–?): Eleonore Zugun was a Romanian woman who began to manifest poltergeist activity just before she turned twelve years old. In a 1999 article in the *Journal of Parapsychology*, researcher Peter Mulacz tells us that "the world famous and much disputed case of Eleonore Zugun has been alternatively called the Talpa Poltergeist Case, due to the name of the Romanian village where it originated."[535] Through the investigation of the phenomena that seemed to surround Zugun, more than three thousand instances of potential recurrent spontaneous psychokinesis were recorded. The origin of the activity seemed to stem from a tense moment between Zugun and her grandmother, who professed a "malediction"[536] upon Zugun when she refused to share some candy with her cousin. A deeply religious family, Zugun was eventually sent to a monastery in the hopes that an exorcism would cease the poltergeist activity that began happening. Things did not settle down, however, and Zugun was eventually transferred to an asylum. She drew the attention of psychical researchers and even royalty. Zoë, Countess Wassilko von Serecki, was greatly intrigued by Zugun and conducted her own series of psychical investigations with her.

This was not the first time Countess Wassilko had engaged in psychical research, however. Some years prior to her meetings with Zugun, the countess had attended séances of a popular medium named Klaus. Through her inquiries, the countess caught the medium engaging in fraudulent acts and exposed his séances as nothing more than trickery.[537] The countess was so intrigued by Zugun that the medium was moved into the countess' household and at one point, they even embarked on a five-month journey through England and Germany where they encountered psychical researchers like Harry Price and Albert von Schrenck-Notzing. Common RSPK phenomena that surrounded Zugun included apported objects like spoons, books moving back and forth on shelves, and sudden appearances of marks upon skin. Upon returning from their five-month journey, Zugun's abilities seemed to cease almost immediately.[538] In addition to the resources found below, you can find numerous mentions of Eleonore Zugun in the archived resources found within Hathi Trust.

Further Reading:

Peter Mulacz, "Eleonore Zugun: The Re-Evaluation of a Historic RSPK Case." *Journal of Parapsychology* 63, no. 1 (March 1999): 15–45.

Harry Price, "Some Account of the Poltergeist Phenomena of Eleonore Zugun." *Journal of the American Society for Psychical Research* 20, no. 8 (August 1926): 449–71.

Z. Wassilko, "The Early History and Phenomena of Eleonore Zugun." *The British Journal of Psychical Research* 1 (1927): 133–50.

Z. Wassilko, "Wer Sie Ist: Das Medium Eleonora Zugun." *Beilage zur Vossischen Zeitung* (January 1, 1927).

NOTES

1. Nandor Fodor, *Between Two Worlds.* New York: Parker Publishing Company, 1964: vi.

2. Arthur S. Berger and Joyce Berger, *The Encyclopedia of Parapsychology and Psychical Research.* New York: Paragon House, 1991: 4–5; Fodor, *Between Two Worlds*, 1–2.

3. Ibid., 5.

4. Ibid., 23.

5. Ibid., 23.

6. Ibid., 25.

7. Shane McCorristine, "William Fletcher Barrett, Spiritualism, and Psychical Research in Edwardian Dublin." *Estudios Irlandeses* no. 6 (January 1, 2011): 40.

8. John Beloff, *Parapsychology: A Concise History*. New York: St. Martin's Press, 1993: 70.

9. McCorristine, "William Fletcher Barrett," 40.

10. J. B. Rhine, *Handbook of Parapsychology*. Edited by Benjamin B. Wolman. New York: Van Nostrand Reinhold Company, 1977: 26.

11. Ibid., 80–83.

12. H. J. Irwin, *An Introduction to Parapsychology*. Jefferson, NC: McFarland and Company, 1989: 58.

13. Beloff, *Parapsychology*, 70.

14. Robert M. Schoch and Logan Yonavjak, *The Parapsychology Revolution: A Concise Anthology of Paranormal and Psychical Research*. New York: Jeremy P. Tarcher, 2008: 15–16.

15. C. E. M. Hansel, *ESP and Parapsychology: A Critical Re-Evaluation*. Buffalo, NY: Prometheus Books, 1980: 29.

16. Sir William F. Barrett, *On the Threshold of the Unseen: An Examination of the Phenomena of Spiritualism and of the Evidence for Survival After Death*. 2nd ed. London: Kegan Paul, Trench, Trubner & Co.: 35.

17. McCorristine, "William Fletcher Barrett," 41.

18. Rufolf Steiner, *The Steinerbooks Dictionary of the Psychic, Mystic, Occult*. Blauvelt, NY: Rudolf Steiner Publications, 1973: 26.

19. Berger and Berger, *The Encyclopedia of Parapsychology*, 29.

20. Eberhard Bauer, "Hans Bender: 'Frontier Scientist'—A Personal Tribute." *Journal of the Society for Psychical Research* 58, no. 825, October 1991): 125.

21. Ibid., 125.

22. Martin Ebon, "Hans Bender: A Life in Parapsychology." *Journal of Religion and Psychical Research* 18, no. 4 (October 1995): 188.

23. Berger and Berger, *The Encyclopedia of Parapsychology*, 28.

24. Bauer, "Hans Bender," 126.

25. Ibid., 126.

26. Berger and Berger, *The Encyclopedia of Parapsychology*, 291–92.

27. Ibid., 369.

28. Bauer, "Hands Bender," 127.

29. Berger and Berger, *The Encyclopedia of Parapsychology*, 32.

30. William G. Barnard, *Living Consciousness: The Metaphysical Vision of Henri Bergson*. Albany: State University of New York Press, 2011: 238.

31. Ibid., xxiii.

32. Berger and Berger, *The Encyclopedia of Parapsychology*, 34, 36.

33. Ibid., 35.

34. Janvier A Juin, "Correspondence," Revue Philosophique de la France et de l'Étranger, 1876, T. 1: 430–31.

35. Berger and Berger, *The Encyclopedia of Parapsychology*, 42.

36. Snezana Lawrence, "Life, Architecture, Mathematics, and the Fourth Dimension." *Nexus Network Journal: Architecture and Mathematics* 17, no. 2 (July 2015): 597–98; 603.

37. Mary E. Boole, *The Message of Psychic Science to the World*. London: C. W. Daniel, 1908: ix.

38. Berger and Berger, *The Encyclopedia of Parapsychology*, 53.

39. Richard Maurice Bucke, *Cosmic Consciousness: A Paper Read before the American Medico-Psychological Association in Philadelphia, 18 May 1894*. Philadelphia: Conservator, 1894.

40. Berger and Berger, *The Encyclopedia of Parapsychology*, 53.

41. Ibid., 58.

42. Ibid., 60–61.

43. Ibid., 62; Beloff, *Parapsychology*, 110–13; Nandor Fodor, *An Encyclopedia of Psychic Science*. Secaucus: Citadel Press, 1974, 41–42.

44. Berger and Berger, *The Encyclopedia of Parapsychology*, 67.

45. Ibid., 67.

46. Ibid., 83, 323.

47. Ibid., 83–84; Fodor, *Between Two Worlds*, 68 and 153.

48. Fodor, *An Encyclopedia*, 69.

49. Ibid., 69–71.

50. Berger and Berger, *The Encyclopedia of Parapsychology*, 102; Carlos S. Alvarado, "Telepathy, Mediumship, and Psychology: Psychical Research at the International Congresses of Psychology, 1889–1905. *Journal of Scientific Exploration* 31, no. 2 (2017): 268.

51. Berger and Berger, *The Encyclopedia of Parapsychology*, 104.

52. Andreas Sommer, "Normalizing the Supernormal: The Formation of the 'Gesellschaft Für Psychologische Forschung' ('Society for Psychological Research')." *Journal of the History of the Behavioral Sciences* 49, no. 1 (Winter 2013): 21.

53. Heather Wolffram, "Parapsychology on the Couch: The Psychology of Occult Belief in Germany, c. 1870–1939." *Journal of the History of the Behavioral Sciences* 42, no. 3 (Summer 2006): 237–39.

54. Sommer, "Normalizing the Supernormal," 19.

55. Wolffram, "Parapsychology on the Couch," 23–25.

56. Sommer, "Normalizing the Supernormal," 25.

57. Berger and Berger, *The Encyclopedia of Parapsychology*, 104.

58. Ibid., 107.

59. Beloff, *Parapsychology,* 98–99.

60. Carlos S. Alvarado, "Musings on Materializations: Eric J. Dingwall on 'The Plasma Theory.'" *Journal of Scientific Exploration* 33, no. 1 (2019): 78–79.

61. Fodor, *An Encyclopedia*, 109.

62. Ibid., 109; Berger and Berger, *The Encyclopedia of Parapsychology*, 114.

63. Stefan Gruner, "Hans Driesch Re-Visited After a Century: On 'Leib Und Seele-Eine Untersuchung Uber Das Psychophysische Grundproblem." *Cosmos and History: The Journal of Natural and Social Philosophy* 13, no. 3 (October 2017): 403.

64. Ibid., 403–5; Berger and Berger, *The Encyclopedia of Parapsychology*, 113.

65. Ibid., 119.

66. "Martin Ebon." In *Gale Literature: Contemporary Authors.* Farmington Hills, MI: Gale, 2002.

67. Paula M. Bortnichak and Edward A. Bortnichak, "Dream Work: The Inner World of *Die Meistersinger.*" *The Wagner Journal* 15, no. 1 (May 2021): 9.

68. Ingrid Kloosterman, "Psychical Research and Parapsychology Interpreted: Suggestions from the International Historiography of Psychical Research and Parapsychology for Investigating its History in the Netherlands," *History of the Human Sciences* 25, no. 2 (2012): 14.

69. Ibid., 14.

70. Ingrid Kloosterman, "'Spiritalismus vincit Mundum:' Dutch Spiritualism and the Beginning of Psychical Research." *Studium* 7, no. 3, (2014): 161.

71. Juan Gimeno, "David Efron: Biography of a Forgotten Pioneer in Psychical Research."*Journal of the Society for Psychical Research* 83, no. 2 (2019): 102–15.

72. Berger and Berger, *The Encyclopedia of Parapsychology*, 123.

73. Júlia Gyimesi, "Why 'Spiritism?'" *The International Journal of Psychoanalysis* 97 (2016): 370–71.

74. Ibid., 366.

75. Ibid., 367–68.

76. Ibid., 370.

77. Frank Podmore, *The Newer Spiritualism.* New York: Henry Holt and Company, 1911: 116.

78. Berger and Berger, *The Encyclopedia of Parapsychology*, 139–40.

79. Fodor, *An Encyclopedia,* 141–42.

80. Elizabeth R. Valentine, "Spooks and Spoofs: Relations Between Psychical Research and Academic Psychology in Britain in the Inter-War Period." *History of the Human Sciences* 25, no. 2 (2011): 77–78.

81. Berger and Berger, *The Encyclopedia of Parapsychology*, 141.

82. Carlos S. Alvarado, "Early Psychological Research Reference Works: Remarks on Nandor Fodor's *Encyclopedia of Psychic Science.*" *Journal of Scientific Exploration* 34, no. 4 (December 2020), 723.

83. Ibid., 723.

84. Michael Nahm, "Out of Thin Air? Apport Studies Performed between 1928 and 1938 by Elemér Chengery Pap." *Journal of Scientific Exploration* 33, no. 4 (2019): 673.

85. Ibid., 688–89.

86. Berger and Berger, *The Encyclopedia of Parapsychology*, 141.

87. Alvarado, "Early Psychological," 724–25.

88. Ibid., 724–25.

89. Adrian Parker and Brian Millar, "Revealing Psi Secrets: Successful Experimenters Seem to Succeed by Using Their Own Psi." *Journal of Parapsychology* 78, no. 1 (2014): 42.

90. Berger and Berger, *The Encyclopedia of Parapsychology*, 144–45.

91. Ibid., 144–45.

92. Miki Takasuna, "The Fukurai Affair: Parapsychology and the History of Psychology in Japan." *History of the Human Sciences* 25, no. 2 (2012): 152.

93. Berger and Berger, *The Encyclopedia of Parapsychology*, 150 and 436.

94. Takasuna, "The Fukarai Affair," 153–56.

95. Fodor, *An Encyclopedia*, 151.

96. Ibid., 151.

97. Gustave Geley, *From the Unconscious to the Conscious*. Translated by S. De Brath. New York: Harper and Brothers, 1919: x.

98. Berger and Berger, *The Encyclopedia of Parapsychology*, 158.

99. Ibid., 391.

100. Ibid., 158.

101. C. D. Broad, "Edmund Gurney." *Man, Myth, & Magic: The Illustrated Encyclopedia of Mythology, Religion and the Unknown*. Vol. 78. Edited by Richard Cavendish (1995): 1097.

102. Broad, "Edmund Gurney," 1097; Andreas Sommer, "Professional Heresy: Edmund Gurney (1847–1888) and the Study of Hallucinations and Hypnotism." *Medical History* 55. no. 3 (July 2011): 385.

103. Berger and Berger, *The Encyclopedia of Parapsychology*, 317.

104. Sommer, "Professional Heresy," 384–85.

105. Fodor, *An Encyclopedia*, 155.

106. Sommer, "Professional Heresy," 386.

107. Kloosterman, "Spiritalismus vincit," 170.

108. Berger and Berger, *The Encyclopedia of Parapsychology*, 179–80.

109. Ibid., 181–82; Fodor, *An Encyclopedia*, 169–70.

110. Berger and Berger, *The Encyclopedia of Parapsychology*, 292.

111. Michael Tymn, "Difficulties in Spirit Communication Explained by Dr. James Hyslop." *The Journal of Spirituality and Paranormal Studies* 33, no. 4 (2010): 196; Michael Tymn. "James Hyslop." In *Psi Encyclopedia London: The Society for Psychical Research*. (2015). Accessed June 5, 2022 from https://psi-encyclopedia.spr.ac.uk/articles /james-hyslop.

112. Tymn, "Difficulties in Spirit Communication, 180.

113. Daniel W. Bjork, *William James: The Center of His Vision*. Washington, DC: American Psychological Association, 1997: xiii.

114. Ibid., 10–12.

115. Ibid., 32.

116. Ibid., 37.

117. Ibid., 108.

118. Ibid., 210–11.

119. Krister Dylan Knapp, *William James: Psychical Research and the Challenge of Modernity*. Chapel Hill: The University of North Carolina Press, 2017: 2.

120. Bjork, *William James*, 210–13.

121. Ibid., 210–12.

122. Knapp, *William James*, 4.

123. Ibid., 3.

124. Ibid., 232.

125. Renaud Evrard, Erika Annabelle Pratte, and Etzel Cardeña, "Pierre Janet and the Enchanted Boundary of Psychical Research." *History of Psychology* 21, no. 2 (2018): 100.

126. Berger and Berger, *The Encyclopedia of Parapsychology*, 206.

127. Ibid., 206.

128. James C. Carpenter, *First Sight: ESP and Parapsychology in Everyday Life*. Lanham, MD: Rowman & Littlefield, 2012: 296–97.

129. Berger and Berger, *The Encyclopedia of Parapsychology*, 207.

130. Ibid., 89, 209; M. Willin. (2021). "Alice Johnson." Psi Encyclopedia London: The Society for Psychical Research. Accessed June 5, 2022 from https://psi-encyclopedia.spr.ac.uk/articles/alice-johnson.

131. Berger and Berger, *The Encyclopedia of Parapsychology*, 216–17.

132. Ibid., 216–17.

133. Michael Fordham, "Editorial Preface," in Carl Jung's *Sychronicity*. New York: Bollingen Foundation, 1960: xi.

134. Berger and Berger, *The Encyclopedia of Parapsychology*, 225.

135. Fodor, *An Encyclopedia*, 204.

136. John Beloff, "Historical Overview," in *Handbook of Parapsychology*, edited by Benjamin B. Wolman. New York: Van Nostrand Reinhold Company, 1977: 11–12.; Berger and Berger, *The Encyclopedia of Parapsychology*, 245.

137. Fodor, *An Encyclopedia*, 204.

138. Berger and Berger, *The Encyclopedia of Parapsychology*, 245.

139. Beloff, "Historical Overview," 13.

140. Berger and Berger, *The Encyclopedia of Parapsychology*, 245.

141. Ibid., 260–61.

142. Daphne Claire Rozenblatt, "Madness and Method: Enrico Morselli and the Social Politics of Psychiatry, 1852–1929." PhD diss., University of California, 2014: 149.

143. Ibid., 150–51.

144. Berger and Berger, *The Encyclopedia*, 274–275.

145. Andreas Sommer, "Psychical Research and the Origins of American Psychology: Hugo Münsterberg, William James and Eusapia Palladino," *History of the Human Sciences* 25, no. 2 (2012): 31.

146. Ibid., 31.

147. Block, *Researching the Paranormal*, 58.

148. Ibid., 52, 58, 108.

149. Fodor, *An Encyclopedia*, 260.

150. Berger and Berger, *The Encyclopedia of Parapsychology*, 284.

151. Fodor, *An Encyclopedia*, 260.

152. Ibid., 261.

153. Dorothy H. Pope, "Obituary: Carroll Blue Nash." *Journal of Parapsychology* 62, no. 4 (December 1998): 361–62.

154. Berger and Berger, *The Encyclopedia of Parapsychology*, 290.

155. Zofia Weaver, "Julian Ochorowicz and His Contribution to Psychical Research." *Journal of Parapsychology* 83, no. 1 (2019): 69–73.

156. Weaver, "Julian Orchorowicz," 302.

157. Ibid., 302.

158. Fodor, *An Encyclopedia*, 270.

159. R. Craig Hogan, "Applying the Science of the Afterlife." *Journal of Spirituality and Paranormal Studies* 32, no. 1 (2009): 10.

160. Carlos Alvarado, "Eugene Osty on Out-of-Body Experiences." *Journal of the Society for Psychical Research* 80, no. 2 (2016): 122.

161. Berger and Berger, *The Encyclopedia of Parapsychology*, 308, 342, 475.

162. Ibid., 308, 342, 475.

163. Nahm, "Out of Thin Air?" 661–62.

164. Ibid., 662–63.

165. Ibid., 674–80.

166. Berger and Berger, *The Encyclopedia of Parapsychology*, 320.

167. Vernon M. Neppe, "Revisiting Survival 37 Years Later: Is the Data Still Compelling?" *The Journal of Spirituality and Paranormal Studies* 33, no. 3 (2010): 143.

168. Berger and Berger, *The Encyclopedia of Parapsychology*, 324–25.

169. Ibid., 44.

170. Ibid., 45.

171. Ibid., 45.

172. Ibid., 287.

173. Margaret M. Price, "A Comparison of Blind and Seeing Subjects in 'ESP' Tests." *Journal of Parapsychology* 2, no. 4 (December 1, 1938): 273–86.

174. Berger and Berger, *The Encyclopedia of Parapsychology*, 334–35.

175. Ibid., 334.

176. Ibid., 334.

177. Ibid., 116, 356–57.

178. Block, *Researching the Paranormal*, 59.

179. Ibid., 102–3.

180. Berger and Berger, *The Encyclopedia of Parapsychology*, 356.

181. Ibid., 357.

182. Block, *Researching the Paranormal*, 102–4.

183. Berger and Berger, *The Encyclopedia of Parapsychology*, 358.

184. Carlos S. Alvarado, "Fragments of a Life in Psychical Research: The Case of Charles Richet." *Journal of Scientific Exploration* 32, no. 1 (2018): 56.

185. Ibid., 58–59.

186. Evraud, Pratt, and Cardeña, "Pierre Janet," 102.

187. Alvarado, "Fragments of a Life," 60.

188. Berger and Berger, *The Encyclopedia of Parapsychology*, 359.

189. Alvarado, "Fragments of a Life," 59–60.

190. Berger and Berger, *The Encyclopedia of Parapsychology*, 363.

191. Ibid., 375.

192. Ibid., 376.

193. Heather Wolffram, "Parapsychology on the Couch: The Psychology of Occult Belief in Germany, c. 1870–1939." *Journal of the History of the Behavioral Sciences* 42, no. 3 (Summer 2006): 239–40.

194. Ibid., 247.

195. Ibid., 247.

196. Ibid., 254.

197. Berger and Berger, *The Encyclopedia of Parapsychology*, 382.

198. Carlos S. Alvarado, "Eleanor M. Sidgwick (1845–1936)." *Journal of Parapsychology* 82, no. 2. (2018): 127.

199. Ibid., 128.

200. Ibid., 128.

201. Block, *Researching the Paranormal*, 57.

202. Christopher Keep, "Evidence in Matters Extraordinary: Numbers, Narratives, and the Census of Hallucinations." *Victorian Studies* 61, no. 4 (Summer 2019): 582.

203. Alvarado, "Eleanor Sidgwick," 129; Berger and Berger, *The Encyclopedia of Parapsychology*, 398.

204. Berger and Berger, *The Encyclopedia of Parapsychology*, 398.

205. Alvarado, "Eleanor Sidgwick," 128–29.

206. Berger and Berger, *The Encyclopedia of Parapsychology*, 398–99.

207. Fodor, *An Encyclopedia*, 343.

208. Arthur Sidgwick, *Henry Sidgwick: A Memoir.* London: Macmillan & Co. Limited, 1906: 203–06.

209. Berger and Berger, *The Encyclopedia of Parapsychology*, 419.

210. Renaud Evrard, "René Sudre (1880–1968): The Metapsychist's Quill." *Journal of the Society for Psychical Research* 73, no. 897. (October 2009): 207–08.

211. Berger and Berger, *The Encyclopedia of Parapsychology*, 420.

212. Ibid., 431; Kloosterman, Ingrid, "Psychical Research and Parapsychology Interpreted: Suggestions from the International Historiography of Psychical Research and Parapsychology for Investigating its History in the Netherlands." *History of the Human Sciences* 25, no. 2 (2012): 15.

213. Berger and Berger, *The Encyclopedia of Parapsychology*, 431.

214. Ibid., 44, 291, 434–35.

215. Ibid., 71, 436–37.

216. Ibid., 438.

217. Ibid., 438; Fodor, *An Encyclopedia*, 386.

218. Berger and Berger, *The Encyclopedia of Parapsychology*, 444.

219. Ibid., 452.

220. Ibid., 452.

221. Ibid., 452.

222. Ibid., 452.

223. Ibid., 454.

224. Fodor, *An Encyclopedia,* 401.

225. Berger and Berger, *The Encyclopedia of Parapsychology*, 459; Fodor, *An Encyclopedia*, 402–03.

226. Berger and Berger, *The Encyclopedia of Parapsychology*, 460.

227. Ibid., 461.

228. Ibid., 461.

229. Ibid., 475; J. Fraser Nicol, "Historical Background." In *Handbook of Parapsychology.* Edited by Benjamin B. Wolman. New York: Van Nostrand Reinhold Company, 1977: 310.

230. Berger and Berger, *The Encyclopedia of Parapsychology*, 476.

231. Helene Pleasants, ed. *Biographical Dictionary of Parapsychology.* New York: Helix Press, 1964: 365

232. Berger and Berger, *The Encyclopedia of Parapsychology*, 476.

233. Richard S. Broughton, *Parapsychology: The Controversial Science.* New York: Ballantine, 1991: 148.

234. Berger and Berger, *The Encyclopedia of Parapsychology*, 3.

235. Berger and Berger, *The Encyclopedia of Parapsychology*, 6.

236. Carlos S. Alvarado, "Mediumship, Psychical Research, Dissociation, and the Powers of the Subconscious Mind," *Journal of Parapsychology* 78, no. 1 (March 2014): 98–114.

237. Alvarado, "Mediumship," 98.

238. "Welcome to the AZIRE." The Alvarado Zingrone Institute for Research and Education. Accessed June 18, 2021 from https://theazire.org/.

239. P. M. H. Atwater, "The Three Near-Death Experiences of P.M.H. Atwater." *Narrative Inquiry in Bioethics* 10, no. 1 (Spring 2020): E13–15; P. M. H. Atwater. "The Website of PMH Atwater" (2018). Accessed June 18, 2021 from http://www.pmhatwater.com/.

240. P. M. H. Atwater, "Children's Near-Death States: New Research, A New Model." *Journal of Spirituality and Paranormal Studies* 30 (2007): 52–53

241. Atwater, "Children's Near-Death States," 54.

242. "Loyd Auerbach," The Parapsychological Association. Accessed June 18, 2021 from https://www.parapsych.org/users/profparanormal/profile.aspx.

243. Loyd Auerbach, Dominic Parker, and Sheila Smith, "Anomalous Cognition/ESP and Psychokinesis Research in the United States." In *Extrasensory Perception: Support, Skepticism, and Science.* Vol. 1. Edited by Edwin C. May and Sonali Bhatt Marwaha. Santa Barbara, CA: Praeger, 2015: 225–49.

244. Zofia Weaver, "A Parapsychological Naturalist: A Tribute to Mary Rose Barrington." *Journal of Scientific Exploration* 34, no. 3 (2020): 599.

245. Berger and Berger, *The Encyclopedia of Parapsychology*, 27.

246. "Obituary: Raymond G. Bayless." *Journal of Near-Death Studies* 22, no. 4 (Summer 2004): 287.

247. Callum E. Cooper, "An Analysis of Exceptional Experiences Involving Telecommunication Technology." *Journal of Parapsychology* 78, no. 2 (September 2014): 209–10.

248. "About Us." Windbridge Research Center (2021). Accessed June 19, 2021 from https://www.windbridge.org/about-us/.

249. Julie Beischel, "Mental Mediumship Research." *Psi Encylopedia.* Society for Psychical Research. (January 2018). Accessed June 19, 2021 from https://psi-encyclopedia.spr.ac.uk/articles/mental-mediumship-research.

250. D. J. Bem, "Feeling the Future: Experimental Evidence for Anomalous Retroactive Influence on Cognition and Affect." *Journal of Personality and Social Psychology* 100 (2011): 407–25.

251. Bem, "Feeling the Future," 407.

252. Ibid., 407

253. Ibid., 417.

254. Ibid., 409–10.

255. Charles M. Judd and Bertram Gawronski, "Editorial Comment." *Journal of Personality and Social Psychology* 100, no. 3 (2011): 406.

256. Ibid., 406.

257. K. M. Wehrstein, "William Bengston and Energy Healing." *PSI Encyclopedia.* (October 2017). (London: The Society for Psychical Research). Accessed June 19, 2021 from https://psi-encyclopedia.spr.ac.uk/articles/william-bengston-and-energy-healing.

258. Ibid.

259. Berger and Berger, *The Encyclopedia of Parapsychology*, 31, 105.

260. M. Duggan, "Dick Bierman." *Psi Encyclopedia* (London: The Society for Psychical Research, February 25, 2020). Accessed July 6, 2021 from https://psi-encyclopedia.spr.ac.uk/articles/dick-bierman.

261. "Massimo Biondi." (The Parapsychological Association: 2021). Accessed December 29, 2021 from https://www.parapsych.org/users/mbiondi/profile.aspx.

262. Berger and Berger, *The Encyclopedia of Parapsychology*, 37.

263. Susan J. Blackmore, "A Psychological Theory of the Out-of-Body Experience." *Journal of Parapsychology* 48, no. 3 (September 1984): 201–18.

264. Susan Blackmore, "First Person—Into the Unknown" (November 4, 2000). Accessed June 20, 2021 from https://www.susanblackmore.uk/journalism/first-person-into-the-unknown/.

265. Berger and Berger, *The Encyclopedia of Parapsychology*, 40–41.

266. Ibid., 47, 268; Rosemarie Anderson, "William G. Braud (1942–2012)." *The Humanistic Psychologist* 41, no. 1 (2013): 94–95.

267. Rosemarie Anderson and William Braud, *Transforming Self and Others through Research: Transpersonal Research Methods and Skills for the Human Sciences and Humanities.* Albany: State University of New York Press, 2011: 233–34.

268. Ibid., 243–45.

269. William G. Braud and Stephen P. Dennis, "Geophysical Variables and Behavior: LVIII. Autonomic Activity, Hemolysis, and Biological Psychokinesis: Possible Relationships with Geomagnetic Field Activity." *Perceptual and Motor Skills* 68, no. 3 (June 1989): 1243–54.

270. Berger and Berger, *The Encyclopedia of Parapsychology*, 48.

271. Stephen Braude, "The Need for Negativity." *Journal of Scientific Exploration* 35, no. 2 (2021): 263.

272. Ibid., 263.

273. Sara R. Feather and Robert Brier, "The Possible Effect of the Checker in Precognition Tests." *Journal of Parapsychology* 32, no. 3 (September 1968): 167.

274. Feather and Brier, "The Possible Effect," 172.

275. M. Duggan, "Richard S. Broughton." *Psi Encyclopedia* (May 25, 2020). (London: The Society for Psychical Research). Accessed June 22, 2021 from https://psi-encyclopedia.spr.ac.uk/articles/richard-s-broughton.

276. Ibid.; Berger and Berger, *The Encyclopedia of Parapsychology*, 51.

277. Berger and Berger, *The Encyclopedia of Parapsychology*, 198.

278. Duggan, "Richard S. Broughton."

279. R. L. Philibert, "Remi Cadoret, M.D.; His Career and Achievements." *Posters.* Paper 22. Samuel B. Guze Symposium on Alcoholism. https://digitalcommons.wustl.edu/guzeposter2006/22/.

280. Berger and Berger, *The Encyclopedia of Parapsychology*, 57.

281. Jarl Fahler and Remi J. Cadoret, "ESP Card Test of College Students with and without Hypnosis." In *Basic Research in Parapsychology*, 2nd edition. Edited by K. Ramakrishna Rao. Jefferson, NC: McFarland and Company, 2001: 251–61.

282. K. M. Wehrstein, "Etzel Cardeña." *Psi Encyclopedia.* (June 9, 2021). (London: The Society for Psychical Research). Accessed June 22, 2021 from https://psi-encyclopedia.spr.ac.uk/articles/etzel-carde%C3%B1a#footnote4_ge27se6.

283. Etzel Cardeña and D. Marcusson-Clavertz, "Changes in State of Consciousness and Psi in Ganzfeld and Hypnosis Conditions." *Journal of Parapsychology* 84, (2020): 66–84.

284. Ibid., 66–84.

285. Berger and Berger, *The Encyclopedia of Parapsychology*, 62.

286. M. Willin, "Manfred Cassirer." *Psi Encyclopedia.* (May 25, 2021). (London: The Society for Psychical Research). Accessed June 22, 2021 from https://psi-encyclopedia.spr.ac.uk/articles/manfred-cassirer.

287. Carlos S. Alvarado, "Psychology and Parapsychology." (October 31, 2017). In *Psi Encyclopedia.* (London: The Society for Psychical Research). Accessed June 22, 2021 from https://psi-encyclopedia.spr.ac.uk/articles/psychology-and-parapsychology; Berger and Berger, *The Encyclopedia of Parapsychology*, 62.

288. Berger and Berger, *The Encyclopedia of Parapsychology*, 68.

289. Renaud Evrard, "Rémy Chauvin." *Journal of Scientific Exploration* 24, no. 2 (2010): 299–303.

290. John Ruch, "This Physicist Saw Promise in the Paranormal, but Now His Legacy Could be Lost." *The Washington Post* (Summer 2019): 9AD.

291. Neil Dagnall, Kenneth G. Drinkwater, Ciarán O'Keeffe, Annalisa Ventola, Brian Laythe, Michael A. Jawer, Brandon Massullo, Giovanni B. Caputo, and James Houran, "Things That Go Bump in the Literature: An Environmental Appraisal of 'Haunted Houses.'" *Frontiers in Psychology* 11 (June 12, 2020): 1.

292. Ibid., 3.

293. Ibid., 6.

294. Gertrude Schmeidler, "Obituary: E. Douglas Dean, 1916–2001." *Journal of Parapsychology* 65, no. 4 (December 2001): 417.

295. Berger and Berger, *The Encyclopedia of Parapsychology*, 99.

296. Ibid., 418.

297. Michael Duggan, "Deborah Delanoy" (February 25, 2020). *Psi Encyclopedia.* (London: The Society for Psychical Research). Accessed June 23, 2021 from https://psi-encyclopedia.spr.ac.uk/articles/deborah-delanoy.

298. David P. Luke, Deborah Delanoy, and Simon J. Sherwood, "Psi May Look Like Luck: Perceived Luckiness and Beliefs about Luck in Relation to Precognition." *Journal of the Society for Psychical Research* 72, no. 4 (October 2008): 193–207.

299. Garret Yount, Arnaud Delorme, Dean Radin, Loren Carpenter, Kenneth Rachlin, Joyce Anastasia, Meredith Pierson, Sue Steele, Heather Mandell, Aimee Chagnon, and Helané Wahbeh, "Energy Medicine Treatments for Hand and Wrist Pain: A Pilot Study." *Explore: The Journal of Science and Healing* 17 (2021): 11–21.

300. Kenneth Drinkwater, Andrew Denovan, Neil Dagnall, and Andrew Parker, "Predictors of Hearing Electronic Voice Phenomena in Random Noise: Schizotypy, Fantasy Proneness, and Paranormal Beliefs." *Journal of Parapsychology* 84, no. 1 (2020): 96–113.

301. Renaud Evrard, "Yvonne Duplessis, 1912–2017." *Journal of Scientific Exploration* 31, no. 4 (2017): 687–90.

302. Rosemarie Pilkington, "Jule Eisenbud, 1908–1999: A Profile in Courage." *Journal of Parapsychology* 63, no. 2 (June 1999): 163–66.

303. Berger and Berger, *The Encyclopedia of Parapsychology*,123–24.

304. Pilkington, "Jule Eisenbud," 163–66.

305. Berger and Berger, *The Encyclopedia of Parapsychology*, 125.

306. M. Willin, "Arthur Ellison." *Psi Encyclopedia.* (London: The Society for Psychical Research, April 26, 2021). Accessed July 6, 2021 from https://psi-encyclopedia.spr.ac.uk/articles/arthur-ellison.

307. Deborah L. Erickson, "Intuition, Telepathy, and Interspecies Communication: A Multidisciplinary Perspective." *NeuroQuantology* 9, no. 1 (March 2011): 145–52.

308. Berger and Berger, *The Encyclopedia of Parapsychology*, 131.

309. Alejandro Parra and Juan Carlos Argibay, "Exploratory Study of the Temperament Theory and Paranormal Experiences." *Journal of the Society for Psychical Research* 80, no. 4. (2016): 216.

310. Ibid., 216.

311. Glynn Custred, "Psychical Research and the Outer Limits of Scientific Inquiry." *Cosmos and History: The Journal of Natural and Social Philosophy* 13, no. 2 (2017): 117.

312. M. Duggan, "Sally Rhine Feather." *Psi Encyclopedia.* (London: The Society for Psychical Research, April 27, 2020). Accessed July 6, 2021 from https://psi-encyclopedia.spr.ac.uk/articles/sally-rhine-feather.

313. Dean I. Radin and D. C. Ferrari, "Effects of Consciousness on the Fall of Dice: A Meta-Analysis." *Journal of Scientific Exploration* 5, no. 1 (1991): 79–80.

314. Guy Lyon Playfair, "Obituaries: David Fontana, 1934–2010." *Journal of the Society for Psychical Research* 75, no. 3 (2011): 168–69.

315. Berger and Berger, *The Encyclopedia of Parapsychology*, 162.

316. M. Willin, "Anita Gregory." *Psi Encyclopedia.* (London: The Society for Psychical Research, June 29, 2021). Accessed July 6, 2021 from https://psi-encyclopedia.spr.ac.uk/articles/anita-gregory.

317. M. Willin, "Maurice Grosse." *Psi Encyclopedia.* (London: The Society for Psychical Research, April 2, 2021). Accessed July 6, 2021 from https://psi-encyclopedia.spr.ac.uk/articles/maurice-grosse.

318. Lance Storm, "In Memory of Erlendur Haraldsson who Died Sunday, November 22, 2020." *Australian Journal of Parapsychology* 20, no. 2 (2020): 201.

319. Erlendur Haraldsson. "Alleged Encounters with the Dead: The Importance of Violent Death in 337 New Cases." *Journal of Parapsychology* 73 (April 2009): 91–118.

320. M. Duggan, "Nicola Holt." *Psi Encyclopedia.* (London: The Society for Psychical Research, July 11, 2020). Accessed July 6, 2021 from https://psi-encyclopedia.spr.ac.uk/articles/nicola-holt.

321. Berger and Berger, *The Encyclopedia of Parapsychology*, 185.

322. "James Houran," Parapsychological Association. Accessed July 6, 2021 from https://parapsych.org/users/jhouran/profile.aspx.

323. James Houran, "Research Note: What's in a Name? The Best Descriptor for People Reporting Anomalous Experiences." *Australian Journal of Parapsychology* 18, no. 2 (2018): 195.

324. Michael A. Jawer, Brandon Massullo, Brian Laythe, and James Houran, "Environmental 'Gestalt Influences' Pertinent to Studies of Haunted Houses." *Journal of the Society for Psychical Research* 84, no. 2 (2020): 65–92.

325. M. Duggan, "Jack Hunter." *Psi Encyclopedia.* (London: The Society for Psychical Research, March 17, 2020). Accessed July 6, 2021 from https://psi-encyclopedia.spr.ac.uk/articles/jack-hunter.

326. Jack Hunter, "Talking with the Spirits: Anthropology and Interpreting Spirit Communications." *Journal of the Society for Psychical Research* 75, no. 904 (2011): 129–41.

327. Berger and Berger, *The Encyclopedia of Parapsychology*, 201.

328. Harvey J. Irwin, "Belief in the Paranormal and a Sense of Control Over Life." *European Journal of Parapsychology* 15 (2000): 68–78.

329. Adrian Parker and Nemo C. Mörck, "Martin Johnson 1930–2011." *Journal of Parapsychology* 75, no. 2 (2011): 353–59.

330. Berger and Berger, *The Encyclopedia of Parapsychology*, 221.

331. Ibid., 221.

332. Yoshishisa Wada, "Chojougenshou No Toraenikusa (The Elusiveness Problem of Psi), Edited by Toshio Kasahara." *Journal of Parapsychology* 57, no. 3 (September 1993): 303.

333. M. Duggan, "Edward F. Kelly." *Psi Encyclopedia.* (London: The Society for Psychical Research, November 19, 2019). Accessed July 6, 2021 from https://psi-encyclopedia.spr.ac.uk/articles/edward-f-kelly.

334. M. Duggan, "Emily Williams Kelly." *Psi Encyclopedia.* (London: The Society for Psychical Research, December 17, 2020). Accessed July 6, 2021 from https://psi-encyclopedia.spr.ac.uk/articles/emily-williams-kelly.

335. Wim H. Kramer, "Experiences with Psi Counseling in Holland." In *Perspectives of Clinical*

Parapsychology: An Introductory Reader. Edited by Wim H. Kramer, Eberhard Bauer, and Gerd. H. Hövelman. Bunnik: Stichting Het Johan Borgman Fonds, 2012: 7–19.

336. Carlos S. Alvarado, "Curso de Parapsicología (Course of Parapsychology)." *Journal of Parapsychology* 61, no. 2 (June 1997): 173–74; Berger and Berger, *The Encyclopedia of Parapsychology*, 230.

337. Block, *Researching the Paranormal*, 225.

338. Jeffrey Kripal, "Secret Lives of the Superpowers: The Remote Viewing Literature and the Imaginal." In *Handbook of Spiritualism and Channeling* Edited by Cathy Gutierrez. Brill: Leiden, 2015: 421.

339. Jeffrey J. Kripal, *Authors of the Impossible: The Paranormal and the Sacred.* Chicago: University of Chicago Press, 2010.

340. K. M. Wehrstein, "Stanley Krippner." *Psi Encyclopedia.* (London: The Society for Psychical Research, February 2, 2021). Accessed July 6, 2021 from https://psi-encyclopedia.spr.ac.uk/articles/stanley-krippner.

341. Rense Lange and James Houran, "Delusions of the Paranormal: A Haunting Question of Perception." *The Journal of Nervous and Mental Disease* 186, no. 10 (October 1998): 63745.

342. Madelaine Lawrence, "Near-Death and Other Transpersonal Experiences Occurring during Catastrophic Events." *American Journal of Hospice and Palliative Medicine* 34, no. 5 (2017): 486–92.

343. Brian Laythe and James Houran, "Concomitant Object Movements and EMF-Spikes at a Purported Haunt." *Journal of the Society for Psychical Research* 83, no. 4 (2019): 222.

344. D. Bierman, H. Gerding, and H. van Dongen, "Psi Research in the Netherlands." *Psi Encyclopedia.* (London: The Society for Psychical Research, December 6, 2019). Accessed July 5, 2021 from https://psi-encyclopedia.spr.ac.uk/articles/psi-research-netherlands.

345. Dean Radin and Eva Lobach, "Toward Understanding the Placebo Effect: Investigating a Possible Retrocausal Factor." *The Journal of Alternative and Complementary Medicine* 13, no. 7 (2007): 734.

346. Pim van Lommel, Ruud van Wees, Vincent Meyers, and Ingrid Elfferich, "Near-Death Experience in Survivors of Cardiac Arrest: A Prospective Study in the Netherlands." *Lancet* 358, no. 9298 (2001): 2039–45.

347. Michaeleen Maher, "Quantitative Investigation of the General Wayne Inn." *Journal of Parapsychology* 64 (December 2000): 365–90.

348. Michaeleen Maher, "Thoughts on Death and Its Survival." *Journal of Religion and Psychical Research* 27, no. 1 (2004): 3.

349. Everton Maraldi, Fatima Regina Machado, and Wellington Zangari, "Importance of a Psychosocial Approach for a Comprehensive Understanding of Mediumship." *Journal of Scientific Exploration* 24, no. 2 (2010): 181–96.

350. M. Duggan, "Experimental Psi Research in Asia and Australia." *Psi Encyclopedia.* (London: The Society for Psychical Research, April 10, 2021). Accessed July 5, 2021 from https://psi-encyclopedia.spr.ac.uk/articles/experimental-psi-research-asia-and-australia.

351. Sonali Bhatt Marwaha and Edwin C. May, "The Multiphasic Model of Precognition: The Rationale." *Journal of Parapsychology* 79, no. 1 (2015): 5–19.

352. Berger and Berger, *The Encyclopedia of Parapsychology*, 259–60.

353. R. A. McConnell and Haakon Forwald, "Psychokinetic Placement I: A Re-Examination of the Forwald-Durham Experiment." *Journal of Parapsychology* 31, no. 1 (March 1967): 51–69.

354. McConnell and Forwald, "Psychokinetic Placement I," 68.

355. M. Duggan, "Julia Mossbridge." *Psi Encyclopedia* (London: The Society for Psychical Research, January 7, 2020). Accessed July 5, 2021 from https://psi-encyclopedia.spr.ac.uk/articles/julia-mossbridge.

356. Julia Mossbridge, Patrizio Tressoldi, and Jessica Utts, "Predictive Physiological Anticipation Preceding Seemingly Unpredictable Stimuli: A Meta-Analysis." *Frontiers in Psychology* 3 (October 2012): 1–18.

357. Julia A. Mossbridge, Marcia Nisam, and Adam Crabtree, "Can Hypnotic Suggestion Induce Feelings of Unconditional Love and Supernormal Performance?" *Spirituality in Clinical Practice* 8 no. 1 (2021): 30, 44.

358. Berger and Berger, *The Encyclopedia of Parapsychology*, 280–81.

359. Sergio A. Rueda, "Tribute to J. Ricardo Musso (1917–1989)." *Journal of Parapsychology* 53 no. 4 (December 1, 1989): 277–80.

360. Ibid., 278.

361. George A. Mashour, Lori Frank, Alexander Batthyany, Ann Marie Kolanowski, Michael Nahm, Dena Schulman-Green, Bruce Greyson, Serguei Pakhomov, Jason Karlawish, and Raj C. Shah, "Paradoxical Lucidity: A Potential Paradigm Shift for the Neurobiology and Treatment of Severe Dementias." *Alzheimer's and Dementia* 15, no. 8 (2019): 1112.

362. M. Duggan, "Roger Nelson." *Psi Encyclopedia* (London: The Society for Psychical Research, February 10, 2020). Accessed July 5, 2021 from https://psi-encyclopedia.spr.ac.uk/articles/roger-nelson.

363. Ibid.

364. M. Willin, "Ralph Noyes." *Psi Encyclopedia.* (London: The Society for Psychical Research, April 26, 2021). Accessed July 5, 2021 from https://psi-encyclopedia.spr.ac.uk/articles/ralph-noyes.

365. M. Duggan, "Ciaran O'Keeffe." *Psi Encyclopedia.* (London: The Society for Psychical Research, July 15, 2020). Accessed July 4, 2021 from https://psi-encyclopedia.spr.ac.uk/articles/ciaran-o%E2%80%99keeffe.

366. Berger and Berger, *The Encyclopedia*, 303.

367. Ibid.

368. Juan Gimeno. "David Efron: Biography of a Forgotten Pioneer in Psychical Research." *Journal of the Society for Psychical Research* 83, no. 2 (2019): 103.

369. Stanley Krippner. "In Memoriam: Michael Persinger." *Journal of Parapsychology* 82, no. 2 (2018): 102–3.

370. Michael A. Persinger. "Geophysical Variables and Behavior: XXX. Intense Paranormal Experiences Occur During Days of Quiet, Global, Geomagnetic Activity." *Perceptual and Motor Skills* 61 (1985): 320–22.

371. Leslie A. Ruttan, Michael A. Persinger, and Stanley Koren. "Enhancement of Temporal Lobe-Related Experiences During Brief Exposures to Milligauss Intensity Extremely Low Frequency Magnetic Fields." *Journal of Bioelectricity* 9, no. 1 (1990): 33–54.

372. Alan Murdie. "Obituary: Guy Lyon Playfair 1935–2018." *Journal of the Society for Psychical Research* 82, no. 3 (2018): 189.

373. Ibid., 189–90.

374. Ibid., 191.

375. Berger and Berger, *The Encyclopedia*, 329.

376. Ibid.

377. Berger and Berger, *The Encyclopedia*, 342–43. H. Jenkins. "Andrija Puharich." *Psi Encyclopedia.* (London: The Society for Psychical Research, June 19, 2020). Accessed July 4, 2021 from https://psi-encyclopedia.spr.ac.uk/articles/andrija-puharich.

378. Russel Targ. "What do We Know About Psi? The First Decade of Remote-Viewing Research and Operations at Stanford Research Institute." *Journal of Scientific Exploration* 33, no. 4 (2019): 569–92.

379. "About: Weaving Together Knowledge and Knowing." (2021). Institute of Noetic Sciences (IONS). Accessed July 4, 2021 from https://noetic.org/about/.

380. R. McLuhan. "Dean Radin." *Psi Encyclopedia.* (London: The Society for Psychical Research, April 2, 2021). Accessed July 4, 2021 from https://psi-encyclopedia.spr.ac.uk/articles/dean-radin.

381. Dean I. Radin. "Unconscious Perception of Future Emotions: An Experiment in Presentiment." *Journal of Scientific Exploration* 11, no. 2 (1997): 163–80.

382. Kennedy, J. E. "New Frontiers of Human Science: A Festschrift for K. Ramakrishna Rao. (Review)." *Journal of Parapsychology* 67, no. 2 (Fall 2003): 395–99.

383. Berger and Berger, *The Encyclopedia*, 350–51.

384. Robert A. Charman and David Ellis. "Mediums and a Possible Source of Communication: A Proposed Experiment." *Journal of the Society for Psychical Research* 79, issue 920 (2015): 190.

385. Berger and Berger, *The Encyclopedia*, 364. And C. E. Cooper. "D. Scott Rogo." *Psi Encyclopedia* (London: The Society for Psychical Research, April 6, 2019). Accessed July 4, 2021 from https://psi-encyclopedia.spr.ac.uk/articles/d-scott-rogo.

386. K. M. Wehrstein. "William Roll." *Psi Encyclopedia.* (London: The Society for Psychical Research, June 29, 2021). Accessed July 4, 2021 from https://psi-encyclopedia.spr.ac.uk/articles/william-roll.

387. William G. Roll. "Poltergeists, Electromagnetism, and Consciousness." *Journal of Scientific Exploration* 17, no. 1 (2003): 76.

388. Berger and Berger, *An Encyclopedia,* 372.

389. John Palmer. "Milan Ryzl: 1928–2011." *Journal of Parapsychology* 75, no. 2 (Fall 2011): 359–61.

390. Berger and Berger, *The Encyclopedia,* 378–79. Ruth Reinsel. "Obituary: Gertrude R. Schmeidler: 1912–2009." *Journal of Parapsychology* 73 (Spring 2009): 163.

391. Berger and Berger, *The Encyclopedia,* 394.

392. Gertrude Raffel Schmeidler and Gardner Murphy. "The Influence of Belief and Disbelief in ESP upon Individual Scoring Levels." *Journal of Experimental Psychology* 36, no. 3 (June 1946): 275.

393. Reinsel, "Obituary," 164.

394. Marilyn Schlitz. "Obituaries: Helmut Schmidt 1928–2011." *Journal of Parapsychology* 75, no. 2 (2011): 349.

395. Ibid., 350.

396. Richard Wiseman, Caroline Watt, and Diana Kornbrot. "Registered Reports: An Early Example and Analysis." *PeerJ* 7 (2019): 4–5.

397. Berger and Berger, *The Encyclopedia,* 389.

398. Jacqueline Amati Mehler. "Letter from Italian Psychoanalytical Association." *The International Journal of Psychoanalysis* 95, no. 2 (2014): 191–93.

399. D. Si Ahmed. "Psychoanalysis and Psi." *Psi Encyclopedia* (London: The Society for Psychical Research, May 9, 2019). Accessed July 3, 2021 from https://psi-encyclopedia.spr.ac.uk/articles/psychoanalysis-and-psi.

400. G. Hayward. "Rupert Sheldrake." *Psi Encyclopedia,* (London: The Society for Psychical Research, March 2, 2020). Accessed July 3, 2021 from https://psi-encyclopedia.spr.ac.uk/articles/rupert-sheldrake.

401. Rupert Sheldrake and Pamela Smart. "Videotaped Experiments on Telephone Telepathy." *Journal of Parapsychology* 67, no. 1 (Spring 2003): 147–66.

402. Andreas Sommer. "Normalizing the Supernormal," 18–44.

403. K. M. Wehrstein. "Russell Targ." *Psi Encyclopedia* (London: The Society for Psychical Research, May 6, 2019). Accessed July 3, 2021 from https://psi-encyclopedia.spr.ac.uk/articles/russell-targ.

404. K. M. Wehrstein. "Charles Tart." *Psi Encyclopedia* (London: The Society for Psychical Research, April 6, 2019). Accessed July 3, 2021

from https://psi-encyclopedia.spr.ac.uk/articles/charles-tart.

405. Charles T. Tart. "The Archives of Scientists' Transcendent Experiences: TASTE." *Journal of Near-Death Studies* 19, no. 2 (Winter 2000): 132–34. "TASTE: The Archive for Scientists' Transcendent Experiences." Academy for the Advancement of Postmaterialist Sciences. Accessed July 2, 2021 from https://www.aapsglobal.com/taste/.

406. M. Duggan. "Michael Thalbourne." *Psi Encyclopedia.* (London: The Society for Psychical Research, March 5, 2020): Accessed July 2, 2021 from https://psi-encyclopedia.spr.ac.uk/articles/michael-thalbourne.

407. Michael A. Thalbourne. "Psychiatry, the Mystical, and the Paranormal." *Journal of Parapsychology* 70, no. 1 (Spring 2006): 143–65.

408. Renaud Evrard. "Institut Métapsychique International." *PSI Encyclopedia.* (August 3, 2017). Accessed June 16, 2021 from https://psi-encyclopedia.spr.ac.uk/articles/institut-m%C3%A9tapsychique-international.

409. Robert Tocquet. *The Magic of Numbers.* New York: A.S. Barnes, 1963: 37.

410. M. Duggan. "Patrizio Tressoldi." *Psi Encyclopedia.* (London: The Society for Psychical Research, January 11, 2020). Accessed July 2, 2021 from https://psi-encyclopedia.spr.ac.uk/articles/patrizio-tressoldi.

411. Enrico Facco, Fabio Fracas, and Patricio Tressoldi. "Moving Beyond the Concept of Altered State of Consciousness: The Non-Ordinary Mental Expressions (NOMEs)." *Advances in Social Sciences Research Journal* 8, no. 3 (March 2021): 615–31.

412. Berger and Berger, *The Encyclopedia,* 146.

413. Erlendur Haraldsson. "Robert L. Van de Castle: 1927–2014." *Journal of Parapsychology* 78, no. 1 (Spring 2014): 126–27.

414. M. Duggan. "Mario Varvoglis." *Psi Encyclopedia.* (London: The Society for Psychical Research, December 14, 2019). Accessed July 2 from https://psi-encyclopedia.spr.ac.uk/articles/mario-varvoglis.

415. Mario Varvoglis and Peter A. Bancel. "Micro-Psychokinesis: Exceptional or Universal?" *Journal of Parapsychology* 80, no. 1 (Spring 2016): 37–44.

416. Ibid.

417. M. Duggan. "Annalisa Ventola." *Psi Encyclopedia* (January 14, 2020). (London: The Society

for Psychical Research). Accessed July 2, 2021 from https://psi-encyclopedia.spr.ac.uk/articles/annalisa-ventola.

418. Brian Laythe, James Houran, and Annalisa Ventola. "A Split-Sample Psychometric Study of 'Haunters.'" *Journal of the Society for Psychical Research* 81, no. 4 (2018): 193–218.

419. Ibid., 210.

420. Ibid., 197 and 210.

421. Annalisa Ventola, James Houran, Brian Laythe, Lance Storm, Alejandro Parra, John Dixon, and John G. Kruth. "A Transliminal 'Dis-Ease' Model of 'Poltergeist Agents.'" *Journal of the Society for Psychical Research* 83, no. 3 (2019): 144–71.

422. Ibid., 147.

423. Ibid., 163.

424. "Scientists: Helané Wahbeh, ND, MCR." (IONS, 2021). Accessed July 2, 2021 from https://noetic.org/profile/helane-wahbeh/.

425. Helané Wahbeh, Dean Radin, Garrett Yount, Arnaud Delorme, and Loren Carpenter. "Effects of the Local and Geocosmic Environment on the Efficacy of Energy Medicine Treatments: An Exploratory Study." *Explore: The Journal of Science and Healing* 17, no. 1 (January 2021): 40–44.

426. M. Duggan. "Caroline Watt." *Psi Encyclopedia.* (February 14, 2020). (London: The Society for Psychical Research). Accessed July 2, 2021 from https://psi-encyclopedia.spr.ac.uk/articles/caroline-watt.

427. C. Watt and R. Wiseman. "'Twitter' as a New Research Tool: Proof of Principle with a Mass Participation Test of Remote Viewing." *European Journal of Parapsychology* 25 (2010): 89–100.

428. Caroline Watt. "Precognitive Dreaming: Investigating Anomalous Cognition and Psychological Factors." *Journal of Parapsychology* 78, no. 1 (Spring 2014): 115–25.

429. M. Willin. "Zofia Weaver." *Psi Encyclopedia.* (2021). Accessed July 2, 2021 from https://psi-encyclopedia.spr.ac.uk/articles/zofia-weaver.

430. Debra H. Weiner and Nancy L. Zingrone. "In the Eye of the Beholder: Further Research on the 'Checker Effect.'" *Journal of Parapsychology* 53 (September 1989): 203–31.

431. Ibid., 229.

432. Zofia Weaver. "In Memoriam: Donald J. West, M.D., D. litt., FRCPsych (1924–2020)." *Journal of Parapsychology* 84, no. 1 (2020): 12–13.

433. Berger and Berger, *The Encyclopedia,* 463.

434. "Obituary: Rhea White, M.L.S." *Journal of Near-Death Studies* 25, no. 3 (Spring 2007): 199.

435. Rhea A. White. "The Human Component in Exceptional Experience." *Journal of Religion and Psychical Research* 20, no. 1 (1997): 23–29.

436. Ibid., 24.

437. "About: Weaving Together Knowledge and Knowing." Accessed July 1, 2021 from https://noetic.org/about/.

438. "Scientists: Garret Yount, Ph.D." Accessed July 1, 2021 from https://noetic.org/profile/garret-yount/.

439. Garret Yount, Shrikant Patil, Umang Dave, Leonardo Alves-dos-Santos, Kimberly Gon, Robert Arauz, and Kenneth Rachlin. "Evaluation of Biofield Treatment Dose and Distance in a Model of Cancer Cell Death." *The Journal of Alternative and Complementary Medicine* 19, no. 2 (2013): 126–27.

440. M. Duggan. "Nancy L. Zingrone." (March 10, 2020). *Psi Encyclopedia* (London: The Society for Psychical Research). Accessed June 29, 2021 from https://psi-encyclopedia.spr.ac.uk/articles/nancy-l-zingrone.

441. Carlos S. Alvarado and Nancy L. Zingrone. "Features of Out-of-Body Experiences: Relationships to Frequency, Wilfulness of and Previous Knowledge about the Experience." *Journal of the Society for Psychical Research* 79, no. 2 (April 2015): 98–111).

442. Ibid., 102–4.

443. Berger and Berger, *The Encyclopedia,* 14.

444. Fodor, *An Encyclopedia,* 25.

445. Berger and Berger, *The Encyclopedia,* 21.

446. Ibid., 128.

447. Carlos S. Alvarado. "Distortions of the Past." *Journal of Scientific Exploration* 26, no. 3. (2012): 616.

448. Berger and Berger, *The Encyclopedia,* 433.

449. Ibid., 39.

450. Fodor, *An Encyclopedia,* 33.

451. Marion Meade. *Madame Blavatsky: The Woman Behind the Myth.* New York: G.P. Putnam's Sons, 1980: 461–62.

452. G. E. Bentley Jr. "Blake and the Paranormal." *Notes and Queries* 64, no. 1 (March 2017): 62.

453. "Our Mission." Edgar Cayce's A.R.E.: Association for Research and Enlightenment. (2021).

Accessed June 24, 2021 from https://www.edgar cayce.org/about-us/our-mission/

454. Berger and Berger, *The Encyclopedia,* 78.

455. Ibid., 78.

456. Michael E. Tymn. "An 'Interview' with Sir William Crookes." *Journal of Spirituality and Paranormal Studies* 30, no. 2 (2007): 85.

457. Berger and Berger, *The Encyclopedia,* 79.

458. Nicol, "Historical Background," 313.

459. Berger and Berger, *The Encyclopedia,* 83.

460. Jack Harrison Pollack, *Croiset the Clairvoyant: The Story of the Amazing Dutchman.* Garden City: Doubleday & Company, 1964: 6.

461. Ibid., 5–7, 62.

462. "Geraldine Dorothy Cummins." In *Gale Literature: Contemporary Authors.* Farmington Hills, MI: Gale, 2002. *Gale Literature Resource Center.* Velma O'Donoghue Greene. "Writing Women for a Modern Ireland: Geraldine Cummins and Susanne Day." In *Women in Irish Drama: A Century of Authorship and Representation.* Edited by Melissa Sihra. Houndmills: Palgrave Macmillan, 2007: 42–43.

463. Robert W. Delp. "Andrew Jackson Davis: Prophet of American Spiritualism." *The Journal of American History* 54, no. 1 (June 1967): 55.

464. Marlene Tromp. *Altered States: Sex, Nation, Drugs, and Self-Transformation in Victorian Spiritualism.* New York: State University of New York Press, 2006: 15–16.

465. Ibid., 81–85.

466. Fodor, *An Encyclopedia,* 90.

467. Berger and Berger, *The Encyclopedia,* 117.

468. Ibid., 138.

469. Ibid., 146.

470. Eileen. J. Garrett. "My Life as a Search for the Meaning of Mediumship." In *The ESP Reader.* Edited by David C. Knight. New York: Grosset & Dunlap, 1969: 191.

471. Ibid., 191–96.

472. Louis Khourey. "Eileen Garrett: The Skeptical Medium." *TAT Journal* 2, no. 2 (1979) Accessed June 25, 2021 from http://www.searchwithin.org/download/eileen_garrett.pdf.

473. Ibid.

474. Berger and Berger, *The Encyclopedia,* 153.

475. Ibid., 155.

476. Ibid., 83–84, 159.

477. Fodor, *An Encyclopedia,* 156.

478. Berger and Berger, *The Encyclopedia,* 183.

479. Ibid., 184.

480. Marco Piccolino and Nicholas J. Wade. "The Frog's Dancing Master: Science, Seances, and the Transmission of Myths." *Journal of the History of the Neurosciences* 22, no. 1 (January 2013): 84.

481. Berger and Berger, *The Encyclopedia,* 190.

482. Norma Lee Browning. *The Psychic World of Peter Hurkos.* Garden City: Doubleday & Company, 1970: 71–73.

483. Rudolf Steiner. *The Steinerbooks Dictionary of the Psychic, Mystic, Occult.* Blauvelt: Rudolf Steiner Publications, 1973: 105.

484. Berger and Berger, *The Encyclopedia,* 197.

485. Ibid.

486. Norman S. Don, Bruce E. McDonough, and Charles A. Warren. "PSI Testing of a Controversial Psychic Under Controlled Conditions." *Journal of Parapsychology* 56, no. 2 (June 1992): 87–96.

487. Ibid., 88, 94–95.

488. Berger and Berger, *The Encyclopedia,* 228.

489. Erlendur Haraldsson. "Extraordinary Physical Phenomena in Poland: A Review of *Other Realities? The Enigma of Franek Kluski's Mediumship.*" *Journal of Parapsychology* 82, no. 2 (2018): 208–9.

490. Ibid., 208.

491. Berger and Berger, *The Encyclopedia,* 228–29.

492. Richard S. Broughton. *Parapsychology: The Controversial Science.* New York: Ballantine, 1991: 144.

493. Ibid., 149–50.

494. Caratelli, Giulio and Maria Luisa Felici. "An Important Subject at the Institut Métapsychique International: Jeanne Laplace. The 1927–1934 Experiments." *Journal of Scientific Exploration* 25, no. 3 (2011): 479–95.

495. *The ESP Reader.* Edited by David C. Knight. New York: Grosset & Dunlap, 1969: 154.

496. Ibid., 157–65.

497. Adam Crabtree. "Mesmerism and the Psychological Dimension of Mediumship." In *Handbook of Spiritualism and Channeling.* Edited by Cathy Gutierrez. Leiden: Brill, 2015: 22.

498. Berger and Berger, *The Encyclopedia,* 265.

499. Tromp, Marlene. "Queering the Séance: Bodies, Bondage, and Touching in Victorian Spiritualism." In *Handbook of Spiritualism and Chan-*

neling, vol. 9, edited by Cathy Gutierrez, 87–115. Leiden: Brill, 2015.

500. Miki Takasuna. "The Fukurai Affair: Parapsychology and the History of Psychology in Japan." *History of the Human Sciences* 25, no. 2 (2012): 153–54.

501. Stephen E. Braude. "The Mediumship of Carlos Mirabelli (1889–1951)." *Journal of Scientific Exploration* 31, no. 3. (2017): 435.

502. Ibid., 436–39.

503. Ibid., 452.

504. Michael Nahm, "Out of Thin Air?" 668–71.

505. Berger and Berger, *The Encyclopedia,* 275.

506. *The ESP Reader,* 356.

507. Michael Nahm. "The Development and Phenomena of a Circle for Physical Mediumship." *Journal of Scientific Exploration* 28, no. 2 (2014): 230.

508. Jan W. Vandersande. "Two Recent Materialization Seances with Kai Muegge." *Journal for Spiritual and Consciousness Studies* 28, no. 1 (2015): 61–66.

509. Ibid., 62–65.

510. Berger and Berger, *The Encyclopedia,* 278–79.

511. Ibid., 301.

512. Andrea Graus. "Discovering Palladino's Mediumship. Otero Acevedo, Lombroso, and the Quest for Authority." *Journal of the History of the Behavioural Sciences* 52, no. 3 (Summer 2016): 212.

513. Eric J. Dingwall. *Very Peculiar People: Portrait Studies in the Queer, the Abnormal, and the Uncanny.* New Hyde Park: University Books, 1962: 178–81.

514. Graus, "Discovering Palladino's Mediumship," 211–12.

515. Ibid., 183–85.

516. Berger and Berger, *The Encyclopedia,* 309–10.

517. Nahm, "Out of Thin Air?" 671–77.

518. Broughton, *Parapsychology,* 148–50.

519. Alan Gauld. "Two Cases from the Lost Years of Mrs. Piper." *Journal of the Society for Psychical Research* 78, no. 915 (April 2014): 65.

520. Berger and Berger, *The Encyclopedia,* 323.

521. Carlos S. Alvarado. "Charles Richet on Leonora Piper." *Journal of the Society for Psychical Research* 79, no. 918 (2015): 57.

522. Berger and Berger, *The Encyclopedia,* 322.

523. Gauld. "Two Cases," 66–68.

524. Paul F. Cunningham. "The Content-Source Problem in Modern Mediumship Research." *Journal of Parapsychology* 76, no. 2 (2012): 314.

525. Berger and Berger, *The Encyclopedia,* 380–81.

526. Nahm, "Out of Thin Air?" 665–67.

527. Berger and Berger, *The Encyclopedia,* 395.

528. Ibid., 401.

529. Richard Milner. "Wallace, Darwin, and the Spiritualism Scandal of 1876." *Skeptic* 20, no. 3 (2015): 27.

530. Ibid., 27 and 31.

531. Berger and Berger, *The Encyclopedia,* 416.

532. Ibid., 422–23.

533. Berger and Berger, *The Encyclopedia,* 435.

534. Michael E. Tymn. "Etta Wriedt: The Best Medium Ever?" *Journal of Spirituality and Paranormal Studies* 34, no. 4 (2011): 229–38.

535. Mulacz, Peter. "Eleonore Zugun: The Re-Evaluation of a Historic RSPK Case." *Journal of Parapsychology* 63, no. 1 (March 1999): 15.

536. Ibid., 17.

537. Ibid., 22–23.

538. Ibid., 26–32.

3

What Does the Research Say?

A Core Annotated Bibliography of Parapsychological Resources through the Decades

One of the most significant advances of science is the discovery that psychic, or psi, ability is real. But the world has heard too little about it and of its meaning for humankind. The question no longer should be "Do you believe in psi" but "Do you know the evidence for it?"[1]

This chapter is a collection of resources on various topics within the field of parapsychology so that you can browse the research, theories, and discussions for yourself. Sources are presented as an annotated bibliography that include citations *and* annotations. To present a unique overview of sources and to highlight the change and growth in research over time, sources are presented decade-by-decade beginning with the 1870s and ending with the 2020s. The resources listed in each decade contain a citation, a brief overview of the book or article, and keyword tags that indicate which aspect(s) of parapsychology are discussed. Keywords will help you locate articles relevant to a particular interest, for example poltergeists. Since many parapsychology resources incorporate multiple aspects of psi simultaneously, I found it useful to use keywords instead of attempting to categorize resources into specific topics.

The sources in this chapter represent a variety of types of research. There are primary research articles in which the authors describe a study or experiment they personally conducted to collect data on a certain topic. Then there are secondary research articles that include metaanalyses and/or literature reviews of primary research articles. Articles are from journals in a wide variety of disciplines: from the obvious parapsychology and psychology to philosophy, neuroscience, biomedicine, and more.

There are also memoirs and biographies of certain people, philosophical discussions, and historical overviews of figures, research, and theories. These resources are primarily books and journal articles, though there are a few popular magazine and newspaper articles sprinkled throughout. Taken together, the sources in this chapter represent the many lenses and disciplines through which parapsychology has been investigated *and* the diverse theories that have developed through the decades. Any omission of work is simply an oversight of mine and does not necessarily represent a criticism or judgment of that work. To be fair, it would take many years to compile *every* resource on parapsychology and it would be a never-ending task since articles and books on psi topics are published every month. My hope is that the sources listed below provide a well-rounded bibliography for those new (or relatively new) to the topic of parapsychology to start their research. Readers are encouraged to take this list and build upon it according to their own specific psi interests.

If you find a source you wish to know more about and/or access the entire document, remember that there are several ways to obtain that information. First, you can search article citations in Google Scholar. For many of the older books and articles, you may be able to find them in the public domain on sites like HathiTrust or Archive.org. If you can't obtain immediate access through any of these avenues, you can ask your local public or academic libraries for a copy, either through their own collections or through a process called interlibrary loan. Remember, too, that state colleges and universities are public universities that are open to visitors—you can access those libraries without necessarily being

1870s

Beard, George M. "Physiology of Mind-Reading." *Popular Science* (February 1877): 459–73.

Doctor George M. Beard presents a discussion on the physiology of mind-reading. He begins his article by discussing the rise of popularity of certain phenomena that have been known to researchers for many years. He reminds us,

> The phenomena of the emotional trance, for example, had been known for ages, but not until Mesmer forced them on the scientific world, by his public exhibitions and ill-founded theory of animal magnetism, did they receive any serious and intelligent study. Similarly the general fact that mind may so act on body as to produce involuntary and unconscious muscular motion was by no means unrecognized by physiologists, and yet not until the "mind-reading" excitement two years ago was it demonstrated that this principle could be utilized for the finding of any object or limited locality on which a subject, with whom an operator is in physical connection, concentrates his mind.[2]

Beard goes on to discuss the rise in popularity of "mesmeric games" and how they can be explained by an understanding of physiology and the subtle, unconscious physical movements of our body in certain situations. In these "games," a person would be removed from the room while all others decided on an object that the person must correctly identify upon their return. The group decides on an object and then calls the person back into the room. At this point, one or two members of the group place their hands upon the player; the idea being that the physical connection helps transmit psychical impressions between players. These games had hugely successful results and many pointed to them as proof of some psychical traits in action.

Beard, however, points to his own research that shows how these "games" can be explained in terms already known, not in unknown psychical concepts yet to be understood. Beard describes experiments that mirror exactly these games and details the various scenarios in which concepts of physiology explain the results. He discusses how physiology results in seemingly psychical performances in a wide range of "game" settings and he concludes by telling us, "It illustrates . . . the general principle of mind acting on body producing muscular tension in the direction of the locality on which the thoughts are concentrated."[3]

Keywords: physiology; mesmeric games; thought-transference

Crookes, William. *Researches in the Phenomena of Spiritualism.* London: J. Burns, 1874.

This work was originally printed in the *Quarterly Journal of Science.* Chemist and psychical researcher William Crookes presents insight into his research on certain psi phenomena such as mediumship and its associated phenomena including psychokinesis, telepathy, and more. He points out his scientific opinion on the value of engaging with psi phenomena when he writes, "I consider it the duty of scientific men . . . to examine phenomena which attract the attention of the public, in order to confirm their genuineness, or to explain, if possible, the delusions of the honest and to expose the tricks of deceivers."[4]

Though he was often targeted and criticized for engaging in psychical research, Crookes nevertheless continued his inquiry. In this work, he presents his research of the mediums Kate Fox, Daniel Dunglas Home, and Florence Cook (otherwise known as her spirit control, Katie King). Crookes tells us that he began this inquiry four years prior and had only intended to give it a passing interest. When he began to dive further into the research, however, he began to realize how complex the situation was. Here he outlines his experiments and findings and toward the end of the book he tells us,

> The phenomena I am prepared to attest are so extraordinary and so directly oppose the most firmly rooted articles of scientific belief . . . that even now, upon recalling the details of what I witnessed, there is an antagonism in my mind between *reason*, which pronounces it to be scientifically impossible, and the consciousness that my senses, both of touch and sight,–and these corroborated, as they were, by the senses of all who were present,–are not lying witnesses when they testify against my preconceptions.[5]

In this work, we get a detailed look into séance research methods of the 1800s, but we also see the complexity of thought and reception of mediums. Some learned people dismissed the notion of any genuine ability while others were entirely convinced. In the Florence Cook case, for example, Crookes tells us,

> To imagine that an innocent school-girl of fifteen should be able to conceive and then successfully carry out for three years so gigantic an imposture as this, and in that time should submit to any test which might be imposed upon her . . .to imagine, I say, the Katie King of the last three years to be the result of imposture does more violence to one's reason and common sense than to believe her to be what she herself affirms.[6]

This book is available via HathiTrust and is a key piece of literature from an early and influential psychical researcher, especially regarding the mediumship of Daniel Dunglas Home, Kate Fox, and Florence Cook.

Keywords: mediumship; Florence Cook; Kate Fox; Daniel Dunglas Home

Fairfield, Francis Gerry. *Ten Years with Spiritual Mediums: An Inquiry Concerning the Etiology of Certain Phenomena Called Spiritual.* New York: D. Appleton and Company, 1875.

Journalist Francis Gerry Fairfield presents here a summary of ten year's inquiry into the phenomena of Spiritualism, including séances and mediumship. This early work captures not only the public appeal of the movement but also the criticisms of the movement. Fairfield outlines very clearly at the beginning, for example,

> In the following pages the author submits the results of ten years of observation and experiment . . . concerning the nature of certain phenomena confidently relied upon by spiritualists as demonstrative of the agency of departed spirits . . . it has not been my intention to produce an elaborate treatise, but simply to make clear to the reader's mind . . . that the phenomena called spiritual are morbid nervous phenomena."[7]

Fairfield goes on to liken the mediums of the Spiritualist era to the priests of any religious order, offering up ideas about life after death. In this book, we see both a philosophical and physiological discussion of mediumship through the lens of a critic, offering a wonderful primary resource for those curious about public perception beyond the spheres of the séance circle.

Keywords: Spiritualism; séance; mediumship

Home, D. D. *Incidents in my Life.* London: Tinsley Brothers, 1872.

This memoir by notable medium Daniel Dunglas Home is an updated edition from the first publishing in the 1860s. In this new edition, Home tells us, "During the years that have since elapsed, although many attacks have been made upon me, and upon the truths of Spiritualism, its opponents have not succeeded in producing one word of evidence to discredit the truth of my statements . . . meantime . . . the subject has been forced upon public attention in a remarkable manner."[8] In this second volume that discusses his work and life, Home picks up where he left off in the first volume and ends with a court case involving Jane Lyon, who sued Home in an attempt to recover large sums of money she had given him. Lyon, while attending one of Home's séances, was convinced that the spirit of her deceased husband told her to treat Home like an adopted son—a decree that she took seriously, and which spurred her to financially support the medium.

This volume of Home's memoirs are mostly responses to allegations brought against him. He begins by issuing some responses to a less-than-favorable newspaper article about his abilities. Following this is a fascinating chapter on his time studying to be a sculptor in Rome and being asked to leave the city for good if he refused to sign a document stating he would not conduct any séances while residing there. This memoir is a firsthand account of Spiritualism and societal attitude toward both the movement and mediums of the day.

Keywords: Daniel Dunglas Home; mediumship; Spiritualism

1880s

Barrett, W. F., A. P. Percival Keep, C. C. Massey, Hensleigh Wedgwood, Frank Podmore, and E. R.

Pease. "First Report of the Committee on Haunted Houses." *Proceedings of the Society for Psychical Research* 1, no. 1 (December 9, 1882): 101–15.

An early committee of the Society for Psychical Research (SPR) was the Committee on Haunted Houses. In this report, the authors tell us that "the object of [this committee] was to investigate the phenomena of alleged hauntings whenever a suitable opportunity and an adequate *prima facie* case for inquiry might be presented."[9] In order to locate suitable haunted house experiences, the committee began their work by soliciting letters from those who believed that they lived (or had lived) in a haunted house. Once the committee received such information, they would follow up in person or even via letter exchange to learn more about the circumstances and determine if it would indeed be a suitable case to pursue. They tell us, "We do not consider that *every* firsthand narration of the appearance of a ghost, even from a thoroughly trustworthy narrator, gives us adequate reason for attempting further investigation."[10] The authors point out, in fact, that one standard for accepting an experience as suitable is that more than one person has witnessed an apparition *or* that the sighting of one person also coincided unknowingly with some notable life event such as a death, wedding, etc. The authors even point out an example of a man who reported seeing an apparition nearly one hundred times in his art studio, but upon their inquiry of previous tenants and a maid, could find no other person who had witnessed anything unusual and so did not pursue the case. The SPR does, however, still have a sketch of the alleged apparition drawn by the witness.

The authors also point out an interesting bit of information. In their research of locations actually deemed suitable, they discovered that there did not appear to be an exaggeration of events from person to person. Instead, they discovered that people tended to downplay their experiences, perhaps due to fear of being mocked or labeled crazy. After outlining their standards for what they would and would not accept, the committee outlines two cases for this first report. In the first case, a gentleman rented a room in an old house that was fairly cheap, perhaps due to the stories of strange experiences that the household staff reported. One evening, on September 22, 1852, as the gentleman was making his way to his bedroom (in complete darkness,

having not taken a candle with him), he saw a brilliant ray of light in a hallway and at the end of that hallway was a hideous old man in a dressing gown. After a few seconds, both the light and the apparition vanished simultaneously. The renter asked about the home's history the next day when he was in town and learned that a former owner had killed his wife and then himself in an upstairs bedroom. Upon further inquiry at the local parish, the renter discovered that the murder-suicide had taken place on September 22. One year later to the day, a friend of the renter came to stay and left after only one night, having claimed being kept awake all night by strange wails and mysterious noises. The committee reports that renovation had been done to the house since the renter vacated in 1856 and they could find no additional reports of continued phenomena. They maintain the case, however, as evidence for haunted houses.

In their second case, they discuss multiple sightings by different eyewitnesses of a female apparition at a home and rectory in Ireland. They conclude their report by discussing some of the perils of investigating haunting experiences, such as the unwillingness of people to share encounters for fear of being thought crazy, denial of homeowners for fear of the former or for fear of public information about their home being leaked, and more. The authors state that they continue to await a case that will allow them to visit a location to engage in further experimentation and that additional cases will be revealed in subsequent journal issues.

Keywords: ghosts; haunting; apparitions; Committee on Haunted Houses; Society for Psychical Research

Barrett, W. F. "On Some Phenomena Associated with Abnormal Conditions of the Mind." *Proceedings of the Society for Psychical Research* 1 (April 24, 1883): 238–44.

Researcher William F. Barrett first presented this paper in a speech to a meeting of the British Association in 1876. In it, he outlines the past ten years of his personal experiences with anomalous encounters of the human mind. Barrett was urging his colleagues to consider giving more attention to these strange events. He lays out the thesis of this speech in the first paragraph when he writes,

There are certain conditions of the mind, either temporarily induced or habitual, which appear to be associated with many remarkable phenomena that have hitherto received but partial attention from scientific men. On various occasions during the last ten years I have had the opportunity of observing some of these singular states, and in the hope of eliciting further information or of stimulating inquiry by those more competent than myself, I venture to bring the following facts under the notice of the British Association.[11]

Barrett goes on to present just such facts to the group, discussing things like hypnotism and mesmerism, and detailing his own experiences witnessing them in action. Barrett discusses the "community of sensation"[12] that he witnessed occurring between operator and subject in hypnosis cases. He witnessed, on multiple occasions, subjects responding to the touch or taste of something the operator was touching or eating. For instance, Barrett outlines the moment an operator put his hand near a hot lamp while in the same moment the subject withdrew their hand, in a motion similar to a reaction to sudden pain. He further observed that in addition to physical stimuli, there seemed to be a connection of thoughts as well. After describing his experiences and the curious phenomena witnessed during hypnosis, Barrett concludes his remark to the associated by saying,

Even as regards the facts I have myself witnessed, I do not pretend that they do more than justify further inquiry, as a large amount of similar evidence must be obtained by well qualified men before these phenomena can be accepted unreservedly. All I wish to urge is, that it is not wise to allow a natural feeling of incredulity on this matter to become a barrier to a possible extension of knowledge."[13]

Keywords: hypnotism; thought-transference; William F. Barrett

Barrett, W. F., C. C. Massey, W. Stainton Moses, Frank Podmore, Edmund Gurney, and F. W. H. Myers. "Report of the Literary Committee." *Proceedings of the Society for Psychical Research* 1 (December 9, 1882): 116–55.

In the early days of the British SPR, various committees were formed and charged with different ob-

jectives. One of these committees was the Literary Committee, composed of William F. Barrett, C. C. Massey, William Stainton Moses, Frank Podmore, and Frederic W. H. Myers. In this report, members of that committee present findings on their work to date. The first objective charged to members of the literary committee was to compile a bibliography of resources already printed within the past two hundred years on various psychical-related topics such as hauntings, extrasensory perception, etc. A second objective, which they state was the more immediate concern, involved asking scholars, colleagues, and journal editors to send in reports that they had heard about and/or published. As word began to spread that the committee was also looking for personal encounters, they also had to deal with the issue of how to verify these cases. In this report, the authors outline their standards for verifying such accounts. Speaking on the cases they received, the authors said, "The point in the evidence that impresses us is not its exciting or terrific quality, but its overwhelming quantity—overwhelming, we mean, to any possibility of further doubting the reality of the class of phenomena."[14]

Another goal of this early work of the SPR and the literary committee was to arrange reported experiences into categories. The report here outlines some of those categories, including "agent and percipient both in a normal condition."[15] This refers to moments of "thought-transference" that occurred through no seemingly explicit force of will. In other words, nobody was intentionally trying to send anyone else psychic images, but impressions were nevertheless received. The next category, "percipient in an abnormal condition," however, *does* include those instances in which someone was intentionally attempting to send psychic messages and the percipient (the received) obtained them either through a dream, trance, or received visions near or at the time of the agent's (sender's) death. These categories are reversed and include situations in which the agent is in an abnormal condition such as sleep, trance, or in a moment close to death. In fact, there are many detailed examples provided of psychical impressions gathered from an agent when they were at or near the time of death.

The next series of cases involved moments when both the agent and percipient were in abnormal conditions, such as *both* being in a dangerous position or even close to death, or both in a state of dreaming, or even one person sleeping while another is in danger. Other categories included coincidences and sightings of apparitions. The authors conclude their report with a philosophical discussion on the merits of psychical research, and they call out the antagonism that had (and still does) plague those who openly investigate these phenomena. The authors tell us,

> If anyone considers the occurrences for which we bring evidence to be supernatural, it is certainly not ourselves. We have no idea what the word can mean in such a connection. We carry our whole instinct of scientific solidarity into every detail of our inquiry . . . we entertain do doubt that orderly laws lie at the basis of *all* observed facts, however remote those laws may be from our present ken. The presumption as to our intellectual habits and attitudes, which the term "supernaturalism" is meant to imply, is therefore wholly without foundation. The phenomena examined by us stand on the same ground as any other phenomena which are widely attested, but are not matters of common experience; any inquiry into such phenomena must not be obstructed by any question-begging term.[16]

This report, from one of the earliest committees of the SPR, offers not only detailed reports of some of the cases gathered, but also provides a glimpse into the thoughts and attitudes of psychical inquiry of the time. It also illustrates some early thought on the merits of psychical research and the implications for knowledge. Anyone interested in psychical history will want to make sure that this resource is on their list.

Keywords: British Society for Psychical Research; literary committee; thought-transference; dreams

Barrett, W. F., Edmund Gurney, and F. W. H. Myers. "Thought-Reading." *The Nineteenth Century: A Monthly Review* 11, no. 64 (June 1882): 890–900.

In this article, researchers William F. Barrett, Edmund Gurney, and Frederic W. H. Myers discuss a popular "psychical" game of the day that seemed to involve thought-transference among players. In this game, a group of people would gather. One would be chosen to be a recipient of some action that others in the group would decide upon. In order to ensure that the recipient was not privy to the agreed-upon

action, they would leave the room and be called back when the discussion was over. Then, after taking a seat, a member of the group would lay their hands on the recipient's shoulder, hands, or elbows, and attempt to psychically deliver the agreed-upon action. The results of this game were fairly accurate, but the authors point out the vast majority could be explained away by subtle conscious or unconscious alterations in the physical pressure of the person's hands upon the recipient. Still, though, the authors acknowledge *some* instances of this game that appear to defy even the explanation of subtle physical cues, such as the rapidity of an action or the correct minutiae of an action, and even those instances when physical touch was not involved. The authors also provide a case study where they, as psychical researchers, interacted with a family whose children seemed to exhibit high success rates in such games. During this inquiry, the researchers conducted more than 380 trials of this "game," and they discuss their thoughts and results within. We know now of many criticisms and even admissions of fraudulent behavior during these games, but the article provides a unique look into the early inquiries into thought-transference. The authors conclude by saying, "The possibility must not be overlooked that further advances along the lines of research here indicated may necessitate a modification of that general view of the relation of mind to matter to which modern science has long been gravitating."[17]

Keywords: thought-reading; early psychical research

Boole, Mary. *The Message of Psychic Science to Mothers and Nurses.* London: Trubner & Co., 1883.

Mary Boole was an early council member of the SPR and its first female member. In this book she attempts to provide an easily accessible discussion of certain psi phenomena and what it might imply about religion, spirituality, and science. She begins by reminding us that just because something is not understood doesn't make it evil, and that religion and psi might be more intermingled than what we believe. Boole wrote this book in part due to the backlash against Spiritualism and psychical topics in the face of Darwin's theory of evolution and the dominance of materialist science that ensued. In 1883, the time of Boole's book, tensions were high between those who saw something potentially genuine happening within the séance rooms and those who dismissed it as nothing more than fraud and charlatanism.

In specifically targeting women as her key audience in this book, Boole naturally focuses her presentations on mothers and nurses. Boole was a staunch supporter of the suffragette movement and part of the goal of this work was to make accessible to women dominant arguments of the day in regard to evolution, Spiritualism, and psi. In chapter 5 specifically she discusses thought-reading and tells us, "Many persons are now familiar with the idea that some children, and even a few adults, are gifted with the power of voluntarily seeing into the thoughts of those around them, and especially of the persons with whom they are in certain close relations."[18] She goes on to discuss the empathic nature of children and her own research into their clairvoyant and telepathic abilities. Mary Boole is an often-overlooked figure in the timeline of psychical research and this work shines a light not only on her contributions but on the tensions between Darwin and spiritualists.

Keywords: Spiritualism; clairvoyance; children and thought-reading

Bowditch, H. P., C. C. Jackson, C. S. Minot, J. M. Peirce, E. C. Pickering, William Watson, and N. D. C. Hodges. "Report of the Committee on Thought-Transference." *Proceedings of the American Society for Psychical Research* 1, no. 1 (July 1885): 6–49.

Similar to its British colleagues, the American SPR also formed a committee on thought-transference. In the report, they compile the results of their first inquiries. In an effort to locate people willing to engage in experimentation, the committee circulated eight hundred copies of an ad asking fellow members to share contact information of anyone they know who may be sensitive to thought-reading. As an additional tactic, the committee also provided several research methods on thought-transference that their colleagues could use, asking that any data be sent their way if they chose to conduct any experiments. The methods they outlined in this call for research were suggested by the French psychical research Charles Richet. The committee was curious what results these particular methods might reveal. Upon receiving enough experimental data from col-

leagues, they applied the results to statistical inquiry and found that the collection as a whole did not suggest any presence of thought-transference.

The committee's report also discussed research done by W. H. Pickering involving the psychic transmission of pictures. In this experiment, one subject would draw a picture and attempt to psychically send that image to the other subject. These experiments resulted in limited success. The authors of this report remark that the *type* of experiment and focus may be a factor in studies of thought-transference. Included in this first report are appendices that list their initial call for participants and research methods for replication.

You can view this resource on HathiTrust.org. In this volume of the *Proceedings of the American Society for Psychical Research*, you can also access additional reports, notes, and items from the American SPR. You can also find additional reports of these (and other) committees.

Keywords: thought-transference; American Society for Psychical Research

Gannon, Peter. *A Spiritual Feast; or, Materialization Extraordinary.* Philadelphia: James A. Bliss, 1881: 3–18.

This entry serves as a primary resource, offering a firsthand account of a séance. The author, Peter Gannon, recounts in this fifteen-page testimony, his experiences at a séance on April 18, 1881. The séance was led by a medium known as Mrs. Bliss. Gannon begins by explaining the circumstances of this event—it was no normal séance. Instead, this gathering was a "guides séance," and as Gannon tells us, was "composed only of persons selected by the spirit guides of the medium."[19] Throughout this essay, Gannon details the events of the séance, which lasted two and a half hours, and describes multiple "spirit manifestations." In fact, Gannon writes, "There were all the comparisons existing between blooming youth and the wrinkled octogenarian—between a boy and a girl of about 13 or 14 years, and a bearded man six feet in height."[20] For those interested in reading a firsthand account of a séance, this resource provides that glimpse and serves as a wonderful primary resource on Spiritualism and its assorted events.

Keywords: séance; mediums; firsthand account; primary source; Spiritualism

Gurney, Edmund, Frederic W. H. Myers, and Frank Podmore. *Phantasms of the Living.* Two volumes. London: Society for Psychical Research, 1886.

Phantasms of the Living is a seminal work in the annals of parapsychology. Early members of the SPR administered a survey asking people about their experiences with anomalous sounds or visions. What they were surveying, of course, were haunting-type experiences—more specifically, moments in which a person saw or heard something that was seemingly unreal. They gathered seven hundred reports from people across England and discovered something quite curious. Many anomalous sounds and visions corresponded to people believed to still be alive at the time of the incident, thus providing the reason for the title *Phantasms of the "Living."*

While each author contributed to this two-volume work, Frank Podmore did the majority of the data collection and analysis, making his efforts particularly crucial for the production of this work. Volume one begins with discussion on the merit of psychical research and outlines the basis of what the British SPR adheres to in a scientific manner. It outlines, essentially, the attitudes and standards to which psychical researchers brought to this topic. Chapter 2 outlines some of the earlier research into thought-transference, providing discussions of research with the Creery family, and experiments done by researchers Charles Richet and Sir Oliver Lodge. The following chapters discuss differences between experimental and spontaneous psi and criticism against spontaneous psi. Chapter 5 is where we first start to see a glimpse of the large survey administered to those seven hundred people, which serves as a template for the various types of experiences that researchers gathered from the survey. It discusses anomalous dream experiences and information seemingly gathered during "borderland" phases between sleep and consciousness. Today, we might recognize those as the hypnagogic and hypnopompic sleep phases, but certainly these were not known facts at the time. They also note that people experienced psi through sight, hearing, *or* touch. The following chapters go into detail on the ways in which psychic impression were manifested, for example, through mental impressions, intense emotional surges or physical effects, or via dreams. The first volume highlights the fact that many of these psychical impressions

coincide with another's moment of peril or death. So, for example, the sighting of someone's aunt who lives miles away coinciding very near to the time of the aunt's death.

The second volume begins with a discussion on how likely these psychical events could be explained away by coincidence, while chapters 2, 3, and 4 dive into more detailed cases involving visual, auditory, and tactile perceptions of apparitions. Following chapters discuss reciprocal and group experiences and include a large supplemental portion that provides case studies of phenomena gathered in this survey. *Phantasms of the Living* is a foundational and seminal publication not only in psychical research, but of the SPR. Anyone interested in apparitions, consciousness, the early days of the SPR, or early psychical research methods will not want to miss this resource.

Keywords: Phantasms of the Living*; hauntings; ghosts; crisis apparitions; thought-transference*

Gurney, Edmund, Frederic W. H. Myers, and William F. Barrett. "Second Report on Thought-Transference." *Proceedings of the Society for Psychical Research* 1, no. 1 (December 9, 1882): 70–99.

This report is the second in the series of reports from the SPR's committee on thought-reading. Gurney and colleagues begin with an overview of what the first report concluded. In the first report, the committee found that many instances of thought-reading were explainable due to subtle and unconscious clues from another's body language. Each person in this instance may not have even realized that they were giving away clues and/or picking up on those subtle physiological hints. The committee pointed out, though, that there were some cases that did seem to be genuine psychical impressions passed from one person to another.

The first report involved tests done with the Creery family where certain thought-reading experiments were done in which one person would leave a room and the remaining group members would choose an object for the person to correctly identify upon their return. It seems very familiar to the popular "mesmeric games" of the day. After that report, members of the committee felt it would be useful to conduct follow-up experiments with the Creery sisters, and this second report discusses those results. In many trials, the results amounted to chance percentages, but in one particular trial, one of the girls correctly identified the suit of cards fourteen times in a row. As the committee reports, the odds of that happening were nearly four million to one. Different from the mesmeric games though, in these experiments with the Creery sisters, the "guesser" was often secluded behind closed doors or opaque curtains in which no physical or visual contact was made.

Some interesting observations from round two of the experiments with the Creery girls involved the role that anxiety plays in thought-reading. Researchers discovered that when the guesser knew that their siblings, along with the researchers, all collectively knew the item to be guessed, psi was lower than those instances in which the guesser did not know who possessed knowledge of the item and/or knew that only a small number of people knew the object at hand. The researchers also pointed out that the results of this second round of experiments were statistically less significant than the first round, leading them to wonder if age had something to do with psi abilities.

The Creery family were not the only study participants in this second report, though. Committee members had received letters from a gentleman in Brighton claiming to have had curious experiences with a mesmerist known as Mr. Smith. Upon traveling to Brighton to investigate the case themselves, Gurney and colleagues write, "The results of these trials give us the most important and valuable insight into the manner of the mental transfer of a picture which we have yet obtained."[21] During these experiments, Mr. Smith was blindfolded. His friend, and the one who initially wrote to the SPR, Mr. Blackburn, took Smith's hand. The researchers showed a slip of paper to Blackburn who would then attempt to psychically send the word to Smith. The results were remarkably accurate but *only* when the two were holding hands. In addition to writing words, the researchers also inflicted pain on Blackburn, and in each instance, Smith was able to identify which part of his friend's body was affected. Still more, researchers drew geometric shapes and Smith, who was blindfolded and had his back to researchers in every one of these experiments, would describe the shape accurately. They even amended this experiment into one where Smith was asked to draw the shape that he intuited, and again displayed remarkable results. It is important to note that Smith and Blackburn had been engaging in these psychical activities for some time and continued to experiment after the SPR researchers conducted their tests. In this report, though, we learn that Smith and Blackburn claim to have developed their skills so precisely that no physical contact between the two were needed, and the authors pointed out that *those* results would be published in part three of the committee's work.

Keywords: thought-transference; Creery sisters; mesmeric games; Society for Psychical Research; committee on thought-reading

Gurney, Edmund and Frederic W. H. Myers. "Visible Apparitions." *The Nineteenth Century: A Monthly Review* 16, no. 89 (July 1884): 68–95.

In this article, psychical researchers Edmund Gurney and Frederic W. H. Myers discuss sightings of apparitions. They begin their work by reminding us that they still classify visual sightings of ghosts under the broader category of telepathy. They write, "Among effects produced on the senses, one particular class . . . concerns the sense of *sight*. . . . Among these we find undoubtedly the furthest and most eccentric of the phenomena which the telepathic theory can be made to embrace; and our account of them will require that the theory, as so far stated, should be somewhat expanded. . . . We are about to treat visible apparitions as 'transferred impressions.'"[22]

They continue to explain the parallels that they draw between telepathy and ghostly sightings. Telepathy, they tell us, occurs when someone focuses on a particular image (like a Zener card, for example), and another person intuits that intense focus from the other. In this sense, Gurney and Myers argue, a dying person is very likely intensely focusing on their lives and others could be picking up on that intense focus at or near the time of their death. In this way, we see a direct parallel between telepathy and visual sightings of ghosts. Gurney and Myers proceeded to expand upon their theory, providing a unique theory on the relationship between two seemingly disparate phenomena.

Keywords: telepathy; ghosts; apparitions

Innes, A. Taylor. "Where are the Letters? A Cross-Examination of Certain Phantasms." *The Nineteenth Century: A Monthly Review* no. 126 (August 1887): 174–94.

Author A. Taylor Innes begins this article describing an event that was recounted to him in which someone had a disturbing dream of their brother being impaled on a fence after a fall from a height. Upon waking, this person wrote a letter home asking for confirmation that all was well, and in the process, a letter *from* his home was being sent to inform him that his brother had indeed taken a grizzly fall. Taylor, after hearing of this, asked the person to produce the letters, but they could not. Taylor expressed frustration at not having any conclusive proof that would confirm that this psychical impression took place, and related this same frustration of proof to the aforementioned publication, *Phantasms of the Living*, where hundreds of case studies are presented in which people report seeing, hearing, or feeling their friends or loved ones at or near the time of peril or death. Hence the word "living" in the title. Taylor discusses how the researchers of that publication verified things like death reports or news reports of accidents, but also discusses how it is much harder to verify that the person receiving the psychical impression *actually did receive* that impression. Taylor notes that handwritten accounts can of course help and points out that Innes realizes this as well, but Taylor also discusses how written reports that remain in the hands of the percipient are much less reliable than if, for example, a percipient had experienced something anomalous and written a letter to a friend, thereby removing the handwritten note entirely from their possession.

Taylor goes on to discuss how, while there are mentions of physical documents existing in the case reports within *Phantasms of the Living*, that there has not been any actually gathered and verified. The cases, they point out, rest on witness testimony and people testifying that they either saw or read the note but could not provide it. Taylor also goes on to point out that he doesn't believe *Phantasms* to be fabricated, especially given the reputation and intelligence of the researchers involved. It is, however, a worthy and interesting critique of this seminal publication and is a must-read for anyone interested in that seminal publication of the SPR.

Keywords: Phantasms of the Living; *firsthand accounts; hauntings; apparitions*

Podmore, F. "Report on the Worksop Disturbances." *Journal of the Society for Psychical Research* 1, no. 11 (December 1884): 199–212.

In this article, psychical researcher Frank Podmore details a poltergeist case at the home of Joe White and his family in Worksop, England. Noting that in March 1883 local newspapers had reported strange occurrences happening, Podmore visited the family in April to conduct his own investigation. The first reported occurrences involved Mrs. White, her two young daughters, and a table that seemingly tilted of its own accord. From here, the activity only escalated, with items being thrown across the room, kitchen items thought to be securely in place being thrown from an upstairs bedroom, items "wafting" across the room and gingerly landing on the floor, and the local doctor and others witnessing a basin levitate about four feet into the air. Part of Podmore's inquiry was interviewing and analyzing reports among eyewitnesses. Podmore points out that three of these eyewitnesses were impartial observers, thus lending even more credence to something strange happening within the home. Podmore concludes that none of the eyewitnesses appeared to be lying and that all seemed baffled by the events themselves. Likewise, Podmore claims that there were simply so many occurrences happening in the home that fraudulent behavior would have been easy to ferret out, though he could find none. This 1884 entry in the journal illustrates some of the early work of the SPR.

Keywords: poltergeists; eyewitness reports

Sidgwick, Eleanor and Richard Hodgson. "On Vision with Sealed and Bandaged Eyes." *Journal of the Society for Psychical Research* 1, no. 5 (June 1884): 84–66.

In 1884, two members of the mesmeric committee of the SPR, Eleanor Sidgwick and Richard Hodgson, set forth to replicate the conditions of a case that was presented to that committee. The committee had learned of a young boy who, when placed under hypnosis and blindfolded, was able to correctly identify objects and cards that were placed in front of his bandaged eyes. In the experiment, a physician placed the boy under hypnosis at which point researchers left the room, leaving the other researchers to place random items in front of the boy. In their replication, Sidgwick and Hodgson discovered small, imperceptible slits in the bandaging and plaster used in the experiment and concluded that the boy was actually able to see more than the researchers assumed. Hypnotism and trance were huge topics in this era of psychical research and this brief report from Sidgwick and Hodgson sheds light on some of the reports and the reality that many inquiries revealed fraudulent and/or explainable conditions.

Keywords: hypnotism; fraud; replication experiments

Taylor, G. L. Le M. "Report on the Alleged Manifestations at Arundel, Sussex." *Journal of the Society for Psychical Research* 1, no. 4 (May 1884): 57–62.

In February 1884, two investigators visited a house in Sussex where a family claimed strange things were happening. The family claimed that strange scratching, moved objects, and apparitions seemed to be happening and focused on their thirteen-year-old daughter. The two investigators performed a thorough investigation and submitted their report to the SPR. Within this report are diagrams of the house and locations of activity, transcripts of communication with witnesses, and the majors' own inquiry. After completing their investigation of the house, interviewing witnesses and the daughter herself, the majors conclude that "on the whole it is most likely that the affair was begun in fun, continued in fraud, and closed in fright."[23] This early report within the journal of the SPR shows some of the work undertaken into the investigation of haunt phenomena.

Keywords: apparitions; fraud

1890s

"Cases Received by the Literary Committee." *Journal of the Society for Psychical Research* 5, no. 84 (November 1891): 147–52.

This entry, from the November 1891 issue of the *Journal of the Society for Psychical Research*, provides direct transcripts of some of the cases gathered by the literary committee, which was tasked with gathering reports from individuals regarding instances of apparitions and thought-transference. These cases helped inform some of the early publications of the SPR. In this article, we see firsthand the types of information gathered by the committee. Examples include that of a photographer, Mr. Dickinson, who, while opening his photo shop one morning, was greeted by a man inquiring about his order and who said he had been traveling all night. Upon telling the man that the order was not yet complete, Mr. Dickinson continued with his work for another week, when a different gentleman came to inquire about the photos. Mr. Dickinson noticed that the negatives were of the man who inquired a week earlier, and he asked about him only to discover that he had passed away one week prior—a week to the day that Mr. Dickinson had seen him in his shop. Further inquiry revealed that the gentleman was unconscious and at home during the hour in which the photographer claimed he visited his shop.

Additional case reports like the one above can be found in subsequent editions of the journal.

Keywords: case reports; Society for Psychical Research; apparitions

Hodgson, Richard. "A Case of Double Consciousness." *Proceedings of the Society for Psychical Research* 7 (1891): 221–57.

In this article, psychical researcher Richard Hodgson discusses the case of Ansel Bourne, a man from Rhode Island. In his sixties, Bourne suffered from memory loss after a particularly notable seizure, and afterward developed a double personality. While in his new personality state, Bourne would act like a different person with different memories and mannerisms. Hodgson outlines other cases in which seizures have seemingly been the catalyst that brought about multiple personalities, and he suggests hypnosis as a possible means to reverse the effects. Within the article, Hodgson even provides transcripts of his own hypnosis upon Bourne. This article is an early inquiry into the study of consciousness as seen through multiple personalities.

Keywords: hypnosis; multiple personality

Hodgson, Richard. "A Further Record of Observations of Certain Phenomena of Trance." *Proceed-*

ings of the Society for Psychical Research 13, no. 33 (1897–1898): 284–582.

This report is the third in Dr. Richard Hodgson's publications of his research with American medium Leonora Piper. The previous two versions that this report builds upon are also published in the *Proceedings of the Society for Psychical Research*, in volumes 6 (pages 436–650) and 8 (pages 1–167), respectively.

Dr. Hodgson begins his report with an overview of reasons why scientists do not think that Piper was producing knowledge fraudulently. Some of these reasons include inviting strangers to have sittings with the medium and also a police investigation that involved trailing the medium and her husband over a period of time to determine if they were somehow involved in secreting information about sitters. Dr. Hodgson refers to his own personal sittings with the medium in which information of very private matters were relayed, and he tells us that, given the inquiries into her behavior *and* the information given at her séances,

> My own conclusion was that—after allowing the widest possible margin for information obtainable under the circumstances by ordinary means, for chance coincidence and remarkable guessing, aided by clues given consciously and unconsciously by the sitters, and helped out by supposed hyperesthesia on the part of Mrs. Piper,—there remained a large residuum of knowledge displayed in her trance state, which could not be account for except on the hypothesis that she had some supernormal power; and this conviction has been strengthened by my later investigations.[24]

Following this, however, is a fascinating discussion of the various reasons that scientists gave to explain the curious abilities of Mrs. Piper. Some believed that her spirit control, known as "Dr. Phinuit," was simply a manifestation of multiple personality and that Piper obtained information from the thought-transference of her sitters. In this scenario, then, there is no implication of communication or channeling with the dead and instead is entirely based on unconscious abilities of the living. Still others thought that there may be some telepathy from distant living persons. Others posited, in perhaps the most spiritualistic of the theories, that Piper was communicating with spirits of the

deceased, who would feed her information about the sitters at her séances.

Dr. Hodgson believed that the answer lied closer to the realm of influence from the living. He posited that Piper's various spirit controls and the spirits of friends and loved ones who seemed to speak through her was the result of an "auto-hypnotic trance"[25] that resulted in multiple personalities that then claimed to be spirits but were really thought-transference (telepathy) from sitters. Dr. Hodgson points to the fact that her main spirit control, Dr. Phinuit, was not able to provide very substantial information about his life when living—the spirit control only ever seemed able to transmit information, thus giving credence to Hodgson's theory that this spirit control was really just a psychological symptom of being in a trance and was further assisted by telepathic abilities of living persons present, both the sitters and the medium herself.

In this report, we learn that the committee on thought-transference had investigated more than five hundred sittings that Piper held. The report also includes updates on the use of automatic writing in séances, a feature of which was not used or reported on in the first two reports. Within this third report are also transcripts of séances and discussions with sitters, along with appendices that detail more of those occurrences. This resource gives a detailed look not only into Leonora Piper's mediumship but also on the methods and thoughts of psychical researchers.

Keywords: Leonora Piper; Dr. Phinuit; mediumship; automatic writing; telepathy

Hodgson, Richard. "Glimmerings of a Future Life." *Forum* (April 1896): 247–57.

In this article written for the magazine *Forum*, Dr. Richard Hodgson references his investigation into the American medium Leonora Piper. He begins by telling us, "The chief object of this paper is to give a brief account of some of the fresh evidence in its relation to the question of man's survival of death."[26] He references the many prior investigations with Mrs. Piper, including his own work alongside psychologist William James as well as the eighty-three sitting she held in England in 1889 and 1890. After giving us a brief overview of prior research, Dr. Hodgson tells us that since 1891 Piper's mediumship seemed to have grown even stronger. He reports that two factors may have contributed to this: a new spirit control (or a spirit speaking through the medium's body) and the incorporation of automatic writing during her trance. After discussing some recent development in the work on Leonora Piper, Hodgson concludes by writing, "We may learn that the consciousness of man is not restricted to the domain of this ordinary earthly life."[27]

Keywords: Leonora Piper; mediumship; automatic writing

Hyslop, James H. "Experiments with Mrs. Piper since Dr. Richard Hodgson's Death." *Journal of the American Society for Psychical Research* 1, no. 2 (February 1907): 93–107.

Psychical researcher Dr. Richard Hodgson spent eighteen years investigating the mediumship of Leonora Piper. In this article, fellow parapsychologist James Hyslop discusses the continuation of research into the American medium in the wake of Dr. Hodgson's death. After his death, the American medium Piper claimed to have received communications coming from the departed researcher. This article discusses the circumstances and possible likelihood of those communications.

Toward the beginning of the article, Hyslop reveals that all manner of rumor and thought had developed making people wonder about Piper's ability to communicate with the deceased researcher—after all, she made regular contact with the deceased, so why not someone she was closely connected to for nearly two decades? Hyslop is quick to dispel rumors though, telling us, "I do not here concern myself with that hypothesis of many unscientific people who think that Mrs. Piper's mind has drawn telepathically into it the personality and memories of Dr. Hodgson previous to his death and can at please afterwards reproduce them and palm them off as spirits. Anyone who can believe such a thing without an iota of evidence for it can believe anything."[28]

Hyslop goes on to tell us, though, that he and Hodgson had contacted a third party medium unknown to Piper. This medium was kept secret as a sort of postdeath control to see if Piper would pick up on any of that communication. Hyslop tells us that there were indeed some curious communications that came through potentially regarding this clandestine third party and in fact, this third-party medium picked up on the death of Hodgson before it was known to the public. Hyslop continues to discuss some curious communications that came through Piper's sittings in the months after Hodgson's death, even including transcripts of some portions. He concludes by telling us, "It will be apparent, I think, to every man that these statements through Mrs. Piper are not due to chance, and that, if we have reason to believe that Mrs. Piper had not previously acquired by normal means the information conveyed, we have facts which do not have an ordinary explanation."[29]

Keywords: Leonora Piper; mediumship; Richard Hodgson

Hughes, C. H. "Psychical or Physical? An Inquiry into the Mind and Matter Problem." *Alienist and Neurologist* 12, no. 2 (April 1, 1891).

Author C. H. Hughes first read this article as a speech at an 1874 convention of the Association of Medical Superintendents of American Institutes for the Insane. In this article, Hughes discusses the efforts at distinguishing the mind from the brain and thoughts and how the psychical and physical could be intertwined. The author also discusses his theories on the ways in which mental disorders affect psychical manifestations and posits that *any* psychological function is a result of some biological change in the brain—via molecules, chemicals, etc. This speech was obviously tailored to those who were concerned with mental disorders, but it offers a unique look into the ways in which the topic of psi and psychical science filtered through to various medical and scientific disciplines.

Keywords: brain physiology; mental health and parapsychology

James, William. "Review of Report on the Census of Hallucinations." *Psychological Review* 2, no. 1 (1895): 69–75.

This 1895 article offers a review of the British SPR's publication titled "Report on the Census of Hallucinations." The father of American psychology himself authors this review and starts by saying,

This extraordinarily thorough and accurate piece of work is understood to be the fruit mainly of

Mrs. Sidgwick's labors; and the present reviewer, who has had a little experience of his own with the "Census," and knows something of its difficulties, may be allowed to pay his tribute of admiration to the energy and skill with which that lady and the other members of the committee have executed their burdensome task.[30]

James goes on to outline the work done within the census, noting that more than seventeen thousand responses had been gathered and that nearly three thousand of them had indicated having had a waking hallucination. These three thousand reports were then followed up to elicit more information. The report concluded that there was a one in forty-three chance of having a visual hallucination of an apparition and stated that this ratio is 440 times higher than chance alone. James also discusses the criticisms that people had lobbied against the survey and said,

This sort of reception by the hard-hearted is inevitable, and it us useless to ask how strictly logical it may be, for belief follows psychological and not logical laws. A single veridical hallucination experienced by oneself or by some friend who tells one all the circumstances has more influence over the mind than the largest calculated numerical probability either for or against. I can testify to this from direct observation. The case will, therefore, still hang pending before public opinion, in spite of the laborious industry of Mrs. Sidgwick and her colleagues.[31]

James is not without his own criticism, of course, though it is nowhere near as harsh as those which others have lobbied. The one criticism that James points out is that he believed the committee was too liberal in including instances of hallucinations that occurred immediately after a person woke up, stating that it was likely that the person was still in a dream-state. This article provides a glimpse into the reception of the Census of Hallucinations from other highly respected and decorated academics.

Keywords: Census of Hallucinations

Myers, Frederic W. H. "A Record of Observations of Certain Phenomena of Trance." *Proceedings of the Society for Psychical Research* 6 (1890): 436–42.

In this article, psychical researcher Frederic W. H. Myers presents an overview of a British inquiry into medium Leonora Piper. At the time of this pub-

lication, Piper was a known medium and had been at the center of experimental inquiry in the United States. For two and a half months, however, Piper was observed by British researchers, and it is those experiments on which Myers focuses. Myers begins his article by reminding readers of the various characteristics of trance, which he refers to as automatism. There are instances of both active and passive automatism, automatic writing and speech being of those respective categories.

Myers then gives an overview of the many instances of automatist utterances that Piper gave forth at séances and the claims by her sitters that she could have had no previous knowledge of such things. Here we also learn of the length to which certain researchers would go to investigate mediums—Piper was trailed by a private detective (paid for by psychical researchers) to ferret out any clandestine meetings or curious bits of mail. They could find no wrongdoing, by the way. In November 1889, Sir Oliver Lodge, Frederic W. H. Myers, Mr. Leaf, and Henry Sidgwick invited Piper to come to England for a series of sittings. The researchers intentionally gave false names of the sitters to Piper and did their best even to ensure that none of the sitters knew each other. During a series of sittings held in various towns across England, Myers wrote, "In my case, as in the case of several other sitters, there were messages purporting to come from a friend who has been dead many years and mentioning circumstances which I believe that it would have been quite impossible for Mrs. Piper to have discovered."[32]

Myers concluded that "we agree only in maintaining that the utterances show that knowledge has been acquired by some intelligence in some supernormal fashion; and in urging on experimental psychologists the duty of watching for similar cases, and of analysing the results in some such way as we have endeavored to do."[33] Though they concur that something strange seems to have happened, they also pointed out the need for further inquiry and that they couldn't say *how* anything happened. The following pages of this edition of the *Proceedings of the Society for Psychical Research* include Sir Oliver Lodge's remarks on the sittings. Anyone interested in either the early research into mediums and/or Leonora Piper herself will want to consult this resource.

Keywords: Leonora Piper; mediumship; trance; Dr. Phinuit

Podmore, Frank. *Apparitions and Thought-Transference: An Examination of the Evidence for Telepathy.* London: Walter Scott, 1894.

This resource, which is publicly available via Project Gutenberg, outlines various psychical experiments on topics relating to thought-transference and apparitions. The work begins by highlighting four main areas that could conceivably explain psychical phenomena: outright fraud, hyperaesthesia, muscle-reading, and thought-forms. However, the author states that sufficient precautions safeguarding against these things have been made in the experiments he lays out in subsequent chapters.

Psychical research and main data collector of *Phantasms of the Living*, Frank Podmore, provides discussions on the experiments of Charles Richet, Henry Sidgwick, Albert von Schrenck-Notzing, Frederic W. H. Myers, and many more. Included in this overview of research are induced and spontaneous telepathy, anomalous dreams, hypnotism, group hallucinations, criticisms and weaknesses of psi research, and much more. Podmore concluded by stating that while there have been some curious revelations, more research was needed.

Readers interested in this work may also wish to consult Podmore's 1897 publication *Studies in Psychical Research*, an almost five hundred-page work that, in addition to the above topics, discusses mediums, haunted houses, and more.

Keywords: thought-transference; hypnotism; hallucinations; apparitions; early psychical research

Podmore, Frank. "What Psychical Research Has Accomplished." *The North American Review* 160, no. 460 (March 1895): 331–44.

In this article, psychical researcher Frank Podmore responds to the criticisms of Professor Minot regarding the work of the British SPR. In the process, Podmore presents research and work done to date not only on exposing fraudulent mediums but on other research that had seemed to yield curious results, like their studies on thought-transference. This article serves as a wonderful primary source that captures the criticism and tension inherent in early psychical research.

Keywords: criticisms of psychical research; fraud; thought-transference

Sidgwick, Henry, Alice Johnson, F. W. H. Myers, Frank Podmore, and Eleanor M. Sidgwick. "Report on the Census of Hallucinations." *Proceedings of the Society for Psychical Research* 10 (1894): 25–422.

This is one of the most-cited documents in the history of psychical research. Alongside *Phantasms of the Living*, these are among the documents you will see referred to time and again. A few short years after *Phantasms* was published, the SPR published the results of their Census of Hallucinations. This survey was administered on an international scale over the course of three years and resulted in seventeen thousand survey responses about hallucinations as the committee referred to them formally, and which today can be thought of as visual, auditory, and physically anomalous experiences, like seeing an apparition, hearing phantom voices, etc.[34] Entrusted mainly to the care of Henry Sidgwick, he and fellow researchers began developing their idea for this study and obtained support and approval from the International Congress of Experimental Psychology in 1899. Similar to *Phantasms*, the researchers were interested in determining whether hallucinations coincided with verifiable, simultaneous events, such as someone being in danger or near death, or some other emotional situation. This wasn't, however, the entire focus of the census, since the researchers remind us, "Apparitions or other sensory hallucinations are not the only kind of spontaneous experiences in which the influence of one mind on another is found operating at a distance."[35]

In their own words, the researchers and administrators of "the Census" as it is often referred, tell us that

> Uur general aim was to ascertain what proportion of persons have had sensory hallucinations while awake, and not suffering from delirium or insanity or any other morbid condition obviously conducive to hallucination; and further, to enquire into the nature of these hallucinations and the conditions under which they occur.[36]

They make clear that they were interested in spontaneous events, not experimental phenomena administered in the course of some formal exercise. In chapters 2 and 3 the researchers outline their methods and present their statistical analysis of data. In chapters 4 through 11 they present a discussion on the ways in which these hallucinations differ from other psychological events, the physiological effects of hallucinations, and the physical traits that may or may not make hallucinations more likely to occur. In the final chapter they focus on data that seem to point to telepathic origins and those reports that seem to have no other known explanation.

Before presenting any of the above, the researchers begin their report with a discussion on definitions of telepathy and a review of telepathy research to date. Following this, they dive into a detailed discussion of the methods of the census. They tell us that they decided to focus primarily on experiences involving sight, sound, and touch. They remind us, however, of their standards for determining which reports were more likely to be the result of some natural occurrence and not of the supernormal nature. They go into great detail outlining the various experiences that they decided to exclude, even listing how many reports of each they had gotten (e.g., visions while waking up that were no longer there when fully conscious, sounds of voices that were not clear, distinguishable words, strange dreams, etc.).

In this section, the authors reveal some of the frustrations of the census—like the 256 respondents who indicated that they had had a waking hallucination but provided no further detail, essentially making these submissions useless. The authors were able to follow up with thirty-nine of these respondents. This section also provides detailed lists and charts of data from the census and a detailed discussion of the possibilities for fraud. For example, the authors address the possibility that some respondents might intentionally lie and say they have had a strange encounter. They tell us, though, that they don't believe this is an issue because of the methods used to gather data. Not only did people have to sign their names as testimony to their report, the data gatherers themselves were often friends or acquaintances of respondents—a tactic that the authors believed would not only ensure more truthful statements but also make people feel more comfortable about sharing such experiences in the first place.

The authors then spend some time discussing pseudo-hallucinations, or those instances that cannot be confidently considered genuinely supernormal. Instances might include seeing an apparition in a darkened room, when even the surroundings of the room are not entirely visible or the strange visions a person sometimes gets upon falling asleep or immediately awakening. The authors do state, however, that there are still some curious cases that fall into these categories that require further consideration. What this illustrates, though, is the thought process and the standards to which the authors held themselves when determining if something potentially falls into the anomalous category. Sprinkled throughout these discussions are personal experiences of strange, hallucinatory events, thus the reader can see firsthand the types of reports gathered by the census.

In the following sections, the authors spend time discussing the various forms that hallucinations seem to take. They illustrate how apparitions tend to appear as normal, as if one were witnessing a person going about their daily lives. In other words, it was rare to witness mangled corpses and gruesome harbingers of death. They go on to discuss the physiological factors of hallucinations and then launch into a discussion of demographic patterns of experiences, such as age of first hallucination, gender, nationality, etc. They then present multiple chapters on visions of apparitions near the time of someone's death *and* other visions that coincide with some traumatic or dangerous events, in addition to experimental hallucinations and group hallucinations.

This comprehensive, international study serves as a seminal resource on psychical research that is still referenced today. The work not only includes an abundant amount of data and personal experiences, it also serves as a reference guide to other prominent researchers, as the authors cite and mention previous studies throughout. If there is any one resource to begin your inquiry, this is a solid starting point.

Keywords: Census of Hallucinations; survey; apparitions; ghosts

"A Society for Psychical Research in Sweden." *Journal of the Society for Psychical Research* 5 (October 1891): 144.

In the correspondences section of the October 1891 issue of the *Journal of the Society for Psychical Research*, we see a brief entry, only a paragraph long, that mentions a branch of the SPR forming in

Sweden—officially known as the Svenska Samfundet för Psykisk Forskning. The article mentions that the Swedish branch had approximately 150 members and was formed under the leadership of Dr. von Bergen. The correspondence and notes portions of this journal (and really of any journal relating to your chosen topic) are useful to browse because in them you will get historical tidbits like this one. What this brief entry reveals to us is the international scope of the SPR and the fact that a desire for more rigorous academic standards on psychical topics was not merely relegated to Britain. Of course, any historical treatment of the rise of psychical science reveals the influence of not just Britain, but also France, Germany, and many others for advancing scientific standards on these topics. This brief article is a reminder of the influence and reach of the SPR and to check the notes embedded in journals for additional information.

Keywords: Sweden; Society for Psychical Research

1900s

Carrington, Hereward. *Eusapia Palladino and Her Phenomena* New York: B. W. Dodge and Company, 1909.

This work by psychical researcher Hereward Carrington details the life and research into noted Italian medium Eusapia Palladino. Carrington tells us, in his preface, "While much has been written in France and Italy concerning the remarkable woman who forms the subject of this book, but little has appeared either in England or America . . . yet the case is one of the most remarkable that has come to the attention of the scientific world for many years."[37] In this work, Carrington details "a summary of all the historic evidence available"[38] that also takes into consideration biological and psychological factors. Additionally, he provides details from his own research with Palladino, conducted with fellow psychical researchers in Naples in 1908. Carrington also discusses the various theories proposed to explain Palladino's ability, including a novel theory of his own.

This book not only provides details of Carrington's own research with Palladino, it serves as a comprehensive text on *all* experiments with the Italian medium. Carrington begins his work with a philosophical discussion on the merits of Palladino's mediumship. If, he claims, her abilities are even *partially* genuine, then it gives a boost of credibility to the field of psychical science and drives a wedge into materialist science. He also discusses how her mediumship is different from those of the trance mediums also popular during the era of Spiritualism. Described as a physical (rather than a trance) medium, Carrington outlines the types of abilities displayed by the medium.

After this discussion, Carrington provides a biographical sketch of Palladino followed by detailed reports of experiments with the medium. This is the largest portion of the book, and readers can view reports of her experiments with figures like Cesare Lombroso, Alexander Aksakof, Charles Richet, Sir Oliver Lodge, Frederic W. H. Myers, Henry and Eleanor Sidgwick, and more. Photos and personal testimony are sprinkled throughout. Remember too, though, that Palladino was caught engaging in fraudulent séance behavior, so pay particular attention to the Cambridge experiments. Carrington follows this section with a detailed report of his own experiments conducted in Naples in 1908. Of these experiments he tells us, "Bearing in mind the results of previous investigators—particularly the reports more recently issued by eminent scientific men in Europe, it became imperative for the Society of Psychical Research, in spite of the past negative results of the Cambridge experiments, to reconsider the question of Eusapia's mediumship."[39] Carrington proceeds to detail the methods and results of these experiments.

In chapter 5, Carrington lays out the various theories (such as fraud or hallucination) used to explain the curious phenomena during Palladino's sittings. In this section, Carrington also presents a theory of his own: that her abilities are explained by spiritistic forces. Carrington addresses the criticisms of his theory further in this chapter.

Those interested in the life and mediumship of Eusapia Palladino, especially a primary source written during Eusapia's life, will want to include this on their list. If interested, you should be able to access this title freely via HathiTrust.

Keywords: Eusapia Palladino; mediumship; séances; Spiritualism

Fielding, Everard, W. W. Baggally, and Hereward Carrington. "Report on a Series of Sittings with Eusapia Palladino." *Proceedings of the Society for Psychical Research* (November 1909): 309–570.

In this book-length publication in the *Proceedings of the Society for Psychical Research*, authors Fielding, Baggally, and Carrington outline the mediumship of Eusapia Palladino. This work is preceded by an introduction to fellow psychical researcher and then-president of the SPR, Eleanor Sidgwick. In this introduction, Sidgwick explains why three researchers headed to Naples to investigate a medium who had, years earlier, been outright caught in fraudulent séance behavior. We learn that while Palladino had indeed been prone to fraud in a few instances, that she nevertheless left researchers stumped in other instances. Additionally, while her reputation was tainted perhaps in the United States, she remained a hugely popular figure abroad where laypeople and researchers alike continued to engage with her. Due in part to her international popularity and the fact that *some* séances left people scratching their heads, researchers headed to Naples in the early 1900s. The three selected researchers were also skilled in ferreting out fraud and had outed others in the past, making them particularly suitable for this continued inquiry into Palladino.

The first thirty pages of the report provided an overview of the researcher's objectives, the physical setup of the séance room, and a general report of phenomena exhibited therein. Some of the phenomena included phantom touches, disembodied hands appearing, objects traveling across the room seemingly of their own accord, table-tiltings, and anomalous musical sounds. After each outline of phenomena, the researchers provide an annotation of which séance that occurred in so that readers can navigate to the second portion of the report that contains detailed transcripts and diagrams of each séance.

At the end of this overview, the researchers state that,

> We limit ourselves here to a statement of opinion, amounting in our own minds to certainty, that to explain Eusapia's manifestations some agency of a kind wholly different from mere physical dexterity on her part must be invoked. The conditions in which the séances were held render absolutely inadmissible the supposition that there was any accomplice. There remains, therefore, in our opinion, only one possible

alternative to the hypothesis of some supernormal *physical* force, namely, the hypothesis that in some way we were collectively hallucinated.[40]

Following this overview are nearly two hundred pages-worth of transcripts and diagrams of each séance with Palladino. Following these detailed transcriptions are the conclusion of each researcher. This work is immensely valuable not only for those interested in the mediumship of Eusapia Palladino, but also for those curious about the exact workings of séances and séance research in the early 1900s.

Keywords: Eusapia Palladino; mediumship; séances; fraud; séance transcripts

Hyslop, James H. "The Immortality of the Soul." *The North American Review* 180, no. 580 (March 1905): 394–409.

In this essay in *The North American Review*, researcher James H. Hyslop presents a discussion of the philosophical and scientific treatments of psychical topics and specifically the question of consciousness beyond death. He compares this topic to the religious notion of immortality. And after outlining his thoughts on these matters, concludes by telling us that "these are the facts and conceptions that suggest the possibility of the survival of consciousness after death, and it only requires such evidence of personal identity as cannot be explained by fraud or illusion."[41] He continues to point out that multiple scientists have engaged in this very research and writes, "Now there is a large body of facts that claim this very character, and they are respectable enough to demand serious attention and investigation . . . and altogether make it a scandal that to science that they are not financially provided for in the scheme of investigation."[42]

This essay illustrates not only the philosophical and scientific ideas surrounding psi topics but also reveals the frustrations of gathering research support for these phenomena.

Keywords: consciousness; survival after death

Hyslop, James H. "Questions for Psychical Research." *The Monist* 18, no. 2 (April 1908): 316–17.

In April 1908, psychical researcher James H. Hyslop published a call for information in *The Monist*. The two-page entry states that the American SPR was looking for people to submit their psi experiences and within the notice is twenty-two questions that Hyslop and his colleagues were particularly interested in. The questions include topics related to psi, such as if a person has ever had any visual or auditory hallucinations, premonitions, thought-transference, sightings of apparitions, hauntings, psychic dreams, and more. This report, while brief, gives a firsthand look into the data-gathering process of the ASPR.

Keywords: American Society for Psychical Research; survey; firsthand experiences

Lodge, Sir Oliver. "Abstract of a Paper on Automatism and Possession." *Journal of the Society for Psychical Research* 13 (1908): 180–86.

At the 131st general meeting of the SPR in January 1908, Sir Oliver Lodge read his paper entitled "Automatism and Possession." In the report of that meeting in volume thirteen of the SPR's journal, we get a glimpse into that article. Lodge's article presents a link between automatism (such as occuring during automatic writing or trance), and possession. Noting that the vast connotation of the word "possession" is something inherently negative, Lodge attempts to "cleanse the word"[43] and remove it of those negative judgments. He states that we can view automatism through the lens of personal possession. He takes this even further when he says that we are possessed of thought each time we have an impulse to perform some physical function and he writes, "By what means the psychical gets out of its region into the physical no one knows, but it is a process on which discovery is possible. The brain is definitely the link between the two universes or modes of existence. It may not be the only link, but it is the only link we know of."[44]

Lodge also presents, in this article, a diagram of the self that shows how we constantly have one foot in the physical world and one foot in the psychical world. Perhaps the most fascinating part of this article are the subsequent diagrams that Lodge produces. He uses these diagrams to show the different ways in which the mind and the external world influence one another through things like psychometry (and its opposite telekinesis), telepathy, ectoplasty, and more. This article is a fascinating look

into the theories of personality, the mind, and their symbiotic relationship with the external world.

Keywords: personality; automatism; Sir Oliver Lodge

Lombroso, Cesare. "What I Think of Psychic Research: A Report on Eusapia Palladino, Most Famous of All Mediums." *Hampton's Magazine* 23, no. 1 (July 1, 1909).

This article is worthy of inclusion to this list for a number of reasons. First, it represents one of the earliest publications from noted psychiatrist and psychical researcher Cesare Lombroso to appear in a US periodical. Second, it serves as a wonderful primary resource that documents reaction to the Italian medium Eusapia Palladino. In the article are detailed descriptions of the phenomena surrounding Palladino and the methods used in her mediumship.

Keywords: Eusapia Palladino; mediums; Cesare Lombroso

Myers, Frederic W. H. *Human Personality and its Survival of Bodily Death.* Two volumes. London: Longmans, Green, & Co., 1903.

In this work, psychical researcher Frederic W. H. Myers provides a summary of the work he discusses in various publications such as the *Journal and Proceedings of the Society for Psychical Research,* and within *Phantasms of the Living.* Putting together a summary of his work here, however, Myers provides an anthology of sorts on the survival of human personality after death. In his preface we see a glimpse into the tensions between psychical researchers and others within the scientific community as Myers tells us,

> I need not say that the attitude of the scientific world . . . then was very much more marked than now. Even now I write in full consciousness of the low value commonly attached to inquiries of the kind which I pursue. Even now a book on such a subject must still expect to evoke, not only legitimate criticisms of many kinds, but also much of that disgust and resentment which novelty and heterodoxy naturally excite."[45]

He begins his work with a glossary of common terms so that readers will have some prior familiarity as they browse. He then provides a discussion on the ways in which human personality is altered among various states such as sleep, hypnosis, and automatism. Appendixes that reference each chapter provide case studies and are essentially an entire book unto themselves. In the second volume, Myers discusses phantasms of the dead, motor automatism, and trance. At the beginning of this second volume, he provides syllabi of key takeaways from each chapter, creating a handy guide for the reader. Within both volumes he stresses the reality that human personality is a much more complex phenomenon than what scientists currently understand, and that consciousness seems to be affected in various states.

Keywords: consciousness after death; automatism; trance; hypnotism

Podmore, Frank. *Modern Spiritualism: A History and a Criticism.* Two volumes. London: Metheun & Co., 1902.

Psychical researcher Frank Podmore wrote this two-volume work on Spiritualism in 1902. In volume 1, he presents a comprehensive discussion of the rise of Spiritualism, the role of mediums, associated phenomena, scientific inquiry, fraudulent behavior, and more. In the introduction Podmore tells us that many people of the time viewed Spiritualism on a spectrum somewhere between faith and religion. The crux of the movement centered around the idea that one could communicate with deceased spirits. He writes, "The primary aim of the present work is to provide the necessary data for determining how far, if at all, that interpretation of the facts is justified . . . if not justified, what is the true interpretation of the facts? And second, how can the origin and persistence of the false interpretation be explained?"[46]

In the first four chapters, Podmore discusses the social and historical contexts predating Spiritualism that had a direct impact on the eventual development of that movement. He discusses social thought on witchcraft, possession, poltergeists, and mesmerism. These chapters all provide a historical context to how Spiritualism gained a foothold in the mid to late 1800s. In chapters 5 and 6, Podmore discusses the rise of trance mediumship in France up to the 1840s. He then proceeds to discuss, in the follow-ing chapter, German thoughts on clairvoyance and trance and follows this with a few chapters on trance and Spiritualism in England.

Book two of this first volume focuses on early American Spiritualism. He begins with a discussion of the infamous Fox sisters and the subsequent boom in popularity of séances of mediums. He also spends a chapter discussing the physical phenomena that occurred during these séances, like apports and levitations, etc. The following few chapters discuss instances of clairvoyance and automatic writing before touching on some social behaviors and beliefs of Spiritualists. He ends volume 1 here and begins volume 2 with "book three" in this set, which is a more detailed discussion of Spiritualism in England. Subsequent chapters include discussions of American mediums who traveled to the United Kingdom in an attempt to make a name for themselves, the rise of private mediumship, materializations, spirit photographs, and clairvoyance. One of the final chapters in book three provides an overview of various thoughts on Spiritualism from a diverse range of scholars and researchers.

Book four in volume 2 is titled "Problems of Mediumship" and points out explanations for various mediumistic phenomena and instances of fraud, such as the case of Eusapia Palladino. Podmore also provides a chapter on the role that hallucination may play, and goes on to discuss dreams, automatism and the role of belief, and a detailed case study of American medium Leonora Piper. An important work by an early psychical researcher, this foundational work was later republished in 1963 in a two-volume work under the title *Mediums of the 19th Century.*

Keywords: history of Spiritualism; mediums; trance; mesmerism; Leonora Piper; Daniel Dunglas Home; Eusapia Palladino

Sheldon, William Henry. "A Case of Psychical Causation?" *Philosophical Review* 11 (January 1, 1902): 578–95.

Author W. H. Sheldon lays out the goal of this article immediately. He tells us, "The aim of this paper is to show that there is possibly such a thing as purely psychical causation."[47] Sheldon begins by acknowledging some of the most prevalent arguments against the reality of psi before digging into a discussion of the conditions under which we can assume that psi might be possible. Sheldon, who was associated with Columbia University, presents a philosophical discussion of the conditions necessary for psi and simultaneously shows how the topic of psychical research branched outward to disciplines beyond psychology.

Keywords: psychical causation; conditions for psi

Vaschide, N. "Experimental Investigations of Telepathic Hallucinations." *The Monist* 12, no. 2 (January 1902): 273–307.

In this article, Vaschide discusses the importance of scientific inquiry into telepathy and points out the dismissive attitudes that some harbor in regards to psi research. Vaschide writes, "The end of the nineteenth century will mark an important date in the history of this branch of science, for never until now have these vague suppositions, these light and tenuous issues of false judgement, of legend, emotions, dreams, and beliefs been subjected to a scientifically methodical and systematic investigation by specialists."[48] Presenting the two biggest hurdles that stand in the way of accepting psi research as legitimate (namely the notion that two physical minds can seemingly connect across distance *and* the retrieval of messages from those no longer living), the author asks, "Why should we not try to classify the facts that have been gathered, to bring a little order into this world of hallucinations, for who knows but there is a great truth here, something that may escape us."[49]

Vaschide focuses on research on thought-transference, or telepathy. They begin with a detailed overview and discussion of the seminal study *Phantasms of the Living*. Along the way they also reference psychical research coming out of France, such as a survey on telepathy done ten years prior to *Phantasms*. The author points out the detailed methods and results in *Phantasms* but also provides a detailed list of their criticisms against the study. The biggest critique Vaschide points out is the lack of adequate inquiry into the respondent's emotional state and intelligence. Vaschide tells us that their colleagues were also collecting research on thought-transference and came to opposite conclusions from these SPR authors. In their experiment, Vaschide

and colleagues studied thirty-four people and their claims of telepathic experiences. They point out that the majority are reconciled as erroneous and perhaps only seemed real due to the power of suggestion and a willingness to believe. They conclude by saying that these phenomena persist across cultures and appear in many forms but calls for more rigorous standards when testing.

Keywords: thought-transference; hallucination; criticism; Society for Psychical Research; Phantasms of the Living

1910s

Baggally, W. W. "Report on Sittings with Charles Bailey, the Australian Apport Medium." *Journal of the Society for Psychical Research* 15, no. 286 (February 1912): 194–208.

Charles Bailey was an Australian medium who garnered a certain amount of fame and attention for his séances in which he would produce apported items. Apports refers to items that seemingly appear as if from thin air. During his séances, Bailey would even apport exotic animals and alleged cuneiform tablets. In addition to his exploits in Australia and Europe, Bailey visited London in 1911, offering public séances of which researcher W. W. Baggally was able to attend.

Baggally begins his report by reminding readers that a commission of European engineers and doctors had found Bailey guilty of fraud in producing these apports, some of which had been published in volume 12 of the *Journal of the Society for Psychical Research*. During his attendance at a number of Bailey's séances, Baggally reports the details of each séance and the ways in which he and his colleagues ferreted out fraudulent behavior. Some of this consisted of requiring complete darkness that would conceal the introduction of apports and animals to the medium by conspirators. In another instance, Baggally brought a handmade satin bag to the séance, waited until Bailey was under the influence of his alleged spirit control, and asked if he would consent to enclosing himself up to his neck in the bag to facilitate proof of genuine ability of apports, but the spirit control refused. Essentially sealing the deal for Baggally, his report details some of the ways in which mediums performed their tricks and offers a firsthand account of séance investigations. Anyone interested in séances and mediums will want to ensure including this (or others like it) that discuss the ways in which mediums created illusions.

Keywords: mediumship; fraud; Australia; Charles Bailey; apports

Barrett, William F. *On the Threshold of the Unseen: An Examination of the Phenomena of Spiritualism and of the Evidence for Survival after Death.* New York: E. P. Dutton & Company, 1918.

William F. Barrett was among the early, founding members of the British SPR. A physicist by training, he was also interested in psychical phenomena. In this work, he presents his more than forty years of research and reflection on the topic. He acknowledges, in the introduction, the struggle that psychical science has had to gain a footing in the academy. In 1918, he mused that this tension was abating and writes, "Many causes have in recent years contributed to lessen this aversion, which is not only passing away but giving place to an earnest desire to know what trustworthy evidence exists on behalf of super-normal—often, but erroneously, called supernatural,—phenomena."[50]

This work is broken into six parts. The first part discusses both public opinion toward psychical science as well as the criticisms lobbied at it from both physical science and religion. Presenting a solid background of social attitudes and responses to the field, part 2 then goes on to discuss Spiritualism, as any discussion of psychical science would be remiss without that era of séances, which motivated the researcher to put these claims to the test. Part 3 presents some of the leading theories on psi phenomena, the "canons" as Barrett calls them. In this part, Barrett lays out some of the most compelling evidence and the dominant theories behind them—theories that also include critiques, like the possibility of fraud. Here Barrett also discusses the particular issues raised by mediumship and the implications of psi on human personality and the notion of a subliminal self.

In part 4, Barrett lays out more detailed evidence in the realm of apparitions, automatic writing, and

the survival of consciousness after death while part 5 discusses clairvoyance and trance phenomena. The final portion, part 6, discusses reincarnation, telepathy, and their implications on notions of the human soul and personality. This work by an early, noted member of the SPR is a key addition in the historical psi literature.

Keywords: survival after death; telepathy; mediumship; Spiritualism; automatism; human personality; criticisms

Barrett, William F. *Psychical Research.* London: Williams and Norgate, 1911.

In this work, physicist and psychical researcher William F. Barrett discusses a wide range of psi phenomena from ghosts to trance to telepathy and even dowsing rods. He tells us in the first chapter that while some may outright dismiss these events, others lean into wholehearted belief. He goes on to state that many people, though, probably exist somewhere in between, and it is his goal in this work to present a comprehensive outline of credible research so that people may reach their own conclusions. He writes,

> The average busy man, who has no time for critical inquiry, probably thinks that there is a good deal of truth in both these statements, and therefore prefers to give the whole subject a wide berth. But the scornful disdain of the *savant* and the credulous belief of the ignorant are now giving way to a more rational attitude of mind. A widespread desire exists to know something about that debatable borderland between the territory already conquered by science and the dark realms of ignorance and superstition; and to learn what trustworthy evidence exists on behalf of a large class of obscure psychical phenomena, the importance of which it is impossible to exaggerate if the alleged facts be incontestably established.[51]

Barrett's work is very nearly an encyclopedic treatment that outlines multiple psychical phenomena, and he tells us, "Even if only a fraction of what is asserted by credible witnesses be true, [it] opens a new and vastly important chapter in the book of human knowledge."[52] He begins by discussing perhaps the most palatable of the phenomena for readers to begin with—unconscious muscular action, or the use of pendulums and the effects upon them of our subconscious through the muscular system. What Barrett points out as most curious is that even if you are intentionally focusing on keeping your muscles as still as possible, your mind still somehow manifests responses to the question or task at hand to make enough minute movements so that a successful result is achieved.

In the following chapter, Barrett presents an overview of the SPR and the scholars who conducted early work, such as Henry and Eleanor Sidgwick and Frederic W. H. Myers. Barrett himself was a member and early researcher, and in this section he discusses the goals of the society, especially in regard to human personality and consciousness. The chapter that follows discuss thought-reading in normal and trance states, clairvoyance, mesmerism and hypnotism, experimental and spontaneous telepathy, phantasms of both the living and the dead, dreams, poltergeists, and automatic writing. Throughout the chapters we learn about the work being done to investigate these topics and also about the different ways in which these events manifest. A comprehensive treatment of psi from a key psychical researcher, this resource lays out an entire compendium of historical thought and research.

Keywords: psychical research; consciousness; telepathy; hypnotism; ghosts; poltergeists; automatic writing

Barrett, W. F. "Poltergeists: Old and New." (1911) *Proceedings of the Society for Psychical Research* 25, no. 64 (August 1911): 377–412.

In this article, psychical researcher and physicist W. F. Barrett presents a discussion on the phenomena known as poltergeists. Barrett tells us the goal of this work when he writes, "I will now pass on to give some of the evidence that exists on behalf of the genuineness of poltergeist phenomena, beginning with recent cases . . . [and] . . . some of the other abundant evidence that exists in different places."[53] At the beginning of the article, Barrett outlines the definition and typical characteristics of poltergeist phenomena. Barrett tells us,

A *poltergeist* [is] a boisterous ghost. It is a convenient term to describe those apparently meaningless noises, disturbances and movements of objects, for which we can discover no assignable cause. The phenomena are especially sporadic, breaking out suddenly and unexpectedly, and disappearing as suddenly after a few days, or weeks, or months of annoyance to those concerned. They differ from hauntings, inasmuch as they appear to be attached to an individual, usually a young person, more than to a place, or rather to *a person in a particular place.*[54]

He also tells us some of the hallmarks of poltergeist cases, like the fact that apparitions are almost never seen and instead that they manifest through strange sounds and movements of objects. A curious quality of these cases is that there is often an intelligence to the sounds and movements, such that they respond to a question for a certain number of raps or the movement of a particular object. He then goes on to outline some of the more recent and noteworthy poltergeist cases, like the Enniscorthy case, which involved strange events that seemed to center around three men who rented a room in a boarding house. In this case, strange knocks and noises would be heard in an upstairs bedroom, beds would be pulled across the room, clothes yanked from beds, and even one boarder himself yanked out of bed while sleeping, sheets and all. It frightened the three men so much, all of whom shared one room, that they often shared one bed with each other, and sometimes *that* bed, with all three boarders in it, would be pulled across the room. Interestingly, no activity had occurred prior to the boarders staying there and they reported no new activity upon leaving the Enniscorthy home.

Barrett then discusses another case from Ireland, the Derrygonnelly case, of which he was an eyewitness to some activity. The home of a widowed farmer and his five children was the focus of this case. Having heard of some strange occurrences, Barrett found himself visiting and witnessed strange knocks and raps when everyone was visible and accounted for in the room. He also witnessed a stone falling from the ceiling onto a bed where everyone was motionless and/or asleep. He conducted experiments to see if the strange raps and knocks would correspond to his mental projections of certain numbers. They did. Barrett eventually invited a colleague to assist in his investigation and the colleague also witnessed the strange activity. The case eventually ended when the family's priest was called to do a blessing. Barrett's conclusion was not *what* was causing the events but an acknowledgment that something strange had indeed occurred at the home.

Barrett then details some cases from the United States, including the case of Mary Carrick, an Irish servant who traveled to work in Massachusetts. Bells would ring and strange knocks and bangs would sound in whatever room she was in. This continued for ten weeks. Then there was a case from Oregon that involved an eleven-year-old boy and the strange movement of objects and levitations of chairs that seemed to center around him while living in his grandparents' home. This case is a rather curious one, though, because while living with a doctor for a few weeks, the boy admitted to faking some of the phenomena, and Barrett concludes that this case perhaps provides more interest in psychology than it does to psychic science.

Barret includes a few other cases before offering his conclusions on what these cases teach us about poltergeists. The cases, he tells us, indicate that there often seems to be some sort of intelligence at work, that phenomena are often associated with young people, that fraud and hallucination can explain some but not *all* phenomena, that poltergeist activity may be accountable for belief in fairies, gnomes, etc. that phenomena doesn't last more than a few months, and that phenomena seem to be affected by suggestion. He concludes his report by writing, "We ourselves and the whole world may be but nucleated cells in a vaster living organism, of which we can form no conception. Some incomprehensible intelligence is certainly at work in the congeries of cells and in the galaxy of suns and stars."[55]

Keywords: poltergeists; Ireland; United States; Vienna

Boirac, Emile. *Psychic Science: An Introduction and Contribution to the Experimental Study of Psychical Phenomena.* Translated by Dudley Wright. London: William Rider and Son, 1918.

This resource written by philosopher Emile Boirac was originally published in French and later translated by Dudley Wright. Most of the chapters in this book were originally published in scholarly journals between 1893 to 1903. The resource here is a compilation of those previously published articles with some new material. Boirac begins his work by pointing out a lack of uniform methodology and a scattershot research approach of various phenomena. In his own (translated) words, he tells us,

Facts multiply but the question of method still awaits solution. So long, however, as it remains unsolved, so long as psychical phenomena are observed and experimented upon at random, no progress will be made, and it will always be possible for new investigators to doubt the validity of the results obtained by their predecessors. Psychical phenomena . . . form a kind of labyrinth which can be entered by a thousand different doors, but wherein we can only walk with assurance if we have taken the right way from the beginning.[56]

What Boirac sets forth to do in this resource is provide a classification of phenomena listed from least complex to most complex. In this schema, each phenomenon requires knowledge of the previous phenomenon in order to successfully research. He classifies events into three categories: hypnoid phenomena (of which is assigned hypnotism and suggestion), magnetoid phenomena (telepathy), and spiritoid phenomena (séances, spiritualist events, etc.).

Keywords: Emile Boirac; early psychical research; hypnotism; telepathy; séances

Coover, J. E. *Experiments in Psychical Research at Leland Stanford Junior University.* Stanford, CA: Stanford University, 1917.

At the time of publication, author J. E. Coover was a psychology professor and psychical research fellow at Stanford University. In this work, he presents a detailed compendium of psychical research methods and experiments. Anyone interested in early psychical experiments must be sure to include this resource on their list. At more than six hundred pages, this work provides a vast amount of information. In addition to research methods on psi topics like thought-transference, though, Coover presents detailed discussions of research into factors that might influence psi, like subliminal symbols, noise assimilation, and more.

In the preface, Coover lays out his feelings on the merits of psi research when he tells us,

It is no adequate defense to claim that science has no time to go out of its way to combat the superstitions and prejudices of men; for no matter to what extent superstition and prejudice may be supported by these alleged phenomena, the phenomena are initially accepted because it is believed they have been repeatedly observed by trustworthy, even eminently qualified, observers.[57]

Broken into parts, the first section deals with experiments involving thought-transference, such as traditional tests that involved the guessing of certain numbers or cards. Coover not only outlines the experiments and the methods, but he also includes information on the data gathered and its statistical implications. In part 2, he discusses subliminal impressions, a theory cited often by scientists as one that could explain thought-transference. Coover details experiments designed to test the impact and effect of subliminal signals on thought-transference. Part 3 continues the discussion of subliminal processes by discussing judgment and mental habits while part 4 discusses how brains might assimilate certain stimuli, like noises, that can result in "malobservation."[58] Included throughout the work are diagrams of experimental setup, charts of statistical information, and more. Anyone looking for a comprehensive discussion on the natural psychological and biological factors that may influence psi phenomena will need to make sure that this work is on their list.

Keywords: subliminal impressions; thought-transference; research methods; statistics; noise assimilation

Crawford, W. J. *Experiments in Psychical Science: Levitation, Contact, and the Direct Voice.* New York: E. P. Dutton & Company, 1919.

W. J. Crawford, a mechanical engineer and professor at Queen's University in Belfast, Ireland, presents in this book an assortment of experiments designed to test levitation, trance channeling, and other phenomena associated with mediums. It can be considered a continuation of the conversations in Crawford's 1917 work *The Reality of Psychic Phenomena*. He tells us, "My purpose in writing these books is to advance our knowledge of psychic phenomena and the laws underlying them," and reminds us that "one needs to take these psychic matters in small doses if they are to have any chance of assimilation."[59]

In this book, Barrett details his work with the Goligher Circle in Belfast in 1916–1917. The Goligher Circle was a group of family members who regularly met to host sittings and during which levitations of objects were claimed to occur. It is those levitations

that Crawford focuses on here. He had presented, in his first book, a cantilever theory that proposed a type of psychic "rod" that extended from the medium during trance, and which would act upon the table, resulting in tilting and levitation. Crawford focuses on various questions surrounding the physics of these supposed psychic rods and diagrams many of them in this book. Offering a detailed look into the early years of the Goligher Circle, and a fascinating entry into the physical phenomena of mediumship during the spiritualist era, this book gives readers a firsthand look into the ways in which people were convinced of and investigated certain mediumistic phenomena. Author Carlos S. Alvarado points out the importance of Crawford's work in the psychical timeline when he tells us,

> While Crawford was a relative latecomer to such theoretical concerns [of the cantilever theories], his contributions were important. His case represents an interesting historical example of process research with physical phenomena. As such, Crawford's work deserves a prominent place in the history of efforts to understand the physical aspects behind telekinesis and materializations.[60]

Keywords: Goligher Circle; mediumship; levitation; psychic rod; ectoplasm

Dallas, Helen A. *Death, the Gate of Life? A Discussion of Certain Communications Purporting to Come from Frederic W. H. Myers.* New York: E.P. Dutton, 1919.

Author Helen A. Dallas tells us that "the object of this little book is to bring before those who are not already familiar with the results of psychical research some small portion of the evidence for survival which has been accumulating within the last few years."[61] This book is unique, however, in that it discusses the efforts to communicate with the "personality" of one particular deceased individual: psychical researcher Frederic W. H. Myers.

Dallas begins with an introduction to Myers and his philosophies on psychical research. We learn in this chapter about Myers's beliefs and dedications, and in the following chapter Dallas launches into a discussion on the various mediums who claimed to receive messages from Myers after his death. One of these mediums was Mrs. Verrall who claimed to have received messages via automatic writing. Other mediums include Mrs. Thompson and Leonora Piper. This book outlines the communications of these mediums and how it connects to Frederic W. H. Myers and the case for the survival of personality beyond bodily death. Anyone interested in the life of Myers, or the notion of cross-correspondences, will want to consider this resource.

Keywords: Frederic W. H. Myers; cross-correspondences; mediumship; automatic writing; Mrs. Thompson; Mrs. Verrall; Leonora Piper

Hill, J. Arthur. *Psychical Investigations: Some Personally-Observed Proofs of Survival.* London: Cassell and Company, 1917.

Researcher Arthur J. Hill presents in this work a summary of his inquiry into mediums and the notion of consciousness beyond death. In this work he provides transcripts of thirteen sittings he had with various mediums, which offer readers a wonderful firsthand look into the experience of mediumship. He provides detailed transcripts because he believes that they will be more impressive in relaying the notion that these events provide proof of life after death than reports and summaries, such as those found in journals and proceedings.

He doesn't overlook the complex nature of the topic at hand, however. In the preface to this work, Hill discusses the importance of questioning an author's bias on the subject matter, particularly when that subject matter is often a divisive one. He writes,

> In debatable matters, such as psychical research, readers may naturally wish for information which shall enable them to estimate the amount of a writer's bias. It may therefore be useful to affirm that, at the beginning of my investigations, my prejudices and wishes were opposed to the conclusions which the facts gradually forced upon me. If I am now biased in favour of the belief in personal life after death, it is objective fact, not subjective preference, that has brought it about. And my judgments have not been hasty. I have worked at the subject for over eleven years.[62]

Thirteen different sittings Hill had and the transcripts from those sittings are then presented, after which Hill provides a bit of discussion. For readers interested in the details of mediumship and what it means to attend a sitting, this work provides a firsthand look into those events.

Keywords: mediumship; transcripts; consciousness beyond death; sittings

Hyslop, James H. "Mrs. Sidgwick's Report on the Piper Trance." *Journal of the American Society for Psychical Research* 11, no. 1 (January 1917): 1–123.

In this article, psychical researcher James H. Hyslop presents an overview of Eleanor Sidgwick's more than six hundred-page report on medium Leonora Piper. Sidgwick's report was compiled after she sifted through the research and notes of the deceased psychical researcher Richard Hodgson, who spent a lot of time investigating Piper's mediumship. Deemed too large to publish in its entirety, Hyslop presents here a (still-lengthy) reaction to Sidgwick's report in which he not only outlines her work but also presents his own thoughts and reactions. Hyslop tells us, "The report is, in fact, a continuation and elaboration of the view which Mrs. Sidgwick advanced in review and criticism of the position taken in Dr. Hodgson's second report on the phenomena of Mrs. Piper's trance."[63]

In this report we learn of Dr. Hodgson's theory of Piper—he believed that her abilities were genuine and that they showed that her physical body was used as a medium for spirit communication. In essence, Hodgson's conclusion draws near to theories of possession. But Hodgson also believed that the subconscious could be at work too, and that it was a unique interplay between the psychological and the physical. Hyslop goes on to discuss the various theories that seem to place the role of the physical body and the role of the subconscious at key junctures in the discussion on the validity of trance mediumship. In this section Hyslop also lays out critiques of Sidgwick's interpretation of Piper's phenomena and compares hers and Hodgson's theories side by side.

Hyslop's report is a detailed response to the previous work and research into Piper's mediumship. Within this document, Hyslop tells us that he is concerned with analyzing three questions: "(1) Do the 'communications' come solely from spirits?; (2) Do they come solely from 'a phase or centre of consciousness of Mrs. Piper herself?' (3) Do they come from both sources at the same time and thus represent an interfusion of two minds? That is, do they issue from A or from B, or from both A and B?"[64] This detailed analysis of various research into Leonora Piper is one not to be missed if you are looking for information on the American medium. Additionally, this resource offers a peek into the various psychical theories and different approaches with which psychical researchers approached topics.

Keywords: Leonora Piper; Eleanor Sidgwick; Richard Hodgson; mediumship; consciousness; spirit control; subconscious

James, William. "What Psychical Research Has Accomplished." In *The Will to Believe: And Other Essays in Popular Philosophy*, 299–327. London: Longmans, Green, & Co., 1912: Originally published in 1896.

Referred to as the father of American psychology, scholar William James presents in this book a compendium of essays that touch on all manner of topics, including belief, rationality, determinism, and religion. He also includes an essay on psychical science. In the introduction, James tells us,

> The paper on Psychical Research is added to the volume for convenience and utility. Attracted to this study some years ago by my love of sportsmanlike fair play in science, I have seen enough to convince me of its great importance, and I wish to gain for it what interest I can. The American Branch of the Society is in need of more support, and if my article draws some new associates thereto, it will have served its turn.[65]

In this article he begins by telling us, "Round about the accredited and orderly facts of every science there ever floats a sort of dust-cloud of exceptional observations, of occurrences minute and irregular and seldom met with, which it always proves more easy to ignore than to attend to."[66] He goes on to discuss the philosophical tensions between what he calls the "mystics" and the "academics" and he dispels some of the assumptions that members of the SPR are not credible and critical scientists. He then tells readers about the history of the SPR. James then provides a summary of research of the early years of the society and the types of publications found within their scholarly journal and proceedings. The result is a summary of psychical research up to the turn of the century—an essay that is a perfect introduction to not only psychical research but the complex scientific and philosophical tensions that come with it.

Keywords: Society for Psychical Research; summary of research to 1900

Joire, Paul. *Psychical and Supernormal Phenomena: Their Observation and Experimentation.* Translated by Dudley Wright. New York: Frederick A. Stokes, Co., 1917.

Dr. Paul Joire was a professor at the Psycho-Physiological Institute in France at the time he wrote this book. He opens with a discussion on hypnotism and the subsequent supernormal abilities that seemed to spring forth from it. He wonders if, just like the supernormal abilities like telepathy can spring forth from induced states, can they also occur during spontaneous moments? These abilities, discovered seemingly unexpectedly, make us question the foundation of what we know about the mind. Joire writes, "We are thus forced to ask ourselves if thought is quite as abstract a phenomenon as we have hitherto believed it to be, and if, in certain instances, it is not capable of creating a durable entity possessing independent force."[67] And from here, he wonders, where does the boundary exist? In addition to telepathy, what about psychokinesis, and poltergeists and haunted houses, and more?

In this work, Joire provides an exhaustive discussion of all of the above . . . and more. Chapters include discussions on some of the expected psychical topics like abnormal dreams, poltergeists, haunted houses, and telepathy. But Joire also includes discussions of topics not found in many other compendiums, like crystal-gazing and crystal-vision. Crystal-gazing, Joire tells us, is an ancient practice that is not *necessarily* supernormal—it invokes a hypnotic, trance-like state in which subconscious images may pop up. Once in this trance-like state, a whole manner of things could happen. Subconscious images may pop up—images perhaps filtered through from things in that person's day or even from deep within their memories. But also, Joire posits, psychical events could be facilitated too, like the telepathic transmission of a sitter to the one crystal-gazing.

Typtology is another topic and is the focus of five chapters. Typtology essentially refers to collective table-tipping. Typtology involves people seated around a table who place their hands lightly atop the table, like how readers today might place their hands gently on a Ouija board's planchette. Eventually, due to the subconscious pressure from the hands and a result of the ideomotor effect, the table would begin tilting one way or another, tapping as it did. At this point, sitters would ask for answers to yes or no questions, requiring a certain number of taps for each.

Another lesser-used word, motricity, which is essentially psychokinesis, or moving objects without physically touching them, is the focus of another chapter. Joire goes on to discuss apparitions, levitations, and various experiments with the mediums Daniel Dunglas Home and Eusapia Palladino. He also spends multiple chapters discussing experimental methods of psychical research and points out the criticisms and instances of fraud within the discipline. Taken as a whole, this work is an encyclopedic treatment of psi phenomena and experimentation and would be an extremely useful resource for anyone looking for a comprehensive overview of psychical science from a historical perspective.

He concludes his work with this passage:

> What we find, in fact, is that with every discovery the extent of our ignorance appears more clearly before our eyes. Each time the light of science enables us to clear up some obscure point of the unknown, we see better the frailty of human theories and we understand more clearly how feeble is the intelligence of man in the presence of the Infinite.[68]

Keywords: research methods; apparitions; telepathy; hypnosis; mediumship; table-tipping; physiology

Ramström, O. M. *Swedenborg on the Cerebral Cortex as the Seat of Psychical Activity.* Presented at the International Swedenborg Congress, July 4–8, 1910.

Author O. M. Ramström presents a discussion of the work of Emanuel Swedenborg, a Swedish philosopher and mystic. During the course of his research, Swedenborg noticed that in cases of trauma to the cerebral cortex, patients displayed changes in sensation and motility. In other words, things that affected the cerebral cortex also affected the ways

in which people were able to sense things physically and mentally. Therefore, he posited that the cerebral cortex was key to understanding psychic phenomena. He even claimed that different types of psychic abilities were located in different areas of the cerebral cortex. In this article, Ramström discusses this theory and in doing so gives us a glimpse into the mind of the Swedish mystic. Though Swedenborg predates both Spiritualism and the timeframe of this bibliography, he is a useful person to know in the history of psychical thought and inquiry.

Keywords: Emanuel Swedenborg; cerebral cortex

1920s

Balfour, Gerald W. *The Ear of Dionysus: Farther Scripts Affording Evidence of Personal Survival.* New York: Henry Holt & Company, 1920.

Gerald W. Balfour was a British earl, politician, and member and past president of the SPR. This book is part of SPR's Psychic Series, which contains a variety of other works as well, on all manner of psychical topics. In this work, Balfour discusses the "scripts" (i.e., transcripts) of both spoken and written text during sittings with the medium Mrs. Willett. In particular, he focuses on a phrase about the ear of Dionysus that came through during one of her sessions and how it led him down a rabbit hole of research about things which the medium could and couldn't have known prior to these sittings. He also discusses cross-correspondences.

Keywords: mediumship; Mrs. Willett; cross-correspondences

Barrett, William and Theodore Besterman. *The Divining-Rod: An Experimental and Psychological Investigation.* London: Methuen & Co., 1926.

In this book, William Barrett and Theodore Besterman discuss the practice of water-dowsing. The ability to "divine" the presence of water in some location was viewed by many as a psychical notion. The author and noted psychical researcher William Barrett wrote upwards of six thousand letters during his inquiries into water dowsing and, in this book, released posthumously for Barrett, the authors discuss the characteristics of and studies into water dowsing. It is a unique entry in the field of psychical research.

Keywords: water-dowsing

Carrington, Hereward. *The Problems of Psychical Research: Experiments and Theories in the Realm of the Supernormal.* New York: Dodd, Mead, and Company, 1921.

In this book, psychical researcher Hereward Carrington presents his thoughts on psychical research and how the discipline might progress forward. He tells us, in his introduction,

> In the following pages I have dealt chiefly with the *mental* or psychological phenomena of psychical research, and have not touched upon the "physical" manifestations to any extent. The book is mostly theoretical and constructive in tone; and because of its speculative character, it may, perhaps, prove of value to future psychical investigators. It represents the author's conclusions after several years' experimentation; and, in a field so new as this, scientific hypotheses and speculations are assuredly helpful—indicating the road we must travel.[69]

Carrington approaches the topic by stating that we can confidently acknowledge that psi phenomena occur and now the task before us is to inquire *how* it occurs. Chapter 2 discusses the various devices and instruments that can (and have) been used during experiments while chapter 4 discusses how the human will is a physical presence itself. In this chapter, Carrington outlines a specific device and experiment, modified from a similar experiment from fellow psychical researcher William Crookes, that seeks to measure the effect of the human will on a physical object. The next few chapters discuss the human mind, evidence for telepathy, and the abuses of psychotherapy or mind-power. The last three chapters are very interesting and include discussions on Ouija boards, witchcraft, and fairy folklore. Carrington's work presents not only a discussion of scientific overviews of psychical research, but also manages to situate these issues within a broader social context.

Keywords: thought-transference; ESP; psychical research methods and devices

Crookes, William. *Researches into the Phenomena of Modern Spiritualism,* 4th ed. Los Angeles: Austin Publishing Company, 1922.

This work, by noted psychical researcher and chemist William Crookes, provides snippets of his research published in the *Quarterly Journal of Science* and from his 1898 speech at the meeting of the British Association. His research involves inquiry into mediums, especially those of Daniel Dunglas Home and Florence Cook. The first article, in fact, discusses his research into the mediumship of Daniel Douglas Home—research of which Crookes writes,

> Of all the persons endowed with a powerful development [of] this Psychic Force, and who have been termed "mediums" . . . Mr. Daniel Douglas [*sic*] Home is the most remarkable, and it is mainly owing to the many opportunities I have had of carrying on my investigation in his presence that I am enabled to affirm so conclusively the existence of this Force. The experiments I have tried have been very numerous, but owing to our imperfect knowledge of the conditions which favor or oppose the manifestations of this force, to the apparently capricious manner in which it is exerted, and to the fact that Mr. Home himself is subject to unaccountable ebbs and flows of the force, it has but seldom happened that a result obtained on one occasion could be subsequently confirmed and tested with apparatus specially contrived for the purpose.[70]

The rest of the article goes on to describe the devices used by Crookes to record the strange phenomena that occurred during Home's séances. In the next article, Crookes outlines the types of phenomena he witnessed during séances he held at his own home with the aforementioned Home and one of the infamous spiritualist sisters, Kate Fox. These phenomena include objects seemingly moving of their own accord, strange sounds and raps, levitation of objects and persons, manifestation of apparitions and disembodied hands, and more. Following this, he provides eight theories which may account for those events. There are also articles on the mediumship of Florence Cook and her spirit control, Katie King. The work concludes with Crookes's remarks to the 1898 meeting of the British Association and an interesting appendix of quotes from prominent figures of the day on the merits of psychical science and Spiritualism.

This work presents primary sources of psychical research that help to paint an accurate picture of some scientific thought and response to certain events and phenomena. Compared to what we now know today of many of the mediums of the spiritualist era, this resource provides the unique perspective of those researchers who watched the events unfold.

Keywords: William Crookes; Daniel Dunglas Home; Katie King; Florence Cook; mediumship; theories

Flammarion, Camille. *Death and its Mystery at the Moment of Death: Manifestations and Apparitions of the Dying, "Doubles," Phenomena of Occultism.* Translated by L. Carroll. New York: The Century Co., 1922.

Author Camille Flammarion was a French astronomer and psychical researcher. In this book, he presents evidence for apparitions and the strange phenomena that surround death. In the introduction, he tells us, "The facts that are to follow will prove superabundantly the truth of our thesis, through manifestations observed round and about death and after death."[71]

Flammarion's thesis is that "The soul [is] an entity independent of the body."[72] He begins his work by addressing some of the most recurrent criticisms of psychical research before diving into a subsequent chapter titled "Phantasms of the Living." In this chapter, Flammarion discusses the cases of apparitions of those known to still be alive, such as those cases laid out in the seminal text *Phantasms of the Living.* Flammarion discusses the conscious and unconscious aspects of this phenomenon, though. The unconscious moments of course being those spontaneously occurring cases wherein a person witnesses (or obtains an intense psychic impression of) someone at the moment of great peril or death. A conscious example of an apparition of the living involves intentional experimentation. Flammarion tells us, "People have tried, with success, to bring about experimental[73] apparitions between the living," like a woman who claimed to successfully send a psychic, a seemingly-real impression of herself to her sister living miles away. Flammarion compares thought to a generator: something that is able to send impressions outward.

In the following chapters, Flammarion provides case reports of specific death or near-death psychical events. For example, there are cases of people seeing apparitions of people shortly before their death and there are cases of people receiving intense psychic impressions of detailed death scenes. He also presents a discussion of cases that deal with physical phenomena, such as psychic impressions that accompany physical touch or sound. This work by a noted French researcher adds to the many discussions on death and near-death psi events of the nineteenth century.

Keywords: apparitions; ghosts; phantasms of the living; consciousness

Lambert, Helen C. *A General Survey of Psychical Phenomena.* New York: Knickerbocker Press, 1928.

In this work, Helen C. Lambert presents a survey of work on psychical topics specifically intended for the "layman," or general reader. A unique aspect of this work is that it is most specifically aimed at laypeople who engage in psychical research. This might be akin to the term "ghost hunters" today. Lambert tells us that to best attempt psi experimentation, even if it is amateurish in nature, knowledge of the research within the field is helpful. She specifically acknowledges that many people are drawn to the topic, perhaps due to a desire to contact their loved ones via a medium. This echoes the allure of the paranormal that exists still today.

In the preface to this work, Stanley De Brath provides a description of Lambert's work when he writes, "Such books as this, by competent, restrained, and cautious investigators, who have not only had personal experience of leading phenomena, but have studied the classical works on the subject and drawn legitimate inferences from them, are of the greatest possible value."[74]

This work is divided into two parts. The first part provides a topical overview of key figures and cases of levitation, ectoplasm, spontaneous psi, telepathy, dreams, and after-death studies. In part 2, Lambert presents personal cases of psi phenomena, even including witness signatures and testimony. Rounding out part 2 are discussions on psychic healing.

Keywords: general bibliography; personal accounts

Lodge, Sir Oliver. *Conviction of Survival: Two Discourses in Memory of F. W. H. Myers.* London: Methuen & Co., 1929.

This resource contains two lectures given in memory of the prominent psychical researcher Frederic W. H. Myers. In these lectures, we get a sense of the impact of Myers's work and his lingering reputation in the field of psychical research. In one essay, author Sir Oliver Lodge discusses the possible postdeath communications of Myers gathered through mediums—one of them being Lodge's own son, Raymond. These essays serve as testimony to the impact of Myers and his contributions.

Keywords: Frederic W. H. Myers; mediumship; survival after death

McDougall, William. "The Need for Psychical Research." *Journal of the American Society for Psychical Research* 17, no. 1 (January 1923): 4–14.

Author William McDougall was a professor at various universities throughout his life, including Harvard, Oxford, and Duke. It was at Duke University, in fact, where he founded the Duke Parapsychology Labs with his colleague and fellow psychical research J. B. Rhine. McDougall was also the president of both the British and American branches of the SPR in the 1920s. This article was originally presented as his president's address to the American Society for Psychical Research in 1922.

In his address, McDougall tells us, "There must be thousands of intelligent people, not now members of the Society, who agree with me in thinking that Psychical Research is in some manner and degree fascinating. My aim is to stimulate that interest—and to try to give the interest a more practical bent than perhaps it has had hitherto."[75] McDougall goes on to address some of the arguments against psychical research, noting certain attitudes that abound in and out of the academy. He also points out the reasons why psychical science is beneficial and necessary for advancing our knowledge about biology and psychology, for example. McDougall also spends a good deal of time addressing ways to get support for continued interest in and funding for psi research. He even points out that the "indifferent" masses, especially the religious ones, should be persuaded to be concerned with psi since it can potentially hold the key for proof of "spirit" after death. McDougall also addresses the role that spiritualist attitudes play in advancing the cause of psychical science and raises the curious involvement of Sir Arthur Conan Doyle within this history. For those looking for a primary source on the early days of psychical research, this presidential address from a seminal figure will prove invaluable.

Keywords: American Society for Psychical Research; public support; public attitudes

Osty, Eugene. *Supernormal Faculties in Man: An Experimental Study.* Translated by Stanley de Brath. London: Methuen & Co., 1923.

Dr. Eugene Osty was a French psychical researcher and physician. In this book, he presents his work investigating "supernormal" abilities and his contributions to what he calls "metanormal psychology."[76] In his own words he tells us, "I now present to informed readers this new book, which has a double-purpose—to trace the main outlines of the problem of supernormal cognition, and to make a general psychological study of the conditions under which that study is most fertile."[77]

He writes, "The phenomenon of supernormal cognition is, as will be seen, reproducible at will, provided that its processes are known. It does not depend on any faith in the witnesses, nor on any beliefs, whether positive or negative, but on exact observations and on experiments that can be renewed at any time."[78] Dr. Osty divides his book into five parts. In the first part he outlines definitions of normal and supernormal cognition. Within this section, he outlines both internal and external supernormal cognition, such as information about the self versus information about external surroundings. The following sections go on to outline what happens during supernormal cognition, what these phenomena might reveal about psychology, and theories on where this supernormal ability might come from. Throughout this work, Dr. Osty includes detailed transcripts from his studies and discussions on how future psychical researchers can benefit from his methods. This work from a prominent French psychical researcher helps illustrate the international scope of psi.

Keywords: metanormal psychology; experimental psychology; research methods; supernormal cognition

Piper, Alta L. *The Life and Work of Mrs. Piper.* London: Kegan, Paul, Trench, Trubner, & Co., 1929.

In this work, author Alta L. Piper presents a comprehensive biography of American medium Leonora Piper. The work traces Leonora Piper and her mediumistic abilities from childhood into her adult life, tracing along the way her involvement with various psychical researchers such as William James, Richard Hodgson, and more. Alta Piper also includes chapters on the medium's experiments abroad in England, administered by the SPR, as well as some of her more noteworthy cases, like the efforts to communicate with Richard Hodgson after his death.

In the foreword to this book, psychical researcher Sir Oliver Lodge reminds us of the way in which Leonora Piper came to the attention of the scientific community. Members of William James's family had attended séances with her and kept encouraging James to attend a sitting with them. After repeated encouragement, James finally attended, and the American medium caught his attention. The rest, as they say, is history.

Keywords: Leonora Piper; biography; mediumship

Rhine, J. B. and Louisa E. Rhine. "One Evening's Observation on the Margery Mediumship." *The Journal of Abnormal and Social Psychology* 21, no. 4 (1927): 401–21.

In July 1926, researchers J. B. and Louisa Rhine were invited to attend a séance with the medium known as Margery. In this article, the Rhines outline their experience as "friendly observers."[79] They take note of the measures taken to prep prior to the séance, such as Margery's use of witnesses as she dressed for the event and the ways in which the medium was tied both to the chair, cabinet, and the wall behind her. The Rhines were even able to analyze a few devices used by Margery prior to the séance, observing them for any possible uses of deceit or trickery.

The article begins with an overview of the types of phenomena that seemingly occurred during the séance. The Rhines go into detail outlining seven different activities that transpired, such as a flower basket levitating, a bell mysteriously ringing, strange voices manifesting, and more. Once they outline the events of the séance and discuss what happened, they dive into their interpretation and analysis. This section starts off with the Rhines telling us,

In spite of our deep interest in psychical research and the spirit hypothesis, and in spite of a predisposition in favor of the genuineness of this case, we could not avoid certain observations which completely altered the character of the performance. These small but very significant data led us to discover that the whole game was a base and brazen trickery, carried out cleverly enough under the guise of spirit manifestations.[80]

What follows next is a detailed analysis of the ways in which the séance phenomena could have been manipulated so as to appear genuine. The Rhines point to three general categories of events that led them to this conclusion: certain conditions of both the lighting and the restraints, inconsistencies throughout the performance, and explicit moments of fraud. One of these examples is the fact that Margery was not able to identify writing on a bank note when a month prior her husband claimed that she was able to make two hundred correct observations of markings on playing cards while in a mediumistic trance. They also pointed to the curious instances in which Margery's husband claimed he needed to be by her side during specific moments in the séance, under the guise of adding his energy to hers for a boost. Other moments of explicit fraud were noticed, such as when J. B. Rhine witnessed the medium's hand tossing out objects said to be psychically manipulated by "Walter."

At another point in the article, the Rhines discuss factors that assisted the Crandon's séances as genuine. First, they point out that Margery and her husband use different techniques to perform the same tricks, thereby potentially making their trickery harder to observe. Additionally, the Rhines note that the Crandon's charm and reputation in society made some visitors perhaps less willing to consider that they had been duped. After a lengthy discussion, the Rhines sum up their thoughts on the nature of this case when they write,

Mrs. Crandon, knowing of her husband's morbid fear of death and intense interest in psychic affairs and needing to create a bond between them to save herself and her interests, started the table tipping which launched the mediumship. Having read considerably on the subject he at once entered into it with thoroughness and enthusiasm and she soon found herself "in deep water." Later he gradually found out that she was deceiving him, the groups of admiring society it brought to his home to hear him lecture and to be entertained . . . he therefore continued to play the game.[81]

This case study by J. B. and Louisa Rhine is an important addition to the case of Margery and her alleged mediumistic abilities.

Keywords: séance, Margery, the Crandons; fraud

Richet, Charles. *Thirty Years of Psychical Research: Being a Treatise on Metaphysics.* New York: Macmillan, 1923.

Dedicated to the memory of his colleagues William Crookes and Frederic W. H. Myers, French physiologist and psychical researcher Charles Richet outlines the past thirty years' worth of psi research in this 1923 work. Richet divides this work into three parts. In part 1 he provides definitions and classifications of the types of psychical phenomena along with a discussion on the source of those phenomena. In this first part he also includes a historical overview of how humans have viewed metaphysical phenomena through the ages. Metaphysics, by the way, is the term Richet uses quite frequently to describe psychical phenomena. In part 2, he focuses on "subjective metaphysics," which include topics like telepathy, hypnotism, crystal vision, and cryptesthesia, just to name a few. This section primarily refers to the inward-focused psi phenomena as opposed to the "objective metaphysics" he discusses in part 3. In this part, Richet discusses the more physical phenomena like psychokinesis, apparitions, direct writing, levitation, ectoplasm, etc. The final part of the book includes Richet's concluding remarks and index. Today this work serves as a historical review that gives us a glimpse into how people thought of and approached psychical phenomena at the turn of the twentieth century.

Keywords: historical review; metaphysics; telepathy; hypnotism; psychokinesis; apparitions

Schrenck-Notzing, A. von. *Phenomena of Materialization: A Contribution to the Investigation of Mediumistic Teleplastics.* London: Kegan, Paul, Trench, Trubner, and Co., 1920.

Baron Albert von Schrenck-Notzing was a German physician and psychical researcher noted for his research into mediumship, especially that of Eva C. (Eva Carrière) and the Schneider Brothers, Rudi and Willie. In this work Schrenck-Notzing focuses on the medium Eva C. and his research into her. This work covers the period of 1909–1919 and includes not only Schrenck-Notzing's research, but also the research of others like Gustave Geley.

The research compiled in this work took place primarily in Paris and employed the use of photography to capture certain moments in Eva's séances. When Schrenck-Notzing wasn't in Paris, his colleague (and Eva's roommate) Juliette Bisson would capture photographs in his place. The first part of this book covers the time period of 1909–1913 and primarily focuses on Eva C., though at the end there is a brief section on the Polish medium known as Stanislava P. Eva and Stanislava were known as physical mediums most noted for their production of ectoplasm. The reliance on photography as the primary tool in these experiments was to ensure capturing the production of this gauzy substance. The reports of sittings include detailed transcripts of attendees and events during each séance, including photos of the cabinet both Eva and Stanislava use and the ectoplasm produced. For anyone interesting in the strange history of ectoplasm and the fascination with it that blossomed during this time period, this work will be very useful.

Keywords: ectoplasm; Eva C.; Stanislava P.; physical mediumship

1930s

Pratt, J. G. "Clairvoyant Blind Matching." *Journal of Parapsychology* 1, no. 1 (1937): 10–17.

In this study, published in the very first issue of the *Journal of Parapsychology*, researcher J. G. Pratt discusses an experiment to test clairvoyance. Inspired by the work of J. B. Rhine and the research coming out of the Duke Parapsychology Labs, Dr. Pratt partnered with his colleague Dr. Gardner Murphy to begin their own studies at Columbia University. Curious to see what would happen when they replicated studies, one of Pratt's goals was to see if any verification could be reached from adhering to the same set of methods.

Pratt begins by outlining the timeline of the study. He had been conducting experiments for fifteen months at the time this article was written. He discusses the number of participants (124), types of experiments, and general results. This article focuses on one study participant referred to as Mrs. M. whose scores quite frequently came in at above-average rates. Between May and December of 1936, Mrs. M. participated in more than eighty-five thousand trials. During these trials, the objective was to guess the correct placement of cards with certain symbols on them—think Zener cards. These methods were conducted using a screened touch matching procedure that involved two people (one of whom was Mrs. M.) separated by a large wooden divider. On one side Mrs. M. would attempt to intuit which card was about to be turned over by the experimenter on the other side. These trials were broken down into four periods, each lasting about a month. The first month, May 1936, Mrs. M.'s success rate was just under 30 percent, a rate that was higher than the percentage of correct guesses that might be attributed to chance. Interestingly, Mrs. M.'s abilities seemed to wane as the study progressed, and Pratt notes that by the end of the study, her success rate plummeted to nothing more than chance levels.

Pratt concludes by stating that Mrs. M. indicated an ability to intuit information in a supernormal manner and that the experiments at Columbia University have succeeded in eliciting information about psi in much the same way of research coming from the Duke Parapsychology Labs.

Keywords: clairvoyance; screened touch matching; Zener cards; Columbia University; Gardner Murphy

Price, Harry. *Confessions of a Ghost-Hunter.* London: Putnam, 1936.

Harry Price was a journalist interested in psychical research. He rose to fame in England for his well-known exploits in haunted houses and ghost investigations, most notably perhaps for his connection to Borley Rectory. In 1925, Price founded the National Laboratory of Psychical Research and in this work he presents some of the most curious cases investigated by the organization. He discusses all manner of phenomena from mediumship, haunted houses, clairvoyance, and more. This work captures not only some of the more popular paranormal cases of the early 1900s, but also provides a look into the work of Harry Price.

Keywords: Harry Price; National Laboratory of Psychical Research

Price, Harry. *Fifty Years of Psychical Research: A Critical Survey.* London: Longmans & Co., 1939.

Famed journalist and psychical researcher Harry Price wrote this book when he was a member of the University of London's Council for Psychical Investigation. In it he presents the past fifty years' worth of research into various psychical matters. Price was inspired by Frank Podmore's 1902 publication *Modern Spiritualism* and wished to publish a work that updated readers on the newer methods and theories that had popped up since Podmore's publication. In *Fifty Years of Psychical Research*, Price lays out the research in language friendly for laypeople, though certainly encouraging people to consult the original sources in journals and proceedings if they are so inclined. His goal, though, was to compile that scholarly literature into a package more palatable for the general public.

Price begins by outlining the beginnings of formal research into psychical matters with the formation of the SPR followed by a number of chapters highlighting various mediums like Rudi Schneider, Leonora Piper, Gladys Osborne Leonard, and more. He then goes on to discuss extrasensory perception, the role of fraud within the spiritualist era and surrounding mediums, and various scientific methods of psi research. Chapter 17 is particularly interesting because Price discusses the criticisms of psychical research. He points out that much of the evidence wouldn't completely satisfy the standards of the scientific method and that much of the research can't be replicated. He also points out, however, that a lack of funding and support impact psychical researchers and keep them from perhaps getting the support they need in order to enhance their methods and scope.

At the end of the work are some helpful appendices. Appendix A is a biographical sketch of key psychical researchers, while appendix B offers a history of the National Laboratory of Psychical Research. Appendix C discusses proposed language for a psychic practitioner's bill, which would place regulations on mediums and psychics. Those interested in the works of Harry Price may also be interested in his 1933 publication *Leaves from a Psychist's Case-Book.*

Keywords: Harry Price; psychical research; National Laboratory of Psychical Research; criticisms

Price, Margaret and Margaret H. Pegram. "Extra-Sensory Perception among the Blind." *Journal of Parapsychology* 1, no. 2 (1937): 143–55.

Researchers Margaret Price and Margaret H. Pegram present their study on extrasensory perception in people with varying degrees of visual impairment. Author Margaret H. Pegram was a researcher with the Duke Parapsychology Labs and worked with her student, Margaret Price, to test the extrasensory abilities of sixty-six blind people ranging between eight and thirty-five years old. During their study, they discovered that 44 percent of participants harbored some above-chance ESP ability that did not seem to correlate with a specific factor like age, gender, or degree of blindness. They warn us of making any conclusions about this, however, when they write, "The high proportion noted cannot be considered significantly unusual until further research has been done with non-blind groups of comparable age and grade and under similar social conditions."[82]

Keywords: extrasensory perception; blindness

Prince, Walter Franklin. *The Enchanted Boundary: Being a Survey of Negative Reactions to Claims of Psychic Phenomena.* Boston: Boston Society for Psychic Research, 1930.

Author Walter Franklin Prince was an executive research officer with the Boston SPR at the time of this publication. In this work, Prince provides an overview and discussion of the critiques and complaints of psychical research. Prince tells us that "this book embodies the first attempt to appraise on a large-scale writings hostile to psychic research. It seeks to deal fairly with persons who, through the course of more than a century, have expressed their disbelief." [83]

Prince divides his discussion into two parts. In book 1, he presents a discussion of books, articles, and letters written by English-speaking authors that present negative viewpoints on psychical phenomena and research from 1820 to 1930. Book 2 is a summary and discussion of data gathered from a questionnaire administered to those who harbor disbelief in psi phenomena. Prince points out that while there have been a number of surveys that ask people about their psychical experiences, there have not been any surveys designed to specifically elicit information and perspectives from those who take a decidedly more skeptical viewpoint. As a whole, this work provides not only a balanced perspective to the topic of psychical phenomena, it also captures the discussions surrounding criticism of psi.

Keywords: criticism; 1820–1930

Rhine, J. B. *Extra-Sensory Perception.* Boston: Bruce Humphries, Inc., 1935.

Parapsychologist and cofounder of the Duke Parapsychology Labs, Dr. J. B. Rhine presents in this 1935 work an overview of the phenomena of extrasensory perception, which is the ability to obtain information in a way other than the normal sensory experiences of sight, sound, touch, etc. This work is divided into three parts. Part 1, "General Introduction," provides readers with an overview of the topic and some historical background. Part 2, "The Experimental Results," presents a discussion of the more than ninety thousand trials conducted at Duke University. Rhine provides general results followed by more detailed vignettes of study participants and details. The final portion, part 3, "Explanation and Discussion, is where Rhine discusses some of the theories of extrasensory perception, addresses common criticisms, and discusses they ways in which psychology, physiology, and biology all impact extrasensory perception. Rhine also presents an appendix for those who wish to engage in replicating his experiments.

Keywords: extrasensory perception; Duke Parapsychology Labs; research methods; replication

Rhine. J. B. *New Frontiers of the Mind: The Story of the Duke Experiments.* New York: Farrar and Rinehart, 1937.

In *New Frontiers of the Mind*, Dr. J. B. Rhine provides a historical overview of the Duke Parapsychology Labs, a twelve-room laboratory located on the Duke University campus. Author, parapsychologist, and cofounder of the labs, Rhine begins with an overview of attitudes and research into psychical phenomena beginning around 1880, setting the stage for the eventual establishment of the Duke Parapsychology Labs in 1930. Once Rhine sets the historical trajectory leading to the establishment of this lab, he then discusses its earliest research and data. Along the way, he discusses criticisms, work being done by other researchers and other laboratories, and theories surrounding who can exhibit ESP and how it might work. Illustrations throughout paint a literal picture of this influential laboratory.

Keywords: Duke Parapsychology Labs; extrasensory perception

Riess, Bernard F. "A Case of High Scores in Card Guessing at a Distance." *Journal of Parapsychology* 1, no. 4 (December 1, 1937): 260–63.

Dr. Bernard F. Riess was a professor at Hunter College in New York when he attended a lecture given by parapsychologist J. B. Rhine. Riess stayed after the lecture to chat with Rhine since his students had been discussing psychical topics in the classroom and he had questions. Reiss obtained Zener cards and instructions for how to conduct his own experiment on ESP. One of Reiss's students claimed she had a friend who exhibited extrasensory abilities and Reiss was persuaded to set up an experiment with this person. What's most unique about this study is the manner in which the test was conducted. Since Dr. Reiss and the study participant both lived in the same neighborhood of New York City and were only about a half mile apart from one another, they actually conducted this study while in their respective homes. Both Dr. Reiss and the subject had a pack of Zener cards. Beginning at the agreed upon time (9:00 p.m.), Dr. Reiss, in his own home, shuffled the deck and turned over one card at a time, focusing on it for one minute. At exactly 9:01 p.m., the subject wrote down her impression of the card, knowing that Dr. Reiss had been attempting to psychically send her the impression for the past minute.

The study went on in this fashion until the deck was exhausted, at which point both participants took a ten-minute break and then Dr. Reiss reshuffled the deck and began again.

This experiment was conducted in two series. The first series began in December 1936 and continued for a number of months until April 1937. This is referred to as Series A, and during that time, more than 1,850 trials were completed. Series B occurred sporadically for about four months during which time the subject moved and was suffering from poor health, rendering Series B incomplete. During Series A, however, the subject displayed a remarkable success rate. Out of 1,850 card pulls Dr. Reiss's notes indicate that the subject had correct guesses in 1,349 instances. This study motivated Dr. Reiss to continue experimenting with ESP and he tells us at the end of this paper that he has another study of sixty-seven female participants who have not yielded any results above chance percentages. Because of the unconventional methods used and the fact that the subject abandoned the study before it was complete, Dr. Reiss concludes merely by telling us that his goal was to simply present and "suggest" what he had done.

Keywords: extrasensory perception; ESP cards; Zener cards; distance ESP

Smith, Burke M. "The Tyrrell Experiments." *Journal of Parapsychology* 1, no. 1 (March 1, 1937): 63–69.

Author Burke M. Smith was working at the Duke Parapsychology Labs when he was tasked with reviewing a machine built by parapsychologist G. N. M. Tyrell. Tyrell, under the support of the SPR, had built a machine specifically designed to use in experiments of extrasensory perception. Tyrell had a friend who exhibited ESP and he had been, since 1922, engaging in experiments with her using cards. After a period of time, however, he began to wonder how else he might be able to test her abilities. He first designed an apparatus that involved five boxes with lids. One side of each box would be in front of the subject while the other side would be facing the experimenter, and both would be separated by a solid screen. The experimenter would randomly choose which box to place an object in and the subject would guess which box contained the item. This was Tyrell's first iteration, but he soon realized that there was a possibility of sound and noise cues that the subject could pick up, even if the experimenter was trying to be as subtle as possible. In the second iteration of this device, Tyrell decided to place bulbs inside each light-proof box that could be triggered to light up. The subject would then choose which box was lit up. Since the light bulbs could be triggered using a mechanical selector, the experiment now involved random selection of which bulb was to be lit versus the subjective selection by a human in the first iteration.

This article sheds light on the creative and inventive methods that psychical researchers began to develop in the lab.

Keywords: G. N. M. Tyrell; mechanical selector; precognition

Taves, Ernest. "A Machine for Research in Extra-Sensory Perception." *Journal of Parapsychology* 3, no. 1 (1939): 11–16.

In this article, author Ernest Taves outlines a machine designed to mechanically randomize objects used in psi experiments. Taves begins by pointing out that some researchers realized that human shuffling of objects, such as with ESP/Zener cards could involve some level of conscious or subconscious patterns. Therefore, they realized that introducing a mechanical selector would help eliminate the potential for any bias, whether that bias be intentional or not. Taves presents a detailed presentation on this device, which can hold and randomize up to 150 items that might be desirable to use in psi tests like dice, coins, cards, etc. Taves provides diagrams and dimensions in the article as well, allowing for replication by fellow researchers. He concludes his article by noting that further adaptations and adjustments continue to be made regarding this mechanical selector.

Keywords: extrasensory perception; mechanical selector

1940s

Dale, L. A. "The Psychokinetic Effect: The First A.S.P.R. Experiment." *Journal of the American Society for Psychical Research* 40 (1946).

Researcher and author L. A. Dale presents here an article which uses dice to test for possible psychokinetic effects. In this study, Dale tested fifty-nine subjects by asking them to roll dice down an inclined platform and testing their landing spots against targeted locations predetermined before each dice roll. Dale concludes that there is evidence of psychokinesis at play in this study, which represents one of the earliest works on PK in the literature.

Keywords: psychokinesis; dice-throwing

Gibson, Edmond P., Lottie H. Gibson, and J. B. Rhine. "The PK Effect: Mechanical Throwing of Three Dice." *Journal of Parapsychology* 8 (1944): 95–109.

In this study, researchers Gibson, Gibson, and Rhine tested whether the landing of dice was somehow dependent upon which side of a die was placed upward into a mechanical selector. Essentially, the researchers tested whether any physical qualities of each side of a die would somehow impact the way in which a die might roll. This question was important to them since the use of dice was being used in studies surrounding psychokinesis. Some of their earlier research involving the use of six dice and a mechanical selector seemed to positively indicate the presence of PK, so they wished to test whether certain sides of a die impacted the presence or absence of PK. They concluded that no special configuration of certain sides of a die would somehow falsely indicate the presence of PK, especially when using multiple runs and throws.

Keywords: psychokinesis; dice-throwing; mechanical selector

Humphrey, Betty. *Handbook of Tests in Parapsychology.* Durham NC: Duke University, 1948.

Dr. Betty Humphrey wrote this book ten years after C. E. Stuart and J. G. Pratt wrote what is considered to be the first textbook on experimental parapsychology, *Handbook for Testing Extrasensory Perception.* In even just ten years' worth of time, methods and theories can change immensely and Dr. Humphrey's work helps update the scientific community where Stuart and Pratt left off.

This work is divided into three parts. In part 1, Humphrey presents an assortment of tests and methods that are used when testing extrasensory perception. Included in this section are things like card-calling tests, matching tests, tests using drawings, etc. In part 2, Humphrey presents tests designed for psychokinesis studies such as the dice tests and more. In part 3, she discusses the specifics and special considerations of administering all of these tests. She starts with a discussion of the necessary training and knowledge required of the experimenter themself and then moves on to a discussion of some key components of successful experiments, proving especially useful for those new to both ESP and PK. Humphrey includes appendices that discuss statistical information like standard deviations that can help determine the presence or absence of phenomena and also provides the reader with a list of further reading.

Keywords: research methods; extrasensory perception; psychokinesis

McMahan, Elizabeth A. and Joan Lauer. "Extrasensory Perception of Cards in an Unknown Location." *Journal of Parapsychology* 12, no. 1 (1948): 47–57.

Duke University students McMahan and Lauer wanted to test the effects of extrasensory perception when the subject was unaware of the location of objects they were trying to intuit. The authors used a deck of cards but did not reveal the location of the cards and the sender to the subject. Using synchronized watches so that the timing of the experiment would match between subject and sender, the authors discovered that ESP did still appear to be present (or at least that correct guesses occurred at higher-than-chance levels). The success rate was not, however, as high as a test in which the subject knew the location of the receiver and the objects in question. The authors were curious what the relation of space-time might be in regard to ESP and considered this a first step in beginning to address that question. They tell us, "All the experimental results so far point to the hypothesis that psi phenomena cannot fit into the present-day picture of the space-time world," but remind us that further research is needed to better understand the whole picture.

Keywords: extrasensory perception; space-time; ESP at a distance

Murphy, Gardner. "What Needs to be Done in Parapsychology." *Journal of Parapsychology* 12, no. 1 (1948): 15–19.

When he wrote this article, Dr. Gardner Murphy was chairman of the research committee of the American SPR and was a psychology professor with the College of the City of New York (today called the City College of New York). In this article, he briefly addresses the future of parapsychological research. In doing so, he begins by pointing out some of the hurdles inherent to studying psi phenomena. In a poignant beginning, he tells us,

First of all, it seems to me that there is a neglect of the raw, tough, primitive stuff that nature gives us. In such sciences as astronomy and geology one does not define first of all what the laboratory can do and then hope that problems will saunter into the laboratory and allow themselves to be studied. . . . One studies in detail the anatomy of the phenomena hurled at us by nature. The data of spontaneous telepathy (and of spontaneous clairvoyance and precognition) are huge granite blocks of irregular shape and variable specific gravity which come hurtling down the mountain side, neither announcing when they are coming nor informing us as to their destination.[84]

Dr. Murphy urges future researchers to take this viewpoint moving forward and to also begin considering the role of the individual personality as a more crucial factor than it had hitherto been treated. Additionally, he urges researchers to consider the personality of the experimenter as well and to contemplate how *their* personality may also affect the results of study on psi phenomena. Lastly, Dr. Murphy discusses the importance of replication of research and securing funding for future experiments.

Keywords: future of research; 1940s

Pratt. J. Gaither, J. B. Rhine, Burke M. Smith, Charles E. Stuart, and Joseph A. Greenwood. *Extrasensory Perception After 60 Years: A Critical Appraisal of the Research in Extra-Sensory Perception.* New York: Henry Holt & Company, 1940.

The authors of this book set forth to document a comprehensive review of research into extrasensory perception when they realized that even though psi was starting to be discussed in college classrooms on experimental psychology, there didn't yet exist any text that provided a complete review of the topic. Divided into four sections, the first section discusses the history of psychical phenomena and roots it in the ancient history of humankind. The authors discuss the presence of ESP in prescientific and scientific eras before discussing some of the experimental methods designed to test the phenomena. They also discuss counterhypotheses to psi. In the second part, the authors present and discus the major criticisms of psi research while in the third part of this work they discuss the physical aspects of ESP. In the fourth section, the authors provide the current situation of ESP research, discussing the statistical problems and critiques of certain methods. There are nearly one hundred pages of appendices that include reviews of statistical methods and various methods for testing psi phenomena.

Keywords: extrasensory perception; research methods; review; statistical methods

Price, Margaret and J. B. Rhine. "The Subject-Experimenter Relation in the PK Test." *Journal of Parapsychology* 8 (1944): 177–86.

In this article, Price and Rhine study the role of the subject's mental state and focus on their ability to exhibit PK behavior. A subject was first tested to determine their average PK levels. When observers were added to the experiment, the subject was still able to exhibit PK abilities. However, when an observer engaged in distracting manners, the subject's PK ability dropped to even less than chance levels, indicating that mental state and focus are key to PK phenomena. The authors conclude by telling us,

> With the PK process entirely unconscious and blind to introspective observation, the subject's effort to direct this ability, especially under strain or distraction, is likely to be disoriented. If the disorientation is prolonged, it may reverse the normally positive scoring ability and cause a significant negative deviation. How this occurs is as obscure to us as is PK itself, but there is evidence that it does occur.[85]

Keywords: psychokinesis; mental state; focus; negative deviation

Rhine, J. B. "Conditions Favoring Success in Psi Tests." *Journal of Parapsychology* 12, no. 1 (1948): 58–75.

In the 1940s, British psychical researchers noticed that their American colleagues seemed to be having more success at replicating conditions needed for psi and so requested a formal discussion of the topic. In this article, then, researcher J. B. Rhine discusses the conditions that he believe enhance the success of psi experiments. Rhine begins by pointing out that the knowledge of psi is still very new, and that psi research is difficult across the board and reminds readers that his article is merely a suggestion of factors based on his own experience. He goes on to discuss four factors that he believes impacts psi success in the laboratory.

The first factor for success lies with the experimenter themself. To be most successful, Rhine tells us, the experimenter must believe in the importance of psi research, even if they are very skeptical of its presence—in other words, they must harbor a certain amount of open-minded scientific respect without being overly zealous or losing sight of research integrity. Just like there must be a genuine interest on the part of the experimenter, so, too, must there be a genuine interest on the part of the subject. However, Rhine points out that experiments tend to be more successful the less the subject is knowledgeable about (or perhaps preoccupied with) the theories and mechanics of the phenomena. The third factor relates to test design and Rhine points out that method rigidity is harmful to psi research. He urges scientists to engage in both formal and informal studies that range from exploratory to very specific. The simple test, he tells us, can be most successful and revealing. Rhine also points out that researchers should ensure that safeguards against fraud or deception are in place. The final point he offers is one of general considerations regarding the test design. He tells us, for example, that friendly demeanors are necessary, and all efforts should be made to make a test site and lab environment as appealing and calming as possible.

Keywords: success factors; extrasensory perception

Rhine, Louisa E. and J. B. Rhine. "The Psychokinetic Effect. I. The First Experiment." *Journal of Parapsychology* 7, no. 1 (1943): 20–43.

In February 1934, the Rhines began experimentation on something known as the Psychokinetic Effect, PK for short. They tell us, "This is the first of a long series of research reports describing experiments on what is called the 'psychokinetic' or 'PK' effect. The PK effect is colloquially called 'mind over matter' and means the direct influencing of a physical system by the action of a subject's effort, without any known intermediate energy or instrumentation."[86]

During the long-term study, dice were used as objects to test for the presence of PK influence. The intention was to manipulate the dice so that their two faces totaled eight or more. The Rhines determined that five out of twelve successful tosses could be attributed to chance. Anything above five, then, could not be attributed to chance alone. Out of more than 560 runs, the average score was just slightly above chance at 5.53. In order to address the possibility of human error when physically rolling the dice, a mechanical device was also used and was also found to a mechanical throw was implemented and still found to elicit results at higher-than-chance rates.

In this report, Louisa and J. B. Rhine also discuss the connection between extrasensory perception and PK. They conclude by reminding readers that though a PK effect seems to exist, they are still not sure *how* it works, and that future research is needed. They also comment about how the PK effect will have implications for our current understanding of psychology. This article will be relevant for anyone interested in the research on psychokinesis, especially the early studies.

Keywords: psychokinesis; extrasensory perception; dice-throwing

Thouless, R. H. "The Present Position of Experimental Research into Telepathy and Related Phenomena." *Proceedings of the Society for Psychical Research* 47 (1942): 1–19.

Author and researcher Robert H. Thouless presents, in this article, his 1942 presidential address to the SPR. In it, Thouless talks about the merits of experimental parapsychology but also the barriers. Many others of this time also realized that the problem of replicability of psi phenomena was a major blow to the topic's future. Thouless also points that out, but suggests, that research begins taking a different focus onto creating those conditions favorable to producing psi which, he says, are provided in the literature. He remarks on his belief that the parapsychological community has shown reasonable data that can lead one to conclude positively in the existence of psi and points out some of the unexpected findings of psi, like the realization that subjects can score significantly *below* chance probability. These realizations, Thouless remarks, illustrate the importance of continuing experimental research. Regarding the future of research, he urges scientists to embark on new questions and studies and build upon what previous generations of researchers have built. This address provides a snapshot in time of the thoughts and attitudes toward experimental psychical research.

Keywords: presidential address; SPR; experimental parapsychology

Thouless, R. H. "Some Experiments on PK Effects in Coin Spinning." *Journal of Parapsychology* 9 (1945): 169–75.

In this article, Robert H. Thouless reports on psychokinesis experiments conducted with coins instead of dice. Leading PK tests of the time tended to use dice quite frequently, so Thouless had an idea to apply the same conditions to different objects. To begin, Thouless points out that this was an independent study that he conducted by himself one summer, reminding us that the study is mostly just a vignette of a particular method an independent researcher tried out one day for the sake of experimentation. To conduct his study, Thouless first determined the statistical chance rates of how a coin would land. Then, Thouless spun the first ten coins focusing on "heads," and then proceeded to spin ten more coins focusing on "tails." After about two months he had accumulated four thousand runs and compiled his data. What Thouless discovered was that while the *entire* four thousand runs evaluated all at once did not reveal any indication of higher-than-chance levels, smaller runs (and especially runs at the beginning of the study) did reveal higher-than-chance levels of placement via heads or tails. This led Thouless to conclude that future PK researchers may wish to disembark from the tendency to only focus on very large data sets and to consider adjusting their focus, pointing out that there may be a trajectory of psi being stronger at the beginning of an experiment then slowly waning over time.

Keywords: psychokinesis; coin spinning

1950s

Anderson, Margaret and Rhea White. "A Further Investigation of Teacher-Pupil Attitudes and Clairvoyance Test Results." *Journal of Parapsychology* 21, no. 2 (June 1957): 81–97.

Authors Margaret Anderson and Rhea White received Ralph Drake Perry fellowships from Duke University's parapsychology labs and a grant from the Parapsychology Foundation for this research. This publication is the third report in a series of experiments that Anderson and White did on clairvoyance. Specifically, they set out to investigate the role that attitude between sender and receiver plays. To test this, they selected seven teachers and administered more than 25,600 tests to 205 high school students. In the tests, each student was given a sealed envelope containing a list of randomized symbols. A sheet on the envelope was attached so that each student could record what their impressions of the objects were. Then, both the teacher and student anonymously filled out a questionnaire regarding their attitudes toward each other. The authors discovered that those students who the teachers liked elicited statistically significant positive results. Interestingly, when the students indicated that they were "moderately positive" toward their teacher, they obtained statistically significant positive results. This study discusses the ways in which attitude between sender and receiver in ESP tests impacts results.

Keywords: clairvoyance; high school students

Blythe, Henry. *The Three Lives of Naomi Henry: An Investigation into Reincarnation.* New York: The Citadel Press, 1956.

Henry Blythe was a British hypnotist who conducted a series of experiments with Naomi Henry in the 1950s. Naomi, a young woman with a family living in Devon, claimed, when placed under hypnosis, to be the reincarnated spirit of two different women. One of the women Naomi claimed to be was a young Irish girl born in 1790 and a woman named Clarice, a nurse from the 1900s. In this book, Blythe presents detailed accounts of his experiments with Naomi, even including transcripts of their sessions. While Henry Blythe is not a parapsychologist, his account of using hypnotism to reveal past lives is an intriguing addition and shows the popularity and school of thought on popular hypnotism at the time.

Keywords: hypnotism; Naomi Henry; reincarnation; past lives

Broad, C. D. "A Half Century of Psychical Research." *Journal of Parapsychology* 20, no. 4 (Dec. 1, 1956): 209–28.

For the twentieth anniversary of the *Journal of Parapsychology*, researcher J. B. Rhine asked his colleague and past president of the SPR, C. D. Broad, to write an article for the edition. Broad presents here a discussion and overview of the past fifty years' worth of psychical research, beginning with the state of psi research in the early 1900s,

when scientists were focused on cross correspondence phenomena. Broad goes on to present his own opinions and outlook on psychical research before diving back into an objective discussion of the current state of the field. He begins by pointing out the technological advancements that have made psychical research easier, such as the invention of tape recorders, which help ensure far less subjective error or oversight from human stenographers. He also points out that the creation of infrared telescopes has made it easier to study mediums and séance phenomena. Broad also points to the enhancement of statistical methods and advanced knowledge of personality psychology as helpful for the future of psychical research.

Keywords: future of psychical research

Cadoret, Remi J. "Effect of Novelty in Test Conditions on ESP Performance." *Journal of Parapsychology* 16, no. 3 (1952): 192–203.

Researcher and medical student Remi J. Cadoret presents in this article his study on extrasensory perception. Specifically, Cadoret was curious to see what would happen in a traditional ESP test using cards if certain unique "novelties" were introduced. For example, during the tests Cadoret, using himself as the subject, would read poetry or sing and evaluate what differences might have cropped up compared to ESP tests that involved no other activity. He was interested to see if any of these novel activities sparked an increase in ESP performance. What he discovered was rather curious. Cadoret discovered that in the first introduction of a novel activity (like singing or reading poetry), there was a statistically significant ESP result, but when that same novel activity was introduced the second time, success rates dropped and eventually plummeted to significantly negative results.

Keywords: extrasensory perception; research methods

Van de Castle, R. L. "An Exploratory Study of Some Variables Relating to Individual ESP Performance." *Journal of Parapsychology* 17, no. 1 (1953): 61–72.

In this article, researcher R. L. Van de Castle (who at the time was a graduate student at the University of Missouri) examined if ESP success would be affected by using various objects *and* by the amount

180   Chapter 3

of time allowed for the subject to intuit the objects at hand. For example, Van de Castle used objects like the traditional Zener cards but also used drawings, letters, numbers, and colors. He also allowed subjects certain amounts of time to intuit objects, ranging in five increments from 0–2 seconds up to 61 seconds or more. He discovered that certain subjects had statistically significant results when allowed shorter time periods whereas other subjects had equal success when given longer periods of time. Castle also discovered that colors seemed to elicit the highest number of successful hits whereas drawings elicited the lowest. Furthermore, this study revealed that when subjects were given between thirty-one and sixty seconds to produce an answer, they scored the highest number of correct hits.

Keywords: extrasensory perception; Zener cards; numbers; drawings

Fahler, Jarl and Remi J. Cadoret. "ESP Card Tests of College Students with and Without Hypnosis." *Journal of Parapsychology* 22, no. 2 (June 1958): 125–36.

Author and researcher Jarl Fahler began conducting ESP research in Finland using hypnotized subjects. His studies indicated a possible relationship between hypnosis and enhanced psychical abilities. Because of that research, he was invited to the Duke Parapsychology Labs in 1957 to build off the work he began in Finland. Using volunteer students from the university, Fahler and Cadoret conducted three rounds of testing using various combinations of hypnosis and waking-state experiments. They discovered, much like Fahler did in his original studies, that hypnosis seemed to impact the success rate of ESP ability. The authors tell us,

> In a word, significant ESP effects did accompany the hypnotic treatment. . . . Perhaps the subjects were usually not equally motivated to perform at their best rate in the waking state. Hypnosis seems to provide the experimenter with a way of concentrating the subject's effort upon his task and improving his interest in his performance. Moreover, with the aid of hypnosis, the subject can be relaxed by the experimenter before the testing begins.[87]

Keywords: hypnosis; extrasensory perception; Finland

Forwald, H. "An Approach to Instrumental Investigation of Psychokinesis." *Journal of Parapsychology* 18, no. 4 (1954): 219–33.

In this article, researcher Haakon Forwald presents an experiment designed to gauge the force needed to psychokinetically drive dice a certain distance down a ramp. In his previous studies, he had tested whether there appeared to be an initial PK effect when mechanically rolling dice down a platform and focusing a psychical effort at getting them to land either to the right or left of a dividing line. In this study, however, Forwald builds upon his previous PK research to inquire what amount of force is needed to get the dice to the locations in which they land. Determining the typical amount of force that *should* be naturally present to get the dice to move, Forwald was then able to compare it to the force that the dice actually generated, discovering that the force present was above what should naturally be occurring, adding yet another layer to the psychokinetic phenomenon.

Keywords: psychokinesis; force; placement tests; placement PK; dice

Forwald, H. "A Further Study of the PK Placement Effect." *Journal of Parapsychology* 16, no. 1 (1952): 59–67.

In this study, Haakon Forwald builds upon his portfolio of research into the phenomenon of psychokinesis. At the beginning of this study, Forwald points out that most PK research involving dice focuses on getting the dice, with their six faces, to land with predetermined sides facing upward. Here, however, Forwald posits that PK can also be tested by attempting to psychically manipulate *where* on a board the objects land. He refers to this as "placement PK." He had begun part one of these placement PK tests a few years prior and here, in part two, he continues the work, but with dice of different substances such as wood, Bakelite, paper, aluminum, and steel. He discovered lower success rates in round two than round one and discusses in this study some of the possible reasons for this, one being intent and motivation levels.

Keywords: psychokinesis; placement PK

Gerber, Rebecca and Gertrude R. Schmeidler. "An Investigation Relaxation and of Acceptance of the

Experimental Situation as Related to ESP Scores in Maternity Patients." *Journal of Parapsychology* 21, no. 1 (March 1957): 47–57.

Author Rebecca Gerber conducted this study under the mentorship of Dr. Gertrude Schmeidler for completion of her master's thesis. In this study, Gerber wanted to test the impact that mood might have on ESP. She specifically chose a population of maternity patients to see if the moods of these women in the immediate aftermath of delivery would positively or negatively impact the presence of psi behavior. This study also incorporated the role that receptivity plays as well. Gerber selected thirty-six patients and ranked them on scales of both relaxation and acceptance through an interview process. In the course of the experiment, the authors discovered that six of the women were still under the effects of anesthesia and therefore only include the thirty not under the influence as part of the formal group. The tests consisted of a deck of twelve cards each having an image of a clock on them. The clock only had one hand which pointed toward a certain hour on the clock. Each subject was asked to go through the deck four times, holding each concealed card and indicating to which hour they believed it corresponded. Subjects who ranked highly relaxed and accepting scored at higher than chance levels while those who were ranked not relaxed and not accepting scored at lower than chance levels. All other groups scored at chance levels. Their research seems to indicate a correlation between mood, receptivity, and psi ability, but the authors conclude by reminding us that their work was exploratory and that more research is needed, especially one which can use objective standards of relaxation and acceptance as opposed to subjective rankings based on brief interviews.

Keywords: extrasensory perception; maternity; mood and psi

Kooy, J. M. J. "Space, Time, and Consciouness." *Journal of Parapsychology* 21, no. 4 (Dec. 1, 1957): 259–72.

Author J. M. J. Kooy begins this article by telling us, "As soon as we start to think about the real essence of precognition, we have to realize that our common conceptions of time and space are completely useless."[88] And he goes on to state that the presence of extrasensory perception blows our concept of physical time to pieces. He writes, "In view of [ESP], we have to start by posing the question: Does an absolute physical time exist, which corresponds to with an absolute Now? The answer is undoubtedly: No, there is no absolute time; no absolute time-interval exists between two events."[89] Anyone looking for a philosophical discussion on the implications of ESP on our concepts of space and time will want to include this work by Kooy.

Keywords: extrasensory perception; space-time

McConnell, R. A. "Why Throw Dice?" *Journal of Parapsychology* 16, no. 3 (1952): 187–91.

In this article, psychical researcher R. A. McConnell discusses the reasons why parapsychologists choose to use dice in their tests of psychokinesis. He points out that dice are associated with a sense of play and therefore induce a sense of curiosity and expectation of certain results. It facilitates belief, in other words. Additionally, because there are six sides to a die, there is a certain amount of control that it offers. Furthermore, dice are easy to use and universally understood. This article helps explain experimental methods of dice-throwing to those interested in psychokinesis.

Keywords: dice-throwing; psychokinesis; research methods

Nielsen, Winnifred. "An Exploratory Precognition Experiment." *Journal of Parapsychology* 20, no. 1 (1956): 33–39.

Researcher Winnifred Nielsen presents their work on an exploratory study to find suitable and scientifically rigorous methods for studying precognition. In this study, the subject, living in New York, recorded eighty runs of intuiting sets of twenty-five symbols. He knew what the symbols might be and was asked to record in each run the order of which he believed they would appear. Meanwhile, six weeks after the subject began recording his intuitions and back at Duke University, Nielson and Rhea White were prepping the decks that would be pulled from. They shuffled entire decks and then used dice to determine how many times a deck would be cut before cards were pulled. In total, the subject had 452 correct hits, which resulted in a higher-than-chance and statistically significant result.

Keywords: precognition

Osis, Karlis. "Precognition Over Time Intervals of One to Thirty-Three Days." *Journal of Parapsychology* 12 (1955): 82–91.

In this article, researcher Karlis Osis tests whether precognition can be impacted by the time period between subject and experimenter. A subject from New York was asked to record her impressions of which objects would be chosen at a later date. One of her recordings corresponded to objects chosen a week later while another set of impressions were noted about a month prior to when objects were selected. There was a statistically significant negative deviation in each case, indicating the potential for "psi missing," but since both results were similar in both the one-week and one-month impressions, it seems to indicate that psi can occur at both of those time periods.

Osis also provides references to multiple other studies regarding precognition and time lapse. Interested readers will want to be sure to consult the references included to learn more.

Keywords: precognition; precognition at a distance; precognition over time; psi missing

Osis, Karlis. "A Test of the Relationship between ESP and PK." *Journal of Parapsychology* 17 (1953): 298–309.

This study examines if there is a potential relationship between extrasensory perception and psychokinesis. Researcher Karlis Osis reminds us that many have wondered if these two items are related. There is even a hypothesis that they are just two components of the same process. In order to test this, predetermined die faces were chosen as targets and not revealed to the subject, or the one throwing the dice. Rather, Osis posits that if the dice landed on the predetermined face (or number) at higher-than-chance levels, then it could indicate the subject exhibited psychokinesis *and* extrasensory perception in the same process. Osis outlines how he sets up the test and the various controls and statistics used. He tells us that the study did reveal statistically significant results that seem to support the theory that PK and ESP work in tandem.

Keywords: extrasensory perception; psychokinesis; dice-throwing

Pratt, J. G. "The Cormack Placement PK Experiments." *Journal of Parapsychology* 15, no. 1 (1951): 57–73.

George Cormack, a retired businessman who had become familiar with and fascinated by the work of the Duke Parapsychology Labs, decided to study his own potential for exhibiting psychokinetic ability. He obtained guidance and feedback from researchers in the lab and in total, he conducted nine series of tests. In five of them, he released dice manually while in the other four, dice were released by an electrical switch. Cormack used multiple types of dice as well, testing to see how their density and dimensions might affect results. In many of his runs, Cormack achieved significantly higher-than-chance results. Throughout the study, he used different types of dice, released them in different ways, and controlled for other variables that might explain naturally why certain dice fell in certain ways. Still, a good deal of his runs scored at rates suggesting something other than chance or coincidence was taking place.

Keywords: psychokinesis; dice-throwing; mechanical selector

Pratt, J. G. "The Reinforcement Effect in ESP Displacement." *Journal of Parapsychology* 15, no. 2 (1951): 103–17.

Psychical researcher J. G. Pratt was interested in the work of S. G. Soal, who had, in the 1930s, discovered a "displacement effect" in a series of experiments on extrasensory perception. What Soal discovered during these tests were two subjects who were able to intuit correct choices one round before or one round after the current round. For example, using ESP cards, the subjects would choose an object that corresponded to the *next* card that would be pulled. It happened with so much frequency that Soal began to notice. He began to study this effect, called ESP displacement, but the statistical methods he used came under critique. In the 1950s, J. G. Pratt worked alongside others to work out the statistical critiques and together they developed a new measure that still indicated that the people in this study score at higher-than-chance levels regarding ESP displacement.

Keywords: extrasensory perception: ESP displacement; reinforcement effect

Pratt, J. G. and W. G. Roll. "The Seaford Disturbances." *Journal of Parapsychology* 22, no. 2 (June 1958): 79–124.

Psychical researchers J. G. Pratt and William G. Roll present their research involving poltergeist phenomena. They begin by reminding the reader of the core characteristics of poltergeist cases and how they often involve psychokinesis. Specifically, poltergeist-related PK is often referred to as recurrent spontaneous psychokinesis, or RK. The authors then provide a historical timeline of research into psychokinesis, pointing out that beginning in the 1920s and through the 1950s, interest in the topic waned before seeming to revive. For those matters, this article will be helpful for anyone interested in understanding the main components of and history into PK research.

Regarding the case that Pratt and Roll report, a family in Seaford, Long Island, began experiencing strange phenomena in their home. At one point they even contacted the local police who could not determine a source for the events. This is when the case was brought to the attention of the Duke Parapsychology Labs. Pratt was sent to investigate and later was joined by colleague William G. Roll. During the course of their investigation, Pratt and Roll noted sixty-seven disturbances that they provide in an appendix to the article. The vast majority include examples of objects moving of their own accord, both large and small items, and sometimes even furniture, occasionally moving so violently that they break. Throughout the investigation, Pratt, Roll, and local police could not identify any natural explanations; they even had the home inspected by a utility company, installed an oscillograph in the home to test for vibrations, sent shattered objects to labs to be tested for foreign materials, and subjected the children to intense interviewing.

Keywords: poltergeist; psychokinesis; recurrent spontaneous psychokinesis; Seaford

Rhine, Louisa E. "Subjective Forms of Spontaneous Psi Experiences." *Journal of Parapsychology* 17 (1953): 77–14.

In this article from the *Journal of Parapsychology*, researcher Louisa E. Rhine discusses the characteristics of spontaneous psi experiences. Rhine begins by reminding readers that many psi phenomena occur at the unconscious level, yet previous psi re-

search has largely overlooked questions surrounding the conscious manifestations of those unconscious processes. Rhine points out that this question of conscious manifestation of psi was largely overlooked due to the focus on experimental parapsychology, which automatically filters the ways in which people exhibit their psi behavior—think of card-guessing experiments, for example.

In her research, Rhine was hoping to discover information about the natural circumstances of spontaneously occurring psi. To uncover this information, she reviewed 1,073 instances of spontaneous psi to see what forms the psi manifested through. What Rhine discovered is that spontaneous cases manifested in one of four ways: intuitive, hallucinatory, realistic dreaming, and unrealistic dreaming. While the details of the psi events run the gamut from general intuitive feelings to very clear and detailed psychic dreams, these four experiences emerged as overall patterned categories of *how* people received information psychically.

This article represents a shift in psi research from "*Does* psi occur?" to '*How* does psi occur?" Rhine goes on to give detailed case studies of each type of psi manifestation, from detailed reports of intuitive (waking) feelings to intense psychic dreams. A key takeaway from this article is Rhine's observation that the four types of experiences are common and familiar. People know what it means to have an intuitive feeling just as they know what it means to have realistic and unrealistic dreams, though the line between psi and non-psi is often blurry, dominated by the subjective meaning and details of each situation. The article further points to additional questions: Is psi somehow mediated by personality? Why does psi show up in different ways? This article, and others by Rhine, occupy a key place in the corpus of psi literature.

Keywords: Louisa Rhine; intuition; dreaming; spontaneous psi; subjective experience of psi

Rhine, J. B. "The Forwald Experiments with Placement PK." *Journal of Parapsychology* 15, no. 1 (1951): 49–56.

In this article, noted researcher J. B. Rhine reinforces the validity of Haakon Forwald's PK tests. Forwald, who conducted forty thousand dice rolls during his experiments, discovered a likelihood of "placement PK," or, the ability to psychically influence *where* an object lands on the test field. Using a device he constructed himself, Forwald's work gained the attention of researchers in the United States. Forwald, who was a member of both the Swedish and British SPRs, was invited by Rhine to visit the Duke Parapsychology Labs to continue research begun in Sweden. While at Duke, Forwald worked with researchers Louisa Rhine, George Cormack, and W. E. Cox, who had all begun work on placement PK and were curious to see what would happen when Forwald tested their theories. In this article, Rhine presents Forwald's work and methods. Those interested in the original studies can search under Forwald's name for additional information.

Keywords: psychokinesis; placement PK; Haakon Forwald; J. B. Rhine

Rhine, J. B. and J. G. Pratt. *Parapsychology: Frontier Science of the Mind: A Survey of the Field, the Methods, and the Facts of ESP and PK Research.* Springfield. MO: Charles C. Thomas, 1957.

In this book, researchers J. B. Rhine and J. G. Pratt present a review on the progress within parapsychology. They tell us that they present it not only as a handy compendium of progress to date, but also in the hopes that it will be useful for teachers, anthropologists, psychologists, ministers, and college students. They specifically tell us that their work is *not* intended for the professional parapsychologist or the seasoned student, but rather for those who are relatively new or entirely unfamiliar with this topic. It is their hope that this work will serve as a core introductory text that will inspire readers to seek out more information.

The book is divided into two parts. The first part provides definitions and overviews of the field, including the various phenomena that are subsumed under the umbrella term "parapsychology." The authors introduce some of the methods used, discuss how psi phenomena interact with both the physical world and psychology, and discuss some of the evidence for psi. To conclude part 1, they include a multidisciplinary discussion of psi and how it affects various fields such as education, psychology, medicine, religion, biology, etc. The second part introduces the reader to specific tests and procedures for measuring psi, along with a discussion of helpful statistical methods to use. An appendix that highlights some of the major events in parapsychology is included along with a glossary of terms.

Keywords: parapsychology; survey; extrasensory perception; psychokinesis

Rhine, J. B. "The Problem of Psi-Missing." *Journal of Parapsychology* 16, no. 2 (1952): 90–129.

Author J. B. Rhine presents a discussion on psi-missing in this article. Psi-missing refers to the phenomenon of statistically significant lower-than-chance results on tests involving some form of psi (like ESP or PK). Just like higher-than-chance results can indicate that something strange is occurring, so, too, do lower-than-chance results indicate that something curious is happening. Multiple researchers, in their psi studies, noticed this effect, and in this article Rhine provides a review of the many experiments in which psi missing is present. He also presents a hypothesis for psi missing and tests it.

Keyword: psi-missing

Rhine, J. B and J. G. Pratt. "A Review of the Pearce-Pratt Distance Series of ESP Tests." *Journal of Parapsychology* 18, no. 3 (September 1, 1954): 165–77.

In the 1930s, a series of tests were conducted that came to be known as the Pearce-Pratt Distance Series of ESP. These tests became well known and at the time this article was written, Rhine and Pratt revisit these seminal tests to apply the current understandings and methods of the interim twenty years. The study was conducted when J. B. Rhine was an assistant professor who, while mentoring J. G. Pratt as a graduate student, developed a series of tests with student (and subject) Hubert Pearce. As a student, Pearce had attended a lecture by Rhine, and afterward approached the professor to tell him that he believed he possessed clairvoyant abilities. Rhine invited Pearce to become involved with the Duke Parapsychology Labs in a series of tests that Pratt and Rhine both administered. In these tests, Pearce scored exceptionally high, his results coming in at a consistent 32 percent success rate, compared to chance-levels, which ranked at 20 percent. In order to control for any visual or sensory cues that Pearce might be picking up on, a Distance Series was introduced in which Pearce was placed in an entirely separate building from the cards with which he was guessing.

Due to the high success rates, multiple researchers through the years studied the case and evaluated its components, analyzing every possible angle to see if some other explanation could be reached. Rhine and Pratt offer those analyses here and conclude by saying, "Viewed twenty years later, the results of the Pearce-Pratt series still appear to allow no interpretation except that they were due to extrasensory perception."[90]

Keywords: Hubert Pearce; Pearce-Pratt Distance Series; ESP at a distance; Duke Parapsychology Labs

Rhine, Louisa E. "Hallucinatory Psi Experiences II: The Initiative of the Percipient in Hallucinations of the Living, the Dying, and the Dead." *Journal of Parapsychology* 21, no. 1 (March 1957): 13–46.

This article is a continuation of research by parapsychologist Louisa E. Rhine on the nature of hallucinatory experiences related to deceased individuals. Analyzing 825 hallucination experiences, Rhine's first report compiled the ways in which these experiences manifested, for example, were they auditory, visual, etc. In that first round of inquiry, Rhine discovered that just over half of the cases involved visual phenomena. In the second round of inquiry, Rhine investigates the triggers for these experiences. In her own words, she writes, "To what extent are such experiences started by action on the part of an agent? As pointed out in the preceding article, the old idea of the nature of psi hallucinations was that they were essentially telepathic transfers. And the assumption in regard to telepathy was that the agent initiated the experience, whether or not he was living, dying, or already dead."[91] But Rhine goes on to state that older notions of origin have been expanded in recent psi research and how it is no longer assumed that the origin doesn't somehow start with the percipient. In her study, Rhine discovers that "psi hallucinations of the living do not depend on the intent and volition of the agent to appear to the percipient."[92] This study presents the continued work of research into phantasms of the living and the role of agent versus percipient and how consciousness is wrapped up in all of this.

Keywords: hallucinations; apparitions; phantasms of the living; auditory hallucinations; visual hallucinations

Rhine, Louisa E. "Placement PK Tests with Three Types of Objects." *Journal of Parapsychology* 15, no. 2 (June 1, 1951): 132–38.

In this article, Louisa E. Rhine presents her work on placement PK, which is the ability to psychically influence where an object will land upon a given surface. Using a divider that separated the right and left sides of a surface, Rhine used three different objects to throw upon the field: marbles, coins, and cubes. While she discovered that some groups scored higher than others, none of the more than 113,000 throws scored above chance levels. Of those groups who did score higher, though, Rhine posits that the conditions of their test environment impacted their psychological state, which in turn impacted their abilities.

Keywords: placement PK; psychokinesis

Schmeidler, Gertrude R. "Rorschachs and ESP Scores of Patients Suffering from Cerebral Concussion." *Journal of Parapsychology* 16, no. 2 (June 1, 1952): 80–89.

In this article, Gertrude R. Schmeidler presents her work on the potential psi abilities of patients who had not yet recovered from a concussion. Of twenty-nine patients, all eighteen of whom were actively healing from some head trauma tested at statistically significant positive ESP rates while all others who were not under the influence of a concussion tested at or below chance levels. Using a set of ten ESP cards that were also painted certain colors, subjects were asked to choose both the color *and* symbol imprinted upon the cards. Schmeidler's results show that all eighteen concussion patients scored at high ESP levels, and she posits that there is some unique effect of a concussion that enabled these scores.

Keywords: concussion; extrasensory perception; ESP cards

Stewart, W. C. "Three New ESP Test Machines and Some Preliminary Results." *Journal of Parapsychology* 23, no. 1 (March 1959): 44–48.

While an engineering student at Duke University, author W. C. Stewart conducted a series of tests using three devices that were built specifically for testing extrasensory perception. Stewart reminds us,

"The need for machines capable of testing for ESP as well as for PK has been recognized for years . . . a machine which would reliably provide a random target, record data accurately, and be foolproof in its operation would relieve the experimenter of several monotonous chores and allow him more flexibility in creating a desirable environment for his experiment."[93] Inspired by the work of one of the electrical engineering faculty in creating a machine designed to do just this, Stewart and two of his colleagues built their own machines and in this article, Stewart tests their efficacy.

The devices were all tested in three different experiments, and Stewart discovered that all but one resulted in statistically significant positive ESP results. He theorizes that the environment in which they were used had an impact as they were tested in group dynamics with the goal of friendly competition among the devices. A playful attitude, it seems, might affect the results. Stewart concludes by telling us that mechanical devices show promise for being incorporated into ESP experiments and that further research is needed.

Keywords: mechanical devices; extrasensory perception; Duke Parapsychology Labs.

Vasse, Paul and Christiane Vasse. "A Comparison of Two Subjects in PK." *Journal of Parapsychology* 15, no. 4 (Dec. 1, 1951): 263–70.

Authors Paul and Christiane Vasse began to notice that Christiane seemed to possess possible psychokinetic abilities shortly after they were married. They began an experiment to study this, which tested Christiane's influence on the germination of seeds. The control seeds, which were left undeterred, grew at a slower rate than the ones in which she focused and they eventually published this work in the French journal *Revue Métapsychique*. During this time, they had been in contact with J. B. Rhine and the Duke Parapsychology Labs and were familiar with some of the methods coming out of them. In particular, they were inspired by the design of Margaret Pegram's research and used her methods to conduct their own study of PK using dice to compare the PK abilities between themselves. Overall, the results of both taken together were statistically significant, but they did note an interesting pattern. Christiane's PK levels started off high and then

declined whereas Paul's PK started out nonexistent and then rose to significant levels before then declining. The authors write, "This difference between us shows clearly enough that these distribution patterns which are now very conspicuous in parapsychology reports are to some extent individual."[94]

Keywords: psychokinesis; Revue Métapsychique

Warner, Lucien. "What the Younger Psychologists Think About ESP" *Journal of Parapsychology* 19, no. 4 (Dec. 1, 1955): 228–35.

Author Lucien Warner was a psychology and biology professor at Claremont Men's College when he wrote this article that discusses the results of a survey of attitudes on extrasensory perception. More specifically, the attitudes in question are those of members of the American Psychological Association (APA). In 1938 and again in 1952, two surveys were administered to APA members to gauge their attitudes and receptivity toward psi research. These were the first in a series of surveys on this topic. In this article, Warner discusses the differences between these first two surveys and how they might reflect the difference in the makeup of the APA in both of these years.

Keywords: attitudes toward psi; American Psychological Association; extrasensory perception

Zorab, George. *Bibliography of Parapsychology.* New York: Parapsychology Foundation, 1957.

In 1953, at the first International Conference of Parapsychological Studies, a board of researchers agreed to form the Committee of Bibliography. George Zorab was placed on that committee and formed the bulk of the work that led to the creation of the 1957 publication, *Bibliography of Parapsychology*. In this work, Zorab presents an unannotated, international compendium of resources ranging from the 1800s to the 1950s. He divides his work into topical categories so that readers can quickly find resources on, for example, telepathy, clairvoyance, crystal gazing, poltergeists, and more. Zorab divides this work into major categories including mental phenomena (in which you can find clairvoyance, telepathy, etc.), physical phenomena (in which you can find telekinesis, levitation, etc.,) and other categories like haunting phenomena, and quantitative experiments. Resources include books and journal articles. This is a wonderful resource that provides citations for a wide variety of historical and international research and would be indispensable especially for those looking for earlier research.

Keywords: bibliography; international

1960s

Bender, Hans. "The Gotenhafen Case of Correspondence Between Dreams and Future Events: A Study of Motivation." *International Journal of Neuropsychiatry* 2, no. 5 (1966): 398–407.

Hans Bender was a psychology professor at Freiburg University when he read this report to those attending the 1964 meeting of the SPR. This article chronicles the dreams and related parapsychic phenomena of a woman who had been regularly sending her dreams to the Freiburg Institute. Along with details of her dreams, she was also asked to send any synchronistic parallels between her dreams and things that happened in waking life. It appeared that 10 percent of her dreams corresponded to some event that happened *after* her dream in her waking life. Bender outlines the methods and procedures in this article and discusses the relationship of dreaming to the psychical world.

Keywords: dreaming; precognition; Freiburg Institute

Cavanna, Roberto and Montague Ullman, eds. *Psi and Altered States of Consciousness: Proceedings of an International Conference on Hypnosis, Drugs, Dreams, and Psi Held at Le Piol, St. Paul de Vence, France, June 9–12, 1967.* New York: Garrett Press, Inc., 1967.

This work, which can be accessed freely online, compiles the proceedings of a 1967 conference on psi and altered states of consciousness held in France. The conference presentations are separated into three main categories. The first category is hypnosis in psi research and includes topics like the history of mesmerism, a historical survey of hypnosis within parapsychology, and more. The second category is psychopharmacological concepts in psi research and discusses the role of psychedelics and psi phenomena. The third category is neurophysiological concepts in psi research and contains discussions of dreaming, dowsing, altered states of consciousness, and more. These presentations include researchers from around the world.

Keywords: consciousness; conference proceedings; hypnosis

Chauvin, Rémy. "ESP and Size of Target Symbols." *Journal of Parapsychology* 25, no. 3 (September 1, 1961): 185–89.

Researcher Rémy Chauvin was the director of the Laboratory of Experimental Ethology in Paris when he published this article in the *Journal of Parapsychology.* He was inspired by research done by Louisa Rhine and others that investigated if the size of an ESP target influenced the success of ESP rates. Chauvin, however, points out that previous researchers focused on sizes that were legible to the naked eye and here, in this research, Chauvin wonders what might happen if target sizes are shrunk to the point of needing visual assistance or magnification. He discovered that normal-sized objects scored positively for ESP while the smaller-sized objects had a statistically significant psi missing effect, meaning that the negative deviation was higher than what should have occurred by chance, indicating that *something* was in effect even during the testing of small objects.

Keywords: psi missing; target objects; extrasensory perception

Dingwall, Eric J. *Very Peculiar People: Portrait Studies in the Queer, the Abnormal, and the Uncanny.* New Hyde Park, NY: University Books, 1962.

Researcher Eric J. Dingwall presents biographical sketches of figures throughout history who have experienced and/or exhibited supernatural phenomena. A diverse set of five figures are selected to not only highlight the supernatural events themselves, but to also shed light on the many diverse ways in which the anomalous shows up throughout history. Of particular relevance among these figures is the biography on Italian medium Eusapia Palladino. Dingwall presents a detailed overview of her early life and rise to fame . . . and infamy.

Keywords: Eusapia Palladino; biographical sketch

Forwald, H. "A PK Experiment with Die Faces as Targets." *Journal of Parapsychology* 25, no. 1 (March 1, 1961): 1–12.

In previous decades, researcher Haakon Forwold was interested in psychokinesis using dice. In particular, he was curious if he could psychically manipulate dice to land on certain sides of a throwing field. In this 1961 article, he builds upon that research and investigates whether PK can manipulate which face of the die turns up. Establishing probability rates for each face before the experience, Forwold conducted this study with dice of different sizes and even threw them onto hard *and* soft surfaces. From 1956–1960, Forwold conducted more than thirty-one thousand dice throws. In conclusion, he tells us,

Positive deviations of strong significance have been obtained in this experiment with die faces as targets, just as they were produced previously in the author's placement experiments, where the target was an area of a dice table within which the subject desired moving cubes to come to rest. In both cases, recognized laws of dynamics cannot account for the results. A factor of a psychological kind must have been involved in the process because the movements of the cubes, when considered in terms of the over-all results, were in accordance with the intentions of the experimenter.[95]

Keywords: psychokinesis; dice-throwing

Freeman, John. "An ESP Test Involving Emotionally-Toned Objects." *Journal of Parapsychology* 25, no. 4 (December 1, 1961): 260–65.

Dr. John Freeman was a research assistant at the Duke Parapsychology Labs and also the director of the parapsychology labs at Wayland College in Texas. In this test of general extrasensory perception (referred to as GESP), Dr. Freeman was interested in seeing if ESP was affected by the introduction of objects to which subjects had an emotional connection. He begins by explaining the motivation for this study when he tells us, "Many of the cases of spontaneous ESP which have been reported involve situations which have strong emotional content. This suggests that the ability to perceive a target through ESP might be facilitated if there were some emotional attachment to the target."[96] Dr. Freeman's experiment did not yield statistically significant results for either the control objects or the emotionally-charged objects, but he did notice that for eleven of the twelve participants, their standard deviations for controls and emotional objects were opposite each other.

Keywords: extrasensory perception; GESP (general extrasensory perception); emotions; spontaneous ESP

Gauld, Alan. *The Founders of Psychical Research.* New York: Schocken Books, 1968.

In this book, historian Alan Gauld provides a biographical overview of the psychical researchers Henry Sidgwick, Edmund Gurney, and Frederic W. H. Myers.

Keywords: biographies; Henry Sidgwick; Edmund Gurney; Frederic W. H. Myers

Knight, David C., ed. *The ESP Reader.* New York: Grosset & Dunlap, 1969.

Author David C. Knight was a member of the American SPR when he compiled this anthology of resources on extrasensory perception. He tells us in his introduction, "Anthologies are somewhat like compasses. Both can point the way, yet neither can actually chart the course. If the present anthology but points the way toward further reading in the expanding literature of psychical research, then it shall have achieved its purpose."[97]

The first part of this work includes two essays by researcher J. B. Rhine that discuss psychical research and Spiritualism. The following part is titled "The Golden Age of the Great Mediums" and includes essays on figures like Eusapia Palladino, the Fox sisters, Leonora Piper, and Eva. C. These essays are written by key figures such as Nandor Fodor, Hereward Carrington, Sir Oliver Lodge, and more. This section covers mediumship and figures during the 1800s. Following this are case studies that discuss spontaneous cases of psi and offers fascinating recountings.

Part 4 is a compendium of essays from modern mediums like Eileen Garrett, Peter Hurkos, Ruth Montgomery. The following five sections focus on specific topics like Ouija boards, automatic writing, out-of-body experiences, reincarnation, and life after death. The work concludes with a glossary of terms and a bibliography for further reading.

Keywords: extrasensory perception; anthology; mediums; near-death experiences

Louwerens, Nicolauda G. "ESP Experiments with Nursery School Children in the Netherlands." *Journal of Parapsychology* 24, no. 2 (June 1, 1960): 75–93.

Author Nicolauda G. Louwerens was a research assistant at the Parapsychological Institute of the University of Utrecht when she conducted this study. In her study, she organized an ESP experiment at a Dutch nursery school. Children between the ages of four and six and a half used cards that had pictures of toys and selected them at certain moments during the reading of a fairy tale. Overall, the results were positive for ESP and the girls skewed more positive than the boys. Interestingly, Louwerens conducted ten trials of this study, serving as a type of control in place of the regular teacher and, even though she was concealed during the study, her results were significantly lower than that of the teacher's, indicating a potential link between the relationship of the sender and the subjects.

Keywords: extrasensory perception and children; the Netherlands; ESP and personality

Nash, Carroll B. "Can Precognition Occur Diametrically?" *Journal of Parapsychology* 24, no. 1 (March 1, 1960): 26–32.

Author Carroll B. Nash points out that some previous research analyzes diametric psi, or the required component of two types of psi in order for an experiment to be successful. Most of these previous studies involve the combination of extrasensory perception and psychokinesis. In this study, however, Nash examines how successful subjects might be if they were required to perform two precognitive tasks, making this the first diametric psi study focusing exclusively on precognition. In this study, subjects had to call out certain number-targets that would not be chosen for another year. They also then had to checkmark those calls in which they felt particularly strongly were correct. Nash found no statistically significant results of precognition but did notice that the hits the subjects checked as strongly correct often turned out to be incorrect.

Keywords: precognition; diametrically psi

Osis, Karlis. *Deathbed Observations by Physicians and Nurses.* New York: Parapsychology Foundation, 1961.

In this study, researcher Karlis Osis investigates the phenomena of spontaneous psi events that happen at or near the time of death. Osis gathered 640 questionnaires sent to physicians and nurses across the United States on the topic of deathbed visions. Osis asked the medical professionals questions about patients who had reported having a deathbed vision and asked them questions about the patient's mood, their level of coherence, amounts of medication, the type of vision they experienced (i.e., visions of non-human things like buildings or landscapes or hallucinations of people known to them such as deceased loved ones), and more. These inquiries examine possible psi hallucinations but also add to the body of literature on survival after death. Osis remarks on the fact that much survival-after-death research focuses on spontaneous psi of relatives and loved ones of dying persons instead of inquiring about any psi phenomena surrounding the dying person, themself. This study attempts to fill in that gap.

The 640 surveys that were returned yielded information on 35,540 dying patients. Of these reports, roughly 10 percent of these patients were reported as conscious in the hours leading up to their death—this is the group that Osis was focused on. In 1,370 cases, terminally ill patients reported seeing apparitions of their dead loved ones. These experiences did not seem to be affected by differences in illness, physiology, or culture and in the vast majority of these cases, patients were not under extreme effects of sedatives or fever. This large-scale study adds to the literature on deathbed visions and the role of consciousness in spontaneous psi events.

Keywords: deathbed visions; near-death visions; spontaneous psi; survival after death

Pleasants, Helene, ed. *Biographical Dictionary of Parapsychology.* New York: Garrett Publications, 1964.

Editor Helene Pleasants compiled this biographical dictionary of key figures in the timeline of parapsychology, including both researchers and mediums. In the introduction, Pleasants points out that up until this point in time no comprehensive work had yet been created that provided biographical sketches of prominent figures. Just under four hundred pages, this work provides brief entries on figures around the world, dating back to the 1700s. This work includes many figures not listed in more recent titles.

Keywords: biographical sketches

Pollack, Jack Harrison. *Croiset the Clairvoyant: The Story of the Amazing Dutchman.* Garden City, NY: Doubleday & Company, 1964.

Gerard Croiset was a medium from Holland who rose to fame in the 1950s and 1960s. In this book, Jack Harrison Pollack presents a biographical account of the noted medium. Most of the book outlines the various cases of missing people and objects that Croiset was involved with, ranging from his home in Holland to elsewhere around the world. Many of these cases involved object reading in which the medium obtains psychic information from handling physical objects. One chapter in this book discusses how a professor took this even further to test if Croiset could intuit historical information from objects, like stone and bone. Chapter 11 is a particularly intriguing addition since it discusses the "chair test." Pollack writes that this test was a "major contribution to modern parapsychological research" and was "perhaps the most original scientific experiment in precognition during this generation."[98] In this test, a random seat location is chosen prior to the beginning of some event (often days in advance) and the medium presents information from psychic impressions on the characteristics and life experiences of the person who will eventually sit there. This biographical treatment of Holland's famed medium is an interesting snapshot from that period.

Keywords: Gerard Croiset; mediumship; Holland; biographical sketch

Pratt, J. G. "Methods of Evaluating Verbal Material." *Journal of Parapsychology* 24, no. 2 (June 1, 1960): 94–109.

Psychical researcher J. G. Pratt delivered this article in June 1959 as part of a conference titled the Symposium on Incorporeal Personal Agency hosted by the Duke Parapsychology Labs. In it, he discusses parapsychology's long, historical focus on incorporeal agency and how important it is to learn

from the past and build upon its new methods and techniques that adhere to scientific standards.

Keywords: research methods; historical overview of methods

Rhine, Louisa E. *Hidden Channels of the Mind.* New York: William Sloane Associates, 1961.

Louisa E. Rhine was a notable researcher who worked at the Duke Parapsychology Laboratory. Many people may have only ever heard her referred to as J. B. Rhine's wife, but Louisa conducted research of her own and published multiple articles and manuscripts. In *Hidden Channels of the Mind,* Louisa specifically presents information in an easily accessible format for those who experience extrasensory perception themselves. She writes in the foreword that the book "is intended, rather, for the untold thousands of persons who have had parapsychical (or psychic) experiences. They have long had questions for which they could find no answers." This book helps laypeople feel legitimized in their own personal experiences. Another goal of this work, though, is to bring a more personal touch to the laboratory experiments. For example, she writes, "The experiences in this book make the data from the laboratory more understandable by demonstrating them, as it were, in action and in life."[99]

She begins with a discussion on the different types of extrasensory perception before moving on to a discussion on the ways in which ESP is experienced by various people. Following this is a section that discusses the nuances of determining if something was a psychic episode or for example, just a normal dream. The book then goes on to discuss the ways in which space and time seem fluid in psychic encounters. Chapter 6 includes detailed examples of psi experiences that show the breadth of subject matter. Additional chapters include differences and similarities among women, children, men, and elderly people. Chapters in the second half of the book discuss potential personality traits of those who experience psi as well as the mental and emotional impact that a psi experience can have on a person. Interspersed throughout this book are quotes from people who have experience psi as well as comments on laboratory research.

Keywords: ESP; Louisa E. Rhine

Rhine, Louisa E. "Psychological Processes in ESP Experiences. Part I: Waking Experiences." *Journal of Parapsychology* 26 (1962): 88–111.

Louisa E. Rhine begins this work by reminding readers of the difficulty of psi research. She tells us, "The general impression one would get from this record of low, even if significant, scoring is that ESP, at least under laboratory conditions, is exercised only with difficulty; that it is somehow restricted, able to function only imperfectly and sporadically."[100] Rhine goes on to discuss her theory that ESP originates from the unconscious and a need to better understand the processes behind it. In this article, Rhine analyses cases of ESP in an attempt to "identify, list, and characterize the mediating vehicles of the ESP process."[101] She analyzed thousands of cases and found that they fell into one of four categories, and she found that spontaneous psi cases were most useful because they revealed more about the psychological process than laboratory-induced psi in which the subject has no context or even awareness of what is happening. She presents her work on what these spontaneous cases reveal about the psychological processes of ESP in this article.

Keywords: extrasensory perception; psychological process of ESP; spontaneous psi

Roll, W. G. "The Contribution of Studies of 'Mediumship' to Research on Survival after Death." *Journal of Parapsychology* 24, no. 4 (December 1, 1960): 258–78.

In this article, W. G. Roll presents an overview of mediumship research and the implications of future usage of mediumistic phenomena to obtain evidence for survival after bodily death. In this article we learn of some of the seminal mediumship cases and along the way, Roll discusses the nuances of methods and psi phenomena. He concludes by telling us,

We can now say what type of finding will indicate an incorporeal personal agent. It would consist in records which have motivational and personality factors foreign to the subject but typical of the deceased personality in question, as well as intellectual or cognitive characteristics that are not part of the furnishings of the subject's mind but were possessed by the supposed communicator. This type of material should be obtained in experiments in which

there is no close linkage with living persons who have the personality traits or the technical knowledge shown in the record.[102]

Keywords: mediumship; mediumship research; research methods

Sanders, Michael S. "A Comparison of Verbal and Written Responses in a Precognition Experiment." *Journal of Parapsychology* 26, no. 1 (March 1962): 23–34.

Author Michael S. Sanders was a research assistant at the Duke Parapsychology Labs when he conducted this experiment. In it, he tested whether there was a difference in success rates between verbally indicating your selection versus writing it. For example, twenty female college students were chosen to test their extrasensory perception. In one group of tests, they wrote down what symbol they believed corresponded to a randomly generated selection while in the other test that verbally called out what they believed the symbol would be. Sanders also investigated how the lab environment and the dynamic between subject and experimenter affects ESP scores. He also discusses how the introduction of a third-party experimenter acting as a neutral control seemed to hamper results.

Keywords: extrasensory perception; experimenter effect

Schmeidler, Gertrude. *ESP in Relation to Rorschach Test Evaluation.* New York: Parapsychology Foundation, 1960.

In this book, researcher Gertrude R. Schmeidler presents a detailed discussion of her sheep-goat hypothesis and the ways in which personality directly impacts the ability for people to display extrasensory perception. Specifically, she discusses what Rorschach personality tests might reveal in those who perform well on ESP tests. For those interested in the sheep-goat effect and the ways in which personality plays a role in ESP, this resource by Schmeidler will be essential.

Keywords: sheep-goat effect; Rorschach tests; ESP and personality

Stevenson, Ian. "The Evidence for Survival from Claimed Memories of Former Incarnations. Part I.

Review of the Data." *Journal of the American Society for Psychical Research* 54, no. 2 (April 1960): 51–71.

In this article, Dr. Ian Stevenson begins by reminding us of the long, philosophical, and cultural history of reincarnation around the world. He then proceeds to outline evidence he has gathered from people who seem to possess memories belonging to deceased individuals. He also outlines what types of information can be presented as potential indicators of reincarnation cases. He then presents specific case studies of individuals exhibiting these characteristics.

Keywords: reincarnation

Advances in Parapsychological Research, vol. 1: Psychokinesis. Edited by Stanley Krippner, Rhea White, Montague Ullman, and Robert O. Becker. New York: Plenum, 1977.

This book is part of the series Advances in Parapsychological Research, that cover other topics like extrasensory perception. Readers interested in seeking out this series should do so, but for purposes of introducing this series, I will just discuss the first volume. This volume specifically focuses on psychokinesis, or the ability of the human mind to impact the physical environment. The first chapter in this work discusses research methods used to investigate PK and the associated limitations and problems associated with that. This is a natural segue to chapter two which discusses research findings on the topic. Chapter three discusses the particular relationship between PK, psi, and psychotherapy.

Chapters four and five 1provide interesting discussions on the implications of PK on both philosophy and religion before concluding with a bibliography of books to consult on the topic that were published between 1974–1976.

Keywords: psychokinesis (PK)

1970s

Ashby, Robert H. *The Guidebook for the Study of Psychical Research.* New York: Samuel Weiser, Inc., 1973.

Researcher Robert H. Ashby presents this guidebook that compiles a variety of resources on psi topics. Chapter 1 gives an overview of the rise of

parapsychology as a discipline and an overview of scientists, theories, and research. Once Ashby presents this introduction of what parapsychology is, chapter 2 presents a bibliography for those completely new to the topic. Chapter 3, however, is dedicated to those who already have some understanding of the topic. In each of these chapters, Ashby arranges resources by type: annotated and unannotated. Those that are annotated, as you may assume, have a summary of that resource while the unannotated portions just include citations. Both are equally helpful, however, and useful for those interested in a variety of psi topics like mediumship, spontaneous psi, etc. Ashby tells us his motivation for writing this guidebook in the introduction:

> It is obvious that the beginning student of psychical research needs some guidance as to where and how to proceed with [their] studies, and those who already have some knowledge of the field need to decide at which point to undertake further study of a very puzzling mass of data, interpretations, theories, and disagreements.[6]

Chapter 4 is especially unique and is titled "Procedures for Sitting with a Medium." In this chapter, Ashby provides information on how you can go about finding a medium, setting up your own session, and what to expect. Chapter 5 provides a list of research organizations, libraries, and publications in both the United States and the United Kingdom that discuss and/or make available psi resources. The last two chapters include a list of key figures and terms. This resource is an essential addition to parapsychology and will be useful for those new to the topic and those who are already somewhat familiar. This resource will be helpful for those interested in researching these topics themselves. Though it is a bit dated, most of the information in this work remains relevant today.

Keywords: general work; reference; history of parapsychology; key figures

Bander, Peter. *Voices from the Tapes: Recordings from the Other World.* New York: Drake Publishers, Inc., 1973.

The author of this work, Peter Bander, was a psychologist and professor at the Cambridge Institute of Education when he first advised a colleague not to publish an English translation of the work of Dr. Konstantin Raudive, a Latvian psychologist who studied electronic voice phenomena (EVP). Bander's colleague convinced him to listen to audio recordings captured using the methods outlined in Raudive's book and, while hesitant, Bander eventually did listen. During those sessions, Bander was convinced that he heard the voice of his deceased mother. This event completely changed Bander's view and he changed his mind, encouraging his colleague to move forward with an English translation, *Breakthrough*, published in 1971. This translation skyrocketed public awareness of electronic voice phenomena.

In this work, Bander coordinates physicists, electronic engineers, and even priests from around the world to engage in EVP experimentation to draw their own conclusions. Bander begins with an overview of the discovery of EVP and the theories surrounding it. The result is a well-rounded discussion that offers a beginning point, especially for the general public, into the topic of electronic voice phenomena.

Keywords: electronic voice phenomena (EVP); Konstantin Raudive

Fodor, Nandor. *An Encyclopedia of Psychic Science.* Secaucus, NJ: The Citadel Press, 1974.

This work, a paperback publication of the original 1966 publication, is an encyclopedic treatment of figures, terms, and cases related to psi phenomena. Author Nandor Fodor was a Hungarian parapsychologist, historian, and journalist who wrote extensively about various psi topics, figures, and cases. In this encyclopedia, Fodor presents more than eight hundred detailed entries on an international scale. In the foreword of this work Leslie Shepard provides some guidance to readers on which entries to begin with for maximum impact. Shepard encourages readers, for example, to start with the comprehensive essays on Spiritualism and psychical research before turning to particular psi phenomena like table-turning and then moving onto notable physical mediums like Eusapia Palladino or the Fox sisters. Since this encyclopedia is an older reference work, it contains references to and information regarding certain cases and figures that may not be included in newer works.

Keywords: encyclopedia; reference

Hartwell, J. W. "Contingent Negative Variation as an Index of Precognitive Information." *European Journal of Parapsychology* 2 (1978): 83–103.

In this article, researcher J. W. Hartwell discusses the relation of a specific brainwave in the context of psychical events. Specifically, they tell us that a certain brainwave referred to as the cognitive negative variation (CNV). Identified in 1964, this brainwave is involved in psychological processes involving expectancy. In this study, Hartwell is curious how and if CNV might be a physiological variable to test precognition.

Keywords: brainwaves; precognition

Johnson, Martin. "A New Technique of Testing ESP in a Real-Life, High-Motivated Context." *Journal of Parapsychology* 37 (1973): 210–17.

Author Martin Johnson begins by telling us some of the limitations of laboratory psi research. He also reminds us that multiple scholars have attempted to use different methods and settings to mitigate for these limitations. In this study, Johnson tells us, "The present study was one more such attempt at measuring the extent to which a person can benefit from extrasensory sources when he finds himself in a compelling real-life situation that calls for a high degree of motivation."[103] In this experiment, university students were given an exam that also simultaneously involved a psi test, even though they were unaware of the psi aspect. Tests had hidden messages below test response areas that either included hints at correct answers, related but incorrect answers, and notes of either encouragement or discouragement. Johnson points out that those who received tests with negative remarks obtained bad test scores at higher-than-chance levels than those who did not receive negative notes. He presents other findings before including suggestions for continued research.

Keywords: extrasensory perception; ESP and motivation

Krippner, Stanley, Rhea White, Montague Ullman, and Robert O. Becker, eds. *Advances in Parapsychological Research, vol. 1: Psychokinesis.* New York: Plenum, 1977.

This book is part of the series Advances in Parapsychological Research, which at nine volumes covers other topics like extrasensory perception.

Readers interested in seeking out this series should do so, but for purposes of introducing it, I will just discuss the first volume, which specifically focuses on psychokinesis, or the ability of the human mind to impact the physical environment. The first chapter in this work discusses research methods used to investigate PK and the associated limitations and problems associated with that. This is a natural segue into chapter 2, which discusses research findings on the topic. Chapter 3 discusses the particular relationship between PK, psi, and psychotherapy.

Chapters 4 and 5 provide interesting discussions on the implications of PK on both philosophy and religion before concluding with a bibliography of books to consult on the topic that were published between 1974–1976.

Keywords: psychokinesis (PK)

Mitchell, Edgar. "An ESP Test from Apollo 14." *Journal of Parapsychology* 35, no. 2 (June 1, 1971): 89–107.

In some studies of extrasensory perception, researchers investigate the impact that distance has on ESP. You could argue that this 1971 study is the most extreme example of those inquiries. The author puts it most effectively in the introduction to this work,

> This is an account of an introductory experiment in ESP made under circumstances that in some respects were uniquely exploratory. So far as is known, no such undertaking has been reported before. It was an attempt to take advantage of the Apollo 14 flight to the moon, of which the author was a crew member, to conduct an ESP experiment in which the targets were in outer space and the participating subjects were on earth.[104]

Astronaut and author Dr. Edgar Mitchell outlines that experiment in this article. Coordinating with friends prior to launch, Mitchell established certain days and times that he would look at a set of ESP cards and focus on them, attempting to have friends back on Earth psychically intuit the targets. While not all sets were able to be completed, Mitchell found that subjects were able to identify targets at a slightly higher rate than in the sample tests he ran while on Earth, indicating that there is perhaps no physical limit to the influence of psi.

Keywords: psi in space; Apollo 14; psi at a distance

Naumov, E. K. and V. Vilenskaya. *Soviet Bibliography on Parapsychology (Psychoenergetics) and Related Subjects.* Arlington, VA: Joint Publications Research Service, 1972.

Russian researchers compiled a work that presented not only an introduction to the topic of parapsychology and a review of prominent cases, but a bibliography of Soviet researchers conducting parapsychological research.

Keywords: Russian parapsychologists

Osis, Karlis and Erlendur Haraldsson. "Deathbed Observations by Physicians and Nurses: A Cross-Cultural Study," *The Journal of the American Society for Psychical Research* 71, no. 3 (July 1977): 237–59.

In this article, parapsychologists Karlis Osis and Erlendur Haraldsson present a survey they administered to medical professionals in both India and the United States. This survey asked doctors and nurses to respond to questions surrounding the deathbed visions of terminal patients. Specifically, the survey asked for information about patients experiencing near-death hallucinations of deceased people. In addition to surveys, the authors also followed up with interviews to obtain more nuanced information. Osis and Haraldsson discovered that the vast majority of hallucinations consisted of deceased loved ones or religious figures that gave patients the impression of being led through the death experience and into the next realm of existence.

Keywords: near-death experiences; deathbed visions; life-after-death; cross-cultural

Pratt, J. Gaither. *ESP Research Today: A Study of Developments in Parapsychology Since 1960.* Metuchen, NJ: Scarecrow Press, 1973.

In this book, parapsychologist J. Gaither Pratt presents a discussion on various cases and developments in parapsychology since 1960. He begins by detailing the different types of psychical events and phenomena. He then introduces modern parapsychology and its progress before diving into a discussion of Russian ESP research followed by two case studies. He continues to discuss psychic photography, poltergeists, and reincarnation.

Keywords: extrasensory perception; poltergeists; reincarnation; psychic photography; ESP in Russia

Pratt, J. Gaither and H. H. J. Keil. "Firsthand Observations of Nina S. Kulagina Suggestive of PK upon Static Objects." *Journal of the American Society for Psychical Research* 67 (1973): 381–90.

Much research on Nina S. Kulagina was only found in Russian publications for quite some time. Eventually, Western researchers, who had been intrigued by Kulagina for years, realized the need to conduct their own research so there could be publications available in English journals. Researchers Pratt and Keil present their research that adds to the international literature on the case of Nina S. Kulagina and her psychokinetic abilities.

Keywords: psychokinesis; Nina Kulagina

Raudive, Konstantin. *Breakthrough: An Amazing Experiment in Electronic Communication with the Dead.* Translated by Nadia Fowler. Gerarrds Cross, England: Colin Smythe, 1971.

Dr. Konstantin Raudive was a Latvian author and researcher who discovered and popularized the concept of electronic voice phenomena (EVP). When he realized that strange noises seemed to be captured on audio tape, he began digging into this phenomenon and eventually wrote a book, translated in 1971, on his work regarding EVP cases.

In this book, Raudive presents a discussion on the first cases where he began to notice that something strange seemed to be happening before jumping into a discussion on some of his early experiments. He also discusses the various mediums through which he conducted his studies, for example he discusses research done using microphones, radios, different frequencies, etc. In the following section he goes into detail on the contents of the EVP recordings, presenting case studies of people involved. Raudive also provides information on his collaborations with other researchers. For those interested in EVPs, this work is a seminal resource.

Keywords: electronic voice phenomena (EVP); Konstantin Raudive

Rhine, J. B., ed. *Progress in Parapsychology.* Durham, NC: The Parapsychology Press, 1971.

J. B. Rhine is the editor of this work that was published in memory of fellow researcher William McDougall on what would have been his one hundredth birthday. Presented as a periodic publication, Rhine states in his introduction that this work presents the newest and best research being done on psi. Additionally, it is an attempt to compile the latest research into one easy-to-find resource. Rhine writes, "For the great many who cannot visit the widely separated research centers and who cannot read all the reports of that work in the scientific periodicals, some way is needed to bring reader and researcher closer together."[105] In this sense, Rhine's work is similar to that of his fellow researcher (and wife) Louisa who wrote multiple books of her own with the goal of spreading psychical awareness to the masses.

This work opens with an overview of new research methods. This particular edition highlights work being done with mice, quantum physics, and EEGs. The book also discusses factors that may impact the outcome of psi experiments and also presents a review of recent psi research. This book also includes appendixes on factors to consider when conducting future research and concludes with a glossary of terms.

Keywords: research methods

Rhine, Louisa E. *Psi: What is It? The Story of ESP and PK.* New York: Harper and Row, 1975.

In this book, researcher Louisa E. Rhine presents information on psi and PK made palatable for the everyday reader. In chapter 1 she tells us that while psi has been researched for decades, "The evidence, however, has not been widely enough or easily enough available to the general public to make widespread appreciation of its meaning possible, or to clarify its application to individuals who need to understand about it for personal reasons."[106] This book is an attempt to rectify that reality. Rhine discusses how, when the Duke Parapsychology Labs began researching psi, they received thousands of letters from people searching for answers. Some of those letters are highlighted within. The first chapter discusses broad definitions of psi and the importance for studying the phenomena. Part 2 discusses various types of psi and any associated personality traits of those who experience it, while part 3 dives into the research on ESP, dreams, and PK. Part 4 details the ways in which someone might experience psi, that is, how it would manifest in their life. Part 5 is entirely devoted to life after death and includes incidences of mediumistic messages from the dead and hauntings. There is also a section on how to pursue parapsychology from a professional standpoint and an appendix of types of ESP and PK tests. Rhine proves herself able once again to help break down the confusing lingo and deliver psi content to the masses, making this work especially useful for those unfamiliar with scientific jargon.

Keywords: extrasensory perception; psychokinesis

Stevenson, Ian. "Research into the Evidence of Man's Survival After Death: A Historical and Critical Survey with a Summary of Recent Developments." *The Journal of Nervous and Mental Disease* 165, no. 3 (1977): 152–70.

Dr. Ian Stevenson was a renowned psychiatrist and parapsychologist known for his work into reincarnation and the survival of personality after bodily death. In this article, Dr. Stevenson provides an overview of the nearly one hundred years of research "on the question of whether human personality survives physical death."[107] He presents a historical overview separated into three major areas and follows this with a discussion on recent developments of the past fifteen years. In Dr. Stevenson's view, research into this topic can be divided into three eras. The first era, the 1880s through the 1930s, was marked by large amounts of collecting and organizing these types of experiences and in dabbling with experimentation, especially as regards mediums. The second era, the 1930s to 1960, sees researchers backing away from the question of life after death in favor of the investigation of ESP. The third era, from the 1960s until 1977, sees the influx of additional parapsychologists who continue to focus on the influence of the living on ESP. Of this era, Dr. Stevenson writes that "most scientists today regard the conjecture that human personality may survive death as unworthy of attention and perhaps even absurd."[108] Throughout the article, Dr. Stevenson discusses these eras in detail and presents research and experiments on reincarnation within the last fifteen years.

Keywords: reincarnation; Ian Stevenson; life-after-death

Ullman, Montague, Stanley Krippner, and Alan Vaughn. *Dream Telepathy.* New York: Macmillan, 1973.

In this work, Montague Ullman and Stanley Krippner discuss their work in leading a dream laboratory at the Maimonides Medical Center in New York. For those interested in telepathy but especially the intersection of dreams and telepathy, this book will be a comprehensive and historical survey.

Keywords: dreams; telepathy; Maimonides Dream Lab

White, Rhea A., ed. *Surveys in Parapsychology: Review of the Literature with Updated Bibliographies.* Metuchen, NJ: Scarecrow Press, 1976.

Librarian and researcher Rhea A. White presents a compilation of resources on various topics in the field of parapsychology. Useful for those new to the topic who want to browse the breadth and scope while locating relevant literature to continue their research. You may also wish to consult White's later work *Parapsychology: New Sources of Information 1973–1989.*

Keywords: bibliography

Wolman, Benjamin B., ed. *Handbook of Parapsychology,* New York: Van Nostrand Reinhold Company, 1977.

This handbook includes entries from such notable parapsychological figures as Gertrude Schmeidler, John Beloff, Louisa Rhine, and Rhea White, just to name a few. Contributors to this nearly one thousand-page work sought to present a comprehensive view of the history and progress and parapsychology. In the words of Howard Zimmerman in the introduction, "The contributors to this volume have brought to this dialogue the history, achievements, scope, and problems as well as the implications and issues of an emerging science."[109]

This work compiles research relating to all manner of psi inquiry including ESP, psychokinesis, reincarnation, poltergeists, altered consciousness, and more. It is broken up into sections that help organize major themes and progressions for the reader. The first part includes three chapters on the history of parapsychology, which include not only a general history but also a history of experimental methods and the influence of William James. The second part takes a detailed look at research methods being used today and includes chapters from Louisa Rhine and Gertrude Schmeidler. Following this, the third section, are chapters that focus on specific topics relating to extrasensory perception such as basic definitions, patterned personality traits, and the experimenter-psi effect. The fourth section discusses some of the more physical psi topics like psychokinesis, poltergeists, and anomalous photographs. The fifth part of this work discusses altered states of consciousness while the sixth part talks about psychical healing. Part 7 discusses the survival of life after death and reincarnation and precedes part 8, which is a fascinating discussion on how parapsychology relates to and intermingles with other fields including physics, biology, anthropology and more. Part 9 presents the dominant theories of psi while part 10 gives an overview of Soviet research into parapsychology.

The concluding portion of this handbook is part 10, which provides a list of common words and terms along with a list of suggested reading. Those who consult this work may benefit from browsing the common terms portion of this section before diving into others. Part 10 also includes a name and subject index, which will help readers navigate to relevant portions if referencing a particular scientist and/or topic. This comprehensive handbook compiled by psi scholars themselves is an essential resource for anyone interested in parapsychology.

Keywords: general reference; history of parapsychology; ESP; psychokinesis; research methods; altered stated of consciousness; multidisciplinary

1980s

Alvarado, Carlos S. "Trends in the Study of Out-of-Body Experiences: An Overview of Developments Since the Nineteenth Century." *Journal of Scientific Exploration* 3, no.1 (1989): 27–42.

Carlos S. Alvarado presents an overview of the research into out-of-body experiences from the mid-1800s to the 1980s. As a result, not only do readers have a comprehensive set of resources to consult, but certain trends are uncovered. For purposes of revealing these trends, Alvarado divides the prior one hundred years into four different eras. He shows that literature reveals a belief in the late 1800s that these events were attributed to a psychic "other," or "double," that acted separate from the physical

person. Beginning in 1900, more case studies were conducted and published, but there is still relatively little experimental research. We start to see that in the next era, beginning in 1940. Additionally, this third era brings with it a concern for phenomenological aspects of psi events. The final era that Alvarado presents in this work is from 1970–1987, which he says is an era of immense growth and research. In this era, there are symposiums on parapsychology and an increase in scientific publications.

Keywords: out-of-body experiences

Batcheldor, Kenneth. "Contributions to the Theory of PK Induction from Sitter-Group Work." *Journal of the American Society for Psychical Research* 78, no. 2 (1984): 105–22.

Kenneth Batcheldor presents a review of his research into the occurrence of psychokinesis within groups. Many of the resources on PK focus on single subjects while in this article, Batcheldor discusses how a group setting affects the phenomenon. This article will be helpful for those interested in PK but specifically interested in how group dynamics might affect psi.

Keywords: psychokinesis (PK); groups; sitter-group

Broughton, Richard S. and James R. Perlstrom. "PK Experiments with a Competitive Computer Game." *Journal of Parapsychology* 50, no. 3 (September 1, 1986): 193–211.

Researchers Broughton and Perlstrom investigated psychokinesis and the concept of competition. To do so, they modified a computer game to be used. In some runs, the tests were labeled as competitive while in others they weren't. They discovered a potential link between anxiety and PK in competitive settings. Additionally, they found that subjects who often enjoyed mental activities scored much lower than others. The authors also discuss that their experiment has implications for psi as well and leave with a recommendation for future research.

Keywords: psychokinesis; psi; anxiety

Corliss, William R. *The Unfathomed Mind: A Handbook of Unusual Mental Phenomena.* Glen Arm, MD: The Sourcebook Project, 1982.

William R. Corliss compiles articles and essays from the annals of general science, psychiatry, and psychology that discuss the strange powers of the mind. In the preface, Corliss tells us that "the general thrust of this book is that the mind has powerful, subtle, often bizarre influences on the human body, human behavior, and perhaps even the so-called objective external world."[110] This work is a bit unique in that Corliss steers away from parapsychology-specific publications in favor of showing how other disciplines treat and discuss topics such as automatic writing, consciousness, hypnotism, anomalous dreams, and more. There are a few sprinklings of essays from both the British and American SPR, but the majority of sources are from other publications such as the *American Journal of Psychiatry*, the *Journal of Abnormal Psychology*, and others. Most of these sources view psi topics through the psychological lens of dissociation. Corliss's work offers readers an avenue to the ways in which psychology and psychiatry view these anomalous events, helping the reader understand how other researchers approach the anomalous.

Keywords: handbook; dissociation; consciousness

Flew, Anthony, ed. *Readings in the Philosophical Problems of Parapsychology*. Buffalo, NY: Prometheus Books, 1987.

This work presents chapters that deal with the philosophical implications of psi phenomena. In the introduction, editor Antony Flew tells us, "Whereas scientists in their working hours always ask what is the case and who do things happen as they do, the philosopher's question is, rather, granting that that was or is or will be so, 'So what?'"[111] The chapters discuss the philosophical underpinnings of psi research and tackle topics such as precognition, ESP, consciousness after death, and more. The chapters also present some critiques of research methods in psi research and even some chapters from scholars on their negative views of the whole prospect. Offering a unique look into what psi means for the reality of the world around us, this work occupies an interesting and useful space in the parapsychological literature. Readers who are interested in critical "so what?" questions of psi may be interested in this work.

Keywords: philosophy of psi; criticisms

Glicksohn, Joseph. "Psi and Altered States of Consciousness: The "Missing" Link." *Journal of Parapsychology* 50, no. 3 (September 1986): 213–33.

Joseph Glicksohn presents a discussion of psi-missing, or the occurrence for psi experiments to discover statistically significant negative results. In other words, it means that the hits or success rates are much lower than what they should be when just attributed to chance. Glicksohn discusses things that could help enhance the quality of psi research, such as figuring out a way to ascertain if an altered state of consciousness had indeed been met. Another factor was the subjects and the importance to also include research that does not just involve volunteers but instead represents a specified set of subjects. For those interested in understanding more about the concept of psi-missing, this resource will be helpful.

Keywords: psi-missing

Greyson, Bruce. "A Typology of Near-Death Experiences," *American Journal of Psychiatry* 142 (1985): 967–69.

Bruce Greyson discusses the eighty-nine cases of near-death experiences he analyzed. He found that NDEs fell into one of three categories. He also discovered that NDEs were not nearly as likely to occur in individuals who anticipated their impending death.

Keywords: near-death experiences (NDEs)

Hansel, C. E. M. *ESP and Parapsychology: A Critical Re-Evaluation*. Buffalo, NY: Prometheus Books, 1980.

This work provides a critique of parapsychological research calling to attention the lack of compelling psi evidence to date. It is useful, of course, to understand the criticisms of a topic just as it is important to understand the advocates and proponents of it. At the time of this publication, Dr. Hansel was the chair of the psychology program at Swansea University in Wales. Though this book takes on a highly critical stance, it provides an amazing amount of information on both the history of parapsychology as an emerging discipline and summarizes many seminal cases in the field's history. Some of the cases presented are the Margery case, the Pearce-Pratt experiments, the Soal-Goldney experiments, the Stanford Research Institute, and the experiments performed at the Duke Parapsychology Labs. Hansel points out some of the weak points of these experiments and offers scientific conclusions. This book, divided into two sections that discuss both the historical and modern timelines, is useful not just as a comprehensive overview of the field, but for the criticism of it as well. To have a holistic understanding of a topic, you must be aware of both its accolades and critiques. This work presents, in an unbiased way, some critiques and would be useful especially for those interested in conducting psi research of their own.

Keywords: criticisms of parapsychological research

Haynes, Renée. *The Society for Psychical Research, 1882–1982: A History.* London: Macdonald, 1982.

For anyone interested in a resource detailing the history of the British SPR, this is a must read. In this work, Haynes provides a detailed discussion of the first one hundred years of this psychical research organization. Haynes begins by explaining the underlying motivations that drove like-minded researchers to gather and establish this group, which is then followed with a discussion on the society's earliest work. Once the fledgling days of the society are outlined, Haynes discusses the importance of mediumship research and some of the seminal research that is still referenced today, such as the Cross Correspondences. A biographical timeline of past SPR presidents is also included. Those interested in the history of the SPR, especially its early years, would be remiss if they did not add this to their reading list.

Keywords: Society for Psychical Research; mediums

Hövelmann, Gerd H. "Beyond the Ganzfeld Debate." *Journal of Parapsychology* 50, no. 4 (December 1, 1986): 365–70.

In this article, Gerd H. Hövelmann presents his submission to the debates surrounding the ganzfeld experiments as given by Ray Hyman, Charles Honorton, and Robert Rosenthal. He focuses on comments surrounding methodology and conducting progressive debates between skeptics and believers.

Keywords: ganzfeld; debate

Irwin, H. J. *An Introduction to Parapsychology.* Jefferson, NC: McFarland and Company, 1989.

Harvey J. Irwin had taught parapsychology courses at the University of New England for ten years when he set forth to write this book. In the introduction, he tells us that "the objective of this book is to provide an introductory survey of parapsychologists' efforts to explore the authenticity and bases of these apparently paranormal phenomena,"[112] but he also makes a point to say that this is not an attempt to "prove" the existence of the paranormal. This leads him into a discussion on the often-tense situation of parapsychology within the broader psychological discipline. Irwin points out that the parapsychologist is merely using the scientific method to determine the boundaries of known science. After this introduction and useful reminder on the precarious nature of psi and the academy, Irwin launches into a discussion of the early days of psychical research and how it developed into the parapsychology programs of his day. In this section, naturally, Irwin discusses the influence of Spiritualism and mediums in helping to pique the curiosity of scholars.

After this chapter, Irwin discusses the hallmarks of an ESP experience and how it is perceived, that is, through intuition, hallucination, or dreaming. Additionally, Irwin discusses other factors like typical length of experience, personal impact, and spontaneous psi. The next chapter provides information on the experimental research being done on ESP, followed by a discussion on the complex relationship between time and ESP. The remainder of the book focuses on additional types of psi like psychokinesis, out-of-body and near-death experiences, and apparitions. Also included in this work is a chapter on the dominant theories of psi. Overall, this book reads like an introductory and layperson-friendly textbook. It would be a useful resource for those new to the topic, but it would also be useful for those already familiar and looking to enhance their understanding of theories and research.

Keywords: psychical theories; extrasensory perception; psychokinesis; near-death experience

Leeds, Morton and Gardner Murphy. *The Paranormal and the Normal: A Historical, Philosophical, and Theoretical Perspective.* Metuchen, NJ: Scarecrow Press, 1980.

Morton Leeds was once a student of Gardner Murphy's and in this work, which was compiled over the course of seven years, the authors present discussions not just on the history of psi research but on the philosophy behind psi events. There is also a review of research into psi that includes types of psi and the conditions that may be conducive to some of them.[113] This work presents a comprehensive discussion of psi research up to 1979, and the addition of philosophical discussions of psi adds to the comprehensiveness of this topic.

Keywords: psi research; philosophy and psi

Mauskopf, Seymour H. "The Origin of The Journal of Parapsychology." *Journal of Parapsychology* 51, no. 1 (March 1, 1987): 9–19.

This article is the published text of a talk given at a gathering of the Foundation for Research on the Nature of Man. Since 1987 represented the fiftieth anniversary of the *Journal of Parapsychology*, Seymour Mauskopf presents a discussion of the journal's history.

Keywords: Journal of Parapsychology

Oppenheim, Janet. *The Other World: Spiritualism and Psychical Research in England, 1850–1914.* Cambridge: Cambridge University Press, 1985.

Researcher Dr. Janet Oppenheim provides a comprehensive portrait of the Spiritualist and psychical science scenes in England from 1850–1914. Focusing on this period of time before World War I, Dr. Oppenheim discusses how the "intellectual and emotional crises of the mid-and-late-Victorian decades" influenced both Spiritualism and psychical research.[114] As she points out, the crisis of faith propelled many into the séance room to appease their spiritual quest, which in turn spurred the scientist to investigate the events happening in the séance room. This work provides a detailed social commentary that not only explains *how* Spiritualism blossomed but also provides information on key figures, organizations, and events in the timeline of psychical research. In her introduction, Dr. Oppenheim sums up this work perfectly when she writes,

> Together with the industrious middle-class professionals and self-educated artisans who joined spiritualist clubs both in London and the provinces, these intellectuals turned to psychic phenomena as courageous pioneers hoping to discover the most

profound secrets of the human condition and of man's place in the universe.[115]

Keywords: Spiritualism; England; 1800s; psychical research; mediums

Persinger, Michael A. "Spontaneous Telepathic Experiences from *Phantasms of the Living* and Low Global Geomagnetic Activity." *Journal of the American Society for Psychical Research* 81 (January 1987): 23–36.

Researcher Michael A. Persinger noticed that within the seminal text *Phantasms of the Living*, which revealed that apparition experiences were not necessarily limited to that of deceased persons, there were 109 reports that contained the day, month, *and* year of occurrence. Using this data, Persinger found the levels of global geomagnetic activity for all of those dates. As the author tells us, "Spontaneous experiences of ESP have been hypothesized to be associated with ELF (extremely low frequency) electromagnetic fields [and that] many ELF fields are generated naturally and are propagated within the spherical wave guide between the earth and the ionosphere."[116] Persinger was inspired to apply this theory to the *Phantasms* cases after initial studies confirmed his theory. In 1985, for example, Persinger discovered,

> An extraordinarily strong statistical relationship . . . between the geomagnetic activity as measured by the average antipodal (aa) index on the days of the experiences and the aa indices for the days immediately before and after the experiences. The days on which the ESP cases occurred were significantly quieter than the days before or after the experiences. Moreover, all the days on which the ESP experience occurred had lower aa values than the average aa value for the months in which the cases occurred.[117]

Using this same inquiry, then, Persinger looked at the 109 cases in *Phantasms* and found very similar results as his initial study, specifically that ESP seemed to occur on days of very low geomagnetic activity. Interestingly, though, Persinger noticed that this did *not* seem to be the case when ESP involved only an auditory experience.

Keywords: geomagnetic fields; ESP; Phantasms of the Living

Research in Parapsychology, 1986. Edited by D. H. Weiner and R. D. Nelson. Metuchen: Scarecrow Press, 1987.

This resource compiles presentations given at the Parapsychological Association's 29th annual convention. Articles include discussion on psychokinesis and experimental studies designed to test it, including one from the Princeton Engineering Anomalies Research (PEAR) project. There are also discussions of energy healing, extrasensory perception, possible relations between ESP and geomagnetic activity, discussions of replication issues, meta-analyses, and more. You can access a digital archive of presentations from all years of this series from the Parapsychological Association's website.

Keywords: Parapsychological Association; psychokinesis; extrasensory perception; replication

Rosenthal, Robert. "Meta-Analytic Procedures and the Nature of Replication: The Ganzfeld Debate." *Journal of Parapsychology* 50 (December 1986): 315–36.

Robert Rosenthal presents a continuation to a debate between parapsychologist Ray Hyman and Charles Honorton. Specifically, Honorton and Hyman debated ganzfeld experiments and the resultant (or not) evidence of psi. Rosenthal adds the concept of replication to their discussions. These scholarly debates not only help present both sides of an issue, but also help to contribute to a general literal review that provides a comprehensive bibliography to a topic. Those interested in ganzfeld experiments and who want to see multiple perspectives on it will want to consult this resource.

Keywords: ganzfeld experiments; replication

Schwartz, B. E. "K: A Presumed Case of Telekinesis." *International Journal of Psychosomatics* 32 (1985): 3–21.

This article presents a case study of a person who displayed psychokinetic abilities. Over the course of eleven days, experiments and observations were made with the subject, which were audio or videotaped. The author discusses the psychological steps that the subject takes in order to prep for engaging in PK. Ultimately, this study found that the subject could only exhibit PK under certain conditions.

Keywords: psychokinesis (PK)

Stokes, Douglas. "Theories of Anomalous Temporal Phenomena." *Parapsychology Review* 16 (1985): 12–15.

In this article, Douglas Stokes discusses various time theories that have been proposed to explain precognition. The notion of retrocausality is discussed as well as alternate futures. For those interested in precognition and the notion of alternate realities and our understanding of time.

Keywords: precognition; retrocausation

Targ, Russell and Keith Harary. *The Mind Race: Understanding and Using Psychic Abilities.* New York: Villard Books, 1984.

Authors Russell Targ and Keith Harary were scientists involved in the Stanford Research Institute (SRI), a US government-funded program designed to study the efficacy of remote viewing. In addition to their work with this program, which ran for ten years, Targ is a physicist and Harary is a psychologist who also studies out-of-body experiences. After their work with SRI, they teamed up to produce this 1984 work. In this book, they detail the experiments they've been part of and conducted regarding remote viewing, telepathy, and precognition.

The Mind Race is divided into three parts. The first part presents a historical overview of psi research, focusing mainly on the United States and the Soviet Union. Targ and Harary present various psi experiments done through the years, not just related to SRI, but certainly focusing on it. In part 2, the authors discuss the stereotypes and misconceptions about psi abilities, while part 3 provides tips and strategies on developing your own psi. The end of this book contains a bibliography of forty-one citations of scholarly works related to psi research.

Keywords: remote viewing; Stanford Research Institute

Tobacyk, Jerome and Gary Milford. "Belief in Paranormal Phenomena: Assessment Instrument Development and Implications for Personality Functioning." *Journal of Personality and Social Psychology* 44, no. 5 (1983): 1029–37.

Researchers Jermo Tobacyk and Gary Milford surveyed 391 college students and discovered seven different attributes that mediated belief in the paranormal. Those attributes are traditional religious belief, psi belief, witchcraft, superstition, Spiritualism, extraordinary life forms, and precognition. Each of these attributes are evaluated in the paranormal scale to determine where a person lands on that scale. As the authors tell us, "Because interest in paranormal phenomena has assumed such a visible role in modern life, it is important that the implications of paranormal belief for the person and for society be empirically evaluated."[118]

Keywords: paranormal belief scale; personality and paranormal belief

Weiner, D. H. and R. D. Nelson, eds. *Research in Parapsychology, 1986.* Metuchen. NJ: Scarecrow Press, 1987.

This resource compiles presentations given at the Parapsychological Association's twenty-ninth annual convention. Articles include discussion on psychokinesis and experimental studies designed to test it, including one from the Princeton Engineering Anomalies Research project. There are also discussions of energy healing, extrasensory perception, possible relations between ESP and geomagnetic activity, discussions of replication issues, meta-analyses, and more.

Keywords: Parapsychological Association; psychokinesis; extrasensory perception; replication

1990s

Berger, Arthur S. and Joyce Berger. *The Encyclopedia of Parapsychology and Psychical Research.* 1st ed. New York: Paragon House, 1991.

Historians and parapsychologists Arthur and Joyce Berger compile in this encyclopedia information on key figures, terms, and cases in the parapsychological timeline. Themselves researchers who investigate psi phenomena, the authors bring a particular perspective and knowledge to the topic. At the time of its publication, for example, Arthur Berger was president of the Survival Research Foundation. The authors state in their introduction their hope that this work provides a gateway to those outside the field to better understand parapsychology, particularly students, journalists, the general public, and those just beginning their own parapsychological research.

In an attempt to provide a comprehensive overview, the entries are international in scope, providing information on researchers and cases from around the world. The authors also include entries on figures designated as "noted witnesses"—famous or prominent figures who experienced spontaneous psychical moments. This encyclopedia also contains an appendix that lists research centers, publications, professional organizations, and educational opportunities found in specific countries. Each of these entries also includes a brief historical overview of parapsychology's development within that country. And while this book is a bit dated and some of these organizations may no longer exist, it remains useful historical information that provides a trajectory of parapsychological organizations throughout time.

Keywords: encyclopedia; international scope

Beloff, John. *Parapsychology: A Concise History.* New York: St. Martin's Press, 1993.

Dr. John Beloff was a psychology fellow at the University of Edinburgh at the time he wrote this book, which provides a concise historical overview of thought from the Renaissance to modern day. In the prologue, Dr. Beloff discusses "magical-thinking" present from the Renaissance through to the mid-1800s, pointing out that people have been interested in and fascinated by the strange, mysterious, and occult for millennia. He then dives into the 1800s, beginning with theories of mesmerism and moving toward Spiritualism and then to psychical science. Along the way he discusses key figures in the timeline, from scientists to those manifesting and experiencing psi phenomena, painting a picture of the modern challenges still faced by parapsychologists today. This book is a perfect choice for anyone who wants a brief historical overview of this topic, and one that situates parapsychology within the broader human record.

Keywords: parapsychology history; general work; mesmerism; Spiritualism; Renaissance magic

Blackmore, Susan. (1996). *In Search of the Light: The Adventures of a Parapsychologist.* Buffalo, NY: Prometheus Books, 1996.

Susan Blackmore presents a revised edition of her 1986 publication *In Search of the Light: The Adventures of a Parapsychologist.* In this work, she outlines her journey to becoming a parapsychologist and the successes and hurdles faced along the way. For those interested in a firsthand report of what parapsychology is like, consider adding Blackmore's book to your list.

Keywords: autobiography; Susan Blackmore

Cook, C. M. and M. A. Persinger. "Experimental Induction of the 'Sensed Presence' in Normal Subjects and an Exceptional Subject." *Perceptual and Motor Skills* 85 (1997): 683–93.

In this article, researchers Cook and Persinger applied three-minute bursts of magnetic fields to participants, after which they sensed a presence. When subjects attempted to intuit the location of the presence, it consistently seemed to move and change locations. The authors also applied this method to one subject who claimed to possess mediumistic abilities, who also sensed a presence they attributed as the origin of their abilities. The authors discuss the implications of this induced sense and the role of the right and left hemispheres of the brain during the process.

Keywords: magnetic fields; sensed presence

Dunne, Brenda J. and Robert G. Jahn, "Experiments in Remote Human/Machine Interaction." *Journal of Scientific Exploration* 6, no. 4 (1992): 311–32.

Authors Brenda J. Dunne and Robert G. Jahn are researchers with the Princeton Engineering Anomalies Research program and present here a discussion of psi experiments involving humans and machines. Specifically, Dunne and Jahn discuss tests where humans and machines are separated by long distances but still display anomalous results. Their research leads them to conclude that remote psi is just as reliable, and sometimes more, as tests where subject and device are in close proximity. Readers interested in learning some of the research involved in the Princeton Engineering Anomalies Research program and/or interested in remote viewing will want to consult this resource.

Keywords: Princeton Engineering Anomalies Research; remote-viewing

Gallagher, Charles, V. K. Kumar, and Ronald J. Pekala. "The Anomalous Experiences Inventory:

Reliability and Validity." *Journal of Parapsychology* 58, no. 4 (December 1, 1994): 402–28.

In 1992, V. K. Kumar and Ronald Pekala created the Mental Experience Inventory. In this article, they join forces with Charles Gallagher to present a revised inventory called the Anomalous Experiences Inventory. This revised scale included information about anomalous and paranormal experiences, paranormal beliefs, fears about having psi abilities, and drug use. The authors discuss its validity as compared with other popular scales for anomalous experiences and how researchers might apply this revised scale in future research.

Keywords: Anomalous Experiences Inventory

Griffin, David Ray. *Parapsychology, Philosophy, and Spirituality: A Postmodern Exploration.* Albany: State University of New York Press, 1997.

At the time of publication, author David Ray Griffin was a religious philosophy professor at the Claremont Graduate School and Claremont School of Theology in California. In this work he presents a discussion of the merits of parapsychology through a postmodern philosophical lens. He begins this resource by introducing us to postmodern theory and how it can be applied to this particular topic. He writes,

> The postmodernism of this series can . . . be called *constructive* or *revisionary.* It seeks to overcome the modern worldview not by eliminating the possibility of worldviews as such, but by constructing a postmodern worldview through a revision of modern premises and traditional concepts. This constructive or revisionary postmodernism involves a new unity of scientific, ethical, aesthetic, and religious institutions. It rejects not science as such but only that scientism in which the data of the modern natural sciences are alone allowed to contribute to the construction of our worldview.[119]

In this book, Griffin focuses on three key areas: information obtained via psychical methods (like ESP), moments when the mind seems to impact the physical world (like psychokinesis), and experiences (like near-death experiences, hauntings, some forms of mediumship, etc). He goes on tell us that "the title and contents of this book reflect my conviction that parapsychology is of utmost importance for both philosophy and the spiritual life."[120] He also tells us that parapsychology often gets overlooked because it is often seen in conflict with dominant and prevailing thoughts of the modern world: atheistic materialism and supernaturalistic dualism. Griffin examines the attitudes toward parapsychology, particularly within the academy and presents his personal experiences with those attitudes as a teacher of the intersection of philosophy and parapsychology.

The first chapter deals primarily with the prevailing thoughts and attitudes toward parapsychology while in the second chapter he presents a general overview of research into and evidence on psi. From here the subsequent chapters take a deep dive into specific psi phenomena and the research and evidence associated with them. Griffin discusses mediumship, possession, reincarnation, ghosts, and out-of-body experiences. Interwoven throughout this book are discussions on the intersection (and implications) of spirituality and parapsychology. This work offers a compelling philosophical argument for the value of psi research and contributes to the multidisciplinary lenses through which we can understand parapsychology.

Keywords: philosophy and parapsychology; postmodernism; mediumship; possession; reincarnation; ghosts; out-of-body experiences

Hagio, Shigeki. "An ESP Experiment on a Mountain-Top." *The Japanese Journal of Parapsychology* 2. no. 2 (November 25, 1997): 100–107.

In this article, parapsychologist Shigeki Hagio discusses an experiment he conducted to determine if location plays a role in the manifestation of psi phenomena. In this case, students with the parapsychology club at Kagoshima-Keizai University engaged in psi experiments in two different locations: one was a mountain top and the other a laboratory setting. One of the theories in this series of experiments is that mountain tops are a setting that contribute to an altered state of consciousness which can facilitate psi phenomena.

In each series of experiments, students from the parapsychology club first engaged in psi tests using Zener cards and then used a device called Perceptron to engage in a similar guessing experiment. The same techniques, cards, and device were used in both a laboratory setting and then on the mountain top. The results were then compared. Hagio tells us that "the results of our experiments supported the hypothesis that the mountain-top situation was more proper for the manifestation of psi than the usual settings in a laboratory-room."[121] Hagio muses on the reasons why a mountain top may more easily facilitate psi: the fact that the setting is outside of the city and far from noise and distraction; feeling a sense of detachment that one doesn't feel in a lab; the effects of fatigue after climbing a mountain; and general relaxation. This research article is an interesting addition to the literature that suggests a relationship between psi and physical setting and location.

Keywords: ESP; Japan; influence of geography

Hansen, George P., Jessica Utts, and Betty Markwick. "Critique of the PEAR Remote-Viewing Experiments." *Journal of Parapsychology* 56 (1992): 97–113.

In this article, the authors present a critique of the research conducted by the Princeton Engineering Anomalies Research (PEAR) program. Specifically, the authors address PEAR's research into remote-viewing. During the 1980s and 1990s, this program conducted multiple experiments involving remote-viewing, but the authors point out multiple weaknesses involving statistical methods, nontraditional criteria, problems with coding, and inadequate safeguards against fraud. They conclude by saying that the PEAR remote-viewing data cannot be considered reliable in light of these weaknesses.

Keywords: Princeton Engineering Anomalies Research (PEAR); criticisms; remote-viewing

Houtkooper, Joop M., Anne Schienle, Rudolf Stark, and Dieter Vaitl. "Geophysical Variables and Behavior LXXXVIII: The Possible Disturbing Influence of Natural Sferics on ESP." *Perceptual and Motor Skills* 89 (1999): 1179–92.

The researchers who wrote this article note that sferics have been shown to impact humans in a number of ways, for example, we all likely know someone who seems to sense, through aches and pains in their joints, when a storm is approaching. Sferics refer to the "electromagnetic impulses generated by electrical discharges during thunderstorms."[122] Citing this and previous parapsychological research done on the relationship between ESP and certain electromagnetic functions, the researchers set forth to determine what relationship, if any, existed between sferics and ESP. They begin by giving readers a helpful breakdown of the different types of electromagnetism and then present an overview of research into the ways in which sferics affects things like the nervous system, weather, EEGs, etc. This overview is helpful not only for those new to the topic of psi but also for those new to the topic of sferics.

To conduct their study, Houtkooper and colleagues gathered one hundred subjects and administered to them a forced-choice ESP test. At the same time, the researchers also gathered sferics data, including the those occurring at the time of testing, twenty-four hours before and after, seven days prior, *and* six days following. The authors conclude that "the sign of the sferics-ESP correlations is in accordance with findings from other studies of geomagnetic as well as sferics effects: the less the sferics activity, the higher the ESP performance."[123]

Keywords: extrasensory perception (ESP); sferics; electromagnetic fields

Palmer, J. "The Challenge of Experimenter-Psi." *European Journal of Parapsychology* 13, (1997): 110–25.

In this article, John Palmer discusses the role of experimenter psi, referred to sometimes as e-psi, and how it can interfere with studies. He presents a discussion of ways on how to measure for e-psi to enhance the validity of future psi research.

Keywords: experimenter psi (e-psi)

Pasricha, Satwant K. "Cases of the Reincarnation Type in Northern India with Birthmarks and Birth Defects." *Journal of Scientific Exploration* 12, no. 2 (1998): 259–93.

Researcher Satwant K. Pasricha worked in the Department of Clinical Psychology at the National Institute of Mental Health and Neurosciences in Bangalore, India. In this article, he presents research into ten cases of potential reincarnation. One aspect of investigating reincarnation cases is through identification and correlation of birthmarks or birth defects. For example, some subjects had birthmarks that physically corresponded to the placement of gunshot or knife wounds from the person they were connected to via reincarnation. Anyone interested in

reincarnation studies and especially relating to India will want to consult this resource.

Keywords: reincarnation; birthmarks; India

Radin, Dean. "Unconscious Perception of Future Emotions: An Experiment in Presentiment." *Journal of Scientific Exploration* 11 (1997): 163–80.

In this article, Dean Radin outlines his experiment on presentiment. In this experiment, subjects were shown a series of photos. Some of the photos displayed calming vistas of landscapes and sunsets while others portrayed explicit or violent images. During the experiment, Radin also captured the subject's heart rate, blood volume, and electrodermal activity. After four runs of this experiment, Radin found that subjects seemed to indicate a presentiment response prior to being shown the explicit or violent photos but not before being shown the calming photos.

Keywords: presentiment; consciousness; physiology and psi

Schmeidler, Gertrude R. "Psi-Conducive Experimenters and Psi-Permissive Ones." *European Journal of Parapsychology* 13 (1997): 83–94.

In this article, Gertrude R. Schmeidler reminds us that some researchers find statistically significant psi results while others, who may even mimic the same design, do not. Schmeidler presents two theories that could account for some of these differences among studies. First, Schmeidler posits that there could be an experimenter effect at play. Specifically, some experimenters are good at creating a warm, friendly, comfortable environment whereas others are much colder and clinical and unconcerned with comfort levels. Those who are warm tend to elicit results that are positive while those who tend to be colder often unveil insignificant results. Additionally, another theory posits that a subconscious psi transfer from experimenter to subject could be involved.

Keywords: experimenter effect; psi

Sheldrake, Rupert and P. Smart. "A Dog that Seems to Know when his Owner is Returning: Preliminary Investigations." *Journal of the Society for Psychical Research* 62 (1998): 220–32.

Rupert Sheldrake studies anticipatory behavior of dogs in this article. Many dog owners note that their pets seem to know when they are coming home, and Sheldrake tests one dog in particular who seems to know far in advance when his owner will return—anticipatory behavior that seemingly falls outside of a dog's natural ability to sense their owners up to 2.5 miles away. This study was conducted over a period of nine months and involved notes and videotaping of the dog's behavior. For instance, the pet seemed to know regardless of how often their owner randomized their return time, means of travel, and even when other members of the household had no awareness of when the owner would arrive home. Sheldrake concludes by theorizing that the dog could be picking up on some psychical influence from their owners.

Keywords: dogs and psi; anticipatory behavior

Stokes, Douglas M. *The Nature of Mind: Parapsychology and the Role of Consciousness in the Physical World.* Jefferson, NC: McFarland and Company, 1997.

Author Douglas M. Stokes presents in this work instances of spontaneous psi and the implications they entail for consciousness. Phenomena discussed includes ESP, poltergeists, out-of-body experiences, hauntings, anomalous dream experiences, and more.

This work not only discusses psi phenomena, but also provides information on theories that attempt to explain these events. Chapter 7, for example, discusses theories involving space, time, physics, and consciousness. The robust bibliography is especially useful to help readers locate additional material on the aforementioned topics and includes citations from many of the seminal parapsychology researchers.

Keywords: spontaneous psi; theories of psi; consciousness

Thalbourne, M. A. "An Attempt to Predict Precognition Scores Using Transliminality-Relevant Variables." *Journal of the Society for Psychical Research* 61 (1996): 129–40.

Michael A. Thalbourne tested ninety-nine incoming psychology students on levels of transliminality and precognition in an attempt to determine what other related variables might also be at play. Vari-

ables relevant to transliminality showed positive correlations while others did not. Thalbourne concludes with a recommendation for diverse testing measures in ESP inquiries.

Keywords: transliminality; precognition

White, Rhea A. *Parapsychology: New Sources of Information, 1973–1989.* Metuchen, NJ: Scarecrow Press, 1990.

In this resource Rhea A. White, librarian and parapsychologist, presents an annotated bibliography of various resources on parapsychological topics published between 1973 and 1989. This 1990 edition is the second volume of a work that White and her colleague Laura A. Dale published in 1973. That first volume of annotated resources only went up until 1972, so White saw a need some years later to come out with another volume, especially given the growth that occurred between 1972 and 1989.

In this work, White cites to books that investigate various topics of psi such as animal psi, altered states of consciousness, psychokinesis, reincarnation, mediumship, and much more. In addition to books, White also indexes more than forty pages worth of parapsychology journals that publish psi articles. Expanding her scope even further, White also presents information on parapsychology organizations, a history of government involvement with psi, current theories about psi, and a glossary of terms you might encounter when researching these topics.

Keywords: general bibliography

Wilkinson, H. P. and Alan Gauld. "Geomagnetism and Anomalous Experiences, 1868–1980." *Proceedings of the Society for Psychical Research* 57, no. 217 (1993): 275–310.

In this article, Wilkinson and Gauld attempt to test the theory of Michael Persinger who suggested a link between spontaneous anomalous experiences and geomagnetic fields. Specifically, Persinger posits that certain events like telepathy are more likely to occur on days of low geomagnetic force while poltergeist activity seems to spike on days of high geomagnetic activity. Wilkins and Gauld, in their analysis, tell us,

> In the end we were left with a residuum of positive findings. The most interesting of these were as fol-

lows: (a) There is a weak but persistent statistical relationship between lowish absolute levels of geomagnetic activity and the occurrence of spontaneous cases of apparent telepathy/clairvoyance. (b) There is a small tendency for the days of onset of cases of poltergeists and hauntings to be days of higher-than-usual geomagnetic activity.[124]

Keywords: geomagnetic activity; spontaneous psi; poltergeists; hauntings; telepathy

Zingrone, Nancy L., Carlos S. Alvarado, and Kathy Dalton. "Psi Experiences and the 'Big-Five': Relating the NEO-PI-R to the Experience Claims of Experimental Subjects." *European Journal of Parapsychology* 14 (1998–1999): 31–51.

In this article, researchers Zingrone, Alvarado, and Dalton discuss an experiment they conducted at the Koestler Parapsychology Lab with a group of artists and musicians. Specifically, they "were particularly interested in testing for a possible positive correlation between psi experiences and Openness to Experience (OE) as measured by"[125] the NEO-PI-R scale. NEO-PI-R is a personality inventory that measures someone's "big-five" personality traits, one of which includes openness to experience. Their theory that psi experiences correlate positively with OE were confirmed and they also found that psi experiences seemed influenced by having family members who experienced psi, and that psi experiences are also correlated with certain altered consciousness events. The authors present a discussion on the ways in which personality data can be useful for parapsychological research and present suggestions for continued research.

Keywords: psi and personality; NEO-PR-I; Openness to Experience (OE)

2000s

Alvarado, Carlos S. "Reflections on Being a Parapsychologist." *Journal of Parapsychology* 67 (Fall 2003): 211–48.

Influential parapsychologist Carlos S. Alvarado presented a version of this article as the Presidential Address at the 46th Annual Convention of the Parapsychological Association. He begins by telling us that "although there is an international community

devoted to the study of psi phenomena, there are few discussions about aspects of parapsychology as a profession and about our experiences as parapsychologists."[126] In the first portion of this article, Alvarado outlines some of the accomplishments in the field of parapsychology, the first of which is that the field and the scholars within serve as constant reminders that we have so much more to learn about the world and our role within it. Additionally, he remarks that the scope of research through the years has revealed just how complex and vast the topic of psi really is, and how some of these complexities help further our understanding of psychology. He then goes into a discussion on seminal figures and organizations in the history of parapsychology, the role of amateur researchers, and education and training. He encourages his fellow parapsychologists to focus on those contributions to help continue the progression of the field.

This article, by a seminal figure in the history of this discipline, serves as a primary source reflection on what life as a parapsychologist is really like.

Keywords: history of parapsychology; contributions of parapsychology; Carlos Alvarado

Barrington, Mary Rose, Ian Stevenson, and Zofia Weaver. *A World in a Grain of Sand: The Clairvoyance of Stefan Ossowiecki.* Jefferson, NC: McFarland & Company, 2005.

This book is a biographical treatment of Polish medium Stefan Ossowiecki. Born in 1877, Ossowiecki "demonstrated clairvoyance of a range and quality no one has exceeded, at least under experimental controls."[127] His clairvoyant abilities earned him the most recognition through the 1920s and 1940s, during which he not only helped provide guidance and answers for those who called upon him, but also worked openly with psychical researchers curious to study his abilities. This goodwill of Ossowiecki's would prove fatal, in fact, when he refused to abandon his home in Poland during World War II, stating that neighbors and friends needed his help locating their missing loved ones.[128] It appears that the medium had no scarcity of goodwill, for he never asked anyone for money and provided his gifts only to those needing it for genuine help, turning down demonstration requests for the sake of entertainment and amusement.

This book provides information not only on Ossowiecki's life, but also the psychical experiments conducted by noted researchers Gustave Geley and Charles Richet, to name a few. In addition to this formal research, the authors also provide transcripts of testimony from others who were affected by Ossowiecki's abilities. These people include other scientists, prominent figures, and even laypeople who recorded their encounters with the medium. As such, this book presents a wonderful array of primary sources, and even includes sketches and photos related to Ossowiecki. A later chapter, written by Mary Rose Barrington, provides a discussion of some of the most dominant criticisms of mediumship and offers an in-depth case study of Ossowiecki.

This work is of particular note since much of the research on Ossowiecki was published in Polish, with very little being published in English. With this publication and the translations of other works into English (especially the work done by coauthor Zofia Weaver), the authors help an even wider audience learn about the remarkable life of Stefan Ossowiecki.

Keywords: biography; Stefan Ossowiecki; Poland; mediums

Beischel, Julie and Adam J. Rock. "Addressing the Survival Versus Psi Debate Through Process-Focused Mediumship Research." *Journal of Parapsychology* 73 (Spring 2009): 71–90.

In this article, Beischel and Rock discuss mediumship and the main arguments surrounding where and how mediums get their information about discarnate entities. Specifically, the two major theories of explaining how mediums get anomalous information reception, points to either a super-psi process or proof of survival of consciousness beyond death. However, the authors also point out that mediumship seems to take a lower priority for modern parapsychology research. They write, "Although parapsychological research most often involves the Big Four—telepathy, clairvoyance, precognition, and psychokinesis,"[129] mediumship is still important because it is "pivotal for our understanding of consciousness, the potential of the mind, and the nature of life in general."[130]

Keywords: anomalous information reception; mediums; survival theory; super psi theory

Biondi, Massimo. "Marco Levi Bianchini: A Forgotten Italian Supporter of Parapsychology." *Journal of Scientific Exploration* 23, no. 3 (2009): 323–28.

Researcher Massimo Biondi presents the work of neuropsychiatrist Marco Levi Bianchini, a figure often omitted from discussions of early Italian psychical researchers. In fact, Biondi points out that there are additional Italian researchers who are often left out of these discussions. Bianchini's contributions are laid out in this article, beginning with the fact that he was among the first to promote psychoanalytic techniques in Italy, even establishing the Italian Society of Psychoanalysis in 1925.

In addition to his interest in that topic, Bianchini wrote many articles about psychical topics and authored more than ten thousand book reviews of various psychical manuscripts, thereby helping introduce these titles to his research colleagues. And because he spoke many languages, he was able to introduce an international spectrum of psychical works. Bianchini also created a handful of academic journals in which he accepted and published articles that discussed and analyzed psychical topics. Though he helped to spread awareness of and access to psychical resources throughout Italy, his role is largely unacknowledged.

Keywords: Marco Levi Bianchini; Italy; biographical sketch

Bösch, Holger, Fiona Steinkamp, and Emil Boller. "Examining Psychokinesis: The Interaction of Human Intention with Random Number Generators—A Meta-Analysis." *Psychological Bulletin* 132, no. 4 (2006): 497–523.

The authors conducted a meta-analysis of 380 studies of psychokinesis to determine the overall significance and results. After conducting their review, they tell us that "the statistical significance of the overall database provides no directive as to whether the phenomena is genuine."[131] The authors note that many of the studies, especially the early PK studies, often had small sample sizes that could present some statistical questions in terms of considering a phenomenon proven or not. They remind researchers to take these criticisms into review and use them to inform the continued research into psychokinetic phenomena.

Keywords: meta-analysis; psychokinesis

Braithwaite, Jason J. and Maurice Townsend. "Research Note: Sleeping with the Enemy—A Quantitative Magnetic Investigation of an English Castle's Reputedly 'Haunted' Bedroom." *European Journal of Parapsychology* 20, no. 1 (2005): 65–78.

Researchers Jason J. Braithwaite and Maurice Townsend tell us that this 2005 article is the first field-based investigation of the amplitude and frequency of the magnetic fields at a reportedly haunted location. Pointing to the idea that magnetic frequencies can impact the way a person perceives a location, Braithwaite and Townsend set out to investigate a haunted English castle. Interestingly, their visual analysis "revealed what appeared to be a number of inverted pulses . . . present at all locations surveyed"[132] that had very low frequencies associated with them. This is interesting because "research has suggested that low-frequency signatures are particularly potent for encouraging neurophysiological shifts and experiential changes in individuals."[133]

Keywords: magnetic fields; haunting

Delanoy, Deborah. "Anomalous Psychophysiological Responses to Remote Cognition: The DMILS Studies." *European Journal of Parapsychology* 16 (2001): 30–41.

Researcher Michael A. Thalbourne reminds us that "direct mental influence on living systems (DMILS)" refers to the ability of an agent to physiologically impact another human or living organism.[134] In this study, Dr. Deborah Delanoy provides an overview of a group of research known as the DMILS studies. She begins by telling us that this article "presents an overview of a group of studies exploring the ability of an individual to interact with the physiological processes of another, sensorially isolated organism/person."[135] Many are likely familiar with intuitively noticing when someone may be looking or staring at us, but DMILS takes this a step further and asks if humans and/or living organisms can be physiologically or behaviorally impacted when they cannot physically *see* if someone is staring at them.

In this article, Dr. Delanoy presents an overview of DMILS research and findings. We learn that DMILS is often measured by electrodermal activity and that a main concern of research is making sure to eliminate all possible sensory cues. Dr. Delanoy concludes that "the findings from the research . . .

presented herein suggest that two organisms may have the ability to interact with each other, by means other than those involving currently understood sensory processes."[136]

Keywords: direct mental influence on living systems (DMILS); electrodermal activity (EDA)

Dobyns, Y. H., B. J. Dunne, R. G. Jahn, and R. D. Nelson. "The MegaREG Experiment: Replication and Interpretation." *Journal of Scientific Exploration* 18 (2004): 369–97.

In this article, the authors, who are all researchers at the Princeton Engineering Anomalies Research (PEAR) lab, discuss their studies on the ways in which consciousness impacts random event generators (REG)—devices that are able to (often electronically) output certain bits of data. A type of psychokinetic phenomena, the PEAR researchers were curious to see what might happen using a MegaREG that could output up to two million data points. They were also curious to see if a MegaREG would reveal data similar to other studies, specifically, that data seem to have an inverse relationship with the subject's intention. Their MegaREG did discover that this attribute continued to be present even in massive REGs.

Keywords: random event generator; MegaREG; Princeton Engineering Anomalies Research (PEAR) lab; psychokinesis

Irwin, Harvey J. and Caroline Watt. *An Introduction to Parapsychology,* 4th ed. Jefferson, NC: McFarland, 2004.

Harvey J. Irwin and Caroline Watt created this work to serve as a university textbook on parapsychology. Within this work, readers can find chapters discussing the history of parapsychology and the emergence of formal research methods, case studies, and laboratory experiments of specific phenomena like ESP, poltergeists, psychokinesis, and more.

Keywords: parapsychology textbook

Luckhurst, Roger. *The Invention of Telepathy: 1870–1901.* Oxford: Oxford University Press, 2002.

In this work, author Roger Luckhurst presents a discussion of the rise of Spiritualism, its associated activities, and the rise of psychical research. Luckhurst tells us that his work has three aims. The first "is to provide an account of the origin and early career of the concept of telepathy."[137] His second aim is "to write a history of telepathy that does not prejudge."[138] And his third aim, he tells us, "is an attempt to follow telepathy into that conjuncture of disciplines where it was formulated, by adopting a multidisciplinary approach."[139] Luckhurst tells us that the "invention" of telepathy is a rather curious one. The idea that there is a connection between minds, he tells us, is an ancient belief, and not necessarily unique to the Victorian era. Yet that era is where we see the birth of a new name and an entirely new approach. Luckhurst tells us, "The reasons for why, when, and where this relation was conceptualized as *telepathy*, an oxymoronic distant (*tele-*) intimacy or touch (*pathos*), are located in the overlapping contexts of late Victorian culture."[140] And it is here in this work that he discusses the circumstances that led to telepathy as we still know it today.

Focusing on the years from 1870–1901, in part 1 Luckhurst focuses on the years up to 1882. In this section, he discusses scientific naturalism and how "the emergence of a scientific culture"[141] created other effects, like a turn to telepathy. In this section Luckhurst also introduces William Crookes and his impact on psychical research. In particular, he discusses how Crookes' work "threatened to erase [the] border"[142] between naturalism and Spiritualism. Part 2 focuses on the emergency of "high" and "low" culture, the influence of W. T. Snead, and the "occult economies"[143] that developed from that. The following chapter discusses the data, case reports, and testimonials gathered by the SPR. Luckhurst discusses how this early body of data "constitutes a set of *doxai*, a shadow-record of beliefs and semi-legitimate knowledges that dealt with material which failed to find sanction in orthodox channels of information."[144] The following chapter discusses the particular reality of psychical research in the late Victorian era and the chapter following that discusses William and Henry James and the rise of mediumship. Offering an academic look into the intersection of Spiritualism, psychical research, culture, and society, Luckhurst's work presents a thorough inquiry into the years between 1870–1901.

Keywords: Spiritualism; psychical research; W. T. Stead; William and Henry James; telepathy

Mulacz, Peter. "Historical Profiles in Poltergeist Research." In *From Shaman to Scientist: Essays on Humanity's Search for Spirits.* Edited by James Houran, 127–90. Lanham, MD: Scarecrow Press, 2004.

Author Peter Mulacz presents historical vignettes of seminal figures in the history of poltergeist research. International in scope, this chapter provides biographical sketches of such figures as Hans Bender, Harry Price, William G. Roll, Albert von Schrenck-Notzing, and more. This chapter will be especially helpful for those new to the topic looking for a friendly introduction to some of the key figures specifically related to poltergeist research. Additionally, the robust bibliography provides an abundance of resources for continued reading.

Keywords: biographies; poltergeist

Noakes, Richard. "The 'Bridge which is Between Physical and Psychical Research': William Fletcher Barrett, Sensitive Flames, and Spiritualism." *History of Science,* 42 no. 4 (2004): 419–64.

In this article, researcher Richard Noakes discusses the psychical investigations of Sir William F. Barrett. Noakes focuses particular attention on the tensions between those who believed in the merits of psychical pursuits and those who did not. As a result, Noakes presents a fascinating (and highly detailed) article that paints a picture of the social context in which early psychical researchers operated. Not only is there a great deal of information on Sir William F. Barrett, we also learn about John Tyndall, Oliver Lodge, and the influence of physics on Barrett's views of the psychical.

Keywords: William F. Barrett; John Tyndall; Oliver Lodge; physics and psychical research

Radin, Dean. *Entangled Minds: Extrasensory Experiences in a Quantum Reality.* New York: Paraview Pocket Books, 2006.

In this book, parapsychologist and chief scientist at the Institute of Noetic Sciences Dr. Dean Radin discusses psi through the lens of quantum physics and, specifically, through quantum entanglement. In the preface he tells us,

One of the most surprising discoveries of modern physics is that objects aren't as separate as they may seem . . . scientists are now finding that there are ways in which the effects of microscopic entanglements "scale up" into our macroscopic world. Entangled connections between carefully prepared atomic-sized objects persist over many miles. . . . Some scientists suggest that the remarkable degree of coherence displayed in living systems might depend in some fundamental way on quantum effects like entanglement. Others suggest that conscious awareness is caused or related in some important way to entangled particles in the brain.[145]

Dr. Radin's book discusses the implications of what quantum entanglement might mean for consciousness and extrasensory abilities. In this work he discusses various topics like conscious and unconscious psi, theories about psi, and begins by providing a historical overview of the development of quantum entanglement discovery. Following this is a chapter that provides a myriad of examples of psi phenomena, followed by a chapter that discusses the assumptions about those who believe in and/or engage in psi research. This chapter also provides references to multiple studies that have examined the intersection of paranormal beliefs, personality, and level of education—studies that often show that highly-educated people have paranormal beliefs *and* that those with paranormal beliefs aren't necessarily more likely to have personality or mental disorders. From here, Radin dives into overviews of psi research, the differences between conscious and unconscious psi, intuition, psi theories, and the ways in which our minds interact with our physical world. This book links quantum physics to the psychical and provides a unique, important entry in the psi literature all while written in an enjoyable, easy-to-read format.

Keywords: consciousness; quantum entanglement

Rauscher, Elizabeth A. and Russell Targ. "The Speed of Thought: Investigation of a Complex Space-Time Metric to Describe Psychic Phenomena." *Journal of Scientific Exploration* 15, no. 3 (2001): 331–54.

Rauscher and Targ provide a discussion of space-time and how it relates to psychical phenomena. Specifically, they tell us, "We present here a theoretical model to elucidate some of the phenomena underlying the remote perception ability, while remaining consistent with modern physics."[146] They begin with a brief discussion of the hundred-year history of laboratory research into such psychical phenomena as precognition, telepathy, remote viewing, and more. The entire crux of their article can be found when they tell us,

One of the most common objections to the existence of psi is that it appears to be in conflict with the laws of physics, because we have not yet found the mechanism for such information transfer. In our investigation we attempt first to demonstrate the compatibility of psi phenomena with the laws and content of physics, and then to develop a theoretical model which is descriptive of the nonlocal properties of psi. In this paper we present a detailed theoretical model describing the properties of psychic phenomena which we have demonstrated to be in agreement with the main body of physics.[147]

The authors go on to detail this model of space-time, which borrows from quantum mechanics, relativity, and the Minkowski theory of space. For those interested in the intersection of physics, space-time, and psi, this article will be resourceful. It also helps shed light on the ways in which parapsychologists have incorporated concepts from other fields to help advance the understanding of psi.

Keywords: space-time; physics; psi

Roe, Chris A., S. J. Sherwood, L. Farrell, L. Savva, and I. Baker. "Assessing the Roles of the Sender and Experimenter in Dream ESP Research." *European Journal of Parapsychology* 22, no. 2 (2007): 175–92.

Chris Roe and coauthors conducted an experiment to investigate the effects of using senders in an extrasensory perception design using dreams. Forty participants agreed to record their dreams on the nights of the study. On some nights, certain video clips would be played while the subject was sleeping and on other nights, a "sender" would be watching the video simultaneously as it played near the sleeping subject. Roe and colleagues discovered that while both sets of experiments (sender and no sender) scored above chance levels, they were not statistically significant, and that the presence of a sender did not necessarily show any impact on any hits in dreaming. They conclude by offering suggestions for future dream ESP research.

Keywords: extrasensory perception; dreams

Roe, Chris A., Russell Davey, and Paul Stevens. "Are ESP and PK Aspects of a Unitary Phenomenon? A Preliminary Test of the Relationship between ESP and PK." *Journal of Parapsychology* 67, no. 2 (Fall 2003): 343–66.

In this study, researchers test the assumption that the same psi processes are applicable to both PK andESP. They remind us that many parapsychologists use the term "psi" to refer to both ESP and PK—this usage, however, assumes that there is a similar process at play for both phenomena. In this study, then, Roe, Davey, and Stevens set out to test the relationship between ESP and PK to better understand if this assumption is valid. They test this by applying both PK and ESP tasks to the same set of subjects in a variety of known and unknown psi tasks. They discovered no statistically significant results, meaning that subjects scored near chance levels. However, the researchers do note that subjects with previous psi experience tend to score at higher levels than those without, but only on those trials in which the psi task was known.

Keywords: Extrasensory perception; psychokinesis

Roll, William G. "Poltergeists, Electromagnetism and Consciousness." *Journal of Scientific Exploration* 17, no. 1 (2003): 75–86.

In this article, William G. Roll outlines the facets of poltergeist cases. He reminds us that they involve both physical and psychological phenomena and are often referred to as recurrent spontaneous psychokinesis (RSPK), which is a type of macro-PK. Macro-PK refers to large objects that, for example, levitate while micro-PK refers to things like dice-throwing experiments in which objects land at a previously agreed-upon goal by means of a random generator.

Roll outlines some of his most memorable cases before launching into a discussion about the role of electromagnetism in poltergeist cases. He poignantly begins this discussion with the statement, "Physics is a way to talk about psychic phenomena in a respectable manner."[148] Roll notes that in the poltergeist cases he's investigated, he's noticed that the effect of movement upon objects decreases the further the affected individual is from those objects. This would seemingly suggest that some sort of physical waves might be at play. He then outlines some of the theories that others have posited regard-

ing how these waves affect objects, like the suspension of gravity due to zero-point energy and electromagnetic fluctuations. Furthermore, Roll discusses the nuances and ethics of observer participance in poltergeist cases and offers some suggestions for future RSPK studies.

Keywords: poltergeists; recurrent spontaneous psychokinesis (RSPK); electromagnetic fields

Schoch, Robert M. and Logan Yonavjak. *The Parapsychology Revolution: A Concise Anthology of Paranormal and Psychical Research.* New York: Jeremy P. Tarcher, 2008.

At the time of publication, author Logan Yonavjak was a researcher with the Rhine Research Center and Dr. Robert Schoch was a professor at Boston University. In this work, they present an annotated bibliography of resources on a wide variety of psi topics. Their resources shed light on the history and abundance of scholarly literature that exists within parapsychology. The authors sort these annotations into categories such as "spontaneous instances of the paranormal," "mediumship," "experimental and laboratory work," "remote viewing," "overviews and reflections," and more. Included within these categories are topics like ESP, psychokinesis, and poltergeists, just to name a few.

In their introduction, Schoch and Yonavjak provide an overview of each type of phenomena they discuss, making this a wonderful resource for those who are relatively new to the topic of parapsychology. Their references at the end of the book also provide a comprehensive list of resources for people to continue their studies.

Keywords: annotated bibliography

Schmied-Knittel, Ina and Michael T. Schetsche. "Everyday Miracles: Results of a Representative Survey in Germany." *European Journal of Parapsychology* 20, no. 1 (2005): 3–21.

This article discusses a survey of paranormal beliefs and experiences conducted in 2000 by the Institut für Grenzgebiete der Psychologie und Psychohygiene (Institute for Frontier Areas of Psychology and Mental Health). This survey gathered responses from 1,500 German citizens. The authors discovered that more than half the respondents reported experiencing paranormal phenomena—

specifically, younger people reported psychical experiences at much higher rates than others. The phenomena that scored lowest in both belief in and personal experience of was psychokinesis while the highest was crisis-ESP. The authors go on to discuss the intersection of belief and experience with other sociodemographic factors and present a discussion on what constitutes an exceptional paranormal experience.

Keywords: paranormal belief; paranormal experience; survey; Germany; crisis-ESP

Smith, Matthew D. "The Psychology of the 'Psi-Conducive' Experimenter: Personality, Attitudes towards Psi, and Personal Psi Experience." *Journal of Parapsychology* 67, no. 1 (Spring 2003): 117–28.

In this article, researcher Matthew D. Smith discusses experimenter effects, which are a prominent concern of many psi studies. The experimenter effect essentially involves the likelihood that an experimenter can subconsciously affect the outcome of a study through psychical processes that may occur between them and subjects. Smith, in this study, focuses on those psi experimenters who seem to consistently obtain data that suggests ESP. Referred to as psi-conducive experimenters, this group of researchers contrasts with those who consistently find no ESP data and who are labeled psi-inhibitory.

Keywords: experimenter effect; psi-conducive; psi-inhibitory; personality and psi

Steinkamp, Fiona. "Does Precognition Foresee the Future? A Postal Experiment to Assess the Possibility of True Precognition." *Journal of Parapsychology* 64, no. 1 (March 2000): 3–18.

In this article, researcher Fiona Steinkamp investigates the possibility that true precognition may not be real. In other words, Steinkamp tests the theory that precognition is not entirely a true process and that seemingly precognitive phenomena are simply the result of other psi processes like clairvoyance and/or psychokinesis. To study this, Steinkamp designed tests that looked at both clairvoyance and precognition. In the clairvoyance sets, a computer was used to identify a target that the subjects were then asked to identify. In the precognition sets, subjects were asked to identify certain stock market targets that could not otherwise be known beforehand

by either human *or* computer. In the study, however, there were no statistically significant precognitive results, which adds to the theory that true precognition may be a stickier subject than realized.

Keywords: precognition; clairvoyance

Storm, Lance. "Remote Viewing by Committee: RV Using a Multiple Agent/Multiple Percipient Design." *Journal of Parapsychology* 67 (Fall 2003): 325–42.

Researcher Lance Storm begins this article with a discussion of the Stanford Research Institute and the work of Russell Targ and Hal Puthoff in regard to remote viewing (RV). He then outlines the experiment undertaken here—a design that tested how the efficacy of remote viewing might be affected with individual versus group agents, or RV by committee. Storm found no significant differences, though, between the use of single remote viewers versus a committee of remote viewers. He also offers guidelines for future research.

Keywords: remote viewing; Stanford Research Institute

Thalbourne, Michael A. *A Glossary of Terms Used in Parapsychology.* Puente Publications: Charlottesville, VA, 2003.

Researcher Michael A. Thalbourne presents, in this book, a compendium of common terms associated with parapsychology. Included are common statistical factors used in experiments, psychical phenomena, and experimental techniques and factors. It will be especially helpful for those new to parapsychology and/or those wanting help deciphering some terms that they encounter in the scholarly literature.

Keywords: glossary

Thalbourne, Michael A. "Transliminality, Anomalous Belief and Experience, and Hypnotisability." *Australian Journal of Clinical and Experimental Hypnosis* 37, no. 2 (2009): 119–30.

Researcher Michael A. Thalbourne provides a discussion on the history of the concept of transliminality and how it might correlate to anomalous experiences. He also discusses how transliminality produces similar states as when in hypnosis. Readers who have come across the term "transliminality" and who are curious about its origin and development will be satisfied by Thalbourne's discussion, which includes not only how it developed as a theory but also the ways in which researchers measure it objectively. Following this is a discussion of how it corresponds with anomalous experiences and how previous research has found links between transliminality and a belief in psychical phenomena. Thalbourne also discusses how transliminality has been found to correlate with other seminal instruments such as the sheep-goat scale and the paranormal belief scale.

Keywords: transliminality; hypnosis

Tobacyk, Jerome J. "A Revised Paranormal Belief Scale." *International Journal of Transpersonal Studies* 23 (2004): 94–98.

In this article, Dr. Tobacyk provides an updated edition of the original 1983 Paranormal Belief Scale. He discusses the changes made that allow for greater cross-cultural application and enhanced reliability. For a discussion of the original scale, consult the 1983 article by Tobacyk and Milford.

Keywords: Paranormal Belief Scale

Tresan, David I. "This New Science of Ours: A More or Less Systematic History of Consciousness and Transcendence: Part I," *Journal of Analytical Psychology* 49 (2004): 193–216.

When it comes to a core bibliography of resources on parapsychology, it is necessary to include resources that discuss consciousness, as one set of parapsychological inquiry concerns itself with the role of consciousness beyond bodily death. This article, by researcher David Tresan, presents a discussion of some overlooked components in the traditional consciousness literature as dominated by Carl Jung and Sigmund Freud. Tresan points out, for example, that one weakness is that "both leaped from the paleolithic to modern mind in one fell swoop, making useful comparisons to present-day man and especially woman difficult."[149] Tresan also points out the need for additional language when discussing psychic functions related to consciousness. A particularly relevant discussion is had regarding Jung's thoughts on "free psychic energy" and psychologies of the unconscious. Part 2 of this article, also published in 2004 in the *Journal of Analytical Psychology*, continues the discussion that Tresan begins here.

Keywords: consciousness; Carl Jung; Sigmund Freud

Vasilescu, Eugen and Elena Vasilescu. "Experimental Study on Precognition." *Journal of Scientific Exploration* 15, no. 3 (2001): 369–77.

In this article, Eugen and Elena Vasilescu conduct an experiment on precognition and radio waves. This research builds upon some of their earlier research of radio waves and telepathy in which they found a potential connection. Using a radio amplifier connected to two copper antennas that each participant pointed at their foreheads, the device was used during an ESP session using Zener cards. The researchers discovered a statistically significant positive rating of ESP scores while using the radio amplifier and noted that the same wavelength (46.20 m) was used in both this experiment and their earlier research into telepathy and radio waves. Readers interested particularly in the use of technology and radio waves alongside psi will want to consult this resource.

Keywords: precognition; extrasensory perception; radio waves; radio amplifier

Wiseman, Richard and Emma Greening. "It's Still Bending: Verbal Suggestion and Alleged Psychokinetic Ability." *British Journal of Psychology* 96 (February 2005): 115–27.

Researchers Wiseman and Greening present, in this article, a discussion on the intersection of eyewitness testimony and suggestion. Taking the popular concept of a psychic metal-bending objects like spoons and keys, they set up an experiment in which two groups watched a fake psychic bend a key and then place it upon a table. In one group, the video included a suggestion from the actor that the key was continuing to bend. The other group's video did not include this statement. Wiseman and Greening found that, via the power of suggestion, the first group reported that they also saw the key continuing to bend, and even in some cases forgot that the actor had suggested that it continued bending. This article also discusses potential roles of paranormal belief when it comes to eyewitness testimony and reports of paranormal experiences, though the authors found no correlation with that in this study.

Keywords: psychokinesis; power of suggestion; eye-witness testimony

Wolffram, Heather. "In the Laboratory of the *Ghost-Baron:* Parapsychology in Germany in the 20th Century." *Endeavor* 33, no. 4 (2009): 151–56.

Researcher Heather Wolffram of the University of Queensland in Brisbane, Australia, presents a biographical sketch of noted psychiatrist Albert von Schrenk-Notzing that particularly focuses on the laboratory he designed to study mediums and psychical phenomena. Wolffram tells us that Schrenk-Notzing's laboratory was "a hybrid space that was symbolic of the irresolvable epistemological and methodological problems at the heart of this aspiring science [parapsychology]."[150] The psychiatrist, who was highly interested in psychical phenomena, recognized the unique experimental needs that were required to adequately study mediums and their associated psi activity. Recognizing that many scientists chalked mediumistic abilities up to nothing more than mere hallucination or outright fraud, Schrenk-Notzing realized that a special type of laboratory and special type of equipment were needed. Specific gadgets were needed to reduce the bias of human perception and error, especially when it came to measuring psi that affected light, temperature, the movement of objects, etc.

He also focused on training mediums to acclimate themselves to a laboratory environment, doing all of this in an effort to try and situate parapsychology as a valid scientific pursuit, distancing it in the process from the fraud rampant within Spiritualism. Schrenk-Notzing worked closely with mediums such as Eva C. and the Schneider brothers. In this article, Wolffram outlines the psychiatrist's unique methods in his attempt to legitimize parapsychology and discusses the ways in which this effort was thwarted.

Keywords: biography; Albert von Schrenk-Notzing; experimental parapsychology; Germany

Wolffram, Heather. "Parapsychology on the Couch: The Psychology of Occult Belief in Germany, c. 1870–1939." *Journal of the History of the Behavioral Sciences* 42, no. 3 (Summer 2006): 237–60.

This article, also written by scholar Heather Wolffram, discusses the role that German scholars played in the construct of a "psychology of occult belief" in the nineteenth and early twentieth centuries. In the late nineteenth century, there existed much tension between scholars who saw the merits of psychical research and those who did not. As a way to *pathologize* those who believed in psychical phenomena, some scholars set out to construct a psychology of occult belief. This effort had an ulterior motive of undermining psi researchers in the hopes of delegitimizing psychical research and thereby widening the chasm between it and the burgeoning discipline of psychology. In retaliation, psi researchers claimed this effort was a symptom of the closed-mindedness of their colleagues.

The tension between the two camps even came before the courts. In 1925, psychiatrist Albert Moll was charged with defamation of the medium Maria Vollhardt after Moll published a work that claimed Vollhardt was merely tricking her audiences. Researchers both for and against psychical science were brought before a judge and jury and while the case was eventually dismissed, it highlighted the deep divide regarding the merits of psychical science at the time. In this article, Wolffram outlines the rhetoric and tactics used by both camps and discusses the three theories that antipsychical researchers developed to explain away the phenomena their psychical colleagues were investigating. In doing so, Wolffram provides key information to anyone interested not only in the history of early psychical research, but especially for those interested in how this played out in Germany. Readers who enjoy this article by Wolffram will want to consult her 2009 book *Stepchildren of Science: Psychical Research and Parapsychology in Germany, c. 1870–1939* for an even more exhaustive treatment of this topic.

Keywords: Germany; Albert Moll; psychology of occult belief; historical tensions

2010s

Alvarado, Carlos S. "Distortions of the Past." *Journal of Scientific Exploration* 26 no. 3 (2012): 611–33.

Carlos S. Alvarado was a prolific parapsychologist. Any bibliography of psychical research would be incomplete without at least a handful of entries discussing his work. In this article, Alvarado discusses the importance of bringing to light lesser-known figures, criticisms of, and unpopular theories and events within the timeline of parapsychology. Not giving equal space to these topics results in a distortion of the reality of the discipline, and especially a distortion of the historical timeline.

This article began as an invited address Alvarado gave during his 2010 Outstanding Contribution Award ceremony hosted by the Parapsychological Association. Alvarado summarizes this work best when he writes,

> These issues are important because, having a more complete grasp of their subject, parapsychologists may improve their writings and may acquire a different sense of the complexity of factors behind their discipline. Furthermore, these new perspectives will affect the views of students and newcomers to the field as well.[151]

Because of the discussions in this article, Alvarado presents a myriad of resources for those new to the topic. The sheer number of references make this article a valuable resource, but the article helps fill in gaps in the psychical timeline as well. This resource is one not to be missed.

Keywords: parapsychological history; lesser-known figures

Alvarado, Carlos S. "Mediumship, Psychical Research, Dissociation, and the Powers of the Subconscious Mind." *Journal of Parapsychology* 78, no. 1 (2014): 98–114.

In this article, preeminent parapsychologist Carlos S. Alvarado provides us with a discussion on the various schools of thought regarding mediums in the late 1800s and early 1900s. Alvarado points out that many psychologists considered mediumship as a form of dissociation associated with the subconscious. Other scholars, however, believed that it was perhaps a combination of this *and* some supernatural abilities of the medium themselves. Alvarado provides information on the work of Frederic W. H. Myers, Eduard von Hartmann, and such mediums as Eusapia Palladino and Leonora Piper. For those interested in learning more about the history of thought on mediums and especially how it played out during the late 1800s when psychology and psy-

chical science were fledgling disciplines vying for dominance, this article will be useful.

Keywords: mediums; dissociation; subconscious; Eusapia Palladino; Leonora Piper

Alvarado, Carlos S. "'Report of the Committee on Mediumistic Phenomena,' by William James (1886)." *History of Psychiatry* 27, no. 1 (2016): 85–100.

In this article, parapsychologist Carlos S. Alvarado presents a snippet of an article written by famed psychologist William James. James's article was published in 1886 in the *Proceedings of the Society for Psychical Research* and focuses on the mediumistic abilities of Leonora Piper. Prior to presenting the snippet of the 1886 article, Alvarado presents a discussion that outlines the viewpoints and theories of mediumship in the 1800s and also presents a brief biography of William James and his interest in psychical phenomena.

Keywords: William James; Leonora Piper; mediums

Alvarado, Carlos S. "Telepathy, Mediumship, and Psychology: Psychical Research at the International Congresses of Psychology, 1889–1905." *Journal of Scientific Exploration* 31, no. 2 (2017): 255–92.

Parapsychologist Carlos S. Alvarado presents an overview of the inclusion of psychical topics into the International Congresses of Psychology. From 1889–1905, the congress allowed these topics before eventually ceasing to include them at gatherings. This article highlights not only the discussions held at these conferences, but also the early and chaotic history of the emerging fields of psychology and psychical science which arose concurrently, both vying for sustainable footing.

Keywords: International Congress of Psychology

Asprem, Egil. "A Nice Arrangement of Heterodoxies: William McDougall and the Professionalization of Psychical Research." *Journal of the History of the Behavioral Sciences* 46, no. 2 (Spring 2010): 123–43.

In this article, researcher Egil Asprem of the University of Amsterdam discusses the attempts to ground parapsychology with a cohesive set of paradigms and standards. Asprem points out that while many point to the work of J. B. Rhine in providing an established set of guidelines and standards, others preceding Rhine attempted this as well. He points to the cases of J. E. Coover, Gardner Murphy, Charles Richet, and Hans Driesch as global precursors who attempted to develop standard programs. Throughout this article, Asprem discusses the professionalization of psychical research and provides readers with an in-depth discussion on the social aspects that morphed the discipline throughout the years.

This article focuses specifically on British researcher William McDougall who had immigrated to the United States when he was offered a position at Harvard University. McDougall was a member of the American Society for Psychical Research (ASPR), eventually becoming its president in 1921. McDougall was a staunch advocate for inserting more scientific standards into psychical research, leading ASPR in that direction. So strong was his conviction, though, that he would even attack colleagues in ASPR who felt that the organization should instead focus on séances and their life-after-death implications. The tension between these groups was so taught that certain members of the ASPR, including McDougall, ended their membership and created their own organization, which they called the Boston Society for Psychic Research. McDougall was eventually offered a position with Duke University in 1927, where he continued his psychical research. This is also where he met J. B. and Louisa Rhine, a partnership that eventually saw the establishment of the Duke Parapsychology Labs. This article provides an important look into the historical tensions among psychical scholars.

Keywords: William McDougall; Duke Parapsychology Labs; American Society for Psychical Research; Boston Society for Psychic Research

Brancaccio, Maria Teresa. "Enrico Morselli's *Psychology* and *'Spiritism'*: Psychiatry, Psychology and Psychical Research in Italy in the Decades around 1900." *Studies in History and Philosophy of Biological and Biomedical Sciences* 48 (2014): 75–84.

Maria Teresa Brancaccio, a researcher at Maastricht University in the Netherlands, presents here an article on the Italian psychiatrist Enrico Morselli. Morselli was an influential scholar who helped advance the cause of experimental psychology in Italy. It was through his interactions and study of the medium Eusapia Palladino that he began to consider the reality of psychical phenomena. Convinced that there was some unknown combination of biology and psychic phenomena at work, Morselli went on to publish his research on the medium in the early 1900s. Using Morselli as an example, Brancaccio goes on to discuss the relationship between psychology, psychiatry, and psychical research in Italy during this time period. She discusses how Morselli saw mediumship as an opportunity to advance new techniques in anomalistic induction. Along the way, Brancaccio discusses multiple other scholars of the time and paints a picture of psychical theory.

Keywords: Enrico Morselli; Italy; Eusapia Palladino; mediums

Caratelli, Giulio and Maria Luisa Felici. "An Important Subject at the Institut Métapsychique International: Jeanne Laplace. The 1927–1934 Experiments." *Journal of Scientific Exploration* 25, no. 3 (2011): 479–95.

In this article, authors Giulio Caratelli and Maria Luisa Felici discuss the French medium Jeanne Laplace. In particular they focus on the eight years that Laplace was involved with the Institut Métapsychique International and its director Eugene Osty. We learn that Laplace began exhibiting mediumistic abilities from childhood and in adulthood she had even worked as a professional medium. After being introduced to the psychical researcher Eugene Osty, Laplace was the center of an eight-year study that also involved other noted researchers like the paranormal investigator Harry Price. In this article, Caratelli and Felici discuss the particulars of Laplace's mediumship and highlight the life of this noted French medium.

Keywords: Jeanne Laplace; Eugene Osty; mediumship; Institut Métapsychique International

Cardeña, Etzel. "The Experimental Evidence for Parapsychological Phenomena: A Review." *American Psychologist* 73, no. 5 (2018): 663–77.

Researcher Etzel Cardeña, of Lund University, provides in this article the prevailing theories surrounding psi. He presents a review of various phenomena including remote viewing, psychokinesis, presentiment, and other manifestations of anomalous cognition. Cardeña begins with a brief historical outline of the trajectory of scholarly inquiry into the psychical and then lays out theories of physics that have been applied to psi phenomena before going into specific examples. This article is a good foundation article that will be especially useful for those new to this topic.

Keywords: anomalous cognition; psi theories; physics; consciousness

Cardeña, Etzel and Michael Winkelman, eds. *Altering Consciousness: Multidisciplinary Perspectives. Volume I: History, Culture, and the Humanities.* Santa Barbara, CA: ABC-CLIO, 2011.

This book is an important addition to this list of parapsychological literature since much of psi involves altered states of consciousness. In this work, editors and consciousness researchers Etzel Cardeña and Michael Winkelman present information on altered consciousness throughout history, in different cultures, and in the humanities disciplines. The result is a multidisciplinary treatment of consciousness that gives a more holistic and nuanced understanding of the overall psi literature.

Topics include lucid dreaming, near-death experiences, meditation, and more. Contributors to this work include those who also contribute to the parapsychological literature. Chapter 5 discusses mesmerism and mediumship and the references in that chapter are particularly useful for those looking for additional reading. Chapter 6 may be of particular interest to those looking for psi overlap since it presents the past fifty years' worth of research on altered consciousness. In it, authors Julie Beischel, Adam J. Rock, and Stanley Krippner remind us that while these phenomena have been around for millennia, Western research into them is new.

Keywords: altered states of consciousness; multidisciplinary

Cunningham, Paul. "A Contribution to the Study of the Possession Trance Mediumship of Jane Roberts." *Journal of Parapsychology* 83, no. 2 (2019): 248–67.

Researcher Paul Cunningham, of Rivier University, presents an overview of the medium Jane Roberts. Roberts, popular from the 1960s through the mid-1980s, claimed to have the ability to channel an entity she called Seth. Those interested in case studies of mediumship will enjoy Cunningham's article.

Keywords: mediumship; Jane Roberts; Seth

Dalkvist, Jan, William Montgomery, Henry Montgomery, and Joakim Westerlund. "Reanalyses of Group Telepathy Data with a Focus on Variability." *Journal of Parapsychology* 74, no. 1 (Spring 2010): 143–71.

In this article, Dalkvist and colleagues discuss the benefits of conducting group studies in parapsychology and provide an overview of past research, including a series of group studies that author Jan Dalkvist has engaged in at Stockholm University since 1993. Following this, the authors discuss their reanalysis of group research focusing on variability, for example, switching around the group roles.

Keywords: group telepathy; variability; Stockholm University

Delorme, Arnaud, Julie Beischel, Leena Michel, Mark Boccuzzi, Dean Radin, and Paul J. Mills. "Electrocortical Activity Associated with Subjective Communication with the Deceased." *Frontiers in Psychology* 4 (November 2013): 1–10.

In this article, researchers gathered psychometric and brain electrophysiology data from six subjects who stated they possessed mediumistic abilities. The authors discovered particular areas of interest in the front theta and gamma band in mediums who gathered highly accurate data about their targets. The authors tell us that "these differences suggest that the impression of communicating with the deceased may be a distinct mental state distinct from ordinary thinking or imagination."[152]

Keywords: psychometry; brain electrophysiology; mediumship

Delorme, Shannon. "Physiology or Psychic Powers? William Carpenter and the Debate Over Spiritualism in Victorian Britain." *Studies in History and Philosophy of Biological and Biomedical Sciences* 48 (2014): 57–66.

Author Shannon Delorme of the University of Oxford presents a discussion of the physiologist William Carpenter and his mostly unknown interest in psychical phenomena like thought-transference and certain cases of mediumship. Though Carpenter was an avid critic of Spiritualism and the rampant fraud that so often accompanied it, he was nevertheless intrigued by certain psychical topics. Delorme points to Carpenter's Unitarian faith as being a mediating factor that allowed him to entertain the possibility of certain psychical phenomena, even though this is rarely (if at all) discussed in other literature on Carpenter. The eminent physiologist could, in fact, be a very combative opponent of psychical research, but Delorme discusses the ways in which he was much more ambivalent than previous literature might suggest. Carpenter entertained notions that trance and hypnotism were indeed very real but were the result of natural physiological forces rather than supernatural occult influences. Still though, Delorme points out that Carpenter's faith allowed him to ponder the mysterious origins of some psi phenomena, like when he attended a séance of Henry Slade and admitted that he could find no immediate "jugglery" to account for what he witnessed.[153] Delorme's case study of Carpenter's life reveals the very tense and very complex nature of early scientific psychical thought.

Keywords: William Carpenter; biographical sketch; Spiritualism; early psychical research, 1800s.

Dixon, John, Lance Storm, and James Houran. "Exploring Ostensible Poltergeist vs. Haunt Phenomena via a Reassessment of Spontaneous Case Data." *Australian Journal of Parapsychology* 18, no. 1 (2018): 7–22.

In this article, researchers Dixon, Storm, and Houran investigate poltergeist phenomena at a bar in Sydney. In this case, certain poltergeist-like phenomena seemed only to occur when a certain employee was physically present and ceased happening when that employee was not present. Instead, when that employee was not present, other staff reported that the activity seemed more similar to hallmarks of a haunting. To define what marks a difference between these two types of phenomena, the authors write, "Haunts tend to consist more of subtle and subjective experiences that transpire sporadically over a long period of time, whereas poltergeists consist more of marked and objective events that occur over a short duration."[154] In this study, phenomena seemed to be related to the presence of a particular person—a factor that might hint at poltergeist phenomena that are a result of recurrent spontaneous psychokinesis on the part of that person. In this article, the authors discuss the overlap and nuances that exist when determining if a case aligns more closely with the haunt or poltergeist phenomena.

Keywords: haunting; poltergeist; recurrent spontaneous psychokinesis

Drinkwater, Kenneth, Brian Laythe, James Houran, Neil Dagnall, Ciarán O'Keeffe, and Sharon A. Hill. "Exploring Gaslighting Effects via the VAPUS Model for Ghost Narratives." *Australian Journal of Parapsychology* 19, no. 2 (2019): 143–79.

In this article, researchers Kenneth Drinkwater and his colleagues discuss the ways in which gaslighting plays a role in haunting experiences, especially when it comes to group experiences. Gaslighting, it is said, can play a role in paranormal investigations and manifest in both positive and negative ways. A positive example would be confirmation bias whereas a negative example would include second-guessing. In fact, they relate this dynamic to Carl Jung's "trickster" archetype, upon which an entire theory of experience has risen. Called trickster theory, the authors write that it "has helped to contextualize and popularize the idea that, by their very nature, anomalous or paranormal experiences orient percipients 'betwixt and between' . . . we sympathize with this assertion and note that it agrees with factors that obfuscate the study or interpretation of witness testimony."[155]

In this article, they combine trickster theory with the VAPUS (versatility, adaptability, participatory nature, universality, and scalability) model, which asserts that there is a brand personality to amateur paranormal investigations. This helps support the author's assertion that "ghost narratives are malleable constructions due to their VAPUS characteristics [and] can elucidate *why* and *how* certain attitudes, circumstances, or powerful social influences can compel or encourage percipients to mistrust, modify, or solidify their perceptions and judgments."[156] These judgments are trickster-like effects and situate the agents of the investigation as active participants in the trickster role. The discussion within this article supports the observation that "people face a basic choice between *fear of an unknown* and an *esoteric explanation for an unknown.*"[157] This article offers a fascinating take on the psychosocial dynamics that are often at play during haunt experiences, especially when applied to group settings.

Keywords: hauntings; ghosts; trickster theory

Evrard, Renaud. "Ghost in the Machine: A Clinical View of Anomalous Telecommunication Experiences." *Journal of Exceptional Experiences and Psychology* 5, no. 2 (Winter 2017): 21–30.

In this article, researcher Renaud Evrard analyzes case studies of events in which people received anomalous phone calls, text messages, and emails in the aftermath of a death of a loved one. Recognizing that in these cases there is some physical material evidence, Evrard questions what the clinical psychological implications are of these cases. He concludes that these anomalous communication events could exist on a spectrum. On one side there are implications of embodiment disorders while on the other there are implications for anomalous, unknown events. Evrard urges researchers to continue studying anomalous communication events in future studies and notes the current lack of clinical considerations of these events. Evrard has also authored historical case studies of various events in parapsychological history. Interested readers will want to consider locating more of Evrard's works beyond the few listed here.

Keywords: anomalous telecommunication; clinical responses to anomalous events

Evrard, Renaud, Erika Annabelle Pratte, and Etzel Cardeña. "Pierre Janet and the Enchanted Boundary of Psychical Research." *History of Psychology* 21, no. 2 (2018): 100–25.

Researchers Evrard, Pratte, and Cardeña present here a biographical sketch of the French psychologist Pierre Janet. The researchers begin by reminding us that when psychology was a fledgling discipline at the end of the 1800s, psychical topics were woven into its fabric—not separated out. They write, "Telepathy, clairvoyance, premonition, and the mental and physical phenomena of mediumship were among the first areas of study in psychological research."[158] To illustrate this early intermingling of topics, the researchers focus on the life of psychologist Pierre Janet. They tell us Janet "claimed to have shown experimentally telepathic communications with a gifted participant, before abandoning this area and trying to erase it from his career. If he really believed that he had achieved the results he described, what could have persuaded him to stop this promising research?"[159] They use Janet as a case study to show

how early French psychologists, though intrigued by psychical phenomena, recanted once they realized that psychical research was associated with a low scientific status. In this article, the authors present information on Janet's experiments at Le Havre, how that research was received, and the eventual backtracking and recanting of his own research. This article presents the reality of the tensions and struggles between psychology and psychical science that began in the late 1800s and will be useful for anyone interested in the history of psi research, the tensions among disciplines, or the life or Pierre Janet.

Readers interested in the history of psychical research in France will want to consult Renaud Evrard's 2010 article "Parapsychology in France after May 1968: A History of GERP."[160]

Keywords: Pierre Janet; early psychical research; boundary science; scientific tension

Graus, Andrea. "Discovering Palladino's Mediumship, Otero Acevedo, Lombroso and The Quest for Authority." *Journal of the History of the Behavioral Sciences* 52, no. 3 (Summer 2016): 211–30.

In this article, Andrea Graus presents an oft-overlooked moment in the timeline of research into Italian medium Eusapia Palladino. In 1888, Eusapia's reputation as a medium was spreading through Naples. She wasn't, however, an international figure quite yet. The spiritist Ercole Chiaia, who also served as her protector, was convinced of Eusapia's talents, and issued a public invitation to well-known psychiatrist Cesare Lombroso. Chiaia's challenge was for Lombroso to come to Naples so he could be convinced of the merit of Eusapia's abilities. Lombroso declined the offer, but in his absence a young physician, Manuel Otero Acevedo, decided to attempt his own research into the medium. Having an interest in psychical phenomena, Acevedo saw this as an opportunity to enhance his reputation as a psychical scholar and challenged Eusapia to a display of mediumistic abilities in broad daylight. Situating a clay mold in front of the medium, Acevedo was shocked when he discovered a child's fingerprints embedded in the clay after her performance.

In this article, Graus discusses the implications of this meeting that occurred in the early careers of both the physicist and the medium. This meeting eventually did attract the attention of Cesare Lombroso who became a convert of mediumship after his encounter. Graus discusses further implications about the role of authority in the history of psychical research and the ways in which early researchers sought to illustrate their psychical expertise.

Keywords: Eusapia Palladino; Manuel Otero Acevedo; Cesare Lombroso; Italy; mediums

Gyimesi, Júlia. "Sándor Ferenczi and the Problem of Telepathy." *History of the Human Sciences* 25, no. 2 (2012): 131–48.

In this article, researcher Júlia Gyimesi provides a look into the psychical interests and research of Sándor Ferenczi, a Hungarian psychoanalyst and prominent member of the Budapest School of Psychoanalysis. Gyimesi tells us that Ferenczi, along with fellow psychoanalysts who had similar interests, advanced our modern understanding of psychoanalysis and its connection with psi. Specifically, "As a result of their efforts, valuable psychoanalytic theories were born, which enriched the understanding of human relationship with innovative ideas. Their main interest remained thought-transference, which they declared relevant in the interpretation of the psychoanalytic situation."[161] Ferenczi conducted multiple experiments with mediums and thought-transference and developed theories surrounding states of mind amenable for both sending and receiving psychic impressions. Throughout this article, Gyimesi delves into Ferenczi's work and contributions and links the history of psychoanalysis and psychical studies.

Keywords: Sándor Ferenczi; Hungary; Budapest School of Psychoanalysis

Further Reading:

S. Ferenczi, "The Phenomena of Hysterical Materialization." In *Further Contributions to the Theory and Technique of Psycho-Analysis.* Edited by J. Rickman, 89–104. London: Hogarth.

Houran, James. "'Sheet Happens!': Advancing Ghost Studies in the Analytics Age." *Australian Journal of Parapsychology* 18, no. 1 (2017): 187–206.

Parapsychologist James Houran presents, in this article, a discussion of factors that hinder the academic advancement of parapsychology. Houran begins by pointing out humankind's constant fasci-

nation with ghosts and haunting experiences. These experiences are often deeply personal. Researching these cases often involve directly interacting with the percipient, and Houran points out that a large portion of research into hauntings takes on a participant-observation style. As such, it can be a daunting task to obtain cohesive standards for investigating these phenomena. Houran posits that there are three major factors that hinder the modern parapsychologist in their research on haunt phenomena.

The first factor that Houran points to is an obsession with technology and gadgets. While technology has certainly allowed us to understand more about our world (psi events included in this), Houran points out that "the downside is that sometimes *style* trumps *substance.*"[162] In other words, sometimes there is misplaced emphasis on having the shiniest, newest gadgets even if they compromise the integrity of the study. The second factor that Houran points to is a sensationalized public image. This results in public awareness of psi concepts being dominated and led not by the scientists themselves, but by popular culture, television programming, ghost clubs, and the like. In turn, this can cast a negative perception on those scholars who pursue psi avenues of research. The third and final factor that Houran points to as a hindrance to haunt research is a lack of cumulative theory-building. In essence, haunt phenomena does not take funding priority and there is a lack of communal resource-sharing since those engaged in haunt research primarily act as siloed researchers.

Following his discussion on factors that hinder haunt phenomena, Houran does not leave the reader on a negative note and provides a discussion on factors that can help improve the quality and reputation of haunt research. His suggestions include more incorporation of quasi-experimental methods, multidisciplinary methods, attempted replication in lab settings, and increased awareness of witness psychology.

Keywords: hauntings; research obstacles; ghosts

Irwin, Harvey J. "The Major Problems Faced by Parapsychology Today: A Survey of Members of the Parapsychological Association." *Australian Journal of Parapsychology* 14, no. 2 (2014): 143–62.

In 2013, parapsychologist Harvey J. Irwin conducted a survey of members of the Parapsychologi-

the brain as held by most physicians, philosophers, and psychologists is too restricted for a proper understanding of [near-death experiences]."[167] Van Lommel began his research in 1986 and in this 2013 article presents a compendium of thought to date on what he's discovered.

Van Lommel begins this article by defining a near-death experience. He tells us, "A near-death experience (NDE) can be defined as the reported memory of a range of impressions during a special state of consciousness, including a number of special elements such as out-of-body experience, pleasant feelings, seeing a tunnel, a light, deceased relatives or a life review, or conscious return into the body."[168] He points out that a variety of situations that induce an NDE result in very similar phenomena, that these phenomena are reported similarly worldwide, and that NDEs have increased in number due to our enhanced technological and medical advances.

Van Lommel then outlines some of his previous research starting with his 1988 Dutch prospective study on NDEs. In this study, 18 percent of respondents claimed to have had an NDE with some recurring themes of seeing a tunnel, encountering dead loved ones, having a life review, and being aware of being dead. Following this, van Lommel also outlines the work of other researchers in the United States and Britain—researchers who found similar results. Upon reviewing the international body of literature on NDEs, van Lommel was able to identify some patterned characteristics like the out-of-body experience, encountering dead loved ones, a life review, etc.

After discussing the research into NDEs, this article discusses some of the leading theories that attempt to explain the phenomena. Among these is the theory of apoxia, or lack of oxygen that results in tunneled retinas and a release of endorphins. Another theory includes heightened levels of carbon dioxide or a side effect of drugs. From here, van Lommel launches into a discussion of brain activity during cardiac arrest. He tells us that there is a "complete cessation of cerebral blood flow"[169] during these events and further outlines the effect that this has on the human body. It is here that van Lommel shows that "there are good reasons to assume that our consciousness does not always coincide with the functioning of our brain: enhanced con-

sciousness, with unaltered self-identity, can sometimes be experienced separately from the body."[170]

Following this discussion, van Lommel presents the concept of neuroplasticity and how the mind can literally shape "the function and the structure of the brain" through things like "mindfulness, emotions, expectations . . . as well as physical activities."[171] After outlining the unique features of brain activity, van Lommel tells us, "In summarizing the aforementioned NDE studies, one can conclude that at present more and more experiences are reported by serious and reliable people who to their own surprise and confusion have experienced an enhanced consciousness independently of their physical body."[172] And it is here that he presents his theory of nonlocal consciousness, which is when the brain merely acts as a "relay station" or a "transmitter"[173] of consciousness, ultimately residing without boundaries and predating our life and death.

Keywords: near-death experience (NDE); consciousness

Marcusson-Clavertz, and David and Etzel Cardeña. "Hypnotizability, Alterations in Consciousness, and Other Variables as Predictors of Performance in a Ganzfeld Psi Task." *Journal of Parapsychology* 75, no. 2 (Fall 2011): 235–59.

In this article, the authors focus on ganzfeld experiments and the various factors that may promote their success. Ganzfeld refers to being in a state of "sensory homogenization,"[174] which many theorize creates an altered state of consciousness that subsequently enables psi functioning. Ganzfeld setups are sometimes seen in pop culture paranormal programming. One example is placing subjects in front of red lights with white, opaque objects (like ping-pong balls) taped to their eyes. The result is a view space awash entirely in red light. Simultaneously, audio input would be introduced so that auditory sense are washed out as well. Once the subject is in this sensory-deprived state, psi experimentation begins. The theory being that sensory deprivation facilitates psi events.

In this study, the authors examined whether things like a proneness to hypnosis, a belief in success, past psi encounters, and dissociation would impact the success of a ganzfeld experiment. They discovered that being prone to hypnosis actually had a negative correlation to a successful psi-ganzfeld experiment and that the most significantly positive factors were a subject's personal belief in success and past encounters with psi.

Keywords: ganzfeld; hypnosis; psi

May, Edwin C. and Sonali Bhatt Marwaha, eds. *Extrasensory Perception: Support, Skepticism, and Science.* 2 volumes. Santa Barbara, CA: Praeger, 2015.

Researchers Edwin C. May and Sonali Bhatt Marwaha are the editors of this two-volume work that compiles various essays from noted parapsychologists on a wide range of topics. Volume 1 focuses on the history, controversies, and research of the field and includes articles by Nancy L. Zingrone, Carlos S. Alvarado, Patrizio Tressoldi, Loyd Auerbach, and more. Specific topics in volume 1 include international psychokinesis studies, an inquiry into the replication problem, ESP, and remote viewing. The second volume focuses on current theories, research organizations, and resources for further reading.

Keywords: extrasensory perception; theories; replication; psychokinesis; remote viewing

McLenon, James. "Secondary Analysis of Sitter Group Data: Testing Hypotheses from the PK Literature." *Journal of Parapsychology* 83, no. 2 (2019): 209–31.

In this article, author James McLenon builds upon research he conducted with his colleagues on the dynamics of psychokinesis. McLenon and colleagues used groups of people (sitters) to test their theories of PK. They discovered that most individuals inhibit PK while certain group dynamics (like rapport and a shared ideology) can enhance the likelihood of PK phenomena. From these initial theories, four additional hypotheses were proposed, and in this article McLenon uses forty years' worth of historical PK data from the Society for Research on Rapport and Telekinesis, to test them.

McLenon's analysis of these cases support the facilitation/suppression theory of PK, which posits that larger groups are less successful because *most* people inhibit PK. McLenon puts forth a synthesis of components from various theories into a PK-dream theory, named as such since PK and REM cycles share similar functions. Discussions of other hypotheses are presented. Those interested in PK

and the theories surrounding it will want to consult this resource.

Keywords: psychokinesis; PK theories; Society for Research on Rapport and Telekinesis

Mülberger, Annette and Mónica Balltondre. "Metapsychics in Spain: Acknowledging or Questioning the Marvelous?" *History of the Human Sciences* 25, no. 2 (2012): 108–30.

In this article, researchers Mülberger and Balltondre discuss the rise of metapsychics in Spain—metapsychics being the term used there (and in other places like France) to refer to psychical research. Charles Richet's 1922 publication *Traité de Métapsychique* was influential to researchers in Spain, particularly Jaume Ferran i Clua, who conducted experiments on thought-transference. Mülberger and Balltondre discuss other psychical research from Spain and also point out the critical voices of the time and the tension between those operating in this borderland of science and those who viewed the topics as unworthy of scientific attention.

Keywords: metapsychics; Spain

Murray, Aja Louise. "The Validity of the Meta-Analytic Method in Addressing the Issue of Psi Replicability." *Journal of Parapsychology* 75, no. 2 (2011): 261–77.

In this article, author Aja Louise Murray addresses one of the major criticisms of parapsychology today: the inability to replicate results. Murray points out the growing use and popularity of meta-analytical techniques and how they have been used to boost the reputation and standing of psi research. However, Murray discusses the weaknesses still left from these techniques and concludes that they still do not satisfy the issue of psi replicability. Murray presents a critical and important discussion, and along the way provides innumerable citations that will be of interest to readers, especially regarding methodology.

Keywords: replication; criticism; meta-analysis; research methods

Nahm, Michael. "Albert Heim (1849–1937): The Multifaceted Geologist Who Influenced Research into Near-Death Experiences and Suggestion Therapy." *Explore* 12, no. 4 (July/August 2016): 256–58.

In this article, researcher Michael Nahm presents a brief article on the Swiss geologist Albert Heim. Nahm points out that many acknowledge Heim's work in geology, but few realize that he also contributed to parapsychology. In fact, Nahm points out that Heim was a pioneer in the field of near-death studies. In addition to this topic, Heim also studied suggestion therapy and even conducted studies where warts were healed by suggestion. As a young boy, Heim's father exhibited the ability to "suggest" warts off his children. As Heim grew older, he had a son of his own who suffered from warts and, remembering the techniques used by his father, performed them on his son to total success. The psychophysiological process of how suggestion therapy works is unknown, but Heim's studies show the unusual treatments to which it can be applied.

Keywords: Albert Heim; Switzerland; suggestion therapy; near-death experiences; biographical sketch

Neppe, Vernon M. "On the Alleged Scientific Evidence for Survival after Bodily Death." *Australian Journal of Parapsychology* 15, no. 2 (2015): 167–96.

The 2015 edition of this article is an updated version of the original 1973 publication. Dr. Vernon M. Neppe tells us that he wrote it while in medical school in South Africa and that his professor, Dr. Lewis Hurst, published it in the school's journal *The Leech.* In addition to being a faculty member at the University of Witwatersrand, Dr. Hurst was a former president of the South African SPR and saw, with this article, a worthy addition to the scholarly literature on consciousness after death.

Neppe outlines various evidence that points to the survival of consciousness after physical death. Drawing from sources like the Cross Correspondences of the SPR (and more), this article argues that taken together, the evidence supports the theory that human consciousness can continue in some matter once physical death has occurred. The crux of Neppe's argument rests on three different types of evidence. The first are physical factors, like an EEG, that indicate some awareness beyond bodily death. Another set of evidence is psychic episodes that include instances of mediumship, out-of-body experiences, and psychical healing.

The third set of evidence stems from the information communicated during these psi episodes. Neppe outlines each of these factors in detail and presents a compelling case for the survival of human consciousness. In addition to the argument espoused, this article is extremely useful for the references to key figures, phenomena, and cases.

Keywords: consciousness; survival after death

Noakes, Richard. "Haunted Thoughts of the Careful Experimentalist: Psychical Research and the Troubles of Experimental Physics." *Studies in History and Philosophy of Biological and Biomedical Sciences* 48 (2014): 46–56.

Richard Noakes, a professor at the University of Exeter in Cornwall, England, discusses the relationship between psychical research and experimental physics during the years 1870–1930. Noakes begins by pointing out that psychical research drew in many scholars from diverse fields because psi was a "field of enquiry [that] appeared to be relevant to, and promise new ways of extending, different sciences."[175] Many different aspects of psi had relevancy to diverse disciplines. For example, ESP and telepathy insighted intriguing questions about psychology while telekinesis was a curious issue for physics. Psi researchers were inspired by the laboratory methods and devices by their contemporaries in other fields, but psi posed its own set of problems within the laboratory. One of the biggest issues was that the clinical lab was not a conducive environment for mediums to exhibit psi phenomena. Because of this, though, experimental physicists could actually sympathize, knowing how difficult it was to replicate conducive lab environments to study certain phenomena. So, too, were physicists sympathetic to psychical research efforts due to the excitement surrounding implications of psi for physics. In this article, Noakes outlines some of the conversations and thoughts of early physicists and psychical researchers and highlights the early relationship between the two fields.

Keywords: physics; psychical physicists; 1800s; laboratory methods

Paraná, Denise, Alexandre Caroli Rocha, Elizabeth Schmitt Freire, Francisco Lotufo Neto, and Alexander Moreira-Almeida. "An Empirical Investigation of Alleged Mediumistic Writing: A Case Study of Chico

Xavier's Letters." *Journal of Nervous and Mental Disease* 207 no. 6 (June 2019): 497–504.

In this article, researchers investigate Chico Xavier, a well-known Brazilian medium. They remind us that "during the last decade, there has been a renewed interest in the research on mediumship, with a number of studies on the phenomenon of anomalous information reception [and that these studies suggest] that different mediums might provide diverse levels of veridical information compared with each other and even the same medium in different occasions."[176] Born in 1910, Xavier displayed curious abilities from a young age, such as psychography, or the ability of writing while in a trance state and alleged to be under the control of a spirit. The researchers located these psychographic letters and chose one from which to base an investigation. They chose a letter based not only on the detail included but also on the amount of contact and awareness that Xavier had with the family involved. Additionally, interviews with the deceased's family were conducted to determine how accurate these psychographic letters were. Overall, the researchers found twenty-nine items that were "highly specific and veridical."[177]

Keywords: mediumship; Chico Xavier; Brazil; veridicality; psychography

Peres, Julio Fernando, Alexander Moreira-Almeida, Leonardo Caixeta, Frederico Leao, and Andrew Newberg. "Neuroimaging During Trance State: A Contribution to the Study of Dissociation." *PLoS ONE* 7, no. 11 (November 2012): 1–9.

In this article, researchers look at the intersection of dissociation, mediumship, and brain activity. They recognize that much of the dissociation literature focuses on pathological conditions but note a comparable lack of research into nonpathological dissociation, such as those types that you often find with spiritual experiences or exercises—mediumship being one of these types of experiences. To investigate this intersection, the researchers gathered ten mediums who engaged in psychography, or produced written works said to be channeled to them from the spirit of a deceased person. All mediums were evaluated to rule out the presence of any psychological disorders. During displays of psychography, the authors note that "experienced mediums spoke of a deeper trance,

with clouded consciousness, often reporting being out of the body, and having little or no awareness of the content of what they were writing. Less expert mediums were in a less pronounced trance state and usually reported writing phases being dictated to them in their minds."[178] The researchers went on to take scans of subject's brains and noted differences in certain portions of the brain during trance states—activity that differed depending on how much experience a medium had. The authors conclude by telling us that "the study of spiritual experiences such as mediumship is seminal to the development of our current understanding of the mind."[179]

Keywords: trance; dissociation; neuroimaging; psychography

Rock, Adam J., Julie Beischel, Mark Boccuzzi, and Michael Biuso. "Discarnate Readings by Claimant Mediums: Assessing Phenomenology and Accuracy Under Beyond Double-Blind Conditions." *Journal of Parapsychology* 78, no. 2 (Fall 2014): 183–94.

In this article, Rock and coauthors set forth to quantitatively examine the phenomenon of mediumship and, specifically, the ability of mediums to contact "discarnates," or spirits of deceased individuals. They developed a series of tests to examine potential accuracy of readings. In total, nineteen mediums were selected to conduct sittings. Each medium was given the same set of questions to answer about their paired discarnate, assigned by the researchers. Just prior to the sitting, each medium was given the Phenomenology of Consciousness Inventory, which essentially measures if conditions conducive to being in an altered state of consciousness are met. Additionally, double-blind (and beyond) measures were taken to ensure that mediums did not know identities of those they were reading for *and* that the sitters and experimenters themselves knew only as little as was necessary. Additionally, sitters were asked to rate how well the mediums did on other sittings not related to them, adding another objective analysis to the mix. In total, there were five levels of blinding in this experiment. The authors conclude that findings "suggest that the claimant mediums were able to demonstrate anomalous information reception under test conditions with five levels of blinding."[180] They caution that other factors could be at play such as precognition and that further research is needed.

Keywords: mediumship; double-blind; anomalous information reception; Phenomenology of Consciousness Inventory

Roll, William G. and William T. Joines. "RSPK and Consciousness." *Journal of Parapsychology* 77, no. 2 (2013): 192–211.

This article, published posthumously one year after the death of parapsychologist William G. Roll, provides a review of three cases involving recurrent spontaneous psychokinesis (RSPK). They review cases involving instances of RSPK during which the subjects were under direct observation, thereby hampering the possibility of fraudulent activity. Focusing on how to explain PK in these moments, the authors were inspired by Puthoff's zero-point energy, or energy that interacts with geomagnetic forces and gravity. Along the way, the authors discuss other theories as well that could account for PK activity.

Keywords: psychokinesis; recurrent spontaneous psychokinesis (RSPK); poltergeists; zero-point energy and PK

Roxburgh, Elizabeth C. and Chris A. Roe. "A Survey of Dissociation, Boundary-Thinness, and Psychological Wellbeing in Spiritualist Mental Mediumship." *Journal of Parapsychology* 75, no. 2 (Fall 2011): 279–99.

Roxburgh and Roe begin their article by outlining the various schools of thought regarding the veracity of mediumship. They note the alternative hypotheses offered and the division between scholars who believe mediums may represent survival theory and those who believe that it is explainable by fraud or ESP. However, that is not the focus here. The authors tell us, "The current research was intended to redress this by putting to one side the issue of the authenticity of mediumship, focusing instead on whether it is possible to generate a character profile of those likely to report such experiences."[181] More specifically, their goal was to "explore . . . whether the occurrence of mediumistic experiences was associated with wellbeing or psychological distress."[182] They discovered, through surveying 159 people (80 of whom identified as mediums), that mediums scored much higher levels of psychological well-being and lower levels of psychological

distress. This research highlights that mediumship cannot be relegated to fantasy-proneness or some form of mental pathology.

Keywords: mediumship; psychological well-being

Sheldrake, Rupert. "Psi in Everyday Life: Nonhuman and Human." In *Parapsychology: A Handbook for the 21st Century*. Edited by Etzel Cardeña, John Palmer, and David Marcusson-Clavertz, 350–63. Jefferson, NC: McFarland and Company, 2015.

Researcher Rupert Sheldrake presents a discussion of psi phenomena from the lens of those everyday things that many of us has likely encountered. For example, how many of us have received a text from someone *just* after we were thinking about them? Or how many of us swear that our animals somehow know when we are coming home? Sheldrake tackles both these questions and in so doing provides a discussion on the ways in which psi manifests in our daily lives. Along the way he provides information about studies designed to test such questions and also provides details on the skeptical claims against psi.

Keywords: psi; skepticism

Shiah, Yung-Jong. "A Proposed Process for Experiencing Visual Images of Targets during as ESP Task." *Journal of Parapsychology* 75, no. 1 (Spring 2011): 129–43.

Researcher Yung-Jong Shiah presents a discussion of the "neural and biophysical mechanisms"[183] at play during extrasensory events. Essentially, Shiah describes the specific processes that are happening in the brain during ESP events. He begins by referencing the work of additional researchers who have also attempted to outline processes and offer theories. Focusing on the parts of the brain that facilitate visual imagery, Shiah presents various tests that examine this part of the brain and its functions, offering, along the way, how these areas of the brain may play a role in ESP events. Anyone interested in a discussion of ESP that focuses on neurology and biophysical mechanisms will want to consult this resource.

Keywords: extrasensory perception; neural and biophysical processes

Slavoutski, Sergei. "Is the Reincarnation Hypothesis Advanced by Stevenson for Spontaneous Past-life Experiences Relevant for the Understanding of the Ontology of Past-life Phenomena?" *International Journal of Transpersonal Studies* 31, no. 1 (2012): 83–96.

In this article, researcher Sergei Slavoutski discusses the reincarnation hypothesis made popular by seminal reincarnation researcher Dr. Ian Stevenson. Slavoutski posits that while the hypothesis neither proves nor disproves the possibility of reincarnation, it does offer a solid framework for understanding spontaneous past-life experiences, and perhaps even those brought on by hypnosis. Slavoutski discusses the merits of this hypothesis and in so doing reminds us of the many situations in which past-life experiences can occur such as during hypnosis, as a result of drugs, sensory deprivation, meditation, certain therapies, etc. This article provides a review of the theory, the history of past-life experiences, research efforts, and more, providing a well-rounded introduction into the theories of reincarnation.

Keywords: reincarnation; Dr. Ian Stevenson; past-life experiences

Sommer, Andreas. "Psychical Research in the History and Philosophy of Science: An Introduction and Review." *Studies in History and Philosophy of Biological and Biomedical Sciences* 48 (2014): 38–45.

In this article, researcher Andreas Sommer of the University of Cambridge outlines psychical literature in the fields of science and medicine—particularly historians who deal specifically with the late nineteenth and early twentieth century. As such, they developed a conference aimed at the topic of gathering historical materials from the fields of science and medicine. Along the way, Sommer discusses the issue of demarcation, determining which topics are worthy of inclusion based on subject matter. This is an issue that continues to this day. The historians tell us, "Editors of mainstream journals have admitted sticking to the rule of rejecting papers reporting positive psi effects irrespective of the quality of submitted manuscripts."[184] Sommer's article illustrates the tension that still exists in regard to the opinions surrounding where parapsychology fits in the broader, scholarly discussions.

Keywords: psychical literature in the late nineteenth and early twentieth centuries

Storm, Lance, Patrizio E. Tressoldi, and Lorenzo Di Risio. "Meta-Analysis of ESP Studies, 1987–2010: Assessing the Success of the Forced-Choice Design in Parapsychology." *Journal of Parapsychology* 76, no. 2 (Fall 2012): 243–73.

In this article the authors present the results of a meta-analysis they conducted of seventy-two extrasensory perception (ESP) studies conducted between 1987 and 2010. They specifically focus on ESP studies that use forced-choice design. In this design, subjects know which targets they are attempting to intuit. For example, Zener cards might be used to test ESP and, in this case, the subject knows the five different symbols within that deck of Zener cards. They tell us that previous meta-analyses of forced-choice studies had shown a small but significant amount of evidence for the existence of ESP. However, "since more than a decade has passed since the last meta-analysis of the forced-choice domain, one of the major aims of the present article is to evaluate the performance of forced-choice studies conducted in the period 1987–2010."[185] Upon completion of their review, they conclude that there *still* exists a small but statistically significant amount of evidence for ESP within forced-choice studies.

Other meta-analyses have been published such as Steinkamp, Milton, and Morris's 1998 article "A Meta-Analysis of Forced-Choice Experiments Comparing Clairvoyance and Precognition"[186] and Storm, Tressoldi, and Di Risio's 2010 article "Meta-Analysis of Free-Response Studies, 1992–2008: Assessing the Noise Reduction Model in Parapsychology."[187]

Keywords: ESP; forced-choice studies; Zener cards; precognition; clairvoyance

Wahbeh, Helané, Dean Radin, Julia Mossbridge, Cassandra Vieten, and Arnaud Delorme. "Exceptional Experiences Reported by Scientists and Engineers." *Explore* 14, no. 5 (September/October 2018): 329–41.

In this article, researchers explore the possible connections between superstition and paranormal experiences, or as they call them, exceptional human experiences (EHEs). They theorized that scientists and engineers may have a lower predisposition toward superstition, so they developed a survey to ask these groups of people about various EHEs. They discovered that 94 percent of their sample of scientists and engineers believed in at least one EHE—in fact, these two groups scored higher than some portions of the general public. Researchers in this study discuss the connections between personality, superstition, belief, and other attributes that factor into exceptional human experiences.

Keywords: exceptional human experiences; belief

Watt, Caroline. *Parapsychology: A Beginner's Guide.* London: Oneworld Publications, 2016.

In this book, Dr. Caroline Watt introduces parapsychology palatable for those new to the topic. Her work is composed of four main parts. In part 1, Watt discusses the historical roots of parapsychology while part 2 focuses specifically on research into those who have exhibited psi abilities like psychokinesis, remote viewing, and mediumship. Part 3 focuses on anomalous experiences like haunting and out-of-body and near-death experiences. The final portion of this book focuses on laboratory research of psi phenomena. Included is an appendix is a test for extrasensory and psychokinetic abilities.

Keywords: general overview; psychokinesis; telepathy; mediumship; hauntings; laboratory research; history of parapsychology

Wolffram, Heather. "Hallucination of Materialization? The Animism versus Spiritism Debate in Late 19th Century Germany." *History of the Human Sciences* 25, no. 2 (2012): 45–66.

Researcher Heather Wolffram provides a discussion of the tensions between the burgeoning fields of psychology and psychical research in late 1800s Germany. Similar to other countries, tensions surrounding these disciplines ran high, with academics on each side vying for footing. In Germany, further debates surrounding those in the animist or spiritist camps raged and tensions among psychologists, psychical researchers, and spiritualists coalesced in this time period. Within this article, Wolffram presents a snapshot in time of the evolution of this border science. Readers will find information on Alexander Askakof, Spiritualism, Eduard von Hartmann, nineteenth-century attitudes on consciousness, and more.

Keywords: Germany; border science; Alexander Askakof; animisms versus spiritism

Zingrone, Nancy L., Carlos S. Alvarado, and Gerd H. Hövelmann. "An Overview of Modern Developments in Parapsychology." In *Parapsychology: A Handbook for the 21st Century.* Edited by Etzel Cardeña, John Palmer, and David Marcusson-Calvertz, 13–29. Jefferson, NC: McFarland and Company, Inc. 2015.

The authors of this chapter provide a discussion of trends and progress in parapsychology since 1977. A comprehensive work done by parapsychologist John Beloff had been written about twenty years prior and, in this chapter, the authors pick up where Beloff left off. Following their introduction, they present a topical overview of research since 1977 on topics such as extrasensory perception, out-of-body experiences, psychokinesis, mediumship, and more. Then they discuss the contributions and influence from other disciplines like philosophy, sociology, and religion. Following this is a discussion of progress in statistical measures to investigate psi.

The authors also provide discussions of criticisms about psi research, institutions that engage in psi research, educational opportunities in parapsychology, and journals that publish parapsychological research. This chapter introduces a wide variety of topics within modern parapsychology research and the bibliography will be useful for readers to locate additional sources. Other chapters include more detailed discussions of research methods, poltergeists, mediumship, electronic voice phenomena, and much more. *Parapsychology: A Handbook for the 21st Century* would be beneficial for readers, as well.

Keywords: parapsychology since 1977

2020s

Acunzo, David, Etzel Cardeña, and Devin B. Terhune. "Anomalous Experiences are More Prevalent Among Highly Suggestible Individuals who are also Highly Dissociative." *Cognitive Neuropsychiatry* 25, no. 3 (2020): 179–89.

In this article, the researchers discuss the connections between high hypnotizability, dissociation, and anomalous experiences. They discovered that people who are highly susceptible to hypnosis often report higher instances of hallucinations and further discovered that people who are highly susceptible to hypnosis and dissociation report higher rates of anomalous experiences. This study (and others like it) highlight the links between anomalous experiences and personality constructs.

Beischel, Julie and Mark Boccuzzi. "Development and Deployment of the Windbridge PSI and Related Phenomena Awareness Questionnaire (WPRPAQ)." *Journal of Scientific Exploration* 34, no. 1 (2020): 36–61.

In this article, Beischel and Boccuzzi discuss their creation of a new survey aimed at investigating psi experiences. They titled it the Windbridge Psi and Related Phenomena Awareness Questionnaire. It was created specifically to address some of the shortcomings of previous survey methods targeted at psi. For example, they note that many previous surveys tend to focus on the negative, dysfunctional aspects of psi experiences such as assumptions about low critical thinking skills or mental disorders. Leading language, vague language, and the use of religious language that is loaded with connotation can also impact survey efficacy. Older surveys may have lost their original intended function with the advancement of technology and for all these reasons (and more), the authors saw a need to develop a new survey methodology for psi.

This new tool, a digital ten-item survey, was sent to both people who identify as mediums and those who do not. The authors included a copy of the survey in appendix A for readers to browse. There are no terms like "telepathy" or "extrasensory perception" so that respondents aren't affected by any biases toward these wordings, but even without using specific wording, the survey tests experiences related to past lives, energy healing, psychokinesis, telepathy, mediumship, precognition, near-death experiences, and remote viewing.

In total, the authors collected surveys from more than 1,300 people, roughly 300 of whom identified as mediums. Respondents were least familiar with micro and macropsychokinesis. Those who identified as mediums reported experiencing all the phenomena at much higher rates than those who did not identify as a medium. The survey also investigated bidirectional (telepathy, energy healing, etc.) and unidirectional phenomena (remote viewing, precognition, microPK, etc.). The authors go on to discuss the benefits and limitations of this new survey methodology for psi.

Keywords: survey; research methodology; Windbridge Institute; mediums; non-mediums

Mossbridge, Julia and Dean Radin. "Psi Performance as a Function of Demographic and Personality Factors in Smartphone-Based Tests: Using a 'SEARCH' Approach." *Journal of Anomalous Experience and Cognition* 1, no. 1–2 (2021): 78–113.

In this article, researchers Julia Mossbridge and Dean Radin discuss their use of an app to gather data regarding psi and personality factors. Specifically, they investigated psychokinesis and precognition through an app that attracted more than 2,600 users. The app was designed to test if users could manipulate an electronic random number generator and/or intuit a future event. The researchers hypothesized that gender and psi belief would be two attributes related to psi ability and their theory was confirmed. Users' expectation of how they would perform was inversely and significantly related to psi performance, something they call "expectation-opposing" rather than the previous, older term "psi-missing."

The researchers were inspired to conduct this study using a smartphone app because, as they tell us, online studies can mitigate certain obstacles to psi research. Those obstacles include replication and small numbers of participants, and the amount of personality and individual differences that seem to impact psi abilities. Mossbridge and Radin gathered data from this smartphone app from 2017 through 2020.

Keywords: psychokinesis; precognition; expectation-opposing; electronic random number generator; app

Olesen, Terry. "Reincarnation Research: I. An Old Idea Re-Examined with New Methods in the 21st Century." *Australian Journal of Parapsychology* 20, no. 2 (2020): 139–60.

Terry Olesen presents an overview of reincarnation research methods. These methods include techniques like child-memory case studies, medium-derived, and hypnotic regression. Olesen calls attention not only to the diverse range of methods, but also to the fact that there are a diverse, though small, range of reincarnation researchers—not all of them necessarily from within the academy. In part 1 (interested readers can search for part 2), Olesen focuses on academic research and the focus on case studys and forensic methods popularized by Dr. Ian Stevenson. Olesen provides summaries of some of Dr. Stevenson's work and also introduces the reader to reincarnation research done at the University of Virginia's Department of Perceptual Studies. One researcher within that department, James Tucker, has developed new questionnaires based on Stevenson's work and Olesen discusses the implications of this new tool for reincarnation research.

Olesen also mentions another reincarnation scholar: Dr. James G. Matlock, a research fellow at the Parapsychology Foundation. An anthropologist by training, Dr. Matlock has written multiple works on reincarnation that present historical overviews, research, and theoretical trends and also offers his own philosophical perspectives. Olesen also includes international scholars in this overview, like the Japanese scholar Ohkado Masayuki, Icelandic researcher Erlendur Haraldsson, and the German Australian researcher Jürgen Keil. This work provides a solid overview of modern reincarnation research and will serve as a useful resource for an introduction to the topic and the scholars involved.

Keywords: reincarnation; Ian Stevenson; Erlendur Haraldsson; James G. Matlock; Ohkado Masayuki; Jürgen Keil

Parker, Adrian. "Thought Forms Gone Rogue: A Theory for Psi-Critics and Parapsychologists." *Journal of Scientific Exploration* 35, no. 1 (2021): 91–128.

Researcher Adrian Parker is a psychology professor at the University of Gothenburg in Sweden. In this article he addresses one of the major criticisms against psi. Parker begins his article by telling us, "A major issue impeding the acceptance of parapsychology is that there is no theoretical conceptual framework linking its diverse phenomena."[188] However, he points out that since consciousness is readily accepted, we can simply view psi phenomena as just one of many different manifestations of dissociative events. Parker posits that by using concepts of consciousness, coconsciousness, and dissociative states, a cause-and-effect relationship can be shown, which seems to be one of the largest criticisms. Parker's article highlights one of the criticisms of the field while also offering insight into the connection between consciousness, dissociation, and psi.

Keywords: dissociative states; consciousness; criticisms of psi

Reber, Arthur S. and James E. Alcock. "Searching for the Impossible: Parapsychology's Elusive Quest." *American Psychologist* 75, no. 3 (2020): 391–99.

Any bibliography of a particular discipline would not be complete if it did not include resources that present criticisms within that discipline. It is not useful to only seek out resources that affirm that which you are personally interested in. It is valuable and necessary to also understand the criticisms that exist. In this article, researchers Arthur S. Reber and James E. Alcock present a critique of parapsychology and psi research in which they state that all claims of parapsychology cannot fundamentally be true.

The entire crux of their article can be summarized when they write that "parapsychology has failed to demonstrate that its claimed phenomena actually exist. Despite the best efforts [there is] still no persuasive evidence that supports the existence of psi."[189] Their major argument relies on the problems of replicability within parapsychology—in other words, the inability of researchers to successfully replicate effects leaves the authors wondering why there is a continued push to study these topics. Additionally, the authors point out the constant flux of methodologies and theories that cycle through every few years, leaving still no cohesive set of guidelines or standards. They discuss some of the reasons why these topics draw scientific attention and while readers may not necessarily agree with some of their arguments, it is a useful article that will provide you with an understanding of the major criticisms of parapsychology within the academy.

Keywords: criticisms and psi research

Storm, Lance and Robb Tilley. "Haunt and Poltergeist Clearing in Australian Residences: A Retrospective Survey." *Australian Journal of Parapsychology* 20, no. 1 (2020): 21–55.

Conducted in Australia, researchers Lance Storm and Robb Tilley surveyed people who experienced haunt or poltergeist activity who subsequently then engaged in a cleansing ritual. Tilley is a member of the Australian Institute of Parapsychological Research and with the help of scholar Lance Storm, the two set forth to determine the relationship between "clearing success and the mental process known as transliminality (the movement of psychological content such as perceptions, emotions, and cognitions, into and out of consciousness) and personal wellbeing."[190] Those who have a high transliminality scale are often physically more sensitive to sensation and touch, which the authors point out could indeed be a factor in paranormal experiences.

Interestingly, Storm and Tilley found that their respondents had, on average, a low transliminality score, meaning that they were less reactive to stress, more introverted, and not prone to having experienced any type of dissociation. Once a home had finally been "cleared," 88 percent of survey respondents stated that they felt the activity had either partially or completely ceased. Poltergeist activity ceased at a slightly higher percentage than hauntings, revealing that there may be a correlation between clearing, low transliminality, and perceived improved quality of life. This article is an interesting look into the psychological effects of clearing in psi phenomena.

Keywords: transliminality; poltergeist; haunting

Wahbeh, Helané, Garret Yount, Cassandra Vieten, Dean Radin, and Arnaud Delorme. "Measuring Extraordinary Experiences and Beliefs: A Validation and Reliability Study." *F1000Research* 8 (2020): 1–25.

The authors, who are researchers at the Institute of Noetic Sciences, explain their efforts in developing the Noetic Experiences and Beliefs Scale. This tool is designed to separately evaluate paranormal beliefs and paranormal experiences. Wahbeh and coauthors discuss the drawbacks of previous surveys that often intermingle both belief and experience, resulting in ambiguous or unclear data. When analyzed separately though, new trends and information can emerge among the two. For example, they found a strong correlation between belief and experience. In this article they review two pilot studies adminis-tered to target groups to test the validity and usefulness of this new tool.

Keywords: Noetic Experiences and Beliefs Scale; Institute of Noetic Sciences; paranormal beliefs

Watt, Caroline, Emily Dawson, Alisdair Tullo, Abby Pooley, and Holly Rice. "Testing Precognition and Alterations of Consciousness with Selected Participants in the Ganzfeld." *Journal of Parapsychology* 84, no. 1 (Spring 2020): 21–37.

Ganzfeld refers to "sensory isolation procedures"[191] designed in the 1970s by researchers Charles Honorton and Adrian Parker. Parapsychologists theorize that psi abilities can be facilitated by the use of sensory deprivation. In this article, Watt and her coauthors designed a study to test precognition within a ganzfeld design. Their design was unique, however, in that they screened their subjects on things like creativity, past psi experience, belief in psi, and whether or not they have a meditation or mental discipline.

Keywords: ganzfeld experiments; precognition; altered states of consciousness

NOTES

1. Louisa E. Rhine, *PSI: What is It? The Story of ESP and PK* (New York: Harper and Row, 1975), 2.
2. Ibid., 459.
3. Ibid., 462.
4. Ibid., 3.
5. Ibid., 82.
6. Ibid., 112.
7. Ibid., 3–4.
8. Ibid., vii.
9. Ibid., 101.
10. Ibid., 101.
11. Ibid., 238.
12. Ibid., 241.
13. Ibid., 244.
14. Ibid., 118.
15. Ibid., 118.
16. Ibid., 150–51.
17. Ibid., 900.
18. Ibid., 131.
19. Ibid., 4.
20. Ibid., 15.

21. Ibid., 78–79.

22. Ibid., 68.

23. Ibid., 62.

24. Ibid., 285.

25. Ibid., 286.

26. Ibid., 247.

27. Ibid., 257.

28. Ibid., 94.

29. Ibid., 107.

30. Ibid., 69.

31. Ibid., 74–75.

32. Ibid., 439.

33. Ibid., 436.

34. Andreas Sommer, "Professional Heresy: Edmund Gurney (1847–1888) and the Study of Hallucinations and Hypnotism," *Medical History* 55, no. 3 (July 2011): 386.

35. Henry Sidgwick, Alice Johnson, F. W. H. Myers, Frank Podmore and Eleanor M. Sidgwick. "Report on the Census of Hallucinations." *Proceedings of the Society for Psychical Research* 10 (1894): 28.

36. Sommer, "Professional Heresy," 33.

37. Ibid., vii.

38. Ibid., vii.

39. Ibid., 152.

40. Ibid., 341.

41. Ibid., 408.

42. Ibid., 409.

43. Ibid., 180.

44. Ibid., 180.

45. Ibid., viii.

46. Ibid., xi.

47. Ibid., 578.

48. Ibid., 274.

49. Ibid., 275.

50. Ibid., vii.

51. Ibid., 9–10.

52. Ibid., 10.

53. Ibid., 380.

54. Ibid., 377.

55. Ibid., 411.

56. Ibid., 2.

57. Ibid., vii.

58. Ibid., 369.

59. Ibid., v.

60. Carlos S. Alvarado, "On W.J. Crawford's Studies of Physical Mediumship," *Journal of Scientific Exploration* 28, no. 2 (2014): 352–53.

61. Ibid., vii.

62. Ibid., preface, unpaginated.

63. Ibid., 2.

64. Ibid., 15.

65. Ibid., xiv.

66. Ibid., 299.

67. Ibid., vi.

68. Ibid., 633.

69. Ibid., v.

70. Ibid., 5–6.

71. Ibid., 3–4.

72. Ibid., 3.

73. Ibid., 59.

74. Helen C. Lambert, *A General Survey of Psychical Phenomena* (New York: Knickerbocker Press, 1928), vii.

75. Ibid., 4.

76. Ibid., viii.

77. Ibid., vii.

78. Ibid., vii.

79. Ibid., 402.

80. Ibid., 406.

81. Ibid., 419.

82. Ibid., 153.

83. Ibid., viii.

84. Ibid., 16.

85. Ibid., 185–86.

86. Ibid., 20.

87. Ibid., 136.

88. Ibid., 259.

89. Ibid., 259–60.

90. Ibid., 174.

91. Ibid., 14.

92. Ibid., 43.

93. Ibid., 44.

94. Ibid., 269.

95. Ibid., 10.

96. Ibid., 260.

97. Ibid., vii.

98. Ibid., 244.

99. Ibid., x.

100. Ibid., 88.

101. Ibid., 90.

102. Ibid., 276.

103. Ibid., 211.

104. Edgar Mitchell, "An ESP Test from Apollo 14," *Journal of Parapsychology* 35, no. 2 (June 1, 1971): 89–90.

105. Ibid., 3.

106. Ibid., 2.

107. Ibid., 152.

108. Ibid., 153.

109. Ibid., xi.

110. Ibid., v.

111. Ibid., 11.

112. Ibid., 1.

113. Robert S. McCully, "'The Paranormal and the Normal' by Morton Leeds and Gardner Murphy (Book Review)," *Journal of Parapsychology* 44, no. 4 (December 1, 1980): 362–65.

114. Ibid., 2.

115. Ibid., 4.

116. Michael A. Persinger, "Spontaneous Telepathic Experiences from *Phantasms of the Living* and Low Global Geomagnetic Activity," *Journal of the American Society for Psychical Research* 81 (January 1987): 23.

117. Ibid., 24.

118. Jerome Tobacyk and Gary Milford, "Belief in Paranormal Phenomena: Assessment Instrument Development and Implications for Personality Functioning," *Journal of Personality and Social Psychology* 44, no. 5 (1983): 1029.

119. Ibid., xii.

120. Ibid., 1.

121. Ibid., 106.

122. Ibid., 1179.

123. Ibid., 1189.

124. Ibid., 276.

125. Ibid., 32.

126. Ibid., 211.

127. Ibid., 1

128. Arthur S. Berger and Joyce Berger, *The Encyclopedia of Parapsychology and Psychical Research*. New York: Paragon House, 1991: 301.

129. Ibid., 71.

130. Ibid., 71.

131. Ibid., 516.

132. Jason J. Braithwaite and Maurice Townsend, "Sleeping With the Enemy—A Quantitative Magnetic Investigation of an English Castle's Reputedly 'Haunted' Bedroom," *European Journal of Parapsychology* 20, no. 1 (2005): 72.

133. Braithwaite and Townsend, "Research Note," 75

134. Michael A. Thalbourne. *A Glossary of Terms Used in Parapsychology*. Charlottesville, VA: Puente Publications, 2003: 30.

135. Deborah Delanoy, "Anomalous Psychophysiological Responses to Remote Cognition: The DMILS Studies," *European Journal of Parapsychology* 16 (2001): 30.

136. Ibid., 30.

137. Ibid., 1.

138. Ibid., 1.

139. Ibid., 5.

140. Ibid., 1.

141. Ibid., 10.

142. Ibid., 27.

143. Ibid., 117.

144. Ibid., 151.

145. Ibid., 1–2.

146. Ibid., 332.

147. Ibid., 333.

148. Ibid., 78.

149. Ibid., 194.

150. Ibid., 151.

151. Ibid., 611–12.

152. Ibid., 1.

153. Ibid., 61.

154. Ibid., 15.

155. Ibid., 144.

156. Ibid., 146.

157. Ibid., 155.

158. Ibid., 100.

159. Ibid., 101.

160. Renaud Evrard, "Parapsychology in France after May 1968: A History of GERP," *Journal of Scientific Exploration* 24, no. 2 (2010): 283–94.

161. Ibid., 132.

162. Ibid., 189.

163. Ibid., 160.

164. Ibid., 2.

165. Ibid., 223.

166. Mark R. Leary and Tom Butler, "Electronic Voice Phenomena," in *Parapsychology: A Handbook for the 21st Century*, eds. Etzel Cardeña, John Palmer, and David Marcusson-Clavertz (Jefferson, NC: McFarland and Company, 2015), 341.

167. Ibid., 7.

168. Ibid., 8.

169. Ibid., 25.

170. Ibid., 29.

171. Ibid., 31.

172. Ibid., 35.

173. Ibid., 38.

174. Ibid., 235.

175. Noakes, Richard. "Haunted Thoughts of the Careful Experimentalist: Psychical Research and the Troubles of Experimental Physics." *Studies in History and Philosophy of Biological and Biomedical Sciences* 48 (2014): 46.

176. Denise Paraná, Alexandre Caroli Rocha, Elizabeth Schmitt Freire, Francisco Lotufo Neto, and Alexander Moreira-Almeida, "An Empirical Investigation of Alleged Mediumistic Writing: A Case Study of Chico Xavier's Letters," *The Journal of Nervous and Mental Disease* 207 no. 6 (June 2019): 497.

177. Ibid., 502.

178. Julio Fernando Peres, Alexander Moreira-Almeida, Leonardo Caixeta, Frederico Leao, and Andrew Newberg, "Neuroimaging During Trance State: A Contribution to the Study of Dissociation," *PLos ONE* 7, no. 11 (November 2012): 4.

179. Ibid., 7.

180. Ibid., 189.

181. Ibid., 280.

182. Ibid., 280.

183. Ibid., 130.

184. Ibid., 43.

185. Lance Storm, Patrizio E. Tressoldi, and Lorenzo Di Risio, "Meta-Analysis of ESP Studies, 1987–2010: Assessing the Success of the Forced-Choice Design in Parapsychology," *Journal of Parapsychology* 76, no. 2 (Fall 2012): 244.

186. Fiona Steinkamp, Julie Milton, and Robert L. Morris, "A Meta-Analysis of Forced-Choice Experiments Comparing Clairvoyance and Precognition," *Journal of Parapsychology* 62, no. 3 (September 1998): 193–218.

187. Lance Storm, Patricio Tressoldi, and Lorenzo Di Risio, "Meta-Analysis of Free-Response Studies, 1992–2008: Assessing the Noise Reduction Model in Parapsychology," *Psychological Bulletin* 136, no. 4 (July 2010): 471–85.

188. Ibid., 91.

189. Ibid., 391.

190. Ibid., 22.

191. Ibid., 21.

4

Criticisms of Parapsychology

To have a well-rounded understanding of a topic, it is important to be aware of its critiques as well. In this chapter, I discuss the historical trajectory of criticisms of parapsychology and some of the main critiques that prevail today. A core annotated bibliography of these criticisms is presented at the end of the chapter as a set of resources to consult as you continue your own inquiry. Use them in tandem with all the other resources in this book to help obtain an even deeper understanding of parapsychology.

As discussed in chapter 1, tension that has been inherent within the field of parapsychology since its inception in the nineteenth century. Even prior, there have been tensions and criticisms aimed at those who sought to scientifically investigate anomalous phenomena. German physician Franz Anton Mesmer, for example, was ridiculed for his theories and research into animal magnetism. In the late 1700s, as a student at the University of Vienna, Mesmer wrote his dissertation on the ways in which planets influence the human body by interacting with an invisible, magnetic field that always surrounds us. This concept piqued the interest of some at the Royal Society of Medicine, but unfortunately Mesmer and his ideas were scorned by the academic community. What's fascinating about Mesmer's case, however, is that though shunned, his ideas inspired the discovery of induced sleepwalking, which further spurred research into and knowledge of hypnotism.[1]

Researcher Heather Wolffram reminds us of the "border science" status of psychical research *and* experimental psychology, and how conflicts taking place in nineteenth-century Germany

highlight the bitter multi-frontal battles that took place during the closing decades of [the nineteenth] century among German spiritists, psychical researchers and psychologists over the meaning and implications of the phenomena of the séance room. At stake in both of these debates was not only the question of whether spirits existed, but the parameters and proper object of the nascent field of psychology.[2]

Specifically, two different debates fanned the flames of attitudes toward psychical research in nineteenth-century Germany. The first major event centered around the infamous American medium Henry Slade. Slade, who fled to Germany in order to avoid legal trouble in England, began performing his séances there and attracted the attention of astrophysicist Johann Karl Friedrich Zöllner. Zöllner began studying Slade, even inviting colleagues to the University of Leipzig to take part and witness for themselves the strange abilities displayed by Slade. Zöllner was so impressed by the medium that he was convinced of the presence of some supernatural ability. A leading psychologist of the day, however, Wilhelm Wundt, published a scathing criticism of Slade and essentially squashed the future of psychical research for Zöllner. Wundt's critique not only established dominance over the competing field of psychical science, it also helped him establish a stronger foothold for his experimental psychology framework. However, Wolffram reminds us that "the Zöllner debate makes evident that the proponents of the new experimental psychology within Germany's universities, who sought to free psychology from philosophy and metaphysics by focusing on quantifiable conscious phenomena, had by no means established a monopoly over the mind by the closing decades of the 19th century."[3]

In addition to the Zöllner-Wundt debate there was also discussion raging, at very nearly the same time, between Alexander Askakow and Eduard von Hartmann. Hartmann, a philosopher, proposed that psychical phenomena are explainable by psychological concepts. For example, Hartmann believed that shared hallucination could account for sightings of apparitions. On the other hand, Alexander Askakow believed in spiritism, or that ghosts were unexplainable yet real manifestations of the spirit world. Here we see the animism versus spiritism debate.[4] Throughout all of this, Wolffram reminds us that each figure was engaging in border science, attempting to define the boundaries of *their* accepted theories while equally trying to affirm what reputable science is *not*.

Germany wasn't the only country navigating the boundaries of psychology, experimental psychology, and psychical science. In fact, a general air of interest in and awareness of supernatural concepts was sweeping across Europe at this time. Author Sofie Lachapelle captures this reality as she tells us,

> During the nineteenth century, numerous technological innovations and scientific advances transformed the consciousness and experience of Europeans. Across the continent, these advances and novelties blurred the lines between the natural and the supernatural. Human inventions seemed to be reaching into the realm of the fantastic. Telegraphs, photographs, and trains, to name a few, had brought about changes that would have appeared impossible to previous generations. Popularizers of science played with the sense of wonder that recent inventions inspired. . . . Science and technology created enchantment; they made the magical seem possible.[5]

Lachapelle goes on to tell us that this interest in the supernatural could be seen through an increased interest among laypeople. More and more people became fascinated by the scientific implications of the paranormal. Simultaneously, there was a growing interest in both spiritism and occultism in the mid-1800s. We see this particularly in France with the teachings of Allen Kardec and the growing popularity of séances. Lachapelle reminds us, though, "Spiritists and occultists were not the only ones interested in supernatural phenomena and mystical experiences. In their own way, turn of the century physicians, psychiatrists, and psychologists were widening their territory of inquiry and developing a sustained interest in the world of the supernatural."[6] However, even though there was a noticeable academic interest in things like mediumship and ghosts, what happened in Germany mirrors the reality of the situation in France as well. Division ensued among those who believed that these phenomena were rooted in mental pathology and those who believed that they carried spiritist implications into the survival of consciousness and life beyond death.

In addition to the tense rivalry between the fledgling disciplines of psychology and psychical science and the division of thought between animists and spiritists, researchers have had to contend with fraud in their studies. In England, one of the early works of the Society for Psychical Research was to ferret through cases that involved outright fraud, mistaken events, and/or just generally unreliable reporters.[7] Of course, people reporting paranormal experiences and/or abilities were not necessarily ill-intentioned. Today, we know that personality traits and belief are just two of the factors that work together to inform the ways in which we interpret various events.[8]

The intensity with which researchers focused on fraud was due largely in part to the activities of the séance room. Dim conditions and trickery proved to be ripe conditions that led many to believe in the veracity of a medium's ability. Notable and prolific psychical researcher Eleanor M. Sidgwick was skeptical of physical mediums. Sidgwick believed that eyewitnesses at séances simply did not consider the potential ways in which they were being fooled.[9]

Not every researcher was dubious of the abilities of mediums, however, and sometimes one medium could stymy researchers, leading some to believe and others not. There was even a huge schism within the American Society for Psychical Research (ASPR) surrounding the medium Mina (Margery) Crandon. She was so divisive that those who were adamant that her mediumship was genuine eventually broke from the ASPR and formed their own society, the Boston Society for Psychic Research (BSPR). The two groups eventually came back together, the BSPR becoming subsumed once again under the ASPR, but this is just one more example of how tense psi research has been, even among researchers who have a shared goal of investigating the anomalous.[10]

A unique perspective on the problems of the scientific study of parapsychology can be seen in an article written by J. B. Rhine in 1947 in the *Journal of Parapsychology*. Rhine points out that many parapsychologists find that the rigors and standards of the scientific method hinder the success of anomalous phenomena. Rhine tells us that some researchers were "not ready to grant that rigorous experimental investigation is adequate to deal with all of the realm of nature that they claim for parapsychology."[11] Naturally, one can imagine the response from critics upon hearing these viewpoints.

In more recent times, Rhine points out that a main concern of researchers still involves the possibility of fraud, specifically fraudulent subjects. This echoes the early work of the British SPR, and particularly the work of Eleanor Sidgwick, who spent a lot of time ferreting out cases that involved outright fraud and mistaken experiences.[12] In a 1974 article in the *Journal of Parapsychology*, Rhine tells us how important this concern was for researchers:

> In the thirties the issue of deception by *subjects* had to be faced. It had become so fiercely controversial in the earlier days of emphasis on mediumship and stage demonstrations of psychic claims that the topic of fraud on the part of the subject was extremely sensitive. The very idea of allowing any possible subject trickery came to be considered as a mockery of science and to be such a dereliction on the part of any experimenter who would allow the loose contributory conditions as to be unthinkable in a department of psychology or on a university campus. Fortunately, at the time the solution was relatively simple to anyone used to the more objective sciences. It was comparable to the insistence on the use of clean glassware or pure substances in a chemical laboratory. At the Duke Parapsychology Laboratory we took the firm position that a subject should not be trusted at all; even if he were a priest or the experimenter's best friend, the conditions must be such that cheating would not be possible. This radical objectivity alienated many workers, but in time it brought dependability on this issue.[13]

Moving on from the concern of fraudulent subjects, researcher John Palmer tells us that the leading critique of parapsychology from the 1960s through 1980 was that both subjects and *experimenters* were engaging in fraud.[14] The main proponent of this argument, Palmer tells us, was psychologist C. E. M. Hansel who published numerous articles and books highly critical of parapsychology. Experimenter fraud, while not a main critique today, has been discovered in some studies. For example, in June 1973, researchers at Rhine's parapsychology lab caught one of their colleagues, Dr. Walter Levy, intentionally manipulating an experiment involving psychokinesis in rats.[15]

Researcher D. Scott Rogo provides a breakdown of some of the most common criticisms in his 1977 article in the *Humanist*. Rogo tells us,

> Criticism could be grouped into nine major objections: that the results . . . are not repeatable; that the possibility of fraud contaminates many allegedly conclusive experiments; that parapsychologists use improper mathematical methods when analyzing their data; that ESP and PK are a priori impossible; that parapsychologists misinterpret their evidence; that the existence of ESP has no relevance to organized science; and that parapsychologists use inadequate experimental designs; disagree on the quality of the evidence; and are biased in favor of the existence of psi.[16]

Rogo offers a rebuttal that many of these criticisms seem emotionally charged and are, at times, incorrect. For example, he tells us that many parapsychologists borrow tried and true designs from their colleagues in the realm of experimental psychology and that professional statistical organizations have reviewed parapsychology data and found no qualms with the data. Rogo goes on to present an example of a well-designed psi study, that of the Maimonides Dream Lab studies.[17]

Rogo's article was written in the 1970s, but even in the 1980s we saw similar criticisms directed at parapsychological studies. For example, C. L. Hardin writes,

> According to skeptics, all of the experiments of parapsychology [can] be divided into two classes. The first class consists of experiments which are . . . poorly controlled and thus inconclusive. Those of the second class are properly controlled according to the standards of 'normal' psychological research, but contain insufficient safeguards against fraud.[18]

A 1996 article in *The New York Times* highlights that another common criticism of parapsychological research is that even if statistically significant data is obtained, it is weak. In other words, it's not overwhelming, and critics point this out. In that same article, however, parapsychologist Dean Radin offers a rebuttal to that argument. He informs us that even though data might be weak, it still tells us that *something* is happening, even if it's on a small scale and even if we don't quite know what it is yet.[19]

Today, to counteract some of these prevailing criticisms, John Palmer tells us that meta-analyses are a high standard for determining the validity and significance of psi research. He points out, however, a disturbing resurgence of critics that seem to be dredging up the experimenter fraud hypothesis.[20] Palmer isn't the only researcher who has noticed a stagnation of critiques from past to present. In a 2017 article in the *Journal of Parapsychology*, Chris A. Roe reviewed and compared critiques of parapsychology from 1993 to 2010 and found that they were primarily still the same.[21] In this same article, Roe discusses one irony surrounding critics of parapsychology. Roe tells us, "[Charles Honorton] . . . reflected on the exceptional situation in parapsychology in which most counter-advocates were not empirical researchers engaged in psi research, so that their counter-explanations tended to be evaluated on the basis of *plausibility* rather than on the basis of *evidence derived from direct empirical tests.*"[22]

As we can see, there are a number of criticisms surrounding parapsychological research. From weak data, possibilities of fraud, and concerns about experimental designs, it is clear that opinions about the value of psi research are extremely divided within the academy. There are even tensions among parapsychologists, though that seems more attributable to simply being a natural byproduct of scholars with differing theories and preferred methods. Constructive criticism and debate are, after all, core components of advancing our understanding of any particular topic. Parapsychology is far from a tidy discipline. As can be seen from the discussion above, it never has been. Today, parapsychologists continue to add to the scientific literature of this liminal discipline and will continue to study all manner of anomalous phenomena where new questions (and critiques) will arise. We should be cautious, though, to not dwell entirely in the realm of criticism, but should rather be aware of the potential weaknesses so we can best understand the topic at hand. The trajectory of any discipline shows how ideas, expectations, and experimental design have changed to allow for a more authentically scientific pursuit, and critique has a natural place within that process. Below are resources you can consult to advance your understanding of the criticisms of parapsychological research.

RESOURCES FOR CRITICISMS WITHIN PARAPSYCHOLOGY

Alcock, James. *Parapsychology: Science or Magic?* New York: Pergamon Press, 1981.

Baptista, Johann and Max Derakhshani. "Beyond the Coin Toss: Examining Wiseman's Criticisms of Parapsychology." *Journal of Parapsychology* 78, no. 1 (Spring 2014): 56–79.

Bauer, Eberhard. "Criticism and Controversies in Parapsychology: An Overview." *European Journal of Parapsychology* 5, no. 2 (1984): 141–65.

Bierman, Dick J., James P. Spottiswoode, and Aron Bijl. "Testing for Questionable Research Practices in a Meta-Analysis: An Example from Experimental Parapsychology." *PLoS One* 11, no. 5 (May 2016): 1–18.

Blackmore S. Psychic Experiences: Psychic Illusions. *Skeptical Inquirer* 16 (1992): 367–76.

Diaconis, Persi. "Statistical Problems in ESP Research." *Science* 201 (July 14, 1978): 131–36.

Girden, Edward. "A Review of Psychokinesis (PK)." *Psychological Bulletin* 59, no. 5 (September 1962): 353–88.

Hardin, C. L. "Table-Turning, Parapsychology and Fraud." *Social Studies of Science* 11, no. 2 (May 1981): 249–55.

Hart, Hornell. "Do Apparitions of the Dead Imply any Intention on the Part of the Agent? A Rejoinder to Louisa E. Rhine." *Journal of Parapsychology* 22, no. 1 (March 1958): 59–63.

Hyman, Ray. "The Case Against Parapsychology." *Humanist* 37, no. 6 (November 1, 1977): 47–49.

Hyman, Ray. "[Replication and Meta-Analysis in Parapsychology]: Comment." *Statistical Science* 6, no. 4 (November 1991): 389–92.

Kennedy, J. E. "Why is Psi So Elusive? A Review and Proposed Model." *Journal of Parapsychology* 65 (2001): 219–46.

———. "Can Parapsychology Move Beyond the Controversies of Retrospective Meta-Analyses?" *Journal of Parapsychology* 77, no. 1 (Spring 2013): 21–37.

Kennedy, John L. and Howard F. Uphoff. "Experiments on the Nature of Extra-Sensory Perception, III: The Recording Error Criticism of Extra-

Chance Scores." *Journal of Parapsychology* 3, no. 2 (December 1, 1939): 226–45.

Musch, Jochen and Katja Ehrenberg. "Probability Misjudgment, Cognitive Ability, and Belief in the Paranormal." *British Journal of Psychology* 93 (May 2002): 169–77.

Pinch, Trevor J. "Normal Explanations of the Paranormal: The Demarcation Problem and Fraud in Parapsychology." *Social Studies of Science* 9, no. 3 (August 1979): 329–48.

Reber, Arthur S. and James E. Alcock. "Searching for the Impossible: Parapsychology's Elusive Quest." *American Psychologist* 75, no. 3 (April 2020): 391–99.

Stanford, Rex G. "Is Scientific Parapsychology Possible? (Some Thoughts on James E. Alcock's 'Parapsychology: Science or Magic?'). *Journal of Parapsychology* 46, no. 3 (September 1, 1982): 231–71.

Stokes, Douglas M. "White Crows Rising: Using Spontaneous Cases to Establish Psi." *Australian Journal of Parapsychology* 17, no. 1 (June 2017): 47–60.

Walker, Evan Harris. "A Review of Criticisms of the Quantum Mechanical Theory of Psi Phenomena." *Journal of Parapsychology* 48 (1984): 277–332.

Wiseman, Richard S. "Heads I Win, Tails You Lose: How Some Parapsychologists Nullify Null Results and What to do About It." In *Debating Psychic Experience: Human Potential or Human Illusion?* Edited by Stanley Krippner and Harris L. Friedman, 169–78. Santa Barbara, CA: Praeger, 2010.

Zingrone, Nancy L. "Controversy and the Problems of Parapsychology." *Journal of Parapsychology* 66, no. 1 (March 2002): 3–30.

NOTES

1. Charles Richet, *Thirty Years of Psychical Research: Being a Treatise on Metaphysics.* New York: Macmillan, 1923: 15–23.

2. Heather Wolffram, "Hallucination or Materialization? The Animism versus Spiritism Debate in Late 19th-Century Germany," *History of the Human Sciences* 25, no. 2 (2012): 46.

3. Ibid., 48–49.

4. Ibid., 48–52.

5. Sofie Lachapelle, *Investigating the Supernatural: From Spiritism and Occultism to Psychical Research and Metaphysics in France, 1853–1931.* Baltimore. MD: Johns Hopkins University Press, 2011: 1–2.

6. Ibid., 5.

7. Renée Haynes, *The Society for Psychical Research, 1882–1982: A History.* London: Macdonald & Co., 1982: 20–29.

8. Kathryn H. Gow, Louise Hutchinson, and David Chant, "Correlations Between Fantasy Proneness, Dissociation, Personality Factors and Paranormal Beliefs in Experiencers of Paranormal and Anomalous Phenomena," *Australian Journal of Clinical and Experimental Hypnosis* 37, no. 2 (November 2009): 169–91.

9. Carlos S. Alvarado, "Eleanor M. Sidgwick (1845–1936)," *Journal of Parapsychology* 82, no. 2 (Fall 2018): 127–31.

10. Arthur S. Berger and Joyce Berger, *The Encyclopedia of Parapsychology and Psychical Research* (New York: Paragon House, 1991), 83.

11. J. B. Rhine, "Impatience with Scientific Method in Parapsychology," *Journal of Parapsychology* 11, no. 4 (December 1, 1947): 283–95.

12. Haynes, *The Society*, 28–29.

13. J. B. Rhine, "Comments: A New Case of Experimenter Unreliability," *Journal of Parapsychology* 38, no. 2 (June 1, 1974): 221.

14. John Palmer, "Hansel's Ghost: Resurrection of the Experimenter Fraud Hypothesis in Parapsychology," *Journal of Parapsychology* 80, no. 1 (Spring 2016): 5–16.

15. Rhine, "Comments," 215–25.

16. D. Scott Rogo, "The Case for Parapsychology," *Humanist* 37, no. 6 (November 1, 1977): 40–44.

17. Ibid., 40–44.

18. C. L. Hardin, "Table-Turning, Parapsychology and Fraud," *Social Studies of Science* 11, no. 2 (May 1981): 249.

19. Chip Brown, "They Laughed at Galileo Too." *New York Times*, August 11, 1996: SM41.

20. Palmer, "Hansel's Ghost," 6.

21. Chris A. Roe, "PA Presidential Address 2017: Withering Skepticism," *Journal of Parapsychology* 81, no. 2 (Fall 2017): 143–59.

22. Ibid., 144.

Appendix A

Topical Bibliographies to Get You Started!

In this appendix, you will find lists of topical citations that serve as a core starting point for various topics. These lists are not comprehensive but serve as a quick, ready-reference list that you can use to begin reading about phenomena in which you are most interested. Many of these citations are found annotated in chapter 3 if you'd like to read a summary of their findings. However, *not all* citations listed below are included in chapter 3. This appendix is, therefore, an attempt to provide even more citations to the overwhelming body of parapsychological literature that exists. Because this appendix serves merely as a place to get started with your reading interests, don't forget to consult chapter 3 to find *even more* topics and research beyond what you find here.

You will also note that some of the citations below could easily be placed into multiple categories, for instance, research on hypnotism and trance can often be categorized with mediumship research. This is another reminder of the fluidity of psi research, so keep this in mind as you consult the brief, quick-start guide below.

Remember, too, that there are numerous ways to access the resources listed here (and throughout this book). Many of the historical resources published prior to the 1920s can be found in at hathitrust.org and/or via Google Scholar. Some of the contemporary citations can also be found in Google Scholar too. Don't forget that you can consult your local libraries as well and if they don't not have immediate access, ask the librarian about the process of interlibrary loan.

EXTRASENSORY PERCEPTION (INCLUDING CLAIRVOYANCE, ESP/GESP, PRECOGNITION, AND TELEPATHY)

Barrington, Mary Rose, Ian Stevenson, and Zofia Weaver. *A World in a Grain of Sand: The Clairvoyance of Stefan Ossowiecki.* Jefferson, NC: McFarland & Company, 2005.

Cook, C. M. and M. A. Persinger. "Experimental Induction of the 'Sensed Presence' in Normal Subjects and an Exceptional Subject." *Perceptual and Motor Skills* 85 (1997): 683–93

Corliss, William R. *The Unfathomed Mind: A Handbook of Unusual Mental Phenomena.* Glen Arm, MD: The Sourcebook Project, 1982.

Franklin, Christine Ladd. "Richet on Mental Suggestion." *Science* 5 no. 106 (February 13, 1885): 132–34.

Hagio, Shigeki. "An ESP Experiment on a Mountain-Top." *Japanese Journal of Parapsychology* 2, no. 2 (November 25, 1997): 100–107.

Houtkooper, Joop M., Anne Schienle, Rudolf Stark, and Dieter Vaitl. "Geophysical Variables and Behavior LXXXVIII: The Possible Disturbing Influence of Natural Sferics on ESP." *Perceptual and Motor Skills* 89 (1999): 1179–92.

Mossbridge, Julia and Dean Radin. "Psi Performance as a Function of Demographic and Personality Factors in Smartphone-Based Tests: Using a 'SEARCH' Approach." *Journal of Anomalous Experience and Cognition* 1, no. 1–2 (2021): 78–113.

Persinger, Michael A. "Spontaneous Telepathic Experiences from *Phantasms of the Living* and

Low Global Geomagnetic Activity." *Journal of the American Society for Psychical Research* 81 (January 1987): 23–36.

Rhine, J. B. *New Frontiers of the Mind: The Story of the Duke Experiments.* New York: Farrar & Rinehart, 1937.

Rhine, Louisa E. "Hallucinatory Psi Experiences I: An Introductory Survey." *Journal of Parapsychology* 20, no. 4 (December 1, 1956): 233–56.

Rhine, Louisa E. *Psi: What is It? The Story of ESP and PK.* New York: Harper and Row, 1975. Schmeidler, Gertrude R. "Psi-Conducive Experimenters and Psi-Permissive Ones." *European Journal of Parapsychology* 13 (1997): 83–94.

Sheldrake, Rupert. "Psi in Everyday Life: Nonhuman and Human." In *Parapsychology: A Handbook for the 21st Century*, edited by Etzel Cardeña, John Palmer, and David Marcusson-Clavertz, 350–63. Jefferson: McFarland and Company, 2015.

Shiah, Yung-Jong. "A Proposed Process for Experiencing Visual Images of Targets during as ESP Task." *Journal of Parapsychology* 75, no. 1 (Spring 2011): 129–43.

Sidgwick, Eleanor Mildred. "Experiments in Thought-Transference." *The New Review* 7, no. 40 (September 1892): 306–15.

Storm, Lance, Patrizio E. Tressoldi, and Lorenzo Di Risio. "Meta-Analysis of ESP Studies, 1987–2010: Assessing the Success of the Forced-Choice Design in Parapsychology." *Journal of Parapsychology* 76, no. 2 (Fall 2012): 243–73.

Thalbourne, M. A. "An Attempt to Predict Precognition Scores Using Transliminality-Relevant Variables." *Journal of the Society for Psychical Research* 61 (1996): 129–40.

Wahbeh, Helané, Dean Radin, Julia Mossbridge, Cassandra Vieten, and Arnaud Delorme. "Exceptional Experiences Reported by Scientists and Engineers." *Explore* 14, no. 5 (September/October 2018): 329–41.

Watt, Caroline, Emily Dawson, Alisdair Tullo, Abby Pooley, and Holly Rice. "Testing Precognition and Alterations of Consciousness with Selected Participants in the Ganzfeld." *Journal of Parapsychology* 84, no. 1 (Spring 2020): 21–37.

GHOSTS AND HAUNTINGS

Barrett, W. F., A. P. Percival Keep, C. C. Massey, Hensleigh Wedgwood, Frank Podmore, and E. R. Pease. "First Report of the Committee on Haunted Houses." *Proceedings of the Society for Psychical Research* 1, no. 1 (1882): 101–15.

Braithwaite, Jason J. and Maurice Townsend. "Research Note: Sleeping With the Enemy—A Quantitative Magnetic Investigation of an English Castle's Reputedly 'Haunted' Bedroom" *European Journal of Parapsychology* 20, no. 1 (2005): 65–78.

Evrard, Renaud. "Ghost in the Machine: A Clinical View of Anomalous Telecommunication Experiences." *Journal of Exceptional Experiences and Psychology* 5, no. 2 (Winter 2017): 21–30.

Gurney, Edmund, Frederic W. H. Myers, and Frank Podmore. *Phantasms of the Living.* London: Kegan Paul, Trench, Trubner, and Co., 1918.

Leary, Mark R. and Tom Butler. "Electronic Voice Phenomena." In *Parapsychology: A Handbook for the 21st Century,* edited by Etzel Cardeña, John Palmer, and David Marcusson-Clavertz, 341–49. Jefferson, NC: McFarland and Company, 2015.

Maher, Michaeleen. "Ghosts and Poltergeists: An Eternal Enigma." In *Parapsychology: A Handbook for the 21st Century,* edited by Etzel Cardeña, John Palmer, and David Marcusson-Clavertz, 327–29. Jefferson: McFarland and Company, 2015.

McCue, P. A. "Theories of Haunting: A Critical Overview." *Journal of the Society for Psychical Research* 60 (2002): 1–21.

Storm, Lance and Robb Tilley. "Haunt and Poltergeist Clearing in Australian Residences: A Retrospective Survey." *Australian Journal of Parapsychology* 20, no. 1 (2020): 21–55.

Wiseman, R., C. Watt, E. Greening, P. Stevens, and C. O'Keeffe. "An Investigation into the Alleged Haunting of Hampton Court Palace: Psychological Variables and Magnetic Fields." *Journal of Parapsychology* 66 (2002): 387–408.

HISTORY OF PSYCHICAL AND PARAPSYCHOLOGICAL RESEARCH (GENERAL DISCUSSIONS BOTH HISTORIC AND MODERN)

Alvarado, Carlos S. "The Concept of Survival of Bodily Death and the Development of Parapsychology." *Journal of the Society for Psychical Research* 67, no. 2 (April 2003): 65–95.

Beloff, John. *Parapsychology: A Concise History.* New York: St. Martin's Press, 1993.

Brancaccio, Maria Teresa. "Enrico Morselli's *Psychology* and *'Spiritism'*: Psychiatry, Psychology and Psychical Research in Italy in the Decades around 1900." *Studies in History and Philosophy of Biological and Biomedical Sciences* 48 (2014): 75–84.

Delgado, L Anne. "Psychical Research and the Fantastic Science of Spirits." In *Strange Science: Investigating the Limits of Knowledge in the Victorian Age.* Edited by Lara Karpenko and Shalyn Claggett, 236–53. Ann Arbor: University of Michigan Press, 2016.

Gissurarson, Loftur Reimar and Erlendur Haraldsson. "History of Parapsychology in Iceland." *International Journal of Parapsychology* 12, no. 1 (2001): 29–50.

Haynes, Renée. *The Society for Psychical Research, 1882–1982, a History.* London: Macdonald, 1982.

James, William. "Address of the President Before the Society for Psychical Research." *Science* 3, no. 77 (June 19, 1896): 881–88.

Kloosterman, Ingrid. "Psychical Research and Parapsychology Interpreted: Suggestions from the International Historiography of Psychical Research and Parapsychology for Investigating its History in the Netherlands," *History of the Human Sciences* 25, no. 2 (2012): 2–22.

Oppenheim, Janet. *The Other World: Spiritualism and Psychical Research in England, 1850–1914.* Cambridge: Cambridge University Press, 1985.

Phelps, Elizabeth Stuart. "The Great Psychical Opportunity." *The North American Review* 141, no. 346 (September 1885): 251–66.

Podmore, Frank. "What Psychical Research Has Accomplished." *The North American Review* 160, no. 460 (March 1895): 331–44.

Sommer, Andreas. "Normalizing the Supernormal: The Formation of the 'Gesellschaft Für Psychologische Forschung' ('Society for Psychological Research')," *Journal of the History of the Behavioral Sciences* 49, no. 1 (Winter 2013): 18–44.

Sommer, Andreas. "Psychical Research and the Origins of American Psychology: Hugo Münsterberg, William James and Eusapia Palladino," in *History of the Human Sciences* 25, no. 2 (April 2012): 23–44.

Takasuna, Miki. "The Fukurai Affair: Parapsychology and the History of Psychology in Japan." *History of the Human Sciences* 25, no. 2 (2012): 149–64.

Timms, Joanna. "Ghost-Hunters and Psychical Research in Interwar England." *History Workshop Journal* no. 74 (Autumn 2012): 88–104.

Wolffram, Heather. *The Stepchildren of Science: Psychical Research and Parapsychology in Germany, c. 1870–1939.* Amsterdam: Rodopi, 2009.

Zingrone, Nancy and Carlos S. Alvarado. "Historical Aspects of Parapsychological Terminology." *Journal of Parapsychology* 51 (March 1987): 49–74.

HYPNOTISM AND TRANCE

Fahler, Jarl and Remi J. Cadoret. "ESP Card Test of College Students with and without Hypnosis." In *Basic Research in Parapsychology,* 2nd edition. Edited by K. Ramakrishna Rao, 251–61. Jefferson: McFarland and Company, 2001.

Gurney, Edmund. "Further Problems of Hypnotism." *Mind* 12, no. 47 (July 1887): 397–422.

Marcusson-Clavertz, David and Etzel Cardeña. "Hypnotizability, Alterations in Consciousness, and Other Variables as Predictors of Performance in a Ganzfeld Psi Task." *Journal of Parapsychology* 75, no. 2 (Fall 2011): 235–59.

Peres, Julio Fernando, Alexander Moreira-Almeida, Leonardo Caixeta, Frederico Leao, and Andrew Newberg. "Neuroimaging During Trance State: A Contribution to the Study of Dissociation." *PLoS ONE* 7, no. 11 (November 2012): 1–9.

Sommer, Andreas. "Professional Heresy: Edmund Gurney (1847–1888) and the Study of Hallucinations and Hypnotism" *Medical History* 55. no. 3 (July 2011): 383–88.

Thalbourne, Michael A. "Transliminality, Anomalous Belief and Experience, and Hypnotisability." *Australian Journal of Clinical and Experimental Hypnosis* 37, no. 2 (November 2009): 119–30.

Wilde, David J. and Craig D. Murray. "An Interpretative Phenomenological Analysis of Out-of-Body Experiences in Two Cases of Novice Meditators." *Australian Journal of Clinical and Experimental Hypnosis* 37, no. 2 (2009): 90–118.

MEDIUMSHIP

Alvarado, Carlos S. "Mediumship, Psychical Research, Dissociation, and the Powers of the Subconscious Mind," *Journal of Parapsychology* 78, no. 1 (March 2014): 98–114.

Alvarado, Carlos S. "'Report of the Committee on Mediumistic Phenomena,' by William James (1886)." *History of Psychiatry* 27, no. 1 (2016): 85–100.

Beischel, Julie and Adam J. Rock. "Addressing the Survival Versus Psi Debate Through Process-Focused Mediumship Research." *Journal of Parapsychology* 73 (Spring 2009): 71–90.

Beischel, Julie. "Contemporary Methods Used in Laboratory-Based Mediumship Research." *Journal of Parapsychology* 71 (Spring 2007): 37–68.

Delorme, Arnaud, Julie Beischel, Leena Michel, Mark Boccuzzi, Dean Radin, and Paul J. Mills. "Electrocortical Activity Associated with Subjective Communication with the Deceased." *Frontiers in Psychology* 4 (November 2013): 1–10.

Graus, Andrea. "Discovering Palladino's Mediumship, Otero Acevedo, Lombroso and The Quest for Authority." *Journal of the History of the Behavioral Sciences* 52, no. 3 (Summer 2016): 211–30.

Hoffmann, Guilia Katherine. "Otherworldly Impressions: Female Mediumship in Britain and America in the Nineteenth and Early Twentieth Centuries." PhD diss., University of California, 2014.

Kelly, Emily Williams. "An Investigation of Mediums who Claim to Give Information About Deceased Persons." *Journal of Nervous and Mental Disease* 199, no. 1 (January 2011).

Paraná, Denise, Alexandre Caroli Rocha, Elizabeth Schmitt Freire, Francisco Lotufo Neto, and Alexander Moreira-Almeida. "An Empirical Investigation of Alleged Mediumistic Writing: A Case Study of Chico Xavier's Letters." *Journal of Nervous and Mental Disease 207,* no. 6 (June 2019): 497–504.

Rock, Adam J., Julie Beischel, Mark Boccuzzi, and Michael Biuso. "Discarnate Readings by Claimant Mediums: Assessing Phenomenology and Accuracy Under Beyond Double-Blind Conditions." *Journal of Parapsychology* 78, no. 2 (Fall 2014): 183–94.

Roxburgh, Elizabeth C. and Chris A. Roe. "A Survey of Dissociation, Boundary-Thinness, and Psychological Wellbeing in Spiritualist Mental Mediumship." *Journal of Parapsychology* 75, no. 2 (Fall 2011): 279–99

Sidgwick, Eleanor M. "An Examination of Book-Tests Obtained in Sittings with Mrs. Leonard." *Proceedings of the Society for Psychical Research* 31 (1921): 241–400.

NEAR-DEATH EXPERIENCES

Fenwick, Peter and Elizabeth. *The Truth in the Light: An Investigation of Over 300 Near-Death Experiences.* London: Headline, 1995.

Greyson, Bruce. "A Typology of Near-Death Experiences," *American Journal of Psychiatry,* 142 (1985): 967–69.

Introvigne, Massimo. "The Social Construction of Near-Death Experiences: The Betty Eadie Case." *La Critica Sociologica* 117–118 (April 1996): 78–88.

Kelly, Emily Williams. "Near-Death Experiences with Reports of Meeting Deceased People." *Death Studies* 25, no. 3 (April/May 2001): 229–49.

Lommel, Pim van. "Non-local Consciousness: A Concept Based on Scientific Research on Near-Death Experiences During Cardiac Arrest." *Journal of Consciousness Studies* 20, no. 1–2 (2013): 7–48.

Osis, Karlis and Erlendur Haraldsson, "Deathbed Observations by Physicians and Nurses: A Cross-Cultural Study," *Journal of the American Society for Psychical Research* 71, no. 3 (July 1977): 237–59.

POLTERGEISTS

Houran, James and Rense Lange. "A Rasch Hierarchy of Haunt and Poltergeist Experiences." *Journal of Parapsychology* 65 (March 2001): 41–58.

Kruth, John G. and William T. Joines. "Taming the Ghost Within: An Approach Toward Addressing Apparent Electronic Poltergeist Activity." *Journal of Parapsychology* 80, no. 1 (Spring 2016): 70–86.

Layard, J. "Psi Phenomena and Poltergeists." *Proceedings of the Society for Psychical Research* 47 (1944): 237–47.

Mulacz, Peter. "Historical Profiles in Poltergeist Research." In *From Shaman to Scientist: Essays on Humanity's Search for Spirits,* edited by James

Houran, 127–90. Lanham, MD: The Scarecrow Press, 2004.

Pratt, J. G. and W. G. Roll. "The Seaford Disturbances." *Journal of Parapsychology* 22, no. 2 (June 1958): 79–124.

Roll, W. G., and M. A. Persinger. "Investigations of Poltergeists and Haunts: A Review and Interpretation. In *Hauntings and Poltergeists: Multidisciplinary Perspectives,* edited by J. Houran and R. Lange, 123–63. Jefferson, North Carolina: McFarland & Company, Inc., 2001.

Roll, William G. "Poltergeists, Electromagnetism, and Consciousness." *Journal of Scientific Exploration* 17, no. 1 (2003): 75–86.

PSYCHOKINESIS

Bösch, H., F. Steinkamp, and E. Boller. "Examining Psychokinesis: The Interaction of Human Intention with Random Number Generators: A Meta-Analysis." *Psychological Bulletin* 132 (2006): 497–523.

Broughton, Richard S. and James R. Perlstrom. "PK Experiments with a Competitive Computer Game." *Journal of Parapsychology* 50, no. 3 (September 1, 1986): 193–211.

Heath, P. R. "The PK Zone: A Phenomenological Study." *Journal of Parapsychology* 64 (2000): 53–72.

Kennedy, J. E. "The Role of Task Complexity in PK: A Review." *Journal of Parapsychology* 42 (1978): 89–122.

Pratt, J. G. "The Case for Psychokinesis." *Journal of Parapsychology* 24, no. 3 (September 1, 1960): 171–88.

Pratt, J. Gaither and H. H. J. Keil. "Firsthand Observations of Nina S. Kulagina Suggestive of PK upon Static Objects." *Journal of the American Society for Psychical Research* 67 (1973): 381–90.

Rhine, J. B. and Betty M. Humphrey. "The PK Effect: Special Evidence from Hit Patterns." *Journal of Parapsychology* 8, no. 1 (March 1, 1944): 18–60.

Roll, William G. and William T. Joines. "RSPK and Consciousness." *Journal of Parapsychology* 77, no. 2 (2013): 192–211.

Thouless, Robert H. "A Report on an Experiment in Psychokinesis with Dice and a Discussion on Psychological Factors Favoring Success." *Journal of Parapsychology* 15, no. 2 (June 1, 1951): 89–102.

Appendix B

Journals Where You Can Find Parapsychology-Related Topics

The list below includes various scholarly journals in which you can find research on parapsychological topics. Some of them are specifically aimed at parapsychology while others merely *include* parapsychological research within their scope. These journals, international in scope, all currently publish editions of research, though some of them are much older than others. Remember that some of these journals (or some of the contents of these journals) are available through hathitrust.org and/or Google Scholar. To access others, consult your local public or academic libraries.

For a list of historic journals and publications that offer a wide range of topics relating to psychical research, Spiritualism, and parapsychology, consult Carlos S. Alvarado, Massimo Biondi, and Wim Kramer, "Historical Notes on Psychic Phenomena in Specialised Journals," *European Journal of Parapsychology* 21, no. 1 (2006): 58–87, which is freely accessible online. In this article, you will find information on historic publications from Italy, England, France, the Netherlands, Germany, Brazil, and the United States. Most of the resources listed in this article are no longer published but are wonderful resources for locating historic psychical scholarship.

American Journal of Hospice and Palliative Medicine
American Psychologist
Australian Journal of Clinical and Experimental Hypnosis
Australian Journal of Parapsychology
Consciousness and Cognition
Cosmos and History: The Journal of Natural and Social Philosophy
Ethos

European Journal of Parapsychology
Explore: The Journal of Science and Healing
F1000Research
Frontiers in Psychology
The Historical Journal
History of the Human Sciences
History of Psychiatry
International Journal of Clinical and Experimental Hypnosis
International Journal of Yoga—Philosophy, Psychology and Parapsychology
The International Journal of Psychoanalysis
Journal for Spiritual and Consciousness Studies
The Journal of Alternative and Complementary Medicine
Journal of American History
Journal of the American Society for Psychical Research
Journal of Anomalous Experience and Cognition
Journal of Exceptional Experiences and Psychology
Journal of Experimental Psychology
Journal of the History of the Behavioural Sciences
Journal of the History of the Neurosciences
Journal of Humanistic Psychology
Journal of Near-Death Studies
Journal of Nervous and Mental Disease
Journal of Parapsychology
Journal of Personality and Social Psychology
Journal of Religion and Psychical Research
Journal of Research into the Paranormal
Journal of the Society for Psychical Research
Journal of Scientific Exploration
Journal of Spirituality and Paranormal Studies
Lancet
Nature

Perceptual and Motor Skills
Proceedings of the American Society for Psychical Research
Proceedings of the Society for Psychical Research
Quaderni di Parapsicologia (Parapsychology Notebooks)

Spirituality in Clinical Practice
Victorian Studies
Zeitschrift für Anomalistik (Journal for Anomalistics)
Zeitschrift für Parapsychologie und Grenzgebiete der Psychologie (Journal for Parapsychology and Frontier Areas of Psychology)

Appendix C

Parapsychological Research Organizations

In this appendix, you will find a list of international parapsychological research organizations that you can consult to find even more information on the topics presented in this book. Some of these organizations are independent institutions while others are affiliated with universities and/or subsumed under other professional institutions. All of them serve as more tools to add to your research toolkit and are especially helpful as many focus on the importance of providing educational resources on the anomalous.

American Society for Psychical Research
Australian Institute of Parapsychological Research
Austrian Society for Parapsychology and Frontier Areas of Science
Center for Research on Consciousness and Anomalous Psychology (CERCEP) at Lund University
Centro Studi Parapsicologici (Center for Parapsychological Studies of Bologna)
Division of Perceptual Studies at the University of Virginia
Gesellshaft fur Psychologische Forschung (Society for Psychological Research)

Heymans Anomalous Cognition Group at the University of Groningen
Institut Métapsychique International (International Metaphysical Institute)
Institut für Grenzgebiete der Psychologie und Psychohygiene (Institute for Frontier Areas of Psychology and Mental Health)
Institute of Noetic Sciences
Japanese Society for Parapsychology
Koestler Parapsychology Unit at the University of Edinburgh
Parapsychological Association
Parapsychology Foundation
Psychical Research Foundation
Public Parapsychology
Rhine Research Center
Society for Psychical Research
Studievereniging der Psychical Research (Dutch Society for Psychical Research)
Windbridge Research Center
Wissenshaftliche Gesellschaft zur Forderung der Parapsychologie (Scientific Society for the Advancement of Parapsychology)

Glossary

While previous chapters introduce prominent figures and seminal research, this glossary provides definitions and overviews of parapsychological phenomena, theories, cases, resources, organizations, and more. Arranged alphabetically, it's designed to provide basic definitions and introductions to a wide variety of items associated with parapsychology. Many of the entries include a "further reading" note in order to locate additional information on various topics.

Like previous chapters, this glossary is not an exhaustive list of all terms associated with parapsychology, but aims, rather, to present a core body of terms for those new or relatively unfamiliar with parapsychology. This glossary includes both historic and modern terms.

Absorption: Absorption is a concept first developed by Tellegen and Atkinson in the 1970s and 1980s. It refers to "an openness to self-altering experiences."[1] Early researchers studying hypnotism began to notice that some subjects seemed to be completely immersed in their imagined realities, which led to the concept and role of absorption within certain altered states. In regard to psi phenomena, many people who have experienced an anomalous event tend to rank high on traits of absorption. For example, researchers Roe and Holt discuss psychokinesis experiments that look at traits relating to absorption and point out that "successful PK [might involve] resonance or absorption and the shutting out of cognitive interference."[2]

Further Reading:

Harvey Irwin, "Parapsychological Phenomena and the Absorption Domain," *Journal of the American Society for Psychical Research* 79, no. 1 (January 1985): 1–11.

Affectability: Affectability is a "psychological condition enhancing the probability of extra-chance scoring,"[3] and in general, refers to factors that affect the outcome of some event. In the 1940s, researcher Charles Stuart was inspired by the card-guessing tests done by J. B. Rhine and colleagues at the Duke Parapsychology Labs and wanted to investigate additional personality traits or factors that might be at play in these experiments. He began to wonder how success rates might be impacted if the subjects were asked to provide guesses at their success or failure after each card guess. Subjects would also know the score on their previous guess, which was a factor in Stuart's study as well. He discovered some relationships between guesses and scoring, spawning interest in future affectability studies.

Further Reading:

Charles E. Stuart, "An Analysis to Determine a Test Predictive of Extra-Chance Scoring in Card-Calling Tests," *Journal of Parapsychology* 5, no. 2 (June 1, 1941): 99–137.

After Death Communication: Researcher Sylvia Hart Wright tells us that after-death communication refers to "spontaneous communications from the dead, received by the living."[4] In other words, it refers to moments in which a person believes they are receiving communication from someone who is no longer living. Quite often, after-death communication is associated with death, dying, and the grieving process,[5] but Phyllis Clay, in a dissertation for Saybrook University, helps us understand that it is not just limited to those instances.[6] In her study, Clay interviewed twelve people who believed that they received communication in the form of mentoring from a deceased person over a long period of time. Researcher Susan Kwilecki tells us that the phrase and concept of after-death communication was especially popularized in the 1990s and that it represents a group of poignant communication received by those personally known to the recipient. These messages can be received in a variety of ways as well, such as in dreams, telephone messages, manifested scents, visions, and more.[7]

Further Reading:

Susan Kwilecki, "Twenty-First Century American Ghosts: The After-Death Communication—Therapy and Revelation from Beyond the Grave." *Religion and American Culture: A Journal of Interpretation* 19, no. 1 (Winter 2009): 101–33.

Sylvia Hart Wright, "Over a Century of Research on After-Death Communication," *Journal of Spirituality and Paranormal Studies* 31, no. 3 (2008): 154–66.

Agent: In experiments, an agent refers to the person who focuses on a target object and attempts to psychically send that target to another person. Not all psychical impressions received by people, however, are done in laboratory settings. In these spontaneous cases of psychic impressions, then, the agent would be a person intuited by another, like in an intuition of a crisis moment, for example.[8] You may sometimes see the term "agent" also referred to as "focus person" (FP).

Altered State of Consciousness: Altered state of consciousness refers to any number of states that allow a person to "dissociate from the normal waking state," and which are "sometimes induced deliberately by means of meditation, drugs or hypnosis"[9] but which can also occur spontaneously such as through stress, emergency situations, and/or illness. Researchers believe that an altered state of consciousness is a central component to such phenomena like extrasensory perception.

American Society for Psychical Research: This organization was established in 1885, three years after the formation of the British Society for Psychical Research. It was established with the help of noted psychologist William James. From the 1900s through the 1920s it was a member of various other groups such as the British Society for Psychical Research and the American Institute for Scientific Research. There was a schism within the group in the 1920s that led to the formation of the Boston Society for Psychic Research.[10]

A group of interested people met to discuss the possibility of creating an American version of the Society for Psychical Research in Boston on September 23, 1884. Impressed by the research being done by the British Society for Psychical Research, these people understood the importance of psychical research and inquiry and believed that the United States should contribute and form its own professional psychical entity. When a large number of people expressed positive reaction at this meeting in Boston, they moved forward with formal establishment, and on January 8, 1885, the American Society for Psychical Research (ASPR) was officially decreed an organization.[11] In their first published proceedings, we learn of their motivation, "The Council of the American society therefore feels that the duty can be no longer postponed of systematically repeating observations similar to those made in England, with a view to confirming them if true, to definitely pointing out the sources of error if false."[12]

The first committees of the ASPR included committees on thought-transference, apparitions, haunted houses, and physical phenomena.[13] Some of the group's other early work focused on cases of mediumship. One notable member, James Hyslop, published one of ASPR's earliest reports—a nearly five hundred-page study of an artist communication with the spirit of a deceased colleague. Hyslop was, in fact, a key member of the ASPR who led the group for many years. The ASPR's work with mediums proved to be detrimental in the 1920s, however, when tensions emerged among members due to diverse opinions of the controversial medium known as Margery (Mina Crandon). The tensions ran so deep, in fact, that certain members broke from the ASPR to form their own research entity, the Boston Society for Psychic Research, which operated until 1941 when it was dissolved and subsumed by the ASPR. The organization's first proceedings was published in 1885 and their journal is still published today. Today, they are an independent institute with headquarters in New York.[14]

Further Reading:

"Formation of the Society," *Proceedings of the American Society for Psychical Research* 1, no. 1 (July 1885): 1–4.

***Annals of Psychical Science*:** The *Annals of Psychical Science* was a monthly journal that was published between 1905 and 1908. Established by Dr. Charles Richet and Dr. Dariex, the journal's board included other notable psychical researchers such as William Crookes, Julien Ochorowicz, Sir Oliver Lodge, Cesar Lombroso, and more.[15] Though it was only published for a few short years, each issue includes hundreds of pages of case studies and experimental research on various psychical topics. All are freely accessible through www.HathiTrust.org.

Anomalous: A word used frequently in parapsychological discussions that refers to something which is not seemingly explainable by any immediately known natural explanations. Readers will also often see variations of this word, such as "anomaly."

Anomalous Cognition: Anomalous cognition is a term that refers to cognition of information "unconstrained by the known biological characteristics of the sense organs and the brain."[16] It is often used to refer to extrasensory perception (ESP) and is credited to researcher Edwin May.[17] Tressoldi and Storm remind us that it is also interchanged with "anomalous perception" and "nonlocal cognition," in addition to being another way to refer to ESP. Multiple international researchers have studied anomalous cognition such as ESP in laboratory settings since the 1800s.

Further Reading:

Edwin May, S. James P. Spottiswoode, and Christine L. James, "Managing the Target Pool Bandwidth: Noise Reduction for Anomalous Cognition Experiments." Presented at the 37th Annual Parapsychological Association at University of Amsterdam, the Netherlands (March 23, 1994): 1–9.
Edwin C. May, Sonali Bhatt Marwaha, Vinay Chaganti, "Anomalous Cognition: Two Protocols for

Data Collection and Analyses," *Journal of the Society for Psychical Research* 75, no. 905 (October 2011): 191–210.

Anomalous Experiences Inventory: The Anomalous Experiences Inventory is "constructed to measure general paranormal belief, experience, ability, drug use, and fear of the paranormal."[18] This inventory was created by modifying the Mental Experience Inventory and is designed to gather information on a range of factors involving paranormal beliefs and experiences. The creators of the inventory point out that "a comprehensive measure including beliefs, experiences, fear, and drug-use subscales will be helpful, not only in survey studies, but also in selecting subjects of particular types for laboratory experiments on psi-related phenomena."[19]

Further Reading:

Charles Gallagher, V. K. Kumar, and Ronald J. Pekala, "The Anomalous Experiences Inventory: Reliability and Validity," *Journal of Parapsychology* 58, no. 4 (December 1, 1994): 402–28.

Anomalous Perturbation: Anomalous perturbation refers to the ways in which intention can influence some factors of an unobservable system, like the psychical phenomenon of psychokinesis.[20]

Apparition: Apparition is a term often used to refer to ghosts, but Arthur and Joyce Berger remind us of a key difference between apparitions and ghosts. An apparition is "the figure of a living *or* dead being (human or animal) seen at a time when in fact no human being or animal is physically present."[21] As such, apparitions include ghosts, but ghosts specifically refer to deceased beings. The Bergers also remind us of the qualities of apparitions: people who see them are certain that it is not a mere memory, they do not appear physical, they seem aware of their surroundings, and there is often an accompanied sense of cold. Perhaps the most famous study of apparitions is the Census of Hallucinations in which researchers examined over a thousand cases of apparitions (though they referred to them as hallucinations). This census formally identified the existence of "crisis apparitions," which confirmed that apparitions can indeed be that of living *or* deceased beings.[22]

Further Reading:

Frederic W. H. Myers, "Report on the Census of Hallucinations," *Proceedings of the Society for Psychical Research* 10 (1894): 25–422.

Apports: Apports refer to objects that seemingly appear out of nowhere during séances. Various items could be apports, from flowers to animals, and nearly everything in between. They are mostly believed to be concealed on the medium's body prior to the gathering.

Further Reading:

Michael Nahm, "Out of Thin Air? Apport Studies Performed between 1928 and 1938 by Elemér Chengery Pap," *Journal of Scientific Exploration* 33, no. 4 (2019): 661–705.

Archetypal Synchronistic Resonance: Archetypal synchronistic resonance is a theory proposed by Drs. Jeffrey Mishlove and Brendan C. Engen. They say that the current state of parapsychological research and knowledge has reached stasis and that there cannot be continual progress without an entirely new paradigm of paranormal experience. They tell us that there seems to be a gray area of paranormal phenomena that cannot be adequately analyzed under current thinking and therefore propose archetypal synchronistic resonance as a new way of thinking about paranormal experience. Specifically, they tell us that it "explains ostensible paranormal experiences that can be neither accepted as literally construed nor dismissed as mere artifact or error."[23] It draws inspiration from the concepts of archetypes, synchronicity (as espoused by Dr. Carl Jung), and resonance.

Further Reading:

Jeffrey Mishlove and Brendan C. Engen, "Archetypal Synchronistic Resonance: A New Theory of Paranormal Experience," *Journal of Humanistic Psychology* 47, no. 2 (April 2007): 223–42.

Artifact Induction: Artifact induction refers to introducing something in order to facilitate a participant's belief that a genuine psychical event is occurring. It is thought that belief in psi facilitates the presence of psi. Artifact induction is used commonly as a tactic in experiments on psychokinesis.

Further Reading:

K. J. Batcheldor, "Contributions to the Theory of PK Induction from Sitter-Work," *Journal of the American Society for Psychical Research* 78, no. 2 (1984): 105–22.

Association for the Scientific Study of Anomalous Phenomena: The Association for the Scientific Study of Anomalous Phenomena is a United Kingdom-based research organization and charity that investigates paranormal claims and helps provide people with skills they can use to conduct their own paranormal inquiry. It holds an annual conference called Seriously Strange,[24] conducts research, performs paranormal investigations, and offers classes to the public on a variety of topics. It publishes a journal called *Anomaly* in which information on topics such as hauntings, electronic voice phenomena, and more can be found.[25]

Astral Projection: Astral projection rests on the theory that there exists an astral body that is psychically connected to our physical body. Arthur and Joyce Berger tell us that "during waking hours, the astral body corresponds precisely to the physical body. But during sleep and at other times the astral body may separate from the physical body and travel to other places."[26] It is often associated with the out-of-body experience (OBE). Some people seem to induce astral projection, or out-of-body experiences during events such as meditation. For example, in a 2009 study in the *Australian Journal of Clinical and Experimental Hypnosis*, researchers interviewed two people who were able to induce this state while in deep meditation. They point out the main characteristic of OBEs: a sensation of disembodiment, seeing the physical body from outside oneself, and a sense of travel. The researchers also point out that this phenomenon can occur during meditation, as is the focus of their article, but can also occur spontaneously, during illness, stress, hypnosis, or in trance.[27]

Further Reading:

Carlos S. Alvarado, "The Psychological Approach to Out-of-Body Experiences: A Review of Early and Modern Developments," *Journal of Psychology* 126 (1992): 237–50.

Pieter F. Craffert, "When is an Out-of-Body Experience (Not) an Out-of-Body Experience? Reflections about Out-of-Body Phenomena in Neuroscientific Research," *Journal of Cognition and Culture* 15 (2015): 13–31.

Australian Institute of Parapsychological Research: The Australian Institute of Parapsychological Research is a nonprofit research group that publishes the *Australian Journal of Parapsychology*. Founded in 1977, their philosophy is described as such, "Psychic experiences (or claims of such) should be studied and treated in the same way as other human experiences [and should be placed] in the broader context of experience, health and illness."[28]

Austrian Society for Parapsychology and Frontier Areas of Science: Established in 1927 in Vienna, the Austrian Society for Parapsychology and Frontier Areas of Science was inspired by the work of Countess Wassilko-Serecki, a psychical researcher noted for their inquiry into the medium Eleanore Zugan. Affiliated with Vienna University, today the institution continues its research but also places emphasis on educational resources.[29]

Automatic Writing: Automatic writing refers to writing done during a trance or trance-like state. It is most commonly associated with mediums. Specifically, Arthur and Joyce Berger tell us that it refers to "writing . . . that is not done consciously or intentionally but nevertheless with purpose and intelligence."[30] Many mediums of the 1800s engaged in automatic writing and you will see it mentioned quite often in the literature. For example, noted medium Leonora Piper engaged in automatic writing and took part in the famous Cross Correspondences investigation of the Society for Psychical Research. In this study, multiple mediums working separately received information through speech or writing that, when pieced together, formed coherent sentences.

Further Reading:

Carlos S. Alvarado, "Mediumship, Psychical Research, Dissociation, and the Powers of the Subconscious Mind," *Journal of Parapsychology* 78, no. 1 (Spring 2014): 98–114.

Basic Technique: This refers to a technique used in studies of clairvoyance and ESP involving cards. In a basic technique, the experimenter takes a face-down card, waits for it to be called by the subject, and then places it facedown on a nearby pile to be checked later. At no time do either the experimenter or the subject see the card.[31]

Bidirectionality: This refers to the scattering of scores in either direction from the mean. In ESP tests, for example, it refers to the fact that some ESP scores scatter significantly higher while others scatter significantly lower. It is sometimes also referred to as the psi-differential effect.[32]

Book Test: This is a technique used in tests of mediumship abilities and consciousness beyond death. In the book test, the idea is that a medium, through channeling the spirit of a deceased individual, will receive a psychical impression urging them to locate a certain book, page number, and passage. That passage will in turn be significant in some way to the deceased individual but otherwise unknown to the medium.[33] In one example of a book test, a medium was attempting to channel the spirit of someone's

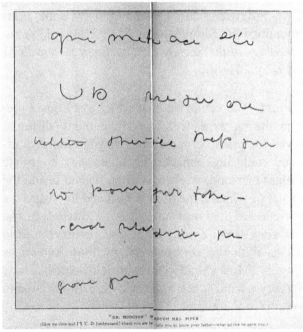

Figure G.1. An Example of Automatic Writing by Medium Leonora Piper

From *Spiritism and Psychology* by Théodore Flournoy (New York: Harper & Brothers, 1911). PD-US

deceased son. During the sitting, the medium directed the father of this individual to a certain book, page, and line. On that line was a reference to an inside joke unknown to the medium.[34]

In a 1921 issue of the *Proceedings of the Society for Psychical Research*, Eleanor Sidgwick wrote a comprehensive review of book tests used in sessions with the medium Mrs. Leonard. In describing the process, Sidgwick tells us,

> In the most typical cases the interior of the sitter's residence, and sometimes even the sitter's name, is unknown to Mrs. Leonard. The sitter himself is unlikely consciously to remember what book occupies the exact place indicated, and even if he has read the book, which he often has not, it is practically certain that he does not know what is on the specified page. A good book-test therefore would exclude ordinary telepathy from the sitter as an explanation and would make it extremely difficult to suppose that Feda (Mrs. Leonard's spirit control), derives her information from any living being.[35]

Further Reading:

T. Besterman, "Further Inquiries into the Elements of Chance in Book Tests," *Proceedings of the Society for Psychical Research* 40 (1931/32): 59–98.

E. M. Sidgwick, "An Examination of Book-Tests Obtained in Sittings with Mrs. Leonard," *Proceedings of the Society for Psychical Research* 31 (1921): 241–400.

Cabinet: The cabinet is that which encloses a medium during a séance. They take many different forms, for example, sometimes they are merely curtained enclosures while other times they are made of glass or wood. A chair is often placed inside the cabinet to which a medium is fastened to ensure the restriction of their movement.[36] A 1926 article in *The New York Times* describes the glass cabinet used in sittings with the controversial medium known as Margery (Mina Crandon). The article describes how Margery's hands, feet, and neck were all fastened to eyebolts in the glass cabinet.[37]

Call: A call is the response of a subject when indicating what they believe a target object to be. For example, in a card-guessing study using a basic technique, the agent lifts a card and the subject "calls" out what they believe that card (target object) to be.[38]

Card-Guessing: This is a research method popularized by J. B. Rhine that dominated psychical experimentation for many years. The idea is straightforward: a deck of cards is used as target objects in tests of extrasensory perception. Various methods are used in card-guessing experiments, such as the basic technique, screened touch matching, and more. Different techniques employed in card-guessing experiments serve to eliminate possibilities of fraud and/or subconscious sensory clues from experimenters.[39] The most popular cards used in card-guessing experiments are Zener cards, often referred to as ESP cards. This deck consists of cards that depict five different geometric shapes: wavy lines, stars, circles, plus signs, and squares. Designed by Dr. Karl Zener of Duke University, the idea is that simplifying the design and choices facilitates the sending and receiving of psychic impressions.[40]

Card-guessing experiments have also involved colored cards, no attached symbols, or shapes. In a 1937 experiment at Columbia University, in fact, two researchers found that subjects scored just as well intuiting colored cards as they did cards with shapes on them.[41] The design of card-guessing experiments varies wildly as well. In some experiments, both the agent and subject are in the same room while in others they are in adjoined rooms, or perhaps even just in the same building. In other tests, though, the agent and subject are located miles apart in completely separate buildings. These experiments test not only general ESP but the impact of distance on ESP.[42]

Further Reading:

C. R. Carpenter and Harold R. Phalen, "An Experiment in Card Guessing," *Journal of Parapsychology* 1, no. 1 (March 1, 1937): 31–43.

Bernard F. Riess, "A Case of High Scores in Card Guessing at a Distance," *Journal of Parapsychology* 1, no. 4 (December 1, 1937): 260–63.

Center for Research on Consciousness and Anomalous Psychology: The Center for Research on Consciousness and Anomalous Psychology, located within the Department of Psychology at Lund

University, conducts and encourages research on "unusual but not pathological experience and events, including reputed parapsychological phenomena."[43]

Centro Studi Parapsicologici (Center for Parapsychological Studies of Bologna): The Centro Studi Parapsicologici (CSP) is an Italian parapsychological research organization that dates back to the early 1950s. Much like other organizations, early researchers at CSP focused on investigating psychics and mediums. The CSP hosts conferences and publishes the *Quaderni di Parapsicologia*.[44]

Further Reading:

Ferdinando Bersani, "The Bologna Center for Parapsychological Studies (CSP): Research Between 1970 and 1985." In abstracts of presented papers from the Parapsychological Association 56th Annual Convention, Viterbo, Italy, August 8–11, 2013, *Journal of Parapsychology* 77, no. 2 (Fall 2013): 189.

Chair Test: A chair test is used in precognition studies. The subject is taken to a venue at which there will be a gathering sometime in the near future. A particular chair is selected and the subject channels information about the person who will end up sitting in that chair.[45]

Channeling: Channeling refers to the act of obtaining information from a deceased individual. Most commonly associated with mediumship, channeling occurs when a medium receives information received from some other nonliving intelligence. During sittings (or séances), a medium's control may channel information through them. A control (in context of mediumship), refers to a spirit that helps connect the medium with other spirits or consciousness and filters messages through them to sitters.[46]

Researcher Michael A. Thalbourne reminds us that this term, when used as a noun, refers primarily to mediums. However, when used as a verb, it refers to the act of channeling,[47] which may or may not be in the presence of a medium or a séance. For example, researcher Dureen J. Hughes tells us that channeling can be induced through trance and is an example of an altered state of consciousness.[48] Hughes even tells us that our ability to engage in altered states of consciousness, such as trance, is part of "our psychobiological heritage as human beings."[49] Hughes points out that trance channeling in today's context is a bit different from that of its emergent late nineteenth-century context, but the idea is still generally the same: that information is downloaded from a source outside of yourself.

Further Reading:

Dureen J. Hughes, "Blending With an Other: An Analysis of Trance Channeling in the United States," *Ethos* 19, no. 2 (June 1991): 161–84.
Luciano Pederzoli, Patrizio Tressoldi, and Helané Wahbeh. "Channeling: A Non-pathological Possession and Dissociative Identity Experience or Something Else?" *Culture, Medicine, and Psychiatry* 46 (2022): 161–69.
Helané Wahbeh, Cedric Cannard, Jennifer Okonsky, and Arnaud Delorme. "A Physiological Examination of Perceived Incorporation During Trance." F1000 Research 8, no. 67 (2019): 1–26.

Checker Effect: The checker effect refers to an experimenter's unintentional ability to influence the results of a psi experiment. Those involved with the experiment at various points can potentially influence results, for example, those who may select targets to be used in ESP tests and/or those who check the data. The theory is that a participant can psychically intuit impressions from those involved in the study, such as obtaining past impressions of targets and/or future impressions of what the data might reveal.[50] It is best outlined as such:

> Because of the apparent tendency of psi processes to transcend both time and space, many bizarre possibilities arise concerning what might be influencing the subject as [they] are taking a precognition test . . . the subject could be reacting differentially (presumably by precognition) to the person or person who will be checking [their] test in the future.[51]

In a 1968 study in *Journal of Parapsychology*, researchers Sara R. Feather and Robert Brier tested the checker effect.[52] In their study, they questioned whether knowledge of the person checking the data would seem to affect a test subject's score. They discovered that subjects scored higher on datasets than they thought the main experimenter was going to score and lower on data sets they didn't believe the main experimenter would score. Multiple studies have been done on various aspects of the checker effect and many have been designed to mitigate any potential impact from checkers.

Further Reading:

Sara R. Feather and Robert Brier, "The Possible Effect of the Checker in Precognition Tests," *Journal of Parapsychology* 32, no. 3 (1968): 167–75.

D. H. Weiner and N. L. Zingrone, "In the Eye of the Beholder: Further Research on the 'Checker Effect,'" *Journal of Parapsychology* 53 (1989): 203–31.

Cipher Test: The cipher test is used to help determine the veracity of communication from deceased individuals. It helps eliminate the possibility that some information about a deceased person is psychically intuited by a medium from the mind of someone living (e.g., information about a deceased person psychically gathered from their living partner). In order to eliminate the possibility that a medium is simply reading the minds of those who were once close to this person, a cipher test is used. When the targeted individual was still alive, they created a cipher and they alone retained knowledge of the key that would reveal that cipher. The information was never written down and stored only in their mind. Upon their death, then, this key would seemingly be impossible for the living to retrieve and therefore any transmission of the key through a medium would be viewed as proof of communication with spirits.[53]

Further Reading:

"Dr. Thouless's Cipher Test," *Journal of Parapsychology* 49, no. 2 (June 1985): 213.

Circle: Circle refers to a group of people sitting with a medium, that is memebers of a séance or sitting.[54] Sometimes a circle is made up of random sitters meeting once for an event whereas other times the sitters may all know each other, and still further some circles may meet regularly with a medium to hold sittings.

Further Reading:

E. E. Fournier d'Albe, *The Goligher Circle: May to August, 1921.* London: John M. Watkins, 1922.

Clairaudience: Clairaudience refers to receiving psychical impressions through sound, usually seeming as if they are generated internally.[55] Sometimes clairvoyance is simply referred to as auditory hallucination. In the 1890 Census of Hallucinations, for example, one-quarter of the respondents indicated they had experienced an anomalous hallucination and that their experience was auditory.[56] Louisa E. Rhine, in a 1963 article in the *Journal of Parapsychology*, refers to clairaudient moments as "spontaneous auditory experiences involving psi"[57] and discusses how people have experienced hearing not only other persons but sounds like phantom doorbells as well. Interestingly, Rhine points out that spontaneous auditory experiences involving objects could potentially be examples of psychokinesis (PK). For example, if a piano key is heard and there is a piano in the room but no natural explanation to explain the noise, she posits that it could be PK instead of ESP. Her theory illustrates how intertwined psi experiences can be.

In a July 2014 article in the *Journal of the Society for Psychical Research*, Renaud Evrard discusses the differences between psi and non-psi auditory experiences.[58] Specifically, Evrard discusses the importance of realizing that certain events (like auditory hallucinations) could be exceptional human experiences and not a mere symptom of a pathological source and urges researchers (and clinicians) to consider this.

Further Reading:

Renaud Evrard, "From *Symptom* to *Difference*: 'Hearing Voices' and Exceptional Experiences," *Journal of the Society for Psychical Research* 78, no. 916 (2014): 129–48.

Louisa E. Rhine, "Auditory Psi Experience: Hallucination or Physical?" *Journal of Parapsychology* 27, no. 3 (1963): 182–97.

Clairsentience: Clairsentience refers to receiving psychical impression through emotions and feelings.[59] It is labeled a type of mental channeling, sometimes also referred to as a form of mental mediumship.[60]

Clairvoyance: Clairvoyance translates to "clear-seeing" and refers to the psychical ability of intuiting information about objects or events. In the past, it has been referred to as cryptesthesia, second sight, and telesthesia.[61] Clairvoyance is often used as a catch-all term to refer to all types of telepathy, but parapsychologist J. B. Rhine reminds us of key differences. He writes,

> When a subject succeeds to a significant degree in identifying objects, such as the cards in a shuffled deck, by some extrasensorial means, we commonly call the performance *clairvoyance*, or the extrasensory perception of objects. If there is similar success in identifying the order of symbols being thought of by a sender, but with no objective target such as a card, we speak of telepathy. If both the card and the sender's thought are possible targets for the subject's extrasensory perception, the test is one of undifferentiated or *general extrasensory perception* (GESP)."[62]

Further Reading:

J. B. Rhine, "Telepathy and Clairvoyance Reconsidered," *Journal of Parapsychology* 9, no. 3 (September 1, 1945): 176–93.

College of Psychic Studies: The College of Psychic Studies was formerly known as the London Spiritualist Alliance and was founded in 1884 by the psychical researcher William Stainton Moses. Existing still today, "The aims of the college are to inquire into psychic phenomena, provide a platform for lectures, hold workshops, give courses, and provide sessions with mediums."[63] Their publication, *Light*, published its first edition in 1881, making it the oldest publication on psychical topics.[64]

Further Reading:

"The College of Psychic Studies: Exploring Consciousness Since 1884," (The College of Psychic Studies, 2021), https://www.collegeofpsychic-studies.co.uk/.

Committee on Haunted Houses: The Committee on Haunted Houses was one of the early committees established by the British Society for Psychical Research. Members of the committee were tasked with identifying not only potential instances of haunt phenomena but also to determine the criteria that might qualify a location as haunted. In volume one of the *Proceedings of the Society for Psychical Research,* the committee's first report is published. In it, we learn a bit about their process and standards. The authors of the report (who include Frank Podmore and William F. Barrett) tell us that they had been amassing a collection of eyewitness testimonies, conducted primarily through in-person interviews and supplemented with cross-examinations via letters. Of their standards, they write,

> We do not consider that *every* first-hand narration of the appearance of a ghost, even from a thoroughly trustworthy narrator, gives us adequate reason for attempting further investigation. On the contrary, our general principle is that *the unsupported evidence of a single witness does not constitute sufficient ground for accepting an apparition as having a prima facie claim to objective reality.*[65]

The authors go on to tell us that there are two other factors that they look for when receiving eyewitness testimonies: Was the apparition/event also experienced by others at the same location and/or was there some extenuating circumstance that could not have been known to the percipient? For example, did the sighting of a ghost coincide with the anniversary of a death or marriage? If so, and if it could not possibly have been known to the percipient, the authors were willing to consider this a more credible candidate for a genuine anomalous experience. In the reports of the committee, you can read their cases for yourself and see, in their own words, the phenomena that they categorized and gathered all across the United Kingdom. The majority of these reports are openly accessible at www.hathitrust.org. The committee was later referred to as the Committee on Apparitions and Haunted Houses.

Further Reading:

W. F. Barrett, A. P. Percival Keep, C. C. Massey, Hensleigh Wedgwood, Frank Podmore, and E. R. Pease, "First Report of the Committee on Haunted Houses," *Proceedings of the Society for Psychical Research* 1, no. 1 (1882): 101–15.

Josiah Royce, "Preliminary Report of the Committee on Apparitions and Haunted Houses," *Proceedings of the Society for Psychical Research* 1, no. 2 (July 1886): 128–31.

Committee on Mediumistic Phenomena: When the Society for Psychical Research was founded in England in 1882, members formed a number of committees tasked with investigating various topics. The Committee on Mediumistic Phenomena was one of those early committees. Carlos S. Alvarado tells us that "the SPR investigators, and other psychical researchers, were also interested in mediumship. The most important of the early investigations into mental mediumship was the work conducted with the American medium Leonora Piper. . . . Her case provided the first systematic opportunity to make repeated observations under controlled conditions."[66] You can find the reports of this committee and read, firsthand, their studies and encounters in the *Proceedings of the Society for Psychical Research*, many of which are openly accessible at www.hathitrust.org.

Further Reading:

Carlos S. Alvarado, "'Report of the Committee on Mediumistic Phenomena,' by William James (1886)," *History of Psychiatry* 27, no. 1 (2016): 85–100.

William James, "Report of the Committee on Mediumistic Phenomena," *Proceedings of the Society for Psychical Research* 1, no. 2 (July 1886): 102–106.

Committee on Thought-Transference: Another early committee of the Society for Psychical Research was the Committee on Thought-Transference (also referred to as the Committee on Thought-Reading). Thought-transference and thought-reading were early ways of describing extrasensory perception, in particular telepathy. In the first report of this committee, published in the *Proceedings of the Society for Psychical Research* in July 1882, we learn of the charge they were tasked with:

> Is there or is there not any existing or attainable evidence than can stand fair physiological criticism, to support a belief that a vivid impression or a distinct idea in one mind can be communicated to another mind without the intervening help of the recognised organs of sensation? And if such evidence be found, is the impression derived from a rare or partially developed and hitherto unrecognised sensory organ, or has the mental percept been evoked directly without any antecedent sense-percept?[67]

In the remainder of the report, the committee members discuss physiological factors that complicate gathering genuine cases of thought-reading as

well as the general skeptical attitude toward the subject by many scholars of the day. They tell us that, after sorting through the various reports given to them, that they were left with *two* cases they thought might warrant further scrutiny. However, one case was tabled since they could not verify the conditions under which an event was said to occur. The one remaining case involved the Creery family from Derbyshire in England. Sir William F. Barrett traveled to the family and engaged in thought-reading games with them. The children (and maid) all seemed to display remarkable abilities, but the Creery case has since been critiqued as nothing more than children picking up on subtle physiological and environmental clues. Barrett's colleagues, including Eleanor and Henry Sidgwick, even discovered the girls cheating in tests of their own. Barrett held fast to his belief in the Creery family, believing that any collusion or cheating only happened once their initial remarkable abilities seemed to wane.[68]

Further Reading:

W. F. Barrett, Edmund Gurney, and F. W. H. Myers, "First Report on Thought-Reading," *Proceedings of the Society for Psychical Research* 1, no. 1 (July 17, 1882): 13–34.

Richard Noakes, "The 'Bridge which is Between Physical and Psychical Research': William Fletcher Barrett, Sensitive Flames, and Spiritualism," *History of Science* 42, no. 4 (2004): 419–64.

Communicator: In mediumship, a communicator refers to a deceased individual who communicates through a medium or the medium's control.[69]

Consciousness: Consciousness is at the core of much of parapsychological research. The earliest psychical researchers were constantly searching for proof of the survival of consciousness beyond physical death. Consciousness refers to a state of awareness. The *Gale Encyclopedia of Psychology* tells us that consciousness is "awareness of external stimuli and of one's own mental activity."[70] This definition reminds us of various seminal figures that shaped the way consciousness has been investigated since the 1800s. Wilhelm Wundt, for example, developed a structuralism approach to consciousness while William James emphasized functionalism, or the ways in which people respond to the environments around them. Then of course there is Sigmund Freud who identified different states of consciousness, like the unconscious.[71] In parapsychology, it is believed that altered states of consciousness facilitate anomalous experiences. Important also for the topic of parapsychology is the concept of nonlocal consciousness, which postulates that consciousness is not bound by the physical confines of our bodies.[72]

Further Reading:

Stanley Krippner, "Parapsychology and Consciousness Research," *Journal of Religion and Psychical Research* 26, no. 2 (2003): 108–13.
Steven A. Schwartz, "Six Protocols, Neuroscience, and Near Death: An Emerging Paradigm Incorporating Nonlocal Consciousness." *Explore* 11, no. 4 (July/August 2015): 252–60.

Control: In mediumship, a control refers to a spirit or entity who controls the speech of a medium. The control delivers messages through the medium and may or may not be the spirit of a deceased person. In some cases, controls claim to be otherworldly intelligences. A control is often referred to as a spirit control and is often given a name. For example, the spirit control of the medium Gladys Osbourne Leonard is Feda, and Leonora Piper referred to her spirit control as Dr. Phinuit.[73]

Further Reading:

Paula Vilaplana de Miguel, "The House that Ghosts Built (And Mediums Performed)," *Invisible Culture* 32, (April 2021).

Covariance Effect: The covariance effect was identified by researchers Gardner Murphy and Ernest Taves. Covariance occurs when "one manifestation of the phenomena [accompanies] another."[74] Specifically, Murphy and Taves tell us that "if conditions are favorable to ESP in general, high scores on one task should be accompanied by high scores on another task."[75] They also point out that various data points should be similarly distributed, whether that is favorably higher than chance or lower than chance. In their study, participants engaged in ESP run with different objects. All conducted as part of one sitting, their theory was that the objects themselves shouldn't necessarily matter so long as conditions in that sitting were favorable to ESP.

Further Reading:

Gardner Murphy and Ernest Taves, "Covariance Methods in the Comparison of Extra-Sensory Tasks," *Journal of Parapsychology* 3, no. 1 (June 1, 1939): 38–78.

Crisis Apparition: A crisis apparition refers to the sighting of an apparition that corresponds to a real-time emergency situation. In other words, a crisis apparition is that of a living person who is, at that moment, encountering a life-threatening (or crisis) situation. The seminal work *Phantasms of the Living* helped recognize the number of people who experienced seeing crisis apparitions.[76]

Further Reading:

Edmund Gurney, Frederic W. H. Myers, and Frank Podmore, *Phantasms of the Living* (London: Kegan Paul, Trench, Trubner, and Co., 1918).

Cross-Correspondences: Cross-correspondences refer to a series of messages received by various mediums. Taken separately, the messages do not appear to have any sensical meaning. It is only when combined across mediums that the pieces form coherent messages when put together. Some of the automatic writers involved in cross-correspondences are Mrs. Willett, Mrs. Holland, and Helen de G. Verrall. Some believed that the messages pieced together among the mediums were received by discarnate spirits, but others believed that the mediums were picking up (telepathically) on the thoughts of living people.[77]

Further Reading:

Frank Podmore, G. Lowes Dickinson, and F. C. Constable, "Private Meeting for Members and Associates," *Journal of the Society for Psychical Research* 14. (January 1909): 3–30.
Helen G. Verrall, "The Element of Chance in Cross-Correspondences," *Journal of the Society for Psychical Research* 15, no. 284 (December 1911): 153–73.

Cultural Source Hypothesis: The cultural source hypothesis postulates that a person's culture influences the ways in which a person experiences and perceives the paranormal. Just as anomalous experiences are mediated by personality traits and cognitive differences, so, too, does culture mediate these experiences. Maraldi and Krippner, in a 2019 article, tell us that "experiences categorized as anomalous vary across cultures, as they are influenced by a range of factors, such as religion and politics"[78] and furthermore remind us that "not all cultures have descriptive terms for anomalous phenomena."[79]

Further Reading:

Everton de Oliveira Maraldi and Stanley Krippner, "Cross-Cultural Research on Anomalous Experiences: Theoretical Issues and Methodological Challenges," *Psychology of Consciousness: Theory, Research, and Practice* 6, no. 3 (2019): 306–307.

Deathbed Visions: Deathbed visions refer to experiences of dying individuals who claim to see the spirits of departed friends and loved ones, or who see surroundings and environments different than their own. While many attribute the role of medicine or drugs as conducive to hallucinations in such a state, researchers have nevertheless pondered these events. For example, scholars Karlis Osis and Erlendur Haraldsson conducted an international survey of deathbed visions and found that in 90 percent of cases, the person experiencing the vision was not under the influence of medicine that would alter their perception.[80]

Further Reading:

Karlis Osis and Erlendur Haraldsson, "Deathbed Observations by Physicians and Nurses: A Cross-Cultural Study," *Journal of the American Society for Psychical Research* 71, no. 3 (July 1977): 237–59.

Decline Effect: The decline effect refers to the gradual decline in positive psi results during some laboratory experiments. In other words, researchers began to notice a steady decline in ESP tests—scores would be much higher at the beginning of an experiment and then, as the same task was repeated with a subject, would decline more and more.[81] The decline effect seems to hint at some correlation between novelty, a sense of play, and psi ability.

Dice Tests: Dice tests were popularized in the 1940s by J. B. and Louisa Rhine and their colleagues at the Duke Parapsychology Labs. Dice tests were used in a series of experiments on psychokinesis to test whether human intention could physically influence the direction (or faces) to which dice landed.[82] Even though the Rhines's are credited with developing dice tests, they were not the first ones to use them in

psychical experiments. Dice tests are also referred to as dice-throwing experiments. There are a number of variations employed to test for possible psychokinetic influence. One method, for example, is to attempt to get two dice to land in such a way that their faces total seven. Another method is to get them to score "high" or "low" so that their combined faces total, respectively, more than eight or six and less.[83]

Further Reading:

J. B. Rhine, "Early PK Tests: Sevens and Low-Dice Series," *Journal of Parapsychology* 9, no. 2 (June 1, 1945): 106–15.
Louisa E. Rhine and J. B. Rhine, "The Psychokinetic Effect: I. The First Experiment," *The Journal of Parapsychology* 7, no. 1 (March 1, 1943): 20–43.
Robert H. Thouless, "A Report on an Experiment in Psychokinesis with Dice and a Discussion on Psychological Factors Favoring Success," *The Journal of Parapsychology* 15, no. 2 (June 1, 1951): 89–102.

Direct Mental Influence on Living Systems: The direct mental influence on living systems (DMILS) refers to a theory that some subjects can psychically influence the biological and physiological characteristics of another living organism, for example, a psychical influence on blood pressure or electrodermal responses.[84] Researchers Stefan Schmidt and Harald Walach remind us that the majority of psi research into DMILS involves tests designed to measure electrodermal activity (EDA) during moments in which a subject is being stared at.[85] While there seems to be a possibility for some correlation, however, the researchers go on to discuss flaws in the methodologies of current psi research into EDA and DMILS.

Further Reading:

D. J. Benor, *Healing Research: Spiritual Healing: Scientific Validation of a Healing Revolution.* Southfield, MI: Vision Publications, 2001.
W. Braud and M. Schlitz, "Consciousness Interactions with Remote Biological Systems: Anomalous Intentionality Effects," *Subtle Energies* 2 (1991): 1–46.
Stefan Schmidt and Harald Walach, "Electrodermal Activity (EDA)—State-of-the-Art Measurement and Techniques for Parapsychological Purposes," *Journal of Parapsychology* 64, no. 2 (June 1, 2000): 139–63.

Direct Voice: Direct voice refers to a common tactic of mediums used in séances. It refers to the seeming appearance of the direct voice of a deceased person, not a voice attributed to any living person in the room. Sometimes these direct voices would be heard coming from a trumpet.[86]

Displacement Effect: Researchers Arthur and Joyce Berger tell us that displacement effect refers to extrasensory (ESP) "responses to targets other than those for which the calls were intended."[87] In other words, subjects may correctly identify targets but out-of-order. For example, backward displacement occurs when a subject correctly calls targets immediately before the current target and forward displacement occurs when subjects correctly identify targets in the immediate positions after the current target.

Further Reading:

Julie Milton, "Critical Review of the Displacement Effect: I. The Relationship Between Displacement and Scoring on the Intended Target," *Journal of Parapsychology* 52, no. 1 (March 1, 1988): 29–55.

Dissociation: Parapsychologist Carlos Alvarado points out that "to this day the term dissociation has different meanings and conceptualizations, but it is frequently used to refer to a misunderstood process underlying disruption or separation of memory, identity and sensations from consciousness."[88] Alvarado goes on to discuss how early psychical researchers viewed trance as a type of dissociation that brought with it supernormal abilities. Today, we have a bit more nuanced understanding of dissociation. It is defined as "the feeling of being detached from the reality of one's body" and is "categorized into two types: depersonalization and derealization."[89] It is an altered state of consciousness that many believe is conducive to the manifestation of psi phenomena.

In a 2017 study in the *Journal of Parapsychology*, researcher John Palmer investigated the relationship between psi, motor automatism, and dissociation. In this article, Palmer reminds us of Frederic W. H. Myer's concept of the "secondary self" as a state conducive to psi and how it is really just a theory of dissociation, even though that term was not used at that time to describe such a state. Inspired by Myers's notions that the secondary self could operate independently from the primary consciousness, Palmer developed an experiment and tells us that "the general hypothesis tested in the experiment is that psi is facilitated by dissociated states of consciousness."[90] Believing that dissociative states can lower mental barriers that inhibit people from manifesting psi, Palmer's experiment asked subjects, using a tablet and pencil, to move their pencil to a chosen location only when they felt like their hand was guided by an outside force. Using a series of psychological scales designed to test certain dissociative traits, Palmer discovered a link between high detachment scores and a sense of being guided by an outside force.[91]

Further Reading:

Carlos S. Alvarado, "Mediumship, Psychical Research, Dissociation, and the Powers of the Subconscious Mind," *Journal of Parapsychology* 78, no. 1 (2014): 98–114.

John Palmer, "Anomalous Cognition, Dissociation, and Motor Automatisms," *Journal of Parapsychology* 81, no. 1 (Spring 2017): 46–62.

Divination: In a traditional sense, divination refers to an act of divining information about something, for example, knowledge about the future or knowledge about the location of water through the usage of dowsing rods. Divination often involves objects like dowsing rods, tarot cards, smoke, water, crystal balls, mirrors, etc. Researchers theorize that divination practices often involve psychical process like clairvoyance or extrasensory perception.[92]

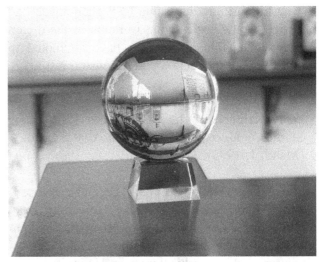

Figure G.2. Crystal Ball at Second Sight Spirits in Ludlow, KY
Author's own photo, 2019

Dreams: One aspect of parapsychology studies the experience of anomalous dreams. Many researchers believe that there is a link between precognition and dreams and that precognitive information can be revealed through dreams. Mark Twain, in fact, had a precognitive dream that foreshadowed his brother's death. Many have experienced precognitive dreams and dreamt of something that happened in the days following a dream. Researchers Arthur and Joyce Berger detail it specifically when they say that anomalous dreams are those "in which the dream imagery corresponds in all material respects to the details of some situation or event that took place prior to, simultaneous with, or subsequent to the dream and of which the dreamer did not know or could not have inferred through any normal means."[93] The dream state can be thought of as an altered state of consciousness, which are states that many researchers theorize are conducive to the manifestation of psi phenomena. Other types of strange dream experiences are sleep paralysis and hallucination that are often experienced in the hypnagogic and hypnopompic states.

One prominent dream study was conducted at the Maimonides Medical Center and is often referred to as the Maimonides Dream Laboratory. Psychiatrist Montague Ullman began noticing that patients seemed to display extrasensory abilities during dream states so much so that he developed a series of studies in a laboratory setting to see what he could learn. Ullman was aided by colleagues Stanley Krippner and Charles Honorton.[94] Out of a total of twelve studies, the researchers found positive results in nine that some ESP phenomena had occurred. Some critics point to faults in the dream experiments while others who have attempted to replicate the design also found promising results.[95]

Further Reading:

Stanley Krippner, "The Maimonides ESP-Dream Studies," *Journal of Parapsychology* 57, no. 1 (March 1, 1993): 39–54.

Duke Parapsychology Labs: The Duke Parapsychology Labs operated at Duke University from 1930–1965. A prominent psychologist, William McDougall, was a faculty member at Duke University interested in psychical matters. He invited botanists Drs. J. B. and Louisa Rhine to Duke University to conduct psychical research under his mentorship. That partnership eventually led to the formal creation of the Duke Parapsychology Laboratory.[96] Under the leadership of Rhine, studies at the lab were mainly comprised of extrasensory perception, and over the course of the Rhines's tenure, upwards of ninety thousand experiments were conducted.[97] It was considered the first North American institute affiliated with higher education dedicated entirely to the pursuit of psychical knowledge. A few years after its founding, in 1937, Rhine and colleagues established the *Journal of Parapsychology*, a scholarly peer-reviewed publication that is still in existence. One notable creation of the Duke Parapsychology Labs is Zener cards. Created by Dr. Karl Zener, these cards use simple geometric shapes designed for use in ESP tests. When J. B. Rhine retired from Duke University in 1965, the lab was disbanded but the Foundation for Research on the Nature of Man was established nearby. This later became the Rhine Education Center, which it is known as today.[98]

Further Reading:

James G. Matlock, "Records of the Parapsychology Laboratory: An Inventory of the Collection in the Duke University Library," *Journal of Parapsychology* 55, no. 3 (September 1, 1991): 301–14.

J. B. Rhine, *New Frontiers of the Mind: The Story of the Duke Experiments* (New York: Farrar and Rinehart, 1937).

Ectoplasm: Ectoplasm is a substance used by physical mediums. Alleged to be spirit-material and spectral "vital energy" emerging from the mouth (or

Figure G.3. Magician Carlos María de Heredia Displaying "Ectoplasm"

From *Spiritism and Common Sense* by Carlos María de Heredia (New York: P.J. Kenedy and Sons, 1922). PD-US

other parts) of the medium's body,[99] ectoplasm is an assortment of gauzy, cheesecloth material secreted by physical mediums and used during séances. It was also a central part in the spirit photography trend of the late 1880s.[100]

Further Reading:

Karl Schoonover, "Ectoplasms, Evanescence, and Photography," *Art Journal* 62, no. 3 (Autumn 2003): 30–43.

Electronic Voice Phenomena: Electronic voice phenomena (EVP) are "anomalous voices or voice-like sounds that are heard using electronic equipment."[101] Electronic voice phenomena is a relatively new concept since, as the name suggests, it manifests through electronic equipment. Almost as soon as various electronic devices emerged, people noticed strange voices and sounds and "the first systematic effort to document these voices [occurred] in 1933 at the World Broadcasting Company."[102] Researchers Mark R. Leary and Tom Butler discuss the various types of EVPs in their 2015 chapter in *Parapsychology: A Handbook for the 21st Century.* They remind us that EVPs are classified into two types: transform or live-voice. Transform (known as Type 1) are EVPs that are recorded on an electronic device but not heard at the time of recording. In other words, transform EVPs are only heard upon playback of a recording. This differs from live-voice EVPs (Type 2), which are simultaneously captured on or through electronic devices *and* heard by a person. Leary and Butler go on to describe that EVPs can be placed into three classes: A, B, or C. Class A EVPs are those that are so clear that there is often no question among listeners as to what the voice is saying. Class B EVPs are identifiable as voices, but listeners often have differing opinions on what is being said. And the final class, Class C EVPs, are those which are anomalous voice-like sounds unable to be interpreted at all.

The story about EVPs rise to fame is particularly interesting. A Swedish artist, Friedrich Jürgenson, who enjoyed recording bird calls in the forest, noticed strange voices and sounds on his audio recordings. He became fascinated with these anomalous voices and eventually went on to publish a book about them in 1964 titled *Voice Transmissions with the Deceased.* People began to hear about EVPs in

popular culture and this interest was further sparked when the Latvian psychologist Konstantine Raudive (who read and was inspired by Jürgenson's book) wrote his own work detailing his research into what he dubbed the "Raudive voices."

EVPs are considered a type of instrumental transcommunication (ITC). Researchers at the Windbridge Institute for Applied Research in Human Potential designed a study to investigate ITC, EVPs, and objectivity.[103] In their study, they investigated the use of EVPMaker, a software designed to randomize bits of text and speech elements. It is used in EVP sessions to capture real-time responses in a live-form EVP setting. Their study looked at the intersection of subjectivity, objectivity, and instrumental transcommunication and provides implications for future EVP and ITC research.

Further Reading:

R. Bayless, *Voices from Beyond* (Secaucus, NJ: University Books, 1959).

Mark Boccuzzi and Julie Beischel, "Objective Analyses of Real-Time Audio Instrumental Transcommunication and Matched Control Sessions: A Pilot Study," *Journal of Scientific Exploration* 25, no. 2 (2011): 215–35.

Mark R. Leary and Tom Butler, "Electronic Voice Phenomena," in *Parapsychology: A Handbook for the 21st Century*, edited by Etzel Cardeña, John Palmer, and David Marcusson-Clavertz, 341–49 (Jefferson, NC: McFarland and Company, 2015).

Konstantin Raudive, *Breakthrough: An Amazing Experiment in Electronic Communication with the Dead* (Gerrards Cross, England: Colin Smythe, 1971).

Energy Healing: Energy healing (which is sometimes referred to as healing touch) "refers to using the hands and intention as the primary instruments of healing . . . the off-the-body execution of interventions, and the premise that this type of healing channels and manipulates energy, has led to it being referred to 'energy healing' or 'energy medicine.'"[104] You may also see it referred to as "remote healing."

Many researchers believe that energy healing involves a psychic process of manipulating energy. Researchers Joines, Baumann, and Kruth discuss various direct effects on living organisms. For example, they cite one study in which scientists discovered that neighboring cell cultures appear to be influenced and impacted by one another—a damaged cell culture would cause the neighboring cell culture to become damaged through what was assumed transmission by ultraviolet light.[105] Joines and his colleagues went on to present their study that investigated the electromagnetic radiation output from energy healers during periods of intense focus and meditation. They discovered that these electromagnetic outputs increased when subjects were in a meditative, intently focused state and decreased when they stopped. Furthermore, the study also discovered that those electromagnetic fields could be detected by light-sensitive equipment.

Further Reading:

William T. Joines, Stephen B. Baumann, and John G. Kruth, "Electromagnetic Emission from Humans during Focused Intent," *Journal of Parapsychology* 76, no. 2 (Fall 2012): 275–94.

Kathryn F. Weymouth, *Healing from a Personal Perspective: Interviews with Certified Healing Touch Practitioners.* PhD diss., Saybrook University, 2012.

Exceptional Human Experience: Exceptional human experience is a term coined by librarian and researcher Rhea White to describe a range of human experiences that are mystical, supernatural, and poignant. White didn't just limit paranormal experiences to this definition though. An exceptional human experience could also be the act of falling in love. This term captures the fact that many psychical events hold poignant meanings for those who have experienced them—they are, in other words, exceptional.[106] A core component of the exceptional human experience is speaking about it. White tells us that "confessional performance means owning your reality even in the face of derision, doubt, and oppression. And the act of owning it plays a seminal part in reinforcing the reality one has glimpsed, not only for others, but for the individual."[107]

Further Reading:

Helané Wahbeh, Dean Radin, Julia Mossbridge, Cassandra Vieten, and Arnaud Delorme, "Exceptional Experiences Reported by Scientists and Engineers," *Explore* 14, no. 5 (September/October 2018): 329–41.

Rhea A. White, "Exceptional Human Experiences as Vehicles of Grace: Parapsychology and the Outlier Mentality," *Academy of Religion and Psychical Research Proceedings Annual Conference* (1993): 46–55

Rhea A. White, "Role Theory and Exceptional Human Experience," *Journal of Religion and Psychical Research* 17, no. 2 (April 1994): 74–77.

Expectancy Effect: The expectancy effect occurs when the data in a study coincide with the expectations theorized by the experimenter. It is, therefore, a type of experimenter effect.[108]

Further Reading:

J. E. Kennedy and Judith L. Taddonio, "Experimenter Effects in Parapsychological Research," *Journal of Parapsychology* 40, no. 1 (March 1, 1976): 1–33.

M. D. Smith, "The Role of the Experimenter in Parapsychological Research," *Journal of Consciousness Studies* 10 (2003): 69–84.

Experient: This term refers to a person who experienced something. In the world of parapsychology, it refers to the person who experienced some phenomena such as psychokinesis, haunting, etc.

Experimental Parapsychology: This term refers to the systematic approach toward studying various parapsychological phenomena. Experimental studies often take place in controlled environments and/or laboratories and differ from instances of spontaneous psi, which are random occurrences of psychical phenomena. An example of experimental parapsychology is the card tests developed at the Duke Parapsychology Labs. These tests, designed to study the possibility of extrasensory perception, involved specific target objects, methods, and conditions.

Further Reading:

Fabio De Sio and Chantal Marazia, "Clever Hans and His Effects: Karl Krall and the Origins of Experimental Parapsychology in Germany," *Studies in History and Philosophy of Biological and Biomedical Sciences* 48 (2014): 94–102.

Donald J. West, "Experimental Parapsychology in Britain: A Survey of Recent Work," *Journal of Parapsychology* 18, no. 1 (March 1, 1954): 10–31.

Experimenter Effect: The experimenter effect is a theory that the experimenters themselves influence the outcomes of a study. Many believe that it could be the result of extrasensory perception, for example, subjects picking up psychically on information about the design in the minds of the experimenters. In a series of experiments, parapsychologists Caroline Watt and Peter Ramakers investigated the experimenter effect and found that "participants tested by believer experimenters had higher scores on the psi task than those tested by disbeliever experimenters, indicating an experimenter effect."[109]

Further Reading:

Caroline Watt and Peter Ramakers, "Experimenter Effects with a Remote Facilitation of Attention Focusing Task: A Study with Multiple Believer and Disbeliever Experiments," *Journal of Parapsychology* 67, no. 1 (Spring 2003): 99–116.

Explore: *Explore* is a peer-reviewed journal in which you can find research conducted by scholars such as Dean Radin, Arnaud Delorme, and more.

Extrasensory Perception: Extrasensory perception, commonly referred to as ESP, refers to "the acquisition of information about, or response to, an external event, object, or influence (mental or physical; past, present, or future) otherwise than through any of the known sensory channels."[110] Researcher Michael Thalbourne reminds us that while many attribute the coining of ESP to J. B. Rhine, it was used earlier by researchers like Rudolph Tischner.[111]

Extrasensory perception can take many specific forms such as clairvoyance (anomalous sight), precognition (knowledge of future events), telepathy (communication between minds), etc. It is a form of "anomalous cognition," a term sometimes used to describe many of the same phenomena. In the United States, ESP research was popularized by the Duke Parapsychology Labs and the work of William McDougall, J. B. Rhine, Louisa Rhine, and many others. *See also, General Extrasensory Perception.*

Fantasy-Proneness: Fantasy-proneness is a personality attribute that refers to people who fantasize so intensely that they actually hallucinate the things that they fantasize and/or can slip in and out of the fantasy state easily. They are often successful subjects in hypnosis studies.[112]

Further Reading:

Michelle M. Dasse, Gary R. Elkins, and Charles A. Weaver III, "Correlates of the Multidimensional Construct of Hypnotizability: Paranormal Belief, Fantasy Proneness, Magical Ideation, and Dissociation," *International Journal of Clinical and Experimental Hypnosis* 63, no. 3 (2015): 274–83.

Kenneth Drinkwater, Andrew Denovan, Neil Dagnall, and Andrew Parker, "Predictors of Hearing Electronic Voice Phenomena in Random Noise: Schizotypy, Fantasy Proneness, and Paranormal Beliefs," *Journal of Parapsychology* 84, no. 1 (2020): 96–113.

Forced Choice Test: A forced-choice test refers to experiments "in which the number of targets as to which a subject is to make calls is limited and sharply defined."[113] Forced choice tests were used quite frequently in the ESP tests of Duke University, for example. In many of those studies, subjects knew the targets that they were attempting to intuit. This differs from subjects having no parameters as to the target objects.

Further Reading:

Fiona Steinkamp, Julie Milton, and Robert L. Morris, "A Meta-Analysis of Forced-Choice Experiments Comparing Clairvoyance and Precognition," *Journal of Parapsychology* 62, no. 3 (September 1998): 193–218.

Free Response Test: In direct comparison to the forced-choice tests, a free response test means that subjects are open to respond with any impressions that they receive about the targets, which are not revealed and often concealed in envelopes, if they are presented at all. Free response tests are also used in mediumship cases.[114]

Further Reading:

Julie Milton, "Meta-Analysis of Free-Response ESP Studies without Altered States of Consciousness," *Journal of Parapsychology* 61, no. 4 (December 1997): 279–319.

Galvanic Skin Response: A galvanic skin response refers to a physiological change in the electrical resistance of the skin.[115] The term is also referred to as an electrodermal response. Researchers have studied galvanic skin responses in extrasensory perception studies to see if the physical body responds to events that a subject is otherwise not consciously aware of.

Further Reading:

Tim Schönwetter, Wolfgang Ambach, and Dieter Vaitl, "Does Autonomic Nervous System Activity Correlate with Events Conventionally Considered as Unperceivable? Using a Guessing Task with Physiological Measurement," *Journal of Parapsychology* 75, no. 2 (2011): 327–48.

Ganzfeld: Researcher Daryl Bem tells us that ganzfeld is "a procedure originally introduced into experimental psychology during the 1930s to test propositions derived from Gestalt theory."[116] It is centered around the idea that blocking sensory input will enhance psi performance. Everyday sensory input, it is theorized, blocks out psi signals that keep most of us from experiencing psi. Researcher Charles Honorton is credited with developing these procedures. In a typical ganzfeld setting a subject will be placed into a sensory deprivation setting. This most often occurs by placing ping-pong ball halves over the eyes, filling the room with red light, and wearing headphones that pump in white noise. This creates a "homogenous perceptual environment"[117] that is potentially conducive for psi. In one example of how ganzfeld is used, after the agent is set up in this sensory deprivation setting, a sender will attempt to transmit photos or images to them. The theory is that the ganzfeld state will allow the agent to obtain psychic downloads more easily.

Further Reading:

Daryl J. Bem, "The Ganzfeld Experiment," *Journal of Parapsychology* 57, no. 2 (June 1, 1993): 101–10.

Joakim Westerlund, Adrian Parker, Jan Dalkvist, and Gergö Hadlaczky, "Remarkable Correspondences Between Ganzfeld Mentation and Target Content—A Psychical or Psychological Effect?" *Journal of Parapsychology* 70, no. 1 (Spring 2006): 23–48.

General Extrasensory Perception: General extrasensory perception refers to ESP that can be intuited from either objects or a sender's thoughts. For example, in a card-guessing test that involves both cards and sender's, it is possible that the subject may be picking up clairvoyantly on the cards as objects or telepathically from the psychical impressions being sent by the sender. This possibility of multiple modes of psychical impression, then, is referred to as general extrasensory perception.[118] It is also referred to as undifferentiated ESP and can involve information gathered from the past or the future.[119]

Further Reading:

Michael A. Thalbourne, "Some Experiments on the Paranormal Cognition of Drawings: With Special Reference to Personality and Attitudinal Variables." PhD diss., Edinburgh Research Archive. Available at https://era.ed.ac.uk/handle/1842/26994.

Gesellschaft für Psychologische Forschung (Society for Psychological Research): The Gesellschaft für Psychologische Forschung is a psychical research group founded by scholars dissatisfied with the dominant stance of psychology proposed by Wilhelm Wundt, who was skeptical toward the value of psychical research. The Gesellschaft, as it is commonly referred, was founded in November 1890 with branches in both Berlin and Munich. The noted psychical researchers Max Dessoir and Albert von Schrenck-Notzing led these branches, respectively. The Gesellschaft was highly influenced by the experimental psychology and hypnosis studies happening in England and France and hoped to bring that same spirit to Germany.

Further Reading:

Andreas Sommer, "Normalizing the Supernormal: The Formation of the 'Gesellschaft Für Psychologische Forschung' ('Society for Psychological Research')," *Journal of the History of the Behavioral Sciences* 49, no. 1 (Winter 2013): 18–44.

Ghost: Ghosts are perhaps the most commonly recognizable symbols of the paranormal. Throughout the history of psychical research, ghosts are also referred to as apparitions, hallucinations, and phantasms. Most commonly believed to be spirits of deceased people, early psychical researchers believed that ghosts could possibly indicate the survival of consciousness beyond bodily death. Mediums, for example, were believed to communicate through spirits to deliver messages to the living, an activity researchers believed could also shed light on survival theories. One of the first committees formed under the British Society for Psychical Research (SPR) was the Committee on Haunted Houses, and members gathered accounts of people who had experienced a variety of ghostly phenomena. Many of which can be found in the historical archives of the *Journal (and Proceedings) of the Society for Psychical Research* at www.hathitrust.org.

Eleanor Sidgwick, a prominent and early member of the SPR compiled scores of ghostly reports and developed guidelines for determining if an experience was something genuinely ghostly. Those guidelines included things like whether the apparition was clearly identifiable, whether it was seen at different times or by different people, if it communicated a message, and if it seemed it was there to serve some purpose.[120] The publication of *Phantasms of the Living* broadened the understanding of ghostly phenomena. Authors Gurney, Podmore, and Myers discovered that ghostly apparitions were not just relegated to deceased people. They obtained hundreds of reports from people who witnessed apparitions of those still living. These apparitions were coined crisis apparitions since many of them were sighted when that person was experiencing an emergency or near-death situation.

Further Reading:

Edmund Gurney, Frederic W. H. Myers, and Frank Podmore, *Phantasms of the Living* (London: Kegan Paul, Trench, Trubner, and Co., 1918).
Michaeleen Maher, "Ghosts and Poltergeists: An Eternal Enigma," in *Parapsychology: A Handbook for the 21st Century*, edited by Etzel Cardeña, John Palmer, and David Marcusson-Clavertz, 327–39 (Jefferson, NC: McFarland and Company, 2015).

The Ghost Society: The Ghost Society was founded in 1851, making it a much earlier organization dedicated to the scientific study of paranormal phenomena. Notable psychical researcher Henry Sidgwick, along with others, was a member.[121]

Further Reading:

Michael E. Tymn, "Heroes and Highlights of Psychical Research Before 1882," *Journal of Spirituality & Paranormal Studies* 29, no. 3 (2006): 162–74.

Global Consciousness Project: The Global Consciousness Project was founded in 1998 by Roger Nelson, a member of the Princeton Engineering Anomalies Research Lab. International in scope, the researchers within this project study the possibility of a unified human consciousness. The online *Psi Encyclopedia* tells us that "the project looks for evidence that thoughts, emotions, and perceptions may potentially cohere in response to major world events, producing detectable effects."[122]

Further Reading:

Roger D. Nelson, "The Global Consciousness Project," *Journal of Parapsychology* 63, no. 3 (September 1, 1999): 213–15.

Goligher Circle: From 1914 to 1920, psychical researcher Dr. William Crawford met in regular sittings with members of the Goligher family. Becoming known as the Goligher Circle, the sittings mainly focused on the mediumship of Kathleen Goligher. Dr. Crawford was convinced that Kathleen used ectoplasmic secretions as cantilevers to levitate objects in the room. After his death, psychical research Dr. E. E. Fournier d'Able conducted sittings with the family but was convinced everything he saw was fraudulent.[123]

Further Reading:

Michael E. Tymn, "William Jackson Crawford on the Goligher Circle," *Journal of Scientific Exploration* 27, no. 3 (2013): 529–39.

Groupe d'Etudes de Recherche en Parapsychologie (Group for the Study and Research of Parapsychology): The Groupe d'Etudes de Recherche en Parapsychologie, or GERP, was established in France in the 1960s.[124] A group of students at the University of Paris recognized that, at the time, the Institut Métapsychique International was in decline and paired with their own interest in the pursuit of parapsychology, decided to form a new organization. Highly inspired by the work of parapsychologist Hans Bender, the students of GERP even traveled to Bender's parapsychology labs for collaboration and inspiration and through Bender's support, GERP was officially established in July 1971. GERP took a "more human-centered approach" to parapsychology, recognizing the need to not only investigate but to disseminate information and acknowledge the social and clinical aspects of psi phenomena.

Further Reading:

Renaud Evrard, "Parapsychology in France after May 1968: A History of GERP," *Journal of Scientific Exploration* 24, no. 2 (2010): 283–94.

Hallucination: Researchers Arthur and Joyce Berger tell us that hallucinations are "the experience of touching, seeing, hearing, or in any other way perceiving a person, object, or event although no physical person or object or event actually is stimulating the sensory organs."[125] Hallucinations can be the result of many things such as illness, meditation, drugs, etc. There are also many types of hallucinations,- for example, seeing a ghost or having an out-of-body experience. Early psychical researchers referred to ghost sightings as hallucination, in fact. One of the most seminal psychical studies is the Census of Hallucinations, which was an international survey gathered over three years. In total, researchers gathered seventeen thousand responses about hallucinatory experiences including sight, sound, touch, and more.

Further Reading:

Frederic W. H. Myers, "Report on the Census of Hallucinations," *Proceedings of the Society for Psychical Research* 10 (1894): 25–422.

Haunted Person Syndrome: Haunted person syndrome "encompasses percipients within the general population who invoke labels of ghosts or other supernatural agencies to explain a specific set of anomalous events that often are perceived recurrently."[126] In other words, there could be specific signs and symptoms that characterize a haunting experience (or *who* might encounter a haunting experience). It also suggests that hauntings are the result of certain people in certain environments or settings.

Further Reading:

Ciarán O'Keeffe, James Houran, Damien J. Houran, Neil Dagnall, Kenneth Drinkwater, Lorraine Sheridan, and Brian Laythe, "The Dr. John Hall Story: A Case Study in Putative 'Haunted Person Syndrome,'" *Mental Health, Religion, and Culture* 23, no. 7 (2020): 532–49.

Haunting: A haunting usually refers to a place that has a reputation of repeated paranormal events. Arthur and Joyce Berger gives us a more specific definition by telling us that "a haunt may be defined more generally as any place, whether house, palace, rectory, garden, or other location, where . . . any or all of the following paranormal phenomena have been experienced over a long period of time by one or more living people."[127] They go on to describe such phenomena as sightings of apparitions, anomalous noises like footsteps, strange sounds like voices or crying, and anomalous sensations like cold spots or cold chills. They also remind us that parapsychologists theorize that visitors to certain locations are psychically picking up on the previous events (and people) that happened throughout that location's history.[128]

Further Reading:

Brian Laythe and Kay Owen, "Paranormal Belief and the Strange Case of Haunt Experiences: Evidence of a Neglected Population," *Journal of Parapsychology* 76, no. 1 (Spring 2012): 79–108.

Heymans Anomalous Cognition Group: The Heymans Anomalous Cognition Group, named in honor of Dutch researcher Gerard Heymans, is a research group embedded within the Department of Psychology at the University of Groningen. According to their website, "The primary mission of the group is to establish and conduct a research programme into anomalous phenomena in order to discover whether such phenomena can be reliably replicated in laboratory studies."[129]

Hit: This refers to a call that is correctly made.[130]

Hypnagogic State: Michael A. Thalbourne tells us that a hypnagogic state (or, hypnagogia) refers to "the transitional state of consciousness experienced while falling asleep, sometimes characterized by vivid hallucinations or imagery of varying degrees of bizarreness."[131] Researchers believe that the hypnagogic state, being a type of altered state of consciousness, is conducive for psi phenomena to manifest. *See also, Dreams.*

Further Reading:

Guido del Prete and Patrizio E. Tressoldi, "Anomalous Cognition in Hypnagogic State with OBE Induction: An Experimental Study," *Journal of Parapsychology* 69, no. 2 (Fall 2005): 329–39.

Hypnopompic State: The hypnopompic state, as the opposite of hypnagogia, refers to the "transitional state of consciousness experience while waking from sleep."[132] In the same manner as the hypnagogic state, researchers believe this state also facilitates psi activity. Researcher Simon J. Sherwood tells us, "A whole range of anomalous experiences has been reported during the hypnagogic or hypnopompic states that surround periods of sleep. It is not uncommon for people to experience brief, vivid, and often strange imagery or to find themselves temporarily unable to move or speak during these periods."[133] Sherwood also points out that children who experience strange experiences in these states go on to report higher than average rates of paranormal experiences as adults.[134]

Further Reading:

Simon J. Sherwood, "Relationship Between the Hypnagogic/Hypnopompic States and Reports of Anomalous Experiences," *Journal of Parapsychology* 66, no. 2 (June 2002): 127–50.

Hypnotism: Hypnotism is described as "an altered state of consciousness bearing a superficial resemblance to sleep."[135] Methods of hypnotism were born from notions of mesmerism, the theory proposed by the physician Franz Mesmer. The theory of mesmerism states that a force existed around our bodies and that he could use that force to induce his patients into trance states. While Mesmer and his notions were highly ridiculed, practitioners curious about the general theory took some of the ideas and developed hypnotism. In addition, in some hypnotic trances, practitioners began to notice that subjects sometimes exhibited curious

psychical abilities. It became so noticeable that the British Society for Psychical Research made sure to include hypnosis as one of their main research subjects upon their founding.[136]

The use of hypnotism as a medical treatment was particularly employed by the French neurologist Jean-Martin Charcot. Researcher Régine Plas tells us, in fact, that "in the late 1870s Charcot, already a celebrated neurologist, 'rehabilitated' hypnotism by turning it into a method for studying hysteria."[137] Charcot's goal was that, by using hypnotism in a clinical way, it would rid this new technique of any lingering bias from its close association with mesmerism. Charcot and his colleagues quickly realized, however, that strange phenomena seemed to accompany their hypnotism work at the Salpêtrière Hospital.[138] This renewed interest in strange phenomena while others advanced our physiological and mental understanding of hypnotism. You can find a plethora of historical research on hypnotism in the archives of the *Journal of the Society for Psychical Research* within www.hathitrust.org.

Further Reading:

Frederic W. H. Myers, "On a Case of Alleged Hypnotic Hyperacuity of Vision," *Mind* 12, no. 45 (January 1887): 154–56.
Frederic W. H. Myers, "Professor Wundt on Hypnotism and Suggestion," *Mind* 2, no. 5 (January 1893): 95–101.
Régine Plas. "Psychology and Psychical Research in France around the end of the 19th Century." *History of the Human Sciences* 25, no. 2 (2012): 91–107.

Institut Général Psychologique: In France, as in other countries, psychology and psychical science emerged simultaneously, often resulting in tensions between the two as both fledgling disciplines fought to secure footing. For a time in France, the psychical and psychological shared the same journals and institutions but near the end of the 1800s and beginning of the 1900s, this collaboration began to change. The Institut Général Psychologique was formed in 1900 and was dedicated to the scientific inquiry of psychical research. It was led by Charles Richet and Pierre Janet and interestingly, the membership in this group was not led by psychologists but rather a diverse mix of others, including biologists, physicians, and others. Though the IGP also examined broader issues of psychology, there existed a subcommittee tasked only with psychical matters.[139]

Institut Métapsychique International: The Institut Métapsychique International (International Metaphysics Institute; IMI) is a French psychological research organization that was founded in 1919 by Gustave Geley and Jean Meyer. Early researchers of the IMI were interested in studying hypnotism and engaged in the emerging field of experimental psychology to study the phenomena. The IMI was formed when researchers recognized the need for a more formal organization that could place standards on researchers and research methods for the study of hypnotism and anomalous cognition. Researcher Sofie Lachapelle tells us that "members of the IMI hoped that it would provide the foundations for a serious and respected future science of metapsychics that would explain séances in terms of yet undiscovered powers in humans (telepathy, telekinesis, clairvoyance, etc.)."[140]

Further Reading:

Sofie Lachapelle, *Investigating the Supernatural: From Spiritism and Occultism to Psychical Research and Metapsychics in France, 1853–1931* (Baltimore, MD: Johns Hopkins University Press, 2011).

Institute for Frontier Areas of Psychology and Mental Health: Founded in 1950 in Germany by psychologist and psychical researcher Hans Bender, the Institute for Frontier Areas of Psychology and Mental Health promotes interdisciplinary research into anomalous phenomena and altered states of consciousness. The institute also promotes educational programs and offers counseling services as well. According to their website, they are the largest nonprofit institute of their kind in the world.[141]

Institute for Parapsychology: After parapsychologist J. B. Rhine retired from Duke University, the parapsychology labs on campus were disbanded and Rhine established his own independent laboratory, called the Institute for Parapsychology. This institute continued the work done at Duke but operated under the auspices of Rhine's organization, Foundation for Research on the Nature of Man. Today, it is known as the Rhine Research Center.[142]

Institute of Noetic Sciences: The Institute of Noetic Sciences (IONS) is a scientific research organization dedicated to the mission of understanding more about profound human experiences. Its website states that its mission is to learn more about the interconnected nature of reality and that "as scientists focused on what are common but not often understood phenomena, we are also aware of the vast historical records of wisdom practices that also speak to the mysteries and possibilities which allow us to access more of our human capacities."[143] Researchers with IONS publish scholarly articles on topics like the genetics of psychic abilities, collective consciousness, channeling, and more.

Instituto de Psicología Paranormal: The Instituto de Psicología Paranormal (IPP) is a nonprofit parapsychological research organization based in Buenos Aires, Argentina. Established in 1994, IPP is "an educational center dedicated to the scientific study of paranormal/anomalous events and experiences" and believes that "parapsychology cannot do without interdisciplinary collaboration."[144] From 1990–2004, IPP published *Revista Argentina de Psicología Paranormal.* That publication ceased to exist in 2004, however, but IPP created *E-Boletin Psi,* a digital newsletter, in its place. Anyone can view the current and past issues of *E-Boletin Psi* and read various research studies contained therein from IPP's website.

Instrumental Transcommunication: Researchers Mark Boccuzzi and Julie Beischel of the Windbridge Institute for Applied Research in Human Potential tell us that instrumental transcommunication (ITC) is "the use of different technologies to facilitate discarnate communication and interaction."[145] ITC can take the shape of various mediums like an audio recorder, a video recorder, special devices, apps, phones, etc. and that the goal is to capture not just voices but also videos, images, or other anomalous aspects that appear to be from discarnate entities. Electronic voice phenomenon (EVP) is one example of instrumental transcommunication. *See also, Electronic Voice Phenomena*

Further Reading:

Callum E. Cooper, "An Analysis of Exceptional Experiences Involving Telecommunication Technology," *Journal of Parapsychology* 78, no. 2 (Fall 2014): 209–22.

Japanese Society for Parapsychology: The Japanese Society for Parapsychology was founded in 1968. It publishes the *Japanese Journal of Parapsychology* and hosts conferences that feature and promote parapsychological research.[146]

Journal of the American Society for Psychical Research: This journal is the scholarly publication of the American Society for Psychical Research, an organization established in 1885 just a few short years after the establishment of the British Society for Psychical Research.[147] The first publication was issued in 1907 and it contains scholarly research articles, case studies, book reviews, and more.[148] Those interested in older issues of this journal will be able to locate them online at www.hathitrust.org.

Journal of Parapsychology: The *Journal of Parapsychology* is a scholarly journal that was first established in 1937 by the Duke University Parapsychology Labs. Today, it is managed by the Rhine Research Center.

Further Reading:

J. B. Rhine, "A Backward Look at Leaving the JP." *Journal of Parapsychology* 41, no. 2 (June 1977): 89–102.

Journal of the Society for Psychical Research: The *Journal of the Society for Psychical Research* is the scholarly journal of the British Society for Psychical Research. Much like the aforementioned journals, this journal publishes primary and secondary research studies, case studies, book reviews, editorial comments, and more. Its first publication was issued in 1884 and was, at the time, a private publication only for members.[149] It serves as a seminal publication in the scholarly literature of parapsychology. You can find some of the historical editions of this journal online at www.hathitrust.org.

"Just One of Those Things": "Just one of those things," or JOTT as it is commonly referred, is a "term coined by Mary Rose Barrington to refer to a collective term for discontinuities in the fabric of observed reality."[150] There are many types of JOTTS, including items that simply disappear and never return (flyaways), items that disappear from normal locations only to be found right in that spot sometime after (comebacks), and walkabouts, or, items that disappear from their normal location and end up somewhere completely unrelated.[151]

Further Reading:

Mary Rose Barrington, "JOTT—Just One of Those Things," *Psi Research* 3 (October 1991).

Koestler Parapsychology Unit: Named after Arthur Koestler and located at the University of Edinburgh, the Koestler Parapsychology Unit (KPU) is a research unit housed within the schools of philosophy and psychology. Dr. Caroline Watt tells us that "the KPU consists of teaching staff, research staff, and postgraduate students whose area of interest and expertise is parapsychology and the psychology of anomalous experiences and beliefs."[152]

Further Reading:

Caroline Watt, "Research Assistants or Budding Scientists? A Review of 96 Undergraduate Student Projects at the Koestler Parapsychology Unit," *Journal of Parapsychology* 70, no. 2 (Fall 2006): 335–55.

Levitation: Levitation occurs when objects seem to raise of their own accord in defiance of known laws of gravity.[153] A staple of the séances of the Spiritualism era, levitation of various objects can be found in reports of sittings with various mediums like Eusapia Palladino, D. D. Home, Nina Kulagina, and more.[154]

Further Reading:

K. J. Batcheldor, "Report on a Case of Table Levitation and Associated Phenomena," *Journal of the Society for Psychical Research* 43 (1966): 339–56.

Figure G.4. Alleged Levitation of Medium Amedee Zuccarini During a Séance
From *After Death–What?* by Cesare Lombroso (Boston: Small, Maynard, and Co., 1909). PD-US

Light: *Light* is the publication of the College of Psychic Studies, the organization formerly known as the London Spiritualist Alliance.

Liminality: Liminality is a concept developed by anthropologists Arnold van Gennep and Victor Turner.[155] The concept of liminality "refers to a transitional or in-between state that occurs during a ritual process—a stage in which the practitioner's understanding, identity, or role is in flux."[156] Others have built upon this concept and tell us that liminality occurs when social structures and hierarchies are held in abeyance.[157] Most relevant to the topic of parapsychology is the concept of transliminality, a "threshold that mediates unconscious-conscious awareness."[158]

Further Reading:

Michael A. Thalbourne, "Transliminality, Anomalous Belief and Experience, and Hypnotisability," *Australian Journal of Clinical and Experimental Hypnosis* 37, no. 2 (November 2009): 119–30.

Linger Effect: The linger effect occurs when psychokinetic activity seems to continue occurring even after the identified agent is no longer at or near the location.[159]

Linkage Design: Sometimes also referred to as a linkage experiment, this is a method used in studies of mediumship. In linkage design, multiple people are placed as "links" between the medium and the intended target and only given certain pieces of information. No one link has all information.[160]

Literary Committee: The Literary Committee was an early committee of the British Society for Psychical Research. Members were tasked with creating a library of core resources on various topics related to psychical research. These resources would indicate the best evidence for a variety of psi phenomena, and members would also provide their view of such evidence. As a result, there was not only a core body of resources made available but in the process these resources were vetted in a type of peer-review process.[161] In an 1887 edition of the *Journal of the Society for Psychical Research*, members of the committee tell us that their first focus was gathering supporting literature on cases of spontaneous telepathy. This was due in large part to the recent publication and success of *Phantasms of the Living*.

Further Reading:

Edmund Gurney and Frederic W. H. Myers, "Statement of the Literary Committee of the Society for Psychical Research," *Journal of the Society for Psychical Research* 3, no. 36 (January 1887): 1–8.

London Dialectical Society: The London Dialectical Society formed a committee to investigate mediumship in the mid and late 1800s. In 1871, they published a report on the medium Daniel Dunglas Home that stated that they could not determine any natural causes to explain his apparent mediumistic abilities.[162]

Macro-Psychokinesis: Macro-psychokinesis, or macro-PK as it is most commonly referred, is a term used to describe the directly observable effects of psychokinesis. For example, a directly observable PK effect could be movement of objects upon a table. A popular example is the many dice-throwing PK experiments.[163] *See also, Psychokinesis.*

Further Reading:

Erlendur Haraldsson and Richard Wiseman, "Two Investigations of Ostensible Macro-PK in India," *Journal of the Society for Psychical Research* 61, no. 843 (April 1, 1996).

Maimonides Dream Labs: In 1962, Dr. Montague Ullman established a dream laboratory in New York at the Maimonides Medical Center with the intent to study telepathy in dreams. One series of experiments was designed as such: a subject (the sleeping person) would briefly meet the agent (the person who would attempt to send images while the subject was asleep). After this brief meeting, the subject would go to sleep and the agent, who remained in a nearby room in the same building, would focus on the random art print that they were assigned and attempt to send their impressions of the art print to the subject. The agent paid particular focus during the times in which the subject was in REM sleep.[164] The dreams would then be reviewed by independent judges for overlap. For example, in one study, the agent was given a painting of ballerinas. The subject, upon waking, said that in their dream they felt like they were at a school and that a girl kept trying to get them to dance.[165]

Additional researchers joined Dr. Ullman in his dream work, such as Charles Honorton, Stanley Krippner, and Robert van de Castle. These researchers all brought unique studies to the dream labs, such as Van de Castle who took a psychoanalytic viewpoint and Krippner, who studied potential links between hypnotic dreaming and clairvoyance.[166]

Further Reading:

Stanley Krippner, "The Maimonides ESP-Dream Studies," *Journal of Parapsychology* 57, no. 1 (March 1, 1993): 39–54.

Montague Ullman and Stanley Krippner, "Experimentally Induced Telepathic Dreams: Two Studies Using EEG-REM Monitoring Technique," *International Journal of Neuropsychiatry* 2, no. 5 (1966): 420–37.

Materialization: This term refers to the presence of an apparition or object that was not in that space previously and which appears seemingly out of thin air. It has most commonly been used to refer to phenomena during séances. For example, Arthur and Joyce Berger tell us that materialization is "the purported appearance during a séance or sitting with a physical medium of visible, tangible objects or human faces, hands, or life-sized forms."[167]

Mean Chance Expectation: The mean chance expectation refers to the average (mean) score in a psi experiment that could be attributed to chance.[168] Knowing this helps researchers understand if their data fall above or below the mean chance expectation.

Medium: A medium is a person who engages in trances and obtains information in an anomalous manner. Most people likely think of the mediums of the Spiritualism era, as this is when their fame and notoriety skyrocketed, but mediums and mediumship practices exist today. There are two main types of mediumship. The first are physical mediums, the class most commonly associated with the 1800s. In physical mediumship, physical effects occur during the medium's trance, like levitations of tables, other psychokinetic effects, apported objects, anomalous voices, etc. The second type is mental mediumship exhibit their abilities through unseen, mental forces like clairvoyance and, some believe, through direct psychical communication with spirits of deceased individuals.[169]

Early psychical researchers recognized the rising trend of mediumship from the mid to late 1800s and realized that mediumistic abilities could have implications for our understanding of consciousness beyond death. If mediums were communicating with deceased individuals, for example, this could be proof of survival. As such, mediums became a large research focus for early psychical researchers. The famed Italian medium Eusapia Palladino drew the attention of Frederic W. H. Myers, Henry and Eleanor Sidgwick, and Sir Oliver Lodge and in 1894 the group met with Palladino in France for a series of investigations. The Sidgwicks were unconvinced while others, like Myers and Lodge, believed Palladino's abilities to be genuine.[170] Many physical mediums like Palladino, it seems, divided researchers into two groups: those who believed *something* anomalous may be occurring and those who did not.

In a 2007 study in the *Journal of Parapsychology*, researcher Julie Beischel discusses the nuances of investigating mediumship in controlled, laboratory settings. In this study, mediums were studied by the Windbridge Institute for Applied Research in Human Potential. The studies involved specific methods that would both facilitate alleged communication with discarnate entities *and* provide some level of controlled, scientific methods. Their methods involved five levels of blinding, screening of all participants, specific protocols and questions, and a detailed formula for scorers to evaluate data. These new protocols can be applied to in-person, phone, or internet readings with mediums, and Beischel discusses the findings using these protocols and how they can help advance the scientific reputation of research into mediums.[171]

Further Reading:

Julie Beischel, "Contemporary Methods Used in Laboratory-Based Mediumship Research," *Journal of Parapsychology* 71 (Spring 2007): 37–68.

Stephen E. Braude, *Immortal Remains: The Evidence for Life After Death* (Lanham, MD: Rowman & Littlefield, 2003).

William Crookes, "Notes of Seances with D.D. Home," *Proceedings of the Society for Psychical Research* 6 (1889): 98–127.

Paul F. Cunningham, "The Content-Source Problem in Modern Mediumship Research," *Journal of Parapsychology* 76, no. 2 (Fall 2012): 295–319.

Armand Martire Diaz, "Divination as a Life Path in Contemporary America: An In-Depth Exploration of the World of Psychic-Mediums," PhD diss., California Institute of Integral Studies, 2011.

Ciarán O'Keeffe and Richard Wiseman, "Testing Alleged Mediumship: Methods and Results," *British Journal of Psychology* 96, no. 2 (May 2005): 165–79.

Mesmerism: Mesmerism is the forerunner to hypnotism and was popularized by the physician Franz Anton Mesmer, who believed that there was an invisible fluid surrounding our bodies that could be manipulated by magnets. Mesmerism also involved placing subjects into a trance through specific movements of the hands over the subject's body. Once

in this trance (which was used at first as a type of sedative for medical procedures), Mesmer and other practitioners noticed that subjects displayed strange psychical abilities like telepathy and clairvoyance.[172]

Further Reading:

John Warne Monroe, *Laboratories of Faith: Mesmerism, Spiritism, and Occultism in Modern France* (Ithaca, NY: Cornell University Press, 2008).

Metapsychics: Metapsychics is a term coined by French researcher Charles Richet and used in France and other European countries to refer to psychical research.[173]

Further Reading:

Annette Mülberger and Mónica Balltondre, "Metapsychics in Spain: Acknowledging or Questioning the Marvelous?" *History of the Human Sciences* 25, no. 2 (2012): 108–30.

Micro Psychokinesis: Micro-psychokinesis, or micro-PK as it is most commonly referred, is a type of psychokinesis in which PK effects are not directly observable to the human eye.[174] It has commonly been applied to studies involving effects on random number generators. Researchers Mario Varvoglis and Peter A. Bancel point out that the studies done by Helmut Schmidt with micro-PK are foundational experiments in our understanding of this phenomenon.[175] *See also, psychokinesis.*

Further Reading:

Azlan Iqbal, "A Replication of the Slight Effect of Human Thought on a Pseudorandom Number Generator," *NeuroQuantology* 11, no. 4 (2013): 519–26.

Mario Varvoglis and Peter A. Bancel, "Micro-Psychokinesis: Exceptional or Universal?" *Journal of Parapsychology* 80, no. 1 (Spring 2016): 37–44.

Muscle Reading: Muscle reading is a physiological process that gives subconscious clues to people regarding, for example, the location of a hidden object. It can sometimes be confused with telepathy and/or clairvoyance.[176] It is responsible for the popularity behind popular parlor games of the 1800s in which a person had to locate an object unknown to them but decided upon by the group. A famous case involving the Creery family is included in the further reading section and helps elucidate this concept.

Further Reading:

W. F. Barrett, Edmund Gurney, and F. W. H. Myers, "First Report on Thought-Reading," *Proceedings of the Society for Psychical Research* 1, no. 1 (July 17, 1882): 13–34.

Near-Death Experience: A near-death experience (NDE) is an event in which a person experiences an emergency situation that involves being very close to death and/or being brought back from clinical, medical death. There are some hallmarks of an NDE including the sensation of traveling through a tunnel, experiencing a life review, a feeling of being out of their body, seeing deceased friends and loved ones, and more.[177] In a 2001 article in the *Lancet*, cardiologist Pim van Lommel and colleagues, also point out that NDEs can occur in people with severe depression and note that the hallmarks of NDEs seem consistent across cultures. Furthermore, the researchers also found that "medical factors cannot account for occurrence of NDE; although all patients had been clinically dead, most did not have NDE."[178]

Further Reading:

Bruce Greyson, "Varieties of Near-Death Experience," *Psychiatry* 56, no. 4 (November 1993): 390–99.

Rense Lange, Bruce Greyson, and James Houran, "A Rasch Scaling Validation of a 'Core' Near-Death Experience," *British Journal of Psychology* 95 (May 2004): 161–77.

Chris A. Roe, Alasdair Gordon-Finlayson, and Michael Daniels, "Transpersonal Psychology and Parapsychology: Lessons from the Near-Death Experience," *Journal of Transpersonal Psychology* 52, no. 2 (2020): 188–203.

Pim van Lommel, Ruud van Wees, and Vincent Myers, "Near-Death Survivors of Cardiac Arrest: A Prospective Study in the Netherlands," *Lancet* 358, no. 9298 (December 15, 2001): 2039–45.

Newspaper Test: The newspaper test is used during studies of mediumship. Mediumship implies that the medium themself is receiving information from a deceased and/or nonliving intelligent entity. Cases of mediumship have implications for consciousness beyond bodily death, then. In an attempt to eliminate the possibility that the medium is picking up on information from the minds of the living sitters in the room, certain tests are sometimes used—the newspaper method being one of them. In this test, a medium's control is asked to communicate via passages and snippets from articles on newspapers. The idea is that neither the sitters nor the medium will have looked at the newspaper so to eliminate the possibility that the medium is picking up telepathically on information in the sitter's minds.[179]

Object Reading: Sometimes referred to as token-object readings, this occurs when an object is used to help induce psychic information about a person. In other words, a medium is given a physical object belonging to the person they're attempting to communicate with in hopes of sparking a connection. Object reading is psychometry, or the ability to psychically intuit information from physical touch.[180]

Further Reading:

Ian S. Baker, Jane Montague, and Abigail Booth, "A Controlled Study of Psychometry using Psychic and Non-Psychic Claimants with Actual and False Readings using a Mixed-Methods Approach," *Journal of the Society for Psychical Research* 81, no. 2 (April 2017): 108–22.

Open Matching: In an experiment involving open matching, a subject is given a pack of ESP cards that remain facedown. On a surface in front of them are five cards, faceup, that represent the various symbols found within the ESP cards. Open-matching involves the subject attempting to match which symbol they believe corresponds to the card they are holding.[181]

Further Reading:

William Russell and J. B. Rhine, "A Single Subject in a Variety of ESP Test Conditions," *Journal of Parapsychology* 6, no. 4 (December 1, 1942): 284–311.

Operator: This term refers to the subject in an experiment. Consider it the person doing the psi activity under question. Michael A. Thalbourne reminds us that it is a term especially used in psychokinesis studies.[182]

Out-of-Body Experience: The out-of-body experience (OOB/OOBE) is an altered state of consciousness. Parapsychologist Michael A. Thalbourne provides a definition of an OOBE as "an experience, either spontaneous or induced, in which one's center of consciousness seems to be in a spatial location outside of one's physical body."[183] Psychologists point to the role of absorption, dissociation, and depersonalization that could play a role in these experiences.[184] Parapsychologist Harvey Irwin tells us that "in phenomenological terms the OBE entails an experient's *impression* that the self has separated from the body, and on this ground the OBE is designated a parapsychological experience, that is, one in which seems to the experient that a paranormal phenomena is involved. It is uncertain, however, that a paranormal process actually does underlie the OBE."[185]

Further Reading:

Harvey J. Irwin, "The Disembodied Self: An Empirical Study of Dissociation and the Out-of-Body Experience," *Journal of Parapsychology* 64, no. 3 (September 1, 2000): 261–77.

David Lindsay, "Out-of-Body Experience: The Definitive Afterlife Research Tool for the 21st Century," *Journal of Spirituality and Paranormal Studies* 30 (July 2007): 109–19.

Joseph Meyerson and Marc Gelkopf, "Therapeutic Utilization of Spontaneous Out-of-Body Experiences in Hypnotherapy," *American Journal of Psychotherapy* 58, no. 1 (2004): 90 102.

D. Scott Rogo, "Psychological Models of the Out-of-Body Experience," *Journal of Parapsychology* 46, no. 1 (March 1, 1982): 29–45.

David Wilde and Craig D. Murray, "Interpreting the Anomalous: Finding Meaning in Out-of-Body and Near-Death Experiences," *Qualitative Research in Psychology* 7, no. 1 (January 2010): 57–72.

Parapsychology: Researchers and parapsychologists Arthur and Joyce Berger tell us that parapsychology is "a division of science that uses experimental and quantitative techniques in the laboratory to investigate paranormal or psychic experiences or events involving living organisms."[186] It differs from the older term "psychical research" in its spe-

cific focus on experimental, scientific methods. Attributed to the German scholar Max Dessoir, it was popularized by William McDougall and J. B. Rhine when they established a parapsychology laboratory at Duke University. Much of parapsychological research focuses on anomalous cognition and anomalous physical behaviors that are not seemingly caused by known sources. As a branch of science, many critics are quick to reduce it to pseudoscience, claiming faulty research methods, lack of replicability, and no statistically significant data.[187]

Further Reading:

John Beloff, *Parapsychology: A Concise History* (London: Athlone Press, 1993).

Parapsychological Association: The Parapsychological Association was established in 1957 through the work of J. B. Rhine and is an affiliate of the American Association for the Advancement of Science. It is an international member organization of scholars interested in parapsychological topics. Their main goals are "the advancement of the field of parapsychology, dissemination of information about parapsychology, and the integration with other branches of science of the findings of parapsychology."[188] The association helps to subsidize the *Journal of Parapsychology*, holds annual conventions, publishes convention abstracts, publishes the *Mindfield Bulletin*, and offers various membership tiers.[189]

Further Reading:

Dean Radin, "Parapsychological Association Presidential Address, 2018," *Journal of Parapsychology* 83, no. 1 (Spring 2019): 5–12.

Parapsychology Foundation: The Parapsychology Foundation was established by Eileen J. Garrett and Frances P. Bolton in 1951 and supports access to and research into parapsychological phenomena. The foundation provides grants for researchers, holds conferences, and maintains a library accessible to any interested.[190] Additionally, the foundation holds lectures, has an outreach program, and cosponsors the *Journal of Anomalous Experience and Cognition.*[191]

Further Reading:

Lynda Richardson, "Gatherings Ponder Other Worlds: Belief and Skepticism Mingle at the

Parapsychology Foundation," *New York Times* (June 5, 2000): B6.

Percipient: The term percipient refers to someone who experiences extrasensory perception and/or who acts as the agent in psi research studies.[192]

Phantasm: Today, most people likely use terms other than "phantasm," but it is a term used to describe an apparition, hallucination, or anomalous sense experience.[193] You may recall its use in the seminal text *Phantasms of the Living.*

Picture Test: Similar to the book test or newspaper test, the picture test is a method used to help verify information from a medium. In the picture test, the medium's spirit control or communicator will identify a picture that is somehow relevant to the sitters and the spirit in question.[194]

Placement Psychokinesis: Placement psychokinesis (PK) refers to a method devised by parapsychologist William Cox. In placement PK studies, objects are thrown upon a surface and attempt to psychokinetically influence *where* on the surface those objects will land, most typically to the left or right side of the field.[195] It is sometimes referred to as the placement test. William Cox recognized in his early studies that a subject may be just as strongly influencing where an object lands *and* where it does not land and worried that these simultaneous efforts may cancel each other out in some traditional left-and-right placement tests. Therefore, he developed revised placement tests that used tiers.[196]

Other PK researchers, like Louisa E. Rhine, investigated how macro-PK is affected when using different types of objects. Dice were the most popular objects, but in a 1951 study Rhine used marbles, coins, and cubes and, though her study did not yield statistically significant results, Rhine did discover a link between success rates and length of runs.[197]

Further Reading:

William E. Cox, "Three-Tier Placement PK," *Journal of Parapsychology* 23, no. 1 (March 1, 1959): 19–29.

Haakon Forwald, "A Further Study of the PK Placement Effect," *Journal of Parapsychology* 16, no. 1 (March 1, 1952): 59–67.

J. G. Pratt, "The Cormack Placement PK Experiments," *Journal of Parapsychology* 15, no. 1 (1951): 57–73.

Louisa E. Rhine, "Placement PK Tests with Three Types of Objects," *Journal of Parapsychology* 15, no. 2 (June 1, 1951): 132–38.

Poltergeist: Poltergeist phenomena refers to cases of anomalous events that typically include movement of objects and which seem to center around one person. Parapsychologists J. G. Pratt and W. G. Roll give us a precise definition of the poltergeist phenomena when they tell us that they involve

a series of unexplained noises and movements of objects [that begin] unexpectedly [and which] continue intermittently in that location for a period which may range from a few days to several months [and which] are observed to be closely associated with a young person . . . and sometimes follow this young person to another location [and which] end as unaccountably as they began.[198]

While many may only associate poltergeist phenomena with young people, researcher Annalisa Ventola and colleagues discovered that it is not only limited to this population and can in fact, even occur among the elderly.[199] There are scores of well-documented cases of alleged poltergeist phenomena. The aforementioned researchers once investigated a case in Long Island in which they documented more than sixty occurrences of items moving on their own accord, strange crashing sounds, and events that seemed to center around one family and their young teenage son.[200] In this case, Pratt and Roll also believed that recurrent spontaneous psychokinesis was causing much of the phenomena (RSPK) and in their study they draw clear connections linking poltergeist phenomena with RSPK. This connection is yet another illustration of the interconnectedness of anomalous phenomena.

A 2016 article in the *Journal of Parapsychology* discusses a peculiar iteration of modern poltergeist phenomena and discusses "electronic poltergeist disturbance." Described as a form of RSPK that manifests through anomalous electronic dis-

Figure G.5. Parapsychologist J. Gaither Pratt Investigating a Poltergeist Case
From "House of Flying Objects" by Robert Wallace in *LIFE Magazine* (March 17, 1958): PD-US-not renewed

turbances, researchers identified the agent and introduced mindfulness techniques to determine their effect on the phenomena.[201]

Further Reading:

H. Bender, "New Developments in Poltergeist Research," *Proceedings of the Parapsychological Association* 6 (1969): 81–109.

John G. Kruth and William T. Joines, "Taming the Ghost Within: An Approach Toward Addressing Apparent Electronic Poltergeist Activity," *Journal of Parapsychology* 80, no. 1 (Spring 2016): 70–86.

J. G. Pratt and W. G. Roll, "The Seaford Disturbances," *Journal of Parapsychology* 22, no. 2 (June 1958): 79–124.

Precognition: Researcher Michael Thalbourne tells us that precognition is "a form of extrasensory perception in which the target is some future event that cannot be deduced from normally known data in the present."[202] In a 1938 article, parapsychology J. B. Rhine discusses the inherent fascination with precognition: "The precognition (or prophecy) hypothesis represents, as is well known, what is for many persons a firm belief, and what has been through the ages an important part of religious and occult creeds and philosophies."[203]

Precognition can manifest in different ways. A 2014 study in the *Journal of Parapsychology*, for example, looked at precognitive dreams.[204] Other researchers have investigated the relationship between ganzfeld environments and precognition.[205] Parapsychologist Louisa Rhine, in her work with the Duke Parapsychology Labs, discovered that nearly 40 percent of all letters sent to the researchers in that lab had to do with precognitive events.[206]

Some researchers, however, argue that true precognition is not possible and that it is the result of some other psi functions, for example, like telepathically obtaining knowledge about an event from someone's mind or psychokinetically affecting an environment or object around you.[207]

Further Reading:

R. L. Morris, "Assessing Experimental Support for True Precognition," *Journal of Parapsychology* 46 (1982): 321–36.

J. B. Rhine, "Experiments Bearing on the Precognition Hypothesis," *Journal of Parapsychology* 2, no. 1 (March 1, 1938): 38–54.

Fiona Steinkamp, "Does Precognition Foresee the Future? A Postal Experiment to Assess the Possibility of True Precognition," *Journal of Parapsychology* 64, no. 1 (March 1, 2000): 3–18

Caroline Watt, "Precognitive Dreaming: Investigating Anomalous Cognition and Psychological Factors," *Journal of Parapsychology* 78, no. 1 (Spring 2014): 115–25.

Presentiment: Having a presentiment refers to having a particular feeling about a future event. It is a type of extrasensory perception rooted in feeling.

Princeton Engineering Anomalies Research Lab: Dr. Robert G. Jahn, dean of Princeton University's engineering school established the Princeton Engineering Anomalies Research (PEAR) lab in 1979. The focus of the PEAR lab was "the exploration of the role of consciousness in the establishment of physical reality."[208] The inspiration came after a student conducted a study on the potential effects of the human mind upon a random number generator. From there, Dr. Jahn and students were curious about other aspects of human and machine interactions and PEAR was established. A series of inventive and creative experiments were designed, ranging from a ten-foot-tall cascade of marbles to a toy frog and "the primary variable in all these experiments was the human operator's pre-stated intentions to shift the output distribution of the random binary events in positive or negative directions."[209] The PEAR lab disbanded in 2007 to become the International Consciousness Research Laboratories.

Further Reading:

Brenda J. Dunne, "Princeton Engineering Anomalies Research Lab," in *Ghosts, Spirits, and Psychics: The Paranormal from Alchemy to Zombies*, edited by Matt Cardin, 231–33 (Santa Barbara, CA: ABC-CLIO, 2015).

Proxy Sitter: In studies of mediums, a proxy sitter is someone who fills in for the regular sitter. Proxy sitters help "blind" the medium from cues that could be gathered from the actual sitter. Researchers have found that mediums still obtain relevant information in the presence of proxy sitters.[210]

Further Reading:

Gertrude R. Schmeidler, "Analysis and Evaluation of Proxy Sessions with Mrs. Caroline Chapman," *Journal of Parapsychology* 22 (1958): 137–55.

D. J. West, "Some Proxy Sittings: A Preliminary Attempt at Objective Assessment," *Journal of the Society for Psychical Research* 35 (1949): 96–101.

Psi: Researcher Robert Thouless proposed the use of "psi" as a broader term to encompass various anomalous phenomena. It is inspired by the word "psyche" and "today, 'psi' has been widely adopted and seems to meet the objections to the terms 'extrasensory perception' and 'psychokinesis.'"[211]

Some researchers have suggested using the terms psi gamma and psi kappa when referring to psi phenomena. Psi gamma would refer to cognitive psi-like clairvoyance and extrasensory perception whereas psi kappa would refer to physical aspects of psi-like psychokinesis.[212]

Psi-Missing: Psi-missing refers to a statistically significant negative result in a psi experiment. Researchers Arthur and Joyce Berger describe it as "when a target at which subjects are directing their ESP is avoided to a significant degree."[213] In designing experiments, researchers establish what the chance levels are for some phenomena to occur. For example, in the popular card-guessing experiments, researchers calculate what the chance

levels are that will result in someone choosing the correct target—after all, there is always a chance, given a set of predetermined targets, that you will guess the correct one. Once a chance level has been established, this will help determine if results fall above, within, or below that average. And it is just as statistically significant when data falls far below the chance levels than when they fall far above. In other words, it is just as curious that something *isn't* happening as when it is.

Belief also plays a role in psi-missing. For example, parapsychologist Gertrude Schmeidler postulated a sheep-goat effect, which states that there is "a tendency for believers in ESP, or sheep, to score above chance and for disbelievers, or goats, to score below."[214]

Further Reading:

Louisa E. Rhine, "Toward Understanding Psi-Missing," *Journal of Parapsychology* 29, no. 4 (December 1, 1965): 259–74.

Psi Open Data: Psi Open Data is an online database managed by the Society for Psychical Research. It is inspired by the open access movement that "initially [focused] on removing access restrictions to articles in scholarly journals [and] has broadened to encompass data and code."[215] Psi Open Data lets researchers upload their datasets and is freely viewable visitors. On their website, you can find datasets from researchers like Marilyn J. Schlitz, Dean Radin, Etzel Cardeña, and more. Topics include a range of psi topics like ganzfeld studies, precognition, hypnosis and more.

Further Reading:

Adrian Ryan, "Open Data in Parapsychology: Introducing *Psi Open Data*," *Journal of Parapsychology* 82, no. 1 (2018): 65–76.

Psychic: Psychic can refer to people who exhibit any number of extrasensory abilities and can also be used to describe psi phenomena.[216]

Psychical: Psychical refers to things that are of or relating to a psychic nature. For example, a common way of referring to the study of these phenomena was "psychical research." It was most commonly used prior to the 1940s.

Psychical Research Foundation: The Psychical Research Foundation (PRF) was created in 1961 and established by Charles E. Ozanne and J. B. Rhine as a means to support parapsychological research. Noted parapsychologists William G. Roll and J. Gaither Pratt were among its first members and through the years the PRF has established international collaborations with researchers on topics like out-of-body experiences, anomalous dreams, recurrent spontaneous psychokinesis, and more.[217]

Psychische Studien: *Psychische Studien* was a publication created in 1874 and published by the psychical researcher Alexander Aksakov. It contained much debate about Spiritualism and was considered an important psychical journal.[218] It was a contemporary publication of (and competitor to) *Sphinx*, another journal that published topics relating to psychical issues.

Further Reading:

Andreas Sommer, "Normalizing the Supernormal: The Formation of the 'Gesellschaft Für Psychologische Forschung' ('Society for Psychological Research'), c. 1886–1890," *Journal of the History of the Behavioral Sciences* 49, no. 1 (Winter 2013): 18–44.

Psychokinesis: Psychokinesis (PK) is defined as "the direct influence of the mind on an external physical system or object without the intermediation of any known physical energy."[219]

Early psychical researchers referred to PK as telekinesis, though that is now a less-favored term.

J. B. and Louisa Rhine popularized the parapsychological study of PK in the 1930s and 1940s with their dice-throwing experiments. In "The Case for Psychokinesis," researcher J. G. Pratt reminds us that the Rhines' set out to investigate the possibility of PK using dice and with the intention of influencing those dice to land so that their sums were either high or low.[220] Pratt tells us, "The first work was exploratory, and the dice were thrown under a variety of circumstances. Some of the trials were made as in ordinary dice games; the cubes were shaken in cupped hands and rolled upon a blanketed surface or bounced off a vertical barrier before they came to rest. For other tests, the dice were shaken in a cup before they were thrown. In still others, the dice were rolled down an inclined chute onto a horizontal table or floor area."[221] Over the course of eight years, the Rhineses and others conducted experiments using a variety of methods and techniques and yielded statistically significant results that seemed to support psychokinesis. Through their studies, researchers also discovered the position effect, a curious effect that indicates scores follow a pattern based on their location (position) in the experimental series.[222]

Other seminal PK researchers include Robert H. Thouless, who conducted a series of PK experiment in 1948 in which he acted as the subject. Using four dice, his goal was to psychokinetically affect the dice so that they landed on certain faces. Thouless conducted the same number of throws for each six sides of the die and used differing methods of throwing for example using a cup versus mechanical throwing. Thouless discovered that, taken as a whole, the results showed a statistically significant result indicated of *some* effect occurring beyond simple chance. Interestingly, Thouless also investigated whether certain attributes impacted PK success. Some of the factors he thought may impact success included motivation, time of day, length of experience, and psychological factors. Perhaps most interestingly, Thouless discovered that having a sense of play seemed to heighten chances for success. He shares a story about his son throwing dice and noticed that the results were higher when he conducted throws on his own controlled attempts.[223]

In addition to the Rhines and Thouless, other researchers have studied psychokinesis. Researchers like William G. Roll and William T. Joines realized that PK is often a factor in cases of poltergeist phenomena. In fact, they labeled PK that occurs in poltergeist cases as recurrent spontaneous psychokinesis.[224] Other subtypes of psychokinesis include macro-psychokinesis (macro-PK), which involve those instances in which PK is noticeable to the observer, for example, an object being moved across a table. This contrasts with micro-psychokinesis (micro-PK), which refers to instances of PK that are not observable with the naked eye, like subtle raises in temperature or effects on random number generators.

Further Reading:

Pamela Rae Heath, *The PK Zone: A Cross-Cultural Review of Psychokinesis* (New York: Universe, 2003).

J. G. Pratt, "The Case for Psychokinesis," *Journal of Parapsychology* 24, no. 3 (September 1, 1960): 171–88.

William G. Roll and William T. Joines, "RSPK and Consciousness," *Journal of Parapsychology* 77, no. 2 (Fall 2013): 192–211.

Robert H. Thouless, "A Report on an Experiment in Psychokinesis with Dice and a Discussion on Psychological Factors Favoring Success," *Journal of Parapsychology* 15, no. 2 (June 1, 1951): 89–102.

Psychologische Gesellschaft: The Psychologische Gesellschaft (Psychological Society) was founded in 1886 by German philosopher Carl du Prel. The organization was interested in psychical research, and members would meet to conduct experiments on phenomena such as thought-transference. For example, during one experiment members of the society invited the well-known "somnambulist" Lina Matzinger to attend a study. Society members would attempt to send psychic impression to Lina, who was seated separately from everyone. The instructions, which Lina carried out correctly, were to obtain a particular book from a table and place it in someone's jacket.[225] Members of the Psychologische Gesellschaft labeled their work as "experimental psychology," which was the psychological study of altered states of consciousness.[226]

Further Reading:

Heather Wolffram, *The Stepchildren of Science: Psychical Research and Parapsychology in Germany, c. 1870–1939* (Amsterdam: Rodopi, 2009).

***Quaderni di Parapsicologia*:** The *Quaderni di Parapsicologia* is an Italian scholarly journal on parapsychology. It is published by the parapsychological organization Centro Studi Parapsicologici. In addition to original research, you can always find works translated into Italian from other publications.[227] For a list of more journals that feature parapsychological articles, see appendix B.

Qualitative Research: Qualitative research refers to research that focuses primarily on nonnumerical data. Some examples of qualitative data in parapsychological research include free-response tests, narratives during séances, personal reports of haunting phenomena, etc. Qualitative data, in other words, has no predetermined and fixed values and focuses on nonnumerical data. Interviews are a form of qualitative research.[228]

Researcher John G. Kruth discusses the importance of qualitative research when he writes, "The rich tapestry of information available from people who have spontaneous psi experiences is essential to expand our knowledge of the field."[229] Further in that same article, Kruth outlines various qualitative methods and their application to parapsychological research.

Further Reading:

John G. Kruth, "Five Qualitative Research Approaches and Their Applications in Parapsychology," *Journal of Parapsychology* 79, no. 2 (Fall 2015): 219–33.

Quantitative Research: In contrast to qualitative research, quantitative research focuses primarily on numerical data, or data that has fixed values. Researcher Michael A. Thalbourne tells us that quantitative experiments include "any test for psi which uses targets each of which has a specific prescribed value for the probability of its occurrence; such a test therefore allows for direct statistical evaluation of the results obtained."[230]

Quantum Mechanics/Physics: Theories of quantum physics and quantum mechanics have been applied to parapsychological topics. "Governing the behavior of matter and radiation,"[231] Arthur and Joyce Berger tell us, quantum theories offer a unique perspective through which to view psi phenomena. They have been applied to retrocausation, positing that particles can move backward in time per the Feynham-Stueckelberg hypothesis.[232] The quantum concept of entanglement suggests that living systems subconsciously communicate with each other, even at a great distance.[233] Researcher Brian Millar points out that quantum theories focus on the potential physical attributes of psi phenomena and illustrate that parapsychology is an interdisciplinary topic.

Further Reading:

C. T. K. Chari, "Quantum Physics and Parapsychology," *Journal of Parapsychology* 20, no. 3 (September 1, 1956): 166–83.

Brian Millar, "Quantum Theory and Parapsychology," in *Parapsychology: A Handbook for the 21st Century.* Edited by Etzel Cardeña, John Palmer, and David Marcusson-Clavertz, 165–80 (Jefferson, NC: McFarland and Company, 2015).

Dean Radin, *Entangled Minds: Extrasensory Experiences in a Quantum Reality* (New York: Paraview, 2006).

Quarter Distribution: The quarter distribution refers to a pattern found in psychokinesis studies in which recorded hits on record sheets appeared to consistently fall predominantly in the upper left quadrant. As J. B. Rhine and Betty M. Humphrey tell us, "The discovery of a characteristic pattern of scoring running through the results of the different researches might serve to identify the hypothetical PK effect and to distinguish it from all other possible causes."[234]

Further Reading:

J. B. Rhine and Betty M. Humphrey, "The PK Effect: Special Evidence from Hit Patterns," *Journal of Parapsychology* 8, no. 1 (March 1, 1944): 18–60.

Random Number Generator: A random number generator (RNG) is a device that generates random outputs: random numbers, colors, noises, etc. It is typically electronic and is used in some studies of ESP to generate target outputs. It is also used in studies of psychokinesis in which a subject attempts to physically make the RNG display a certain output.[235] Multiple variations of RNGs have been used in studies. For example, researcher Helmut Schmidt used a high-speed RNG in a psychokinesis study. In his study, the RNG could deliver outputs at speeds up to three hundred numbers per second. This RNG study sought not only to investigate the presence of PK, but the role that speed of outputs played as well. Schmidt was, in fact, a leading researcher of RNG-PK studies and many of his experiments yielded statistically significant results.[236]

Mario Varvoglis and Peter A. Bancel give us a brief overview of RNGs when they tell us,

PK studies on probabilistic systems were carried out in various laboratories during the 1940s and 1950s, typically employing mechanical devices with tumbling dice or coin tosses. In the early 1970s hardware random number generators (RNGs) began to replace mechanical systems and quickly became widespread in parapsychology, first as self-standing units and later in computer controlled configurations.[237]

Further Reading:

Helmut Schmidt, "PK Tests with a High-Speed Random Number Generator," *Journal of Parapsychology* 37, no. 2 (June 1, 1973): 105–18.

Michael A. Thalbourne, "Kundalini and the Output of a Random Number Generator," *Journal of Parapsychology* 70, no. 2 (Fall 2006): 303–33.

Reading: This term is most commonly associated with mediums and refers to the act of obtaining messages from discarnate entities. It can also be applied to other instances of extrasensory perception in which a person provides a "reading" of the impressions they are receiving.[238]

Receiver: Though it is preferred to use the term percipient or subject, the term "receiver" refers to the person "receiving" anomalous sensory inputs, such as in studies of telepathy.[239]

Recurrent Spontaneous Psychokinesis: Recurrent spontaneous psychokinesis, or RSPK, refers to psychokinetic events that continue to spontaneously happen in a location and that are often centered around a particular person. As such, RSPK is an attribute of much poltergeist research. Researchers William G. Roll and William T. Joines tell us that "RSPK primarily consists of movements of household objects and furniture, that is, objects weighing a few ounces to several pounds. In other words, the occurrences are energetic displays involving material objects that ordinarily are constrained by inertia and gravitation."[240] It was William G. Roll in fact, who along with his colleague J. G. Pratt, coined the term recurrent spontaneous psychokinesis after their case study of a family suffering poltergeist activity in Long Island.

Many instances of RSPK occur in people's homes and/or buildings that are frequented by the person at the center of the phenomenon, but researchers have also attempted to study RSPK in controlled laboratory settings. One instance of this occurred at the Spring Creek Institute in North Carolina and was administered by neurophysiologist Stephen Baumann. Baumann had previously investigated a case in Ohio surrounding RSPK events that centered around a teenager. After investigating the case, the teenage girl was invited to the institute. During the study, RSPK phenomena occurred at the institute and Baumann began wondering if PK could be used in a medical context. To test this theory, he asked the teenager, Tina, to try and prompt electrical discharges in nerve cells and certain crystal minerals found in the body. While there were some evaluation hurdles, Baumann indicated that the results were promising.[241] *See also poltergeist and psychokinesis.*

Further Reading:

J. G. Pratt and W. G. Roll, "The Seaford Disturbances," *Journal of Parapsychology* 22, no. 2 (June 1958): 79–124.

William G. Roll and William T. Joines, "RSPK and Consciousness," *Journal of Parapsychology* 77, no. 2 (Fall 2013): 192–211.

Reichenbach Phenomena: This term refers to the work and theory of Baron Karl von Reichenbach, who proposed that certain individuals could see a radiating glow surrounding humans and certain objects, like crystals. This is akin to our idea of an aura today. Reichenbach's ideas sparked the interest of early researchers in both the British and American Societies for Psychical Research, who eventually concluded that there was no sufficient evidence for these forces.[242]

Further Reading:

Jules Regnault, "Odic Phenomena and New Radiations," *The Annals of Psychical Science* 1, no. 3 (March 1905): 145–63.

Remote Viewing: Researcher Etzel Cardeña, in an article written for *American Psychologist*, tells us that remote viewing "is a technique in which in individual describes a place, chosen at random, where a *sender* is located at the present or at a future time (there may also be just a location chosen without any observer there)."[243] Remote viewing, often abbreviated as RV, involves the process of anomalous cognition and can, at times, even involve precognition, for example, when a viewer attempts to view something that will occur in the future.

Many remote viewing studies were conducted at the Stanford Research Institute (SRI) by Russell Targ, Edwin May, and Hal Puthoff. Russell Targ had, in fact, been interested in ESP research and built an ESP-teaching machine that drew the attention of NASA. This ESP machine was instrumental in securing financial support from NASA for conducting studies at the Stanford Research Institute, a nonprofit research group located in California. At SRI, Targ and his colleagues conducted remote viewing experiments and their studies indicated statistically significant positive results—in other words, participants were able to successfully identify, through anomalous cognition, information about targets either physically far away and/or in the future. They discovered that remote viewing was successful up to 10,000 kilometers and that it appeared easier for subjects to intuit shapes and settings rather than numbers. The remote viewing experiments conducted by Targ and colleagues eventually drew the interest of the US government, especially the CIA, who contracted SRI remote viewers with help in national security matters. In one example, the CIA recruited SRI remote viewers to help locate a crashed Soviet plane in order to retrieve confidential information from it. Remote viewers focused on the task, provided information, and when agents were dispatched to the area, they found the plane almost immediately.[244]

Not all remote viewing research is limited to the SRI, of course. For example, researchers at Saybrook University, The University of Northampton, and California State University banded together in 2019 to study the effects of darkness on remote viewing.[245] In their article, they also remind us that remote viewing, though it was not referred to as such, is a practice that can be found even in ancient times, for example, Greek oracles divining future information. In their 2019 study, though, they recruited twenty remote viewers from the Energy Medicine University in California and had them perform remote viewing activities under both light and dark conditions. Though they discovered that successful RV did occur in dark conditions, it was not any more significant than RV in light conditions, and the authors point out suggestions for continued study.

Further Reading:

J. Baptista, M. Derakhshani, and P. E. Tressoldi, "Explicit Anomalous Cognition: A Review of the Best Evidence in Ganzfeld, Forced Choice, Remote Viewing, and Dream Studies," in *Parapsychology: A Handbook for the 21st Century.* Edited by E. Cardeña and J. Palmer, 192–214 (Jefferson, NC: McFarland, 2015).

Edwin C. May, "Star Gate: The U.S. Government's Psychic Spying Program," *Journal of Parapsychology* 78, no. 1 (Spring 2014): 5–18.

Russell Targ, "What do We Know about PSI? The First Decade of Remote-Viewing Research and Operations at Stanford Research Institute," *Journal of Scientific Exploration* 33, no. 4 (2019): 569–92.

Replication: Replication is an important concept of scientific research and "means to obtain the same findings when a sufficiently similar experimental procedure is followed designed to yield that effect."[246] It can be used as a noun and refer to something being a "replication" study. It is a primary critique of parapsychology. Many point to problems of replication as one of the major downfalls of the field. Some parapsychologists counter that critique, however, by suggesting that the very nature of psi phenomena make them inherently difficult to replicate. This counterpoint rests on the inherently spontaneous nature of much psi phenomena.

Further Reading:

David Luke, Chris A. Roe, and Jamie Davison, "Testing for Forced-Choice Precognition Using a Hidden Task: Two Replications," *Journal of Parapsychology* 72 (Spring 2008): 133–54.

Jessica Utts, "Replication and Meta-Analysis in Parapsychology," *Statistical Science* 6, no. 4 (November 1991): 363–78.

Jessica Utts, "What Constitutes Replication in Parapsychology?" in *Extrasensory Perception: Support, Skepticism, and Science.* Volume 1: History, Controversy, and Research. Edited by Edwin C. May and Sonali Bhatt Marwaha, 179–92 (Santa Barbara, CA: Praeger, 2015).

Retrocognition: Credited to the psychical researcher Frederic W. H. Myers, retrocognition refers to "a form of extrasensory perception in which the target is some past event which could not have been learned or inferred by normal means."[247]

Further Reading:

Andrew MacKenzie, *Adventures in Time* (London: Athlone Press, 1997).

Frederic W. H. Myers, "The Subliminal Self. Chapter VIII: The Relation of Supernormal Phenomena to Time—Retrocognition," *Proceedings of the Society for Psychical Research* 11, no. 29 (December 1895): 334–407.

Revue Métapsychique: *Revue Métapsychique* was the journal of the research organization, Institute Métapsychique International in France. Its first issue was published in 1919 and ceased publication in 1982.[248]

Further Reading:

Carlos S. Alvarado, Massimo Biondi, and Wim Kramer, "Historical Notes on Psychic Phenomena in Specialised Journals," *European Journal of Parapsychology* 21, no. 1 (2006): 58–87.

Rhine Research Center: The Rhine Research Center grew out of the Duke Parapsychology Labs and the work of Dr. J. B. Rhine. From 1935 to 1965, Rhine conducted parapsychological research at the labs of Duke University. In 1965, when Rhine retired, he wished to continue to support parapsychological research and founded the Foundation for Research into the Nature of Man. This foundation, however, was renamed the Rhine Research Center in 1995, a center that still exists. You can visit its website to report a personal paranormal experience, read research on ESP, and even take online courses.[249]

Run: A run refers to one cycle of an experiment. For example, in a study involving ESP, one run of ESP cards means one cycle of making calls for each of the twenty-five cards in that set. In a dice-throwing experiment, on the other hand, a typical run consists of making twenty-four throws of a dice.[250] There can be as few as a handful of runs or as many as hundreds, depending on the scope of the study.

Scole Mediumship Circle: In the 1990s, a trio of couples in Norfolk met regularly to hold séances and engage in mediumship practices. During their sessions, the group claimed to experience apported objects, manifestations of anomalous lights and figures, and even obtained rolls of strange words and objects on film, which was thought to be evidence of spirit thoughtography. The group attracted the attention of the British Society for Psychical Research, and three members visited the group to see what they could discover. This inquiry led to the Scole Report, which was published in the 1999 *Proceedings of the Society for Psychical Research.* In this report, researchers note that they saw strange lights that seemed to respond to both verbal and mental cues, and, in one case, they witnessed the levitation of a crystal on the table.[251]

Further Reading:

Montague Keen, "The Scole Investigation: A Study in Critical Analysis of Paranormal Physical Phenomena," *Journal of Scientific Exploration* 15, no. 2 (2001): 167–82.

M. A. Ellison Keen and D. Fontana, "The Scole Report," *Proceedings of the Society for Psychical Research* 58 (1999): 150–452.

Screened Touch Matching: The screened touch matching method refers to an experiment of extrasensory perception in which the two participants are separated by an opaque screen. On one side, the agent holds a deck of cards (or chosen object) and on the other side of the screen, the subject attempt to intuit what that item is and respond by pointing to the symbol of their choice, which are displayed on their side of the screen.[252] Screened touch studies can use open or blind matching, terms which refer to whether a range of target symbols are available to the subject or not.[253]

Further Reading:

J. L. Woodruff and R. W. George, "Experiments in Extra-Sensory Perception," *Journal of Parapsychology* 1, no. 1 (March 1, 1937): 18–30.

Séance: A séance refers to the setting in which a medium and sitters gather together in an attempt to make communication with discarnate entities. The séance was a common practice that rose to fame during the Spiritualist era in the mid to late 1800s.

A core tenet of Spiritualists is, in fact, that certain people can make communication with the dead. As such, Spiritualists believed in the survival hypothesis, or that human consciousness transcends physical death. A way that this spirit communication could be achieved is through the use of mediums and the séance provided a public forum for which mediums could deliver messages from their spirit controls.[254] Séances, mediums, and the belief in survival became so popular that it is part of what motivated the formation of the British Society for Psychical Research. In fact, researcher Carlos S. Alvarado points out that between 1882 and 1900, 23 percent of the reports within the society's journal involved séances.[255] Common occurrences at séances would include apported objects, levitation of objects, strange figures and sounds, and messages delivered through the medium from discarnate entities.

Though séances are most commonly associated with the spiritualist era, séances occur today and researchers even continue to investigate them. In a 2003 study in the *British Journal of Psychology*, for example, the role between paranormal belief and suggestion in subsequent claims of paranormal activity was studied. Researchers in the study held a séance, though it was operated by a fake medium. Staged for the purpose of the study, the medium claimed to levitate objects during the sessions and nearly 30 percent of participants, when interviewed after the séance, stated that they saw and felt the objects levitate.[256]

Further Reading:

Brian R. Laythe, Elizabeth Cooper Laythe, and Lucinda Woodward, "A Test of an Occult-Themed Séance: Examining Anomalous Events, Psychosomatic Symptoms, Transliminality, and Electromagnetic Fields," *Journal of Scientific Exploration* 31, no. 4 (2017): 572–624.

Richard Wiseman, Emma Greening, and Matthew Smith, "Belief in the Paranormal and Suggestion in the Séance Room," *British Journal of Psychology* 94 (August 2003): 285–97.

Sender: The term "sender" refers to the agent in parapsychological studies. The agent is the person who attempts to send psychical impressions to a subject (who could be referred to as the receiver).

Set: A set refers to a group of trials, or runs, conducted during a study.[257] One set could involve ten runs of attempting to guess twenty-five cards, for example.

Sheep-Goat Effect: The sheep-goat effect was posited in the 1940s by parapsychologist Dr. Gertrude R. Schmeidler. Schmeidler, during her inquiries into the role of attitude and belief when it comes to anomalous experiences, concluded that experiencers are in one of two camps. Someone is either a sheep (a person who believed in the paranormal) or a goat (someone who rejects the idea of the paranormal). Essentially, Schmeidler discovered that those who believe in certain phenomena (in her case, ESP), were more likely to report having had an ESP-related experience than those who do not believe in ESP (goats).[258]

Further Reading:

T. R. Lawrence, "Gathering in the Sheep and Goats: A Meta-Analysis of Forced-Choice Sheep-Goat ESP Studies, 1947–1993," *Proceedings of the 36th Annual Convention of the Parapsychological Association* (Durham: Parapsychological Association, 1993): 75–86.

Barbara E. Lovitts, "The Sheep-Goat Effect Turned Upside Down," *Journal of Parapsychology* 45, no. 4 (December 1, 1981): 293–309.

Gertrude R. Schmeidler, "Additional Data on Sheep-Goat Classification," *Journal of the Society for Psychical Research* 40 (June 1, 1959).

Gertrude R. Schmeidler and R. A. McConnell, *ESP and Personality Patterns* (New Haven, CT: Yale University Press, 1958).

Sitter-Group: Sitter-groups refer to groups of people who, like the Scole Mediumship Circle mentioned above, meet regularly to conduct sittings in the hopes that mediumistic phenomena manifests. Modern parapsychologists posit that phenomena in these groups could be the result of psychokinesis.[259]

Further Reading:

Kenneth Batcheldor, "Contributions to the Theory of PK Induction from Sitter-Group Work," *Journal of the American Society for Psychical Research* 78 (1984): 105–22.

Society for Psychical Research: The Society for Psychical Research (SPR) was formed in Britain in 1882. Driven partly by a desire to investigate and respond to the phenomena coming from the séance rooms of the spiritualist era, a group of researchers gathered together with a common goal of researching anomalous phenomena. Some of its founding members include Frederic W. H. Myers, Henry Sidgwick, and William F. Barrett. Author and mathematician Mary Boole was the first female member of the SPR and Eleanor Sidgwick, president of Newnham College, was an early and prominent member.[260] Author and SPR historian Renée Haynes tells us that the SPR's goal was "to examine without prejudice or prepossession and in a scientific spirit those faculties of man, real or supposed, which appear to be inexplicable in terms of any generally recognized hypotheses."[261] The SPR exists to this day and continues their scholarly pursuit into understanding more about anomalous phenomena. Additionally, multiple other countries established their own branches of the SPR, such as the United States and the Netherlands. Other countries, like Germany and France, had very similar research institutions dedicated to investigating anomalous phenomena.[262]

Some of the earliest topics of interest to the British SPR were hypnotism, telepathy, and mediumship. Various committees were formed and tasked with specific topics. For example, the Committee on Haunted Houses worked to collect personal experiences of ghosts and apparitions and to outline the guidelines for acceptable eyewitness reports. The Literary Committee's goal was to compile a core body of literature on psychical topics and to provide their own educated thoughts on the literature to date.[263]

A huge part of the society's early work, however, was ferreting out fraudulent activity and reports. It is widely recognized that the spiritualist era was rife with fraudulent performances of mediums, and the SPR did their fair share of debunking in studies with multiple mediums. Sometimes, though, even the researchers became divided on whether they believed an event to be genuine or not and perhaps the most intense example of this is the schism that resulted from the investigation into the mediumship of Mina

Crandon. Referred to as "Margery," researchers within the American Society for Psychical Research (ASPR) became so heated that a group of members left the ASPR to form their own society, the Boston Society for Psychic Research.[264]

Today the SPR continues to publish its research in both the *Journal of the Society for Psychical Research* and the *Proceedings of the Society for Psychical Research.* You can find many of the historical issues of both British and US editions of the *Journal (and Proceedings) of the Society for Psychical Research* online at www.hathitrust.org. In these issues you can read for yourself the earliest committee reports, case studies, and experiments of the SPR.

Further Reading:

Renée Haynes, *The Society for Psychical Research, 1882–1982: A History* (London: Macdonald & Co., 1982).

Sphinx: The *Sphinx* was a publication established in 1886 by the German theosophist Wilhelm Hübbe-Schleiden. This journal was heavily inspired by the transcendental psychology espoused by Carl du Prel, who believed that consciousness existed independently from the physical body. Articles within the *Sphinx* discussed hypnotism, mediums, clairvoyance, and more. Researcher Andreas Sommer tells us that "the *Sphinx* became one of the most important—if not the most important—early German periodicals serving as a conduit for the latest works in hypnotism from France and England."[265]

Further Reading:

Andreas Sommer, "Normalizing the Supernormal: The Formation of the 'Gesellschaft Für Psychologische Forschung' ('Society for Psychological Research')," *Journal of the History of the Behavioral Sciences* 49, no. 1 (Winter 2013): 18–44.

Spiricom: The Spiricom refers to a device made by George Meek, an engineer fascinated with the electronic voice phenomena. Upon retirement, Meek began creating a device he claimed would allow users to communicate with spirits. Coining it spiricom, Meek claimed that his colleague William O'Neil used it to communicate with the spirit of Dr. George Mueller. Critics have pointed out that O'Neil had already exhibited clairvoyant abilities and note that the device might *rely* on the user having some pre-existing psychical ability.[266]

Spiritualism: Spiritualism is a movement that was born in the mid-1800s. At that time, especially in Britain, people had lost their certainty regarding the nature of God and religion. It is specifically defined as a religion (or even philosophy) in which people believe in a higher power *and* "a world of spirits who communicate with living people through mediums."[267] The roots of Spiritualism can be traced back to Emanuel Swedenborg and his claims of supernormal abilities obtained during trance. The book of Spiritualism, however, really took off when the Fox sisters of New York claimed to receive strange raps and knocks in their home and eventually held séances for curious neighbors and then, eventually, across the nation.[268]

Researcher Janet Oppenheim tells us,

> Victorians themselves were fully aware that the place of religion in the cultural fabric of their times was scarcely secure. In an effort to counter that insecurity, to calm their fears, and to seek answers where contemporary churches were ambiguous, thousands of British men and women in the Victorian and Edwardian eras turned to spiritualism and psychical research.[269]

It should be no surprise, then, that Oppenheim goes on to tell us that "no study of the spiritualist boom in the second half of the nineteenth century would be complete without the mediums—the men, women, and children who claimed to function as channels of communication between the living and the dead."[270]

The phenomena exhibited by mediums and happening in the séance room is partly what drew scientists to form professional research organizations dedicated to investigating the question of survival, or consciousness beyond death. Much of the work done by these institutions, especially the British Society for Psychical Research, was ferreting out instances of fraudulent behavior, which was rampant during this era. Keep in mind, however, that even amid the fraudulent behavior in séances and mediumship, researchers have pointed out the importance of mediumship to performative expression and challenging the power dynamics of the Victorian era.[271]

Further Reading:

Janet Oppenheim, *The Other World: Spiritualism and Psychical Research in England, 1850–1914* (Cambridge: Cambridge University Press, 1985).

Alex Owen, *The Darkened Room: Women, Power and Spiritualism in Late Victorian England* (Philadelphia: University of Pennsylvania Press, 1990).

Michael P. Richard and Albert Adato, "The Medium and Her Message: A Study of Spiritualism at Lily Dale, New York," *Review of Religious Research* 22, no. 2 (December 1980): 186–97.

Spontaneous Psi: Cases of spontaneous psi refer to those seemingly random moments that someone has a psi experience. They differ from experimental psi experiences, which occur in controlled laboratory settings. Spontaneous psi, in other words, represent those anomalous experiences that occur randomly in everyday, uncontrolled situations. It might be like you having a precognitive dream of something before it happens or another person with an apparition experience. Spontaneous cases are important to researchers, especially when gathered in large scale inquiries. Not only can large data sets of spontaneous experiences help unveil patterns, it they also capture the reality that thousands of people are experiencing something strange at random points in their lives. Parapsychologist Louisa Rhine was a forerunner in collecting mass quantities of personal experiences, with which she studied to analyze potential patterns. This is similar to the early work of the British Society for Psychical Research, who amassed large quantities of personal experiences on various topics like hauntings, telepathy, etc. The difference between Rhine and the early psychical researchers, though, is in the qualifications which they weighed personal reports against.[272]

In a June 1953 article in the *Journal of Parapsychology*, for example, Rhine collected a thousand personal reports of people who claimed to have spontaneous psychic experiences. After analyzing a data set that large, Rhine was able to identify some patterns. She found that spontaneous psychic experiences took one of four forms: intuitive, hallucinatory, unrealistic dreaming, or realistic dreaming.[273] After Rhine identified this, she began to wonder what role personality might play in the ways in which people process their spontaneous psi experiences. This is important to analyze, Rhine tells us, because "this observation suggests that the form may have a rationale [and] may be the result of general underlying principles."[274]

Further Reading:

JoMarie Haight, "Spontaneous Psi Cases: A Survey and Preliminary Study of ESP, Attitude, and Personality Relationship," *Journal of Parapsychology* 43, no. 3 (September 1, 1979): 179–204.

J. B. Rhine, "Editorial: The Value of Reports of Spontaneous Psi Experiences," *Journal of Parapsychology* 12, no. 4 (December 1, 1948): 231–35.

Louisa E. Rhine, "Subjective Forms of Spontaneous Psi Experiences," *Journal of Parapsychology* 17, no. 2 (June 1, 1953): 77–114.

Studievereniging der Psychical Research: The Studievereniging der Psychical Research is the Dutch Society for Psychical Research. Established in 1920 through the work of Dr. Gerard Heymans, it has had a bit of a tumultuous history. During World War II, the society shuttered its efforts. When it regrouped after the war, the society suffered from tensions surrounding then director, researcher Wilhelm Tenhaeff.[275] The Dutch SPR was supported by the University of Utrecht and the University of Humanistic Studies until 2011, when the partnership was disbanded. It exists still today, though, as a nonprofit organization.[276]

Subconscious: According to the American Psychological Association, the subconscious is "a lay term that is widely used to denote the unconscious or preconscious mind as described by Sigmund Freud or the general idea of subliminal consciousness. It is also popularly associated with autosuggestion and hypnosis."[277]

In terms of parapsychology, much of the subconscious was informed by the early work of Frederic W. H. Myers and his notion of the subliminal self.[278] Particularly, "Myers assumed that a subliminal self manifested in disintegrations of personality as well as in more positive phenomena such as creativity and mediumship [and] argued that mediumship and other phenomena such as creativity and telepathy were expressions of the subliminal mind."[279]

Further Reading:

Carlos S. Alvarado, "Mediumship, Psychical Research, Dissociation, and the Powers of the Subconscious Mind," *Journal of Parapsychology* 78, no. 1 (2014): 98–114.

Subliminal Self: The subliminal self is a concept developed by psychical researcher Frederic W. H. Myers. Myers believed that the soul could continue to exist beyond bodily death but also believed that "supernormal" phenomena emanated forth from the psychic self of the living person. From his beliefs he developed a theory of the subliminal self which he also referred to as ultra-marginal consciousness. This subliminal self, Myers posited, facilitated dreaming, hypnosis, *and* the ability to tap into psychical abilities like telepathy. Through all of these states, the subliminal self passes messages to our conscious waking selves.[280]

Further Reading:

Carlos S., "On the Centenary of Frederic W.H. Myers's *Human Personality and its Survival of Bodily Death,*" *Journal of Parapsychology* 68, no. 1 (Spring 2004): 3–43.
Frederic W. H. Myers, *Human Personality and Its Survival of Bodily Death* (London: Longmans, Green, and Co., 1906), 470.

Subjective Paranormal Experience: Parapsychologist Michael A. Thalbourne tells us that subjective paranormal experiences "refer to those experiences of individuals which are judged by them to be psychic or paranormal [but] there is no implication that the experiences are necessarily objectively paranormal."[281] In the 1980s, researcher Vernon Neppe realized that many anomalous experiences were expressed by subjects as feelings, strange dreams, intuition, and other perceptual expressions. Neppe began studying what he coined the "subjective paranormal experience," or SPE. SPE research "[examines] the ways in which individuals make sense of and account for their extraordinary experiences"[282] and recognizes various social and cultural factors that influence a person's subjective experience of a paranormal event.

Further Reading:

Kenneth Drinkwater, Neil Dagnall, Sarah Grogan, and Victoria Riley, "Understanding the Unknown: A Thematic Analysis of Subjective Paranormal Experiences," *Australian Journal of Parapsychology* 17, no. 1 (June 2017): 23–46.
Rachael Ironside, "Feeling Spirits: Sharing Subjective Paranormal Experience Through Embodied Talk and Action," *Text and Talk* 38, no. 6 (2018): 705–28.
Vernon Neppe, "Déjà vu: Origins and Phenomenology: Implications of the Four Subtypes for Future Research," *Journal of Parapsychology* 74, no. 1 (Spring 2010): 61–97.
Vernon Neppe, "Subjective Paranormal Experience Psychosis." *Parapsychology Review* 15, no. 2 (1984): 7–9.
Michael A. Persinger, "Propensity to Report Paranormal Experiences is Correlated with Temporal Lobe Signs," *Perceptual and Motor Skills* 59, no. 2 (1984): 583–86.

Super-psi: Super-psi refers to a theory that posits since we do not know the parameters and boundaries of psi phenomena, instances of what we think might be spirit communication could really just be an example of some form of extrasensory perception. In other words, super-psi suggests that the survival theory is null because it *could* be an instance of ESP and not communication with discarnate spirits.[283] You may also see this referred to as super-ESP or living agent psi.

Further Reading:

Stephen E. Braude, "Survival or Super-psi?" *Journal of Scientific Investigation* 6, no. 2 (1992): 127–44.

Survival Hypothesis: Survival hypothesis relies on the notion that consciousness transcends bodily death. Survival research, then, includes research that investigates that possibility. This research includes studies on after-death communication, reincarnation, mediumship, cross correspondences, and more. You will often come across phrases such as "survival studies" or "the survival question" in parapsychological literature. Survival questions were at the heart of early psychical research. One of the seminal psychical researchers, in fact, Frederic W. H. Myers, wrote a book entitled *Human Personality and its Survival of Bodily Death.* Some modern parapsychologists, however, question the survival hypothesis' value to promoting the scientific merit of the field.[284]

Further Reading:

"Editorial: ESP, PK, and the Survival Hypothesis." *Journal of Parapsychology* 7, no. 4 (December 1943): 223–27.

Harvey Irwin, "Is Scientific Investigation of Post-mortem Survival an Anachronism? The Demise of the Survival Hypothesis," *Australian Journal of Parapsychology* 2, no. 1 (June 2002): 19–27.

Adam J. Rock, *The Survival Hypothesis: Essays on Mediumship* (Jefferson, NC: McFarland and Co., 2013), 309.

Synchronicity: Synchronicity is a concept identified by Dr. Carl Jung. Researcher Lance Storm reminds us of that, "according to Jung, two or more events constitute synchronicity when a meaningful connection—meaningful association—can be made between the events, but it is only synchronicity when meaningfulness is the connecting principle between the events with no causal connections."[285] According to Jung, synchronicity also implies that space and time are "psychically relative"[286] because quite often, in a synchronicity, one event is physical while the other occurs psychically. One example would be someone who has a premonition of something happening at the same time that event is happening, unbeknownst to that person.

Further Reading:

Lance Storm, "Synchronicity, Causality, and Acausality," *Journal of Parapsychology* 63, no. 3 (September 1999): 247–69.

T-test: A t-test is a statistical tool used to help determine if data and scores in a study are statistically significant. Statistically significant means that those scores fall significantly above or below the mean (average) of where the data should be distributed.[287] You will come across various statistical language as you read through the parapsychological literature and the text in the further reading section below may be helpful for those new to statistics or who may need a refresher.

Further Reading:

Isadore Newman, Carole Newman, Russell Brown, and Sharon McNeely, *Conceptual Statistics for Beginners.* (Lanham, MD: University Press of America, 2006).

Table-Tipping: Table-tipping is a common occurrence during séances and sittings with mediums. A manifestation of physical mediumship, table-tipping is also referred to as table-tilting and table-turning. During a séance, sitters place their hands upon a table and cause it to move, levitate, and/or make knocking sounds in correspondence to questions or morse-code like communication.[288] Though the practice predates Spiritualism, it boomed in popularity during the 1800s. Researchers point to unconscious physical movements and/or psychokinesis as possible explanations for the phenomena.[289]

Further Reading:

Kenneth Batcheldor, "Contributions to the Theory of PK Induction from Sitter-Group Work," *Journal of the American Society for Psychical Research* 78, no. 2 (April 1984).

Michael Faraday, "Experimental Investigation of Table-Moving," in *Parapsychology*, edited by Richard Wiseman and Caroline Watt, 373–76 (London: Routledge, 2005).

Target: The target in a parapsychological experiment is the object that the subject is attempting to psychically perceive. Likewise, it is the object which the agent is attempting to send, as in the case of ESP studies. In other studies, like psychokinesis, the target is the object that the subject is attempting to manipulate.[290]

Tambov Experiments: The Tambov Experiments refer to an 1898 case involving a séance, hypnotism, and extrasensory perception. Dr. Khovrin, a Russian, worked with a patient referred to as Miss M., who had suffered from nervous conditions her whole life that seemed to worsen drastically after she attended a séance. Throughout his treatment of Miss M., Khovrin noticed that hypnotism and suggestion seemed to make some of her symptoms disappear almost entirely. But throughout the course of treatment, he also witnessed strange abilities displayed by Miss M., like the time she was handed a sealed letter and began immediately crying, proclaiming to the doctor that the letter contained news of her nephew's death even though she hadn't even opened the envelope. Khovrin eventually submitted Miss M. to additional tests in which she continued to exhibit ESP abilities.[291]

Further Reading:

Eric J. Dingwall, ed., "Dr. A.N. Khovrin and the Tambov Experiments," in *Abnormal Hypnotic Phenomena: A Survey of Nineteenth-Century Cases*, Volume 3 (London: J. & A. Churchill, 1968), 33–75.

Telekinesis: Telekinesis is an older term used to describe what researchers most commonly now refer to as psychokinetic phenomena. It is credited to Frederic W. H. Myers.[292] In a 1923 issue of the *Proceedings of the Society for Psychical Research*, Sir Oliver Lodge writes that "the facts of telekinesis and materialisation tend to show that the human organism can exert force beyond its recognised periphery, and that temporary emanations from that organism can not only exert force on distance objects, but can also mold themselves into strange simulacra, which for a time can be seen, felt, and photographed."[293]

Telepathy: Telepathy refers to communication between minds. It was popularized by Frederic W. H. Myers who stated that telepathy includes any impressions between minds that are not made via normal channels. Telepathy was one of the first topics of inquiry made by the British Society for Psychical Research.[294] You will sometimes see it referred to as thought-reading or thought-transference, especially in older literature. Today, it is less commonly used than other terms such as psi, anomalous cognition, and extrasensory perception.

In 2003, researchers investigated the possibility that nervous systems could be signaled between two people separated by distance.[295] In their study, they used two subjects who first engaged in meditation and then attempted to telepathically send and receive images. Throughout the experiment, both sub-

jects were placed in MRI machines so that researchers could capture various brain data. The researchers discovered that "the brain activity observed in the visual association cortex suggests that the receiver 'processed' a signal from the sender."[296] In other words, some anomalous communication appeared to occur between subjects.

Further Reading:

W. F. Barrett, Edmund Gurney, and F. W. H. Myers, "First Report on Thought Reading," *Proceedings of the Society for Psychical Research* 1, no. 1 (July 17, 1882): 13–34.
Leanna J. Standish, L. Clark Johnson, Leila Kozak, and Todd Richards, "Evidence of Correlated Functional Magnetic Resonance Imaging Signals Between Distant Human Brains," *Alternative Therapies in Health and Medicine* 9, no. 1 (January/February 2003): 122–28.

Thoughtography: The concept of thoughtography was popularized by Japanese parapsychologist Tomokichi Fukurai. Thoughtography is a psychokinetic process that "denotes the apparent ability of a subject, deliberately and without using any photographic process, camera lens, or shutter, to imprint pictures on film plates or the film of a camera."[297] In a 2012 article in the *History of the Human Sciences*, author Miki Takasuna tells us more of Fukurai and his research. Having written his dissertation on hypnosis, Fukurai went on to teach abnormal psychology, where he frequently taught about hypnosis. He eventually began conducting his own research into thoughtography. In some of his experiments, he would insert dry film plates inside envelopes and ask one of his subjects to psychically manipulate the images that would then develop.[298]

Further Reading:

Miki Takasuna, "The Fukurai Affair: Parapsychology and the History of Psychology in Japan," *History of the Human Sciences* 25, no. 2 (2012): 149–64.

Trance: Trance refers to "an altered state of consciousness resembling a condition of deep hypnosis."[299] It is associated with mental mediumship and some figures in the literature are even referred to as trance mediums. In trance mediumship, the medium engages in a state similar to hypnosis and channels messages from discarnate entities. Mediums might also have spirit controls, or entities that they regularly communicate with who help filter messages between other intelligences and the medium. Psychical researcher Eleanor Sidgwick investigated mental mediumship, particularly that of the medium Leonora Piper. Sidgwick believed that spirit controls were simply subconscious manifestations of the medium's personality but also believed that the medium could still receive their messages telepathically.[300] Of course, scholars also note that trance mediumship also carried with it a performative, entertainment aspect, especially in the 1800s when it exploded in popularity.[301]

It is also important to note that trance mediumship is not merely a product of the spiritualist era, and it is not relegated to the Western world, either. In a 1995 article in *Asian Folklore Studies*, researchers remind us of the annual Laru Festival held in Tibet. The festival is centered around a trance medium through whom the mountain gods participate in the celebration.[302]

Further Reading:

Sarasvati Ann S. Buhrman, "Trance in America: A Comparison of Trance Types and Trance Experience in Two Religious Communities." PhD diss., University of Colorado, 1996: 330.

Simone Natale, "The Medium on the Stage: Trance and Performance in Nineteenth-Century Spiritualism," *Early Popular Visual Culture* 9, no. 3 (2011): 239–55.

Steward Edward White, "The Process of Mental Mediumship," *Journal of the American Society for Psychical Research* 27, no. 10 (October 1933): 283.

Transliminality: Transliminality is a concept that suggests that certain processes can transcend thresholds. Specifically, transliminality is "the hypothesized tendency for psychological material to cross thresholds into, or out of, consciousness."[303] Though credited to parapsychologist Michael A. Thalbourne, researchers in the first decade of the 1900s were pondering notions of transliminality in their theories on telepathy. They believed, for example, that aspects of consciousness might leak through from one mind into another, causing the phenomena of telepathy.

In the 1990s, Thalbourne and his colleagues gave personality scales to subjects and noticed an overlap between some paranormal belief and mysticism attributes, further suggesting the transliminal concept of attributes crossing into and out of consciousness. In other words, these scales, and the notion of transliminality, suggest that some people's thresholds are more open to paranormal belief than others. Thalbourne tells us, for example, "Persons high in transliminality will, relatively speaking, experience a much larger number of different types of input from the subliminal regions, whereas others, lower in transliminality, may hear from that region on considerably fewer occasions. Thus, paranormal belief and experience can be said to be one consequence amongst many of a mind high in transliminality."[304]

Further Reading:

R. Lange, M. A. Thalbourne, J. Houran, and L. Storm, "The Revised Transliminality Scale: Reliability and Validity Data from a Rasch Top-Down Purification Procedure," *Consciousness and Cognition* 9, no. 4 (December 2000): 591–617.

Michael A. Thalbourne, "Transliminality, Anomalous Belief and Experience, and Hypnotisability," *Australian Journal of Clinical and Experimental Hypnosis* 37, no. 2 (November 2009): 119–30.

M. A. Thalbourne, "Transliminality as an Index of the Sheep-Goat Variable," *European Journal of Parapsychology* 18 (2003): 3–14.

Transpersonal Consciousness: Parapsychologist Michael A. Thalbourne provides us with a definition of transpersonal consciousness. He tells us that it is an "altered state of consciousness in which awareness of the personal self is lost in, or identified with, an awareness of the world at large or other living beings [and it can be] inducible by meditation."[305] Researcher Ervin Laszlo, in an article in the *International Journal of Transpersonal Studies*, reminds us that the foundation for transpersonal consciousness was laid out by Dr. Carl Jung and his theories of interconnections between people. The idea of connections between subjects, even when subjects are far apart, was further explored in remote viewing studies, anomalous dream studies, and other psi experiments. All of these point to the notion of a transpersonal consciousness that is aware of and can communicate with other living beings.[306]

Further Reading:

Roberto Assagioli, "Symbols of Transpersonal Experiences," *Journal of Transpersonal Psychology* 1, no. 1 (Spring 1969): 33–45.

Ervin Laszlo, "Cosmic Connectivity: Toward a Scientific Foundation for Transpersonal Consciousness," *International Journal of Transpersonal Studies* 23 (2004): 21–31.

Undifferentiated ESP: Undifferentiated ESP is another term used to indicate general extrasensory perception (GESP). In much the same way that GESP is a broad term that allows for multiple modes of ESP, so, too, does undifferentiated ESP refer to cases in which anomalous cognition might be the result of psi between two people and/or between a person and an object, future event, etc.[307]

Up-Through: The up-through technique refers to a method used in extrasensory perception tests (clairvoyance, for example) in which a stack of cards (or similar target objects stacked upon each other) is guessed by the subject, beginning from the bottom, and working upward. A similar technique that moves from the top of the stack of target objects downward is referred to as the down-through method.[308]

Utrecht University: In a 2012 article in the *History of the Human Sciences*, author Ingrid Kloosterman tells us that "it is in the Netherlands that the first professor in parapsychology worldwide was appointed at Utrecht University in 1953."[309] Professor Wilhelm Tenhaeff became the first chair of parapsychology, and for a period of time Utrecht University had two parapsychology research labs and cochairs of the program. Most recently, though the parapsychology labs and chair have been disbanded, the essence of the program continues as part of the exceptional human experiences program taught at the University for Humanistics in Utrecht.[310]

Further Reading:

Ingrid Kloosterman, "Psychical Research and Parapsychology Interpreted: Suggestions from the International Historiography of Psychical Research and Parapsychology for Investigating its History in the Netherlands," *History of the Human Sciences* 25, no. 2 (2012): 2–22.

Variance: Variance is a statistical tool used to measure dispersion, or the range difference from the mean (average) of something.[311] When applied to tests of extrasensory perception, variance is used to "test the significance of the scatter of ESP scores above or below the expected chance mean. Usually, the scores are those of standard runs of 25 trials, but larger and even smaller units"[312] can be used.

Further Reading:

Rudolf J. Freund and William J. Wilson, *Statistical Methods*, 2nd ed. (Amsterdam: Academic Press, 2003).

Veridical: Veridical is a quality of being truthful and rooted in actual events. Researchers Arthur and Joyce Berger tell us that "in psychical research when a percipient comes by information, perhaps in a dream, whose details correspond with the details of an actual event that, at the time of the experience, the percipient could not have known by any normal means, the experience is called veridical."[313] This is the term that you will frequently encounter when reading the parapsychological literature.

Visual Cortical Hyperexcitability: In a 2019 article in the journal *Consciousness and Cognition*, researchers investigated the link between visual cortical hyperexcitability and hallucinations, or "aberrant visual experiences."[314] This research explores the connections between neurocognition and consciousness and can be useful for understanding the various neurobiological processes that affect our consciousness and visual experiences. Since so much of parapsychology focuses on consciousness, this research could have implications for future studies in the psychical realm. This article represents just one of the many benefits of taking a multidisciplinary approach when studying parapsychology-related topics like consciousness and neurocognition.

Further Reading:

Chun Yuen Fong, Chie Takahashi, and Jason J. Braithwaite, "Evidence for Distinct Clusters of Diverse Anomalous Experiences and their Selective Association with Signs of Elevated Cortical Hyperexcitability," *Consciousness and Cognition* 71 (2019): 1–17.

Waiting Technique: A method used in extrasensory perception experiments that describes the intentional waiting period used by the percipient to clear their mind and receive target objects.[315]

Further Reading:

John Beloff and I. Mandleberg, "An Attempted Validation of the 'Waiting Technique,'" *Journal of the Society for Psychical Research* 45 (1970): 82–88.

Rhea A. White, "A Comparison of Old and New Methods of Response to Targets in ESP Experiments," *Journal of the American Society for Psychical Research* 58 (1964): 21–56.

Watseka Wonder: The Watseka Wonder refers to a famous case out of Watseka, Illinois, in the late 1800s. Lurancy Vennum, a teenager living in Watseka with her family, began to exhibit strange personality changes and eventually claimed to be channeling the spirit of Mary Roff, the deceased daughter of a neighboring family. Eventually, this spirit took over control of Lurancy's body, leading many to speculate that it was a case of spirit possession. Frederic W. H. Myers contends that the case supports the notion of a subliminal self and the survival of consciousness beyond bodily death.[316]

Further Reading:

E. Winchester Stevens, *The Watseka Wonder* (Los Angeles: Austin Publishing Company, 1928).

William McDougall Award for Distinguished Work in Parapsychology: In 1957, J. B. Rhine and his colleagues at the Duke Parapsychology Labs established the William McDougall Award for Distinguished Work in Parapsychology.[317] Dr. Carroll Nash of St. Joseph's College in Philadelphia was the first recipient of this award. Interestingly, Dr. Nash was a first in many other ways—to teach parapsychology for college credit *and* utilize dice in psychokinesis experiments a few years prior to J. B. and Louisa Rhine.[318]

Windbridge Research Center: The Windbridge Research Center is an organization with a mission of easing "suffering around dying, death, and what comes next by performing rigorous scientific research and sharing the results and other custom-ized content with the general public, clinicians, scientists, and practitioners."[319] Founded by Dr. Julie Beischel and Mark Bocuzzi, the research center not only conducts scholarly research on consciousness beyond death, it also engages the public and medical communities. In addition to conducting research and offering information to the general public, the Windbridge Research Center publishes a scholarly journal, *Threshold*. It even has a group of people referred to as the Windbridge Certified Research Mediums. Since much of its research involves mediums, this certified program has curated a group of credible mediums that the organization enlists for research purposes.

Wissenshaftliche Gesellschaft zur Forderung der Parapsychologie (Scientific Society for the Advancement of Parapsychology): According to its website, the Wissenshaftliche Gesellschaft zur Forderung der Parapsychologie (Scientific Society for the Advancement of Parapsychology) is "a non-profit association [that] maintains the parapsychological counseling center in Freiburg. Another purpose of the association is the organizational, financial and journalistic promotion of qualified parapsychological research at universities and university-related institutes."[320]

Zener cards: Zener cards are used in experiments on extrasensory perception. Named after their creator, the psychologist Karl E. Zener, they were used frequently in the Duke Parapsychology Labs. Dr. Zener was a psychologist at Duke, in fact, which could explain why many people incorrectly attribute the creation of these cards to J. B. Rhine. Zener cards are sometimes simply referred to as "ESP cards." They have five different geometric designs including a star, circle, square, plus sign, and wavy lines.[321] Zener cards were used in card-guessing studies that utilized forced-choice design. Forced-choice refers to a limited number of targets that are known to the subjects prior to the experiment.[322]

Further Reading:

Lance Storm, Patrizio E. Tressoldi, and Lorenzo Di Risio, "Meta-Analysis of ESP Studies, 1987–2010: Assessing the Success of the Forced-Choice Design in Parapsychology," *Journal of Parapsychology* 76, no. 2 (Fall 2012): 243–73.

Zero-Point Energy: Zero-point energy is a physics concept that states that no empty space is actually ever empty and that there is still some energy within a space, even at absolute zero. It has been applied to instances of poltergeist and recurrent spontaneous psychokinesis phenomena to suggest a possible explanation for psychokinetic events.[323]

Further Reading:

William G. Roll and William T. Joines, "RSPK and Consciousness," *Journal of Parapsychology* 77, no. 2 (Fall 2013): 192–211.

NOTES

1. Suzanne M. Roche and Kevin M. McConkey, "Absorption: Nature, Assessment, and Correlates," *Journal of Personality and Social Psychology* 59, no. 1 (1990): 91.

2. Chris A. Roe and Nicola J. Holt, "The Effects of Strategy ('Willing' Versus Absorption) and Feedback (Immediate versus Delayed) on Performance at a PK Task," *Journal of Parapsychology* 70, no. 1 (Spring 2006): 73.

3. Charles E. Stuart, "An Analysis to Determine a Test Predictive of Extra-Chance Scoring in Card-Calling Tests," *Journal of Parapsychology* 5, no. 2 (June 1, 1941): 100.

4. Sylvia Hart Wright, "Over a Century of Research on After-Death Communication," *Journal of Spirituality and Paranormal Studies* 31, no. 3 (2008): 154.

5. Susan Kwilecki, "Twenty-First Century American Ghosts: The After-Death Communication—Therapy and Revelation from Beyond the Grave," *Religion and American Culture: A Journal of Interpretation* 19, no. 1 (Winter 2009): 101–33.

6. Phyllis L. Clay, "Understanding the Experiences of Individuals who Believe they are Mentored by Someone who is no Longer Living." PhD diss., Saybrook University: 2011.

7. Kwilecki, "Twenty-First Century American Ghosts," 101.

8. Arthur and Joyce Berger, *The Encyclopedia of Parapsychology and Psychical Research* (Paragon House: New York, 1991), 4.

9. Ibid., 6

10. Ibid., 8.

11. "Formation of the Society," *Proceedings of the American Society for Psychical Research* 1, no. 1 (July 1885): 1–4.

12. Ibid., *Proceedings*, 4.

13. Ibid., *Proceedings*, 5.

14. Guy Lyon Playfair, "An American Institution in Low Spirits," *Fortean Times* 320 (November 2014): 52–53.

15. *The Annals of Psychical Science* 1, (January–June 1905): front matter.

16. Patrizio Tressoldi and Lance Storm, "Anomalous Cognition: An Umbrella Review of the Meta-Analytic Evidence," *Journal of Anomalous Experience and Cognition* 1, no. 1 (2021): 56.

17. Michael A. Thalbourne, *A Glossary of Terms Used in Parapsychology.* Charlottesville, VA: Puente Publications, 2003, 4.

18. James Houran and Rense Lange, "A Rasch Hierarchy of Haunt and Poltergeist Experiences," *Journal of Parapsychology* 65 (March 2001): 42.

19. Charles Gallagher, V. K. Kumar, and Ronald J. Pekala, "The Anomalous Experiences Inventory: Reliability and Validity," *Journal of Parapsychology* 58, no. 4 (December 1, 1994): 403.

20. Etzel Cardeña, "The Experimental Evidence for Parapsychological Phenomena: A Review," *American Psychologist* 73, no. 5 (2018): 670.

21. Berger and Berger, *The Encyclopedia*, 11.

22. Ibid., 11.

23. Jeffrey Mishlove and Brendan C. Engen, "Archetypal Synchronistic Resonance: A New Theory of Paranormal Experience," *Journal of Humanistic Psychology* 47, no. 2 (April 2007): 223.

24. Dave Wood and Christian Jensen Romer, "Where do we go From Here? The Future of Ghost Investigation," *Journal of Research into the Paranormal* 47 (January 2014): 11–23.

25. "ASSAP: Association for the Scientific Study of Anomalous Phenomena," Accessed November 28, 2021 from http://www.assap.ac.uk/index.html.

26. Berger and Berger, *The Encyclopedia*, 15.

27. David J. Wilde and Craig D. Murray, "An Interpretative Phenomenological Analysis of Out-of-Body Experiences in Two Cases of Novice Meditators," *Australian Journal of Clinical and Experimental Hypnosis* 37, no. 2 (2009): 90–118.

28. "Home: Welcome to the Website of the Australian Institute of Parapsychological Research," The Australian Institute of Parapsychological Re-

search (2016). Accessed January 13, 2022, from aiprinc.org.

29. "The Austrian Society for Parapsychology and Frontier Areas of Science," Accessed January 13, 2022, from parapsychologie.ac.at/eng-info.htm.

30. Berger and Berger, *The Encyclopedia*, 18.

31. Thalbourne, *A Glossary*, 9.

32. James C. Carpenter and David Price Rogers, "A Review of Recent Work on ESP Score Variation," in *Parapsychology Today: New Writings on ESP, Telepathy, Clairvoyance, Precognition, PK, and Mind Over Matter*, eds. J. B. Rhine and Robert Brier (New York: The Citadel Press, 1968), 36.

33. Berger and Berger, *The Encyclopedia*, 44.

34. William G. Roll, "Survival After Death: Alan Gauld's Examination of the Evidence," *Journal of Parapsychology* 48 (June 1984): 130.

35. E. M. Sidgwick, "An Examination of Book-Tests Obtained in Sittings with Mrs. Leonard." *Proceedings of the Society for Psychical Research* 31 (1921): 242.

36. Berger and Berger, *The Encyclopedia*, 57.

37. "Book Defends Boston Medium," *New York Times* (February 17, 1926): 19.

38. Thalbourne, *A Glossary*, 15.

39. Berger and Berger, *The Encyclopedia*, 59.

40. Ibid., 474.

41. C. R. Carpenter and Harold R. Phalen, "An Experiment in Card Guessing," *Journal of Parapsychology* 1, no. 1 (March 1, 1937): 31–43.

42. Bernard F. Riess, "A Case of High Scores in Card Guessing at a Distance," *Journal of Parapsychology* 1, no. 4 (December 1, 1937): 260–63.

43. "CERCAP," Lund University: Department of Psychology. Accessed January 13, 2022, from psy.lu.se/en/research/research-networks/cercap.

44. "History," Centro Studi Parapsicologici. Accessed January 13, 2022, from http://www.cspbo.it/b/storia%201.html.

45. Thalbourne, *A Glossary*, 15.

46. Berger and Berger, *The Encyclopedia*, 66–67.

47. Thalbourne, *A Glossary*, 16.

48. Dureen J. Hughes, "Blending With an Other: An Analysis of Trance Channeling in the United States," *Ethos* 19, no. 2 (June 1991): 161–84.

49. Huges, "Blending With an Other," 161.

50. J. E. Kennedy, "Why is PSI So Elusive? A Review and Proposed Model," *Journal of Parapsychology*, 65 (September 2001): 234.

51. Sara R. Feather and Robert Brier, "The Possible Effect of the Checker in Precognition Tests," *Journal of Parapsychology* 32, no. 3 (1968): 167.

52. Feather and Brier, "The Possible Effect," 167–75.

53. Berger and Berger, *The Encyclopedia*, 71.

54. Ibid., 71; Thouless, *A Glossary*, 17.

55. Berger and Berger, *The Encyclopedia*, 71.

56. Renaud Evrard, "From *Symptom* to *Difference*: 'Hearing Voices' and Exceptional Experiences," *Journal of the Society for Psychical Research* 78, no. 916 (2014): 129.

57. Louisa E. Rhine, "Auditory Psi Experience: Hallucination or Physical?" *Journal of Parapsychology* 27, no. 3 (1963): 182.

58. Evrard, "From *Symptom* to *Difference*," 129–48.

59. Thalbourne, *A Glossary*, 18.

60. Helané Wahbeh, Cedric Cannard, Jennifer Okonsky, and Arnaud Delorme, "A Physiological Examination of Perceived Incorporation During Trance," *F1000Research* 8, no. 67 (2019): 1.

61. Ibid., 72.

62. J. B. Rhine, "Telepathy and Clairvoyance Reconsidered," *Journal of Parapsychology* 9, no. 3 (September 1, 1945): 176.

63. Berger and Berger, *The Encyclopedia*, 75.

64. Ibid., 243.

65. W. F. Barrett, A. P. Percival Keep, C. C. Massey, Hensleigh Wedgwood, Frank Podmore, and E. R. Pease, "First Report of the Committee on Haunted Houses," *Proceedings of the Society for Psychical Research* 1, no. 1 (1882): 101.

66. Carlos S. Alvarado, "'Report of the Committee on Mediumistic Phenomena,' by William James (1886)," *History of Psychiatry* 27, no. 1 (2016): 88.

67. W. F. Barrett, Edmund Gurney, and F. W. H. Myers, "First Report on Thought-Reading," *Proceedings of the Society for Psychical Research* 1, no. 1 (July 17, 1882): 13.

68. Richard Noakes, "The 'Bridge Which is Between Physical and Psychical Research': William Fletcher Barrett, Sensitive Flames, and Spiritualism," *History of Science* 42, no. 4 (2004): 444–46.

69. Berger and Berger, *The Encyclopedia*, 77.

70. "Consciousness," In *Gale Encyclopedia of Psychology*, ed. Bonnie Strickland, 2nd ed. (Detroit, MI: Gale, 2001), 150.

71. Ibid.

72. Steven A. Schwartz, "Six Protocols, Neuroscience, and Near Death: An Emerging Paradigm Incorporating Nonlocal Consciousness," *Explore* 11, no. 4 (July/August 2015): 252.

73. Berger and Berger, *The Encyclopedia*, 77–78.

74. Gardner Murphy and Ernest Taves, "Covariance Methods in the Comparison of Extra-Sensory Tasks," *Journal of Parapsychology* 3, no. 1 (June 1, 1939): 39.

75. Ibid., 38.

76. Berger and Berger, *The Encyclopedia*, 11; Gurney, Edmund, Frederic W. H. Myers, and Frank Podmore, *Phantasms of the Living* (London: Kegan Paul, Trench, Trubner, and Co., 1918), 520.

77. Berger and Berger, *The Encyclopedia*, 89.

78. Everton de Oliveira Maraldi and Stanley Krippner, "Cross-Cultural Research on Anomalous Experiences: Theoretical Issues and Methodological Challenges," *Psychology of Consciousness: Theory, Research, and Practice* 6, no. 3 (2019): 306–307.

79. Ibid., 306–307.

80. Berger and Berger, *The Encyclopedia*, 100–101.

81. Ibid., 101.

82. Louisa E. Rhine and J. B. Rhine, "The Psychokinetic Effect: I. The First Experiment," *Journal of Parapsychology* 7, no. 1 (March 1, 1943): 20–43.

83. Berger and Berger, *The Encyclopedia*, 105.

84. Chris A. Roe, "Clients' Influence in the Selection of Elements of a Psychic Reading," *Journal of Parapsychology* 60, no. 1 (March 1996): 46–47.

85. Stefan Schmidt and Harald Walach, "Electrodermal Activity (EDA)—State-of-the-Art Measurement and Techniques for Parapsychological Purposes," *Journal of Parapsychology* 64, no. 2 (June 1, 2000): 139–63.

86. Berger and Berger, *The Encyclopedia*, 108.

87. Ibid., 109.

88. Carlos S. Alvarado, "Mediumship, Psychical Research, Dissociation, and the Powers of the Subconscious Mind," *Journal of Parapsychology* 78, no. 1 (2014): 98

89. "Dissociation and Dissociative Disorders," in *Gale Encyclopedia of Psychology*, ed. Bonnie Strickland, 2nd ed. (Detroit, mI: Gale, 2001), 189–90.

90. John Palmer, "Anomalous Cognition, Dissociation, and Motor Automatisms," *Journal of Parapsychology* 81, no. 1 (Spring 2017): 46.

91. Palmer, "Anomalous Cognition," 46.

92. Berger and Berger, *The Encyclopedia*, 109.

93. Ibid., 113.

94. Irvin L. Child, "Psychology and Anomalous Observations: The Question of ESP in Dreams," *American Psychologist* 40, no. 11 (November 1985): 1220.

95. Berger and Berger, *The Encyclopedia*, 254.

96. "Early Studies in Parapsychology at Duke," Duke University Libraries. Accessed December 14, 2021, from https://library.duke.edu/exhibits/2020 /parapsychology.

97. Courtney M. Block, *Researching the Paranormal: How to Find Reliable Information about Parapsychology, Ghosts, Astrology, Cryptozoology, Near-Death Experiences, and More* (Lanham. MD: Rowman & Littlefield, 2020), 59.

98. Ibid., 104.

99. Berger and Berger, *The Encyclopedia*, 119.

100. Karl Schoonover, "Ectoplasms, Evanescence, and Photography," *Art Journal* 62, no. 3 (Autumn 2003): 30–43.

101. Mark R. Leary and Tom Butler, "Electronic Voice Phenomena," in *Parapsychology: A Handbook for the 21st Century*, eds. Etzel Cardeña, John Palmer, and David Marcusson-Clavertz (Jefferson, NC: McFarland and Company, 2015), 341.

102. Leary and Butler, "Electronic Voice Phenomena," 42.

103. Mark Boccuzzi and Julie Beischel, "Objective Analyses of Real-Time Audio Instrumental Transcommunication and Matched Control Sessions: A Pilot Study," *Journal of Scientific Exploration* 25, no. 2 (2011): 215–35.

104. Kathryn F. Weymouth, *Healing from a Personal Perspective: Interviews with Certified Healing Touch Practitioners.* PhD diss, Saybrook University, 2012: 15.

105. William T. Joines, Stephen B. Baumann, and John G. Kruth, "Electromagnetic Emission from Humans during Focused Intent," *Journal of Parapsychology* 76, no. 2 (Fall 2012): 277.

106. Thalbourne, *A Glossary*, 38.

107. Rhea A. White, "Role Theory and Exceptional Human Experience," *Journal of Religion and Psychical Research* 17, no. 2 (April 1994): 76.

108. Thalbourne, *A Glossary*, 39.

109. Caroline Watt and Peter Ramakers, "Experimenter Effects with a Remote Facilitation of Attention Focusing Task: A Study with Multiple

Believer and Disbeliever Experiments," *Journal of Parapsychology* 67, no. 1 (Spring 2003): 99.

110. Thalbourne, *A Glossary*, 40.

111. Ibid., 40.

112. Ibid., 43.

113. Berger and Berger, *The Encyclopedia*, 142.

114. Ibid., 148.

115. Thalbourne, *A Glossary*, 45.

116. Daryl J. Bem, "The Ganzfeld Experiment," *Journal of Parapsychology* 57, no. 2 (June 1, 1993): 102.

117. Bem, "The Ganzfeld Experiment," 102.

118. J. B. Rhine, "Telepathy and Clairvoyance Reconsidered," 176.

119. Berger and Berger, *The Encyclopedia*, 155.

120. Michaeleen Maher, "Ghosts and Poltergeists: An Eternal Enigma," in *Parapsychology: A Handbook for the 21st Century*, eds. Etzel Cardeña, John Palmer, and David Marcusson-Clavertz (Jefferson, NC: McFarland and Company, 2015), 347.

121. Berger and Berger, *The Encyclopedia*, 156.

122. "Global Consciousness Project," *Psi Encyclopedia* (Society for Psychical Research). Accessed December 16, 2021, from https://psi-encyclopedia .spr.ac.uk/articles/global-consciousness-project.

123. Berger and Berger, *The Encyclopedia*, 159.

124. Renaud Evrard, "Parapsychology in France after May 1968: A History of GERP," *Journal of Scientific Exploration* 24, no. 2 (2010): 286.

125. Berger and Berger, *The Encyclopedia*, 170.

126. Ciarán O'Keeffe, James Houran, Damien J. Houran, Neil Dagnall, Kenneth Drinkwater, Lorraine Sheridan, and Brian Laythe, "The Dr. John Hall Story: A Case Study in Putative 'Haunted Person Syndrome,'" *Mental Health, Religion, and Culture* 23, no. 7 (2020): 532.

127. Berger and Berger, *The Encyclopedia*, 175.

128. "The Ganzfeld Experiment," 175.

129. "Mission Statement: Mission Continued," University of Groningen: Heymans Anomalous Cognition Group. Accessed January 13, 2022, from https://sites.google.com/a/rug.nl/heymans-anoma lous-cognition-group/home/mission-continued.

130. Berger and Berger, *The Encyclopedia*, 180.

131. Thalbourne, *A Glossary*, 52.

132. Ibid., 52.

133. Simon J. Sherwood, "Relationship Between the Hypnagogic/Hypnopompic States and Reports of Anomalous Experiences," *Journal of Parapsychology* 66, no. 2 (June 2002): 127.

134. Sherwood, "Relationship Between," 127–28.

135. Berger and Berger, *The Encyclopedia*, 193.

136. Ibid., 266.

137. Régine Plas, "Psychology and Psychical Research in France around the end of the 19th Century," *History of the Human Sciences* 25, no. 2 (2012): 92.

138. Ibid., 92.

139. Renaud Evrard, "Anomalous Phenomena and the Scientific Mind: Some Insights from 'Psychologist' Louise Favre (1868–1938?)," *Journal of Scientific Exploration* 31, no. 1 (2017): 71–73.

140. Sofie Lachapelle, *Investigating the Supernatural: From Spiritism and Occultism to Psychical Research and Metapsychics in France, 1853–1931* (Baltimore, MD: Johns Hopkins University Press, 2011), 5–6.

141. "Institute for Frontier Areas of Psychology and Mental Health," Institute for Frontier Areas of Psychology and Mental Health. Accessed January 13, 2022, from https://www.igpp.de/allg/welcome.htm.

142. Michael R. McVaugh, "Rhine Research Center" (2006), Accessed December 16, 2021, from https://www.ncpedia.org/rhine-research-center.

143. About: Weaving Together Knowledge and Knowing" (2021), Institute of Noetic Sciences (IONS). Accessed December 16, 2021, from https://noetic.org/about/.

144. "About Us," Instituto de Psicología Paranormal. Accessed January 14, 2022, from http://www .alipsi.com.ar/quienes-somos/.

145. Mark Boccuzzi and Julie Beischel, "Objective Analyses of Real-Time Audio Instrumental Transcommunication and Matched Control Sessions: A Pilot Study," *Journal of Scientific Exploration* 25, no. 2 (2011): 216.

146. "Japanese Society for Parapsychology," Japanese Society for Parapsychology. Accessed January 14, 2022, from http://j-spp.umin.jp/english /jspp_e.htm.

147. Berger and Berger, *The Encyclopedia*, 8.

148. Ibid., 215.

149. Ibid., 215.

150. Thalbourne, *A Glossary*, 59.

151. Ibid., 59.

152. Caroline Watt, "Research Assistants or Budding Scientists? A Review of 96 Undergraduate Stu-

dent Projects at the Koestler Parapsychology Unit," *Journal of Parapsychology* 70, no. 2 (Fall 2006): 336.

153. Thalbourne, *A Glossary*, 63.

154. Berger and Berger, *The Encyclopedia*, 242.

155. Arthur van Gennep, *The Rites of Passage* (Chicago: University of Chicago Press, 1960); Victor Turner, *The Ritual Process: Structure and Anti-Structure* (Chicago: Aldine, 1969).

156. Block, *Research the Paranormal*, xiv.

157. James Seale-Collazo, "Charisma, Liminality, and Freedom: Toward a Theory of the Everyday Extraordinary," *Anthropology of Consciousness* 23, no. 2 (2012): 175–91.

158. Michael A. Thalbourne, "Transliminality, Anomalous Belief and Experience, and Hypnotisability," *Australian Journal of Clinical and Experimental Hypnosis* 37, no. 2 (November 2009): 120.

159. Thalbourne, *A Glossary*, 63.

160. Ibid., 64; Berger and Berger, *The Encyclopedia*, 244.

161. Edmund Gurney and Frederic W. H. Myers, "Statement of the Literary Committee of the Society for Psychical Research," *Journal of the Society for Psychical Research* 3, no. 36 (January 1887): 1–8.

162. Peter Lamont, "Spiritualism and a Mid-Victorian Crisis of Evidence," *The Historical Journal* 47, no. 4 (December 2004): 911.

163. Berger and Berger, *Encyclopedia*, 253.

164. Jon Tolaas and Montague Ullman, "Extrasensory Communication and Dreams," in *Handbook of Dreams—Research, Theories, and Application,* ed. Benjamin B. Wolman (New York: Van Nostrand Reinhold, 1979.

165. Tolas and Ullman, "Extrasensory Communicatio."

166. Stanley Krippner, "The Maimonides ESP-Dream Studies," *Journal of Parapsychology* 57, no. 1 (March 1, 1993): 39–54.

167. Berger and Berger, *The Encyclopedia*, 258.

168. Thalbourne, *A Glossary*, 68.

169. Berger and Berger, *The Encyclopedia*, 264.

170. Janet Oppenheim, *The Other World: Spiritualism and Psychical Research in England, 1850–1914* (Cambridge: Cambridge University Press, 1985), 150.

171. Julie Beischel, "Contemporary Methods Used in Laboratory-Based Mediumship Research," *Journal of Parapsychology*, 71 (Spring 2007): 37–68.

172. Berger and Berger, *The Encyclopedia*, 266.

173. Thalbourne, *A Glossary*, 72.

174. Berger and Berger, *The Encyclopedia*, 268.

175. Mario Varvoglis and Peter A. Bancel, "Micro-Psychokinesis: Exceptional or Universal?" *Journal of Parapsychology* 80, no. 1 (Spring 2016): 38.

176. Berger and Berger, *The Encyclopedia*, 282.

177. Ibid., 287.

178. Pim van Lommel, Ruud van Wees and Vincent Myers, "Near-Death Survivors of Cardiac Arrest: A Prospective Study in the Netherlands," *Lancet* 358, no. 9298 (December 15, 2001): 2043.

179. Thalbourne, *A Glossary*, 78.

180. Ibid., 99, 127.

181. Ibid., 80.

182. Ibid., 80.

183. Ibid., 81.

184. Harvey J. Irwin, "The Disembodied Self: An Empirical Study of Dissociation and the Out-of-Body Experience," *Journal of Parapsychology* 64, no. 3 (September 1, 2000): 261–77.

185. Ibid., 262.

186. Berger and Berger, *The Encyclopedia*, 312.

187. Ibid., 311–12.

188. Ibid., 311.

189. "History of the Parapsychological Association" (The Parapsychological Association, 2021). Accessed December 22, 2021, from https://www.parapsych.org/articles/1/14/history_of_the_parapsychological.aspx.

190. Berger and Berger, *The Encyclopedia*, 312.

191. "About the Parapsychology Foundation" (Parapsychology Foundation, 2021). Accessed December 22, 2021, from https://parapsychology.org/about-us/.

192. Berger and Berger, *The Encyclopedia*, 315.

193. Ibid., 317.

194. Ibid., 319.

195. Ibid., 323.

196. William E. Cox, "Three-Tier Placement PK," *Journal of Parapsychology* 23, no. 1 (March 1, 1959): 19–29.

197. Louisa E. Rhine, "Placement PK Tests with Three Types of Objects," *Journal of Parapsychology* 15, no. 2 (June 1, 1951): 132–38.

198. J. G. Pratt and W. G. Roll, "The Seaford Disturbances," *Journal of Parapsychology* 22, no. 2 (June 1958): 79–80.

199. Annalisa Ventola, James Houran, Brian Laythe, Lance Storm, Alejandro Parra, John Dixon,

and John G. Kruth. "A Transliminal 'Dis-Ease' Model of 'Poltergeist Agents.'" *Journal of the Society for Psychical Research* 83, no. 3 (2019): 144–71.

200. Pratt and Roll, "The Seaford Disturbances, 79–80.

201. John G. Kruth and William T. Joines, "Taming the Ghost Within: An Approach Toward Addressing Apparent Electronic Poltergeist Activity," *Journal of Parapsychology* 80, no. 1 (Spring 2016): 70–86.

202. Thalbourne, *A Glossary*, 90.

203. J. B. Rhine, "Experiments Bearing on the Precognition Hypothesis," *Journal of Parapsychology* 2, no. 1 (March 1, 1938): 40.

204. Caroline Watt, "Precognitive Dreaming: Investigating Anomalous Cognition and Psychological Factors," *Journal of Parapsychology* 78, no. 1 (Spring 2014): 115–25.

205. Caroline Watt, Emily Dawson, Alisdair Tullo, Abby Pooley, and Holly Rice, "Testing Precognition and Alterations of Consciousness with Selected Participants in the Ganzfeld," *Journal of Parapsychology* 84, no. 1 (Spring 2020): 21–37.

206. Berger and Berger, *The Encyclopedia*, 331.

207. Fiona Steinkamp, "Does Precognition Foresee the Future? A Postal Experiment to Assess the Possibility of True Precognition," *Journal of Parapsychology* 64, no. 1 (March 1, 2000): 3–4.

208. Brenda J. Dunne, "Princeton Engineering Anomalies Research Lab," in *Ghosts, Spirits, and Psychics: The Paranormal from Alchemy to Zombies*, ed. Matt Cardin (Santa Barbara, CA: ABC-CLIO, 2015), 232.

209. Ibid., 232.

210. Julie Beischel, "Contemporary Methods Used in Laboratory-Based Mediumship Research," *Journal of Parapsychology* 71 (Spring 2007): 41.

211. Berger and Berger, *The Encyclopedia*, 338.

212. Ibid., 338.

213. Ibid., 339.

214. Louisa E. Rhine, "Toward Understanding Psi-Missing," *Journal of Parapsychology* 29, no. 4 (December 1, 1965): 272–73.

215. Adrian Ryan, "Open Data in Parapsychology: Introducing *Psi Open Data*," *Journal of Parapsychology* 82, no. 1 (2018): 65.

216. Berger and Berger, *The Encyclopedia*, 339.

217. "About the PRF," Psychical Research Foundation. Accessed January 13, 2022, from https://www.psychicalresearchfoundation.com/about.

218. Andreas Sommer, "Normalizing the Supernormal: The Formation of the 'Gesellschaft Für Psychologische Forschung' ('Society for Psychological Research'), c. 1886–1890," *Journal of the History of the Behavioral Sciences* 49, no. 1 (Winter 2013): 20–21.

219. Berger and Berger, *The Encyclopedia*, 341.

220. J. G. Pratt, "The Case for Psychokinesis," *Journal of Parapsychology* 24, no. 3 (September 1, 1960): 171–88.

221. Ibid., 173.

222. Ibid., 173.

223. Robert H. Thouless, "A Report on an Experiment in Psychokinesis with Dice and a Discussion on Psychological Factors Favoring Success," *Journal of Parapsychology* 15, no. 2 (June 1, 1951): 89–102.

224. William G. Roll and William T. Joines, "RSPK and Consciousness," *Journal of Parapsychology* 77, no. 2 (Fall 2013): 192–211.

225. Heather Wolffram, *The Stepchildren of Science: Psychical Research and Parapsychology in Germany, c. 1870–1939* (Amsterdam: Rodopi, 2009), 33–34.

226. Ibid., 35.

227. "History," Centro Studi Parapsicologici. Accessed January 13, 2022, from http://www.cspbo.it/b/storia%201.html.

228. Thalbourne, *A Glossary*, 103.

229. John G. Kruth, "Five Qualitative Research Approaches and Their Applications in Parapsychology," *Journal of Parapsychology* 79, no. 2 (Fall 2015): 219.

230. Thalbourne, *A Glossary*, 103.

231. Berger and Berger, *The Encyclopedia*, 345.

232. C. T. K. Chari, "Quantum Physics and Parapsychology," *Journal of Parapsychology* 20, no. 3 (September 1, 1956): 167.

233. Dean Radin, *Entangled Minds: Extrasensory Experiences in a Quantum Reality* (New York: Paraview, 2006). 1–2.

234. J. B. Rhine and Betty M. Humphrey, "The PK Effect: Special Evidence from Hit Patterns," *Journal of Parapsychology* 8, no. 1 (March 1, 1944): 19.

235. Thalbourne, *A Glossary*, 105.

236. Mario Varvoglis and Peter A. Bancel, "Micro-Psychokinesis: Exceptional or Universal?"

Journal of Parapsychology 80, no. 1 (Spring 2016): 38–39.

237. Ibid., 37.

238. Thalbourne, *A Glossary*, 106.

239. Ibid., 106.

240. William G. Roll and William T. Joines, "RSPK and Consciousness," *Journal of Parapsychology* 77, no. 2 (Fall 2013): 192.

241. Ibid., 195–96.

242. Berger and Berger, *The Encyclopedia*, 353.

243. Etzel Cardeña, "The Experimental Evidence for Parapsychological Phenomena: A Review," *American Psychologist* 73, no. 5 (2018): 670.

244. Russell Targ, "What do We Know about PSI? The First Decade of Remote-Viewing Research and Operations at Stanford Research Institute." *Journal of Scientific Exploration* 33, no. 4 (2019): 56–592.

245. Stanley Krippner, David T. Saunders, Angel Morgan, and Alan Quan, "Remote Viewing of Concealed Target Pictures Under Light and Dark Conditions," *Explore* 15, no. 1 (2019): 27–37.

246. Thalbourne, *A Glossary*, 108.

247. Ibid., 109.

248. Carlos S. Alvarado, Massimo Biondi, and Wim Kramer, "Historical Notes on Psychic Phenomena in Specialised Journals," *European Journal of Parapsychology* 21, no. 1 (2006): 68.

249. "What is the Rhine?" (Rhine Research Center, 2021). Accessed December 29, 2021, from https://www.rhineonline.org/about-us.

250. Berger and Berger, *The Encyclopedia*, 370.

251. Montague Keen, "The Scole Investigation: A Study in Critical Analysis of Paranormal Physical Phenomena," *Journal of Scientific Exploration* 15, no. 2 (2001): 167–69.

252. Berger and Berger, *The Encyclopedia*, 386.

253. J. L. Woodruff and R. W. George, "Experiments in Extra-Sensory Perception," *Journal of Parapsychology* 1, no. 1 (March 1, 1937): 18–30.

254. Carlos S. Alvarado, "The Concept of Survival of Bodily Death and the Development of Parapsychology," *Journal of the Society for Psychical Research* 67, no. 2 (April 2003): 68.

255. Ibid., 69.

256. Richard Wiseman, Emma Greening, and Matthew Smith, "Belief in the Paranormal and Suggestion in the Séance Room," *British Journal of Psychology* 94 (August 2003): 285–97.

257. Berger and Berger, *The Encyclopedia*, 389.

258. Ibid., 394.

259. Thalbourne, *A Glossary*, 116.

260. Renée Haynes, *The Society for Psychical Research, 1882–1982: A History* (London: Macdonald & Co., 1982), xiii–5.

261. Haynes, *The Society for Psychical Research* xiii.

262. Andreas Sommer, "Normalizing the Supernormal: The Formation of the 'Gesellschaft Für Psychologische Forschung' ('Society for Psychological Research')," *Journal of the History of the Behavioral Sciences* 49, no. 1 (Winter 2013): 18–44.

263. W. F. Barrett, A. P. Percival Keep, C. C. Massey, Hensleigh Wedgwood, Frank Podmore, and E. R. Pease, "First Report of the Committee on Haunted Houses," *Proceedings of the Society for Psychical Research* 1, no. 1 (1882): 101–15; Edmund Gurney and Frederic W. H. Myers, "Statement of the Literary Committee of the Society for Psychical Research," *Journal of the Society for Psychical Research* 3, no. 36 (January 1887): 1–8

264. Berger and Berger, *The Encyclopedia*, 83.

265. Andreas Sommer, "Normalizing the Supernormal: The Formation of the 'Gesellschaft Für Psychologische Forschung' ('Society for Psychological Research')," *Journal of the History of the Behavioral Sciences* 49, no. 1 (Winter 2013): 21.

266. Berger and Berger, *The Encyclopedia*, 264, 408–409.

267. Ibid., 410.

268. Ibid., 410.

269. Janet Oppenheim, *The Other World: Spiritualism and Psychical Research in England, 1850–1914*, (Cambridge: Cambridge University Press, 1985), 1.

270. Ibid., 7.

271. Alex Owen, *The Darkened Room: Women, Power and Spiritualism in Late Victorian England* (Philadelphia: University of Pennsylvania Press, 1990), 314.

272. JoMarie Haight, "Spontaneous Psi Cases: A Survey and Preliminary Study of ESP, Attitude, and Personality Relationship," *Journal of Parapsychology* 43, no. 3 (September 1, 1979): 179–81.

273. Louisa E. Rhine, "Subjective Forms of Spontaneous Psi Experiences," *Journal of Parapsychology* 17, no. 2 (June 1, 1953): 77–114.

274. Ibid., 78.

275. Berger and Berger, *The Encyclopedia*, 420.

276. "History," (Dutch Society for Psychical Research, 2021). Accessed December 29, 2021, from https://dutchspr.org/spr/overdespr/geschiedenis.

277. "Subconscious," American Psychological Association. Accessed December 15, 2021, from https://dictionary.apa.org/subconscious.

278. Carlos S. Alvarado, "Mediumship, Psychical Research, Dissociation, and the Powers of the Subconscious Mind," *Journal of Parapsychology* 78, no. 1 (2014): 98–114.

279. Ibid., 100.

280. Carlos S. Alvarado, "On the Centenary of Frederic W.H. Myers's *Human Personality and Its Survival of Bodily Death*," *Journal of Parapsychology* 68, no. 1 (Spring 2004): 7–9.

281. Thalbourne, *A Glossary*, 120.

282. Rachael Ironside, "Feeling Spirits: Sharing Subjective Paranormal Experience Through Embodied Talk and Action," *Text and Talk* 38, no. 6 (2018): 706.

283. Thalbourne, *A Glossary*, 121.

284. Harvey Irwin, "Is Scientific Investigation of Postmortem Survival an Anachronism? The Demise of the Survival Hypothesis," *Australian Journal of Parapsychology* 2, no. 1 (June 2002): 19–27.

285. Lance Storm, "Synchronicity, Causality, and Acausality," *Journal of Parapsychology* 63, no. 3 (September 1999): 249.

286. Ibid., 250.

287. Thalbourne, *A Glossary*, 129.

288. Ibid., 123.

289. Berger and Berger, *The Encyclopedia*, 426.

290. Ibid., 428.

291. "Dr. A.N. Khovrin and the Tambov Experiments," in *Abnormal Hypnotic Phenomena: A Survey of Nineteenth-Century Cases*, ed Eric J. Dingwall, Volume 3 (London: J. & A. Churchill, 1968), 33–75.

292. Berger and Berger, *The Encyclopedia*, 430.

293. Sir Oliver Lodge, "A Textbook of Metapsychics: Review and Critique by Sir Oliver Lodge," *Proceedings of the Society for Psychical Research* 34 (October 1923): 75.

294. Berger and Berger, *The Encyclopedia*, 430.

295. Leanna J. Standish, L. Clark Johnson, Leila Kozak, and Todd Richards, "Evidence of Correlated Functional Magnetic Resonance Imaging Signals Between Distant Human Brains," *Alternative Therapies in Health and Medicine* 9, no. 1 (January/February 2003): 122–28.

296. Standish et al., "Evidence of Correlated," 123.

297. Berger and Berger, *The Encyclopedia*, 436.

298. Miki Takasuna, "The Fukurai Affair: Parapsychology and the History of Psychology in Japan," *History of the Human Sciences* 25, no. 2 (2012): 149–64.

299. Berger and Berger, *The Encyclopedia*, 440.

300. Carlos S. Alvarado, "Eleanor M. Sidgwick (1845–1936)," *Journal of Parapsychology* 82, no. 2. (2018): 128.

301. Simone Natale, "The Medium on the Stage: Trance and Performance in Nineteenth-Century Spiritualism," *Early Popular Visual Culture* 9, no. 3 (2011): 239–55.

302. Kevin Stuart, Banmadorji, and Huangchojia, "Mountain Gods and Trance Mediums: A Qinghai Tibetan Summer Festival," *Asian Folklore Studies* 54, no. 2 (1995): 219–37.

303. Michael A. Thalbourne, "Transliminality, Anomalous Belief and Experience, and Hypnotisability," *Australian Journal of Clinical and Experimental Hypnosis* 37, no. 2 (November 2009): 119.

304. Ibid., 120.

305. Thalbourne, *A Glossary*, 128.

306. Ervin Laszlo, "Cosmic Connectivity: Toward a Scientific Foundation for Transpersonal Consciousness," *The International Journal of Transpersonal Studies* 23 (2004): 21–31.

307. Thalbourne, *A Glossary*, 131.

308. Ibid., 131.

309. Ingrid Kloosterman, "Psychical Research and Parapsychology Interpreted: Suggestions from the International Historiography of Psychical Research and Parapsychology for Investigating its History in the Netherlands," *History of the Human Sciences* 25, no. 2 (2012): 14.

310. Ibid., 14–15.

311. Rudolf J. Freund and William J. Wilson, *Statistical Methods*, 2nd ed (Amsterdam: Academic Press, 2003), 24.

312. J. B. Rhine, "Introductory Comments," in *Parapsychology Today: New Writings on ESP, Telepathy, Clairvoyance, Precognition, PK, Mind Over Matter*, eds. J. B. Rhine and Robert Brier (New York: Citadel Press, 1968), 26.

313. Berger and Berger, *The Encyclopedia*, 453.

314. Chun Yuen Fong, Chie Takahashi, and Jason J. Braithwaite, "Evidence for Distinct Clusters of Diverse Anomalous Experiences and their Selective Association with Signs of Elevated Cortical Hyperexcitability," *Consciousness and Cognition* 71 (2019): 1–17.

315. Thalbourne, *A Glossary*, 135.

316. Jeffrey Mishlove, *Roots of Consciousness* (Da Capo Press: Boston, 1997). 186–88.

317. Arthur S. Berger, *Lives and Letters in American Parapsychology: A Biographical History, 1850–1987* (Jefferson, NC: McFarland & Co., 1988), 141.

318. Ibid., 315.

319. "About Us." Windbridge Research Center. Accessed November 29, 2021, from https://www.windbridge.org/about-us/.

320. "Scientific Society for the Promotion of Parapsychology eV." WGFP. Accessed January 13, 2022, from https://www.parapsychologische-beratungsstelle.de/WGFP/.

321. Berger and Berger, *The Encyclopedia*, 474.

322. Lance Storm, Patrizio E. Tressoldi, and Lorenzo Di Risio, "Meta-Analysis of ESP Studies, 1987–2010: Assessing the Success of the Forced-Choice Design in Parapsychology," *Journal of Parapsychology,* 76, no. 2 (Fall 2012): 243.

323. William G. Roll and William T. Joines, "RSPK and Consciousness," *Journal of Parapsychology,* 77, no. 2 (Fall 2013): 197–98.

Bibliography of Resources Found in Glossary

This bibliography compiles all citations of resources that you can find in the 'further reading' sections of the Glossary. Citations are arranged alphabetically by topic. While you can view these citations in their respective sections in the Glossary, this appendix is provided so you can use it as another handy compilation of reading to jumpstart your own research into parapsychology. Remember that the resources listed below are by no means comprehensive and merely representation a sample to help get you started!

Absorption:
Irwin, Harvey. "Parapsychological Phenomena and the Absorption Domain," *Journal of the American Society for Psychical Research* 79, no. 1 (January 1985): 1–11.

Affectability:
Stuart, Charles E. "An Analysis to Determine a Test Predictive of Extra-Chance Scoring in Card Calling Tests," *Journal of Parapsychology* 5, no. 2 (June 1, 1941): 99–137.

After Death Communication:
Kwilecki, Susan. "Twenty-First Century American Ghosts: The After-Death Communication—Therapy and Revelation from Beyond the Grave." *Religion and American Culture: A Journal of Interpretation* 19, no. 1 (Winter 2009): 101–33.

Wright, Sylvia Hart, "Over a Century of Research on After-Death Communication," *Journal of Spirituality and Paranormal Studies* 31, no. 3 (2008): 154–66.

American Society for Psychical Research:
"Formation of the Society," *Proceedings of the American Society for Psychical Research* 1, no. 1 (July 1885): 1–4.

Anomalous Cognition:
May, Edwin, S. James P. Spottiswoode, and Christine L. James, "Managing the Target Pool Bandwidth: Noise Reduction for Anomalous Cognition Experiments." Presented at the 37th Annual Parapsychological Association at University of Amsterdam, the Netherlands (March 23, 1994): 1–9.

May, Edwin C., Sonali Bhatt Marwaha, Vinay Chaganti, "Anomalous Cognition: Two Protocols for Data Collection and Analyses," *Journal of the Society for Psychical Research* 75, no. 905 (October 2011): 191–210.

Anomalous Experiences Inventory:
Gallagher, Charles, V. K. Kumar, and Ronald J. Pekala, "The Anomalous Experiences Inventory: Reliability and Validity," *Journal of Parapsychology* 58, no. 4 (December 1, 1994): 402–28.

Apparition:
Myers, Frederick W. H. "Report on the Census of Hallucinations," *Proceedings of the Society for Psychical Research* 10 (1894): 25–422.

Apports:
Nahm, Michael. "Out of Thin Air? Apport Studies Performed between 1928 and 1938 by Elemér Chengery Pap," *Journal of Scientific Exploration* 33, no. 4 (2019): 661–705.

Archetypal Synchronistic Resonance:

Mishlove, Jeffrey and Brendan C. Engen, "Archetypal Synchronistic Resonance: A New Theory of Paranormal Experience," *Journal of Humanistic Psychology* 47, no. 2 (April 2007): 223–42.

Artifact Induction:

Batcheldor, K. J. "Contributions to the Theory of PK Induction from Sitter-Work," *Journal of the American Society for Psychical Research* 78, no. 2 (1984): 105–22.

Astral Projection:

Alvarado, Carlos S. "The Psychological Approach to Out-of-Body Experiences: A Review of Early and Modern Developments," *Journal of Psychology* 126 (1992): 237–50.

Craffert, Pieter F. "When is an Out-of-Body Experience (Not) an Out-of-Body Experience? Reflections about Out-of-Body Phenomena in Neuroscientific Research," *Journal of Cognition and Culture* 15 (2015): 13–31.

Automatic Writing:

Alvarado, Carlos S. "Mediumship, Psychical Research, Dissociation, and the Powers of the Subconscious Mind," *Journal of Parapsychology* 78, no. 1 (Spring 2014): 98–114.

Book Test:

Besterman, T. "Further Inquiries into the Elements of Chance in Book Tests," *Proceedings of the Society for Psychical Research* 40 (1931/32): 59–98.

Sidgwick, E. M. "An Examination of Book-Tests Obtained in Sittings with Mrs. Leonard," *Proceedings of the Society for Psychical Research* 31 (1921): 241–400.

Card-Guessing:

Carpenter, C. R. and Harold R. Phalen, "An Experiment in Card Guessing," *Journal of Parapsychology* 1, no. 1 (March 1, 1937): 31–43.

Riess, Bernard F. "A Case of High Scores in Card Guessing at a Distance," *Journal of Parapsychology* 1, no. 4 (December 1, 1937): 260–63.

Centro Studi Parapsicologici (Center for Parapsychological Studies of Bologna):

Bersani, Ferdinando. "The Bologna Center for Parapsychological Studies (CSP): Research Between 1970 and 1985." In abstracts of presented papers from the Parapsychological Association 56th Annual Convention, Viterbo, Italy, August 8–11, 2013, *Journal of Parapsychology* 77, no. 2 (Fall 2013): 189.

Channeling:

Hughes, Dureen J. "Blending With an Other: An Analysis of Trance Channeling in the United States," *Ethos* 19, no. 2 (June 1991): 161–84.

Checker Effect:

Feather, Sara R. and Robert Brier, "The Possible Effect of the Checker in Precognition Tests," *Journal of Parapsychology* 32, no. 3 (1968): 167–75.

Weiner, D. H. and N. L. Zingrone, "In the Eye of the Beholder: Further Research on the 'Checker Effect,'" *Journal of Parapsychology* 53 (1989): 203–31.

Cipher Test:

"Dr. Thouless's Cipher Test," *Journal of Parapsychology* 49, no. 2 (June 1985): 213.

Circle:

Fournier d'Albe, E. E. *The Goligher Circle: May to August, 1921*. London: John M. Watkins, 1922.

Clairaudience:

Evrard, Renaud. "From Symptom to Difference: 'Hearing Voices' and Exceptional Experiences," *Journal of the Society for Psychical Research* 78, no. 916 (2014): 129–48.

Rhine, Louisa E. "Auditory Psi Experience: Hallucination or Physical?" *Journal of Parapsychology* 27, no. 3 (1963): 182–97.

Clairvoyance:

Rhine, J. B. "Telepathy and Clairvoyance Reconsidered," *Journal of Parapsychology* 9, no. 3 (September 1, 1945): 176–93.

College of Psychic Studies:

"The College of Psychic Studies: Exploring Consciousness Since 1884," (The College of Psychic Studies, 2021), https://www.collegeofpsychic studies.co.uk/.

Committee on Haunted Houses:

Barrett, W. F., A. P. Percival Keep, C. C. Massey, Hensleigh Wedgwood, Frank Podmore, and E. R. Pease, "First Report of the Committee on Haunted

Houses," *Proceedings of the Society for Psychical Research* 1, no. 1 (1882): 101–15.

Royce, Josiah. "Preliminary Report of the Committee on Apparitions and Haunted Houses," *Proceedings of the Society for Psychical Research* 1, no. 2 (July 1886):128–31.

Committee on Mediumistic Phenomena:

Alvarado, Carlos S. "'Report of the Committee on Mediumistic Phenomena,' by William James (1886)," *History of Psychiatry* 27, no. 1 (2016): 85–100.

James, William. "Report of the Committee on Mediumistic Phenomena," *Proceedings of the Society for Psychical Research* 1, no. 2 (July 1886): 102–6.

Committee on Thought-Transference:

Barrett, W. F., Edmund Gurney, and F. W. H. Myers, "First Report on Thought-Reading," *Proceedings of the Society for Psychical Research* 1, no. 1 (July 17, 1882): 13–34.

Noakes, Richard. "The 'Bridge which is Between Physical and Psychical Research': William Fletcher Barrett, Sensitive Flames, and Spiritualism," *History of Science* 42, no. 4 (2004): 419–64.

Consciousness:

Krippner, Stanley. "Parapsychology and Consciousness Research," *Journal of Religion and Psychical Research* 26, no. 2 (2003): 108–13.

Schwartz, Steven A. "Six Protocols, Neuroscience, and Near Death: An Emerging Paradigm Incorporating Nonlocal Consciousness." *Explore* 11, no. 4 (July/August 2015): 252–60.

Control:

de Miguel, Paula Vilaplana. "The House that Ghosts Built (And Mediums Performed)," *Invisible Culture* 32, (April 2021).

Covariance Effect:

Murphy, Gardner and Ernest Taves, "Covariance Methods in the Comparison of Extra-Sensory Tasks," *Journal of Parapsychology* 3, no. 1 (June 1, 1939): 38–78.

Crisis Apparition:

Gurney, Edmund, Frederic W. H. Myers, and Frank Podmore, *Phantasms of the Living* (London: Kegan Paul, Trench, Trubner, and Co., 1918).

Cross-Correspondences:

"Private Meeting for Members and Associates," *Journal of the Society for Psychical Research* 14. (January 1909): 3–30.

Verrall, Helen G. "The Element of Chance in Cross Correspondences," *Journal of the Society for Psychical Research* 15, no. 284 (December 1911): 153–73.

Cultural Source Hypothesis:

Maraldi, Everton de Oliveira and Stanley Krippner, "Cross-Cultural Research on Anomalous Experiences: Theoretical Issues and Methodological Challenges," *Psychology of Consciousness: Theory, Research, and Practice* 6, no. 3 (2019): 306–7.

Deathbed Visions:

Osis, Karlis and Erlendur Haraldsson, "Deathbed Observations by Physicians and Nurses: A Cross-Cultural Study," *Journal of the American Society for Psychical Research* 71, no. 3 (July 1977): 237–59.

Dice Tests:

Rhine, J. B. "Early PK Tests: Sevens and Low-Dice Series," *Journal of Parapsychology* 9, no. 2 (June 1, 1945): 106–15.

Rhine, Louisa E. and J. B Rhine, "The Psychokinetic Effect: I. The First Experiment," *Journal of Parapsychology* 7, no. 1 (March 1, 1943): 20–43.

Thouless, Robert H. "A Report on an Experiment in Psychokinesis with Dice and a Discussion on Psychological Factors Favoring Success," *Journal of Parapsychology* 15, no. 2 (June 1, 1951): 89–102.

Direct Mental Influence on Living Systems (DMILS):

Benor, D. J. *Healing Research: Spiritual Healing: Scientific Validation of a Healing Revolution.* Southfield, MI: Vision Publications, 2001.

Braud, W. and M. Schlitz, "Consciousness Interactions with Remote Biological Systems: Anomalous Intentionality Effects," *Subtle Energies* 2 (1991): 1–46.

Schmidt, Stefan and Harald Walach, "Electrodermal Activity (EDA)—State-of-the-Art Measurement and Techniques for Parapsychological Purposes," *Journal of Parapsychology* 64, no. 2 (June 1, 2000): 139–63.

Displacement Effect:

Milton, Julie. "Critical Review of the Displacement Effect: I. The Relationship Between Displacement and Scoring on the Intended Target," *Journal of Parapsychology* 52, no. 1 (March 1, 1988): 29–55.

Dissociation:

Alvarado, Carlos S. "Mediumship, Psychical Research, Dissociation, and the Powers of the Subconscious Mind," *Journal of Parapsychology* 78, no. 1 (2014): 98–114.

Palmer, John. "Anomalous Cognition, Dissociation, and Motor Automatisms," *Journal of Parapsychology* 81, no. 1 (Spring 2017): 46–62.

Dreams:

Krippner, Stanley. "The Maimonides ESP-Dream Studies," *Journal of Parapsychology* 57, no. 1 (March 1, 1993): 39–54.

Duke Parapsychology Labs:

Matlock, James G. "Records of the Parapsychology Laboratory: An Inventory of the Collection in the Duke University Library," *Journal of Parapsychology* 55, no. 3 (September 1, 1991): 301–14.

Rhine, J. B. *New Frontiers of the Mind: The Story of the Duke Experiments* (New York: Farrar and Rinehart, 1937).

Ectoplasm:

Schoonover, Karl. "Ectoplasms, Evanescence, and Photography," *Art Journal* 62, no. 3 (Autumn 2003): 30–43.

Electronic Voice Phenomena:

R. Bayless, Voices from Beyond (Secaucus, NJ: University Books, 1959).

Boccuzzi, Mark and Julie Beischel, "Objective Analyses of Real-Time Audio Instrumental Transcommunication and Matched Control Sessions: A Pilot Study," *Journal of Scientific Exploration* 25, no. 2 (2011): 215–35.

Leary, Mark R. and Tom Butler, "Electronic Voice Phenomena," in *Parapsychology: A Handbook for the 21st Century*, edited by Etzel Cardeña, John Palmer, and David Marcusson-Clavertz, 341–49 (Jefferson, NC: McFarland and Company, 2015).

Raudive, Konstantin. *Breakthrough: An Amazing Experiment in Electronic Communication with the Dead* (Gerrards Cross, England: Colin Smythe, 1971).

Energy Healing:

Joines, William T. Stephen B. Baumann, and John G. Kruth, "Electromagnetic Emission from Humans during Focused Intent," *Journal of Parapsychology* 76, no. 2 (Fall 2012): 275–94.

Weymouth, Kathryn F. *Healing from a Personal Perspective: Interviews with Certified Healing Touch Practitioners*. PhD diss., Saybrook University, 2012.

Exceptional Human Experience:

Wahbeh, Helané, Dean Radin, Julia Mossbridge, Cassandra Vieten, and Arnaud Delorme, "Exceptional Experiences Reported by Scientists and Engineers," *Explore* 14, no. 5 (September/October 2018): 329–41.

White, Rhea A. "Exceptional Human Experiences as Vehicles of Grace: Parapsychology and the Outlier Mentality," *Academy of Religion and Psychical Research Proceedings Annual Conference* (1993): 46–55

White, Rhea A. "Role Theory and Exceptional Human Experience," *Journal of Religion and Psychical Research* 17, no. 2 (April 1994): 74–77.

Expectancy Effect:

Kennedy, J. E. and Judith L. Taddonio, "Experimenter Effects in Parapsychological Research," *Journal of Parapsychology* 40, no. 1 (March 1, 1976): 1–33.

Smith, M. D. "The Role of the Experimenter in Parapsychological Research," *Journal of Consciousness Studies* 10 (2003): 69–84.

Experimental Parapsychology:

De Sio, Fabio and Chantal Marazia, "Clever Hans and His Effects: Karl Krall and the Origins of Experimental Parapsychology in Germany," *Studies in History and Philosophy of Biological and Biomedical Sciences* 48 (2014): 94–102.

West, Donald J. "Experimental Parapsychology in Britain: A Survey of Recent Work," *Journal of Parapsychology* 18, no. 1 (March 1, 1954): 10–31.

Experimenter Effect:

Watt, Caroline and Peter Ramakers, "Experimenter Effects with a Remote Facilitation of Attention Focusing Task: A Study with Multiple Believer and Disbeliever Experiments," *Journal of Parapsychology* 67, no. 1 (Spring 2003): 99–116.

Fantasy-Proneness:

Dasse, Michelle M., Gary R. Elkins, and Charles A. Weaver III, "Correlates of the Multidimensional Construct of Hypnotizability: Paranormal Belief, Fantasy Proneness, Magical Ideation, and Dissociation," *International Journal of Clinical and Experimental Hypnosis* 63, no. 3 (2015): 274–83.

Drinkwater, Kenneth, Andrew Denovan, Neil Dagnall, and Andrew Parker, "Predictors of Hearing Electronic Voice Phenomena in Random Noise: Schizotypy, Fantasy Proneness, and Paranormal Beliefs," *Journal of Parapsychology* 84, no. 1 (2020): 96–113.

Forced Choice Test:

Steinkamp, Fiona, Julie Milton, and Robert L. Morris, "A Meta-Analysis of Forced-Choice Experiments Comparing Clairvoyance and Precognition," *Journal of Parapsychology* 62, no. 3 (September 1998): 193–218.

Free Response Test:

Milton, Julie. "Meta-Analysis of Free-Response ESP Studies without Altered States of Consciousness," *Journal of Parapsychology* 61, no. 4 (December 1997): 279–319.

Galvanic Skin Response:

Schönwetter, Tim, Wolfgang Ambach, and Dieter Vaitl, "Does Autonomic Nervous System Activity Correlate with Events Conventionally Considered as Unperceivable? Using a Guessing Task with Physiological Measurement," *Journal of Parapsychology* 75, no. 2 (2011): 327–48.

Ganzfeld:

Bem, Daryl J. "The Ganzfeld Experiment," *Journal of Parapsychology* 57, no. 2 (June 1, 1993): 101–10.

Westerlund, Joakim, Adrian Parker, Jan Dalkvist, and Gergö Hadlaczky, "Remarkable Correspondences Between Ganzfeld Mentation and Target Content—A Psychical or Psychological Effect?" *Journal of Parapsychology* 70, no. 1 (Spring 2006): 23–48.

General Extrasensory Perception (GESP):

Thalbourne, Michael A. "Some Experiments on the Paranormal Cognition of Drawings: With Special Reference to Personality and Attitudinal Variables." PhD diss., Edinburgh Research Archive. Available at https://era.ed.ac.uk/handle/1842/26994.

Gesellschaft für Psychologische Forschung (Society for Psychological Research):

Sommer, Andreas. "Normalizing the Supernormal: The Formation of the 'Gesellschaft Für Psychologische Forschung' ('Society for Psychological Research')," *Journal of the History of the Behavioral Sciences* 49, no. 1 (Winter 2013): 18–44.

Ghost:

Gurney, Edmund, Frederic W. H. Myers, and Frank Podmore, *Phantasms of the Living* (London: Kegan Paul, Trench, Trubner, and Co., 1918).

Maher, Michaeleen, "Ghosts and Poltergeists: An Eternal Enigma," in *Parapsychology: A Handbook for the 21st Century*, edited by Etzel Cardeña, John Palmer, and David Marcusson-Clavertz, 327–39 (Jefferson, NC: McFarland and Company, 2015).

The Ghost Society:

Tymn, Michael E. "Heroes and Highlights of Psychical Research Before 1882," *Journal of Spirituality & Paranormal Studies* 29, no. 3 (2006): 162–74.

Global Consciousness Project:

Nelson, Roger D. "The Global Consciousness Project," *Journal of Parapsychology* 63 no. 3 (September 1, 1999): 213–15.

Goligher Circle:

Tymn, Michael E. "William Jackson Crawford on the Goligher Circle," *Journal of Scientific Exploration* 27, no. 3 (2013): 529–39.

Groupe d'Etudes de Recherche en Parapsychologie (Group for the Study and Research of Parapsychology):
Evrard, Renaud, "Parapsychology in France after May 1968: A History of GERP," *Journal of Scientific Exploration* 24, no. 2 (2010): 283–94.

Hallucination:
Myers, Frederick W. H. "Report on the Census of Hallucinations," *Proceedings of the Society for Psychical Research* 10 (1894): 25–422.

Haunted Person Syndrome:
O'Keeffe, Ciarán, James Houran, Damien J. Houran, Neil Dagnall, Kenneth Drinkwater, Lorraine Sheridan, and Brian Laythe, "The Dr. John Hall Story: A Case Study in Putative 'Haunted Person Syndrome,'" *Mental Health, Religion, and Culture* 23, no. 7 (2020): 532–49.

Haunting:
Laythe, Brian and Kay Owen, "Paranormal Belief and the Strange Case of Haunt Experiences: Evidence of a Neglected Population," *Journal of Parapsychology* 76, no. 1 (Spring 2012): 79–108.

Hypnagogic State:
Prete, Guido del and Patrizio E. Tressoldi, "Anomalous Cognition in Hypnagogic State with OBE Induction: An Experimental Study," *Journal of Parapsychology* 69, no. 2 (Fall 2005): 329–39.

Hypnopompic State:
Sherwood, Simon J. "Relationship Between the Hypnagogic/Hypnopompic States and Reports of Anomalous Experiences," *Journal of Parapsychology* 66, no. 2 (June 2002): 127–50.

Hypnotism:
Myers, Frederic W. H. "On a Case of Alleged Hypnotic Hyperacuity of Vision," *Mind* 12, no. 45 (January 1887): 154–56.
Myers, Frederic W. H. "Professor Wundt on Hypnotism and Suggestion," *Mind* 2, no. 5 (January 1893): 95–101.
Plas, Régine Plas. "Psychology and Psychical Research in France around the end of the 19th Century." *History of the Human Sciences* 25, no. 2 (2012): 91–107.

Institut Métapsychique International:
Lachapelle, Sofie. *Investigating the Supernatural: From Spiritism and Occultism to Psychical Research and Metaphysics in France, 1853–1931* (Baltimore, MD: Johns Hopkins University Press, 2011).

Instrumental Transcommunication:
Cooper, Callum E. "An Analysis of Exceptional Experiences Involving Telecommunication Technology," *Journal of Parapsychology* 78, no. 2 (Fall 2014): 209–22.

Journal of Parapsychology:
Rhine, J. B. "A Backward Look at Leaving the JP." *Journal of Parapsychology* 41, no. 2 (June 1977): 89–102.

"Just One of Those Things:"
Barrington, Mary Rose, "JOTT—Just One of Those Things," *Psi Research* 3 (October 1991).

Koestler Parapsychology Unit:
Watt, Caroline. "Research Assistants or Budding Scientists? A Review of 96 Undergraduate Student Projects at the Koestler Parapsychology Unit," *Journal of Parapsychology* 70, no. 2 (Fall 2006): 335–55.

Levitation:
Batcheldor, K. J. "Report on a Case of Table Levitation and Associated Phenomena," *Journal of the Society for Psychical Research* 43 (1966): 339–56.

Liminality:
Thalbourne, Michael A. "Transliminality, Anomalous Belief and Experience, and Hypnotisability," *Australian Journal of Clinical and Experimental Hypnosis* 37, no. 2 (November 2009): 119–30.

Literary Committee:
Gurney, Edmund and Frederic W. H. Myers, "Statement of the Literary Committee of the Society for Psychical Research," *Journal of the Society for Psychical Research* 3, no. 36 (January 1887): 1–8.

Macro-Psychokinesis:
Haraldsson, Erlendur and Richard Wiseman, "Two Investigations of Ostensible Macro-PK in India,"

Journal of the Society for Psychical Research 61, no. 843 (April 1, 1996).

Maimonides Dream Labs:
Krippner, Stanley. "The Maimonides ESP-Dream Studies," *Journal of Parapsychology* 57, no. 1 (March 1, 1993): 39–54.
Ullman, Montague and Stanley Krippner, "Experimentally Induced Telepathic Dreams: Two Studies Using EEG-REM Monitoring Technique," *International Journal of Neuropsychiatry* 2, no. 5 (1966): 420–37.

Medium:
Beischel, Julie. "Contemporary Methods Used in Laboratory-Based Mediumship Research," *Journal of Parapsychology* 71 (Spring 2007): 37–68.
Braude, Stephen E. *Immortal Remains: The Evidence for Life After Death* (Lanham, MD: Rowman & Littlefield, 2003).
Crookes, William. "Notes of Seances with D.D. Home," *Proceedings of the Society for Psychical Research* 6 (1889): 98–127.
Cunningham, Paul F. "The Content-Source Problem in Modern Mediumship Research," *Journal of Parapsychology* 76, no. 2 (Fall 2012): 295–319.
Diaz, Armand Martire. "Divination as a Life Path in Contemporary America: An In-Depth Exploration of the World of Psychic-Mediums," PhD diss., California Institute of Integral Studies, 2011.
O'Keeffe, Ciarán and Richard Wiseman, "Testing Alleged Mediumship: Methods and Results," *British Journal of Psychology* 96, no. 2 (May 2005): 165–79.

Mesmerism:
Monroe, John Warne. *Laboratories of Faith: Mesmerism, Spiritism, and Occultism in Modern France* (Ithaca, NY: Cornell University Press, 2008).

Metapsychics:
Mülberger, Annette and Mónica Balltondre, "Metapsychics in Spain: Acknowledging or Questioning the Marvelous?" *History of the Human Sciences* 25, no. 2 (2012): 108–30.

Micro-Psychokinesis:
Iqbal, Azlan. "A Replication of the Slight Effect of Human Thought on a Pseudorandom Number Generator," *NeuroQuantology* 11, no. 4 (2013): 519–26.
Varvoglis, Mario and Peter A. Bancel, "Micro-Psychokinesis: Exceptional or Universal?" *Journal of Parapsychology* 80, no. 1 (Spring 2016): 37–44.

Muscle-Reading:
Barrett, W. F., Edmund Gurney, and F. W. H. Myers, "First Report on Thought-Reading," *Proceedings of the Society for Psychical Research* 1, no. 1 (July 17, 1882): 13–34.

Near-Death Experience:
Greyson, Bruce. "Varieties of Near-Death Experience," *Psychiatry* 56, no. 4 (November 1993): 390–99.
Lange, Rense, Bruce Greyson, and James Houran, "A Rasch Scaling Validation of a 'Core' Near-Death Experience," *British Journal of Psychology* 95 (May 2004): 161–77.
Roe, Chris A., Alasdair Gordon-Finlayson, and Michael Daniels, "Transpersonal Psychology and Parapsychology: Lessons from the Near-Death Experience," *Journal of Transpersonal Psychology* 52, no. 2 (2020): 188–203.
Lommel, Pim van, Ruud van Wees, and Vincent Myers, "Near-Death Survivors of Cardiac Arrest: A Prospective Study in the Netherlands," *Lancet* 358, no. 9298 (December 15, 2001): 2039–45.

Object Reading:
Baker, Ian S., Jane Montague, and Abigail Booth, "A Controlled Study of Psychometry using Psychic and Non-Psychic Claimants with Actual and False Readings using a Mixed-Methods Approach," *Journal of the Society for Psychical Research* 81, no. 2 (April 2017): 108–22.

Open Matching:
Russell, William and J. B. Rhine, "A Single Subject in a Variety of ESP Test Conditions," *Journal of Parapsychology* 6, no. 4 (December 1, 1942): 284–311.

Out-of-Body Experience:
Irwin, Harvey J. "The Disembodied Self: An Empirical Study of Dissociation and the Out-of-Body Experience," *Journal of Parapsychology* 64, no. 3 (September 1, 2000): 261–77.

Lindsay, David. "Out-of-Body Experience: The Definitive Afterlife Research Tool for the 21st Century," *Journal of Spirituality and Paranormal Studies* 30 (July 2007): 109–19.

Meyerson, Joseph and Marc Gelkopf, "Therapeutic Utilization of Spontaneous Out-of-Body Experiences in Hypnotherapy," *American Journal of Psychotherapy* 58, no. 1 (2004): 90– 102.

Rogo, D. Scott, "Psychological Models of the Outof-Body Experience," *Journal of Parapsychology* 46, no. 1 (March 1, 1982): 29–45.

Wilde, David and Craig D. Murray, "Interpreting the Anomalous: Finding Meaning in Out-of-Body and Near-Death Experiences," *Qualitative Research in Psychology* 7, no. 1 (January 2010): 57–72.

Parapsychology:

Beloff, John. *Parapsychology: A Concise History* (London: Athlone Press, 1993).

Parapsychological Association:

Radin, Dean. "Parapsychological Association Presidential Address, 2018," *Journal of Parapsychology* 83, no. 1 (Spring 2019): 5–12.

Parapsychology Foundation:

Richardson, Lynda. "Gatherings Ponder Other Worlds: Belief and Skepticism Mingle at the Parapsychology Foundation," *New York Times* (June 5, 2000): B6.

Placement Psychokinesis:

Cox, William E. "Three-Tier Placement PK," *Journal of Parapsychology* 23, no. 1 (March 1, 1959): 19–29.

Forwald, Haakon. "A Further Study of the PK Placement Effect," *Journal of Parapsychology* 16, no. 1 (March 1, 1952): 59–67.

Pratt, J. G. "The Cormack Placement PK Experiments," *Journal of Parapsychology* 15, no. 1 (1951): 57–73.

Rhine, Louisa E. "Placement PK Tests with Three Types of Objects," *Journal of Parapsychology* 15, no. 2 (June 1, 1951): 132–38.

Poltergeist:

Bender, H. "New Developments in Poltergeist Research," *Proceedings of the Parapsychological Association* 6 (1969): 81–109.

Kruth, John G. and William T. Joines, "Taming the Ghost Within: An Approach Toward Addressing Apparent Electronic Poltergeist Activity," *Journal of Parapsychology* 80, no. 1 (Spring 2016): 70–86.

Pratt, J. G. and W. G. Roll, "The Seaford Disturbances," *Journal of Parapsychology* 22, no. 2 (June 1958): 79–124.

Precognition:

Morris, R. L. "Assessing Experimental Support for True Precognition," *Journal of Parapsychology* 46 (1982): 321–36.

Rhine, J. B. "Experiments Bearing on the Precognition Hypothesis," *Journal of Parapsychology* 2, no. 1 (March 1, 1938): 38–54.

Steinkamp, Fiona. "Does Precognition Foresee the Future? A Postal Experiment to Assess the Possibility of True Precognition," *Journal of Parapsychology* 64, no. 1 (March 1, 2000): 3–18.

Watt, Caroline. "Precognitive Dreaming: Investigating Anomalous Cognition and Psychological Factors," *Journal of Parapsychology* 78, no. 1 (Spring 2014): 115–25.

Princeton Engineering Anomalies Research Lab:

Dunne, Brenda J. "Princeton Engineering Anomalies Research Lab," in *Ghosts, Spirits, and Psychics: The Paranormal from Alchemy to Zombies*, edited by Matt Cardin, 231–33 (Santa Barbara, CA: ABC-CLIO, 2015).

Proxy Sitter:

Schmeidler, Gertrude R. "Analysis and Evaluation of Proxy Sessions with Mrs. Caroline Chapman," *Journal of Parapsychology* 22 (1958): 137–55.

West, D. J. "Some Proxy Sittings: A Preliminary Attempt at Objective Assessment," *Journal of the Society for Psychical Research* 35 (1949): 96–101.

Psi-Missing:

Rhine, Louisa E. "Toward Understanding Psi-Missing," *Journal of Parapsychology* 29, no. 4 (December 1, 1965): 259–74.

Psi Open Data:

Ryan, Adrian. "Open Data in Parapsychology: Introducing Psi Open Data," *Journal of Parapsychology* 82, no. 1 (2018): 65–76.

Psychische Studien:
Sommer, Andreas. "Normalizing the Supernormal: The Formation of the 'Gesellschaft Für Psychologische Forschung' ('Society for Psychological Research'), c. 1886–1890," *Journal of the History of the Behavioral Sciences* 49, no. 1 (Winter 2013): 18–44.

Psychokinesis:
Heath, Pamela Rae. *The PK Zone: A Cross-Cultural Review of Psychokinesis* (New York: Universe, 2003).

Pratt, J. G. "The Case for Psychokinesis," *Journal of Parapsychology* 24, no. 3 (September 1, 1960): 171–88.

Roll, William G. and William T. Joines, "RSPK and Consciousness," *Journal of Parapsychology* 77, no. 2 (Fall 2013): 192–211.

Thouless, Robert H. "A Report on an Experiment in Psychokinesis with Dice and a Discussion on Psychological Factors Favoring Success," *Journal of Parapsychology* 15, no. 2 (June 1, 1951): 89–102.

Psychologische Gesellschaft:
Wolffram, Heather. *The Stepchildren of Science: Psychical Research and Parapsychology in Germany, c. 1870–1939* (Amsterdam: Rodopi, 2009).

Qualitative Research:
Kruth, John G. "Five Qualitative Research Approaches and Their Applications in Parapsychology," *Journal of Parapsychology* 79, no. 2 (Fall 2015): 219–33.

Quantum Mechanics/Physics:
Chari, C. T. K. "Quantum Physics and Parapsychology," *Journal of Parapsychology* 20, no. 3 (September 1, 1956): 166–83.

Millar, Brian. "Quantum Theory and Parapsychology," in *Parapsychology: A Handbook for the 21st Century*. Edited by Etzel Cardeña, John Palmer, and David Marcusson-Clavertz, 165–80 (Jefferson, NC: McFarland and Company, 2015).

Radin, Dean. *Entangled Minds: Extrasensory Experiences in a Quantum Reality* (New York: Paraview, 2006).

Quarter Distribution:
Rhine, J. B. and Betty M. Humphrey, "The PK Effect: Special Evidence from Hit Patterns," *Journal of Parapsychology* 8, no. 1 (March 1, 1944): 18–60.

Random Number Generator:
Schmidt, Helmut. "PK Tests with a High-Speed Random Number Generator," *Journal of Parapsychology* 37, no. 2 (June 1, 1973): 105–18.

Thalbourne, Michael A. "Kundalini and the Output of a Random Number Generator," *Journal of Parapsychology* 70, no. 2 (Fall 2006): 303–33.

Recurrent Spontaneous Psychokinesis:
Pratt, J. G. and W. G. Roll, "The Seaford Disturbances," *Journal of Parapsychology* 22, no. 2 (June 1958): 79–124.

Roll, William G. and William T. Joines, "RSPK and Consciousness," *Journal of Parapsychology* 77, no. 2 (Fall 2013): 192–211.

Reichenbach Phenomena:
Regnault, Jules. "Odic Phenomena and New Radiations," The Annals of Psychical Science 1, no. 3 (March 1905): 145–63.

Remote Viewing:
Baptista, J., M. Derakhshani, and P. E. Tressoldi, "Explicit Anomalous Cognition: A Review of the Best Evidence in Ganzfeld, Forced Choice, Remote Viewing, and Dream Studies," in *Parapsychology: A Handbook for the 21st Century*. Edited by E. Cardeña and J. Palmer, 192–214 (Jefferson, NC: McFarland, 2015).

May, Edwin C. "Star Gate: The U.S. Government's Psychic Spying Program," *Journal of Parapsychology* 78, no. 1 (Spring 2014): 5–18.

Targ, Russell. "What do We Know about PSI? The First Decade of Remote-Viewing Research and Operations at Stanford Research Institute," *Journal of Scientific Exploration* 33, no. 4 (2019): 569–92.

Replication:
Luke, David, Chris A. Roe, and Jamie Davison, "Testing for Forced-Choice Precognition Using a Hidden Task: Two Replications," *Journal of Parapsychology* 72 (Spring 2008): 133–54.

Utts, Jessica. "Replication and Meta-Analysis in Parapsychology," *Statistical Science* 6, no. 4 (November 1991): 363–78.

Utts, Jessica. "What Constitutes Replication in Parapsychology?" in *Extrasensory Perception: Support, Skepticism, and Science. Volume 1: History, Controversy, and Research.* Edited by Edwin C. May and Sonali Bhatt Marwaha, 179–92 (Santa Barbara, CA: Praeger, 2015).

Retrocognition:

MacKenzie, Andrew. *Adventures in Time* (London: Athlone Press, 1997).

Myers, Frederic W. H. "The Subliminal Self. Chapter VIII: The Relation of Supernormal Phenomena to Time—Retrocognition," *Proceedings of the Society for Psychical Research* 11, no. 29 (December 1895): 334–407.

Revue Métapsychique:

Alvarado, Carlos S., Massimo Biondi, and Wim Kramer, "Historical Notes on Psychic Phenomena in Specialised Journals," *European Journal of Parapsychology* 21, no. 1 (2006): 58–87.

Scole Mediumship Circle:

Keen, Montague. "The Scole Investigation: A Study in Critical Analysis of Paranormal Physical Phenomena," *Journal of Scientific Exploration* 15, no. 2 (2001): 167–82.

Keen, M. A. Ellison and D. Fontana, "The Scole Report," *Proceedings of the Society for Psychical Research* 58 (1999): 150–452.

Screened Touch Matching:

Woodruff, J. L. and R. W. George, "Experiments in Extra-Sensory Perception," *Journal of Parapsychology* 1, no. 1 (March 1, 1937): 18–30.

Séance:

Laythe, Brian R., Elizabeth Cooper Laythe, and Lucinda Woodward, "A Test of an Occult-Themed Séance: Examining Anomalous Events, Psychosomatic Symptoms, Transliminality, and Electromagnetic Fields," *Journal of Scientific Exploration* 31, no. 4 (2017): 572–624.

Wiseman, Richard, Emma Greening, and Matthew Smith, "Belief in the Paranormal and Suggestion in the Séance Room," *British Journal of Psychology* 94 (August 2003): 285–97.

Sheep-Goat Effect:

Lawrence, T.R. "Gathering in the Sheep and Goats: A Meta-Analysis of Forced-Choice Sheep-Goat ESP Studies, 1947–1993," *Proceedings of the 36th Annual Convention of the Parapsychological Association* (Durham: Parapsychological Association, 1993): 75–86.

Lovitts, Barbara E. "The Sheep-Goat Effect Turned Upside Down," *Journal of Parapsychology* 45, no. 4 (December 1, 1981): 293–309.

Schmeidler, Gertrude R. "Additional Data on Sheep-Goat Classification," *Journal of the Society for Psychical Research* 40 (June 1, 1959).

Schmeidler, Gertrude R. and R. A. McConnell, *ESP and Personality Patterns* (New Haven, CT: Yale University Press, 1958).

Sitter-Group:

Batcheldor, Kenneth. "Contributions to the Theory of PK Induction from Sitter-Group Work," *Journal of the American Society for Psychical Research* 78 (1984): 105–22.

Society for Psychical Research:

Haynes, Renée. *The Society for Psychical Research, 1882–1982: A History* (London: Macdonald & Co., 1982).

Sphinx:

Sommer, Andreas. "Normalizing the Supernormal: The Formation of the 'Gesellschaft Für Psychologische Forschung' ('Society for Psychological Research')," *Journal of the History of the Behavioral Sciences* 49, no. 1 (Winter 2013): 18–44.

Spiritualism:

Oppenheim, Janet. *The Other World: Spiritualism and Psychical Research in England, 1850–1914* (Cambridge: Cambridge University Press, 1985).

Owen, Alex. *The Darkened Room: Women, Power and Spiritualism in Late Victorian England* (Philadelphia: University of Pennsylvania Press, 1990).

Richard, Michael P. and Albert Adato, "The Medium and Her Message: A Study of Spiritualism at Lily Dale, New York," *Review of Religious Research* 22, no. 2 (December 1980): 186–97.

Spontaneous Psi:

Haight, JoMarie. "Spontaneous Psi Cases: A Survey and Preliminary Study of ESP, Attitude, and Personality Relationship," *Journal of Parapsychology* 43, no. 3 (September 1, 1979): 179–204.

Rhine, J. B. "Editorial: The Value of Reports of Spontaneous Psi Experiences," *Journal of Parapsychology* 12, no. 4 (December 1, 1948): 231–35.

Rhine, Louisa E. "Subjective Forms of Spontaneous Psi Experiences," *Journal of Parapsychology* 17, no. 2 (June 1, 1953): 77–114.

Subconscious:

Alvarado, Carlos S. "Mediumship, Psychical Research, Dissociation, and the Powers of the Subconscious Mind," *Journal of Parapsychology* 78, no. 1 (2014): 98–114.

Subliminal Self:

Alvarado, Carlos S. "On the Centenary of Frederic W.H. Myers's Human Personality and Its Survival of Bodily Death," *Journal of Parapsychology* 68, no. 1 (Spring 2004): 3–43.

Myers, Frederic W. H. *Human Personality and Its Survival of Bodily Death* (London: Longmans, Green, and Co., 1906).

Subjective Paranormal Experience:

Drinkwater, Kenneth, Neil Dagnall, Sarah Grogan, and Victoria Riley, "Understanding the Unknown: A Thematic Analysis of Subjective Paranormal Experiences," *Australian Journal of Parapsychology* 17, no. 1 (June 2017): 23–46.

Ironside, Rachael. "Feeling Spirits: Sharing Subjective Paranormal Experience Through Embodied Talk and Action," *Text and Talk* 38, no. 6 (2018): 705–28.

Neppe, Vernon. "Déjà vu: Origins and Phenomenology: Implications of the Four Subtypes for Future Research," *Journal of Parapsychology* 74, no. 1 (Spring 2010): 61–97.

Neppe, Vernon. "Subjective Paranormal Experience Psychosis." *Parapsychology Review* 15, no. 2 (1984): 7–9.

Persinger, Michael A. "Propensity to Report Paranormal Experiences is Correlated with Temporal Lobe Signs," *Perceptual and Motor Skills* 59, no. 2 (1984): 583–86.

Super-psi:

Braude, Stephen E. "Survival or Super-psi?" *Journal of Scientific Investigation* 6, no. 2 (1992): 127–44.

Survival Hypothesis:

"Editorial: ESP, PK, and the Survival Hypothesis." *Journal of Parapsychology* 7, no. 4 (December 1943): 223–27.

Irwin, Harvey. "Is Scientific Investigation of Postmortem Survival an Anachronism? The Demise of the Survival Hypothesis," *Australian Journal of Parapsychology* 2, no. 1 (June 2002): 19–27.

Rock, Adam J. *The Survival Hypothesis: Essays on Mediumship* (Jefferson, NC: McFarland and Co., 2013).

Synchronicity:

Storm, Lance. "Synchronicity, Causality, and Acausality," Journal of Parapsychology 63, no. 3 (September 1999): 247–69.

T-test:

Newman, Isadore, Carole Newman, Russell Brown, and Sharon McNeely. *Conceptual Statistics for Beginners.* (Lanham, MD: University Press of America, 2006).

Table-Tipping:

Batcheldor, Kenneth. "Contributions to the Theory of PK Induction from Sitter-Group Work," *Journal of the American Society for Psychical Research* 78, no. 2 (April 1984).

Faraday, Michael. "Experimental Investigation of Table-Moving," in *Parapsychology*, edited by Richard Wiseman and Caroline Watt, 373–76 (London: Routledge, 2005).

Tambov Experiments:

Dingwall, Eric J. ed., "Dr. A.N. Khovrin and the Tambov Experiments," in *Abnormal Hypnotic Phenomena: A Survey of Nineteenth-Century Cases*, Volume 3 (London: J. & A. Churchill, 1968), 33–75.

Telepathy:

Barrett, W. F., Edmund Gurney, and F. W. H. Myers, "First Report on Thought Reading," *Proceedings of the Society for Psychical Research* 1, no. 1 (July 17, 1882): 13–34.

Standish, Leanna J., L. Clark Johnson, Leila Kozak, and Todd Richards, "Evidence of Correlated Functional Magnetic Resonance Imaging Signals Between Distant Human Brains," *Alternative*

Therapies in Health and Medicine 9, no. 1 (January/February 2003): 122–28.

Thoughtography:
Takasuna, Miki. "The Fukurai Affair: Parapsychology and the History of Psychology in Japan," *History of the Human Sciences* 25, no. 2 (2012): 149–64.

Trance:
Buhrman, Sarasvati Ann S. "Trance in America: A Comparison of Trance Types and Trance Experience in Two Religious Communities." PhD diss., University of Colorado, 1996: 330.

Natale, Simone. "The Medium on the Stage: Trance and Performance in Nineteenth-Century Spiritualism," *Early Popular Visual Culture* 9, no. 3 (2011): 239–55.

White, Steward Edward. "The Process of Mental Mediumship," *Journal of the American Society for Psychical Research* 27, no. 10 (October 1933): 283.

Transliminality:
Lange, R., M. A. Thalbourne, J. Houran, and L. Storm, "The Revised Transliminality Scale: Reliability and Validity Data from a Rasch Top-Down Purification Procedure," *Consciousness and Cognition* 9, no. 4 (December 2000): 591–617.

Thalbourne, Michael A. "Transliminality, Anomalous Belief and Experience, and Hypnotisability," *Australian Journal of Clinical and Experimental Hypnosis* 37, no. 2 (November 2009): 119–30.

Thalbourne, M. A. "Transliminality as an Index of the Sheep-Goat Variable," *European Journal of Parapsychology* 18 (2003): 3–14.

Transpersonal Consciousness:
Assagioli, Roberto. "Symbols of Transpersonal Experiences," *Journal of Transpersonal Psychology* 1, no. 1 (Spring 1969): 33–45.

Laszlo, Ervin. "Cosmic Connectivity: Toward a Scientific Foundation for Transpersonal Consciousness," *The International Journal of Transpersonal Studies* 23 (2004): 21–31.

Utrecht University:
Kloosterman, Ingrid. "Psychical Research and Parapsychology Interpreted: Suggestions from the International Historiography of Psychical Research and Parapsychology for Investigating its History in the Netherlands," *History of the Human Sciences* 25, no. 2 (2012): 2–22.

Variance:
Freund, Rudolf J. and William J. Wilson, *Statistical Methods,* 2nd ed. (Amsterdam: Academic Press, 2003).

Visual Cortical Hyperexcitability:
Fong, Chun Yuen, Chie Takahashi, and Jason J. Braithwaite, "Evidence for Distinct Clusters of Diverse Anomalous Experiences and their Selective Association with Signs of Elevated Cortical Hyperexcitability," *Consciousness and Cognition* 71 (2019): 1–17.

Waiting Technique:
Beloff, John and I. Mandleberg, "An Attempted Validation of the 'Waiting Technique,'" *Journal of the Society for Psychical Research* 45 (1970): 82–88.

White, Rhea A. "A Comparison of Old and New Methods of Response to Targets in ESP Experiments," *Journal of the American Society for Psychical Research* 58 (1964): 21–56.

Watseka Wonder:
Stevens, E. Winchester. *The Watseka Wonder* (Los Angeles: Austin Publishing Company, 1928).

Zener cards:
Storm, Lance, Patrizio E. Tressoldi, and Lorenzo Di Risio, "Meta-Analysis of ESP Studies, 1987–2010: Assessing the Success of the Forced-Choice Design in Parapsychology," *Journal of Parapsychology* 76, no. 2 (Fall 2012): 243–73.

Zero-Point Energy:
Roll, William G. and William T. Joines, "RSPK and Consciousness," *Journal of Parapsychology* 77, no. 2 (Fall 2013): 192–211.

Bibliography

"About the Parapsychology Foundation." (Parapsychology Foundation, 2021). Accessed December 22, 2021, from https://parapsychology.org/about-us/.About the PRF. Psychical Research Foundation. Accessed January 13, 2022, from https://www.psychicalresearchfoundation.com/about.

"About Us." Instituto de Psicología Paranormal. Accessed January 14, 2022, from http://www.alipsi.com.ar/quienes-somos/.

"About Us." Windbridge Research Center. Accessed November 29, 2021, from https://www.windbridge.org/about-us/.

"About: Weaving Together Knowledge and Knowing." (2021). Institute of Noetic Sciences (IONS). Accessed July 1, 2021, from https://noetic.org/about/.

Ahmed, D. Si. "Psychoanalysis and Psi." In *Psi Encyclopedia* (London: The Society for Psychical Research, May 9, 2019). Accessed July 3, 2021, from https://psi-encyclopedia.spr.ac.uk/articles/psychoanalysis-and-psi.

Alvarado, Carlos S. "Charles Richet on Leonora Piper." *Journal of the Society for Psychical Research* 79, no. 918 (2015): 56–59.

Alvarado, Carlos S. "The Concept of Survival of Bodily Death and the Development of Parapsychology." *Journal of the Society for Psychical Research* 67, no. 2 (April 2003): 65–95.

Alvarado, Carlos S. "Curso de Parapsicología (Course of Parapsychology)." *Journal of Parapsychology* 61, no. 2 (June 1997): 173–74.

Alvarado, Carlos S. "Distortions of the Past." *Journal of Scientific Exploration* 26, no. 3 (2012): 611–33.

Alvarado, Carlos S. "Early Psychological Research Reference Works: Remarks on Nandor Fodor's *Encyclopedia of Psychic Science. Journal of Scientific Exploration* 34, no. 4 (December 2020): 717–54.

Alvarado, Carlos S. "Eleanor M. Sidgwick (1845–1936)." *Journal of Parapsychology* 82, no. 2 (2018): 127–31.

Alvarado, Carlos S. "Eugene Osty on Out-of-Body Experiences." *Journal of the Society for Psychical Research* 80, no. 2 (2016): 122–25.

Alvarado, Carlos S. "Fragments of a Life in Psychical Research: The Case of Charles Richet." *Journal of Scientific Exploration* 32, no. 1 (2018): 55–78.

Alvarado, Carlos S. and Nancy L. Zingrone. "Features of Out-of-Body Experiences: Relationships to Frequency, Willfulness of and Previous Knowledge about the Experience." *Journal of the Society for Psychical Research* 79, no. 2 (April 2015): 98–111.

Alvarado, Carlos S., Massimo Biondi, and Wim Kramer. "Historical Notes on Psychic Phenomena in Specialised Journals." *European Journal of Parapsychology* 21, no. 1 (2006): 58–87.

Alvarado, Carlos S. "Mediumship, Psychical Research, Dissociation, and the Powers of the Subconscious Mind." *Journal of Parapsychology* 78, no. 1 (March 2014): 98–114.

Alvarado, Carlos S. "Musings on Materializations: Eric J. Dingwall on 'The Plasma Theory.'" *Journal of Scientific Exploration* 33, no. 1 (2019): 73–113.

Alvarado, Carlos S. "On the Centenary of Frederic W.H. Myers's *Human Personality and Its Survival of Bodily Death." Journal of Parapsychology,* 68, no. 1 (Spring 2004): 3–43.

Alvarado, Carlos S. "On W.J. Crawford's Studies of Physical Mediumship." *Journal of Scientific Exploration* 28, no. 2 (2014): 351–57.

Alvarado, Carlos S. "Psychology and Parapsychology." (October 31, 2017). In *Psi Encyclopedia.* (London: The Society for Psychical Research). Accessed June 22, 2021, from https://psi-ency clopedia.spr.ac.uk/articles/psychology-and-para psychology.

Alvarado, Carlos S. "'Report of the Committee on Mediumistic Phenomena,' by William James (1886)." *History of Psychiatry* 27, no. 1 (2016): 85–100.

Alvarado, Carlos S. "Telepathy, Mediumship, and Psychology: Psychical Research at the International Congresses of Psychology, 1889–1905." *Journal of Scientific Exploration* 31, no. 2 (2017): 255–92.

Anderson, Rosemarie. "William G. Braud (1942–2012)." *The Humanistic Psychologist* 41, no. 1 (2013): 94–96.

Anderson, Rosemarie and William Braud. *Transforming Self and Others through Research: Transpersonal Research Methods and Skills for the Human Sciences and Humanities.* Albany: State University of New York Press, 2011.

The Annals of Psychical Science, 1, (January–June 1905): front matter.

"ASSAP: Association for the Scientific Study of Anomalous Phenomena." (Association for the Scientific Study of Anomalous Phenomena). Accessed November 28, 2021, from http://www .assap.ac.uk/.

Atwater, P. M. H. "Children's Near-Death States: New Research, A New Model." *Journal of Spirituality and Paranormal Studies* 30 (2007): 51–60.

Atwater, P. M. H. "The Three Near-Death Experiences of P.M.H. Atwater." *Narrative Inquiry in Bioethics* 10, no. 1 (Spring 2020): E13–15.

Atwater, P. M. H. "The Website of PMH Atwater." (2018). Accessed June 18, 2021, from http:// www.pmhatwater.com/.

Auerbach, Loyd, Dominic Parker, and Sheila Smith. "Anomalous Cognition/ESP and Psychokinesis Research in the United States." In *Extrasensory Perception: Support, Skepticism, and Science,* vol. 1. Edited by Edwin C. May and Sonali Bhatt Marwaha, 225–49. Santa Barbara: Praeger, 2015.

"The Austrian Society for Parapsychology and Frontier Areas of Science." Accessed January 13, 2022, from parapsychologie.ac.at/eng-info.htm.

Baptista, Johann and Max Derakhshani. "Beyond the Coin Toss: Examining Wiseman's Criticisms of Parapsychology." *Journal of Parapsychology* 78, no. 1 (2014): 56–79.

Barnard, William G. *Living Consciousness: The Metaphysical Vision of Henri Bergson.* Albany: State University of New York Press, 2011.

Barrett, W. F., A. P. Percival Keep, C. C. Massey, Hensleigh Wedgwood, Frank Podmore, and E. R. Pease. "First Report of the Committee on Haunted Houses." *Proceedings of the Society for Psychical Research* 1, no. 1 (1882): 101–15.

Barrett, William F. *On the Threshold of the Unseen: An Examination of the Phenomena of Spiritualism and of the Evidence for Survival After Death.* 2nd Ed. London: Kegan Paul, Trench, Trubner & Co., 1918.

Barrett, W. F., Edmund Gurney, and F. W. H. Myers. "First Report on Thought-Reading." *Proceedings of the Society for Psychical Research* 1, no. 1 (July 17, 1882): 13–34.

Bauer, Eberhard. "Hans Bender: 'Frontier Scientist'—A Personal Tribute." *Journal of the Society for Psychical Research* 58, no. 825 (October 1991): 124–27.

Bauer, Eberhard, Gerd H. Hövelmann, and Walter von Lucadao. "Betraying the Present by Distorting the Past: Comments on Parker's Tendentious Portrait of German Psychical Research." *Journal of the Society for Psychical Research* 77, no. 910 (January 2013): 32–42.

Beischel, Julie. "Contemporary Methods Used in Laboratory-Based Mediumship Research." *Journal of Parapsychology* 71 (Spring 2007): 37–68.

Beloff, John. *Parapsychology: A Concise History.* New York: St. Martin's Press, 1993.

Beloff, John. "Historical Overview." In *Handbook of Parapsychology,* edited by Benjamin B. Wolman, 4–7. New York: Van Nostrand Reinhold Company, 1977.

Bem, Daryl J. "The Ganzfeld Experiment." *Journal of Parapsychology* 57, no.2 (June 1, 1993): 101–10.

Bentley Jr., G. E. "Blake and the Paranormal." *Notes and Queries* 64, no. 1 (March 2017): 57–62.

Berger, Arthur S. and Joyce Berger. *The Encyclopedia of Parapsychology and Psychical Research.* New York: Paragon House, 1991.

Berger, Arthur S. *Lives and Letters in American Parapsychology: A Biographical History, 1850–1987.* Jefferson, NC: McFarland & Co., 1988.

Bierman, D., H. Gerding, and H. van Dongen. "Psi Research in the Netherlands." *Psi Encyclopedia.* (London: The Society for Psychical Research, December 6, 2019). Accessed July 5, 2021, from https://psi-encyclopedia.spr.ac.uk/articles/psi-research-netherlands.

Bjork, Daniel W. *William James: The Center of His Vision.* Washington, DC: American Psychological Association, 1997.

Blackmore, Susan. "First Person—Into the Unknown." (November 4, 2000). Accessed June 20, 2021, from https://www.susanblackmore.uk/journalism/first-person-into-the-unknown/.

Blackmore, Susan J. "A Psychological Theory of the Out-of-Body Experience." *Journal of Parapsychology* 48, no. 3 (September 1984): 201–18.

Block, Courtney. *Researching the Paranormal: How to Find Reliable Information about Parapsychology, Ghosts, Astrology, Cryptozoology, Near-Death Experiences, and More.* Lanham, MD: Rowman & Littlefield, 2020.

Boccuzzi, Mark and Julie Beischel. "Objective Analyses of Real-Time Audio Instrumental Transcommunication and Matched Control Sessions: A Pilot Study." *Journal of Scientific Exploration* 25, no. 2 (2011): 215–35.

"Book Defends Boston Medium." *New York Times* (February 17, 1926): 19.

Boole, Mary E. *The Message of Psychic Science to the World.* London: C.W. Daniel, 1908.

Bortnichak, Paula M. and Edward A. Bortnichak. "Dream Work: The Inner World of *Die Meistersinger.*" *The Wagner Journal* 15, no. 1 (May 2021): 4–25.

Braithwaite, Jason J., and Maurice Townsend. "Research Note: Sleeping with the Enemy—A Quantitative Magnetic Investigation of an English Castle's Reputedly 'Haunted' Bedroom." *European Journal of Parapsychology* 20, no. 1 (2005): 65–78.

Braud, William G. and Stephen P. Dennis. "Geophysical Variables and Behavior: LVIII. Autonomic Activity, Hemolysis, and Biological Psychokinesis: Possible Relationships with Geomagnetic Field Activity." *Perceptual and Motor Skills* 68, no. 3 (June 1989): 1243–54.

Braude, Stephen E. "The Mediumship of Carlos Mirabelli (1889–1951)." *Journal of Scientific Exploration* 31, no. 3. (2017): 435–56.

Braude, Stephen. "The Need for Negativity." *Journal of Scientific Exploration* 35, no. 2 (2021): 261–66.

Broad, C. D. *Man, Myth, & Magic: The Illustrated Encyclopedia of Mythology, Religion and the Unknown.* Vol. 78. Edited by Richard Cavendish. New York: Marshall Cavendish, 1995.

Brown, Chip. "They Laughed at Galileo Too." *New York Times,* August 11, 1996: SM41.

Browning, Norma Lee. *The Psychic World of Peter Hurkos.* Garden City, NY: Doubleday & Company, 1970.

Bucke, Richard Maurice. *Cosmic Consciousness: A Paper Read before the American Medico-Psychological Association in Philadelphia, 18 May 1894.* Philadelphia: Conservator, 1894.

Caratelli, Giulio and Maria Luisa Felici. "An Important Subject at the Institut Métapsychique International: Jeanne Laplace. The 1927–1934 Experiments." *Journal of Scientific Exploration* 25, no. 3 (2011): 479–95.

Cardeña, Etzel. "The Experimental Evidence for Parapsychological Phenomena: A Review." *American Psychologist* 73, no. 5 (2018): 663–77.

Carpenter, C. R. and Harold R. Phalen. "An Experiment in Card Guessing." *Journal of Parapsychology* 1, no. 1 (March 1, 1937): 31–43.

Carpenter, James C. *First Sight: ESP and Parapsychology in Everyday Life.* Lanham, MD: Rowman & Littlefield, 2012.

Carpenter, James C. and David Price Rogers. "A Review of Recent Work on ESP Score Variation." In *Parapsychology Today: New Writings on ESP, Telepathy, Clairvoyance, Precognition, PK, and Mind Over Matter.* Edited by J. B. Rhine and Robert Brier, 36–45. New York: The Citadel Press, 1968.

"CERCAP." Lund University: Department of Psychology. Accessed January 13, 2022, from psy.lu.se/en/research/research-networks/cercap.

Chari, C. T. K. "Quantum Physics and Parapsychology." *Journal of Parapsychology* 20, no. 3 (September 1, 1956): 166–83.

Charman, Robert A. and David Ellis. "Mediums and a Possible Source of Communication: A Proposed Experiment." *Journal of the Society for Psychical Research* 79, no. 920 (2015): 186–92.

Child, Irvin L. "Psychology and Anomalous Observations: The Question of ESP in Dreams." *American Psychologist* 40, no. 11 (November 1985): 1219–30.

Clay, Phyllis. "Understanding the Experiences of Individuals who Believe they are Mentored by Someone who is no Longer Living." PhD diss., Saybrook University, 2011.

"Consciousness." In *Gale Encyclopedia of Psychology* edited by Bonnie Strickland, 150. 2nd ed. Detroit: Gale, 2001.

Cooper, C. E. "D. Scott Rogo." *Psi Encyclopedia* (London: The Society for Psychical Research, April 6, 2019). Accessed July 4, 2021, from https://psi-encyclopedia.spr.ac.uk/articles/d-scott-rogo.

Cox, William E. "Three-Tier Placement PK." *Journal of Parapsychology* 23, no. 1 (March 1, 1959): 19–29.

Crabtree, Adam. "Mesmerism and the Psychological Dimension of Mediumship." In *Handbook of Spiritualism and Channeling.* Edited by Cathy Gutierrez, 7–31. Leiden: Brill, 2015.

Cunningham, Paul F. "The Content-Source Problem in Modern Mediumship Research." *Journal of Parapsychology* 76, no. 2 (2012): 295–319.

Custred, Glynn. "Psychical Research and the Outer Limits of Scientific Inquiry." *Cosmos and History: The Journal of Natural and Social Philosophy* 13, no. 2 (2017): 111–25.

Dagnall, Neil, Kenneth G. Drinkwater, Ciarán O'Keeffe, Annalisa Ventola, Brian Laythe, Michael A. Jawer, Brandon Massullo, Giovanni B. Caputo, and James Houran. "Things That Go Bump in the Literature: An Environmental Appraisal of 'Haunted Houses.'" *Frontiers in Psychology* 11 (June 12, 2020): 1–15.

Davies, Owen. *Cunning-Folk: Popular Magic in English History.* London: Hambledon and London, 2003.

Delanoy, Deborah. "Anomalous Psychophysiological Responses to Remote Cognition: The DMILS Studies." *European Journal of Parapsychology* 16 (2001): 30–41.

Delp, Robert W. "Andrew Jackson Davis: Prophet of American Spiritualism." *Journal of American History* 54, no. 1 (June 1967): 43–56.

Dingwall, Eric J. *Very Peculiar People: Portrait Studies in the Queer, the Abnormal, and the Uncanny.* New Hyde Park, NY: University Books, 1962.

Dingwall, Eric, J. "Dr. A.N. Khovrin and the Tambov Experiments." In *Abnormal Hypnotic Phenomena: A Survey of Nineteenth-Century Cases,* 33–75. Volume 3. London: J. & A. Churchill, 1968.

Don, Norman S., Bruce E. McDonough, and Charles A. Warren. "PSI Testing of a Controversial Psychic Under Controlled Conditions." *Journal of Parapsychology* 56, no. 2 (June 1992): 87–96.

Drinkwater, Kenneth, Andrew Denovan, Neil Dagnall, and Andrew Parker. "Predictors of Hearing Electronic Voice Phenomena in Random Noise: Schizotypy, Fantasy Proneness, and Paranormal Beliefs." *Journal of Parapsychology* 84, no. 1 (2020): 96–113.

Duggan, M. "Annalisa Ventola." In *Psi Encyclopedia.* London: The Society for Psychical Research. (January 14, 2020). Accessed July 2, 2021, from https://psi-encyclopedia.spr.ac.uk/articles/annalisa-ventola.

Duggan, M. "Caroline Watt." In *Psi Encyclopedia.* London: The Society for Psychical Research. (March 10, 2020). Accessed July 2, 2021, from https://psi-encyclopedia.spr.ac.uk/articles/caroline-watt.

Duggan, M. "Ciaran O'Keeffe." In *Psi Encyclopedia.* London: The Society for Psychical Research. (July 15, 2020). Accessed July 4, 2021, from https://psi-encyclopedia.spr.ac.uk/articles/ciaran-o%E2%80%99keeffe.

Duggan, Michael. "Deborah Delanoy." In *Psi Encyclopedia.* London: The Society for Psychical Research. (February 25, 2020). Accessed June 23, 2021, from https://psi- encyclopedia.spr.ac.uk/articles/deborah-delanoy.

Duggan, M. "Dick Bierman." In *Psi Encyclopedia.* London: The Society for Psychical Research. (February 25, 2020). Accessed July 6, 2021, from https://psi-encyclopedia.spr.ac.uk/articles/dick-bierman.

Duggan, M. "Edward F. Kelly." In *Psi Encyclopedia.* London: The Society for Psychical Research.

(November 19, 2019). Accessed July 6, 2021, from https://psi-encyclopedia.spr.ac.uk/articles/edward-f-kelly.

Duggan, M. "Emily Williams Kelly." In *Psi Encyclopedia*. London: The Society for Psychical Research. (December 17, 2020). Accessed July 6, 2021, from https://psi-encyclopedia.spr.ac.uk/articles/emily-williams-kelly.

Duggan, M. "Experimental Psi Research in Asia and Australia." In *Psi Encyclopedia*. London: The Society for Psychical Research. (April 10, 2021). Accessed July 5, 2021, from https://psi-encyclopedia.spr.ac.uk/articles/experimental-psi-research-asia-and-australia.

Duggan, M. "Jack Hunter." In *Psi Encyclopedia*. London: The Society for Psychical Research. (March 17, 2020). Accessed July 6, 2021, from https://psi-encyclopedia.spr.ac.uk/articles/jack-hunter.

Duggan, M. "Julia Mossbridge." In *Psi Encyclopedia*. London: The Society for Psychical Research. (January 7, 2020). Accessed July 5, 2021, from https://psi-encyclopedia.spr.ac.uk/articles/julia-mossbridge.

Duggan, M. "Mario Varvoglis." In *Psi Encyclopedia*. London: The Society for Psychical Research. (December 14, 2019). Accessed July 2, 2021, from https://psi-encyclopedia.spr.ac.uk/articles/mario-varvoglis.

Duggan, M. "Michael Thalbourne." In *Psi Encyclopedia*. London: The Society for Psychical Research. (March 5, 2020). Accessed July 2, 2021, from https://psi-encyclopedia.spr.ac.uk/articles/michael-thalbourne.

Duggan, M. "Nancy L. Zingrone." In *Psi Encyclopedia*. London: The Society for Psychical Research. (March 10, 2020). Accessed June 29, 2021, from https://psi-encyclopedia.spr.ac.uk/articles/nancy-l-zingrone.

Duggan, M. "Nicola Holt." In *Psi Encyclopedia*. London: The Society for Psychical Research. (July 11, 2020). Accessed July 6, 2021, from https://psi-encyclopedia.spr.ac.uk/articles/nicola-holt.

Duggan, M. "Patrizio Tressoldi." In *Psi Encyclopedia*. London: The Society for Psychical Research. (January 11, 2020). Accessed July 2, 2021, from https://psi-encyclopedia.spr.ac.uk/articles/patrizio-tressoldi.

Duggan, M. "Richard S. Broughton." In *Psi Encyclopedia*. London: The Society for Psychical Research. (May 25, 2020). Accessed June 22, 2021, from https://psi-encyclopedia.spr.ac.uk/articles/richard-s-broughton.

Duggan, M. "Roger Nelson." In *Psi Encyclopedia*. London: The Society for Psychical Research. (February 10, 2020). Accessed July 5, 2021, from https://psi-encyclopedia.spr.ac.uk/articles/roger-nelson.

Duggan, M. "Sally Rhine Feather." In *Psi Encyclopedia*. London: The Society for Psychical Research. (April 27, 2020). Accessed July 6, 2021, from https://psi-encyclopedia.spr.ac.uk/articles/sally-rhine-feather.

Dunne, Brenda J. "Princeton Engineering Anomalies Research Lab." In *Ghosts, Spirits, and Psychics: The Paranormal from Alchemy to Zombies* edited by Matt Cardin, 231–33. Santa Barbara, CA: ABC-CLIO, 2015.

"Early Studies in Parapsychology at Duke." Duke University Libraries. Accessed December 14, 2021, from https://library.duke.edu/exhibits/2020/parapsychology.

Ebon, Martin. "Hans Bender: A Life in Parapsychology." *Journal of Religion and Psychical Research* 18, no. 4 (October 1995): 187–95.

Erickson, Deborah L. "Intuition, Telepathy, and Interspecies Communication: A Multidisciplinary Perspective." *NeuroQuantology* 9, no. 1 (March 2011): 145–52.

The ESP Reader. Edited by David C. Knight. New York: Grosset & Dunlap, 1969.

Evrard, Renaud. "Anomalous Phenomena and the Scientific Mind: Some Insights from 'Psychologist' Louise Favre (1868–1938?)." *Journal of Scientific Exploration* 31, no. 1 (2017): 71–83.

Evrard, Renaud. "From *Symptom* to *Difference*: 'Hearing Voices' and Exceptional Experiences." *Journal of the Society for Psychical Research* 78, no. 916 (2014): 129–48.

Evrard, Renaud, Erika Annabelle Pratte, and Etzel Cardeña. "Pierre Janet and the Enchanted Boundary of Psychical Research." *History of Psychology* 21, no. 2 (2018): 100–25.

Evrard., Renaud. "Institut Métapsychique International." In *Psi Encyclopedia*. (August 3, 2017). Accessed June 16, 2021, from https://psi-encyclopedia.spr.ac.uk/articles/institut-m%C3%A9tapsychique-international.

Evrard, Renaud. "Parapsychology in France after May 1968: A History of GERP." *Journal of Scientific Exploration* 24, no. 2 (2010): 283–94.

Evrard, Renaud. "Rémy Chauvin." *Journal of Scientific Exploration* 24, no. 2 (2010): 299–303.

Evrard, Renaud. "René Sudre (1880–1968): The Metapsychist's Quill." *Journal of the Society for Psychical Research* 73, no. 897. (October 2009): 207–22.

Evrard. Renaud. "Parapsychology in France after May 1968: A History of GERP." *Journal of Scientific Exploration* 24, no. 2 (2010): 283–94.

Evrard, Renaud. "Yvonne Duplessis, 1912–2017." *Journal of Scientific Exploration* 31, no. 4 (2017): 687–90.

Facco, Enrico, Fabio Fracas, and Patricio Tressoldi. "Moving Beyond the Concept of Altered State of Consciousness: The Non-Ordinary Mental Expressions (NOMEs)." *Advances in Social Sciences Research Journal* 8, no. 3 (March 2021): 615–31.

Fahler, Jarl and Remi J. Cadoret. "ESP Card Test of College Students with and without Hypnosis." In *Basic Research in Parapsychology,* 2nd edition. Edited by K. Ramakrishna Rao, 251–61. Jefferson, NC: McFarland and Company, 2001.

Feather, Sara R. and Robert Brier. "The Possible Effect of the Checker in Precognition Tests." *Journal of Parapsychology* 32, no. 3 (September 1968): 167–75.

Fodor, Nandor. *Between Two Worlds.* New York: Parker Publishing Company, 1964.

Fodor, Nandor. *An Encyclopedia of Psychic Science.* Secaucus: Citadel Press, 1974.

Fong, Chun Yuen, Chie Takahashi, and Jason J. Braithwaite. "Evidence for Distinct Clusters of Diverse Anomalous Experiences and their Selective Association with Signs of Elevated Cortical Hyperexcitability." *Consciousness and Cognition,* 71 (2019): 1–17.

Fordham, Michael. "Editorial Preface." In Carl Jung's *Sychronicity.* New York: Bollingen Foundation, 1960.

"Formation of the Society." *Proceedings of the American Society for Psychical Research,* 1, no.1 (July 1885): 1–4.

Gallagher, Charles, V. K. Kumar and Ronald J. Pekala. "The Anomalous Experiences Inventory: Reliability and Validity." *Journal of Parapsychology* 58, no. 4 (December 1, 1994): 402–28.

Garrett, Eileen. J. "My Life as a Search for the Meaning of Mediumship." In *The ESP Reader,* edited by David C. Knight, 190–206. New York: Grosset & Dunlap, 1969.

Gauld, Alan. "Two Cases from the Lost Years of Mrs. Piper." *Journal of the Society for Psychical Research* 78, no. 915 (April 2014): 65–84.

Geley, Gustave. *From the Unconscious to the Conscious.* Translated by S. De Brath. New York: Harper and Brothers, 1919.

Gennep, Arthur van. *The Rites of Passage.* Chicago: Chicago: University of Chicago Press, 1960.

"Geraldine Dorothy Cummins." In *Gale Literature: Contemporary Authors.* Farmington Hills, MI: Gale, 2002. Gale Literature Resource Center.

Gimeno, Juan. "David Efron: Biography of a Forgotten Pioneer in Psychical Research." *Journal of the Society for Psychical Research* 83, no. 2 (2019): 102–15.

"Global Consciousness Project." In *Psi Encyclopedia* (Society for Psychical Research). Accessed December 16, 2021, from https://psi-encyclopedia.spr.ac.uk/articles/global-consciousness-project.

Gow, Kathryn H., Louise Hutchinson, and David Chant. "Correlations Between Fantasy Proneness, Dissociation, Personality Factors and Paranormal Beliefs in Experiencers of Paranormal and Anomalous Phenomena." *Australian Journal of Clinical and Experimental Hypnosis* 37, no. 2 (November 2009): 169–91.

Graus, Andrea. "Discovering Palladino's Mediumship. Otero Acevedo, Lombroso, and the Quest for Authority." *Journal of the History of the Behavioural Sciences* 52, no. 3 (Summer 2016): 211–30.

Greene, Velma O'Donoghue. "Writing Women for a Modern Ireland: Geraldine Cummins and Susanne Day." In *Women in Irish Drama: A Century of Authorship and Representation,* edited by Melissa Sihra, 42–54. London: Palgrave Macmillan, 2007.

Gruner, Stefan. "Hans Driesch Re-Visited After a Century: On 'Leib Und Seele-Eine Untersuchung Uber Das Psychophysische Grundproblem.'" *Cosmos and History: The Journal of Natural and Social Philosophy* 13, no. 3 (October 2017): 401–24.

Gurney, Edmund, Frederic W. H. Myers, and Frank Podmore. *Phantasms of the Living.* London: Kegan Paul, Trench, Trubner, and Co., 1918.

Gurney, Edmund and Frederic W. H. Myers. "Statement of the Literary Committee of the Society for Psychical Research." *Journal of the Society for Psychical Research* 3, no. 36 (January 1887): 1–8.

Gyimesi, Júlia. "Why 'Spiritism?'" *The International Journal of Psychoanalysis* 97 (2016): 357–83.

Haight, JoMarie. "Spontaneous Psi Cases: A Survey and Preliminary Study of ESP, Attitude, and Personality Relationship." *Journal of Parapsychology* 43, no. 3 (September 1, 1979): 179–204.

Hansel, C. E. M. *ESP and Parapsychology: A Critical Re-Evaluation.* Buffalo, NY: Prometheus Books, 1980: 29.

Haraldsson, Erlendur. "Alleged Encounters with the Dead: The Importance of Violent Death in 337 New Cases." *Journal of Parapsychology* 73 (April 2009): 91–118.

Haraldsson, Erlendur. "Extraordinary Physical Phenomena in Poland: A Review of *Other Realities? The Enigma of Franek Kluski's Mediumship.*" *Journal of Parapsychology* 82, no. 2 (2018): 208–209.

Haraldsson, Erlendur. "Robert L. Van de Castle: 1927–2014." *Journal of Parapsychology* 78, no. 1 (Spring 2014): 126–27.

Hardin, C. L. "Table-Turning, Parapsychology and Fraud." *Social Studies of Science* 11, no. 2 (May 1981): 249–55.

Haynes, Renée. *The Society for Psychical Research: 1882–1982, A History.* London: Macdonald & Co., 1982.

Hayward, G. "Rupert Sheldrake." In *Psi Encyclopedia.* London: The Society for Psychical Research. (March 2, 2020). Accessed July 3, 2021, from https://psi-encyclopedia.spr.ac.uk/articles/rupert-sheldrake.

Hennessy, Kathryn. *A History of Magic, Witchcraft, and the Occult.* New York: DK Publishing, 2020.

"Historical Overview of IMI's Activities." (2021). Institut Métaphysique International. Accessed March 31, 2021, from https://www.metapsychique.org/apercu-historique-des-activites-de-limi/.

"History." Centro Studi Parapsicologici. Accessed January 13, 2022, from http://www.cspbo.it/b/storia%201.html.

"History." (Dutch Society for Psychical Research, 2021). Accessed December 29, 2021, from https://dutchspr.org/spr/overdespr/geschiedenis.

"History of CSICOP." Center for Inquiry, Inc. (2021). Accessed April 1, 2021 from https://skepticalinquirer.org/history-of-csicop/.

"History of the Parapsychological Association." (The Parapsychological Association, 2021). Accessed December 22, 2021, from https://www.parapsych.org/articles/1/14/history_of_the_parapsychological.aspx.

Hogan, R. Craig. "Applying the Science of the Afterlife." *Journal of Spirituality and Paranormal Studies* 32, no. 1 (2009): 6–23.

"Home: Welcome to the Website of the Australian Institute of Parapsychological Research." The Australian Institute of Parapsychological Research. (2016). Accessed January 13, 2022, from aiprinc.org.

Houran, James and Rense Lange. "A Rasch Hierarchy of Haunt and Poltergeist Experiences." *Journal of Parapsychology* 65 (March 2001): 41–58.

Houran, James. "Research Note: What's in a Name? The Best Descriptor for People Reporting Anomalous Experiences." *Australian Journal of Parapsychology* 18, no. 2 (2018): 195–200.

Hughes, Dureen J. "Blending with an Other: An Analysis of Trance Channeling in the United States." *Ethos* 19, no. 2 (June 1991): 161–84.

Hunter, Jack. "Talking with the Spirits: Anthropology and Interpreting Spirit Communications." *Journal of the Society for Psychical Research* 75, no. 904 (2011): 129–41.

"Institute for Frontier Areas of Psychology and Mental Health." Institute for Frontier Areas of Psychology and Mental Health. Accessed January 13, 2022, from https://www.igpp.de/allg/welcome.htm.

Ironside, Rachael. "Feeling Spirits: Sharing Subjective Paranormal Experience Through Embodied Talk and Action." *Text and Talk* 38, no. 6 (2018): 705–28.

Irwin, H. J. *An Introduction to Parapsychology.* (Jefferson, NC: McFarland and Company, 1989).

Irwin, Harvey J. "The Disembodied Self: An Empirical Study of Dissociation and the Out-of-Body

Experience." *Journal of Parapsychology* 64, no. 3 (September 1, 2000): 261–77.

Irwin, Harvey. "Is Scientific Investigation of Postmortem Survival an Anachronism? The Demise of the Survival Hypothesis." *Australian Journal of Parapsychology* 2, no.1 (June 2002): 19–27.

"J.B. Rhine." The Parapsychological Association (2021). Accessed March 30, 2021 from https://www.parapsych.org/articles/0/257/jb_rhine.aspx.

"James Houran." (2021). Parapsychological Association. Accessed July 6, 2021, from https://parapsych.org/users/jhouran/profile.aspx.

"Japanese Society for Parapsychology." Accessed April 1, 2021, from http://j-spp.umin.jp/english/jspp_e.htm.

Jawer, Michael A., Brandon Massullo, Brian Laythe, and James Houran. "Environmental 'Gestalt Influences' Pertinent to Studies of Haunted Houses." *Journal of the Society for Psychical Research* 84, no. 2 (2020): 65–92.

Jenkins, H. "Andrija Puharich." In *Psi Encyclopedia.* London: The Society for Psychical Research. (June 19, 2020). Accessed July 4, 2021, from https://psi-encyclopedia.spr.ac.uk/articles/andrija-puharich.

Joines, William T., Stephen B. Baumann, and John G. Kruth. "Electromagnetic Emission from Humans during Focused Intent." *Journal of Parapsychology* 76, no. 2 (Fall 2012): 275–94.

Jones, David E. H. *Why Are We Conscious? A Scientist's Take on Consciousness and Extrasensory Perception* (Singapore: Pan Stanford Publishing, 2017).

Judd, Charles M. and Bertram Gawronski. "Editorial Comment." *Journal of Personality and Social Psychology* 100, no. 3 (2011): 406.

Juin, Janvier A. "Correspondence," *Revue Philosophique de la France et de l'Étranger*, 1876: T.1: 430–31.

Keep, Christopher. "Evidence in Matters Extraordinary: Numbers, Narratives, and the Census of Hallucinations." *Victorian Studies* 61, no. 4 (Summer 2019): 582–607.

Keen, Montague. "The Scole Investigation: A Study in Critical Analysis of Paranormal Physical Phenomena." *Journal of Scientific Exploration* 15, no. 2 (2001): 167–82.

Kennedy, J. E. "New Frontiers of Human Science: A Festschrift for K. Ramakrishna Rao. (Review)." *Journal of Parapsychology* 67, no. 2 (Fall 2003): 395–99.

Kennedy, J. E. "Why is PSI So Elusive? A Review and Proposed Model." *Journal of Parapsychology* 65 (September 2001): 219–46.

Khourey, Louis. "Eileen Garrett: The Skeptical Medium." *TAT Journal* 2, no. 2 (1979). Accessed June 25, 2021, from http://www.searchwithin.org/download/eileen_garrett.pdf.

Kloosterman, Ingrid. "Psychical Research and Parapsychology Interpreted: Suggestions from the International Historiography of Psychical Research and Parapsychology for Investigating its History in the Netherlands." *History of the Human Sciences* 25, no. 2 (2012): 2–22.

Kloosterman, Ingrid. "'Spiritalismus vincit Mundum:' Dutch Spiritualism and the Beginning of Psychical Research." *Studium* 7, no. 3, (2014): 157–72.

Knapp, Krister Dylan. *William James: Psychical Research and the Challenge of Modernity.* Chapel Hill, NC: The University of North Carolina Press, 2017.

Knight, David C., ed. *The ESP Reader.* New York: Grosset & Dunlap, 1969.

Kohler, Kaufmann and Louiz Ginzberg, "Cabala." Accessed March 10, 2021, from https://www.jewishencyclopedia.com/articles/3878-cabala.

Kramer, Wim H. "Experiences with Psi Counseling in Holland." In *Perspectives of Clinical Parapsychology: An Introductory Reader,* edited by Wim H. Kramer, Eberhard Bauer, and Gerd. H. Hövelman, 7–19. Bunnik: Stichting Het Johan Borgman Fonds, 2012.

Kripal, Jeffrey J. *Authors of the Impossible: The Paranormal and the Sacred.* Chicago: University of Chicago Press, 2010.

Kripal, Jeffrey J. *The Flip: Epiphanies of Mind and the Future of Knowledge* (New York: Bellevue Literary Press, 2019).

Kripal, Jeffrey J. "Life." 2018. Accessed March 29, 2021, from https://jeffreyjkripal.com/life/.

Kripal, Jeffrey. "Secret Lives of the Superpowers: The Remote Viewing Literature and the Imaginal." In *Handbook of Spiritualism and Channeling,* edited by Cathy Gutierrez, 421–43. Brill: Leiden, 2015.

Krippner, Stanley. "In Memoriam: Michael Persinger." *Journal of Parapsychology* 82, no. 2 (2018): 102–103.

Krippner, Stanley. "The Maimonides ESP-Dream Studies." *Journal of Parapsychology* 57, no. 1 (March 1, 1993): 39–54.

Krippner, Stanley, David T. Saunders, Angel Morgan, and Alan Quan. "Remote Viewing of Concealed Target Pictures Under Light and Dark Conditions." *Explore* 15, no. 1 (2019): 27–37.

Kruth, John G. "Five Qualitative Research Approaches and Their Applications in Parapsychology." *Journal of Parapsychology* 79, no. 2 (Fall 2015): 219–33.

Kruth, John G. and William T. Joines. "Taming the Ghost Within: An Approach Toward Addressing Apparent Electronic Poltergeist Activity." *Journal of Parapsychology* 80, no. 1 (Spring 2016): 70–86.

Kwilecki, Susan. "Twenty-First Century American Ghosts: The After-Death Communication—Therapy and Revelation from Beyond the Grave." *Religion and American Culture: A Journal of Interpretation* 19, no. 1 (Winter 2009): 101–33.

Lachapelle, Sofie. *Investigating the Supernatural: From Spiritism and Occultism to Psychical Research and Metapsychics in France, 1853–1931.* Baltimore, MD: Johns Hopkins University Press, 2011.

Lamont, Peter. "Spiritualism and a Mid-Victorian Crisis of Evidence." *The Historical Journal* 47, no. 4 (December 2004): 897–920.

Lange, Rense and James Houran. "Delusions of the Paranormal: A Haunting Question of Perception." *Journal of Nervous and Mental Disease* 186, no. 10 (October 1998): 637–45.

Laszlo, Ervin. "Cosmic Connectivity: Toward a Scientific Foundation for Transpersonal Consciousness." *International Journal of Transpersonal Studies* 23 (2004): 21–31.

Lawrence, Madelaine. "Near-Death and Other Transpersonal Experiences Occurring during Catastrophic Events." *American Journal of Hospice and Palliative Medicine* 34, no. 5 (2017): 486–92.

Lawrence, Snezana. "Life, Architecture, Mathematics, and the Fourth Dimension." *Nexus Network Journal: Architecture and Mathematics* 17, no. 2 (July 2015): 597–603.

Laythe, Brian and James Houran. "Concomitant Object Movements and EMF-Spikes at a Purported Haunt." *Journal of the Society for Psychical Research* 83, no. 4 (2019): 212–29.

Laythe, Brian, James Houran, and Annalisa Ventola. "A Split-Sample Psychometric Study of 'Haunters.'" *Journal of the Society for Psychical Research* 81, no. 4 (2018): 193–218.

Leary, Mark R. and Tom Butler. "Electronic Voice Phenomena." In *Parapsychology: A Handbook for the 21st Century,* edited by Etzel Cardeña, John Palmer, and David Marcusson-Clavertz, 341–49. Jefferson, NC: McFarland and Company, 2015.

Lodge, Sir Oliver. "A Textbook of Metapsychics: Review and Critique by Sir Oliver Lodge." *Proceedings of the Society for Psychical Research* 34 (October 1923): 70–106.

Lommel, Pim van. "Consciousness Beyond Life, the Science of the Near-Death Experience." Accessed March 29, 2021, from https://pimvanlommel.nl /en/consciousness-beyond-life/.

Lommel, Pim van, Ruud van Wees, Vincent Meyers, and Ingrid Elfferich. "Near-Death Experience in Survivors of Cardiac Arrest: A Prospective Study in the Netherlands." *Lancet* 358, no. 9298 (2001): 2039–45.

Lommel, Pim van, Ruud van Wees and Vincent Myers. "Near-Death Survivors of Cardiac Arrest: A Prospective Study in the Netherlands." *Lancet* 358, no. 9298 (December 15, 2001): 2039–45.

"Loyd Auerbach." The Parapsychological Association. Accessed June 18, 2021, from https://www .parapsych.org/users/profparanormal/profile.aspx.

Luke, David P., Deborah Delanoy, and Simon J. Sherwood. "Psi May Look Like Luck: Perceived Luckiness and Beliefs about Luck in Relation to Precognition." *Journal of the Society for Psychical Research* 72, no. 4 (October 2008): 193–207.

Maher, Michaeleen. "Ghosts and Poltergeists: An Eternal Enigma." In *Parapsychology: A Handbook for the 21st Century.* Edited by Etzel Cardeña, John Palmer, and David Marcusson-Clavertz, 327–39. Jefferson, NC: McFarland and Company, 2015.

Maher, Michaeleen. "Quantitative Investigation of the General Wayne Inn." *Journal of Parapsychology* 64, no. 4 (December 2000): 365–90.

Maher, Michaeleen. "Thoughts on Death and Its Survival." *Journal of Religion and Psychical Research* 27, no. 1 (2004): 2–3.

Maraldi, Everton de Oliveira and Stanley Krippner. "Cross-Cultural Research on Anomalous Experiences: Theoretical Issues and Methodological Challenges." *Psychology of Consciousness: Theory, Research, and Practice* 6, no. 3 (2019): 306–19.

Maraldi, Everton, Fatima Regina Machado, and Wellington Zangari. "Importance of a Psychosocial Approach for a Comprehensive Understanding of Mediumship." *Journal of Scientific Exploration* 24, no. 2 (2010): 181–96.

"Martin Ebon." In *Gale Literature: Contemporary Authors.* Farmington Hills, MI: Gale, 2002. *Gale Literature Resource Center.*

Marwaha, Sonali Bhatt and Edwin C. May. "The Multiphasic Model of Precognition: The Rationale." *Journal of Parapsychology* 79, no. 1 (2015): 5–19.

Mashour, George A., Lori Frank, Alexander Batthyany, Ann Marie Kolanowski, Michael Nahm, Dena Schulman-Green, Bruce Greyson, Serguei Pakhomov, Jason Karlawish, and Raj C. Shah. "Paradoxical Lucidity: A Potential Paradigm Shift for the Neurobiology and Treatment of Severe Dementias." *Alzheimer's and Dementia* 15, no. 8 (2019): 1107–14.

"Massimo Biondi." (The Parapsychological Association: 2021). Accessed December 29, 2021, from https://www.parapsych.org/users/mbiondi/profile.aspx.

May, Ashley. "How Many People Believe in Ghosts or Dead Spirits?" *USA Today,* (October 25, 2017). Retrieved February 23, 2021 from How many people believe in ghosts or spirits of the dead? (usatoday.com).

McConnell, R. A. and Haakon Forwald. "Psychokinetic Placement I: A Re-Examination of the Forwald-Durham Experiment." *Journal of Parapsychology* 31, no. 1 (March 1967): 51–69.

McCorristine, Shane. "William Fletcher Barrett, Spiritualism, and Psychical Research in Edwardian Dublin." *Estudios Irlandeses* no. 6 (January 1, 2011): 39–53.

McCully, Robert S. "'The Paranormal and the Normal' by Morton Leeds and Gardner Murphy (Book Review)." *Journal of Parapsychology* 44, no. 4 (December 1, 1980): 362–65.

McLuhan, R. "Dean Radin." In *Psi Encyclopedia.* London: The Society for Psychical Research. (April 2, 2021). Accessed July 4, 2021, from https://psi-encyclopedia.spr.ac.uk/articles/dean-radin.

McVaugh, Michael R. "Rhine Research Center." (2006). Accessed December 16, 2021, from https://www.ncpedia.org/rhine-research-center.

Mehler, Jacqueline Amati. "Letter from Italian Psychoanalytical Association." *The International Journal of Psychoanalysis* 95, no. 2 (2014): 191–93.

Milner, Richard. "Wallace, Darwin, and the Spiritualism Scandal of 1876." *Skeptic* 20, no. 3 (2015): 27–33.

Mishlove, Jeffrey and Brendan C. Engen. "Archetypal Synchronistic Resonance: A New Theory of Paranormal Experience." *Journal of Humanistic Psychology* 47, no. 2 (April 2007): 223–42.

Mishlove, Jeffrey. *Roots of Consciousness.* Boston: Da Capo Press, 1997.

"Mission Statement: Mission Continued." University of Groningen: Heymans Anomalous Cognition Group. Accessed January 13, 2022, from https://sites.google.com/a/rug.nl/heymans-anomalous-cognition-group/home/mission-continued.

Mitchell, Edgar. "An ESP Test from Apollo 14." *Journal of Parapsychology* 35, no. 2 (June 1, 1971): 89–107.

Moss, Thelma. *The Body Electric: A Personal Journey into the Mysteries of Parapsychological Research, Bioenergy, and Kirlian Photography.* Los Angeles: J.P. Tarcher, 1979.

Mossbridge, Julia A., Marcia Nisam, and Adam Crabtree. "Can Hypnotic Suggestion Induce Feelings of Unconditional Love and Supernormal Performance?" *Spirituality in Clinical Practice* 8 no. 1 (2021): 30–50.

Mossbridge, Julia, Patrizio Tressoldi, and Jessica Utts. "Predictive Physiological Anticipation Preceding Seemingly Unpredictable Stimuli: A Meta-Analysis." *Frontiers in Psychology,* 3 (October 2012): 1–18.

Mulacz, Peter. "Eleonore Zugun: The Re-Evaluation of a Historic RSPK Case." *Journal of Parapsychology* 63, no. 1 (March 1999): 15–45.

Mülberger, Annette and Mónica Balltondre. "Metaphysics in Spain: Acknowledging or Questioning the Marvellous?" *History of the Human Sciences* 25, no. 2 (2012): 108–30.

Murdie, Alan. "Obituary: Guy Lyon Playfair 1935–2018." *Journal of the Society for Psychical Research* 82, no. 3 (2018): 189–92.

Murphy, Gardner and Ernest Taves. "Covariance Methods in the Comparison of Extra-Sensory Tasks." *Journal of Parapsychology* 3, no. 1 (June 1, 1939): 38–78.

Myers, Frederic W. H. "Report on the Census of Hallucinations." *Proceedings of the Society for Psychical Research* 10 (1894): 25–422.

Nahm, Michael. "The Development and Phenomena of a Circle for Physical Mediumship." *Journal of Scientific Exploration* 28, no. 2 (2014): 229–83.

Nahm, Michael. "Out of Thin Air? Apport Studies Performed between 1928 and 1938 by Elemér Chengery Pap." *Journal of Scientific Exploration* 33, no. 4 (2019): 661–705.

Natale, Simone. "The Medium on the Stage: Trance and Performance in Nineteenth-Century Spiritualism." *Early Popular Visual Culture* 9, no. 3 (2011): 239–55.

Neppe, Vernon M. "Revisiting Survival 37 Years Later: Is the Data Still Compelling?" *The Journal of Spirituality and Paranormal Studies* 33, no. 3 (2010): 123–46.

Nicol, J. Fraser Nicol. "Historical Background." In *Handbook of Parapsycholoy,* edited by Benjamin B. Wolman, 305–23. New York: Van Nostrand Reinhold Company, 1977.

Noakes, Richard. "The 'Bridge Which is Between Physical and Psychical Research': William Fletcher Barrett, Sensitive Flames, and Spiritualism." *History of Science* 42, no. 4 (2004): 419–64.

"Obituary: Raymond G. Bayless." *Journal of Near-Death Studies* 22, no. 4 (Summer 2004): 287.

"Obituary: Rhea White, M.L.S." *Journal of Near-Death Studies,* vol. 25, no. 3 (Spring 2007): 199.

O'Keeffe, Ciaran, James Houran, Damien J. Houran, Neil Dagnall, Kenneth Drinkwater, Lorraine Sheridan, and Brian Laythe. "The Dr. John Hall Story: A Case Study in Putative "Haunted People Syndrome", *Mental Health, Religion & Culture* 23, no. 7 (2020): 532–49.

Oppenheim, Janet. *The Other World: Spiritualism and Psychical Research in England, 1850–1914.* London: Cambridge University Press, 1985.

"Our History." (2018). The Incorporated Society for Psychical Research. Accessed March 29, 2021, from https://www.spr.ac.uk/about/our-history.

"Our Mission." Edgar Cayce's A.R.E.: Association for Research and Enlightenment. (2021). Accessed June 24, 2021, from https://www.edgar cayce.org/about-us/our-mission/.

Owen, Alex. *The Darkened Room: Women, Power and Spiritualism in Late Victorian England.* Philadelphia: University of Pennsylvania Press, 1990.

Palmer, John "Anomalous Cognition, Dissociation, and Motor Automatisms." *Journal of Parapsychology* 81, no. 1 (Spring 2017): 46–62.

Palmer, John. "Hansel's Ghost: Resurrection of the Experimenter Fraud Hypothesis in Parapsychology." *Journal of Parapsychology* 80, no. 1 (Spring 2016): 5–16.

Palmer, John. "Milan Ryzl: 1928–2011." *Journal of Parapsychology* 75, no. 2 (Fall 2011): 359–61.

Paraná, Denise, Alexandre Caroli Rocha, Elizabeth Schmitt Freire, Francisco Lotufo Neto, and Alexander Moreira-Almeida. "An Empirical Investigation of Alleged Mediumistic Writing: A Case Study of Chico Xavier's Letters." *Journal of Nervous and Mental Disease* 207, no. 6 (June 2019): 497–504.

Parker, Adrian and Nemo C. Mörck. "Martin Johnson 1930–2011." *Journal of Parapsychology* 75, no. 2 (2011): 353–59.

Parker, Adrian and Brian Millar. "Revealing Psi Secrets: Successful Experimenters Seem to Succeed by Using Their Own Psi." *Journal of Parapsychology* 78, no. 1 (2014): 39–55.

Parra, Alejandro and Juan Carlos Argibay. "Exploratory Study of the Temperament Theory and Paranormal Experiences." *Journal of the Society for Psychical Research* 80, no. 4. (2016): 214–22.

Peres, Julio Fernando, Alexander Moreira-Almeida, Leonardo Caixeta, Frederico Leao, and Andrew Newberg. "Neuroimaging During Trance State: A Contribution to the Study of Dissociation." *PLoS ONE* 7, no. 11 (November 2012): 1–9.

Perry, Jim and Tim Rothschild. "Dr. Dean Radin on Real Magic and the Secret Power of the Universe." *Nite Drift* October 19, 2020.

Persinger, Michael A. "Geophysical Variables and Behavior: XXX. Intense Paranormal Experiences Occur During Days of Quiet, Global, Geomagnetic Activity." *Perceptual and Motor Skills* 61 (1985): 320–22.

Persinger, Michael A. "Spontaneous Telepathic Experiences from *Phantasms of the Living* and Low Global Geomagnetic Activity." *Journal of the American Society for Psychical Research* 81 (January 1987): 23–36.

Philibert, R. L. "Remi Cadoret, M.D.: His Career and Achievements." *Posters.* Paper 22. Samuel B. Guze Symposium on Alcoholism. https://digital commons.wustl.edu/guzeposter2006/22/.

Piccolino, Marco and Nicholas J. Wade. "The Frog's Dancing Master: Science, Seances, and the Transmission of Myths." *Journal of the History of the Neurosciences* 22, no 1. (January 2013): 79–95.

Pilkington, Rosemarie. "Jule Eisenbud, 1908–1999: A Profile in Courage." *Journal of Parapsychology* 63, no. 2 (June 1999): 163–66.

Plas, Régine. "Psychology and Psychical Research in France around the End of the 19th Century." *History of the Human Sciences* 25, no. 2 (2012): 91–107.

Playfair, Guy Lyon. "An American Institution in Low Spirits." *Fortean Times* 320 (November 2014): 52–53.

Playfair, Guy Lyon. "Obituaries: David Fontana, 1934–2010." *Journal of the Society for Psychical Research* 75, no. 3 (2011): 168–69.

Pleasants, Helene, ed. *Biographical Dictionary of Parapsychology.* New York: Helix Press, 1964.

Podmore, Frank. *The Newer Spiritualism.* New York: Henry Holt and Company, 1911.

Pollack, Jack Harrison. *Croiset the Clairvoyant: The Story of the Amazing Dutchman.* Garden City, NY: Doubleday & Company, 1964.

Pope, Dorothy H. "Obituary: Carroll Blue Nash." *Journal of Parapsychology* 62, no. 4 (December 1998): 361–62.

Pratt, J. G. "The Case for Psychokinesis." *Journal of Parapsychology* 24, no. 3 (September 1, 1960): 171–88.

Pratt, J. G. and W. G. Roll. "The Seaford Disturbances." *Journal of Parapsychology* 22, no. 2 (June 1958): 79–124.

Price, Margaret M. "A Comparison of Blind and Seeing Subjects in 'ESP' Tests." *Journal of Parapsychology* 2, no. 4 (December 1, 1938): 273–86.

Qamar, Azher Hameed. "Tona, the Folk Healing Practices in Rural Punjab, Pakistan." *Journal of Ethnology & Folkloristics* 9, no. 2 (July 2015): 59–74.

Radin, Dean I. and D. C. Ferrari. "Effects of Consciousness on the Fall of Dice: A Meta-Analysis." *Journal of Scientific Exploration* 5, no. 1 (1991): 61–83.

Radin, Dean. *Entangled Minds: Extrasensory Experiences in a Quantum Reality.* New York: Paraview, 2006.

Radin, Dean I. "Unconscious Perception of Future Emotions: An Experiment in Presentiment." *Journal of Scientific Exploration* 11, no. 2 (1997): 163–80.

Radin, Dean, Garret Yount, Arnaud Delorme, Loren Carpenter, and Helané Wahbeh. "Spectroscopic Analysis of Water Treated by and in Proximity to Energy Medicine Practitioners: An Exploratory Study." *Explore: The Journal of Science and Healing* 17, no. 1 (2021): 27–31. doi:10.1016/j.explore.2020.10.005.

Radin, Dean and Eva Lobach. "Toward Understanding the Placebo Effect: Investigating a Possible Retrocausal Factor." *Journal of Alternative and Complementary Medicine* 13, no. 7 (2007).

Reinsel, Ruth. "Obituary: Gertrude R. Schmeidler: 1912–2009." *Journal of Parapsychology* 73 (Spring 2009): 159–71.

Rhine, J. B. "Comments: A New Case of Experimenter Unreliability." *Journal of Parapsychology* 38, no. 2 (June 1, 1974): 215–25.

Rhine, J. B. "Experiments Bearing on the Precognition Hypothesis." *Journal of Parapsychology* 2, no.1 (March 1, 1938): 38–54.

Rhine, J. B. *Handbook of Parapsychology.* Edited by Benjamin B. Wolman. New York: Van Nostrand Reinhold Company, 1977.

Rhine, J. B. "Impatience with Scientific Method in Parapsychology." *Journal of Parapsychology* 11, no. 4 (December 1, 1947): 283–95.

Rhine, J. B. "Introductory Comments." In *Parapsychology Today: New Writings on ESP, Telepathy, Clairvoyance, Precognition, PK, Mind Over Matter,* edited by J. B. Rhine and Robert Brier, 25–28. New York: Citadel Press, 1968.

Rhine, J. B. and Betty M. Humphrey. "The PK Effect: Special Evidence from Hit Patterns." *Journal of Parapsychology* 8, no. 1 (March 1, 1944): 18–60.

Rhine, J. B. "Telepathy and Clairvoyance Reconsidered." *Journal of Parapsychology* 9, no. 3 (September 1, 1945): 176–93.

Rhine, Louisa E. "Auditory Psi Experience: Hallucination or Physical?" *Journal of Parapsychology* 27, no. 3 (1963): 182–97.

Rhine, Louisa E. "Placement PK Tests with Three Types of Objects." *Journal of Parapsychology* 15, no. 2 (June 1, 1951): 132–38.

Rhine, Louisa. *PSI: What is It? The Story of ESP and PK.* New York: Harper & Row, 1975.

Rhine, Louisa E. and J. B. Rhine. "The Psychokinetic Effect: I. The First Experiment." *Journal of Parapsychology* 7, no. 1 (March 1, 1943): 20–43.

Rhine, Louisa E. "Subjective Forms of Spontaneous Psi Experiences." *Journal of Parapsychology* 17, no. 2 (June 1, 1953): 77–114.

Rhine, Louisa E. "Toward Understanding Psi-Missing." *Journal of Parapsychology* 29, no. 4 (December 1, 1965): 259–74.

Richet, Charles. *Thirty Year of Psychical Research: Being a Treatise on Metaphysics.* New York: Macmillan Company, 1923.

Riess, Bernard F. "A Case of High Scores in Card Guessing at a Distance." *Journal of Parapsychology* 1, no. 4 (December 1, 1937): 260–63.

Roche, Suzanne M. and Kevin M. McConkey. "Absorption: Nature, Assessment, and Correlates." *Journal of Personality and Social Psychology* 59, no. 1 (1990): 91–101.

Roe, Chris A. "Clients' Influence in the Selection of Elements of a Psychic Reading." *Journal of Parapsychology* 60, no. 1 (March 1996): 43–70.

Roe, Chris A. and Nicola J. Holt. "The Effects of Strategy ('Willing' Versus Absorption) and Feedback (Immediate versus Delayed) on Performance at a PK Task." *Journal of Parapsychology* 70, no. 1 (Spring 2006): 69–90.

Roe, Chris A. "PA Presidential Address 2017: Withering Skepticism." *Journal of Parapsychology* 81, no. 2 (Fall 2017): 143–59.

Rogo, D. Scott. "The Case for Parapsychology." *Humanist* 37, no. 6 (November 1, 1977): 40–44.

Roll, William G. "Poltergeists, Electromagnetism, and Consciousness." *Journal of Scientific Exploration* 17, no. 1 (2003): 75–86.

Roll, William G. and William T. Joines. "RSPK and Consciousness." *Journal of Parapsychology* 77, no. 2 (Fall 2013): 192–211.

Roll, William G. "Survival After Death: Alan Gauld's Examination of the Evidence." *Journal of Parapsychology* 48 (June 1984): 127–48.

Rozenblatt, Daphne Claire. "Madness and Method: Enrico Morselli and the Social Politics of Psychiatry, 1852–1929." PhD diss., University of California, 2014.

Ruch, John. "This Physicist Saw Promise in the Paranormal, but Now His Legacy Could be Lost." *The Washington Post.* (Summer 2019): 9AD.

Rueda, Sergio A. "Tribute to J. Ricardo Musso (1917–1989)." *Journal of Parapsychology* 53, no. 4 (December 1, 1989): 277–80.

Ruffle, Libby. "Vessels of the Gods: The Oracle at Delphi." *History Today* 67, no. 5 (May 2017): 50–61.

Ruickbie, L. "Helen Salter." In *Psi Encyclopedia London: The Society for Psychical Research* (2022). Accessed June 5, 2022 from https://psi-encyclopedia.spr.ac.uk/articles/helen-salter.

Ruttan, Leslie A., Michael A. Persinger, and Stanley Koren. "Enhancement of Temporal Lobe-Related Experiences During Brief Exposures to Milligauss Intensity Extremely Low Frequency Magnetic Fields." *Journal of Bioelectricity* 9, no. 1 (1990): 33–54.

Ryan, Adrian. "Open Data in Parapsychology: Introducing *Psi Open Data.*" *Journal of Parapsychology* 82, no. 1 (2018): 65–76.

Schlitz, Marilyn. "Obituaries: Helmut Schmidt 1928–2011." *Journal of Parapsychology* 75, no. 2 (2011): 349–53.

Schmeidler, Gertrude Raffel and Gardner Murphy. "The Influence of Belief and Disbelief in ESP upon Individual Scoring Levels." *Journal of Experimental Psychology* 36, no. 3 (June 1946): 271–76.

Schmeidler, Gertrude. "Obituary: E. Douglas Dean, 1916–2001." *Journal of Parapsychology* 65, no. 4 (December 2001): 417–19.

Schmidt, Stefan and Harald Walach. "Electrodermal Activity (EDA)—State-of-the-Art Measurement and Techniques for Parapsychological Purposes." *Journal of Parapsychology* 64, no. 2 (June 1, 2000): 139–63.

Schoch, Robert M. and Logan Yonavjak. *The Parapsychology Revolution: A Concise Anthology of Paranormal and Psychical Research.* New York: Jeremy P. Tarcher, 2008.

Schoonover, Karl. "Ectoplasms, Evanescence, and Photography." *Art Journal* 62, no. 3 (Autumn 2003): 30–43.

Schwartz, Steven A. "Six Protocols, Neuroscience, and Near Death: An Emerging Paradigm Incorporating Nonlocal Consciousness." *Explore* 11, no.4 (July/August 2015): 252–60.

"Scientists: Garret Yount, Ph.D." Accessed July 1, 2021, from https://noetic.org/profile/garret-yount/.

"Scientific Society for the Promotion of Parapsychology eV." WGFP. Accessed January 13, 2022, from https://www.parapsychologische-beratungsstelle.de/WGFP/.

"Scientists: Helané Wahbeh, ND, MCR." (Institute of Noetic Sciences, 2021). Accessed July 2, 2021, from https://noetic.org/profile/helane-wahbeh/.

Seale-Collazo, James. "Charisma, Liminality, and Freedom: Toward a Theory of the Everyday Extraordinary." *Anthropology of Consciousness* 23, no. 2 (2012): 175–91.

Sheldrake, Rupert and Pamela Smart. "Videotaped Experiments on Telephone Telepathy." *Journal of Parapsychology* 67, no. 1 (Spring 2003): 147–66.

Sherwood, Simon J. "Relationship Between the Hypnagogic/Hypnopompic States and Reports of Anomalous Experiences." *Journal of Parapsychology* 66, no. 2 (June 2002): 127–50.

Sidgwick, E. M. "An Examination of Book-Tests Obtained in Sittings with Mrs. Leonard." *Proceedings of the Society for Psychical Research* 31 (1921): 241–400.

Sidgwick, Eleanor. "Notes on the Evidence, Collected by the Society, for Phantasms of the Dead." *Proceedings of the Society for Psychical Research* 3 (April 24, 1885): 69–150.

Sommer, Andreas. "Normalizing the Supernormal: The Formation of the 'Gesellschaft Für Psychologische Forschung' ('Society for Psychological Research')," *Journal of the History of the Behavioral Sciences* 49, no. 1 (Winter 2013): 18–44.

Sommer, Andreas. "Professional Heresy: Edmund Gurney (1847–1888) and the Study of Hallucinations and Hypnotism." *Medical History* 55. no. 3 (July 2011): 383–88.

Sommer, Andreas. "Psychical Research in the History and Philosophy of Science." *Studies in History and Philosophy of Biological and Biomedical Sciences* 48 (2014): 38–45.

Sommer, Andreas. "Psychical Research and the Origins of American Psychology: Hugo Münsterberg, William James and Eusapia Palladino." *History of the Human Sciences* 25, no. 2 (April 2012): 23–44.

Standish, Leanna J., L. Clark Johnson, Leila Kozak, and Todd Richards. "Evidence of Correlated Functional Magnetic Resonance Imaging Signals Between Distant Human Brains." *Alternative Therapies in Health and Medicine* 9, no. 1 (January/February 2003): 122–28.

Steiner, Rudolf. *The Steinerbooks Dictionary of the Psychic, Mystic, Occult.* Blauvelt, NY: Rudolf Steiner Publications, 1973.

Steinkamp, Fiona. "Does Precognition Foresee the Future? A Postal Experiment to Assess the Possibility of True Precognition." *Journal of Parapsychology* 64, no. 1 (March 1, 2000): 3–18.

Steinkamp, Fiona, Julie Milton, and Robert L. Morris. "A Meta-Analysis of Forced-Choice Experiments Comparing Clairvoyance and Precognition." *Journal of Parapsychology* 62, no. 3 (September 1998): 193–218.

Storm, Lance. "In Memory of Erlendur Haraldsson who Died Sunday, November 22, 2020." *Australian Journal of Parapsychology* 20, no. 2 (2020): 201–202.

Storm, Lance Storm, Patrizio E. Tressoldi, and Lorenzo Di Risio. "Meta-Analysis of ESP Studies, 1987–2010: Assessing the Success of the Forced-Choice Design in Parapsychology." *Journal of Parapsychology* 76, no. 2 (Fall 2012): 243–73.

Storm, Lance, Patricio Tressoldi, and Lorenzo Di Risio. "Meta-Analysis of Free-Response Studies, 1992–2008: Assessing the Noise Reduction Model in Parapsychology." *Psychological Bulletin* 136, no. 4 (July 2010): 471–85.

Storm, Lance. "Synchronicity, Causality, and Acausality." *Journal of Parapsychology* 63, no. 3 (September 1999): 247–69.

Stuart, Charles E. "An Analysis to Determine a Test Predictive of Extra-Chance Scoring in Card-Calling Tests." *Journal of Parapsychology* 5, no. 2 (June 1, 1941): 99–137.

Stuart, Kevin, Banmadorji, and Huangchojia. "Mountain Gods and Trance Mediums: A Qinghai Tibetan Summer Festival." *Asian Folklore Studies* 54, no. 2 (1995): 219–37.

"Subconscious." American Psychological Association. Accessed December 15, 2021, from https://dictionary.apa.org/subconscious.

Takasuna, Miki. "The Fukurai Affair: Parapsychology and the History of Psychology in Japan." *History of the Human Sciences* 25, no. 2 (2012): 149–64.

Targ, Russel. "What do We Know About Psi? The First Decade of Remote-Viewing Research and Operations at Stanford Research Institute." *Journal of Scientific Exploration* 33, no. 4 (2019): 569–92.

Tart, Charles T. "The Archives of Scientists' Transcendent Experiences: TASTE." *Journal of Near-Death Studies* 19, no. 2 (Winter 2000): 132–34.

"TASTE: The Archive for Scientists' Transcendent Experiences." Academy for the Advancement of Postmaterialist Sciences. Accessed July 2, 2021, from https://www.aapsglobal.com/taste/.

Thalbourne, Michael A. *A Glossary of Terms Used in Parapsychology.* Charlottesville, VA: Puente Publications, 2003.

Thalbourne, Michael A. "Psychiatry, the Mystical, and the Paranormal." *Journal of Parapsychology* 70, no. 1 (Spring 2006): 143–65.

Thalbourne, Michael A. "Transliminality, Anomalous Belief and Experience, and Hypnotisability." *Australian Journal of Clinical and Experimental Hypnosis* 37, no. 2 (November 2009): 119–30.

Thouless, Robert H. "A Report on an Experiment in Psychokinesis with Dice and a Discussion on Psychological Factors Favoring Success." *Journal of Parapsychology* 15, no. 2 (June 1, 1951): 89–102.

Thouless, R. H. "Experiments on Paranormal Guessing." *British Journal of Psychology* 33, no. 1 (July 1, 1942): 22.

Tobacyk, Jerome and Gary Milford. "Belief in Paranormal Phenomena: Assessment Instrument Development and Implications for Personality Functioning." *Journal of Personality and Social Psychology* 44, no. 5 (1983): 1029–37.

Tocquet, Robert. *The Magic of Numbers.* New York: A.S. Barnes, 1963.

Tolaas, Jon and Montague Ullman. "Extrasensory Communication and Dreams." In *Handbook of Dreams—Research, Theories, and Application,* edited by Benjamin B. Wolman. New York: Van Nostrand Reinhold, 1979. Accessed December 22, 2021, from https://siivola.org/monte/papers_grouped/copyrighted/Parapsychology_&_Psi/Extrasensory_Communication_and_Dreams.htm.

Tressoldi, Patrizio and Lance Storm. "Anomalous Cognition: An Umbrella Review of the Meta-Analytic Evidence." *Journal of Anomalous Experience and Cognition* 1, no. 1 (2021): 55–72.

Tromp, Marlene. *Altered States: Sex, Nation, Drugs, and Self-Transformation in Victorian Spiritualism.* New York: State University of New York Press, 2006.

Tromp, Marlene. "Queering the Séance: Bodies, Bondage, and Touching in Victorian Spiritualism." In *Handbook of Spiritualism and Channeling,* vol. 9, edited by Cathy Gutierrez, 87–115. Leiden: Brill, 2015.

Turner, Victor. *The Ritual Process: Structure and Anti-Structure.* Chicago: Aldine, 1969.

Tymn, Michael. "Difficulties in Spirit Communication Explained by Dr. James Hyslop." *The Journal of Spirituality and Paranormal Studies* 33, no. 4 (2010): 195–209.

Tymn, Michael E. "An 'Interview' with Sir William Crookes." *Journal of Spirituality and Paranormal Studies* 30, no. 2 (2007): 80–86.

Tymn, Michael E. "Etta Wriedt: The Best Medium Ever?" *Journal of Spirituality and Paranormal Studies* 34, no. 4 (2011): 229–38.

Tymn, Michael. "James Hyslop." In *Psi Encyclopedia London: The Society for Psychical Research.* (2015). Accessed June 5, 2022 from https://psi-encyclopedia.spr.ac.uk/articles/james-hyslop.

"University Education in Parapsychology." (2021). The Parapsychological Association. Accessed April 1, 2021, from University Education in Parapsychology–The Parapsychological Association.

Valentine, Elizabeth R. "Spooks and Spoofs: Relations Between Psychical Research and Academic Psychology in Britain in the Inter-War Period." *History of the Human Sciences* 25, no. 2 (2011): 67–90.

Vandersande, Jan W. "Two Recent Materialization Seances with Kai Muegge." *Journal for Spiritual and Consciousness Studies* 28, no. 1 (2015): 61–66.

Varvoglis, Mario and Peter A. Bancel. "Micro-Psychokinesis: Exceptional or Universal?" *Journal of Parapsychology* 80, no. 1 (Spring 2016): 37–44.

Ventola, Annalisa, James Houran, Brian Laythe, Lance Storm, Alejandro Parra, John Dixon, and John G. Kruth. "A Transliminal 'Dis-Ease' Model of 'Poltergeist Agents.'" *Journal of the Society for Psychical Research* 83, no. 3 (2019): 144–71.

Wada, Yoshishisa. "Chojougenshou No Toraenikusa (The Elusiveness Problem of Psi), edited by Toshio Kasahara." *Journal of Parapsychology* 57, no. 3 (September 1993): 303–306.

Wahbeh, Helané, Dean Radin, Garrett Yount, Arnaud Delorme, and Loren Carpenter. "Effects of the Local and Geocosmic Environment on the Efficacy of Energy Medicine Treatments: An Exploratory Study." *Explore: The Journal of Science and Healing,* 17, no. 1 (January 2021): 40–44.

Wahbeh, Helané, Cedric Cannard, Jennifer Okonsky, and Arnaud Delorme. "A Physiological Examination of Perceived Incorporation During Trance." *F1000Research* 8, no. 67 (2019): 1–26.

Watt, Caroline and Peter Ramakers. "Experimenter Effects with a Remote Facilitation of Attention

Focusing Task: A Study with Multiple Believer and Disbeliever Experiments." *Journal of Parapsychology* 67, no. 1 (Spring 2003): 99–116.

Watt, Caroline. "Precognitive Dreaming: Investigating Anomalous Cognition and Psychological Factors." *Journal of Parapsychology* 78, no. 1 (Spring 2014): 115–25.

Watt, Caroline. "Research Assistants or Budding Scientists? A Review of 96 Undergraduate Student Projects at the Koestler Parapsychology Unit." *Journal of Parapsychology* 70, no. 2 (Fall 2006): 335–55.

Watt, Caroline, Emily Dawson, Alisdair Tullo, Abby Pooley, and Holly Rice. "Testing Precognition and Alterations of Consciousness with Selected Participants in the Ganzfeld." *Journal of Parapsychology* 84, no. 1 (Spring 2020): 21–37.

Watt, C. and R. Wiseman. "'Twitter' as a New Research Tool: Proof of Principle with a Mass Participation Test of Remote Viewing." *European Journal of Parapsychology* 25 (2010): 89–100.

Weaver, Zofia. "In Memoriam: Donald J. West, M.D., D. litt., FRCPsych (1924–2020)." *Journal of Parapsychology* 84, no. 1 (2020): 12–13.

Weaver, Zofia. "Julian Ochorowicz and His Contribution to Psychical Research." *Journal of Parapsychology* 83, no. 1 (2019): 69–78.

Weaver, Zofia. "A Parapsychological Naturalist: A Tribute to Mary Rose Barrington." *Journal of Scientific Exploration* 34, no. 3 (2020): 597–601.

Wehrstein, K. M. "Charles Tart." In *Psi Encyclopedia.* London: The Society for Psychical Research. (April 6, 2019). Accessed July 3, 2021, from https://psi-encyclopedia.spr.ac.uk/articles/charles-tart.

Wehrstein, K. M. "Russell Targ." In *Psi Encyclopedia.* London: The Society for Psychical Research. (May 6, 2019). Accessed July 3, 2021, from https://psi-encyclopedia.spr.ac.uk/articles/russell-targ.

Wehrstein, K. M. "Stanley Krippner." In *Psi Encyclopedia.* London: The Society for Psychical Research. (February 2, 2021). Accessed July 6, 2021, from https://psi-encyclopedia.spr.ac.uk/articles/stanley-krippner.

Wehrstein, K. M. "William Bengston and Energy Healing." In *PSI Encyclopedia.* London: The Society for Psychical Research. (October 2017). Accessed June 19, 2021, from https://psi-encyclopedia.spr.ac.uk/articles/william-bengston-and-energy-healing.

Wehrstein, K. M. "William Roll." In *Psi Encyclopedia.* London: The Society for Psychical Research. (June 29, 2021). Accessed July 4, 2021, from https://psi-encyclopedia.spr.ac.uk/articles/william-roll.

Weiner, Debra H. and Nancy L. Zingrone. "In the Eye of the Beholder: Further Research on the 'Checker Effect.'" *Journal of Parapsychology* 53 (September 1989): 203–31.

"Welcome to the AZIRE." The Alvarado Zingrone Institute for Research and Education." Accessed June 18, 2021, from https://theazire.org/.

Weymouth, Kathryn F. "Healing From a Personal Perspective: Interviews with Certified Healing Touch Practitioners" PhD diss., Saybrook University, 2012.

"What is Parapsychology?" (February 11, 2011). Parapsychological Association. Accessed January 4, 2021 from https://parapsych.org/articles/36/76/what_is_parapsychology.aspx.

White, Rhea A. "The Human Component in Exceptional Experience." *Journal of Religion and Psychical Research* 20, no. 1 (1997): 23–29.

White, Rhea A. "Role Theory and Exceptional Human Experience." *Journal of Religion and Psychical Research* 17, no. 2 (April 1994): 74–77.

Wilde, David J. Wilde and Craig D. Murray. "An Interpretative Phenomenological Analysis of Out-of-Body Experiences in Two Cases of Novice Meditators." *Australian Journal of Clinical and Experimental Hypnosis* 37, no. 2 (2009): 90–118.

Willin, M. "Alice Johnson." In *Psi Encyclopedia London: The Society for Psychical Research.* (2021). Accessed June 5, 2022 from https://psi-encyclopedia.spr.ac.uk/articles/alice-johnson.

Willin, M. "Anita Gregory." In *Psi Encyclopedia.* London: The Society for Psychical Research. (June 29, 2021). Accessed July 6, 2021, from https://psi-encyclopedia.spr.ac.uk/articles/anita-gregory.

Willin, M. "Arthur Ellison." In *Psi Encyclopedia.* London: The Society for Psychical Research. (April 26, 2021). Accessed July 6, 2021, from https://psi-encyclopedia.spr.ac.uk/articles/arthur-ellison.

Willin, M. "Manfred Cassirer." In *Psi Encyclopedia.* London: The Society for Psychical Research. (May 25, 2021). Accessed June 22, 2021, from https://psi-encyclopedia.spr.ac.uk/articles/manfred-cassirer.

Willin, M. "Maurice Grosse." In *Psi Encyclopedia.* London: The Society for Psychical Research. (April 2, 2021). Accessed July 6, 2021, from https://psi-encyclopedia.spr.ac.uk/articles/maurice-grosse.

Willin, M. "Ralph Noyes." In *Psi Encyclopedia.* London: The Society for Psychical Research. (April 26, 2021). Accessed July 5, 2021, from https://psi-encyclopedia.spr.ac.uk/articles/ralph-noyes.

Willin, M. "Zofia Weaver." In *Psi Encyclopedia.* (2021). Accessed July 2, 2021, from https://psi-encyclopedia.spr.ac.uk/articles/zofia-weaver.

Wiseman, Richard, Emma Greening, and Matthew Smith. "Belief in the Paranormal and Suggestion in the Séance Room." *British Journal of Psychology* 94 (August 2003): 285–97.

Wiseman, Richard, Caroline Watt, and Diana Kornbrot. "Registered Reports: An Early Example and Analysis." *PeerJ* 7 (2019): 1–13.

Wolffram, Heather. "Hallucination or Materialization? The Animism versus Spiritism Debate in Late 19th-Century Germany." *History of the Human Sciences* 25, no. 2 (2012): 45–66.

Wolffram, Heather. "Parapsychology on the Couch: The Psychology of Occult Belief in Germany, c. 1870–1939." *Journal of the History of the Behavioral Sciences* 42, no. 3 (Summer 2006): 237–60.

Wolffram, Heather. *The Stepchildren of Science: Psychical Research and Parapsychology in Germany, c. 1870–1939.* Amsterdam: Rodopi, 2009.

Wood, Dave and Christian Jensen Romer. "Where do we go From Here? The Future of Ghost Investigation." *Journal of Research into the Paranormal* 47 (January 2014): 11–23.

Woodruff, J. L. and R. W. George. "Experiments in Extra-Sensory Perception." *Journal of Parapsychology* 1, no.1 (March 1, 1937): 18–30.

Wright, Sylvia Hart Wright. "Over a Century of Research on After-Death Communication." *Journal of Spirituality and Paranormal Studies* 31, no. 3 (2008): 154–66.

Yount, Garret, Arnaud Delorme, Dean Radin, Loren Carpenter, Kenneth Rachlin, Joyce Anastasia, Meredith Pierson, Sue Steele, Heather Mandell, Aimee Chagnon, and Helané Wahbeh. "Energy Medicine Treatments for Hand and Wrist Pain: A Pilot Study." *Explore: The Journal of Science and Healing* 17 (2021): 11–21.

Yount, Garret, Shrikant Patil, Umang Dave, Leonardo Alves-dos-Santos, Kimberly Gon, Robert Arauz, and Kenneth Rachlin. "Evaluation of Biofield Treatment Dose and Distance in a Model of Cancer Cell Death." *Journal of Alternative and Complementary Medicine* 19, no. 2 (2013): 124–27.

Index

Page references to figures are italicized.

American Society for Psychical Research (ASPR), 11, 15, 17, 33, 35, 37–38, 41, 46–47, 51, 53, 55, 57–58, 65, 67, 69, 71, 73–75, 80, 82, 89, 94, 96, 101, 106, 110, 114, 118–19, 122–23, 145, 151, 156–57, 164–65, 169 176, 188, 197, 216–17, 222, 238, 254, 287, 291, 299n11; publications in *Journal of American Society for Psychical Research,* 175, 192, 194, 197, 200, 235n116, 244, 246–47, 253, 255–56, 264, 290, 294, 296, 298
animals and psi, 75–77, 95, 114, 205–6, 228
anomalous experiences inventory, 255, 299n19
apparition, 7, 11, 20, 32, 36, 41, 54, 56–57, 61, 76, 82, 114, 142, 144, 146–49, 153–54, 157, 160–61, 166–68, 171, 185, 199–200, 238, 240, 254–56, 261, 269, 281, 290; crisis apparition, 44–45; 263, 271, during seances, 104–6, 116, 277. *See also* ghost; haunting
apport, 37, 41–42, 55, 65, 103–4, 109, 113, 117, 119, 123, 125n86, 158–60, 256, 277, 289
ASPR. *See* American Society for Psychical Research

Bender Institute. *See* Institute for Border Areas of Psychology and Mental Hygiene
book test, 63, 257–58
Boston Society for Psychic Research, 26, 58, 66, 107, 173, 238, 254, 291
Budapest School of Psychoanalysis, 40, 221

cabinet, 258
Center for Research on Consciousness and Anomalous Psychology, 18, 76, 251, 258–59
Centro Studi Parapsicologici (Center for Parapsychological Studies), 76, 251, 259, 285, 300n44, 304n226
channeling, 85, 100, 115, 120, 136n497, 163, 257, 259, 274, 298, 300n48

clairaudience, 260
clairsentience, 260
clairvoyance, 11, 30, 49, 53–54, 59, 63–64, 101, 116, 122, 158–61, 171–72, 176, 178–79, 186, 206–8, 213, 220, 229, 236n85, 243, 257, 260–61, 265, 269, 274, 277–78, 283, 300n32, 300n62, 302n118, 306n311
Committee on Haunted Houses, 142, 244, 261, 271, 290, 300n65, 305n262
Committee on Mediumistic Phenomena, 216, 246, 261–62, 300n66
Committee on Thought-Reading, 146, 147
Committee on Thought-Transference, 145–47, 150, 262
consciousness, 1–2, 11, 13, 18–19, 23n101, 30, 33, 45, 47–49, 52, 68, 72–73, 80, 88–90, 95, 98, 110, 124n32, 131n313, 205–6, 262–66, 271–74, 277, 279–80, 282–83, 285, 289, 291, 293–94; altered states of, 51, 53, 59, 76–77, 82, 85, 130n284, 134n411, 149, 156–58, 187, 196–97, 204, 269, 274; non-local consciousness, 223–24, 246, 262–63, 301n72; phenomenology of consciousness inventory, 227; and poltergeist cases, 133n387. *See also* survival theory
crisis apparitions, 44–45, 54, 255, 263, 271. *See also* Phantasms of the Living
crisis-esp, 213

deathbed visions, 32, 189, 194, 246, 264
dice-test, *16*, 42, 81, 88, 99, 114, 131n313, 175, 177–78, 180–82, 186, 188, 247, 264, 277, 281, 284, 286, 288, 298, 304n222. *See also* psychokinesis; J.B. Rhine; Louisa Rhine
direct mental influence on living systems (DMILS), 209, 264
displacement effect, 265. *See also* placement effect

dissociation, 17, 36, 67, 76, 97, 129n236, 197–98, 216, 224, 227–28, 231–32, 236n177, 241n8, 245-46, 257, 265

DMILS. *See* direct mental influence on living systems

dreams, 49, 53, 73, 77, 80, 95, 98, 100, 103, 119, 125n69, 135n428, 143–46, 152, 158, 168, 183, 187, 196, 211, 266, 282; lucid dreaming, 38–39, 218; Maimonides Dream Lab, 82, 85, 98–99, 239, 277. *See also* Frederik van Eeden, Jules Eisenbud

Duke Parapsychology Labs, 15–16, 35, 42, 46, 51, 57–59, 62, 68, 75, 84, 88, 91, 93, 98, 107, 112–14, 169–76, 181–85, 188–90, 195, 217, 239, 253, 264, 266, 269, 282. *See also* Rhine Research Center

electromagnetic fields, 67, 78, 86, 87, 90, 204, 212, 267–68, 301n105

electronic voice phenomena (EVP), 223, 230, 236n166, 256, 267, 269, 274, 291, 301n101, 301n102. *See also* instrumental transcommunication

ESP. *See* extrasensory perception

EVP. *See* electronic voice phenomena

exceptional human experience, 15, 73, 98, 101–2, 229–30, 260, 268, 297, 301n107

expectancy effect, 268

experimenter effect, 72, 191, 205, 213, 268–69. *See also* experimenter-psi

experimenter-psi, 196, 204–5, 222. *See also* experimenter effect

extrasensory perception (ESP), 11, 16–17, 129n244, 143, 173–83, 185–91, 195, 199, 201, 204, 212, 214, 225, 228–31, 243–44, 256, 269, 281, 288; in dreams, 211, 266; and the

experimenter effect, 269; general extrasensory perception (GESP), 188, 261, 270, 297; research methods, 258, 268, 289, 297–98; researchers who studied, 27–28, 32–33, 38, 46, 57, 58, 62–63, 65, 68–69, 74, 76–77, 92, 101

Fukurai Institute of Psychology, 14

ganzfeld, 75–76, 79, 82, 99, 199–201, 224, 233, 244–45, 270, 282, 288, 302nn116–117, 128, 204

general extrasensory perception (GESP), 188, 261, 270, 297

geomagnetic activity, 74, 90, 100, 129n269, 200, 201, 204, 206, 228, 235n116

Gesellschaft für Experimental-Psychologie (Society for Experimental Psychology), 13

GESP. *See* general extrasensory perception

ghosts, 11, 19, 21n10, 56–57, 83, 86–87, 100, 142, 146–49, 154, 161, 168, 172, 203, 214–15, 219–21, 238, 244–45, 254–56, 261, 270–72, 299n24. *See also* apparition; crisis apparition; haunting

haunted person syndrome, 272, 302n126

haunting, 11, 19–20, 29, 32, 39, 44, 56–57, 61, 69, 76–78, 83, 86–87, 91, 99–100, 114, 130n292, 132n343, 142, 146, 149, 161, 165, 172, 206, 208, 219, 221, 233, 244, 247, 254, 261, 272, 290, 299n18. *See also* apparition; crisis apparition; ghost

hypnotism, 4, 5, 12–14, 16, 27, 34, 36–37, 53, 60, 81, 88, 94, 126n104, 143, 149, 153, 161, 179, 218, 237, 245–45, 273, 274, 278–79

Institut Métapsychique International, 39, 62, 66, 99, 134n408, 136n494, 217, 251, 271, 274

Institute for Border Areas of Psychology and Mental Hygiene (The Bender Institute), 29

Institute of Noetic Sciences, 92, 97, 133n379, 210, 233, 251, 269, 274

Instituto Argentino de Parapsicología, 89

instrumental transcommunication, 274. *See also* electronic voice phenomena (EVP)

Japanese Society for Parapsychology, 22n76, 90, 251, 275

Koestler Parapsychology Unit, 18, 79, 100, 251, 275, 302n152

levitation, 6–7, 35, 62, 69, 99, 105–6, 111, *112,* 116–17, 121, 158, 162–63, 166–68, 171, 186, 275, *276,* 277

Literary Committee, 143, 149, 276, 290, 303n161, 305n262

mechanical selector, 89, 174, 175, 178, 180, 182, 186, 284, 286

mediums, 5–9, 11, 13, 20, 41–43, 50, 53–55, 277–78; biographical sketches of, 65, 103–23; publications involving, 26, 31, 49, 67, 70, 76, 81, 88, 101. *See also* séance

mesmerism, 4–5, 18, 32, 34, 65, 108–9, 136n497, 143, 158, 187, 202, 218, 273, 278. *See also* hypnotism

morphic resonance, 95

near-death experience, 19, 23n101, 49, 68, 84–85, 87, 89, 96, 101, 132n346, 188–89, 194, 198, 223–24, 225–26, 246, 279. *See also* deathbed visions

out-of-body experience, 54, 72, 80, 83, 86, 93, 98, 102, 117, 122, 129n263, 135n441, 188, 197, 199, 203, 205, 224, 226, 230, 245, 256–57, 272, 280

paranormal belief scale, 202, 213–14
Parapsychological Association, 16, 21, 22nn85–86, 29, 58, 68, 70, 72–73, 75, 77–79, 93–94, 98, 102, 201, 207, 215, 221–22, 251, 255, 259, 280, 303n189
Parapsychology Foundation, 38, 67, 78, 83, 93, 96, 110, 178, 232, 251, 280–81
Phantasms of the Living, 11, 44–45, 52, 54, 67, 146–48, 153, 157–59, 185, 200, 263, 271, 281. *See also* crisis apparitions
phenomenology of consciousness inventory, 227
PK. *See* psychokinesis
placement effect, 180, 182–85, 281, 303n196. *See also* displacement effect, psychokinesis
poltergeist, 29–30, *41,* 42, 57, 69, 74, 76, 81–82, 86, 90–91, 93, 99–100, 116, 123, 133n387, 158, 194, 196, 206, 210, 228, 244, 246–47, 271, 281–*282,* 284–85, 286–87, 299n18, 302n120, 304n200; case studies, 148, 161–62, 183, 212, 219, 232–33. *See also* J. G. Pratt; recurrent spontaneous psychokinesis (RSPK); William Roll
precognition, 59, 71, 74–75, 78–79, 82, 88–89, 95, 129n274, 132n351, 174–76, 181–82, 187–93, 198, 201, 206, 208, 213–14, 229, 231–33, 236n185, 243–44, 282; and chair test, 259; and checker effect, 259; and dreams, 266; and forced-choice tests, 269; and remote viewing, 287; and replication, 288; 300n32, 300n51, 304n202, 304n204, 304n206, 306n311
Princeton Engineering Anomalies Research Lab (PEAR), 89, 201, 203–4, 209, 271, 282–83, 304n208
psi-gamma, 63
psi-kappa, 63
psi-missing, 182, 184, 187, 198, 231, 283, 304n213
Psychokinesis (PK), 35, 42, 59, 65, 67, 69, 73–75, 78, 81, 86, 88–89, 95, 98–99, 111, 114, 116, 123, 128n243, 129n269, 166, 171, 175–76, 178, 180–88, 193–201, 208–9, 212, 219, 225, 230–31; in animals, 239; 247, 253, 256, 260, 264, 284–85, 290, 294, 304n219; bio-PK, 90; ESP and PK, 128n243; macro-PK, 276–77; micro-PK, 88, 102, 134n415, 278, 303n175, 304nn235–236; placement PK, 281; recurrent spontaneous psychokinesis (RSPK), 93, 228, 286–87, 299. *See also* dice-test; Haakon Forwald; poltergeist; J. B Rhine; Louisa Rhine
psychometry, 58, 71, 107, 110, 118, 157, 218, 279
Psychologische Gesellschaft (Psychological Society), 285

quantum entanglement, 210–11

random event generator, 89, 209
random number generator, 208, 231, 247, 286

recurrent spontaneous psychokinesis (RSPK) 93, 228, 286–87, 299. *See also* poltergeist; psychokinesis
remote viewing, 73, 85, 88, 92, 96–97, 100, 122, 132n338, 133n378, 201, 203–4, 213, 287–88. *See also* Stanford Research Institute
replication, 97–98, 102, 149, 173, 199, 201, 209, 225, 240, 278, 288
retrocausation, 285
retrocognition, 70, 78, 288
Rhine Research Center, 16, 75, 107, 212, 251, 274, 288
RSPK. *See* recurrent spontaneous psychokinesis

séance, 6–7, 9, 26, 33, 41, 54–55, 61, 81, *106,* 112, 118–20, 123, 136n480, 137n508, 141, 150, 155–56, 162, 167, 274, 278, 285, 291. *See also* cabinet; mediums; Spiritualism
sheep-goat effect, 94, 191, 213, 283, 290. *See also* Gertrude Schmeidler
sitter-group, 69, 197, 290, 294
Society for Experimental Psychology, 14, 36–37
Society for Psychical Research, 4, 8, 15, 22n43, 143–44, 147, 149, 165, 199, 238, 251, 254, 261, 271, 273, 275–76, 289, 290–91; members of 26–27, 31, 35, 37, 41, 62–63, 65, 69, 75, 91, 101; in Sweden, 154
Society for the Study of Supernormal Pictures, 27
spiritscope, 8–9. *See also* Robert Hare
Spiritualism, 4–15, 22n29; in Japan, 14; mediums of the era, 103–12, 115–23; and psychical
research, 17–18, 27–29, 33–41, 55–56, 64–66; in Spain, 15. *See also* cabinet; mediums; séance
spontaneous psi, 69, 72, 146, 168, 183, 189, 191–92, 199, 205–6, 268, 285, 292, 305n271
Stanford Research Institute, 92, 97, 111, 122, 133n378, 198, 201, 213, 287, 288, 305n243. *See also* Russell Targ
subconscious, 5, 12, 29, 40, 53–54, 62, 67, 88, 95, 128n236, 161, 164–66, 175, 213, 216, 222, 258, 292–23, 296
super-psi, 208, 293
survival theory, 208, 228
synchronicity, 49, 256, 294. *See also* Carl Jung

target objects, 122, 187, 254, 258, 268–69, 297–98
telekinesis, 40, 157, 163, 186, 201, 225–26, 274, 284, 295. *See also* psychokinesis; recurrent spontaneous psychokinesis (RSPK)
telepathy, 11, 15, *18,* 28, 30, *120,* 150, 220, 221, 295; dreams and, 98, 277; and geomagnetic activity, 206; and ghosts, 147; research articles about, 39, 63, 80, 89, 124n52, 131n307, 134n401, 153, 159, 160–61, 166, 176, 178, 196, 201, 209, 214, 216, 218, 231, 243–44, 261; researchers interested in,

30, 33, 37, 48, 49, 52, 56, 62, 64–66, 78, 92, 95, 99. *See also* thought-transference

thoughtography, 14, 42, 80, 289, 295

thought-transference, 27–28, 31, 140, 143–47, 149–50, 153, 157, 159, 162–63, 167, 218, 221. *See also* Committee on Thought-Transference, telepathy

transliminality, 97, 99, 206, 213, 233, 244–45, 276, 289, 296

trickster theory, 219

Utrecht University, 63, 72, 84–85, 95, 107, 189, 222, 292, 297

Wissenschaftliche Gesselschaft zur Förderung der Parapsychologie (Scientific Society for the Furtherance of Parapsychology, or WGFP), 21

Person Index

Page references to figures are italicized.

Adamenko, Victor G., 67
Aksakof, Alexander, 26, 108, 155
Allison, Lydia Winterhalter, 26
Alvarado, Carlos S., 32, 41–42, 54, 59, 67–68, 72, 102–3, 119, 163, 197, 206–7, 215–16, 225, 230, 249, 256, 257, 261–62, 265, 288–89, 293
Anderson, Margaret L., 68, 178
Arigo, José, 103
Atwater, P. M. H., 68
Auerbach, Loyd, 68–69, 225

Bailey, Charles, *103*–4, 159
Balfour, Arthur, 26–27
Balfour, Gerald, 27, 56, 166
Barlow, Fred, 27
Barrett, Sir William, 10, 27–29, 108, 111, 121, 123, 141–43, 146, 160–61, 166, 210, 244, 261–62, 279, 290, 295
Barrington, Mary Rose, 69, 101, 111, 118, 207, 243, 275
Bayless, Raymond, 69–70, 267
Beloff, John, 4–6, 9, 25, 70, 75, 79, 111, 196, 202, 230, 244
Bem, Daryl, 70–71, 270, 310
Bender, Hans, 29–30, 82, 111, 117, 187, 210, 272, 274, 282
Bengston, William, 71–72
Béraud, Marthe (Eva C/Eva Carriere), 43, 61, *104*
Berger, Arthur S., 72, 123n2, 202, 241n10
Bergson, Henri, *30,* 31
Besterman, Theodore, 31, 121, 166, 258
Bierman, Dick, 72
Biondi, Massimo, 72, 208, 249, 288
Bird, James Malcolm, 31
Bisson, Juliette, 104
Blackburn, Charles, 105

Blackmore, Susan, 72–73, 130nn263–264, 202, 240
Blavatsky, Helena Petrovna, 46, 104–5, 120
Bleksley, Arthur E. H., 73
Boirac, Emile, *31,* 32, 162
Boole, Mary, 10, 32, 124n37, 144–45, 290
Bozzano, Ernesto, 31, *32*
Braid, John, 5
Braud, William G., 73–74, 130nn267–269, 264
Braude, Stephen E., 74, 116, 130n271, 137n501, 278, 293
Brier, Robert, 74–75, 130n273, 259, 300n32, 300n51
Broughton, Richard S., 75, 114, 129n233, 130n274, 136n492, 197, 247
Bucke, Richard Maurice, 32–33, 124n39

Cadoret, Remi, 75, 130n281, 179–80, 245
Canavesio, Orlando, 33
Cardeña, Etzel, 49, 75–76, 126n125, 130nn283–284, 217-18, 220, 223-4, 228, 230, 236n166, 244–45, 267, 271, 283, 286–88, 299n20, 305n242
Carington, Walter, 33
Carriere, Eva (Eva C.). *See* Marthe Beraud
Carrington, Hereward, 33, *34,* 40, 106, 117, 119, 155–56, 167, 188
Cassirer, Manfred, 76
Cayce, Edgar, 105, 135n453
Charcot, Jean-Martin, 34, 273
Chari, Cadambur T. K. (C. T. K.), 34–35, 286, 304n231
Chauvin, Rémy, 76–77, 187
Cook, Florence, 7, 35–36, 64, 67, 70, 105, *106,* 109, 140–41, 167–68
Corliss, William R., 77, 197, 243
Cox, William, 35, 184, 281, 303n196
Crandon, Mina, 31, 33, 37, 51, 56, 58, 64, 70, 106, *107,* 170–71, 238, 254, 258, 290–91
Crawford, William Jackson, *35,* 111, 163, 234n60, 271

344   *Person Index*

Creery family, 27–28, 146–47, 262, 279
Croiset, Gerard, 53, 63, 84, 107, 190
Crookall, Robert, 77
Crookes, William, 35–36, 64, 105–6, 110, 112,
    136n456, 140–41, 167–68, 171, 210, 255, 278
Cummins, Geraldine, 107–8

Dagnall, Neil, 23n107, 77–79, 83, 90, 130n291,
    130n301, 219, 269, 272, 293, 302n126
Dalkvist, Jan, 78, 218, 270
Davis, Andrew Jackson, 108, 110
Dean, E. Douglas, 78
Delanne, Gabriel, 36
Delanoy, Deborah, 78–79, 208–9, 235n135
Delorme, Arnaud, 23n104, 79, 102, 131n299, 135n425,
    218–19, 229, 233, 244, 246, 268, 300n60
D'Esperance, Elizabeth *108*, 109
Dessoir, Max, 12, 36–37, 96, 270, 280
Didier Brothers, Alexis and Adolph, 109
Dingwall, Eric, 22n36, 27, 37–38, 106, 137n513, 187,
    295, 306n290
Driesch, Hans, 12, 38, 53, 216
Drinkwater, Kenneth, 23n107, 78–79, 83, 90, 130n291,
    131n300, 219, 269, 272, 293, 302n126
Duncan, Helen V., 76, *109*

Ebon, Martin, 30, 38, 124n22
Eeden, Frederik van, 15, *38,* 39
Efron, David, 39
Ehrenwald, Jan, 39, 80
Erickson, Deborah L., 80, 131n307
Eysenck, Hans, 80

Fahler, Jarl, 75, 130n281, 180, 245
Feather, Sally Rhine, 81
Ferenczi, Sándor, *39,* 40
Ferrari, Diane C., 81, 131n313
Fielding, Everard, 40, 156
Fleming, Alice M., 109–10
Flournoy, Theodore, 8, 9, 40–41, 110, 257
Flügel, John Carl, 41
Fodor, Nandor, 38, *41,* 42, 45, 50, 52, 54, 103–5,
    123nn1–2, 188, 193
Fontana, David, 81, 289
Forthuny, Pascal, 53–54, 110
Forwald, Haakon, 42, 88, 132nn353–54, 180, 183–84,
    188, 281
Fox Sisters (Kate, Leah, Margaret): 4, *6,* 7, 64, 67, 108,
    110, 140–41, 158, 167, 188, 193, 291
Fukurai, Tomokichi, 42, *43,* 116, 295

Garrett, Eileen, 44, 92, 110, 136n470, 188, 280
Gasparin, Count Agenor de, 9

Gauld, Alan, 5, 81, 84, 120, 137n519, 188, 206, 300n34
Geley, Gustave, 12, 36, *43,* 62, 104, 111, 114, 118,
    126n97, 171, 207, 274
Geller, Uri, 80, 110–11
Goldney, Kathleen M., *44,* 198
Goligher, Kathleen, 35, *111,* 163, 260, 271
Gregory, Anita K., 81
Grosse, Maurice, 69, 81–82, 91, 131n317
Gurney, Edmund, 10–11, 44–45, 50, 61–62, 95, 117,
    143–44, 146–47, 188, 234n34, 244–45, 262–63,
    271, 276, 279, 295, 300n67, 301n76, 303n161,
    305n262
Guzyk, Jan, 111

Haraldsson, Erlendur, 82, 89, 113, 131nn319, 134n413,
    136n489, 194, 232, 246, 264, 277
Hare, Robert, *8,* 9
Hauffe, Friedericke, 5
Heim, Albert, 225–26
Heymans, Gerardus, 15, *45,* 222, 251, 272, 292,
    302n129
Heywood, Rosalind, 45, *46*
Hodgson, Richard, 46, 94, 104, 118, 120, 148–51,
    164–65, 170
Holt, Nicola, 82, 253, 299n2
Home, Daniel Dunglas, 6, *7,* 8–9, 111, *112,* 140–41,
    158–59, 166–68, 276, 278
Honorton, Charles, 82, 99, 119, 200, 233, 240, 266, 270,
    277
Houdini, Harry, 15, 34, 106, 112
Houran, James, 23n107, 82–83, 86, 90, 100, 130n291,
    131nn323–324, 132n341, 132n343, 132n341,
    132n343, 219, 221, 246–47, 272, 279, 296,
    299n18, 302n126
Humphrey, Betty, 46, 58, 175–76, 247, 286, 304n233
Hunter, Jack, 83
Hurkos, Peter, 92, 112–13, 188
Hyslop, James, 46–47, 53, 58, 151, 156–57, 164, 254

Indridason, Indridi, 113
Irwin, Harvey J., 83, 124n12, 131n328, 199, 209, 221–
    22, 253, 280, 294, 303nn184–185, 306n283

James, William, 9, 11–12, 14, 17, 22n89, 37, 40, 42, 45,
    47–48, 51–52, 95–96, 119–20, 150, 165, 170, 196,
    216, 222–23, 245–46, 254, 262, 300n66
Janet, Pierre, 12, 29, 34, *48,* 49, 65, 220, 273
Jephson, Ina, 49
Johnson, Alice, 49, 52, 56, 61, 153
Johnson, Martin, 83–84, 95, 193
Jonsson, Olof, 113
Jung, Carl, 29, 49, 81, 126n133, 214, 219, 256, 294,
    296. *See also* synchronicity

Kappers, Jan, 84
Karagulla, Shafica, 84
Kasahara, Toshio, 84
Keil, Jürgen, 84, 115, 194, 232, 247
Kelly, Edward F., 84
Kelly, Emily W., 49, 84–85, 89, 246
Kerner, Justus, 5
Kilner, Walter John, 50
King, Katie. *See* Florence Cook
Kiyota, Masuaki, 113
Kluski, Franek, 12, 36, 43, 53–54, 59, 101, 114
Kramer, Wim H., 72, 85, 131n335, 249, 288, 305n247
Krieman, Naum, 85
Kripal Jeffrey J., viii, 19, 23n105, 85, 132nn338–339, 222–23
Krippner, Stanley, 85, 98, 133n369, 193, 196, 218, 241, 263–64, 266, 277, 301n78, 303n166, 305n244
Kulagina, Nina, 84, 114–15, 119, 194, 247, 275

Lange, Rense, 83, 85–86, 132n341, 246–47, 279, 296, 299n18
Laplace, Jeanne, 115
Lawrence, Madelaine, 86, 132n342
Laythe, Brian, 23n107, 83, 86, 90, 99–100, 130n291, 131n324, 132n343, 135n418, 135n421, 219, 272, 289, 302n126
Leonard, Gladys Osborne, 26, 50, 63, *115*, 172, 246, 258, 300n35
Lobach, Eva, 86, 132n345
Lodge, Sir Oliver, *50*, 83, 115, 146, 152, 155, 157, 168–70, 188, 210, 255, 277, 295, 306n292
Lommel, Pim van, 19, 23n101, 25, 87, 133n346, 223–24, 246, 279, 303n178

Maher, Michaeleen, 20, 23n110, 87, 133nn347–348, 244, 271, 302n120
Maraldi, Everton, 87–88, 133n349, 263–64, 301nn78–79
Margery. *See* Mina Crandon
Marwaha, Sonali, 88, 133n351, 225, 255, 288
Masayuki, Ohkado, 232
Matlock, James G., 232, 266
McConnell, Robert A., 42, 68, 88, 94, 133nn353–354, 181, 290
McDougall, William, 15, 34, 42, 51, 58, 68, 169, 195, 216–17, 266, 269, 280, 298
Mellon, Annie F., 116
Mifune, Chizuko, 14, 26, 116
Mirabelli, Carlos, 38, 70, 116, 137n501
Mita, Koichi, 14
Molnar, Tibor, 55, 116–17, 119
Morselli, Enrico, 51, 217, 245
Moser, Fanny Hoppe, 51

Moses, William Stainton, 10, 35, 117, 120, 143, 261
Mossbridge, Julia, 88–89, 132n356–357, 229, 231, 243–44, 268
Mügge, Kai, 117
Muldoon, Sylvan, 117
Münsterberg, Hugo, 17, 51, *52*, 96, 245
Murphy, Gardner, 66, 85, 89, 94, 98, 132n393, 171–72, 176, 199, 216, 235n113, 263, 301n74
Musso, J. Ricardo, 25, 89
Myers, Frederic W. H., 10–11, 38, 43–45, 50, 52–53, 61–62, 67, 85, 110, 122, 143–47, 152–53, 155, 157–58, 161, 163–64, 168–69, 171, 188, 216, 223, 244, 256, 262-3, 265, 271–73, 276–77, 279, 288, 290, 292–96, 298, 300n67, 301n76, 303n161, 305n262, 306n279

Nagao, Ikuko, 14, 42
Nahm, Michael, 55, 89, 117, 119, 125nn84–85, 133n362, 137n504, 137n507, 225, 256
Nash, Carroll Blue, 53, 189, 298
Nelson, Roger, 89–90, 133nn361, 201, 209, 271
Newbold, William R., 53
Noyes, Ralph, 90

Ochorowicz, Julian, 53, 101, 255
O'Keeffe, Ciarán, 23n107, 83, 90, 130n291, 219, 244, 272, 278, 302n126
Ossowiecki, Stefan, 37, 101, 118, 207, 243
Osterreich, Traugott Konstantin, 53
Osty, Eugene, 53, *54*, 115, 121, 169, 217
Otani, Soji, 90

Pagenstecher, Gustav, 54–55
Palladino, Eusapia, 7, *8,* 9, 17, 22n89, 26, 32–33, 36–37, 40, 48, 50–52, 59–61, 76, 95–96, 118–20, 155–58, 166, 187–88, 193, 216–17, 220, 223, 245–46, 275, 277
Pap, Elemér Chengery, 42, 55, 116–17, 119, 121, 256
Pap, Lajos, 26, 41–42, 55, 119
Parise, Felicia, 119
Paulí, E. Novillo, 90
Pearce, Hubert, 16, 91, 184–85, 198
Persinger, Michael, 90–91, 122, 133nn370–371, 200, 202, 206, 235n116, 243, 247, 293
Piddington, John George, 55–56
Piper, Leonora, *9,* 26, 37, 46–50, 53, 62, 65, 115, 119, *120*, 150–53, 158, 164–65, 169–70, 188, 216, 222, *257,* 262–63, 296
Playfair, Guy Lyon, 81–82, 91, 131n314, 133n372, 299n14
Podmore, Frank, 11, 40, 44, 56, 109, 112, 125n77, 141–43, 146, 148, 153, 158–59, 172, 244–45, 261, 263, 271, 300n65, 301n76, 305n262

346   *Person Index*

Pratt, J. Gaither, 42, 51, 57, 84, 88, 91–92, 93–94, 110, 115, 122, 171–72, 175–77, 182–85, 190, 194, 198, 247, 281–82, 284–87, 303nn197–199, 304nn219–221

Price, Harry, *17,* 41, 56–57, 109, 115, 123, 172, 210, 217

Price, Margaret M., 57, 127n173, 173, 177

Prince, Walter Franklin, 31, 55, 57–58, 173

Puharich, Andrija, 92, 103, 112

Puységur, Marquis de, 5

Puthoff, Harold E., 92, 96, 111, 213, 228, 287

Radin, Dean, 2–3, 19, 21n6, 23n104, 25, 72, 79, 81, 86, 89, 92, 102, 130n299, 131n313, 132n345, 133nn381, 205, 210–11, 218, 229, 231, 233, 240, 243–44, 246, 268, 280, 283, 286, 304n232

Rao, K. Ramakrishna, 75, 92–93, 130n281, 245

Raudive, Konstantin, 93, 193, 195, 223, 267

Rhine, J. B., 11–12, 15, *16,* 22n85, 29, 39, 42, 46, 51, 57–58, 62, 65, 74–76, 84–85, 91, 93, 106, 110, 112–14, 124n10, 170–71, 173–77, 183–91, 195, 216, 239, 241n11, 241n13, 244, 247, 253, 258, 260–61, 264, 266, 274–75, 279–80, 282, 284, 286, 292, 298, 300n62, 304n202, 306n311

Rhine, Louisa, 25, 58, *59,* 101, 107, 170–71, 177–78, 183–91, 195–96, 217, 244, 260, 264, 281, 283, 292, 300n57, 301n82, 303n197, 304n213, 305n272

Richet, Charles, 4, 7, 12, 21n12, 32, 40, 53, 59–61, 85, 104–5, 118–20, 145–46, 153, 155, 171, 207, 216, 223, 225, 241n1, 243, 255, 273, 278

Roberts, Jane, 120, 218

Rochas, Albert de, 60

Rogo, Douglas Scott, 69–70, 93, 239, 241nn16–17, 280

Roll, William George Jr., 93–94, 122, 134nn387, 183, 191, 210, 212, 228, 247, 281–82, 284–87, 299, 300n34, 303nn198–199, 304n223, 305nn239–240, 307n322. *See also* poltergeist

Ryzl, Milan, 94

Salter, Helen, 60

Saltmarsh, H. F., 60

Schmeidler, Gertrude, 78, 88, 94, 122, 131n294, 134n392, 180–81, 185, 191, 196, 205, 283, 290

Schmidt, Helmut, 94–95, 278, 286

Schneider Brothers: Rudi & Willi, 38–39, 53, 56, *57,* 60, 65, 81, 121, 171–72, 215

Schouten, Sybo A., 95

Schrenck-Notzing, Albert von, 36–37, 40, 60–61, 65, 96, 104, 118, 121, 123, 153, 171, 210, 214–15, 270

Servadio, Emilio, 95

Sheldrake, Rupert, 95, 134nn401, 205, 228, 244

Sherman, Harold, 121

Sidgwick, Eleanor, 10–11, 27, 49, 56, *61,* 62, 110, 120, 148–49, 152–53, 155–56, 161, 164–65, 238–39, 241n9, 244, 246, 258, 262, 271, 277, 290, 296, 300n35, 306n299

Sidgwick, Henry, 10, 26, 45, 52, 62, 128n208, 152–53, 155, 161, 188, 262, 271, 277, 290

Silbert, Maria, 55, 121

Slade, Henry, 13, 66, *121,* 122, 219, 237

Sommer, Andreas, 17, 22n89, 37, 45, 51–52, 61, 95–96, 125n52, 125n54, 125n56, 126n102, 126n104, 126n106, 127nn145–146, 134n402, 229, 245, 270, 284, 291, 304n217, 305n261, 305n264

Stepanek, Pavel, 91, 94, 122

Stevenson, Ian, 84, 96, 101, 118, 191–92, 195–96, 207, 228–29, 232, 243

Stuart, Charles E., 62, 91, 175–76, 253, 299n3

Sudre, René, 62–63, 128n210

Sugishita, Morihiro, 96

Swann, Ingo Douglas, 94, 122

Takahashi, Sadako, 14, 297, 307n313

Targ, Russell, 92, 96–97, 111, 201, 211, 213, 287–88, 305n243. *See also* Stanford Research Institute

Tart, Charles, 92, 97

Tenhaeff, Wilhelm, 15, 63, 83–84, 107, 292, 29

Thalbourne, Michael, 97, 99, 134nn407, 206, 209, 213, 235n134, 244–45, 259, 269–70, 272, 276, 279–80, 282, 285–86, 293, 296–97, 299n17, 300n31, 300n38, 300n45, 300n47, 300n59, 301n106, 301n108, 302nn110–112, 302n115, 303n153, 303n158, 303nn159–160, 303n168, 303n173, 303nn179–183, 304n201, 304n227, 304n229, 04n234, 305n238, 305nn245–246, 305n258, 306n280, 306n282, 306nn286–287, 306nn302–304, 306nn306–307, 307n314

Thomas, Charles D., 63

Thompson, Rosalie, 52–53, 122

Thouless, Robert Henry, 63, 178, 247, 260, 264, 283–85, 300n54

Thury, Marc, 9

Tillyard, Robin, 64

Tischner, Rudolf, 64, 269

Tocquet, Robert, 97–98, 134n409

Tressoldi, Patrizio E., 98, 132n356, 135nn411, 225, 229, 236n184, 236n186, 244, 255, 273, 288, 298, 299n16, 307n321

Tyrell, G. N. M., 64, 174–75

Ullman, Montague, 85, 98, 115, 187, 193, 196, 266, 277, 303nn164–165. *See also* Maimonides dream lab

Van de Castle, Robert L., 98–99, 179–80, 277
Varley, Cromwell Fleetwood, *64*
Varvoglis, Mario, 99, 134nn415, 278, 286, 303n175, 304nn235–236
Vasiliev, Leonid L., 64–65, 114
Ventola, Annalisa, 99–100, 130n291, 134nn418–419, 135n421
Verrall, Helen G., 263
Verrall, Margaret, 60, 65, 163–64

Wahbeh, Helané, 79, 100, 102, 131n299, 135nn425, 229, 233, 244, 268, 300nn60–61
Wallace, Alfred Russell, 65, 121
Walther, Gerda, 65–66
Warcollier, René, 66, 80
Watt, Caroline, 25, 100–1, 134n396, 135nn427–428, 209, 230, 233, 244, 269, 275, 282, 294, 301n109, 302n152, 304nn203–204

Weaver, Zofia, 53, 69, 101, 114, 118, 127n156, 136n432, 207, 243
Weiner, Debra H., 101, 135n430, 201
West, Donald J., 101, 269, 283
White, Rhea A., 68, 101–2, 135nn435, 178, 181, 193, 196, 206, 268, 298, 301n107. *See also* exceptional human experience
Wriedt, Etta, *122,* 123

Xavier, Chico, 20, 23n111, 226–27, 236n175, 246

Yount, Garret, 23n103, 79, 102, 131n299, 135n425, 135nn439, 233

Zingrone, Nancy, 67–68, 101–3, 135n430–431, 135nn441, 206, 225, 230, 241, 245, 260
Zöllner, Johann Karl Friedrich, *66,* 237–38
Zugun, Eleonore, 123

About the Author

Courtney M. Block is the reference, instruction, and user engagement librarian at Indiana University Southeast in New Albany, Indiana. She received her master's of library science from Indiana University in Bloomington in 2010 and has worked in both public and academic libraries. An advocate of challenging the status quo whenever possible, Courtney focuses on the intersection of the paranormal and information literacy to help students not only unpack stereotypes surrounding what it means to be an academic person, but to help them gain a deeper understanding of information literacy. Courtney has also conducted research on library/librarian stereotypes, how social media can mitigate library anxiety, and has presented her work both nationally and internationally at conferences such as UX in Libraries, the Pop Culture Association, and more. Courtney believes that all who are curious, college students or not, should have access to a wide range of resources, such as those presented in this work.

She is the author of *Researching the Paranormal: How to Find Reliable Information about Parapsychology, Ghosts, Astrology, Cryptozoology, Near-Death Experiences, and More.* You can also find Courtney's work on the perils of representation in the historic psychical literature in *The Feminine Macabre*, volume 3.

Printed in the USA
CPSIA information can be obtained
at www.ICGtesting.com
LVHW081928291123
764582LV00001B/1